SIXTH EDITION

APPLIED STATISTICS
FOR PUBLIC AND NONPROFIT ADMINISTRATION

SIXTH EDITION

APPLIED STATISTICS
FOR PUBLIC AND NONPROFIT ADMINISTRATION

KENNETH J. MEIER
TEXAS A&M UNIVERSITY

JEFFREY L. BRUDNEY
THE UNIVERSITY OF GEORGIA

JOHN BOHTE
UNIVERSITY OF WISCONSIN–MILWAUKEE

THOMSON

WADSWORTH

Australia • Canada • Mexico • Singapore • Spain • United Kingdom • United States

THOMSON
™
WADSWORTH

Applied Statistics for Public and Nonprofit Administration
Kenneth J. Meier, Jeffrey L. Brudney, John Bohte

Publisher: Clark Baxter
Executive Editor: David Tatom
Assistant Editor: Rebecca F. Green
Editorial Assistant: Cheryl C. Lee
Technology Project Manager: Michelle Vardeman
Marketing Manager: Janise Fry
Marketing Assistant: Teresa Jessen
Marketing Communications Manager: Kelley McAllister
Project Manager, Editorial Production: Matt Ballantyne
Art Director: Maria Epes

Print Buyer: Doreen Suruki
Permissions Editor: Kiely Sisk
Production Service: G & S Book Services, Inc.
Copy Editor: Laura Larson, Leap for Words
Illustrator: G & S Book Services, Inc.
Cover Designer: Jeanette Barber
Cover Image: © Chad Baker/Getty Images
Compositor: International Typesetting and Composition
Text and Cover Printer: Transcontinental Printing, Louisville

Printed in Canada
1 2 3 4 5 6 7 09 08 07 06 05

For more information about our products, contact us at:
Thomson Learning Academic Resource Center
1-800-423-0563

For permission to use material from this text or product, submit a request online at
http://www.thomsonrights.com.
Any additional questions about permissions can be submitted by email to
thomsonrights@thomson.com.

Library of Congress Control Number: 2005920218
ISBN 0-534-60268-1

Thomson Higher Education
10 Davis Drive
Belmont, CA 94002-3098
USA

Asia (including India)
Thomson Learning
5 Shenton Way
#01-01 UIC Building
Singapore 068808

Australia/New Zealand
Thomson Learning Australia
102 Dodds Street
Southbank, Victoria 3006
Australia

Canada
Thomson Nelson
1120 Birchmount Road
Toronto, Ontario M1K 5G4
Canada

UK/Europe/Middle East/Africa
Thomson Learning
High Holborn House
50–51 Bedford Road
London WC1R 4LR
United Kingdom

Latin America
Thomson Learning
Seneca, 53
Colonia Polanco
11560 Mexico
D.F. Mexico

Spain (including Portugal)
Thomson Paraninfo
Calle Magallanes, 25
28015 Madrid, Spain

To Diane and Nancy

About the Authors

Kenneth J. Meier (Ph.D., Syracuse University) is currently the Charles Puryear Professor of Liberal Arts and professor of political science at Texas A&M University. He is also a professor of public management at the University of Cardiff (Wales). Meier is the director of the Project for Equity, Representation and Governance at Texas A&M, which conducts research on the politics and administration of public policies such as education, health care, and criminal justice. He is president of the Public Management Research Association (2003–2005) and president of the Midwest Political Science Association (2005–2006). He has served as president of the Southwest Political Science Association and the Public Administration, the Public Policy, and the State Politics sections of the American Political Science Association. He was a member and chair of the Oklahoma State Ethics and Merit Commission and a member of the Governor's Commission on Professional Licensing and Discipline (Wisconsin) and the Task Force on Property and Liability Insurance (Wisconsin). He is the author or coauthor of several books including *Politics and the Bureaucracy* (Harcourt, 2000), *What Works: A New Approach to Program and Policy Analysis* (Westview, 2000), *The Politics of Fertility Control Policy* (Chatham House, 2001) and *The Scientific Study of Bureaucracy* (University of Michigan, 2003). Dr. Meier's current research projects involve building empirical theories of public management, examining the relationship between democratic governance and bureaucratic organizations, how political and bureaucratic processes affect minorities in the United States and the United Kingdom, and whatever topic strikes his fancy on a given day. His hobbies include serving as the resident humorist for the discipline and seeking the perfect California zinfandel.

Jeffrey L. Brudney is a professor of public administration and policy at the University of Georgia. He is the cofounder and codirector of the Institute for Nonprofit Organizations and the Master of Arts in Nonprofit Organizations (MNPO) program at Georgia. He received his B.A. degree in political science from the University of California at Berkeley and his M.A. and Ph.D. degrees, also in political science, from the University of Michigan at Ann Arbor. Dr. Brudney has published widely in journals in political science, public administration, and nonprofit sector studies, and he is a member of several editorial boards in these fields. He is the author of *Fostering Volunteer Programs in the Public Sector: Planning, Initiating, and Managing Voluntary Activities* (Jossey-Bass, 1990), for which he won the John Grenzebach Award for Outstanding Research in Philanthropy for Education. He received the Mentor Award from the Women's Caucus for Political Science of the American Political Science Association "in recognition of his exceptional guidance of women graduate students and junior faculty members." Dr. Brudney has also received the Herbert Kaufman Award from the American Political Science Association, the Mosher Award from the *Public Administration Review,* and the Harriet Naylor Distinguished Member Service Award from the Association for Volunteer Administration (AVA). In 1994, he was selected as the Fulbright-Kahanoff Scholar at York University, Toronto, Canada. Dr. Brudney has served twice as chairperson of the American Society for Public Administration's (ASPA) Section on Public Administration Education and twice as chairperson of the American Political Science Association's (APSA) Section on Public Administration. He coached more than twenty youth baseball and basketball teams before being retired from this activity for excessive sportsmanship.

John Bohte is currently an assistant professor of political science at the University of Wisconsin–Milwaukee. He received his Ph.D. in political science from Texas A&M University. Dr. Bohte has published articles in *Public Administration Review* and a variety of other public administration and political science journals. Dr. Bohte enjoys teaching courses on public budgeting and finance, research methods and statistics, and public administration. He agreed to be a coauthor on this text so that he could have a longer "about the author" section in his next book.

Brief Contents

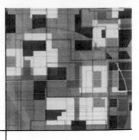

Contents

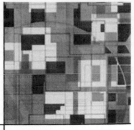

List of Symbols

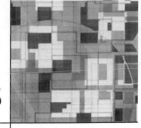

μ	population mean
σ	population standard deviation
Σ	summation of all listed numbers
P	probability
$\cup$	union of two events
$\cap$	intersection of two events
$\mid$	conditional probability [for example, $P(A\mid B)$ means the probability of A given B]
$!$	factorial
C_r^n	combination of n things taken r at a time
p^r	probability p raised to the rth power
EV	expected value
$\bar{X}$	sample mean
s	sample standard deviation
n	size of the sample
$\mathbf{N}$	size of the population
λ	lambda for the Poisson distribution
α	population regression intercept
β	population regression slope
a	sample regression intercept
b	sample regression slope
$\hat{Y}$	predicted value of Y
e	error
s.e.	standard error of the mean
$S_{y\mid x}$	standard error of the estimate
r^2	coefficient of determination (bivariate)
R^2	multiple coefficient of determination (multivariate)
Adj. R^2	adjusted R^2 (coefficient of determination adjusted for variables with little or no explanatory power)
s.e.$_b$	standard error of the slope
Z	standard normal score
t	t distribution score

Preface

The first edition of this book was not the product of years of planning. It was written out of necessity. Assigned to teach a course entitled "Measurement and Analysis for Public Administrators," the original two authors could find no suitable text. So, we wrote one. Since the initial publication of this book in 1981, a few other textbooks have appeared intended for the "methods" course(s) in master's of public administration (MPA) degree programs. With this sixth edition, we believe that *Applied Statistics for Public and Nonprofit Administration* still possesses unique advantages for study and practice in this field.

The first advantage—long a hallmark of the book—is accessibility. Because MPA students as well as those with an interest in the nonprofit sector come from disparate backgrounds, their prior exposure to statistics and quantitative methods is generally weak and varies widely. For many MPA students, the last time they took a mathematics course was in high school. Given this audience, a rigorous presentation of statistical methods would have proved too threatening, difficult, and off-putting. Instead, we wanted a volume that would assume little familiarity with the subject but one that would teach quantitative novices a great deal in very little time. We also wanted to adopt a tone that would invite readers rather than intimidate them.

A second advantage of the book is that it addresses substantive problems illustrative of those faced by practicing administrators in the public and nonprofit sectors. Methods and statistics textbooks in political science and sociology and other disciplines rely predominantly on academic rather than practitioner-oriented examples. Although a number of excellent methods textbooks for business administration are available, they typically focus, understandably, on a different set of issues and problems (for example, manufacturing production, market analysis) than those that normally concern and activate public and nonprofit administrators. We wanted a methods–statistics book with examples that would relate to this audience.

In preparing this sixth edition, we have again followed these guidelines. In fact, the sixth edition is more faithful to them than was the original, for in the past quarter century we have had the opportunity to use this book—and receive valuable feedback from a great many students and practitioners—at several major research universities as well as at numerous off-campus locations. The new edition benefits from this experience and "field testing."

Over the years since initial publication, a constituency of valued students and colleagues has arisen around *Applied Statistics for Public and Nonprofit Administration.* We are grateful for their guidance and help. They have kindly provided us with comments and suggestions, both positive and negative, but always with an eye toward improving the book for students of public affairs and nonprofit management. We welcome you to join this group by contacting us either individually or through the publisher Wadsworth/Thomson Learning.

New to This Edition

At the suggestion of this group and the reviewers, we have incorporated several changes into the sixth edition. We thank them for the suggestions. Two changes are especially noteworthy.

First, in this sixth edition we have continued to make substantial headway on a process that schools and departments of public administration and affairs are also undertaking: incorporating greater recognition and discussion of problems and examples relevant and important to the nonprofit sector and organizations. More than any other academic unit (such as social work or business administration), public administration schools and departments offer their students concentrations in nonprofit management, leadership, or organizations in the curriculum and attract students with these interests. A few universities also have free-standing master's degree programs in this burgeoning domain of research and practice. We feel that this book should reflect as much as possible emerging trends in public administration and affairs. Accordingly, we have tried to make the discussion and examples in this sixth edition more responsive and interesting to students with a background in nonprofit organizations or aspirations to work in the nonprofit sector. Our growing appreciation of the problems and processes important to the nonprofit sector makes the book more relevant for these students as well as for MPA students who will interact with them.

In recognition of the increasing role played by the nonprofit sector in interacting and working with the public sector as well as its importance to many other facets of American life, we have renamed this sixth edition *Applied Statistics for Public and Nonprofit Administration.*

Second, we have added two new chapters to the book. Based on our experiences in the classroom, we have found that students often have difficulty making the transition from the presentation of regression analysis in a textbook to the presentation of regression results in statistical software packages. In a new Chapter 23, "Regression Output and Data Management," we present several detailed examples of regression output generated using SPSS so that students will be better equipped to interpret actual regression output from statistical software packages.

A particularly important issue that cuts across both the public and nonprofit sectors is the use of performance measurement techniques as a means for improving organizational performance and ensuring accountability to the public and other stakeholders. In a new Chapter 24, "Performance Measurement Techniques," we highlight some of the major issues that both nonprofit and government officials must address when designing and implementing performance measurement systems. Chapter 24 compliments Chapter 2, "Measurement," in that many of the general methodological issues in measurement theory are discussed specifically in the context of performance measurement issues.

Our guiding philosophy continues to be to make the book *accessible, practical,* and *useful,* even at the expense of statistical rigor. In their program of study, MPA students and those with an interest in the nonprofit sector will have plenty of time to pick up that *second* course in statistics, if they are interested. But first they must get through their *initial* exposure. We wrote this book to assist them in this endeavor. The goal of the text is to help students make good sense and good use of data with appropriate statistics, recognize the strengths as well as the limitations of the results obtained, and communicate these findings and insights clearly and persuasively to others.

Toward these ends, the sixth edition maintains the tone, level of presentation, and approach featured in the five previous editions. We have also updated, corrected, amended, clarified, and elaborated the material as necessary to make it more readable, current, and interesting. We have also tried to streamline the presentation by restructuring some of the chapters.

In this sixth edition, we have also done more of the things that faculty and students tell us they like about the book. We have incorporated more examples and step-by-step procedures to guide calculation and interpretation of statistics for public and nonprofit managers. We have added more examples to the text, and we have tried to present them more completely with intermediate steps and answers. This edition also includes more figures and other graphical displays. The summary sections for several chapters have been improved.

We remind instructors that you can find answers to the problems, as well as much additional worthwhile material for teaching, on the Instructor's Resource CD-ROM, available free from Wadsworth/Thomson Learning. For each chapter, the Instructor's Manual on the CD discusses the objectives, major points, and difficult points in instruction. It contains a Test Bank with problems for examinations and solutions fully elaborated. The CD also includes a diskette with actual data sets. The final section of the CD explains how to access and analyze these data on a personal computer and presents sample problems for student use. Also, please check the Wadsworth/Thomson website for this book at http://politicalscience.wadsworth.com/meier06/ for these and other teaching enhancements.

We are grateful to students, colleagues, and reviewers for suggesting many of these changes. We look forward to hearing your ideas.

Acknowledgments

A task of this magnitude could not have been accomplished without the assistance of others. We are grateful to colleagues who have kindly given us feedback that informs this sixth edition. A great many students at Texas A&M University, the University of Georgia, the University of Oklahoma, Oakland University, and the University of Wisconsin–Milwaukee have provided us with a diverse teaching laboratory. They, too, have offered comments and suggestions that proved helpful. We appreciate their tolerance not only for errors that appeared in earlier editions but also for a sense of humor that occasionally goes awry on the printed page. (Otherwise reasonable people may disagree over the frequency of the latter occurrence).

The authors give special thanks to Beth Gazley, Indiana University, for her excellent work and dedication in the revision process. Her assistance with editing, production, and communications among the authors and the publisher was valuable to completing this edition.

Thanks are due to the reviewers of this sixth edition for their very helpful comments and suggestions: R. M. Bittick, California State University, Dominguez Hills; Paul J. Culhane, Northern Illinois University; Jon R. Taylor, University of St. Thomas (Houston, TX); and Meredith Weinstein, North Carolina State University.

We are also grateful to a lengthy list of colleagues who have reviewed and improved previous editions of the book: William C. Adams, George Washington University; Robert Aldinger, Valdosta State University; Akpan Akpan, Texas Southern University; Nolan J. Argyle, Valdosta State University; Charles Barrilleaux, Florida State University; Cindy Bennett-Boland, University of Arkansas; Gary Copeland, University of Oklahoma; Mark Daniels, University of Memphis; Jody Fitzpatrick, University of Colorado, Colorado Springs; Barry D. Friedman, North Georgia College and State University; John Forrester, University of Missouri–Columbia; James F. Guyot, Baruch College–City University of New York; Tom Holbrook, University of Wisconsin–Milwaukee; Steve Percy, University of Wisconsin–Milwaukee; John Piskulich, Oakland University; Steven Rhiel, Ole Dominion University; Arthur Sementelli, Stephen F. Austin State University; Soo Geun Song, West Virginia University; Brian Stipak, Portland State University; and Robert Wrinkle, University of Texas, Pan American.

We thank our editor, David Tatom, for his commitment to this book. We are also grateful to Rebecca Green, assistant editor; Michelle Vardeman, technology project manager; Matt Ballantyne, project manager, Wadsworth/Thomson Learning; Michael Bass, president, Michael Bass Associates, Aline Magee, project editor, Michael Bass Associates; Laura Larson, copy editor, Leap for Words; and the staff of G & S Book Services, Inc.

Although we appreciate the help rendered by all of these people, they share none of the blame for any errors of commission or omission. That responsibility rests solely with us.

Kenneth J. Meier
Texas A&M University

Jeffrey L. Brudney
The University of Georgia

John Bohte
University of Wisconsin–Milwaukee

PART

I

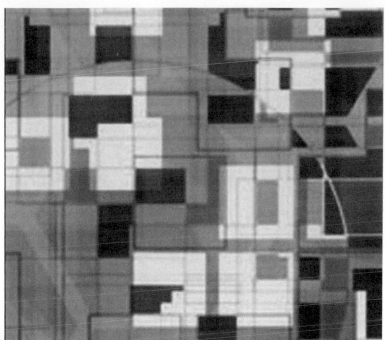

Foundations of Quantitative Analysis

CHAPTER 1

Statistics and Public and Nonprofit Administration

The Advantages of a Statistical Approach

S tatistics have many advantages for the study and practice of public and nonprofit administration and other applied fields. We can summarize these advantages simply by noting that statistics offer insight into issues and problems in a field that would otherwise go unnoticed and unheeded. Although each book on the subject appraises statistics somewhat differently, we can briefly relate the major advantages of this approach.

First, statistics have great power to describe systematically a body of information or data. No other approach matches the precision and quantification that statistics bring to this task. Statistics can elucidate very precisely the main tendencies, as well as the spread of the data about them, in a subset or sample of a population or the population as a whole. This task is the descriptive function of statistics.

Second, statistics are very useful for subjecting our intuitive ideas about how a process or phenomenon operates to empirical test. *Empirical* means observable or based on data. This confrontation of informed conjecture and speculation with actual data and observation is called *hypothesis testing*. A *hypothesis* is an informed guess or conjecture about an issue or problem of interest—for example, that developing skills in statistics in a MPA program or a concentration in nonprofit management will enhance a student's prospects in the job market upon graduation. Statistics are helpful not only for determining the extent to which the data available support or refute our hypotheses but also for generating the kind of hypotheses that can be tested. Hypotheses should be clear, observable, and falsifiable. This perspective expresses the hypothesis-testing function of statistics.

Third, statistics are the foremost method for drawing an accurate inference from a subset or sample of data to its parent, the full population. Rarely does the public or nonprofit administrator have the luxury of working with the complete population; instead, the data available are almost always a sample of observations. For example, the analyst may have a sample of all agency employees, clients, audits, or records—whatever the units of analysis might be—and may want to generalize to the entire population. Public and nonprofit administrators need to know what the sample suggests about the population. Statistics provide an excellent methodology for drawing this linkage. They allow the analyst to evaluate the risk of error when making an inference from sample to population. They also allow us to derive a confidence band or interval about an estimate that expresses the inherent uncertainty in generalizing from a sample of data to the full population. Because we do not have the data from the entire population, we can still make an error in inferring from the sample. Yet, statistics are valuable, for they enable the analyst to estimate the probability or extent of this error. This is the essence of statistical inference.

To these classic uses of statistics we can add two others. First, in public and nonprofit administration, managers face situations and challenges of daunting complexity, such as homelessness, poverty, illiteracy, crime, drug and alcohol dependency, and child and spousal abuse. We entrust to public and nonprofit managers some of the most difficult problems in society. A major benefit of statistics is that they can help the manager keep track of an almost innumerable collection of measured characteristics or attributes, called *variables,* at the same time. The ability to examine a large number of variables simultaneously—and to sort out and make sense of the complicated relationships among them—is a great advantage of statistical methods for dealing with highly complex situations.

Second, an appreciation of statistics can help the public and the nonprofit manager become a much more discerning consumer of quantitative information. Like it or not, managers in all sectors are bombarded with "facts" or assertions based on statistical analysis. There is no escape from them. They appear regularly in myriad sources, including reports, evaluations, memoranda, briefings, hearings, press releases, newspaper accounts, electronic communications, books, academic journals, and many other outlets. Public and nonprofit managers need the skills to evaluate the conflicting claims and representations often made and to avoid being misled. Statistics offer major benefits in this area. Perhaps this reason is the best one of all for the study of statistics in public and nonprofit administration.

As reflected in the master's of public administration curriculum, statistics are certainly not all there is to know about public or nonprofit organizations and management. One must acquire or hone additional skills as well as develop a general understanding of broader political, legal, economic, and social forces. But statistics, too, have a rightful place in the program of study for the master's degree in public administration as well as in academic concentrations and degree programs in nonprofit organizations and management.

Statistics and Options for Managers

For these reasons, statistics and quantitative analysis have become a major element of public management. Agencies that only a few years ago made decisions based on seat-of-the-pants guesses and convenient assumptions now routinely use computer print-outs, contingency tables, regression analyses, decision trees, and other statistical techniques to help understand complex situations and make decisions. Personnel managers receive personnel projections to schedule recruitment efforts. Transportation planners rely on complex computer simulations to design urban transportation systems. Budget officers and accountants scour economic projections and analyses. Program evaluators are charged with making quantitative assessments of a program's effectiveness. Quantitative analyses have become so prevalent that no midlevel manager in the public or nonprofit sector can (or should) hope to avoid them.

The increasing sophistication of quantitative techniques affords public and nonprofit managers few options. At one extreme, a manager untutored in these methods can act as if they did not exist and refuse to read reports containing statistics. Unfortunately, this option is exercised all too often and at considerable cost: The manager loses valuable information presented in quantitative form. This option is not acceptable.

At the other extreme, public and nonprofit managers may choose to accept uncritically the findings of the data analyst rather than reveal to others an ignorance of statistics. This option leads to an error as serious as the first. Although quantitative analysts will almost certainly possess a stronger background in statistics than does the manager (that's their job), the analysts lack the experience, management skills—and the responsibility—to make the decisions. Those decisions rest with public and nonprofit managers, based on the best statistical (and other) advice available. This book is intended for students who consider public or nonprofit management their current or future job.

The third option open to the manager—and the one favored by the authors—is to receive training in quantitative techniques. The training advocated and offered in this book, however, is *not* a standard course in statistics, which in recent years has become a required (and dreaded) element of most master's of public administration programs. Instead, we seek to develop appreciation for and intuitive understanding of basic elements of statistics and quantitative analysis for managers in the public and nonprofit sectors.

Reading this book and working the problems at the end of the chapters will not transform public and nonprofit managers from quantitative novices into master statisticians. Such a transformation is neither desired nor necessary. By and large, public managers do not set up research designs and select and calculate appropriate statistical measures. Far more often they receive information of this kind and are expected to make reasoned and responsible decisions based upon it. For this task, a course in mathematical statistics is not required. However, it is essential that managers become intelligent and critical consumers of quantitative information. Toward that end, this book stresses the application, interpretation, and evaluation of basic statistics.

This book is intended primarily for students who have no or only a very limited background in mathematics, statistics, or other quantitative methods. Material is presented in an applied, nonrigorous, easily readable format centered around practical problems of public and nonprofit management. The text is designed to involve readers in the discussion of these problems and to encourage students to seek and understand numerical answers to them. Statistical theory is discussed only rarely, and the computational formulae that pepper most statistics books are reserved for those instances in which they enlighten rather than mystify.

We have elaborated some of the advantages of our approach, and we hope that they will become evident as you read the book. However, we would be remiss were we to overlook its shortcomings. The most obvious is that this is not a comprehensive text in formal statistics. As noted before, the book is not rigorous, and we have ignored and probably violated many elements of standard statistical theory. Whereas this approach may arouse the disapproval of some professional colleagues, we believe that it has its place—as an introduction to statistics for managers in the public and nonprofit sectors. Too often, students are alienated by more formal courses that emphasize precision over application, and a first course in statistics becomes an eminently disliked and forgettable last one. We have endeavored to develop a text that will engage and hold the interest of public and nonprofit sector managers and at the same time present fundamental applied statistics—and, perhaps, whet the appetite for further training in this area. For those who seek a more mathematical and theoretical approach to managerial statistics, several good books are available (see the Annotated Bibliography at the end of this text).

The Role of Calculation

Whenever possible in this book, we have provided step-by-step instructions for performing statistical procedures and evaluating the results. We strongly recommend that you do these calculations and follow along. Statistics is not a spectator sport: You learn by doing.

If you do not own a hand calculator, we suggest that you purchase an inexpensive one. A hand calculator not only will take much of the anxiety out of learning statistics but also will allow you to concentrate on understanding statistics instead of computing them. Most keys on an inexpensive hand calculator are fairly standard, but we strongly recommend that you find one that also has keys for square root, factorial, and exponentiation (powers).

But, you may be wondering, with microcomputer programs featuring an entire repertoire of statistics available at the push of a button or the click of a computer mouse, why worry about calculating statistics? Why go to the trouble?

Our answer is that, precisely because statistics have become so immediately accessible, it is all the more important to see how they are derived and computed. We know of no better way to understand the various statistics, their advantages and limitations, their assumptions and anomalies, than to experiment with a few observations or data points, make the appropriate calculations, and observe what values of the statistic are generated in return. Whatever the strengths or peculiarities of the statistic, they will soon become apparent to you.

Given the profusion of user-friendly statistical package programs loaded onto microcomputers, however, many students and managers in the public and nonprofit sectors are likely becoming exposed to them through a different mechanism: Instead of learning about the statistics beforehand, they may plunge into using them because they are readily obtainable on their microcomputers, rather than readily understood by them. We do not want to discourage healthy curiosity or interest in statistics; nurturing it is difficult enough. But, in effect, these students practice a tempting statistical version of the popular television quiz show *Jeopardy;* for those who aren't aware, in this quiz show, contestants are given the answer but must state the question (instead of the reverse—fun, huh?).

With statistical package programs increasingly loaded onto microcomputers, students untrained in quantitative techniques can easily generate the statistical "answers" on their computer monitor at the click of a computer mouse—but then can only guess at the question, use, or purpose behind those answers. In our judgment, these students have not learned statistics for public and nonprofit managers; they have acquired a potentially useful computer skill. There is a big difference. In this book, we place our emphasis on building knowledge of the former.

NASPAA Standards for Professional Master's Degree Programs in Public Affairs, Policy, and Administration

If we have still not persuaded you of the advantages—or at least the need—for learning and using applied statistics in public administration, we can offer you one more reason: the accreditation standards in the field. The National Association of Schools of Public Affairs and Administration (NASPAA) has formulated standards for accreditation of master's-level programs in public affairs, policy, and administration. Many public administration programs also offer concentrations or certificates in nonprofit administration and include pertinent courses in the curriculum. In fact, public administration schools and departments most often provide nonprofit management education.

In accrediting schools to grant the MPA degree, NASPAA stipulates that the "common curriculum components shall enhance the student's values, knowledge, and skills to act ethically and effectively in the application of quantitative and qualitative techniques of analysis." These components call for developing background and skills in policy and program implementation and evaluation as well as in decision making and problem solving. Statistics are very important to these tasks. The publication by NASPAA of "Curriculum Recommendations for Public Management Education in Computing" (*Public Administration Review,* November 1986, Special Issue) reinforces the emphasis on analytic methods in graduate programs in public affairs, policy, and administration.

This book can form the basis for courses that satisfy the NASPAA accreditation standards relating to quantitative techniques of analysis and requisite skills in program evaluation, decision making, and problem solving. The book elaborates statistical methods as a tool for assisting public and nonprofit managers in making decisions. By focusing on the assumptions underlying the various techniques, the careful interpretation of results, and the limitations as well as the strengths of the information conveyed, the text stresses the ethical and effective utilization of statistics and quantitative analysis.

With respect to the competencies identified by NASPAA, Part I of the book addresses "Foundations of Quantitative Analysis." The chapters in this section set out the rationale for a statistical approach in public and nonprofit administration and provide essential background in measurement and research design. The chapters are strong in the methodology of research and treat a wide range of issues, including problem diagnosis, the logic of inquiry, causal inference, and threats to the validity of a quantitative study.

Part II, "Descriptive Statistics," introduces basic statistical analysis. The chapters here are also useful for acquainting students with the presentation and interpretation of statistical charts, graphs, and tables to inform themselves as well as other decision makers.

Part III, "Probability," explores the many uses of this tool in public and nonprofit management. The chapters in this section assist students in defining and diagnosing decision situations and selecting and evaluating a course of action.

The chapters in Part IV, "Inferential Statistics," not only develop sophisticated analytic skills but also help in the definition of problems, formulation of alternatives, choice of decision, and evaluation of results. They help the manager to understand the promise—and the limitations—of a sample of data for reaching conclusions about the entire population.

Part V, "Analysis of Nominal and Ordinal Data," introduces another set of quantitative skills useful for the public and nonprofit administrator. This type of analysis is employed very frequently in written memoranda and technical reports and in the evaluation of survey data. These data distinguish public administration (and other social science fields) from the natural, physical, and biological sciences in which measurement is typically much more precise.

Part VI presents "Regression Analysis." Regression is both one of the most flexible and the most utilized statistical techniques. The chapters in this section greatly enhance the decision-making, analytic, and evaluative capabilities of public and nonprofit managers. The first five chapters in this section discuss the methods of regression analysis and the varied applications that regression-based techniques have for public and nonprofit management. The last chapter in this section explains how to interpret regression output generated by statistical software packages.

The final part of the book discusses three "Special Topics in Quantitative Management:" performance measurement, linear programming, and decision theory. These chapters expose students to techniques for measuring organizational performance, different models of logical analysis, bases for decisions, and evaluation of alternatives.

A Road Map for This Book

This book is designed so that each of its parts is self-contained yet builds on the other parts.

Part I lays the foundations for the use of statistics and quantitative analysis in public and nonprofit administration. Chapter 1 explains why statistics have become important to this enterprise, and Chapter 2 elaborates how to measure critical concepts in these fields. The chapter shows that measurement of key concepts such as organizational effectiveness, job satisfaction, and public trust in an agency can be difficult but necessary. It also provides twin evaluative criteria for measurement: reliability and validity. Chapter 3 explains how to model or depict a problem or issue of importance (for example, service delivery by a public or nonprofit agency) and to follow up with a systematic study based on data. The chapter elaborates different research plans called *research designs* that direct how and when data are to be collected, analyzed, and interpreted to answer questions about topics or issues of interest, such as improvements in service delivery and effective methods to recruit volunteers.

Part II covers basic descriptive statistics. This part of the book is devoted to the analysis of one variable at a time, or *univariate statistics*. Chapter 4, "Frequency Distributions," begins this discussion with a treatment of how to categorize and display a large volume of data, or a (frequency) distribution, in a graphical format, such as a table, chart, or graph. The chapter following, "Measures of Central Tendency," is concerned with finding and interpreting the average in a distribution of data: You may be familiar with the main measures of central tendency, the mean, median, and mode. The chapter shows how to calculate these statistics both for data that have been arranged in a table or chart, and for data that have not, or so-called raw data. Once you have calculated or read the average for a group or distribution of data, the next question to ask is how closely the data cluster about this average—that is, whether the observed values or observations are relatively concentrated or dispersed about the measure of central tendency. Chapter 6, "Measures of Dispersion," introduces the two major statistics for measuring dispersion in a sample of data, the variance and its close relative, the standard deviation.

The next part of the book is about probability. Probability can be confusing for students to understand; do not become discouraged. To learn the basic rules and applications of probability, please see Chapter 7, which presents an introduction to the topic. In that chapter you will learn the basic law of probability as well as what is meant by *a priori probabilities, posterior probabilities, joint probabilities,* and *conditional probabilities.* With this background, the remaining chapters on probability will be much easier to follow.

Chapter 8 presents the most common probability distribution, the normal curve. The familiar bell-shaped curve has numerous uses and applications in public and nonprofit administration. For example, what percentage of job applicants fall above or below a criterion score on a test of job-related skills? Or, what is the score that would distinguish the top 5% of applicants for further consideration, such as an interview?

Have you ever wanted to know the probability that an agency could hire 3 minorities for 10 positions when 50% of the job applicants were minorities? For problems similar to this one, Chapter 9 introduces the binomial probability distribution. The chapter also shows how the normal distribution can be applied to simplify complex binomial problems provided certain conditions are met. The following chapter discusses other useful probability distributions for public and nonprofit managers. The hypergeometric probability distribution is used when the manager wants to make a generalization from a sample to a finite population. The Poisson and the exponential distributions are used whenever the manager needs to include time or distance in a probability statement—for example, 1.2 computer failures per day or 15 potholes per 100 meters.

Part IV elaborates statistical inference: This part focuses on the issue of how one can generalize results from a small sample of data to the much larger population from which the sample was drawn. This technique is useful in its own right and also to support advanced statistical procedures presented later in the book, such as regression analysis. Because the public or nonprofit manager must work almost always with a sample rather than the full population of data—but seeks reliable information about the entire population—knowledge of statistical inference is essential. To learn how to estimate the value of the mean or average for a population from a sample of data, consult Chapter 11. This chapter also discusses procedures for constructing confidence bands or intervals around the mean estimate.

Chapter 12 applies the techniques of statistical inference to testing hypotheses. Although there is no way to infer from a sample of data to the population without error, public or nonprofit managers may be willing to take an acceptable risk in drawing an inference. The chapter shows how by using the techniques of classical hypothesis testing on a small sample of data, the manager can make a decision regarding the full population—for example, that the average number of times the population of agency clients seeks assistance is four times or more per year, or that the average is less—at the risk of error of, say, 5%. You will thus learn a technique that in the long run will allow you to make the correct decision 95% of the time, but be in error the remaining 5% (remember, because we do not know the "answers" in the population, we cannot be right all the time). Chapter 13 shows how to estimate population proportions, rather than mean or average values, from a sample—for example, the proportion (or percentage) of motorists in a county who drive faster than 65 miles per hour on a stretch of highway. For those situations in which the manager needs to compare the performance or characteristics of two groups (for example, experimental and control groups, groups before or after an intervention or treatment, and so forth), Chapter 14 explains how to test for these differences using the statistical technique called *analysis of variance.*

Beginning with Part V, the remainder of the book deals with relationships between two or more variables. The study of relationships between two variables is called *bivariate analysis.* Bivariate statistical techniques can help to answer myriad research and practical questions: Is agency budget related to performance? Do police patrols reduce crime? Does greater inclusiveness in governmental hiring lead to a more responsive bureaucracy? Does government contracting with nonprofit organizations produce more efficient delivery of services? Do employees in nonprofit organizations display greater job motivation than those in others sectors of the economy? Is there a relationship between delegating decision-making authority to lower levels of the organization and innovativeness of employees?

Part V explains how to construct tables and analyze data at the nominal and ordinal levels of measurement—that is, information measured in terms of categories (for example, gender) or rating scales (for example, attitude toward balancing the federal budget or clients' evaluations of the training provided by a volunteer center). Chapter 15 shows how to use percentages to analyze and interpret tables called *contingency tables* or *cross-tabulations* that pair data from two variables. Chapter 16 builds on this foundation to provide more sophisticated techniques for analyzing tables, including statistical inference (chi-square) and measures of association (gamma, lambda, and so forth). Chapter 17 elaborates statistical control table analysis, a procedure for examining the relationship between two variables while taking into account or "controlling for" or "holding constant" a third variable. The analysis of three or more variables at a time presented in this chapter introduces multivariate analysis, a topic covered more extensively later in the text.

Part VI is concerned with relationships between variables measured on equal interval scales, such as in years, dollars, or miles. Chapter 18 begins the discussion with an "Introduction to Regression Analysis," a highly flexible and often used statistical technique helpful in a variety of management situations. The chapter shows how a line can summarize the relationship between two interval variables—for instance, the relationship between the number of intake workers at a government facility and the number of clients who receive service in a given day. Chapter 19 explains the assumptions and limitations of regression analysis. Estimating and predicting trends in the future based on past data is the subject of Chapter 20 on time series analysis. To forecast such trends as future population, the number of people likely to volunteer to government agencies, service usage, sewage output, the number of organizations that will participate in the community walk-a-thon to raise cancer awareness, and other information important to public and nonprofit managers, consult this chapter. Chapter 21, "Multiple Regression," extends this technique to the multivariate context: It shows how to use regression to analyze and understand relationships among three or more variables. For example, how well can the average age of housing and the percentage of renter-occupied buildings in a neighborhood explain or predict the incidence of fires across a city? To what extent do the number of volunteers working in nonprofit agencies and the number of community events sponsored by these organizations affect the amount of money collected in their annual fund-raising campaigns?

Chapter 22 on interrupted time series analysis explains how to estimate the impact of a program or policy over time. The manager can use this technique to evaluate whether a program, such as a senior citizens' center or a municipal volunteer office, has had a short-term, long-term, or short-term temporary impact (or perhaps no impact) on the health and welfare of city residents.

Chapter 23 centers on the interpretation of regression output from statistical software packages. Chapters 18 through 22 present a variety of regression examples in equation form to illustrate how relationships between independent and dependent variables can be summarized using linear equations. Statistical software packages generally do not present regression results in equation form, which can make the leap from textbook to computer applications confusing. Although it is perfectly acceptable to write up regression results in either equation or summary table form (the format used by most statistical software packages), managers need to have a clear understanding of the similarities and differences of each format. Regression analysis is almost always performed with computers. As a result, managers need exposure to how regression is carried out and presented in statistical software packages before conducting such analyses on their own.

Part VII presents three special topics in quantitative management that are sometimes useful to public and nonprofit managers. From years of teaching as well as feedback from instructors who have been kind enough to adopt this book (thank you!) and their students (thank you, too!), we know that not all students will be exposed to this part. But some students are—and we include treatment of these topics as an aid and courtesy to them.

Statistical techniques are often used as tools for measuring and improving organizational performance in both governmental and nonprofit settings. Chapter 24 provides an overview of some of the key issues that managers in both sectors need to know when designing performance measurement systems and reporting performance results to external audiences.

If you are interested in how to make decisions given various amounts of information, Chapter 25 on decision theory can be very helpful. The chapter presents useful ways to evaluate alternatives and select among them. For decision situations that involve maximizing or minimizing some output under certain constrains, please see Chapter 26 on linear programming.

Following the chapters, you will find other materials useful for the study of applied statistics for public and nonprofit administration. For those motivated to learn more about statistics (don't laugh—by the time you have read a chapter or two, this student could be you!), we have included an Annotated Bibliography. The bibliography contains a wide range of texts valuable for assistance and reference. For ease of use of the book, you will also find at the back a Glossary of key terms that have been boldfaced in the text at first appearance. Finally, you will quickly make friends with the section containing answers to the odd-numbered questions from the problem sets at the end of each chapter.

Whenever possible, we have attempted to include problems faced by public and nonprofit administrators in the real world. Many of our midcareer as well as more senior students suggested problems and examples. Although all the data and problems are hypothetical, they represent the types of situations that often confront practicing public and nonprofit administrators. We hope that you find them useful and interesting.

Now you have a road map for the book. Good luck on the journey!

CHAPTER 2

Measurement

U sing a statistical approach in public and nonprofit administration begins with measurement. **Measurement** is the assignment of numbers to some phenomenon that we are interested in analyzing. For example, the effectiveness of army officers is measured by having senior officers rate junior officers on various traits. Educational attainment may be measured by how well a student scores on standardized achievement tests. Good performance from a city bus driver might be measured by the driver's accident record and by his or her record of running on time. The success of a nonprofit agency's fund-raising drive might be measured by the amount of money raised.

Frequently, the phenomenon of interest cannot be measured so precisely, but only in terms of categories. For example, public and nonprofit administrators are often interested in characteristics and attitudes of the general populace and of various constituency groups. We can measure such things as the racial and gender composition of the individuals in these groups; their state of residence or their religious preferences; their attitudes toward a particular agency or government in general; their views on space exploration, public spending, or the tax treatment of nonprofit organizations; and so on. Although such variables do not have quantitative measurement scales, it is still quite possible to measure them in terms of categories—for instance, white versus nonwhite; female versus male; favor tax decrease, favor no change, favor tax increase; and so on. Although these phenomena cannot be measured directly with numerical scales, they are important variables nonetheless. Public and nonprofit administrators need to know how to measure, describe, and analyze such variables statistically.

In many managerial situations the manager does not consciously think about measurement. Rather, the manager takes some data and subjects them to analysis. There are problems in this approach. In Chapter 12 we will discuss an example in which the Prudeville police crack down on prostitution in the city. The police chief increases daily arrests by the vice squad from 3.4 to 4.0. Based on these numbers, the police chief claims a successful program. This example illustrates a common measurement problem. The city council of Prudeville was concerned about the high level of prostitution activity, not the low level of prostitution arrests. Conceivably the number of prostitution arrests could be positively related to the level of prostitution activity. In this situation, the police chief's data may reveal increased prostitution, not decreased prostitution. In fact, the only thing an analyst can say, given the police chief's data, is that the number of prostitution arrests increased.

In this chapter, we will discuss some of the important aspects of measurement, both in theory and in application.

Theory of Measurement

Measurement theory assumes that a concept representing some phenomenon that the analyst is concerned about cannot be directly measured. Army officer effectiveness, educational achievement, bus driver performance, level of prostitution activity, and program success are all concepts that cannot be measured directly. Such concepts are measured indirectly through indicators specified by operational definitions. An **operational definition** is a statement that tells the analyst how a concept will be measured. An **indicator** is a variable or set of observations that results from applying the operational definition. Examples of operational definitions include the following:

1. Educational attainment for Head Start participants is defined by the achievement scores on the Iowa Tests of Basic Skills.

2. Officer effectiveness is defined by subjective evaluations by senior officers using form AJK147/285-Z.

3. Program success for the Maxwell rehabilitation program is defined as a recidivism rate of less than 50%.

4. A convict is considered a recidivist if, within 1 year of release from jail, the convict is arrested and found guilty.

5. Clients' satisfaction with the service of the Department of Human Resources is measured according to the response categories clients check on a questionnaire item (high satisfaction; medium satisfaction; low satisfaction).

6. An active volunteer in the Environmental Justice Association is defined as a person who donates her or his time to the association at least 5 hours per week, on average.

7. One measure of board director activity of the Nature Society is the number of hours devoted by board members to this organization each month.

Operational definitions are often not stated explicitly but implied from the research report, the memo, or the briefing. A manager should always encourage research analysts to state explicitly their operational definitions. Then the manager can focus on these definitions and answer a variety of measurement questions, such as the ones we will discuss later. It is important for public and nonprofit managers to know how the complicated concepts they deal with are measured.

Reading the preceding operational definitions, you may have been troubled by the lack of complete congruence between the concept and the indicator. For example, assume the city transit system evaluates the job performance of its bus drivers by examining each one's accident record and on-time rate. A driver may well have a good accident record and be on time in her bus runs, and yet be a bad bus driver. Perhaps the on-time record was achieved by not stopping to pick up passengers when the driver was running late. Or perhaps the driver's bus was continually in the shop because the driver did not maintain the bus properly.

This example suggests that indicators may not be a complete measure of a concept. Most students of measurement accept the following statement:

$$\text{Indicator} = \text{concept} + \text{error}$$

A good indicator of a concept has very little error; a poor indicator is only remotely related to the underlying concept.

In many cases several indicators are used to measure a single concept. One reason for using **multiple indicators** is that a concept may have more than one dimension. For example, the effectiveness of a receptionist may be related to the receptionist's efficiency and the receptionist's courtesy to people. To measure effectiveness adequately in this instance, we would need at least one indicator of efficiency and one of courtesy. The term *triangulation* is sometimes used to describe how multiple indicators enclose or "hone in" on a concept.

Multiple indicators are also needed when the indicators are only poor representations of the underlying concept. The success of a neighborhood revitalization program would require several indicators. The increase in housing values might be one indicator. The decrease in crime, reduction in vandalism, willingness to walk outside at night, and general physical appearance might be other indicators. The start of a neighborhood association or day care cooperative might be additional indicators. Each indicator reflects part of the concept of "neighborhood revitalization" but also reflects numerous other factors, such as economic growth in the entire city, pressure for housing, street lighting, and so on. The theory behind multiple indicators in this situation is that the errors in one indicator will cancel out the errors in another indicator. What remains will measure the concept far better than any single indicator would. For these reasons, a "multiple indicator strategy" to measure important concepts comes highly recommended.

Measurement Validity

A **valid indicator** accurately measures the concept it is intended to measure. In other words, if the indicator contains very little error, then the indicator is a valid measure of the concept. The measurement validity of an indicator often becomes a managerial problem. For example, many governments give civil service exams that are supposed to be valid indicators of on-the-job performance. If minorities or women do not do as well as white males do on these exams, the manager is open to discrimination suits. The manager's only defense in such a situation is to prove that the civil service exam is a valid indicator of on-the-job performance (not an easy task).

Validity can be either convergent or discriminant. In the preceding paragraph, we were discussing **convergent validity**—do the indicator and the concept converge? Does the indicator measure the concept in question? **Discriminant validity** asks whether the indicator allows the concept to be distinguished from other similar, but different, concepts. For example, using achievement scores on standardized tests may lack discriminant validity if the tests have some cultural bias. A good indicator of educational achievement will distinguish that concept from the concept of white middle-class acculturation. A culture-biased test will indicate only educational achievement that corresponds with the dominant culture. As a result, such an indicator may not be valid.

Social scientists have long grappled with the idea of **measurement validity.** They have suggested several ways that validity can be established. An indicator has **face validity** if the manager using the indicator accepts it as a valid indicator of the concept in question. An indicator has **consensual validity** if numerous persons in different situations accept the indicator as a valid indicator of the concept. The recidivism rate, for example, has consensual validity as a good measure of a prison's ability to reform a criminal. Often, consensual validity is established through finding a research study in which the indicator has been used. An indicator has **correlational validity** if it correlates strongly with other indicators that are accepted as valid. For example, community satisfaction with a nonprofit organization as assessed in a survey might be strongly related to the amount of monetary donations received by the agency or the number of donors. Finally, an indicator has **predictive validity** if it correctly predicts a specified outcome. For example, if scores on a civil service exam accurately predict on-the-job performance, the exam has predictive validity.

These four types of validity offer ways that a manager can argue that an indicator is valid. However, they do not guarantee that the indicator is a particularly effective measure of the concept in question. An indicator may have face validity, consensual validity, correlational validity, and predictive validity and still not be as effective as other measures. Consider the Law School Admission Test (LSAT). The LSAT has face validity and consensual validity (numerous law schools use it to screen applicants). It also has correlational validity (it correlates with undergraduate grades) and predictive validity (it correlates with law school grades). Yet, the LSAT is not as strong a predictor of law school performance as is the socioeconomic status of the student's family.

With all the tests for validity and all the different ways an indicator can be validated, developing valid indicators of concepts is still an art. It requires all the skills that a manager has at his or her disposal. To be sure, in some cases, such as finding indicators of lawn mower efficiency, valid indicators are easy to derive. On the other hand, developing valid indicators of community police effectiveness or of the "health" of the nonprofit community in a city are very difficult tasks.

One way to ease this task is to review the published literature in a field. In general, if an indicator is used in the literature, it has at a minimum both face and consensual validity, and it may meet other validity criteria as well. Before (or while) you create your own indicators of an important concept, it is a good idea to consult the relevant literature. This approach carries additional benefits, such as making you aware of how other researchers have approached relevant problems and what they have found. Such information can make your analytical task easier.

Measurement Reliability

A **reliable indicator** consistently assigns the same number to some phenomenon that has not, in fact, changed. For example, if a person measures the effectiveness of the police force in a neighborhood twice over a short period of time (short enough so that change is very unlikely) and arrives at the same value, then the indicator is termed *reliable*. If two different people use an indicator and arrive at the same value, then, again, we say that the indicator is reliable. Another way of defining a reliable indicator is to state that an indicator is a reliable measure if the values obtained by using the indicator are not affected by who is doing the measuring, by where the measuring is being done, or by any other factors other than variation in the concept being measured.

Increasing Reliability

The two major threats to **measurement reliability** are subjectivity and lack of precision. A **subjective measure** is a measure that relies on the judgment of the measurer or of a respondent in a survey. A general measure that requires the analyst to assess the quality of a neighborhood or the performance of a nonprofit board of directors is a subjective measure. Subjective measures have some inherent unreliability because the final measures must incorporate judgment. Reliability can be improved by rigorous training of individuals who will do the measuring. The goal of this training is to develop consistency. Another method of increasing reliability is to have several persons assign a value and then select the consensus value as the measure of the phenomenon in question. Some studies report a measured interrater reliability based on the consistency of measurement performed by several raters. Often, judgments about the effectiveness of nonprofit boards of directors are based on the ratings provided by multiple knowledgeable actors—for example, the board chairperson, the chief executive officer of the nonprofit, and nonprofit stakeholders such as founders, donors, and other similar nonprofits in the community.

Reliability can also be improved by eliminating the subjectivity of the analyst. Rather than providing a general assessment of the quality of the neighborhood, the analyst might have to answer a series of specific questions. Was there trash in the streets? Did houses have peeling paint? Were dogs running loose? Did the street have potholes? How many potholes?

Reliability problems often arise in survey research. For example, suppose that you were asked to respond to survey questions concerning the performance of one of your instructors—or a local political figure, or "bureaucrats," or the volunteers assisting in your agency—on a day that had been especially frustrating for you. You might well evaluate these subjects more harshly than on a day when all had seemed right with the world. Although nothing about these subjects had changed, extraneous factors could introduce volatility into the ratings, an indication of unreliability. By contrast, if your views of these subjects actually did change and the survey instrument picked up the (true) changes, the measurement would be considered reliable. (For that reason, reliability is often assessed over a short time interval.)

Unfortunately, although removing the subjective element from a measure will increase reliability, it may decrease validity. Certain concepts important to public and nonprofit managers—employee effectiveness, citizen satisfaction with services, the impact of a recreation program—are not amenable to a series of objective indicators. In such situations a combination of objective and subjective indicators may well be the preferred means of measurement.

Lack of precision is the second major threat to reliability. To illustrate this problem, let us say that Barbara Kennedy, city manager of Barren, Montana, wants to identify the areas of Barren with high unemployment so that she can use her federal job funds in those areas. Kennedy takes an employment survey and measures the unemployment rate in the city. Because her sample is fairly small, neighborhood unemployment rates have a potential error of ±5%. This lack of precision makes the unemployment measure fairly unreliable. For example, neighborhood A might have a real unemployment rate of 5%, but the survey measure indicates 10%. Neighborhood B's unemployment rate is 13.5%, but the survey measure indicates 10%. Clearly the manager has a problem.

The precision of these measures can be improved by taking larger samples. But in many cases, this task is not so easy. Let us say the city of Barren has a measure of housing quality that terms neighborhood housing as "good," "above average," "average," and "dilapidated." Assume that 50% of the city's housing falls into this last category, dilapidated. If the housing evaluation were undertaken to designate target areas for rehabilitation, the measure lacks precision. No city can afford to rehabilitate 50% of its housing. Barren needs a more precise measure that can distinguish among houses in the dilapidated category. This need can be met by creating measures that are more sensitive to variations in dilapidated houses (the premise is that some dilapidated houses are more dilapidated than others; for example, "dilapidated" and "uninhabitable"). Improvement of precision in this instance is far more difficult than increasing the sample size.

Measuring Reliability

Unlike validity, the reliability of a measure can be determined objectively. A common method for assessing measurement reliability is to measure the same phenomenon or set of variables twice over a reasonably short time period and to correlate the two sets of measures. The correlation coefficient is a measure of the statistical relationship or association between two characteristics or "variables" (see Chapter 18). This procedure is known as **test-retest reliability.**

Another approach to determining reliability is to prepare alternative forms that are designed to be equivalent to measure a given concept and then to administer both of them at the same time. For example, near the beginning of a survey, a researcher may include a set of five questions to measure attitudes toward government spending or trust in nonprofit fund-raisers, and toward the end of the survey, he or she may present five more questions on the same topic, all parallel in content. The correlation between the responses obtained on the two sets of items is a measure of **parallel forms reliability.** Closely related is **split-half reliability,** in which the researcher divides a set of items intended to measure a given concept into two parts or halves; a common practice is to divide the even-numbered questions and the odd-numbered questions. The correlation between the responses obtained on the two halves is a measure of split-half reliability. Cronbach's alpha, a common measure of reliability, is based on this method.

In all three types of reliability measurement—test-retest, parallel forms, and split-half—the higher the intercorrelations among the items, the higher the reliability of the indicators.

If several individuals are responsible for coding and collecting data, it is also a good idea to assess **interrater reliability.** Interrater reliability is based on the premise that the application of a measurement scheme should not vary depending on who is doing the measuring. For example, in screening potential applicants for a food and clothing assistance program, a nonprofit community center might have a 10-item checklist for assessing the level of need for each client. To determine whether agency staff are interpreting and applying the checklist consistently, we could ask five employees to screen the same group of 20 clients using the checklist. High interrater reliability would exist if all five employees came up with very similarly scored checklists for each client. If the scored checklists for each client looked dramatically different, we would have low interrater reliability. Low interrater reliability can indicate that confusion exists over how a measurement instrument should be interpreted and applied.

Types of Measures

We have already discussed two types of indicators—subjective and objective. The **subjective indicator** requires some judgment to assign a value, whereas the **objective indicator** seeks to minimize discretion. Assume that the city manager wants to know the amount of city services delivered to each neighborhood in the city. Objective measures of city services would be acres of city parks, number of tons of trash collected, number of police patrols, and so on. Subjective measures of city services could be obtained by asking citizens whether the levels of various city services were adequate. A subjective measure of nonprofit organizational effectiveness—a difficult concept to assess—might be the reputation of these organizations, as assessed by local funding agencies.

A third type of measure, an **unobtrusive indicator,** is intended to circumvent the so-called Hawthorne effect, in which the act of measuring a phenomenon can alter the behavior being assessed. For example, asking city residents about the quality of police services may sensitize them to police actions. If an individual is asked his or her opinion again, the answer may be biased by earlier sensitizing. A city employment counselor, for example, will likely know that her evaluation is based on the number of individuals who are placed in jobs. She may then focus her efforts on the easiest persons to place, to build up a favorable record. Any reactive measure (a measure that affects behavior when it is taken) has some inherent reliability and validity problems.

One way to circumvent this problem is through the use of unobtrusive measures (see Webb et al. 1973). A library, for example, could determine its most useful reference books by asking patrons which reference books they use most frequently. Among the problems in this situation is that many people who never use reference books might answer the question. An unobtrusive measure of reference book popularity would be the amount of wear on each book (since these volumes normally cannot be checked out).

Suppose the head of the Alcohol Beverage Control Board in a state wants to know how much liquor is consumed "by the drink." Because it is illegal to serve liquor by the drink in many counties in certain states, sending a survey questionnaire to private clubs would yield little response. An unobtrusive measure would be to examine the trash of all private clubs and count the number of empty liquor bottles found in their trash. An unobtrusive measure of the interest of service volunteers in the governance of a nonprofit board would be a simple count of how many volunteers attend open board sessions over a year.

Unobtrusive measures can be used in a variety of situations and can take on as many different forms as the creative manager can devise. They do have some limitations, however. Unless care is taken in selection, the measures may lack validity. For example, a manager may decide that she can determine the amount of time an office spends in nonproductive socializing by measuring the office's consumption of coffee and fountain water (this fountain uses bottled water). She assumes that more coffee and more water fountain meetings imply less productivity. In fact, one office might consume more coffee than another because it has older workers (thus more likely to drink coffee) or because the office puts in more overtime and needs coffee to make it through the night.

Levels of Measurement

In many cases, we have been discussing data that are actual numbers—tons of garbage collected in a given town, number of arrests made by the police per week, response times in minutes of a local fire department, number of children attending a daily church after-school program, miles driven in a week by Meals on Wheels volunteers, and so forth. Because this information consists of real numbers, it is possible to perform all types of arithmetic calculations with them—addition, subtraction, multiplication, and division. As we will learn in Chapter 5 on measures of central tendency, when this is the case, we can readily compute mean or average scores, such as the mean or average number of tons of garbage collected per week as well as the average response time of the fire department.

Unfortunately for public and nonprofit administrators, available data are often not measured in nearly as precise a fashion as are these variables. There are several reasons for the lack of precision. In some cases, it is a reflection of the state of the art of measurement. For instance, although it may be possible to say that a citizen is very satisfied, satisfied, neutral, dissatisfied, or very dissatisfied with a new job training program contracted out to a nonprofit agency, it usually is *not* possible to state that his or her level of satisfaction is exactly 2.3—or 5 or 9.856 or 1.003. Most measures of attitudes and opinions do not allow this level of exactitude. In other instances, loss of precision results from errors in measurement or, perhaps, from lack of foresight. For example, you may be interested in the number of traffic fatalities in the town of Berrysville over the past few years. As a consequence of incomplete records or spotty reporting in the past, you may not be able to arrive at the exact number of fatalities in each of these years, but you may be quite confident in determining that there have been *fewer* fatalities this year than *last* year.

Finally, some variables inherently lack numerical precision: One could classify the citizens of a community according to race (white, African American, Hispanic, or other), sex (male, female), religion (Protestant, Catholic, Jewish, Buddhist, or other), or any of a number of other attributes. However, it would be futile to attempt to calculate the arithmetic average of race or religion, and it would be meaningless to say that a citizen is more female than male: a person is either one or the other.

In discussing these different types of variables, social scientists usually refer to the concept of **levels of measurement.** Social scientists conventionally speak of three levels of measurement. The first or highest (most precise) level is known as the **interval level** of measurement. The name derives from the fact that the measurement is based on a unit or interval that is accepted as a common standard and that yields identical results in repeated applications. Weight is measured in pounds or grams, height in feet and inches, distance in miles. The variables discussed at the beginning of this section are all measured at the interval level: *tons* of garbage, *number* of arrests, response times in *minutes*. As a consequence of these standard units, it is possible to state not only that there were more arrests last week than this week but also that there were exactly *18* more arrests. (Some texts discuss a fourth level of measurement—*ratio*—but for our purposes it is effectively the same as interval measurement.)

The second level of measurement is called **ordinal.** At this level of measurement, it is possible to say that one object (or event or phenomenon) has *more* or *less* of a given characteristic than another, but it is not possible to say *how much* more or less. Generally, we lack an agreed-upon standard or unit at this level of measurement. Almost all assessments of attitudes and opinions are at the ordinal level.

Consider the previous example that focused on citizen satisfaction with a new job training program contracted out to a nonprofit agency specializing in this area. At this writing, no one is quite sure how to measure satisfaction or how a unit of satisfaction may be defined. Nevertheless, an interviewer could be dispatched to the field to ask participants, "How satisfied are you with the new job training program recently instituted in this community? Very satisfied, satisfied, neutral, dissatisfied, or very dissatisfied?" To create an ordinal-level variable, we would need to attach numbers to the response categories for this survey question. The numbered categories might look like those displayed in Table 2.1.

Table 2.1

An Ordinal Measure of the Concept "Satisfaction"

1 = very satisfied
2 = satisfied
3 = neutral
4 = dissatisfied
5 = very dissatisfied

Table 2.2

What an Ordinal Variable Looks Like

Name	Satisfaction
Jones	2
R. Smith	3
Franklin	1
Barnes	2
A. Smith	3

A participant who is "very satisfied" is assigned a score of one. A participant who is "satisfied" is assigned a score of two, and so on. Table 2.2 shows what the satisfaction variable would look like if we inputted data for a number of participants into a spreadsheet or statistical software package.

Of course, it would not be possible to ascertain from a citizen his or her exact numeric level of satisfaction (e.g., 4.37; 16.23). For example, if a "1" is assigned to the response of one participant and a "3" to another, the precise magnitude of difference between the participants cannot be determined (for more on why precise distances across cases cannot be determined using nominal and ordinal level measures, see the section titled "Some Cautions" in Chapter 5). However, if one citizen answers that he is "very satisfied" with the program, it is safe to conclude that he is *more* satisfied than if he had stated that he was "satisfied" (or "neutral," "dissatisfied," or "very dissatisfied"); similarly, a response of "very dissatisfied" indicates *less* satisfaction than one of "dissatisfied" (or "neutral," "satisfied," or "very satisfied"). How *much* more or less remains a mystery. As another example, a polling firm might ask a representative sample of citizens how good a job they believe the mayor is doing in running the city (very good, good, average, poor, or very poor) and to what extent they are interested in community affairs (very interested, interested, neutral, uninterested, or very uninterested). These also are ordinal-level variables and are subject to the same limitations as is the measure of satisfaction with the job training program.

The name *ordinal measurement* derives from the ordinal numbers: first, second, third, and so on. These numbers allow the *ranking* of a set of objects (or events or

	Table 2.3

A Nominal Measure of Employment Status

1 = full-time employee
0 = part-time employee

	Table 2.4

What a Nominal Variable Looks Like

Name	Employment Status
Jones	1
R. Smith	0
Franklin	1
Barnes	1
A. Smith	0

phenomena) with respect to some characteristic, but they do not indicate the exact distances or differences between the objects. For example, in an election, the order of finish of the candidates does not say anything about the number of votes each one received. The order of finish indicates only that the winner received more votes than did the runner-up, who in turn received more votes than the third-place finisher. By contrast, the exact vote totals of the candidates are interval information.

At the third level of measurement, one loses not only the ability to state exactly how much of a trait or characteristic an object or event possesses (interval measurement) but also the ability to state that it has more or less of the characteristic than has another object or event (ordinal measurement). In short, the **nominal level** of measurement totally lacks any sense of relative size or magnitude: It allows one to say only that things are the same or different. Some of the most important variables in the social sciences are nominal. These were mentioned before: race, sex, and religion. It is easy to expand this list to management: occupation, type of housing, job classification, sector of the economy, employment status. A nominal coding scheme for employment status appears in Table 2.3.

If we inputted data for a number of employees into a spreadsheet or statistical software package, the values for the employment status variable would look like those displayed in Table 2.4. In this example, employee Jones is clearly a full-time employee, whereas R. Smith is a part-time employee.

Now that you have some idea of the three levels of measurement, write several examples of interval, ordinal, and nominal variables on a separate piece of paper. After you have finished, fill in the level of measurement for each of the variables listed in Table 2.5.

Table 2.5

Some Variables: What Is the Level of Measurement?

Variable	Level of Measurement

1. Number of children
2. Opinion of the way the president is handling the economy (strongly approve; approve; neutral; disapprove; strongly disapprove)
3. Age
4. State of residence
5. Mode of transportation to work
6. Perceived income (very low; below average; average; above average; very high)
7. Income in dollars
8. Interest in statistics (low; medium; high)
9. Sector of economy in which you would like to work (public; nonprofit; private)
10. Hours of overtime per week
11. Your comprehension of this book (great; adequate; forget it)
12. Number of memberships in clubs or associations
13. Dollars donated to nonprofit organizations
14. Perceived success of animal rights association in advocacy (very high; high; moderate; low; very low)
15. Years of experience as a supervisor
16. Your evaluation of the level of "social capital" of your community (very low; low; moderate; high; very high)

Whether you were aware of it or not, if you are like most people, before you read this chapter, you probably assumed that measurement was easy and accurate: All you needed to do was to count whatever it is that interests you or rely on technology to do the same thing. From the number of dollars a person makes (income) to the number of people in your city (population) to the amount of degrees registered on a thermometer (temperature) to the number of miles recorded by your automobile odometer as you drive to and from work (commute mileage), measurement was straightforward and precise. In (management) practice, it is not that easy.

The Implications of Selecting a Particular Level of Measurement

When deciding what level of measurement to use, keep in mind that variables originally coded at a higher level of measurement can be transformed into variables at lower levels of measurement. The opposite is generally not true. Variables originally coded at lower levels of measurement cannot be transformed into variables at higher levels of measurement.

Table 2.6

Different Levels of Measurement for the Same Concept

Cost per Client (interval)	Cost per Client (ordinal)	
$57	2	where 1 = low (less than $50)
$38	1	2 = moderate ($50 to $100)
$79	2	3 = high ($100 or more)
$105	3	
$84	2	
$159	3	
$90	2	
$128	3	
$103	3	

For example, let's say that the director of a nonprofit organization decides to collect data on the dollar amount of supplies and services spent on each client, to get a sense of how efficiently services are being provided. He can measure the cost per client at either the interval or ordinal level. The director takes data for 10 recent clients and constructs both ordinal and interval variables, just to see what the different data would look like. The results are displayed in Table 2.6.

If you were the director, how would you measure the cost variable? Think about the advantages of measuring costs at the interval level. With the interval-level variable, we know exactly how much money was spent on each client. With the ordinal-level variable, we only know that a client falls into a particular cost range. If we construct the measure at the interval level, we can also determine the exact distance between individual cases. For example, it cost $19 more to serve the first client than it did to serve the second client. In contrast, the ordinal-level measure would only tell us that the first client was in the "moderate" cost range, whereas the second client was in the "low" cost range.

In terms of flexibility, note that we can always recode the interval-level version of the variable into the ordinal-level variable if we want to present the data differently at a later point in time. But what if we originally constructed the variable at the ordinal level and later found it necessary to obtain data on the actual dollar amount spent per client? We would be unable to obtain this information because ordinal-level data cannot be transformed into interval-level data. Although we would know that the cost per client was between $50 and $100 in four cases, we would be unable to determine the exact cost per client if our data were originally measured at the ordinal level.

As a data analyst, sometimes you will not be able to choose the level of measurement for the variables to be examined. This is especially true when working with data originally collected by another party, such as a government agency. In those cases where you are able to choose, keep in mind the many advantages of constructing variables at higher rather than lower levels of measurement.

When you reach Parts V and VI of this book, you will see that levels of measurement have important implications for data analysis. If you plan on using a particular statistical method to analyze data, you need to make sure to use an appropriate level of measurement when constructing your variables. Otherwise you may spend a lot of time collecting data only to find that you are unable to analyze the data with a particular statistical technique. Contingency tables (Chapters 15–18) are used to analyze nominal- and ordinal-level data. Regression analysis (see Chapter 18), one of the most commonly used techniques in statistical analysis, generally requires the use of interval-level data.

When you study public or nonprofit administration or become a practicing administrator, the measurement situation changes dramatically. In the first place, as elaborated in the theory of measurement discussed earlier in the chapter, measurement often contains error. We do not have perfect measures of bureaucratic or organizational performance or employee morale or citizen satisfaction—or many of the other concepts that you may want to measure and use. Evaluating the quality and accuracy of measurement through validity and reliability assessment is desirable and frequently challenging. In the second place, the richness of public and nonprofit administration calls for several different types of measures. Thus, you will need to use subjective, objective, and unobtrusive indicators. In addition, you will confront different levels of measurement. The interval level corresponds most closely to our typical understanding of measurement as counting things—for example, the number of hours of class attended in a week or the number of pages of reading required in an assignment is an interval measure. The other two levels of measurement, ordinal and nominal, do not allow such ready accounting. Nevertheless, you may have to assess work attitudes in your organization (ordinal) for an organizational development effort or identify five areas of social need in your community (nominal) for a grant proposal. Bringing the full menu of measurement concepts to bear on a problem or issue is a useful technique in public and nonprofit administration.

Chapter Summary

Measurement is the assignment of numbers to some phenomenon. Some variables cannot be measured so precisely but only in terms of categories. An operational definition tells the analyst how a concept will be measured. An indicator is a variable linked to a concept through an operational definition. The two key issues in measurement are reliability or consistency of measurement and validity or meaningfulness (are we measuring what we think we are measuring?). Several kinds of validity and types of reliability as well as three types of measures (subjective, objective, and unobtrusive) are discussed in the chapter.

In management, we use three levels of measurement: interval, ordinal, and nominal. Interval measurements are based on a standard unit or interval. Ordinal measurements lack such an agreed-upon standard or unit. Nominal measurements lack any sense of relative size or magnitude; they only allow one to say that things are the same or different.

Problems

2.1 A prominent social scientist believes that she can measure the effectiveness of police departments by asking citizens how effective they feel their police department is. What are the advantages and disadvantages of this measure?

2.2 Compile a list of indicators that could be used to evaluate the quality of a city's sanitary landfill (garbage dump).

2.3 A campus safety program requires all volunteer safety officers to be 5 feet, 8 inches tall and to be able to chin themselves on an 8-foot bar. What concept does the program seem to measure? Evaluate these indicators.

2.4 Compile a list of indicators that could be used to evaluate a building maintenance crew.

2.5 What are the relative advantages of subjective and objective indicators of a concept?

2.6 Evaluate the validity and reliability of the survey question, "To what extent does this department have waste and inefficiency in its operations?" as a measure of the waste and inefficiency in the department. Suggest other measures that the department could use to measure waste and inefficiency, and explain why they would be an improvement over the survey question.

2.7 The head of a municipal recreation department is not satisfied with the city's standardized performance evaluation form for employees. The form consists largely of a rating system consisting of five categories: far above expectations, above expectations, meets expectations, below expectations, and far below expectations. The department head wants to develop improved measures of employee performance. Help him by suggesting improved measures and by evaluating their validity and reliability. Consider objective as well as subjective measures and obtrusive as well as unobtrusive measures of employee performance.

2.8 Identify a crucial concept in public administration, such as bureaucracy, professionalism, or responsiveness, and explain how this concept has been measured in the literature.

(a) What are some of the ways that researchers have measured the concept?

(b) To what degree have they established valid and reliable measures of the concept?

(c) Suggest new indicators that might improve upon the measurement of the concept.

2.9 The director of the Art Institute would like to present some data on the size of donations in this year's annual report. He selects the following four categories to summarize donations:

Friend of the Institute	($25 to $99)
Silver Member	($100 to $249)
Gold Member	($250 to $499)
Platinum Member	($500 and above)

To get a sense of what the data will look like, the director gives you a sample of donations measured at the interval level and asks you to apply the coding scheme. Create an ordinal-level variable for donations using the data below. (Hint: To get started, you first need to assign a numeric code to each category.)

Interval Version	Ordinal Version
$25	
$150	
$75	
$450	
$100	
$750	
$90	
$175	
$250	
$50	

2.10 The director of the West Arbor Senior Center decides to put together a database on the center's activities. The center currently takes written records of services provided to clients, but the director feels that program information will be easier to access and analyze if the records are computerized. The program director generates the following sample data for 10 current clients:

	Service Provided	
Gender	Home Delivery of Meals	Assistance with Transportation
Male	Yes	Never
Female	Yes	Frequently
Female	No	Never
Male	No	Rarely
Female	Yes	Never
Male	Yes	Rarely
Male	Yes	Frequently
Female	No	Never
Male	Yes	Never
Female	No	Frequently

The director asks you to develop a measurement scheme and turn the data into numbers that can be put into a computerized database. Show the director how much you know about measurement, and develop a numerical coding scheme for each of the variables. Is a nominal-level coding scheme sufficient for all three variables, or does one variable need to be constructed using a higher level of measurement?

2.11 The Wildlife Conservation Center has put together a database to keep track of the attributes of its employees. Specifically, numeric codes are assigned to variables as follows:

Gender	1 = female	2 = male	
Job Status	1 = full-time	2 = part-time	
Job Description	1 = professional	2 = administrative	3 = general labor

Employee	Gender	Job Status	Job Description
1	1	1	1
2	2	1	3
3	1	2	2
4	2	1	2
5	1	2	1
6	1	2	1
7	2	2	3
8	1	1	3

Use the variable codes above to describe in words the attributes of each employee.

2.12 The city manager of Snook, Texas, wants to generate some statistics on a voluntary free flu shot clinic for city employees. Specifically, she has the following data on whether employees received shots and whether they took sick leave during the winter months:

Received Shot	Took Sick Leave
Yes	No
No	Yes
No	Yes
Yes	No
Yes	Yes
Yes	No
No	No
Yes	No
Yes	No
No	Yes

The city manager asks you to come up with a numerical coding scheme so that these data can be placed in a statistical program for analysis. Develop a coding scheme for each variable.

CHAPTER 3

Research Design

Winston Lewis, mayor of the city of Bison, Kansas, is upset. The showcase of his community pride program, "Stand Up for Bison," is a failure. The program was intended to upgrade the quality of life of senior citizens in Bison by relocating those living below the poverty line to new federally subsidized public housing. Because termination of the program means a loss not only of federal funds but also of local jobs to Bison, Mayor Lewis is especially perturbed.

To add to the mayor's problems, in a blistering front-page editorial, the local newspaper, the *Bison News,* blamed the failure on the incompetence of Lewis and his staff. The editorial claimed that the mayor did not take a personal interest in running the program, instead leaving its administration largely to cronies, none of whom had education or training in the needs and problems of senior citizens. As a result, the editorial contends, the senior citizens were treated shabbily—"as a product"—by the program, and insufficient attention was paid to their rights, convenience, and welfare. The editorial also made vague allegations that some of the federal funds tied to the program were skimmed by the mayor and his staff.

Lewis's initial reaction was to counterattack in the public media. He and his staff assembled information intended to refute the charges made in the editorial, and a press conference was tentatively scheduled.

Before the press conference took place, however, the mayor's chief strategist, Dick Murray, informed Lewis of his misgivings about this type of response to the editorial.

In the first place, argued Murray, it would be certain to occasion a rejoinder from the newspaper, further publicity, and perhaps an official investigation of the program. Understandably, the mayor would prefer to avoid all of these. Second, even if the mayor were able to refute the newspaper charges, the nagging question would remain: What *did* cause the program to fail? Murray maintained that if he could demonstrate that *factors other* than those pertaining to the mayor and his staff were responsible for the failure of the program, then he could limit the adverse publicity and take the heat off Lewis—a nice solution to the mayor's problems. Suitably impressed, Lewis canceled the press conference and told Murray to proceed.

Murray first undertook his research. A telephone call to Washington, D.C., yielded the information that the federal government had funded the same program for senior citizens in Virtuous, Montana, a city similar to Bison in area, population, and other crucial characteristics (economic base, form of government, and so forth). In contrast to the experience in Bison, however, the federal government was quite pleased with the program in Virtuous; the Washington bureaucrat quipped that the program has enjoyed a success "as big as the sky." Murray reasoned that if Lewis and his staff have a level of interest and a level of competence in running the program comparable to their counterparts in Virtuous, then these factors *cannot* be the cause of the failure of the program in Bison, for the program has succeeded in Virtuous with the *same* level of official involvement. Murray checked with the Virtuous authorities and found that, in both cities, the levels of interest and of competence of the mayor and staff were very similar. Thus, Murray concluded that some other factor must be responsible for the failure of the program in Bison.

What might this factor be? Murray had been around long enough to feel that in administering a program, the bottom line is always money: The more money, the greater is the likelihood of success. He checked again with the Virtuous authorities and learned that Bison was awarded far less in federal funds to run the senior citizen program than was Virtuous. This information provided support for Murray's hunch. He concluded that the program in Bison failed *not* because of lack of official involvement—recall that the program in Virtuous succeeded with the same level of involvement—but because of a lack of federal funding. He reasoned that had the program in Bison received the same level of funding as had that in Virtuous, it would have been a success. After all, look at the experience in Virtuous, where more money was made available.

Murray delivered his findings to Mayor Lewis, who naturally was pleased. At a newly scheduled press conference, the mayor presented Murray's evidence to refute the allegations of the *Bison News* editorial and to establish a new possible cause of the failure of the program in Bison: federal funding. The press conference had the desired impact. Murray was given a raise.

The process in which Murray was engaged—attempting to determine the cause of a relationship or event—is at the core of all social research. Social scientists seek to discover the causes of phenomena and rule out possible rival causes. The nature of this enterprise provides the focus for this chapter.

The first section of the chapter introduces the process and terminology commonly used by social scientists in constructing causal explanations. The second portion of the chapter discusses the formal criteria necessary to establish a relationship as causal. In other words, what evidence must the researcher present in order to demonstrate that A causes B? The final chapter segment is devoted to research design. A research design is a systematic program intended to evaluate proposed causal explanations on the basis of data. The two major types of design—experimental and quasi-experimental—are distinguished and elaborated.

Constructing Causal Explanations

In contrast to Mayor Lewis's strategist Dick Murray—who sought the causes of a single event (the failure of the senior citizens program in Bison)—social scientists typically are interested in accounting for *entire classes* of events or relationships. For example, what are the causes of success or failure of social programs? Does congressional oversight lead to a more responsive bureaucracy? Does regulation of utilities result in lower prices? Does government contracting with nonprofit agencies for service delivery lead to greater efficiency? Does contracting weaken public sector accountability, however? Does government spending on social services tend to lessen nonprofit activity—or increase it? Does mandated community service (for example, as a requirement for high school graduation) increase—or decrease—volunteering later in life? These broad questions go far beyond isolated outcomes and lead us to think more generally about causation. Do more open and fluid structures in public and nonprofit organizations lead to more effective agencies?

The basic building block in answering these questions and, more generally, in constructing causal explanations is the **concept.** From the mass of detail, and often confusion, surrounding the particular events in a class, the concept pinpoints an idea or element thought to be essential in accounting for the entire class. Concepts abstract or summarize the critical aspects in a class of events. For example, in his research, Murray isolated official involvement and level of funding as important elements in the senior citizens program in Bison. These are concepts on the basis of which he might have attempted to explain the success or failure of *all* social programs. The concept points out a common trait or characteristic shared by the members of a class: In this case, social programs have varying levels of official involvement and funding.

To provide a more complete explanation of program success, Murray could have highlighted more abstract concepts. These might include power, social class (of clientele groups), and organizational goals. Because broader concepts potentially allow the researcher to account for a greater number of events, the more abstract the concept, and the more applicable to a wide range of phenomena, the more useful it is. Thus, a relatively small array of concepts tends to appear repeatedly in social science research, such as power, role, motivation, environment, system, exchange, and organization.

Concepts act as a perceptual screen that sensitizes researchers to certain aspects of objects or events and leaves them oblivious to others. For this reason, the process of abstraction to arrive at concepts is perhaps the most critical element in the research process. In one sense, it is a process similar to those used in everyday life: Inevitably we tune in to some characteristics and tune out others. For example, after you meet a person for the first time, you are almost certain to remember his or her sex; you are less likely to recall elements of personal appearance, and less likely still to recall specific attitudes, opinions, and preferences. However, in another sense it is quite different, because in scientific research, conceptualization is a much more self-conscious, painstaking endeavor.

To construct explanations of events or relationships, concepts must be defined. Two types of definitions are necessary for empirical or data-based research. The first is called a **nominal** or **conceptual definition.** It is the standard dictionary definition that defines the concept in terms of other concepts. For example, *patriotism* may be defined as love for one's country; *intelligence* may be defined as mental capacity; *occupation* may be defined as the type of work that an individual primarily performs; *volunteer* may be defined as donating one's time without pay.

In social research, nominal definitions must satisfy a set of conditions. Concepts should be defined as clearly and precisely as possible. A concept must not be defined in terms of itself. For example, to define *happiness* as the state of being happy is meaningless. Also, the definition should say what the concept is, rather than what it is not. For example, to define *duress* as the absence of freedom does not distinguish it from several other concepts (coercion, imprisonment, compulsion, and so on). Inevitably many other concepts will fit the description of what the concept is not. Furthermore, unless there is good reason, the definition should not constitute a marked departure from what has generally been accepted in the past. A good reason might be that you feel that previous definitions have misled research in the area. Whereas nominal definitions are arbitrary—they are neither right nor wrong—in order to advance knowledge, researchers attempt to make definitions as realistic and sensible as possible. Although it could not be proven incorrect to define a cat as a dog, it would be counterproductive.

The second type is called an **operational definition** (sometimes called a *working definition*). The operational definition translates the nominal definition into a form in which the concept can be measured empirically—that is, with data. As discussed in Chapter 2, the process of operationalizing a concept results in indicators, or variables designed to measure the concept.

By converting abstract ideas (concepts) into a form in which the presence or absence, or the degree of presence or absence, of a concept can be measured for every individual or case in a sample of data, operational definitions play a vital role in research. They allow researchers to assess the extent of empirical support for their theoretical ideas. For example, *civic involvement* might be defined as the number of clubs, groups, or associations to which a person belongs.

In the prior example, Dick Murray felt that the degree of success attained by federal programs is determined by the level of funding rather than by local involvement. He operationalized these concepts as the size of the federal allotment to each city in the program, and the level of interest and training of the local mayor and staff in the program, respectively. Program success is a difficult concept to operationalize, but Murray might have used a variety of indicators: the perceived satisfaction with the program (assessed in a survey) felt by public housing residents and by the larger community, the number of new housing units constructed, the cost per square foot, the

Table 3.1

Data for Five Bureaucrats

| | | | Variable | |
Case	Race	Sex	Time Wasted on Job (minutes)	Attitude toward Job
Bureaucrat 1	White	Female	62	Dislike
Bureaucrat 2	White	Male	43	Neutral
Bureaucrat 3	African American	Male	91	Like
Bureaucrat 4	Hispanic	Male	107	Like
Bureaucrat 5	White	Female	20	Dislike

degree to which the housing met federal standards, and so forth. He would be using a multiple indicator strategy, as explained in Chapter 2. By comparing the cities of Bison and Virtuous, he was then able to demonstrate that although local involvement seemed to make no difference in the success of the senior citizens program (because the cities rated about the same on this dimension), the level of funding (here the cities differed) did make a difference.

Once a concept has been operationalized and measured in a sample of data, it is called a **variable.** A variable assigns numerical scores or category labels (such as female, male; married, single) to each case in the sample on a given characteristic. For example, in a study examining the job-related behavior of bureaucrats, a researcher may obtain data for five bureaucrats on the variables "race," "sex," "time wasted on the job per day" (minutes), and "attitude toward the job" (like, neutral, dislike). These data are displayed in Table 3.1, with each column representing a variable.

Often in research, variables are classified into two major types. It is the goal of most research to explain or account for changes or variation in the **dependent variable.** For example, Dick Murray sought to explain the failure of the senior citizens program in Bison (and implicitly, to understand how the program might be made a success). What factors could account for the different outcomes of the programs in Bison and Virtuous? A variable thought to lead to or produce changes in the dependent variable is called independent. An **independent variable** is thought to affect or have an impact on the dependent variable. Murray examined the effects on program success of two independent variables: interest and training of mayor and staff and federal funding. For terminological convenience, independent variables are sometimes referred to as *explanatory, predictor,* or *causal* variables, and the dependent variable as the *criterion.*

To account for changes in the dependent variable, researchers link the criterion explicitly to independent variables in a statement called a **hypothesis.** A hypothesis formally proposes an expected relationship between an independent variable and a dependent variable.

The primary value of hypotheses is that they allow theoretical ideas and explanations to be tested against actual data. To facilitate this goal, hypotheses must meet two

2 Requirements of Hypotheses

requirements. First, the concepts and the variables that they relate must be measurable. Although propositions connecting unmeasurable concepts (or those for which data are currently unavailable) are important in research, they cannot be evaluated empirically and must be treated as assumptions. Second, hypotheses must state in precise language the relationship expected between the independent and dependent variables. For example, two hypotheses guided the research of Dick Murray:

1. The greater the local involvement in a program, the greater is the chance of program success.
2. The greater the level of federal funding for a program, the greater is the chance of program success.

In both hypotheses, the expected relationship is called *positive,* because increases (decreases) in the independent variable are thought to lead to increases (decreases) in the dependent variable. In contrast, a *negative* or *inverse* relationship proposes that increases in the independent variable will result in decreases in the dependent variable, or vice versa. An example of a negative relationship is this hypothesis:

3. The higher the degree of federal restrictions on administering a program, the less is the chance of program success.

Once the concepts specified by these hypotheses have been operationalized (measured), data can be brought to bear on them to evaluate the degree of empirical support for the anticipated relationships.

Hypotheses intended to provide an explanation for a phenomenon of interest (for example, success or failure of federal programs) most often propose a positive or a negative relationship between an independent and a dependent variable. One merit of this procedure is that because the direction of the relationship (positive or negative) is made explicit, it is relatively easy to determine the degree of confirmation for (or refutation of) the hypothesis. However, researchers are not always this circumspect in stating hypotheses, and it is not unusual to find in the literature examples in which the independent variable is said to "affect," "influence," or "impact" the dependent variable, without regard for direction. This practice not only condones imprecision in thinking and hypothesis formulation, but also creates difficulties in assessing empirical support for a hypothesis. For these reasons, this practice should be avoided.

An integrated set of propositions intended to explain or account for a given phenomenon is called a **theory.** The propositions link the important concepts together in anticipated relationships so that the causal mechanisms underlying the phenomenon are elucidated. In some of these propositions, it will be possible to operationalize the concepts and collect the data necessary to evaluate the hypothesized relationships empirically. However, as a consequence of difficulties in measuring some concepts or lack of available data, it may not be possible to test all propositions. Untested propositions constitute **assumptions.** Although assumptions lie outside the boundaries of empirical testing, they should not be accepted uncritically. Evidence from past research, as well as logical reasoning, can be used to assess their validity. For example, budget projections based on an assumption that all Americans will give contributions to charitable organizations in the next year are unreasonable. Also untenable is an assumption that the amount of volunteer hours will quadruple next year, even if a nonprofit needs them.

Figure 3.1

Arrow Diagram and Model

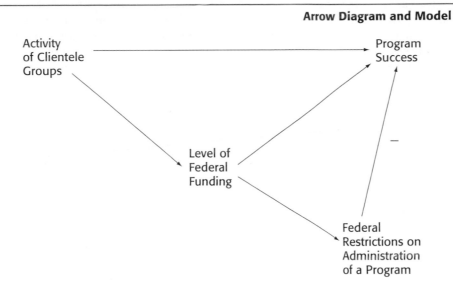

A full-blown theory to explain an important phenomenon, such as representativeness in public bureaucracy, relationships between political appointees and career civil servants, or the effect of volunteering on building social capital, can be highly abstract and comprehensive. It may contain numerous assumptions not only about how concepts are related but also about how they are measured. Because of difficulties in specifying and operationalizing all relevant elements and collecting all necessary data, theories are rarely, if ever, tested directly against actual data or observations. Instead, a simplified version of the theory called a **model** is developed and put to an empirical test. Usually the relationships proposed by the theory are depicted as a set of equations or, equivalently, as an arrow diagram (see Figure 3.1). Regardless of the form, the model is a compact version of the theory intended for an empirical test. It identifies the essential concepts and the interrelationships among them that are proposed by the theory, and it presumes the existence of adequate measurement and relevant data (see Chapter 2). Ultimately, it is the model that is tested statistically, but the results will be brought to bear indirectly on the validity and utility of the theory.

As an example of a model, consider again the question of the determinants of success of social programs. Perhaps the activity of clientele groups leads to high levels of federal funding, which, in turn, increase the likelihood of program success. In addition, the activity of clientele groups may help to achieve program success directly through support at the local level. Federal funding, however, may be a mixed blessing. Although high levels of funding may enhance the prospects of success, they may also bring increased federal restrictions on administration of the program. These restrictions may reduce the chance of program success. This heuristic theory is by no means complete. To yield a more satisfactory explanation, we might want to add several components, such as the interest of elected officials in the program (recall the example of Bison, Kansas, and Dick Murray with which this chapter began), the organizational structure of the program, and the degree to which the means of achieving program success are well understood (for example, issuing checks for unemployment compensation versus improving mental health). The relationships with program success that have been proposed formally here can be displayed schematically in an arrow diagram, in which each arrow represents an expected causal linkage between a pair of concepts. A negative sign above an arrow indicates an inverse relationship, and an unmarked arrow corresponds to a positive relationship. Figure 3.1 presents the resulting heuristic model of the success of social programs.

To the extent that data provide confirmation for the relationships proposed by a theory and tested in the model, support is obtained for the theory, and its validity is enhanced. Analogously, the failure to find empirical support for a theory detracts from its validity and suggests the need for revisions. However, researchers usually are more willing to subscribe to the first of these principles than to the second. Whereas they rarely question data that offer support for their theoretical ideas, in the face of apparent empirical disconfirmation, revision of the theory is seldom their immediate response. Instead, operational definitions are critically evaluated; possible problems in the selection, collection, and recording of the sample of data are considered; numerical calculations are checked; and so on. As a result of the state of the art of social science research, these are reasonable steps to take prior to revising the theory. However, if these measures fail to lead to alternative explanations for the lack of empirical support obtained (such as a biased sample of data) or possible procedures to amend this situation (for instance, by devising new operational definitions for some concepts), the researcher has no choice but to reconsider and revise the theory.

The revision usually leads to new concepts, definitions, operationalizations, and empirical testing, so that the process begins all over again. Generally, it is through a series of repeated, careful studies, each building on the results of earlier ones, that researchers come to understand important subject areas.

Causal Relationships

In the preceding discussion of theory, repeated reference was made to the concept of causality, the idea that one phenomenon is the cause of another. A theory may be considered a system of interrelated causal statements intended to account for or explain a given phenomenon. However, these are tentative (hypothesized) statements of a relationship whose validity cannot be taken for granted but must be tested. The purpose of this section is to discuss the four formal criteria identified by most social scientists as necessary to establish a relationship as causal. The criteria are time order, covariation, nonspuriousness, and theory.

Probably the most intuitive of these criteria is the notion of **time order.** If A is the cause of B, then A must precede B in time; that is, changes in A must occur before changes in B. This stipulation is just another way of saying that cause must precede effect.

In many hypothesized relationships, the question of time order between variables is obvious. For example, if the researcher is interested in the effect of sex, race, country of birth, or other so-called ascribed characteristics on certain attitudes and behaviors, it is clear that the former set of variables precedes the latter. Unfortunately, this issue cannot always be resolved so easily. Consider the relationship between tenure on the job and job satisfaction: Does tenure lead to satisfaction, or does satisfaction lead to tenure? Both viewpoints seem reasonable. Or consider the relationship between attitude toward bureaucrats and attitude toward a particular government agency. Which variable comes first? Again the question of temporal priority is problematic. In most relationships between attitudes and behaviors, it is difficult to establish time order with certainty. For this reason, causal statements linking these types of variables should be considered carefully.

The second criterion that must be satisfied for the relationship between two variables to be considered causal is **covariation,** or statistical *association* between the variables. *Covariation* means that the two variables move or vary together. That is, if A changes and B also changes, this covariation provides some evidence that A is the cause of B. Analogously, if changes in A are never accompanied by changes in B (no covariation), then A cannot be the cause of B. One way to understand this idea is to consider that, if as A changes, B always remains constant, then A can have no impact on B. In that case, changes in A do not matter with respect to B.

For example, suppose a researcher hypothesized that higher salaries lead to more productive workers. If in a sample of data she found that salary and productivity covaried—that is, those paid higher salaries were more productive than those paid less—then she would have evidence for a causal relationship. However, if she found that as salaries increased, productivity showed no concomitant change, then the hypothesized causal relationship would be in jeopardy.

Of the four criteria of causality, perhaps the most difficult to comprehend is **nonspuriousness.** A nonspurious relationship is a covariation or association between two variables or phenomena that cannot be explained by a third factor. A nonspurious relationship implies that there is an *inherent* link between the two variables in the sense that changes in one produce changes in the other, and that their observed covariation is not the result of an accidental connection with some associated (third) variable.

For example, just about everyone knows someone who claims to predict the weather—usually rain—based on "a feeling in their bones." Interestingly enough, these predictions may turn out to be correct more often than not. Thus, one would observe a covariation between the prediction and the weather. However, a moment's reflection will show that there is no inherent link between these two phenomena. Instead, changes in pressure and moisture in the atmosphere cause both changes in the state of the human body (such as a feeling in the bones) and changes in the weather (such as rain). The original covariation between feeling in the bones and rain is observed not because the variables are causally related, but because both of them are associated with a third factor, changes in the atmosphere. Hence, the original relationship is **spurious:** It can be explained by the effects of a third variable.

Although it may be relatively easy to think of examples of likely nonspurious relationships (fertilizer use and crop yield, exposure to sunlight and tan skin), it is far more difficult to *demonstrate* that an observed covariation is nonspurious. Establishing a relationship as nonspurious is an inductive process that requires that the researcher take into account *all* possible sources of an observed covariation between two variables. If, after the effects of all third factors are eliminated, the original covariation remains, then the relationship is nonspurious.

Because the stipulation requiring the elimination of all possible third variables is based on logical grounds (one would be incorrect in claiming a causal relationship between two variables if it could be explained by the effects of *any* other factor), nonspuriousness cannot be proved by data analysis alone. However, to the extent that a researcher explicitly takes into account possible sources of an observed covariation between two variables and is able to eliminate them as alternative explanations for the covariation, the validity of the causal inference is enhanced. In other words, the greater the number of relevant third variables considered and eliminated, the greater is the confidence that the original relationship is causal. For example, the researcher who finds that a covariation between interest in public affairs and performance in a master's of public administration program persists after the effects of prior undergraduate education, occupation, amount of time available for study, and so on, have been taken into account would have more confidence in the causal inference than if only one of these third factors had been considered.

The final criterion for establishing a relationship as causal is *theory.* As discussed earlier in the chapter, theories are meant to explain important phenomena. To establish a causal relationship, not only must the conditions of time order, covariation, and nonspuriousness be satisfied, but also a theoretical or substantive justification or explanation for the relationship must be provided. Theory interprets the observed covariation; it addresses the issue of how and why the relationship occurs. In one sense, theory serves as an additional check on nonspuriousness. It lends further support to the argument that the link between two phenomena is inherent rather than the artifact of an associated third factor.

Many of the techniques used to assess causal relationships can be performed on computers using statistical software packages. Although computers can quickly generate sophisticated statistical analyses, they do not have the capability to judge whether results are plausible or meaningful in real-world settings. Statistical software packages see numbers for what they are—numbers. They cannot tell you whether a relationship between two variables is actually plausible. This is why theory is such an important component of causality.

Parts IV through VII of the text deal with statistical techniques used to test hypotheses. As you learn about these techniques, you should remember that even if a relationship is *statistically* significant, that does not necessarily mean it is *meaningfully* significant. The job of a data analyst is to explain the substantive meaning of statistical relationships; computers are not capable of making such judgments on their own.

As this discussion has illustrated, the criteria necessary for proof of a causal relationship are demanding. It is essential to balance this view with the idea that the determination of causation is not a yes-no question but is a matter of degree. Satisfaction of each criterion lends further support to the causal inference. Additionally, for each criterion, there are varying levels of substantiation. Confidence in the time order of phenomena is variable, observed covariations can assume a range of magnitude from small to large, demonstrating nonspuriousness is nearly always problematic, and the validity of a given theory is usually the subject of debate. Evidence for a causal relationship is based on the extent to which these criteria are satisfied.

In this context, two final points merit consideration. First, social scientists accept the concept of **multiple causation.** It is widely acknowledged that an event or phenomenon may have several causes, all of them contributing to the result. For example, explanations of why a person continues to volunteer for an agency are complicated, based on a variety of organizational, social, and personal factors. Consequently, social researchers rarely speak of *the* cause; instead, they seek the causes or determinants of a phenomenon. Thus, it can and does happen that an observed covariation between an independent variable and a dependent variable turns out to be neither totally nonspurious nor totally spurious, but partially spurious. Data analysis frequently suggests that both the independent variable and a third variable (as well as other explanatory variables) are potential causes of the dependent variable. The chapters on multivariate statistical techniques explain how to assess such effects.

Second, in developing and evaluating causal explanations, it can be extremely useful to construct an arrow diagram like the one in Figure 3.1. Depicting graphically a system of proposed causal relationships helps to uncover possible interrelationships among expected causes, sources of spuriousness, and omitted variables whose effects should not be ignored. It is also a quick and easy procedure. For all these reasons, the arrow diagram is a highly recommended technique, no matter how simple or complicated the model may be.

Research Design

A **research design** is a systematic program for empirically evaluating proposed causal relationships. The design specifies a model of proof for testing the validity of these relationships. The research design guides the collection, analysis, and interpretation of the relevant data. There are many types of research design, and they differ in their ability to generate reliable inferences concerning causality.

The concept of causality has long been a source of controversy among social scientists. Partly for this reason, several different conceptions of the validity or viability of a causal relationship have been proposed and utilized. The two most important of these are internal validity and external validity. **Internal validity** addresses the question of whether, *in a given study or research project,* the independent variable did indeed cause or lead to changes in the dependent variable. The criteria for assessing internal validity are those considered in the previous section: time order, covariation, nonspuriousness, and theory.

External validity captures a different idea: It is concerned with the issue of whether and to what extent results obtained in a given study can be *inferred* or generalized to hold true in settings, time periods, and populations different from the ones used in the study. For instance, are the findings of a study of college sophomores generalizable to the population of all U.S. citizens? Are the results of a study conducted 20 years ago still applicable today? To what extent might findings from a program evaluation in one state be generalizable to the same type of program in a different state? To what degree are supervisory techniques that seem to work well in a study of paid employees equally effective for volunteers? With what confidence can findings of a report on nonprofit agencies in the arts be extended to other domains, such as literacy, adult recreation, and nutrition? The names of the two key types of validity can be remembered easily because they refer to contexts that are internal and external to a study, respectively.

A major distinction can be made between *experimental* research designs and *quasi-experimental* designs. Nearly everyone has some familiarity with the setup of an experiment. A researcher assembles two groups of subjects; to ensure a valid comparison, the groups should be as similar as possible. The *experimental* group receives some treatment or stimulus, whereas the second or *control* group does not; instead, it serves as a baseline or reference point for evaluating the behavior of the first group. Before and after administration of the experimental stimulus, both groups are measured on relevant variables, particularly the dependent variable or criterion. By comparing the scores of the experimental group with those of the control group, the researcher is able to determine whether the treatment led to a difference in areas of interest (attitude, behavior, performance). This procedure is called the classical **experimental design.**

For example, suppose that a researcher wanted to examine whether inspection of automobiles reduced the rate of traffic accidents. One way to do so would be to select two random samples of drivers in a given state. The first group would be required to have their automobiles inspected within 6 months (experimental group); the second group would be left alone (control group). Data would be collected regarding the past driving records of the drivers in both groups, and, after 2 years, data would be collected again to encompass the period of the study. If in this period the rate of accidents decreased in the experimental (inspection) group relative to the rate in the control group, then the researcher would have some evidence for inferring that automobile inspections reduce traffic accidents. Conversely, if the data failed to show this pattern, the proposed causal relationship would be rejected.

Quasi-experimental designs of research have been given this appellation because they fail to incorporate one or more of the features of experimental designs. In particular, in many research designs it is difficult to control exposure to the experimental stimulus or independent variable. Consider a television information program funded by the federal government and intended to promote energy conservation. To examine the effectiveness of this program, the researcher would ideally want to study the behavior of two random samples of people: one that viewed the program and another that did not. In this situation, it would be relatively easy to determine whether the program led to energy conservation. In actuality, however, people interested in conservation will tend to watch the program, and those not interested in conservation will tend to seek other diversion—and there is little reason to assume that these two groups are random or matched in any sense. (For one thing, the groups differ dramatically in interest in energy conservation.) Thus, although the researcher may find that those who viewed the program were subsequently more likely to conserve energy than those who did not, it is not clear whether the program—or initial attitude—was responsible for the impact.

A second aspect of the classical experimental research design that is often lacking in quasi-experimental designs is repeated measurement. To evaluate whether the independent variable produces changes in the dependent variable, it is very helpful to know respondents' scores on the variables prior to a change in the independent variable. Then one can determine whether this change is accompanied by a change in the dependent variable. In the experiment, this function is served by measurement before and after the experimental treatment, which is intended to affect or change the level of the independent variable in the experimental group (for instance, auto inspections are intended to increase the safety of automobiles).

Unfortunately, repeated measurements are not always available or feasible. For example, a researcher may be interested in the determinants of the effectiveness of an agency, but data on effectiveness may not have been collected until very recently, or relevant data from the past may not be comparable to current information. Or a researcher may be interested in the determinants of public opinion toward a nonprofit agency, but funding may limit the study to a single survey of respondents, so that repeated measurement is not possible. In both situations, the researcher is likely to obtain only one set of data for one point in time. Although it may be possible with such data to observe covariations between variables (such as between the funding of agency divisions and their performance), establishing time order between variables is necessarily problematic.

In the following sections, we discuss experimental and quasi-experimental designs of research in greater detail. Our primary objective is to assess the internal and external validity of these two major families of design. Within the category of the quasi-experiment, some texts further distinguish designs, such as "descriptive" and "pre-experimental" designs. If that distinction is important in your work, consult an advanced text in research methods.

Experimental Designs of Research

Internal Validity

Experimental research designs offer the strongest model of proof of causality. The basic components of the classical experimental design can be summarized briefly.

Step 1: Assign subjects to two or more groups, with at least one "experimental" and one "control," so that the groups are as comparable as possible. The best way to assemble comparable groups is through random assignment of subjects to groups. *Random* means that there is no bias in the assignment so that within the limits of statistical probability, the groups should not differ.

Step 2: Measure all subjects on relevant variables. Although a preexperiment measurement or pretest is usually administered, some experimental designs do not require a pretest. We present some of these designs below.

Step 3: Expose the experimental group(s) to a treatment or stimulus, the independent variable. Ensure that the other control group(s) is not exposed. Exposure to the treatment should constitute the only difference between the groups.

Step 4: Measure the groups again on the requisite variables in a postexperiment measurement, or posttest.

Step 5: Compare the measurements of the groups. If the independent variable does lead to changes in the dependent variable, this result should be evident in pretest-posttest comparisons between the experimental and control groups. Or, if the groups are large and known to be equivalent through random assignment, the analyst can simply compare posttest scores between the two groups. If the causal inference is valid, these comparisons should bear out predicted differences between the experimental and control groups.

The classical experimental design is outlined in Table 3.2. In the table, O stands for observation or measurement, X for administration of the experimental treatment, R for random assignment, c for control group, e for experimental group, time subscript 1 for pretest, and time subscript 2 for posttest.

Intuitively, we know that the strength of experimental research designs with respect to internal validity arises from the fact that when these experiments are conducted properly, the experimental and control groups are identical except for a single factor—exposure to the experimental treatment. Thus, if at the conclusion of the experiment, the former group is significantly different than the latter with respect to the dependent variable, the cause *must* be the treatment or the independent variable. After all, this factor was the only one that distinguished the two groups.

The strength of the experimental design in internal validity can be shown more formally in connection with the elements of causality discussed before. First, consider the criterion of time order. Because the researcher controls administration of the experimental stimulus and measurements are obtained prior to and after its introduction, the time order of variables is clear. Through exposure to the stimulus, the level of the independent variable is first altered (for subjects in the experimental group) and then, through pretest-posttest comparison, any resulting changes in the dependent variable are readily observed.

Second, consider the criterion of covariation. If the independent variable is the cause of the dependent variable, then subjects exposed to higher levels of the former should manifest greater change in the latter. Operationally, this means that the experimental group should show greater change in the dependent variable than does the control group—or, equivalently, that exposure to the experimental treatment *covaries* with change in the dependent variable. The analyst can establish covariation by comparing pretest and posttest scores (if both are available) or by comparing the posttest scores alone.

Table 3.2

Classical Experimental Design

Group	Random Assignment	Observation 1	Treatment	Observation 2	Comparison
Experimental	R_e	O_{e1}	X	O_{e2}	$O_{e2} - O_{e1}$
Control	R_c	O_{c1}		O_{c2}	$O_{c2} - O_{c1}$

Third, consider the criterion of nonspuriousness. As noted earlier, if the experimental and control groups are identical, with the exception of exposure to the treatment, then observed differences between the groups with respect to changes in the dependent variable can reliably be attributed to the independent variable rather than to other potential causes.

You may ask why the control group should manifest *any* changes in the dependent variable since these subjects are denied exposure to the experimental treatment. It is in this area especially that the advantages of the control group become apparent. With the passage of time, subjects in both the experimental and control groups may show changes in the dependent variable for reasons quite unrelated to the independent variable. For example, subjects may develop biologically and emotionally; they may react to the fact that they are being observed or measured; they may learn of dramatic events that transpire outside the experimental setting that may affect their scores on the dependent variable. The general name for developments such as these that could potentially jeopardize the causal inference is *threats to internal validity.* The three threats just delineated refer to the threats of "maturation," "reactivity," and "history," respectively. (This listing is illustrative; refer to research design texts for a more complete inventory.)

The impact of these threats may be felt in any experiment, but assuming that the experimental and control groups are equated to begin with (through a procedure such as random assignment of subjects to groups), there is no reason to suspect that the threats should affect the groups differently. Hence, when the measurements of the two groups are compared, these effects should *cancel* one another. However, if the independent variable is a cause of the dependent variable, the effect of the treatment should be manifested in an *additional* increment of change in the dependent variable—but only in the experimental group. Thus, although both groups may exhibit change, the experimental group should demonstrate greater change. In this manner, the control group serves as an essential baseline for interpreting and evaluating change in the experimental group.

Care must be taken in assembling experimental and control groups that are as comparable as possible. In particular, assigning subjects to the experimental or control groups arbitrarily, or segregating them according to scores on a criterion (low achievers versus high achievers, regular voters versus occasional voters), or allowing them to volunteer for either group creates obvious *selection biases* that result in a priori differences between the groups. Consequently, if the experiment reveals a difference on the dependent variable between the experimental group and the control group, the researcher cannot rule out the possibility that it was the initial differences between the groups—rather than the experimental stimulus (independent variable)—that led to this result. Because the causal inference is thereby weakened, these selection procedures must be avoided.

The technique of choice in constructing equivalent experimental and control groups is **random assignment** of subjects to those groups. Random assignment removes *any* systematic difference between the groups. Randomization is an extremely powerful technique, for it controls for factors both known *and* unknown to the researcher. For good reason, then, random assignment is the foremost method for equating experimental and control groups.

Random assignment does not mean haphazard or arbitrary assignment. It has a precise statistical meaning: Each subject or case has an equal chance of being assigned to the experimental group or to the control group. As a result, the groups will have very similar (if not equivalent) composition and characteristics, within the limits of statistical probability. It is this quality that leads to the comparability of the experimental and control groups. If you ever need to draw a random sample for research or other purposes, consult a table of random numbers (contained in the appendices of most statistics texts) or an expert in the field of sampling.

The final criterion of causality is theory. Unfortunately, no research design—and no statistical technique—can establish a causal relationship as substantively meaningful, credible, or important. This evaluation must be made on other grounds, such as logic, experience, and previous research. The criterion of theory reinforces the adage that statistics are no substitute for substantive knowledge of a field.

External Validity

The preceding discussion supports the conclusion that experimental designs of research are relatively strong with respect to internal validity—the causal inference based on the experimental setting and the selected sample of subjects. However, they are not as strong with respect to external validity—the ability to generalize the results of a study to other settings, other times, and other populations. Primarily two factors limit the external validity of experimental designs.

The first is the **context** of these designs. To isolate subjects from extraneous variables, experimenters frequently place them in a laboratory setting. Although the laboratory works admirably in sealing off subjects from possibly confounding factors, it also removes them from a real-life setting, to which the researcher usually seeks to generalize results. Thus, one can question how closely the situation simulated in the laboratory resembles the processes of everyday life. For example, as part of the experimental treatment, the researcher may systematically expose subjects to new ideas, problems, information, or people. However, in the normal course of events, people exercise a great deal more personal choice and control regarding their exposure to and handling of these influences. Consequently, the results obtained in the experiment may hold under the experimental conditions, but their application to less artificial (more realistic) situations may be problematic.

Closely related to this type of difficulty is the argument that because premeasurement (pretesting) may sensitize subjects to the experimental treatment, results may apply only to pretested populations. This problem, however, is more tractable than the first. If the experimental and control groups have been randomly assigned, then the researcher can eliminate the pretest procedure altogether since random assignment should remove any initial differences between the groups; a posttest is then sufficient to assess the effect of the experimental treatment. This research design is called the *posttest only-control group design.* Or, if time and resources allow, an additional set of experimental and control groups that are *not* pretested can be incorporated into the classical experimental design. With this addition, it is possible to determine not only whether the experimental stimulus has an effect on nonpretested samples but also the magnitude of any reactive effects of premeasurement. This design is known as the

Table 3.3

Posttest Only–Control Group Design

Group	Randomization	Treatment	Observation 1
Experimental	R_e	X	O_{e1}
Control	R_c		O_{c1}

Table 3.4

Solomon Four-Group Design

Group	Randomization	Observation 1	Treatment	Observation 2
Experimental	R_{ep}	O_{ep1}	X	O_{ep2}
Control	R_{cp}	O_{cp1}		O_{cp2}
Experimental	R_e		X	O_{e2}
Control	R_c			O_{c2}

Solomon four-group design. Letting O stand for observation or measurement, X for administration of the experimental treatment, R for random assignment of subjects to groups, c for control group, e for experimental group, and p for pretest, these two experimental designs can be outlined as shown in Tables 3.3 and 3.4.

The second factor that threatens the external validity of experimental designs of research is the sample of subjects on which findings are based. Because of ethical and financial considerations, experiments conducted on a random sample of individuals drawn from a well-defined population (such as U.S. citizens) have been rare. Institutional review boards (IRBs) are in place at most universities and research centers to evaluate ethical issues in research. They weigh the advantages and disadvantages of research carefully and probe the use of deception, which may be employed in order to make an experimental setting seem more realistic to participants. Sometimes the potential knowledge to be gained by the experiment is judged so vital that these objections are put aside (as with medical research on life-threatening diseases). In addition, the cost and practical problems of conducting an experiment on a random sample of subjects can be prohibitive. As a result, experiments traditionally have been conducted on "captive" populations—prison inmates, hospital patients, and especially students. The correspondence between these groups and more heterogeneous, "natural" populations is necessarily problematic, thus threatening the external validity of many experiments.

It is important to note, however, that this situation is beginning to change. As social science researchers have grown more familiar with the use and advantages of experimental designs, they have become attuned to naturally occurring experiments— such as changing traffic laws and their enforcement, implementing new government programs, turning over a part of nonprofit agency operations to volunteers, contracting with a fund-raising firm to increase donations to an agency, and so on. With adequate foreknowledge of such developments, the severity of threats to the external validity of experimental designs posed by problems of sampling and context can be attenuated significantly. In the future, social science researchers will probably become increasingly adept at warding off threats to the external validity of experiments.

Quasi-Experimental Designs of Research

Internal Validity

The most fundamental difference between quasi-experimental research designs and experimental designs centers on the ability of the researcher to control exposure to the experimental treatment or independent variable. This control is much greater in experimental designs than in quasi-experimental designs. This section discusses the internal validity of several of the most common quasi-experimental designs.

Perhaps the most widely used quasi-experimental design is the **cross-sectional study** (sometimes called a *correlational study*). This type of study is based on data obtained at one point in time, often from a large sample of subjects. Most surveys of public opinion or attitudes toward government or nonprofit agencies are cross-sectional studies. A **case study** is an in-depth examination of an event or locale, usually undertaken after something dramatic has transpired (such as the *Challenger* explosion or the Chernobyl nuclear accident). Although a case study may rest (at least partially) on data obtained from a random sample of respondents, more often the researcher relies on information from carefully selected individuals (informants) and archival records. A **panel study** is a series of cross-sectional studies based on the same sample of individuals over time; that is, a group of individuals is surveyed repeatedly over time. An examination of the effects of college that followed incoming students until their graduation would be a panel study. Finally, **trend studies** monitor and attempt to account for over-time shifts in various indicators, such as gross national product, unemployment, attitude toward the president, number of nonprofit organizations registered with the Internal Revenue Service (IRS), and so on. Examples are plentiful; regularly published reports chart the course of myriad economic measures (consumer price index, inflation rate), as well as indicators of public opinion (Harris poll, Gallup poll).

These quasi-experimental research designs can be evaluated with respect to three of the four criteria for establishing a relationship as causal (internal validity): covariation, time order, and nonspuriousness. The remaining criterion is theory. As discussed before, the substantive plausibility of a causal relationship stands apart from considerations of research design or statistical techniques. Examples of these four quasi-experimental designs are diagrammed in Table 3.5. In the table, X represents the independent variable, O stands for observation or measurement, and the subscripts 1, 2, 3, . . . refer to time points at which relevant variables are measured.

Quasi-experimental designs are relatively strong in demonstrating covariation between independent and dependent variables. Many statistics have been developed for assessing the magnitude of covariation or association between two variables

Table 3.5

Some Common Quasi-Experimental Designs of Research

Design	Design Diagram						
Cross-sectional study	X	O					
Case study	X	O					
Panel study	O_1	X	O_2				
Trend study	O_1	O_2	O_3	X	O_4	O_5	O_6

(see Chapters 15 through 21). As long as the independent and dependent variables are measured across a sample of subjects, the researcher can use statistics to assess the degree of covariation.

An exception to this general conclusion should be noted. Because most case studies are based on a single unit of analysis (the case), establishing covariation may be problematic. For example, in a given case study, both the independent and the dependent variables may assume high values, thus tempting the researcher to conclude that one is the cause of the other. However, because other cases in which the independent variable takes on different values are *not* examined, it is not possible to observe how the dependent variable changes with changes in the independent variable—the essence of the concept of covariation. This situation resembles an experiment in which a control group is mistakenly omitted: Without the control group, it is very difficult to evaluate the effect of the experimental treatment on the dependent variable.

In quasi-experimental designs that employ repeated measurements over time—called *longitudinal studies*—the time order of the independent and dependent variables is relatively clear. Thus, in panel studies, the criterion of time order for demonstrating causality is usually substantiated since changes can be tracked over time. In-depth studies that seek to reconstruct the chronology of important events may also be able to establish time order.

This conclusion does *not* hold for static or single-point-in-time studies, however. In cross-sectional studies especially, because of the lack of over-time data, except in the most obvious cases (relationships between ascribed characteristics such as sex or race and various attitudes and behaviors), the time order of a relationship may be a matter of faith or assumption (such as relationships between attitudes or between attitudes and behaviors). As a consequence, in many static (that is, cross-sectional) studies the causal inference is weakened. For example, if all variables are measured just once, it is unclear whether employee work motivation leads to self-confidence or vice versa, or whether either variable is the cause or the result of employee productivity.

The major threat to the internal validity of quasi-experimental designs is non-spuriousness. This criterion requires that the relationship between the independent variable and the dependent variable hold in the presence of all third variables. In experimental designs, control over exposure to the experimental treatment, random assignment of subjects to experimental and control groups, and isolation of subjects from extraneous influences enhance significantly the ability of the researcher to satisfy this condition. In quasi-experimental designs, circumstances are not as fortuitous. Exposure to the independent variable is beyond the control of the investigator; there is no reason to assume that those exposed are otherwise identical to those not exposed; and in the real world, confounding factors abound.

For example, a researcher interested in the determinants of efficiency in public organizations may conduct a survey of state agencies. The results of the survey may show that efficiency covaries with agency size, measured according to personnel and budget. Might this relationship be causal? The answer is complicated. Many other variables covary with efficiency and may be responsible for the observed relationship. The type of technology used in an agency will affect both its efficiency and its size. Similarly, the training of agency employees will affect how efficiently the agency operates and the amount of personnel and budget needed. The structure of the agency may influence the degree of efficiency attained, as well as the level of personnel and budget. In order to determine whether the relationship between agency size and efficiency is nonspurious, the researcher would have to show that even after the effects of third variables such as agency technology, employee training, and organization structure have been taken into account, this relationship persists in the survey data. Chapter 17 presents an extensive discussion of nonspuriousness and appropriate statistical procedures.

To test for nonspuriousness in a quasi-experimental design, researchers attempt to compensate statistically for their lack of control over the actual situation. They employ *statistical control techniques* that assess the magnitude of relationship between the independent and dependent variables, taking into account (controlling for) the effects of plausible third variables (see Chapters 17 and 21). Unfortunately, these techniques are complex. Also, it is not possible *logically* to eliminate all third variables as the putative cause of an observed relationship. Moreover, to control statistically for their effects, the researcher must hypothesize in advance the likely third variables and collect data on them. This task is difficult, time-consuming, and expensive—but essential nonetheless. Because statistical control techniques require data from several cases or subjects, case studies are especially vulnerable with respect to the nonspuriousness criterion of causality.

External Validity

Although quasi-experimental designs of research must overcome serious challenges to internal validity, they tend to be relatively strong with respect to external validity. Two major reasons account for this fact. First, it is easier to obtain representative samples of the population for quasi-experimental designs. Consequently, in these designs more confidence can be placed in inferring findings from sample to population.

Second, in general, quasi-experimental designs are conducted in more natural (less artificial) settings than are experimental designs. Experiments often place subjects in a contrived environment controlled and monitored by the researcher. In contrast, in quasi-experimental designs, subjects may not realize that they are the focus of study (as in the use of highly aggregated statistics pertaining to the economy, traffic fatalities, and so on), or relevant information may be ascertained from them in comfortable and familiar surroundings (as in surveys of public attitudes and behaviors administered in the home or office). Whereas few would contend that these settings are totally free of bias, there is consensus that they are less reactive than most experimental designs—subjects are less likely to react to the context of the study itself. Hence, the results obtained are more likely to hold outside the study in other settings, thereby increasing external validity.

Again, exceptions must be appended to these conclusions. Because in panel studies the same respondents are interviewed repeatedly over time, they may grow sensitized to the fact that they are under study and thus become less typical of the population they were originally chosen to represent. This problem may be alleviated by limiting participation in the panel to a short period of time. Case studies are less tractable with respect to external validity. The case is usually selected precisely because there is something distinctive, atypical, or particularly interesting about it. As a consequence, it is difficult to judge the extent to which the results of a case study have relevance for other cases. Case study researchers should devote serious attention to considering the population of cases to which they may legitimately generalize their results. Unfortunately, researchers and readers alike often are so captivated by the details of an arresting case that they fail to ask the important question: What can be learned from this case to apply to other cases?

Research Designs and Validity

In the discussion of research design, two general points stand out. First, there is a trade-off between internal validity and external validity. In a given design, it is very difficult to increase one type of validity without decreasing the other. In experimental designs, although the control exercised by the researcher enhances internal validity, it jeopardizes external validity. In quasi-experimental designs, more natural settings and representative samples contribute to external validity, but these same factors make it more difficult to establish internal validity. In a given study, the researcher should work to achieve an acceptable balance between the two types of validity.

Some research procedures can enhance both internal validity and external validity simultaneously. For example, larger samples increase both internal validity and external validity. Replication increases internal and external validity. Mixed designs combining elements of experimental and quasi-experimental designs can also assist. So the researcher can take steps, but they are expensive and require additional care and effort.

Second, drawing reliable causal inferences is a serious, painstaking, and difficult enterprise. For example, after decades of research and thousands of studies on job attitudes and performance, experts continue to disagree over the causes and effects. This instance is not an isolated one; in many other fields in the social sciences, the causes of important phenomena remain elusive. By contrast, in everyday life one hears a great deal of loose talk regarding the cause or causes of an event or a phenomenon. Most of it is just that—talk. Nevertheless, critical decisions are often made on this basis. Remember that the same criteria used to establish a relationship as causal in research apply as well *outside* this environment. Unless these criteria are reasonably satisfied, one can—and should—question the causal inference.

Chapter Summary

Research designs involve setting up a research project so that research questions can be answered as unambiguously as possible. The objective of a good research design is to establish causal relationships and to assess their generalizability.

The basic building block in constructing causal explanations is the concept, which pinpoints an idea or element thought to be essential in accounting for the class of events under study. Concepts are defined in two ways: with a nominal definition, which is the standard dictionary definition, and with an operational definition, which translates the nominal definition into a form in which the concept can be measured empirically. Once concepts have been operationalized and measured in a sample of data, they are called variables. The two major types of variables are independent (anticipated causes) and dependent (the variables thought to be affected by them). A hypothesis formally proposes an expected relationship between an independent and dependent variable.

Social scientists have identified four criteria as necessary for establishing a relationship as causal: time order, covariation, nonspuriousness, and theory. A research design is a program for evaluating empirically proposed causal relationships. The evaluation is based on two criteria: internal validity (did the independent variable lead to changes in the dependent variable?) and external validity (can the results obtained in the study be generalized to other populations, times, and settings?). Two major families of research design were outlined: experimental designs and quasi-experimental designs. Both types were evaluated with regard to the four criteria for causal relationships that define internal validity and with regard to external validity. Briefly, the experimental design has its primary strengths in internal validity, and the quasi-experimental design has its strengths in external validity.

Problems

3.1 A researcher asserts that the relationship between *attitude toward the field of public administration* and *taking courses in a public administration degree program* is causal.

 (a) What evidence must the researcher provide about this relationship to prove that it is causal?

 (b) Given your answer, what aspects of the researcher's argument are likely to be strongest, and what aspects of her argument are likely to be weakest? Your discussion should include clear definitions of each element of a causal relationship.

3.2 Develop a model that includes at least four concepts. Elaborate any theoretical or literature support underlying it. Present the model in an arrow diagram that shows schematically the relationships the model proposes. Provide operational definitions for all concepts, and state hypotheses derived from the model.

(a) Which types of research design would be best suited to testing the model?

(b) Which types of research design would be least suited to testing the model?

3.3 Professor George A. Bulldogski has taught social graces to athletic teams at a major southeastern university for the past 15 years. Based on this experience, he insists that table manners are causally related to leadership. Professor Bulldogski has data showing that athletes who have better table manners also demonstrate greater leadership in athletic competition. The university gymnastics coach, who wants to build leadership on her team, is considering asking Professor Bulldogski to meet regularly with her team. She hopes that by having him teach table manners to team members, they will become better leaders. Should she invite Professor Bulldogski to meet with the gymnastics team? If she does so, can she expect his involvement to develop greater leadership on the team? Explain your answers.

3.4 For the entire month of January 2004, the local domestic violence shelter ran a series of ads on the government access cable television channel. The director of the shelter hypothesized that the ads would bring more attention to the problem of domestic violence and make victims of domestic violence more aware of the shelter's programs. The director has monthly data on the number of new clients. At the end of April 2004, the director asks you to come up with a research design to help assess whether the ads had an effect on the number of clients served.

(a) What type of research design would you use to test the hypothesis?

(b) The director has monthly figures for the number of clients served in 2003. Are these data relevant for testing the above hypothesis? If so, why?

3.5 The head of the Teen Intervention Center believes that troubled youth are not getting the message if they complete the center's 5-week education program but still have subsequent encounters with law enforcement. When they first come to the center, teens are broken up into groups of 15 to meet with a counselor and answer questions about what society defines as acceptable versus unacceptable behaviors.

(a) If you were the head of counseling at the center, what knowledge might you gain by asking each group of teens similar questions at the end of the 5-week program?

(b) Is there any reason to expect different responses from the initial question and the one at the end of the program? Explain.

(c) What type of research design would you be using if you administered a questionnaire to the same group of individuals at the outset of treatment, the end of treatment, and 6 months after treatment?

PART II

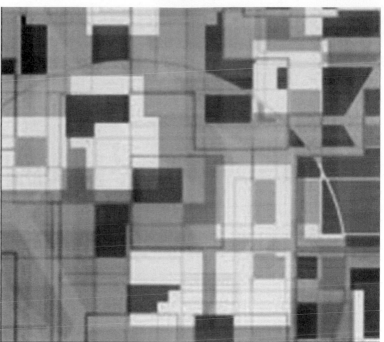

Descriptive Statistics

CHAPTER 4

Frequency Distributions

Descriptive statistics is nothing more than a fancy term for numbers that summarize a group of data. These data may be the number of arrests each police officer makes, the amount of garbage collected by city work crews, the number of fund-raising events held by a nonprofit organization in a year, the number of volunteers assisting a government agency, the number of high school students participating in community service projects, or the size of various government agencies. In their unsummarized or nontabulated form, data (affectionately known as "raw data") are difficult to comprehend. For example, the list below gives the number of tons of trash collected by the Normal, Oklahoma, sanitary engineer teams for the week of June 8, 2004. Each entry is the number of tons of trash collected by a team during the week.

57	70	62	66	68	62	76	71	79	87
82	63	71	51	65	78	61	78	55	64
83	75	50	70	61	69	80	51	52	94
89	63	82	75	58	68	84	83	71	79
77	89	59	88	97	86	75	95	64	65
53	74	75	61	86	65	95	77	73	86
81	66	73	51	75	64	67	54	54	78
57	81	65	72	59	72	84	85	79	67
62	76	52	92	66	74	72	83	56	93
96	64	95	94	86	75	73	72	85	94

Table 4.1

Arrests per Police Officer: Morgan City, March 2004

Number of Arrests	Number of Police Officers
1–5	6
6–10	17
11–15	47
16–20	132
21–25	35
25+	7
	244

Clearly, presenting these data in their raw form would tell the administrator little or nothing about trash collection in Normal. For example, how many tons of trash do most teams collect? Do the teams seem to collect about the same amount, or does their performance vary?

The most basic restructuring of raw data to facilitate understanding is the **frequency distribution.** A frequency distribution is a table that pairs data values—or ranges of data values—with their frequency of occurrence. For example, Table 4.1 is a frequency distribution of the number of arrests each Morgan City police officer made in March 2004. Note that the entire table is labeled, as is each column. Here, the data values are the number of arrests, and the frequencies are the number of police officers. This procedure makes it easy to see that most Morgan City police officers made between 16 and 20 arrests in March 2004.

Some definitions are in order. A **variable** is the trait or characteristic on which the classification is based; in the preceding example, the variable is the number of arrests per police officer. A **class** is one of the grouped categories of the variable. The first class, for example, is from 1 to 5 arrests. Classes have **class boundaries** (the lowest and highest values that fall within the class) and **class midpoints** (the point halfway between the upper and lower class boundaries). The class midpoint of the third class, for example, is 13—which is 11, the lower class boundary, plus 15, the upper class boundary, divided by 2, or $(11 + 15) \div 2$. The **class interval** is the distance between the upper limit of one class and the upper limit of the next higher class. In our example, the class interval is 5. The **class frequency** is the number of observations or occurrences of the variable within a given class; for example, the class frequency of the fourth class (16–20) is 132. The **total frequency** is the total number of observations or cases in the table—in this case, 244. In the remainder of this chapter, we will discuss some important characteristics of frequency distributions and the procedures for constructing them.

Constructing a Frequency Distribution

Constructing a frequency distribution is a relatively simple task. To illustrate this process, we will use the Normal, Oklahoma, garbage collection data listed previously.

Step 1: Scan the data to find the lowest and highest values. The lowest value in these data is 50 (column 3, the third value), and the highest value is 97 (column 5, the fifth value).

Step 2: Make a list of the values from the lowest to the highest and then mark as follows: the number of times each value appears. This process is illustrated below:

50 /	60	70 //	80 /	90
51 ///	61 ///	71 ///	81 //	91
52 //	62 ///	72 ////	82 //	92 /
53 /	63 //	73 ///	83 ///	93 /
54 //	64 ////	74 //	84 //	94 ///
55 /	65 ////	75 ##/	85 //	95 ///
56 /	66 ///	76 //	86 ////	96 /
57 //	67 //	77 //	87 /	97 /
58 /	68 //	78 ///	88 /	98
59 //	69 /	79 ///	89 //	

Step 3: The tabulations in Step 2 could actually be called a frequency distribution, because each data value (tons of trash) is paired with its frequency of occurrence. For a better visual presentation, however, the data should be grouped into classes. The rule of thumb is to collapse data into no fewer than 4 or no more than 20 classes. Fewer than 4 classes obscures the variation in the data; more than 20 presents too complex a picture to grasp quickly. The analyst chooses the actual number of classes in a table so that the table reflects the data as closely as possible. Other tips for constructing frequency distribution classes are as follows:

1. Avoid classes so narrow that some intervals have zero observations.

2. Make all the class intervals equal unless the top or bottom class is open-ended. An open-ended class has only one boundary. In the Morgan City arrest table, for example, the last category (25+) is an open-ended category.

3. Use open-ended intervals only when closed intervals would result in class frequencies of zero. This usually happens when some values are extremely high or extremely low.

4. Try to construct the intervals so that the midpoints are whole numbers.

For the present example, let us collapse the data into five categories. Constructing the remainder of the table results in the frequency distribution shown in Table 4.2.

Note in the table that the upper limit of every class is also the lower limit of the next class; that is, the upper limit of the first class is 60, the same value as the lower limit of the second class. This format is typically used when the data are continuous.

Table 4.2

Tons of Garbage Collected by Sanitary Engineer Teams in Normal, Oklahoma, Week of June 8, 2004

Tons of Garbage	Number of Crews
50–60	16
60–70	24
70–80	30
80–90	20
90–100	10
	100

A **continuous variable** can take on values that are not whole numbers (the whole numbers are 1, 2, 3, . . .); some examples are temperature, miles per gallon, and time spent at work. In the situation given in Table 4.2, statisticians interpret the first interval as running from 50 tons up to but not including 60 tons (that is, 59.999 tons). In this way, no data value can fall into more than one class. When you see tables like this one, in which interval limits appear to overlap, remember that the upper limit means up to but not including the value, and that the lower limit begins with this value. Tables 4.3 and 4.4 are constructed in the same manner.

The Percentage Distribution

Suppose the Normal city manager wants to know whether Normal sanitary engineer crews are picking up more garbage than the city crews in Moore. The city manager may want to know because Moore crews only collect garbage that residents place curbside in front of their houses, whereas Normal crews collect trash cans located in

Table 4.3

Tons of Garbage Collected by Sanitary Engineer Teams, Week of June 8, 2004

Tons of Garbage	Numbers of Crews	
	Normal	Moore
50–60	16	22
60–70	24	37
70–80	30	49
80–90	20	36
90–100	10	21
	100	165

Table 4.4

Tons of Garbage Collected by Sanitary Engineer Teams, Week of June 8, 2004

	Percentage of Work Crews	
Tons of Garbage	Normal	Moore
50–60	16	13
60–70	24	22
70–80	30	30
80–90	20	22
90–100	10	13
	100	100
	N = 100	**N** = 165

residents' yards. The city manager's goal is to collect more garbage, while holding down garbage collection costs.

Table 4.3 shows the frequency distributions of garbage collection in both cities. But from the frequency distributions, the city manager cannot tell which method of trash collection is more efficient. Because Moore has a larger workforce, it has a larger number of crews in all five of the classes. The data must be altered so that the two cities can be compared. The easiest way to do this is to convert both columns of data into percentage distributions. A **percentage distribution** shows the percentage of the total observations that fall into each class. To convert the data of Table 4.3 to percentage distributions, the frequency in each class should be divided by the total frequency for that city. In this instance, all Normal class frequencies should be divided by 100, and all Moore class frequencies should be divided by 165. (Chapter 15 presents a more detailed discussion of percentage distributions.) Table 4.4 shows the resulting percentage distributions. Is the Moore method of trash collection more efficient?

Table 4.4 pairs each class with the percentage of time the class occurs. Notice that some new items are included in the percentage table that were not included in the frequency table. At the bottom of each column, a number is found (**N** = 100 or **N** = 165). **N** stands for the total number of observations; it represents the total frequency (or number of observations) on which the percentages are based. Given this number, you can calculate the original class frequencies. Try it. You should get the frequency distributions shown in Table 4.3.

Cumulative Frequency Distributions

Frequency distributions and percentage distributions show the number or percentage of observations that fall in each class of a variable. Sometimes the administrator needs to know how many observations (or what percentage of observations) fall below or

Table 4.5

Response Times of the Metro Fire Department, 2004

Response Time (Minutes)	Number of Calls	Running Total	Cumulative Percentage
0–1	7		
1–2	14		
2–3	32		
3–4	37		
4–5	48		
5–6	53		
6–7	66		
7–8	73		
8–9	42		
9–10	40		
10–11	36		
11–12	23		
12–13	14		
13–14	7		
14–15	2		
15–20	6		
	500		

above a certain standard. For example, the fire chief of Metro, Texas, is quite concerned about how long it takes his fire crews to arrive at the scene of a fire. The *Metro Morning News* has run several stories about fires in which it claimed the Metro fire department was slow in responding. Since the Metro fire department automatically records the time of fire calls on computer tape and also records the dispatched fire truck's report that it has arrived at the fire, the response times to all fires can be found. An analyst has made a frequency distribution of these response times (Table 4.5). The Metro fire chief considers 5 minutes to be an excellent response time, 10 minutes to be an acceptable response time, 15 minutes to be an unsatisfactory response time, and 20 minutes to be unacceptable. As a result, the fire chief wants to know the percentage of fire calls answered in under 5 minutes, under 10 minutes, under 15 minutes, and under 20 minutes. To provide the fire chief with the information he wants, the analyst must construct a cumulative percentage distribution.

The first step in developing a **cumulative percentage distribution** is to prepare a running total of responses to fire calls. To the right of the "Number of Calls" column, you will find a blank column labeled "Running Total." In this column, we will calculate the total number of responses made that were less than each interval's upper limit. For example, how many fires were responded to in less than 1 minute? From the table, we can see seven fires had response times of under a minute. Enter the number 7 for the first class in the running total column. How many fire responses were under

Table 4.6

Response Times of Metro Fire Department, 2004

Response Time	Percentage (Cumulative) of Response Times
Under 5 minutes	27.6
Under 10 minutes	82.4
Under 15 minutes	98.8
Under 20 minutes	100.00

$$N = 500$$

2 minutes? There were 21: 7 under 1 minute, plus 14 between 1 and 2 minutes. Enter 21 as the value for the second class. Using this logic, fill in the rest of the values.

The second step is to construct a cumulative percentage column. This step is performed by dividing each frequency in the "Running Total" column by the total frequency (in this case, 500). In the fourth column of the table, "Cumulative Percentage," enter the following numbers. The first entry should be 1.4 (7 ÷ 500); the second entry should be 4.2 (21 ÷ 500); the third entry should be 10.6 (53 ÷ 500). Fill in the remaining values for this column.

You now have a **cumulative frequency distribution** (and cumulative percentage distribution) for the fire chief. The distribution is a bit awkward, however, because it has so many categories. The next step would be to collapse the cumulative percentage distribution into fewer categories. Because the fire chief is concerned with response times of 5, 10, 15, and 20 minutes, these times would be the best categories. Table 4.6 should result from your calculations. From this table, what can you tell the chief about fire department response times in Metro?

Graphic Presentations

Often a public or nonprofit administrator wants to present information visually so that leaders, citizens, and staff can get a general feel for a problem without reading a table. Two methods of visual presentation will be described here: the frequency polygon and the histogram.

Let us say that the Normal city manager, as part of her budget justification, wants to show the city council the number of complaints that the city dog pound receives about barking dogs. An assistant has prepared the frequency distribution shown in Table 4.7.

To construct a **frequency polygon,** follow these steps.

Step 1: On a sheet of graph paper, write the name of the variable across the bottom and the frequency along the side. Here, the variable is the number of complaints about dogs, and the frequency is the number of weeks. Make sure that the scale for the variable encompasses all values in the distribution, so that the frequency of each value can be graphed. (See Figure 4.1.)

Table 4.7

Complaints Per Week about Barking Dogs, 2004

Number of Complaints	Number of Weeks
5–9	7
10–14	6
15–19	15
20–24	17
25–29	5
30–34	2
	52

Step 2: Calculate the midpoint for each class interval. To do so, add the two boundaries for each class and divide by 2. For the first class, the midpoint is $(5 + 9) \div 2$, or 7. The midpoints for the other classes are 12, 17, 22, 27, 32.

Step 3: On the horizontal dimension or axis of the graph, find the first class midpoint (7). From this point, move your pencil straight up until you find the value equal to the frequency for this class (also 7). Make a dot. Repeat this process for the five other classes. At this point, your graph should look like the one in Figure 4.2.

Figure 4.1

First Step in Constructing a Frequency Polygon

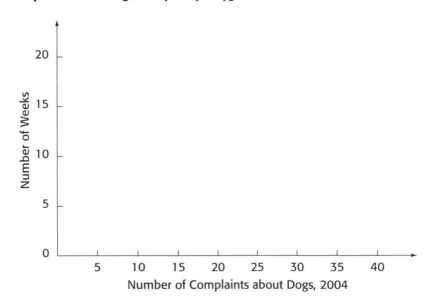

Figure 4.2

Third Step in Constructing a Frequency Polygon

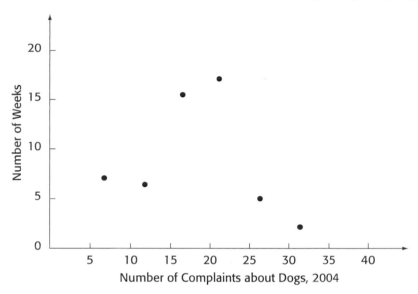

Step 4: Pretend that two more classes exist: one the class lower than the lowest class (this class would be 0–4 complaints), and one higher than the highest class (35–39). Calculate the midpoints for these make-believe classes, and plot their midpoints with a frequency of 0 on your graph. This procedure makes the graph touch the horizontal axis for both imaginary classes.

Step 5: Staring from the leftmost point, draw a line connecting the points in sequence. You have now completed your first frequency polygon. If it looks like the one in Figure 4.3, congratulations. (Note that whereas the frequency polygon presents a useful visual representation of the data, the line segments do not correspond to actual data points.)

One nice aspect of frequency polygons is that the analyst can draw more than one on the same graph. For example, suppose that the Normal city manager wants to show how complaints about barking dogs have changed over time. The city manager gives you the data shown in Table 4.8. In Figure 4.4, graph frequency polygons for both years on the same graph. What does the graph tell you about barking dog complaints in 2004 as opposed to those in 2003?

Note: Whenever two or more frequency polygons are drawn on the same set of axes, each polygon should be drawn in a different color or with a different type of line (such as solid, broken, bold) to tell them apart. Be sure to label each line. Figure 6.1 in Chapter 6 presents an example of using different types of lines on the same set of axes.

Figure 4.3

The Frequency Polygon

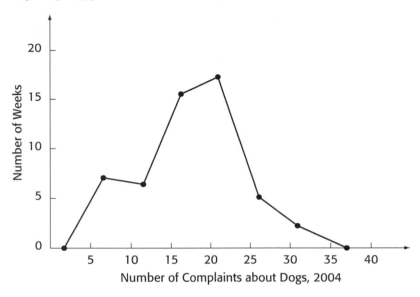

Number of Complaints about Dogs, 2004

Table 4.8

Complaints per Week about Barking Dogs, 2003 and 2004

Number of Complaints	Number of Weeks	
	2003	2004
5–9	8	7
10–14	12	6
15–19	14	15
20–24	10	17
25–29	6	5
30–34	2	2
	52	52

A **histogram** is a bar graph for a variable that takes on many values (such as income or gross national product [GNP]). The term **bar chart** is sometimes used when a variable can take on only a very limited set of values (for example, a variable assessing an opinion that calls for the responses "agree," "undecided," or "disagree"). Our intention is not to multiply terms (or confusion), but some statistical package programs loaded onto computers, such as the Statistical Package for the Social Sciences (SPSS), do make this distinction. You may need to use it on the job.

Figure 4.4

Frequency Polygons for Number of Complaints about Dogs, 2003 and 2004

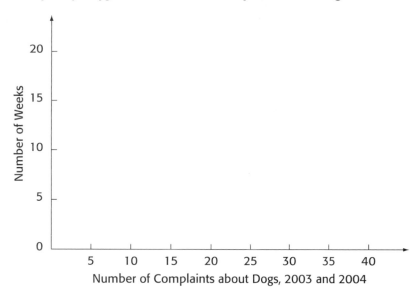

To construct a histogram of barking dog complaints in Normal for 2004, complete the following steps.

Steps 1–3: Follow the same procedures given for constructing frequency polygons in Steps 1, 2, and 3 above. Following this procedure should yield the graph shown in Figure 4.5.

Step 4: Using the points on the graph, first draw a horizontal line from the lower to the upper class boundary for each class. Then draw in the vertical lines along the class boundaries from these horizontal lines to the horizontal axis of the graph. Each class is now represented by a bar.

Step 5: Shade in the bars you have drawn in Step 4. Your graph should appear as shown in Figure 4.6.

You should use histograms rather than frequency polygons whenever you want to emphasize the distinctiveness of each class. As you can see by looking at the graphs, the frequency polygon tends to smooth out class differences. Frequency polygons should be used whenever you want to emphasize a smooth trend or when two or more graphs are placed on a single chart, table, or axes.

Cumulative frequency distributions can also be graphed. For example, the cumulative distribution for the Metro fire department response times shown in Table 4.6 can be made into a frequency polygon. For each response time in the table (under 5 minutes, under 10 minutes, and so on), simply plot the corresponding percentage, and connect the consecutive points. Your graph should look like the one in

Figure 4.5

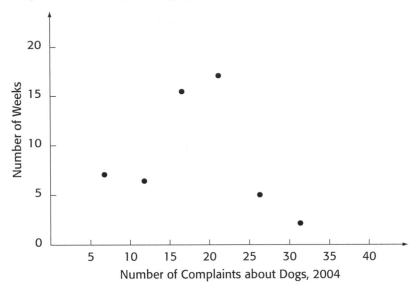

Third Step in Constructing a Histogram

Figure 4.6

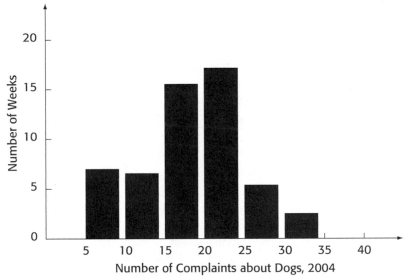

The Histogram

Figure 4.7. For comparative purposes, make a second frequency polygon in Figure 4.7 for the city of Atlantis fire department; the response times are presented in Table 4.9. Be sure to label the two lines for clarity.

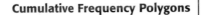

Figure 4.7

Cumulative Frequency Polygons

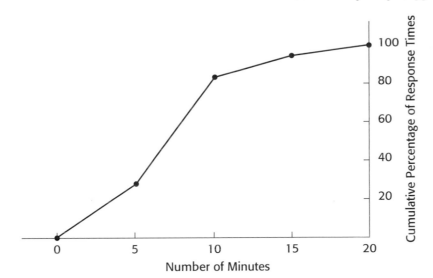

Table 4.9

Response Times of Atlantis Fire Department, 2004

Response Time	Percentage (Cumulative) of Response Times
Under 5 minutes	21.2
Under 10 minutes	63.9
Under 15 minutes	86.4
Under 20 minutes	100.0

A frequency polygon for a cumulative distribution is called an **ogive.** Compare the ogives in Figure 4.7. Which fire department appears to respond more quickly to fires? Why do you think so?

Chapter Summary

Descriptive statistics summarize a body of raw data so that the data can be more easily understood. Frequency distributions, percentage distributions, and cumulative frequency distributions are three ways to condense raw data into a table that is easier to read and interpret. A frequency distribution displays the number of times each value, or range of values, of a variable occurs. The frequency distribution shows classes appropriate for the variable under study and the number of data points falling into each class. A percentage distribution shows the percentage of total data points that fall into each class. A cumulative frequency (or percentage) distribution displays the number (or percentage) of observations that fall above or below a certain class.

To add visual appeal and to increase interpretability, graphic presentations of data are used. Graphic techniques discussed in this chapter include the frequency polygon, the histogram and bar chart, and the ogive. The frequency polygon is a plot of the frequency distribution information (class versus frequency), with the plotted points connected in sequence by line segments. The histogram is a bar graph of a frequency distribution; each class is represented by a horizontal bar, whose frequency corresponds to the height of the bar from the horizontal axis. The term *bar chart* is sometimes used in place of *histogram* when the variable can take on only a very limited set of values. An ogive is a frequency polygon for a cumulative frequency distribution.

Problems

4.1 You are the research assistant to the administrator of a small bureau in the federal government. Your boss has received some criticism that the bureau does not respond promptly to Congressional requests. The only information you have is the day the agency received the request and the day the agency mailed the response. From those figures, you have calculated the number of days the agency took to respond.

Days Necessary to Respond to Congressional Requests

9	1	6	10	8	12	9	14	15	7
19	8	21	10	50	37	9	4	28	44
9	18	8	39	7	1	4	15	7	28
47	9	6	7	24	10	41	7	9	29
6	4	12	7	9	15	39	24	9	2
20	31	18	9	33	8	6	3	7	16
20	26	9	9	16	5	3	12	36	11
8	6	28	35	8	10	11	20	3	10
16	8	12	4	6	9	10	10	9	16
4	14	11	8	5	8	11	9	7	6
11	9	7	8	10	9	11			

Do the following:

(a) Prepare the frequency distribution.

(b) Present the distribution graphically.

(c) Prepare a cumulative frequency distribution.

(d) Present the cumulative distribution graphically.

(e) Write a paragraph explaining what you have found.

4.2 Allan Wiese, the mayor of Orva, South Dakota, feels that the productivity of meter butlers has declined in the past year. Mayor Wiese's research assistant provides him with the accompanying data. Convert the frequency distributions to comparable distributions. What can you tell Mayor Wiese about the productivity of his meter butlers?

Parking Tickets Issued per Meter Butler	Number of Butlers	
	May 2003	May 2004
21–30	5	6
31–40	7	9
41–50	9	12
51–60	5	7
61–70	3	1
	29	35

4.3 Scotty Allen, the civil service director for Maxwell, New York, compiles the accompanying frequency distribution of scores on the Maxwell civil service exam. Construct a cumulative frequency distribution and a cumulative frequency polygon for Mr. Allen.

Exam Score	Number of Applicants
61–65	20
66–70	13
71–75	47
76–80	56
81–85	33
86–90	27
91–95	41
96–100	34

4.4 The incumbent governor of a large state is campaigning on the platform that he eliminated a great many large, "do-nothing" bureaucracies. As the research assistant for the challenger, you are asked to present the accompanying data (numbers are the size of bureaus eliminated under the incumbent and under his predecessor) graphically in the most favorable manner for the challenger.

Incumbent		Predecessor
6	16	15
14	5	28
7	3	48
3	7	104
24	19	37
6	21	56
3	12	15
1	4	6
2	3	3
21	6	27
41	1	39

4.5   Refer to Problem 4.4. Construct a frequency distribution, and present it to reflect favorably on the incumbent.

4.6   The city clerk has received numerous complaints over the past year that couples applying for a marriage license have to wait too long to receive one. Although the clerk is skeptical (couples applying for a license are usually young and impatient), she pulls a representative sample of marriage licenses issued in the past year. Because a machine stamps each license application with the time the application is received and the time it is issued, she can tell how long the young (and old) lovers had to wait for the marriage license. The clerk considers service received in less than 10 minutes good and service received in less than 15 minutes acceptable. Her tabulation of the license data shows the following:

Minutes Waited for Marriage License	Number of Couples
Less than 5	28
5–9	36
10–14	60
15–19	82
20–24	44
25–29	39

Prepare the percentage distribution for the marriage license data and the appropriate graphical displays. Write a short memorandum explaining the results and addressing the issue of whether couples have to wait too long for marriage licenses.

4.7   The city clerk from Problem 4.6 is intrigued by the findings of her survey of marriage licenses issued in the past year (data analysis often has this effect). Accordingly, she decides to pull another representative sample of marriage licenses, this time from 2 years ago. She is interested in determining whether service to the public from her unit has improved or declined over the past 2 years. As before, the clerk considers service received in less than 10 minutes good and service received in less than 15 minutes acceptable. Her tabulation of the sample of marriage licenses issued 2 years ago shows the following:

Minutes Waited for Marriage License	Number of Couples
Less than 5	112
5–9	87
10–14	31
15–19	27
20–24	29
25–29	3

Prepare the percentage distribution for the marriage license data and the appropriate graphical displays. Write a short memorandum explaining the results and addressing the question whether service to the public from her unit has improved or declined over the past 2 years.

4.8 Because of cutbacks in agency funding, the United Way of Megopolis has had to forego routine maintenance of its computer terminals for the past 5 years. (The equipment is made by the Indestructible Computer Company.) The head of the agency is concerned that the agency will face a major equipment crisis this year, because the recommended maintenance schedule for the terminals is once every 3 years. Over the past 5 years, the agency has been able to purchase new terminals. In an effort to obtain more funding from the state legislature, the agency chief compiles the following data. The data show the time since the last routine maintenance of the terminal or, if the terminal was purchased in the last 2 years, the time since the terminal was purchased.

Years since Last Maintenance	Number of Terminals
1 or less	103
2	187
3	97
4	56
5	37
6	12
7 or more	5

Prepare the percentage distribution for the terminal maintenance data and the appropriate graphical displays. Write a short memorandum both explaining the results and trying to convince the state legislature to provide funding for routine maintenance of computer terminals.

4.9 Assume that you are a staff analyst to the head of the United Way of Megopolis in Problem 4.8. Write a short memorandum both explaining the results of the data tabulation in Problem 4.8 and trying to convince the agency head that the equipment "crisis" at the agency is overblown.

4.10 The local Humane Society is concerned about available space for impounded animals. The agency keeps careful count of the number of animals it shelters each day. To determine the load on the agency, its head, Anna Trueheart, selects a representative sample of days from the last 2 years and records the number of animals impounded on each day. Her data appear as follows:

65	49	84	72	43	91
57	46	77	69	90	64
85	67	52	44	95	79
48	63	55	96	75	48

88	81	93	67	58	72
51	49	96	79	73	80
65	54	86	98	42	63
92	71	79	84	59	45

Prepare the frequency and percentage distributions for the animal impoundment data and the appropriate graphical displays for Ms. Trueheart. Write a short memorandum explaining both the results and the demands on the Humane Society to shelter animals.

4.11 The director of the state Department of Public Works wants to upgrade the department's automobile fleet; she claims that the fleet is too old. The governor appoints a staff analyst to investigate the issue. The analyst compiles data on both the age and the odometer readings (mileage) of the department's automobile fleet. Her data appear as follows:

Age (in years)	Number of Automobiles
Less than 2	16
2–4	24
4–6	41
6–8	57
8–10	64
10 or more	39

Mileage	Number of Automobiles
Less than 10,000	76
10,000–20,000	63
20,000–30,000	51
30,000–40,000	32
40,000–50,000	12
50,000 or more	7

Prepare percentage distributions for the age and mileage data and the appropriate graphical displays. Write a short memorandum to the governor both explaining the results and making a recommendation regarding whether the department's automobile fleet should be upgraded.

CHAPTER 5

Measures of Central Tendency

The most commonly used descriptive statistics are measures of central tendency. As you can guess from this title, measures of central tendency attempt to locate the middle or center point in a group of data. For example, what was the average starting salary of the students who graduated from the MPA program last year? On average over the past 5 years, how many MPA students accepted job offers from nonprofit organizations? On last week's midterm exam, what was the middle score? On the average, how many employees of the Mechanicsburg city government report job-related accidents every month? The measures of central tendency give a shorthand indication of what is going on in the data.

A **measure of central tendency** is a number or score or data value that represents the average in a group of data. Three different types of average are calculated and used most often. The first is the *mean,* which is the arithmetic average of the observations; the second is the *median,* which is the observation that falls exactly in the middle of the group; and the third is the *mode,* or the data value that occurs with greatest frequency. This chapter shows how to calculate the three measures of central tendency for both ungrouped and grouped data (data that have been assembled into a frequency distribution) and discusses the use and interpretation of these measures. It concludes with a discussion of the relationship between the measures of central tendency and the different levels of measurement—interval, ordinal, and nominal—you learned about in Chapter 2.

The Mean

The first measure of central tendency is the mean. The **mean** is the arithmetic average of a set of numbers. To calculate the mean, add all the numbers (the data points or observations), and divide this new number (the sum) by the total number of observations in the set, which we labeled **N** in Chapter 4.

To illustrate, suppose that the head of the Bureau of Records wants to know the mean length of government service of the employees in the bureau's Office of Computer Support. Table 5.1 displays the number of years that each member of the office has been employed in government.

To calculate the mean length of government service of the employees in the bureau's Office of Computer Support, add the years of service of each of the employees. You should come up with a total of 118 years. Divide this sum by the number of employees in the office (8). This procedure will give you the mean number of years of government service of the employees in the office (14.75).

The procedure for calculating the mean can be presented as a formula:

$$\mu = \frac{\sum_{i=1}^{N} X_i}{N}$$

This formula is not as formidable as it seems. The Greek letter μ on the left side of the equal sign is the statistician's symbol for the population mean; it is pronounced "mu." The mean μ is equal to the formula on the right side of the equal sign. Σ is another statistician's symbol; it means add (or sum) all the values of X (in our example, these were years of government service). The subscripts below and above the Σ indicate to sum all the X's from the first X_1, all the way through X_N, the last observation (here, the years of government service of the eighth employee). Finally, the formula says to divide the sum of all the X's by **N,** the number of items being summed.

The formula for calculating the mean of a sample or subset of data, rather than the entire population, is identical except different symbols are used to distinguish sample and population. The sample mean is denoted $\overline{X}$ ("x-bar"), and the number of observations in the sample **n.** Chapter 11 reviews these distinctions and elaborates their importance. That chapter introduces the topic of how the analyst can use a sample of data to make an inference to the larger population from which it is drawn.

Table 5.1

Years of Government Service

Employee	Years	Employee	Years
Bush	8	Jackson	9
Clinton	15	Gore	11
Reagan	23	Cheney	18
Kerry	14	Carter	20

The mean has several important characteristics:

1. Every item in a group of data is used to calculate the mean.

2. Every group of data has one and only one mean; as mathematicians would say, the mean is rigidly determined.

3. The mean may take on a value that is not realistic. For example, the average U.S. family had exactly 1.7 children, 2.2 pets, and made financial contributions to 3.4 charitable organizations.

4. An extreme value, sometimes called an **outlier,** has a disproportionate influence on the mean and thus may affect how well the mean represents the data. For example, suppose that the head of the Bureau of Records decides to shake up the Office of Computer Support by creating a new position in the office with responsibility to expedite operations. To fill the position, the head appoints a newly graduated MPA with a fine background in computers but only 1 year of prior service in government. In the space provided, calculate the mean of years of government service of the employees in the expanded Office of Computer Support.

If you performed the calculations correctly, you should get a mean length of government service of 13.22 years. (The sum of the observations is 119, divided by 9, the number of observations, yields a mean of 13.22.) This number tends to understate the years of government service of the employees in the Office of Computer Support. Why?

The Median

The second measure of central tendency is the median. The **median** is the middle observation in a set of numbers when the observations are ranked in order of magnitude. For example, the Stermerville City Council requires that all city agencies include an average salary in their budget requests. The Stermerville City Planning Office has seven employees. The director is paid $42,500; the assistant director makes $39,500. Three planning clerks are paid $22,600, $22,500, and $22,400. The secretary (who does all the work) is paid $17,500, and a receptionist is paid $16,300.

The planning director calculates the mean salary and finds that it is $26,186. Check this result (you should get a total payroll of $183,300 for seven employees). This result disturbs the director, because it makes the agency look fat and bloated. The secretary points out that the large salaries paid to the director and the assistant director are distorting the mean. The secretary then calculates the median, following these steps:

Step 1: List the salaries in order of magnitude. You may start with the largest or the smallest; you will get the same answer. The secretary prepares the following list:

Director	$42,500
Assistant Director	39,500
Clerk 1	22,600
Clerk 2	22,500
Clerk 3	22,400
Secretary	17,500
Receptionist	16,300

Step 2: Locate the middle item. With seven persons, the middle observation is easy to find; it is the fourth item, or the salary paid to clerk 2 ($22,500). For larger data sets, the rule is to take the number of observations (7, in this case) and add 1 to it (7 + 1 = 8). Divide this number by 2, and that number (8 ÷ 2 = 4) tells you that the median is the fourth observation (once data values have been put in order). Note that it makes no difference whether you use the fourth item from the top or the fourth from the bottom.

The planning director reports the median salary to the Stermerville City Council. It is lower than the mean—why? Nevertheless, the Stermerville mayor tells the planning director that, because of the local tax revolt, the planning office must fire one person. The planning office responds as all bureaucracies do by firing the receptionist. After this action, what is the median salary of the planning office? Calculate in the space provided.

After arranging the salaries in order, you may have discovered that with six observations, no middle item exists. The formula $(N + 1) ÷ 2$ seems to offer no help because $(6 + 1) ÷ 2 = 3½$. But the median is actually that, the 3½th item from the top (or bottom). Because observations cannot be split in half, we define 3½ as halfway between the third and fourth items, in this case halfway between the salaries of clerk 2 and clerk 1. Because clerk 2 makes $22,500 and clerk 1 makes $22,600, the median is $22,550 [(22,600 + 22,500) ÷ 2]. Whenever the number of items (**N**) is an even number, the median will be halfway between the middle observations. This is easy to remember if you think of the median as the measure of central tendency that divides a set of numbers so that exactly half are smaller than the median and exactly half are larger than the median.

The median has several important characteristics:

1. The median is not affected by extreme values.

2. Although every observation is used to determine the median, the actual value of every item is not used in the calculations. At most, only the two middle items are used to calculate the median.

3. If items do not cluster near the median, the median will not be a good measure of the group's central tendency.

4. The median usually does not take on an unrealistic value. The median number of children per family in the United States, for example, is 2.

5. The median is the 50th percentile in a distribution of data, because half the observations fall above it and half fall below it. (Percentiles are measures of relative ranking. You may have seen them reported on a standardized test, such as the Graduate Record Examination, or GRE. As with the median, they express what percentage of the scores fall below a given score.) In percentage distributions, you can use this fact to locate the median quickly by observing the data value at which the distribution crosses the 50th percentile.

Although the median conveys less precise information than the mean (knowing where the middle of a set of observations falls is less exact than is the precise numerical average), as you will see later in the chapter, the median is sometimes used in preference to the mean. In certain distributions of data, the median is more descriptive of the central tendency. In addition, when a phenomenon cannot be measured on an (equal) interval scale (for example, job attitudes, client satisfaction, quality of life, volunteer interest in career development, and so forth), the median is especially useful as a measure of central tendency.

The Mode

The final measure of central tendency is the mode. The **mode** is simply the data value that occurs most often (with greatest frequency) in any distribution. In the frequency distribution in Table 5.2, what is the mode number of tickets issued? The value that occurs most often is 3 tickets issued, so 3 is the mode.

The distribution in Table 5.2 has only one mode; thus, it is called unimodal. The distribution in Table 5.3 is bimodal; it has two modes. Because Kapaun had 9 arrests for 14 weeks and 11 arrests for 14 weeks, the modes are 9 and 11. Distributions also can be trimodal, tetramodal, and so on.

Table 5.2

Tickets Issued by Woodward Police, Week of January 28, 2004

Number of Tickets	Number of Police Officers
0	2
1	7
2	9
3	14
4	3
5	2
6	1
	38

Table 5.3

Arrests per Week, Kapaun Air Station, 2004

Number of Arrests	Number of Weeks
7	2
8	4
9	14
10	8
11	14
12	10
	52

Table 5.4

Number of Required Courses in Research Methods and Statistics

Number of Courses	Number of Schools
0	3
1	23
2	5
3	19
	50

Statisticians generally relax the definition of the mode(s) to include the distinct peaks or clusters in the data that occur with high frequency. You should, too. Table 5.4 presents an example—the number of research methods and statistics courses required for graduation by a sample of MPA-granting schools. The distribution is bimodal, with modes at one and three courses. Even though the latter mode occurs slightly less often, it would be misleading to ignore it.

The mode has several important characteristics:

1. Because the most common value in a distribution of data can occur at any point, the mode need not be "central" or near the middle.

2. Unlike the mean and the median, the mode can take on more than one value. No other measure of central tendency has this characteristic. As a result, in some complex data distributions, such as a bimodal or trimodal distribution, the mode is the statistic of choice for summarizing the *central tendencies.* When a distribution has more than one distinct mode, it usually indicates something important in the data that cannot be captured so well by the mean or median.

3. More often than not, when a variable is measured on a numerical or interval scale (number of arrests, feet of snow plowed, and so forth), the mode may be of little interest. However, with variables measured at less precise levels— nominal (classifications) and ordinal (rank orderings)—the mode is much more useful as a measure of central tendency. We return to this issue later in the chapter.

Means for Grouped Data

Even with the tremendous increase in microcomputers in work organizations, you may still encounter a situation in public or nonprofit management in which you must calculate statistics by hand using someone else's data. Often these data are in the form of a frequency distribution. As we explained in Chapter 1, having a facility with a microcomputer is not the same thing as understanding statistics and using them appropriately.

Measures of central tendency can be calculated from frequency distributions, whether the data have been grouped into classes or not. Raw ungrouped data should be collected and retained at every opportunity, but sometimes archival data and sensitive survey data require that **grouped data** be used. Because grouped data collapse frequencies and thus lose information, statistics calculated by using grouped data are less accurate than statistics calculated from ungrouped data. As a result, *never calculate statistics from grouped data if the ungrouped data are available.*

Sometimes, however, the analyst does not have a choice. Suppose the director of the Oklahoma Highway Department knows that the average (mean) speed on Oklahoma highways is 62.4 miles per hour. Federal Department of Transportation officials are upset, charging Oklahoma with lax enforcement of speed limits. The Oklahoma director feels that Oklahoma is no worse than any other state. But the information the director has is the frequency distribution shown in Table 5.5. The director asks the analyst to calculate the mean speed on Texas highways.

By applying the logic of calculating means for ungrouped data, we find that the calculations for grouped data are straightforward. The mean is nothing more than the sum of all the values divided by the number of values. Examining the first class, we see that 26 drivers were clocked between 45 and 50 miles per hour, although we do not

Table 5.5

Frequency Distribution of Texas Motorists' Speeds

Miles per Hour	Number of Drivers
45–50	26
50–55	123
55–60	273
60–65	319
65–70	136
70–75	84
75–80	7
	968

know their exact speeds. Whenever grouped data are used for calculations, statisticians assume that all values are spread evenly throughout the interval. Thus, the mean of the first class, or any class, is equal to the midpoint of the class (in this case, $[45 + 50]$ $\div 2 = 47.5$). For purposes of calculating the mean, we can then treat the first class as if it contained 26 items all equal to the class midpoint. With this assumption, the mean can be calculated by the following steps.

Step 1: Make a new column in the frequency table for class midpoints and fill in the midpoints. (See Table 5.6.)

Table 5.6

Motorists' Speeds and Class Midpoints

Class	Frequency	Midpoint
45–50	26	47.5
50–55	123	52.5
55–60	273	57.5
60–65	319	62.5
65–70	136	67.5
70–75	84	72.5
75–80	7	77.5
	968	

Step 2: Multiply the frequency in each class by the *class midpoint,* and place this value in a column labeled $F \times M$. This first value, for example, is 26×47.5, or 1,235. In the space next to the midpoint column, calculate these values.

Step 3: Sum all the values in the $F \times M$ column. This sum is equivalent to the sum of the values in the calculations for ungrouped data. At this point, your table should look like Table 5.7.

Table 5.7

Motorists' Speeds

Class	Frequency	Midpoints	$F \times M$
45–50	26	47.5	1,235
50–55	123	52.5	6,457.5
55–60	273	57.5	15,697.5
60–65	319	62.5	19,937.5
65–70	136	67.5	9,180
70–75	84	72.5	6,090
75–80	7	77.5	542.5
	968		$\Sigma F \times M = 59,140$

Step 4: Divide the sum of all values (the sum of the $F \times M$ column) by the number of values or **N.** This number is the mean ($59,140 \div 968 = 61.1$). How does the average speed in Texas compare with the average speed in Oklahoma? What should the Oklahoma highway director do with this information?

Following the steps just outlined, calculate the mean number of serious crimes per precinct for Metro, Texas. The data are given in Table 5.8.

If you worked the example correctly, you should get a mean of 11.0. (**Hint:** Did you use midpoints of 3, 8, 13, 18, and 23?)

When the data have been aggregated into a frequency distribution but not grouped into classes (as they have been in Tables 5.5 through 5.8), it is much easier to calculate the mean. Table 5.9 presents an example using the frequency distribution of the number of letters received by employees of the Evanapolis recreation department from adult and youth league teams expressing thanks and appreciation to them over

Table 5.8

Serious Crimes per Precinct, Metro, Texas, Week of March 7, 2004

Number of Crimes	Number of Precincts	Class Midpoints	$F \times M$
1–5	6		
6–10	9		
11–15	14		
16–20	5		
21–25	1		
	35		

$\Sigma F \times M =$ _____

Mean number of serious crimes = _____

Table 5.9

Letters Received by Employees of Evanapolis Recreation Department

Number of Letters (X)	Number of Employees (F)	F × X
0	3	
1	4	
2	6	
3	5	
4	2	
Σ = _____	Σ = _____	

the past year. The letters are highly prized. The department head wants to calculate the average number of letters received by employees to show the mayor how responsive her department is to the community.

To calculate the mean, we need to divide the total number of letters received by the number of employees. How many letters were received in all? Table 5.9 shows that three employees each received zero letters for a total of zero (3 × 0), four employees each received one letter for a total of four (4 × 1), and so on. The logic is the same as stated earlier, except you do not have to calculate midpoints since the data values are not grouped into classes. In the column of Table 5.9 labeled "$F \times X$" (frequency × data value), calculate and write each cross-product; sum the cross-products to find the total number of letters received (you should get 39). As before, **N**, the number of employees, is equal to the sum of the frequencies (20). The mean is 1.95 or almost 2 letters received per employee (39 ÷ 20).

Medians for Grouped Data

Medians can also be calculated for grouped data. The logic is similar to that for ungrouped data; for grouped data, the median is the middle value. For the data listed in Table 5.8, the median can be calculated in a manner similar to that for ungrouped data. There are 35 precincts in Metro; the median precinct is the 18th one in order of magnitude (35 + 1 = 36; 36 ÷ 2 = 18).

Step 1: Find the 18th (the middle) item. There are six precincts with 5 or fewer crimes and nine with 6 to 10 crimes. This means 15 precincts have 10 or fewer crimes, so the median is greater than 10. The 18th item is in the third class. In fact, it is the 3rd item in the third class.

Step 2: Calculate how far into the class the median item is. Remember that for grouped data, we assume that the items are equally distributed throughout the class interval. Because there are 14 items in the third class and the median is the 3rd item, the median is ¾ths of the distance into the class. So in this case, the median is 11 + ¾ of the third class.

Step 3: Calculate how far ¾ths is into the third class. To do this, simply multiply this fraction by the class interval (in this case, 5). The resulting number ($\frac{3}{14} \times 5 = 1.07$) should be added to the lower limit of this class (in this case, 11) for a median of 12.07. The procedure you used to calculate how far into an interval a particular value (in this case, the median) lies is called **interpolation.**

Some practice is in order. In the space provided, calculate the median score on the Morgan City civil service exam. The data are given in Table 5.10.

Calculate here.

Class median is in which class? _____

How far is the median into the class? _____

Multiply fraction by class interval = _____

Add to lower limit of this class to get the median = _____

_____

If you got a median civil service score of 82.6, congratulations. If not, check your calculations. Did you find the 45½th item?

What is the median number of letters received by employees of the Evanapolis recreation department? (Refer back to Table 5.9.) With a sample of 20 employees, the middle of the distribution lies midway between the 10th and the 11th observations in order of magnitude, or 10.5 ($20 + 1 = 21$; $21 \div 2 = 10.5$). Both of these values fall in the category of two letters received—and that value is accurate enough to express the median for most purposes.

Table 5.10

Distribution of Morgan City Civil Service Scores, July Exam

Civil Service Score	Number of Applicants
50–60	14
60–70	11
70–80	12
80–90	33
90–100	20
	90

Modes for Grouped Data

The crude mode (so named because it is a rough approximation) for grouped data is the midpoint of the class with the greatest frequency. For the Metro crimes example, the mode is 13. For the Morgan City example, the mode is 85.

The Mean versus the Median

In most situations, numerical data can be summarized well with the mean. However, situations can arise in which the mean gives a misleading indication of central tendency, and so the median is preferred. When extreme values or outliers occur on a variable, the mean is distorted or pulled toward them. The statistical term is *skewed*. By contrast, because the median is the value of the middle case—once the data points have been arranged in order—it will remain in the middle of the distribution even if the variable has an extreme value. In this situation, the median is the preferred measure of central tendency. (Chapter 6 returns to this issue.)

For example, suppose that a nonprofit administrator needed to estimate the average price of houses in a city in order to apply for a federal grant. She pulls a random sample of 10 homes sold recently and discovers 9 of them sold for between $180,000 and $220,000, and 1 home sold for well over $1 million. The mean housing price will be grossly inflated by the one outlying case and will yield a value unrepresentative of the price of houses in the city. The median will not be affected by the deviant case, however, and will have a value near the middle of housing prices, between $180,000 and $220,000.

Levels of Measurement and Measures of Central Tendency

Chapter 2, "Measurement," introduced the concept of levels of measurement. Students of public and nonprofit administration are most accustomed to interval measurement: variables that can be measured on a numerical scale, such as the budget of an agency or work group in dollars, or the amount of overtime hours logged by the cafeteria staff last week. Public and nonprofit managers (and those employed in business) also use variables measured at other, less precise levels. In discussing the median and the mode, we referred to these levels earlier in the chapter: Ordinal variables allow rank ordering of information—for example, how satisfied a client is with a nonprofit organization's response to her inquiry (very satisfied, satisfied, neutral, dissatisfied, or very dissatisfied) or a citizen's overall assessment of the services provided by the public library (very good, good, neutral, poor, or very poor). Nominal variables are classifications that have no metric information—for example, the gender of employees, their religion, their marital status, and so forth.

Why devote so much attention to the levels of measurement of the variables encountered in public and nonprofit administration? The answer is both simple and important: The statistics that can be appropriately calculated to summarize the distribution of single variables (the subject of this chapter) and to describe the relationship between variables (the subject of later chapters) differ from level to level. It is easy to see the source of the differences. Each of the levels expresses a different amount of information about a variable, and this idea is reflected directly in the kind of statistics that may be calculated and used.

For example, if a variable is measured at the interval level, we usually know everything about it that we may wish to know. It is possible to locate precisely all the observations along a scale: $17,529 yearly income; 4.57 prostitution arrests per week; 38 years of age; 247 cubic feet of sewage; 10,106 hours volunteered to United Way agencies last month. Because for these variables an equal distance separates each whole number on the measurement scale (dollars, arrests, years, cubic feet, and hours), all mathematical operations can be performed. Thus, as we saw earlier in the chapter, the scores of a group of cases or observations can be added and the sum divided by the number of observations to obtain the mean income, number of arrests, age, cubic feet of sewage, and hours volunteered. It is also possible to find the *median* or the middle score of the group for each of these variables. And, of course, the *mode*—the value occurring most frequently in a distribution—presents no problem.

Table 5.11 displays the number of pilots at selected air bases. At what level of measurement are these data? Be sure that you can calculate the mean (a total of 11,886 pilots ÷ 7 air bases = 1,698), median (896), and mode (0) for this distribution. If you have any problems, review the earlier portions of the chapter where these statistics are discussed. With interval level data, the manager can calculate and use all three measures of central tendency.

Now consider *ordinal* data. At this level of measurement we are able to rank objects or observations, but it is not possible to locate them precisely along a scale. A citizen may "strongly disapprove" of the Springhill mass transit system's performance, but no number is available that expresses her exact level of disapproval or how much less she approves than if she had said "disapprove." Because there are no numerical scores or numbers attached to the responses—which, in the case of interval variables, are added and divided to compute the mean—*it is not possible to calculate the mean for a variable measured at the ordinal level.*

Table 5.11

Pilots at Selected Air Bases

Air Base	Number of Pilots
Minot	0
Torrejon	2,974
Kapaun	896
Osan	0
Andrews	6,531
Yokota	57
Guam	1,428

Table 5.12

Citizens' Responses to Question about Springhill's Mass Transit System

Citizen	Response
1	Strongly disapprove
2	Approve
3	Neutral
4	Strongly disapprove
5	Disapprove
6	Strongly disapprove
7	Strongly approve
8	Strongly disapprove
9	Neutral
10	Approve
11	Disapprove

How about the median? Can it be calculated for ordinal data? Suppose an interviewer obtains from 11 citizens their responses to the question, "Do you approve or disapprove of the Springhill mass transit system's performance? Strongly approve, approve, neutral, disapprove, strongly disapprove?" Table 5.12 shows the results. To find the median with ordinal data, follow the steps below. We presented the steps earlier in the chapter.

Step 1: Arrange the responses in rank order. This ordering is possible because ordinal data preserve the ranking of cases. That is, you can rank the responses in order of expressing strongest approval of the mass transit system's performance to expressing least approval. Alternatively, you can order them from least approval to strongest. If you did it the first way, your data will look like those shown in Table 5.13.

Table 5.13

Rank Ordering of Citizen's Responses Concerning Springhill's Mass Transit System

Citizen	Response
7	Strongly approve
2	Approve
10	Approve
3	Neutral
9	Neutral
5	Disapprove
11	Disapprove
1	Strongly disapprove
4	Strongly disapprove
6	Strongly disapprove
8	Strongly disapprove

If you ranked the citizens in the other direction, read the list from the bottom up.

Step 2: Now that the cases have been arranged in order with respect to the variable (opinion regarding the Springhill mass transit system's performance), it is a simple matter to find the median. The median is the middle score, or the score of the case that falls in the middle. Because there are 11 cases, the sixth score falls in the middle. (The rule is to add 1 to the number of cases and divide this result by 2. So 11 + 1 = 12, and 12 ÷ 2 = 6.) Counting from either the top or the bottom of the list (it makes no difference), the middle score belongs to citizen 5: *Disapprove* is the median response of the group.

Be sure to note that the median is *not* citizen 5. She is just one of the respondents, not a score on the variable of interest (opinion about the Springhill transit system's performance). Also, make sure that you understand that the median is *not* the score of citizen 6. He just happened to be the sixth person interviewed. After the scores have been arranged in order, his score falls 10th in the list (or 2nd, if you count up from the bottom). Clearly his is not the middle response.

Ordinal data are commonly displayed in a frequency distribution. Table 5.14 presents the frequency distribution for the Springhill mass transit system. Note that the median still corresponds to the middle or the sixth case. Just as before, counting either up or down the list shows that the sixth case gave the response "disapprove," so it is the median.

It is important to note that the median is *not* "neutral." Although "neutral" is the middle response category, it does not tell us anything about the middle response given by the 11 citizens. "Neutral" falls in the middle of the scale but not in the middle of the 11 citizens. Note also that the median is the middle score of the 11 citizens, or the response "disapprove."

We have now shown that the median can be calculated for ordinal variables. So can the mode. In Table 5.14, the most frequently mentioned response is "strongly disapprove," given by four citizens. Therefore, it is the mode or modal response.

Finally, at the *nominal* level of measurement, it is not possible to assign numerical scores to cases (interval level). A score of 1.7 on religion or 458 on nationality would be arbitrary and would make no sense. *Thus, it is not possible to calculate the mean for nominal data.*

Table 5.14

Frequency Distribution of Citizens' Responses Concerning Springhill's Mass Transit System

Response	Number of Citizens
Strongly approve	1
Approve	2
Neutral	2
Disapprove	2
Strongly disapprove	4

Table 5.15

Civil Service Commission Employees by Occupation

Occupation	Number of People	Percentage
Lawyer	192	61
Butcher	53	17
Doctor	41	13
Baker	20	6
Candlestick maker	7	2
Indian chief	3	1
	N = 316	100

Furthermore, the values of a group of cases on a nominal variable cannot be ranked in any kind of meaningful ordering of least to most, or vice versa (ordinal level). There is no meaningful or correct way to order the categories of race, religion, sex, or any other nominal variable. (Usually, we place them in alphabetical order for convenience, but that ordering is not a numerical or measurement scale.) Because the median is predicated on the ability to rank cases or observations of a variable so that the middle or median value may be found, *it is not possible to calculate the median for nominal data.*

However, the mode can be found for nominal data. For the data in Table 5.15, which is the modal occupation of the employees of the Civil Service Commission?

The mode is "lawyer," because it is the occupation of the largest number of people (192) in the distribution. Usually, the percentage of observations in the modal category is given, here 61%. Make sure that you can calculate the percentage distribution. If you have any difficulty, see Chapter 4.

Hierarchy of Measurement

We can summarize this discussion of levels of measurement and measures of central tendency in a convenient table. In Table 5.16, place an X in the column of a row if the

Table 5.16

Hierarchy of Measurement

Measure of Central Tendency	Level of Measurement		
	Nominal	Ordinal	Interval
Mean			
Median			
Mode			

designated measure of central tendency (mean, median, mode) can be calculated for a given level of measurement (nominal, ordinal, and interval).

If you have completed the table correctly, X's will appear in the triangle of the table below the main diagonal that slopes upward from left to right. If you did not find this pattern, you should review earlier parts of the chapter.

The lesson of Table 5.16 is that any statistic that can be calculated for a variable at a lower (less precise) level of measurement can also be calculated at all higher (more precise) levels of measurement. Thus, the mode is available at all three levels, the median at the ordinal and the interval levels, and the mean only at the interval level. This rule is usually stated as the "hierarchy of measurement" to indicate the ascending power of the higher levels of measurement. To the degree possible, then, it is always to your advantage to construct and use variables measured at higher levels.

With this knowledge, you are now in a position to describe phenomena of interest in quantitative terms. For example, consider your work organization. The mean age of employees may be 37.1 years, the median 35, and the mode 39. The median opinion of employees with respect to the in-house information system's performance may be "disapprove"; perhaps the modal opinion is "strongly disapprove." Most of the employees may be white and male; and so on.

Some Cautions

Two cautions regarding this discussion of levels of measurement should be kept in mind. First, most of the time you will not calculate statistics yourself; instead, a computer program will compute them for you. In order to store information compactly in a computer, the substantive category labels or names for ordinal variables—such as strongly agree, agree, neutral, disagree, and strongly disagree—as well as for nominal variables—such as white, African American, Hispanic—are entered and stored in the computer as numbers. These numbers are usually called *codes*. The computer may also store the labels or names for the codes, but it performs all calculations based on the codes, not the value labels assigned to them. For example, the coding schemes in Table 5.17 may apply.

| Table 5.17 |

Examples of Two Coding Schemes

Coding Scheme 1		Coding Scheme 2	
Code	Response	Code	Response
1	Strongly agree	1	White
2	Agree	2	African American
3	Neutral	3	Hispanic
4	Disagree		
5	Strongly disagree		

Because the computer calculates all statistics based on the numerical codes entered for the variables, strange things can happen to the unwary analyst. For example, if instructed to do so, the computer can and will calculate a mean or a median for nominal variables or a mean for ordinal variables based on the codes—even though these statistics have no meaning at these levels of measurement. It is up to you as the analyst to recognize such statistics as a mean attitude of 2.7 or a median race of 1 for what they are: garbage. Note that for interval variables the codes are the actual data values (7.123, 5.6, 10075.9, 14, and so forth) so that this problem does not arise.

The second caution is in part a consequence of the first. Because ordinal variables frequently are coded for computer utilization in the manner shown earlier—1 = strongly agree, 2 = agree, 3 = neutral, and so on—some students have jumped to the incorrect conclusion that these codes are actually meaningful numbers on a scale that expresses the precise level of an individual's agreement or disagreement with an interviewer's question. In other words, they have assumed that the coding categories are actual numbers and can be treated as such for statistical calculations—just as if they were interval data. This practice, which is rather common in all the social sciences, including political science and public administration, has led to the ordinal-interval debate. (Don't feel bad if you have missed it; it is not exactly a household term.) As the title suggests, the debate has focused on the justification for —or the lack of it— and the advantages of treating ordinal data as interval. Both sides have produced some persuasive evidence, and the debate has yet to be resolved definitively.

Our recommendation for students just starting out in quantitative work in public or nonprofit management is that you adopt the stance of the statistical purist—that you calculate and use for ordinal data only those statistics that are clearly appropriate for that level of measurement. For now, when you need to summarize or describe the distribution of an ordinal variable, rely on the median and mode. In the future, if you decide to continue your work in statistics, you can read some of the literature in the ordinal-interval debate and come to your own conclusions.

You may be wondering why we are placing such emphasis on the ordinal-interval debate. When you see the steps involved in examining and interpreting *relationships* among ordinal variables—as compared with those involved in the analysis of interval data (see the chapters on regression)—the significance of this debate will grow. But that is the purpose of Chapters 15 through 17.

Chapter Summary

Measures of central tendency are values used to summarize a body of data by indicating middle (or central) points in the distribution. Each measure of central tendency has a distinct meaning and method of calculation. The mean is the arithmetic average of all data points. The median is the data value that is greater than 50% of all the data points and less than 50% of all the data points. The mode is the data value that occurs most often in the distribution. This chapter illustrates the calculations for all three measures of central tendency for both grouped (frequency distribution) and ungrouped data. The chapter also shows how the level of measurement of a variable (interval, ordinal, nominal) determines the measures of central tendency that can appropriately be calculated for it. The hierarchy of measurement illustrates this concept. The level of measurement determines the statistics that can be calculated. More specifically, the hierarchy of measurement shows that the more precise the measurement, the more numerous the statistics that can be calculated and used. Thus, the mean, the median, and the mode can be calculated for internal-level data. The median and the mode can be calculated for ordinal-level data. Only the mode can be calculated for nominal-level data.

In the examples in this chapter and in the problems that follow, we use small numbers of cases to ease the burden of calculation of measures of central tendency, while still illustrating the crucial concepts and points. In actual situations in public and nonprofit administration, you will typically deal with much larger numbers of cases, and a computer will perform the necessary calculations. The concepts and points for proper use and interpretation remain the same, however.

Problems

5.1   During a recent crackdown on speeding, the Luckenbach, Texas, police department issued the following number of citations on seven consecutive days: 59, 61, 68, 57, 63, 50, and 55. Calculate the mean and median number of speeding citations.

5.2   The dean of Southwestern State University is concerned that many faculty members at SSU are too old to be effective teachers. She asks each department to send her information on the average age of its faculty. The head of the sociology department does not wish to "lie" with statistics, but, knowing the preference of the dean, he would like to make the department appear youthful. The names and ages of the sociology department's members are listed in the accompanying table. Calculate both the mean age and the median age. Should the department send the dean the mean age or the median age?

Member	Age
Durkheim	64
Campbell	31
Weber	65
Likert	27
Stanley	35
Katz	40
Lazarsfeld	33

5.3   The average number of sick leave days used per employee per year in Normal, Oklahoma, is 6.7. The city manager feels the public works department is abusing its sick leave privileges. The only information available is the frequency distribution given in the accompanying table. Calculate the mean and median number of sick days used by the public works employees. Is the department abusing its sick leave?

Number of Days of Sick Leave Taken	Number of Employees
0–2	4
3–5	7
6–8	7
9–11	14
12–14	6

5.4 The U.S. Army is allowed only five test firings of the Lance missile. The following figures represent the number of feet the missiles missed the target by: 26, 147, 35, 63, and 51. Calculate the mean and the median. Which should the army report?

5.5 The Department of Welfare wants to know the average outside income for all welfare recipients in the state. Calculate both the mean and the median from the data in the accompanying table.

Income	Number of Families
0–300	25
300–600	163
600–900	354
900–1200	278
1,200–1,500	421
1,500–1,800	603
1,800–2,100	211
2,100–2,400	84
2,400–2,700	32
2,700–3,000	5

5.6 When should the median be used in preference to the mean?

5.7 From the data in the accompanying table, calculate the mean and median age for the Quechan Indian Tribe. Which is the more appropriate measure?

Age	Persons
0–4	213
5–9	215
10–14	242
15–19	194
20–24	168
25–29	162
30–34	111
35–39	82
40–44	74

Age	Persons
45–49	50
50–54	53
55–59	46
60–64	24
65–85	86

5.8   The legislature has limited the Bureau of the Audit to a monthly average of 34 employees. For the first 9 months of the year, the employment figures were 31, 36, 34, 35, 37, 32, 36, 37, and 34. Does it appear that the bureau will make the target? How many employees can the bureau have over the next three months and still meet the target?

5.9   The collective bargaining agreement between Family Services Agency and the Federation of Social Workers specifies that the average case load for case-workers cannot exceed 45. Using the accompanying data, the agency claims compliance, yet the union argues that the agency has violated the agreement. Who is correct?

Caseworker	Case Load
A	43
B	57
C	35
D	87
E	36
F	93
G	45
H	48
I	41
J	40

5.10   Refer to Problem 5.7. What is the modal age? Is this an appropriate measure of central tendency in this case?

5.11   Calculate the mean and median for the marriage license data in Problem 4.6 (Chapter 4).

5.12   Calculate the mean and median for the marriage license data in Problem 4.7 (Chapter 4). Compare these results with those obtained in Problem 5.11. Write a short memorandum addressing the question of whether service to the public has improved or declined over the past 2 years.

5.13   The director of the Doctor of Public Administration (DPA) program at Federal University is developing a report to the faculty on the entering class of DPA students. The director wants to present a statistical profile of the new students, including their grade point average (GPA) earned in master's de-gree programs. The GPAs for the eight entering students are 3.1, 3.7, 3.6,

3.2, 3.8, 3.5, 2.9, and 4.0. Calculate the mean and median GPA earned by these students in their master's degree studies.

5.14 Some faculty at Federal University have complained to the director of the Doctor of Public Administration program that DPA students typically have strong verbal skills but lack mathematical preparation. (Fortunately, a statistics book is available in public administration to meet the needs of these students.) In response to the complaint, the DPA director assembles the scores on the verbal and quantitative sections of the Graduate Record Examination (GRE) for the class of eight entering DPA students. Each section is scored on a scale of 200 to 800. The GRE scores of each student are listed below.

GRE Verbal	GRE Quantitative
590	620
680	510
630	550
700	600
610	540
650	570
620	590
670	580

Based on your analysis of these data, evaluate the complaint lodged by the faculty members at Federal University.

5.15 The head of the data processing department in Springhill wants to estimate the amount of waste and inefficiency in her department. She conducts a survey of employees in the department. One question asks, "To what extent does this department have waste and inefficiency in its operations?" The responses to the item are given in the accompanying table.

Response	Number of Employees
To a very great extent	42
To a great extent	31
To a moderate extent	19
To some extent	12
Not at all	7

(a) At what level of measurement are these data?

(b) Calculate the percentage distribution and the appropriate measures of central tendency.

(c) According to these data, does the department appear to have a problem with waste and inefficiency? Explain your answer.

5.16   The civic center of Kulture City is badly in need of refurbishment. However, before the city council allocates funds for this purpose, its members want to get a better idea of how frequently the residents of Kulture City actually use the center. To find out, they hire a public opinion polling firm to survey citizens. The pollsters ask a random sample of residents the following question: "In the last year, how many times have you attended performances or activities at Kulture City civic center?" The responses of the sample are listed in the accompanying table.

Number of Performances or Activities Attended	Number of Citizens
0	587
1	494
2	260
3	135
4	97

(a) At what level of measurement are these data?

(b) Calculate the appropriate measures of central tendency and the percentage distribution.

(c) Should the city council allocate money to refurbish the civic center?

(d) Write a short memorandum in which you use these results to make a recommendation to the city council.

5.17   The head of a city's recreation department feels that the employees of the department are the best in the city. Each year, all city employees receive a standardized performance evaluation that rates them on a scale of performance: "far above expectations," "above expectations," "meets expectations," "below expectations," and "far below expectations." (Each rating has an operational definition.) The department head feels that his assessment of employees will be justified if at least 90% of them fall into the top two categories. The ratings received by department employees are shown in the accompanying table.

Rating	Number of Employees
Far above expectations	15
Above expectations	22
Meets expectations	77
Below expectations	9
Far below expectations	8

(a) At what level of measurement are these data?

(b) Calculate the percentage distribution and the appropriate measures of central tendency.

(c) What can you tell the head of the recreation department?

5.18   The director of a city's personnel office is concerned that the city have a diverse workforce. One variable she uses to measure diversity is race. According to records kept by the personnel office, the city employs 59 African Americans, 73 whites, 41 Hispanics, 38 Asians, and 17 from other ethnic groups.

(a) At what level of measurement are these data?

(b) Prepare the percentage distribution for these data, and calculate appropriate measures of central tendency.

(c) What can you tell the director of the personnel office?

CHAPTER 6

Measures of Dispersion

A useful descriptive statistic complementary to the measures of central tendency is a measure of dispersion. A **measure of dispersion** tells how much the data do or do not cluster about the mean. For example, the data listed in Table 6.1 show the number of daily arrests in Wheezer, South Dakota, for 2002, 2003, and 2004. The mean number of daily arrests for all 3 years is the same (2.75). How much the daily arrests cluster about the mean, however, varies. In 2003, the numbers cluster less about the mean than they do in 2002. In 2004, the arrests cluster closer to the mean than do either the 2003 or the 2002 arrests. This clustering is illustrated by the frequency polygons in Figure 6.1; the mean is depicted vertically to facilitate interpretation. Clearly the dispersion of the data is a valuable descriptive statistic in analyzing a set of data.

Most statistics texts discuss a variety of dispersion measures, such as the range, the average deviation, the interquartile deviation, and the standard deviation. Of all these measures, only the standard deviation has broad use and great value statistically, and hence this statistic is the only one we will discuss in this chapter. The only thing you need to remember about the other measures of dispersion is what they are. The **range** is the difference between the largest value and the smallest value in a distribution of data. The **interquartile deviation** is the difference between two numbers. These two numbers are selected so that the middle 50% of all values fall between them. The **average deviation** is the average difference between the mean and all other values. If these measures of dispersion seem appropriate for any projects you are interested in,

Table 6.1

Number of Daily Police Arrests in Wheezer, South Dakota

Number of Arrests	Number of Days		
	2002	2003	2004
0	24	36	10
1	36	54	36
2	95	65	109
3	104	74	118
4	66	84	66
5	40	52	26
	365	365	365

Figure 6.1

Frequency Polygons for the Data in Table 6.1

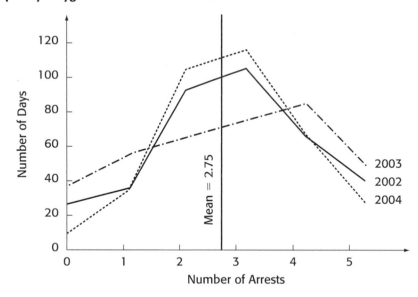

consult a general statistics book to find out how to calculate them [for example, see the text by Johnson (1995); a list of other suitable texts is given in the bibliography at the end of the book].

The Standard Deviation

The standard deviation is the most common measure of dispersion. The **standard deviation** is the square root of the average squared deviation of the data from the mean; that is, the standard deviation is based on the squared differences between every item in a data set and the mean of that set.

Table 6.2

Blocks of Streets Cleaned by Work Crews

Work Crew	Number of Blocks
A	126
B	140
C	153
D	110
E	136
	665

An example can explain this process far better than words. Normal, Okalahoma, has five street-cleaning crews. Because we have data for all five crews, we are working with the population and will calculate the population standard deviation. Later, we will explain the adjustment you would need to make if the five crews were a sample of the Normal, Oklahoma, street-cleaning crews (sample standard deviation). Listed in Table 6.2 are the numbers of blocks of city streets cleaned by the five crews. To determine the (population) standard deviation for these data, follow these steps:

Step 1: From the data, calculate the mean. Recall from Chapter 5 that to calculate the mean, you need to add the data values across cases (here, the sum of the data values is 665 blocks) and divide that sum by the number of cases or **N** (here, the number of work crews, 5). The mean is 133.

Step 2: Subtract the mean from every item in the data set. In this situation, subtract 133 from the number of streets cleaned by each crew. Often a table like Table 6.3 is helpful in performing these calculations. Note that the sum of these differences equals *zero*. In fact, in any distribution of data, the sum of the differences of the data values from the mean will *always* equal zero. The reason is that the positive deviations above the mean will just balance the negative deviations below the mean such that the sum of the deviations is zero.

Table 6.3

Calculating the Differences

Number of Blocks	Subtract the Mean	Difference
126	133	−7
140	133	7
153	133	20
110	133	−23
136	133	3
		0

Step 3: Square the difference between each number and the mean (the third column). As noted in Step 2, the differences sum to zero, regardless of how condensed or dispersed the data values are about the mean. The reason is that

the positive and negative differences will always balance each other out. Squaring the differences avoids this problem and is instrumental in measuring the actual amount of dispersion in the data (see Table 6.4).

Table 6.4

Calculating the Difference Squared

Blocks	Mean	Difference	Difference Squared
126	133	−7	49
140	133	7	49
153	133	20	400
110	133	−23	529
136	133	3	9

Step 4: Sum the squared differences. You should get a sum of 1,036.

Step 5: Divide the sum by the number of items (N = 5). This number (207.2) is called the **variance.** The variance is the arithmetic average of the squared differences of the data values from the mean.

Step 6: Take the square root of the variance to find the standard deviation (here, the standard deviation is 14.4). If you do not have a calculator to calculate the square root, look up the value in a square root table. Because we squared the differences between the mean and the data values in Step 3 (so that the differences would not sum to zero), it now makes sense to take the square root. In this manner, the standard deviation converts the variance from squared units to the original units of measurement.

After calculating this relatively simple statistic, you should not be surprised to learn that statisticians have a complex formula for the standard deviation. The formula for σ (the Greek letter sigma, which statisticians use as the symbol for the standard deviation of a population) is

$$\sigma = \sqrt{\frac{\sum_{i=1}^{N} (X_i - \mu)^2}{N}}$$

This formula is not as formidable as it seems: $(X_i - \mu)$ is nothing more than Step 2, subtracting the mean of the population from each data value. $(X_i - \mu)^2$ is Step 3, the squaring of the differences. $\sum_{i=1}^{N} (X_i - \mu)^2$ is Step 4, the summing of all the squared differences. The entire formula within the square root sign completes Step 5, the division by the number of items (N). Finally, the square root sign is Step 6.

How would the calculations change if the five street-cleaning crews were a sample of the crews from Normal, Oklahoma, rather than the entire population? You would then need to calculate the sample standard deviation, denoted by the symbol s. To do so, you would follow the steps in the formula for the standard deviation, replacing μ with $\bar{X}$, the sample mean, and $\mathbf{N}$ with $n - 1$, the number of cases in the sample (n) less 1. There are sound statistical reasons for making this adjustment, which we will discuss in Chapter 11 on statistical inference. There are also good practical reasons. Dividing by $n - 1$ rather than n will yield a slightly larger standard deviation, which is the appropriate measure of care to take when you are using a sample of data to represent the population. In this example, the sample standard deviation would be 16.1 ($1,036 \div 4 = 259$; the square root of $259 = 16.1$). When you are working with the population rather than a sample, there is no need to add this extra measure of caution. Thus, if the five Normal, Oklahoma, street-cleaning crews constitute the population, the (population) standard deviation is smaller, 14.4. You need to be aware that statistical package programs, spreadsheets, and hand calculators may assume that you are using the sample standard deviation rather than the population standard deviation and thus make the appropriate adjustment.

The smaller the standard deviation, the more closely the data cluster about the mean. For example, the standard deviations for the Wheezer, South Dakota, police arrests are 1.34 for 2002, 1.55 for 2003, and 1.16 for 2004. This calculation reinforces our perception that the 2003 data were the most dispersed and the 2004 data were the least dispersed.

Standard Deviations for Grouped Data

As we saw in Chapter 5, in public and nonprofit management you sometimes receive grouped data and need to calculate statistics from the frequency distribution. Just as you can calculate the mean for grouped data, you can calculate the standard deviation.

The logic for calculating standard deviations from grouped data is the same as that for calculating a standard deviation from ungrouped data. *Again, never calculate a standard deviation from grouped data if the ungrouped data are available.* The data shown in Table 6.5 on Metro serious crimes per precinct will be used to illustrate this process.

Table 6.5

Serious Crimes per Precinct, Metro, Week of March 7, 2004

Number of Crimes	Number of Precincts
1–5	6
6–10	9
11–15	14
16–20	5
21–25	1
	35

Step 1: Calculate the mean. Using the steps outlined in Chapter 5 and illustrated in Table 6.6, you should find the mean to be 11.

Table 6.6

Calculating the Mean

Class	Frequency	Midpoint	$F \times M$
1–5	6	3	18
6–10	9	8	72
11–15	14	13	182
16–20	5	18	90
21–25	1	23	23

Sum $F \times M = 385$

Mean $= 385 \div 35 = 11$

Step 2: Subtract the mean from the midpoint of each class. Note that the value of each item in the class is now considered to be the midpoint of the class (refer to Table 6.7).

Step 3: Square the differences between the mean and the class midpoints, and enter them in Table 6.7. You should get the following values: 64, 9, 4, 49, and 144.

Table 6.7

Calculating the Differences

Frequency	Midpoint	Mean	Difference	Squared Difference
6	3	11	−8	
9	8	11	−3	
14	13	11	+2	
5	18	11	+7	
1	23	11	+12	

Step 3½: This step is unique to grouped data. Step 4 is to sum the squared differences. But for the first class, there are six precincts with three crimes each (using the class midpoint). For these six precincts, the squared difference is 64. To get the correct sum of the squared differences, multiply the squared difference by the frequency for that class. You should get the results shown in Table 6.8.

Step 4: Sum the squared differences. In this case, sum the numbers in the $F \times S$ column (frequency $\times$ squared differences). The answer is 910.

Step 5: Divide this sum by **N** (in this case, 35) to get the variance (26).

Table 6.8

Squared Difference Times Frequency

Frequency	Squared Difference	$F \times S$
6	64	384
9	9	81
14	4	56
5	49	245
1	144	144

Step 6: The square root of the variance is the standard deviation; in this case, the standard deviation is 5.1.

Shape of a Frequency Distribution

In addition to measuring the central tendency (see Chapter 5) and dispersion of a variable, public and nonprofit managers also need to know something about the "shape" of the frequency distribution of data values. The shape arises from plotting the values of the variable horizontally against their corresponding frequency of occurrence, plotted vertically. Several distinctive shapes of data distributions appear regularly in public and nonprofit administration.

Figure 6.2 shows a **symmetric distribution.** The data are evenly balanced on either side of the center or middle of the distribution. As you can see, each side is a reflection of the other. When a distribution is basically symmetric, the mean, median, and mode will have very similar values.

Figure 6.2

A Symmetric Distribution

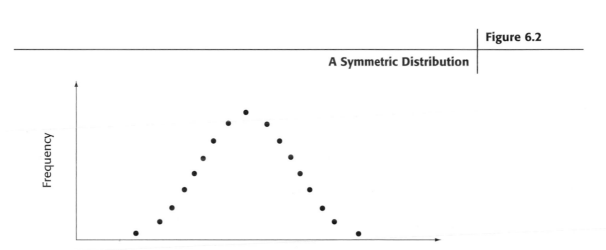

Values of Variable

Figure 6.3

A Uniform Distribution

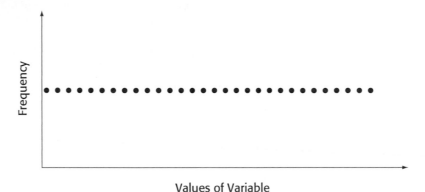

Figure 6.4

A Bimodal Distribution

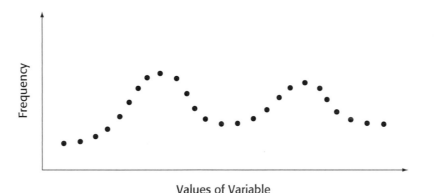

Figure 6.3 shows a **uniform distribution.** In a uniform distribution, each data value occurs with the same (or nearly the same) frequency. Because the data do not cluster around the middle or center of the distribution but are evenly spread across the variable, the dispersion, as measured by the standard deviation, will be large.

Chapter 5 introduced the idea of a **bimodal distribution.** The shape of such a distribution has two distinct peaks, corresponding to data values that occur with high frequency, separated by other values that occur much less often. Figure 6.4 presents an example of a bimodal distribution.

In an **asymmetric distribution,** the data fall more on one side of the center or middle than on the other side. In that case, skewness exists in the data.

Figure 6.5

Negatively Skewed Data

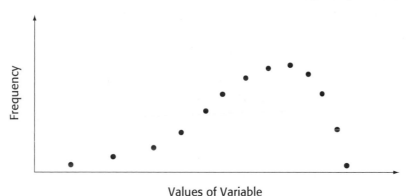

Figure 6.6

Positively Skewed Data

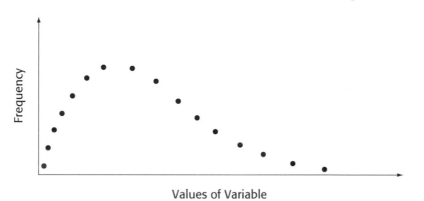

Negatively skewed data have a few extremely low numbers that distort the mean. Negatively skewed data form a frequency distribution like the one pictured in Figure 6.5.

Positively skewed data have a few very large numbers that distort the mean. The frequency distribution of positively skewed data resembles the one shown in Figure 6.6.

If data are strongly skewed, the mean is not a good measure of central tendency. The reason is that the mean is "pulled" or skewed in the direction of the skewness away from the center of the distribution. A few very high or low values in a very asymmetric distribution will skew the mean. In that case, the median is the preferred measure of central tendency because it is basically unaffected by skewness. Recall that in calculating the median, the relative positions of the values are what matters, rather than the actual magnitudes.

Skewness is a difficult statistic to calculate by hand. If you are sane, you will rely on a computer program to do it. Many programs of descriptive statistics will print out something similar to the following:

$$skewness = 1.34$$

This value indicates that the data are positively skewed and, therefore, the mean is artificially high. Skewness figures around zero indicate an unskewed (or symmetric) distribution. Negative numbers indicate negative skewness and, therefore, a mean that is artificially low.

The Importance of Using Measures of Dispersion and Measures of Central Tendency Together

The standard deviation is an important complement to the mean. It's so important, in fact, that an analyst should be extremely cautious in making conclusions about data if she is only given the mean but not the standard deviation. A mean without a standard deviation has limited value because without a standard deviation, it is difficult to see how much volatility or variability exists in the data.

For example, let's say that a supervisor is informed that the mean score for a group of employees on a job skills test is 90%. The supervisor is very pleased with the test scores. Without a standard deviation, however, how much does the supervisor really know about the mean score? To illustrate the value of the standard deviation when interpreting the mean, let's look at a couple of different scenarios.

$$\mu = 90 \qquad \sigma = 2$$
$$\mu = 90 \qquad \sigma = 9$$

In the first scenario where the standard deviation is 2, most individual test scores are tightly clustered around the mean. In the second scenario where the standard deviation is 9, the individual test scores are far more dispersed around the mean.

The supervisor might reach far different conclusions about her employees' performance depending on which of these standard deviations was associated with the mean. A standard deviation of 2 suggests that most employees have scores close to the mean, whereas a standard deviation of 9 suggests that the performance of individual employees is much more variable. The two situations are highly different—yet indistinguishable without the standard deviation to accompany the mean.

It is hard to know how good a measure of central tendency the mean is without seeing the value of the standard deviation as well. As a rule of thumb, an analyst should always provide both the mean and the standard deviation when describing data or reporting results.

Recall our discussion in Chapter 5 regarding the use of the median as a measure of central tendency. If the standard deviation for a set of data approaches or exceeds the value of the mean itself, the mean may not be a very representative measure of central tendency. When the standard deviation exceeds the mean, extreme values in the data are often to blame. Consider using the median in cases like this, because it is not as sensitive to extreme values in the data.

Chapter Summary

Measures of dispersion indicate how closely a set of data clusters around the midpoint or center of the data distribution. Measures of dispersion include the range, the interquartile deviation, the average deviation, the variance, and the standard deviation. The first three of these measures are not as useful statistically as the last two.

For descriptive purposes, the standard deviation is used most often. The standard deviation is the square root of the average squared difference of the data values from the mean. It is the square root of the variance. This chapter illustrates the calculation of the standard deviation for both grouped and ungrouped data. A small standard deviation (and variance) indicates that the data cluster closely around the mean.

The chapter discussed the characteristic shape of several data distributions common in public and nonprofit administration. The distributions include symmetric, uniform, bimodal, and asymmetric.

In an asymmetric distribution, skewness can present a problem. Negatively skewed data have a few very low values that distort the mean; conversely, positively skewed data have a few very large values that will also distort. Because it is basically unaffected by skewness, the median is the preferred measure of central tendency in this situation.

Problems

6.1 Charles Jones, the local fire chief, wants to evaluate the efficiency of two different water pumps. Brand A pumps an average of 5,000 gallons per minute with a standard deviation of 1,000 gallons. Brand B pumps 5,200 gallons per minute with a standard deviation of 1,500 gallons. What can you say about the two types of pumps that would be valuable to Chief Jones?

6.2 Bobby Gene England, a research analyst for the United Way of Chickasaw, is asked to provide information on the number of daily visits to food banks in Chickasaw for the past two weeks. For the accompanying data, calculate the mean, median, and standard deviation for Bobby Gene.

6	9	0
11	12	5
4	7	10
3	3	12
9	8	

$$\text{median} = \underline{\hspace{2in}}$$
$$\text{mean} = \underline{\hspace{2in}}$$
$$\text{standard deviation} = \underline{\hspace{2in}}$$

6.3 Helen Curbside, the chief custodial engineer for Placerville, has entered into the department computer the number of tons of garbage collected per day by all work crews in the city during a 1-week period. One statistic on the computer puzzles her: "Skewness $= -2.46$." Interpret this result for Helen. What does it suggest about the performance of the city work crews?

6.4 Scotty Allen, whom you met in Chapter 4, now wants to know the mean, median, and standard deviation for Maxwell, New York, civil service exam scores. Using the accompanying data, perform the necessary calculations.

Exam Score	Number of Applicants
61–65	20
66–70	13
71–75	47
76–80	56
81–85	33
86–90	27
91–95	41
96–100	34

6.5 Refer to Problem 5.4 (Chapter 5) on the Lance missile system. Five shots missed the target by 26, 147, 35, 63, and 51 feet, respectively. What is the standard deviation of the data?

6.6 The chief operating officer (COO) for Healthy Hills Hospital is concerned that certain orders are not filled within a uniform time period. She believes that requests for equipment should have a standard deviation no greater than 2.0 days. Calculate the standard deviation for the COO from the accompanying data. Also calculate all measures of central tendency. What can you tell the COO?

Days to Fill Order	Number of Items
0–1	10
2–3	14
4–5	17
6–7	12
8–9	4

6.7 The head of research and development for the U.S. Army must select one of the antitank weapons from the accompanying listing for procurement. The listed results indicate the distance away from the intended target that 100 test rounds fell. Which system should the army select, and why?

Weapon	Mean	Standard Deviation
A	22.4	15.9
B	18.7	36.5
C	24.6	19.7

6.8 The Whitehawk Indian Tribe believes the Bureau of Indian Affairs responds faster to grant applications from the Kinsa Tribe than it does to grants for the Whitehawk Tribe. From the accompanying data, what can you tell the Whitehawks?

Days to Respond to Grant Applications

Whitehawk	Kinsa
64	50
58	72
66	74
54	46
70	75
66	81
51	43
56	46

6.9 An audit of the Community Rehabilitation Agency reveals that the average 26 closures (rehabilitation talk for a successful effort) takes 193 days with a standard deviation of 49 days and a skewness of 3.15. What does this mean in English?

6.10 The U.S. Postal Service is concerned with the time it takes to deliver mail. It would like not only to deliver mail as quickly as possible but also to have as little variation as possible. Twenty letters are mailed from New York collection boxes to Cutbank, Montana. From the following number of days for delivery, what can you tell the Postal Service? Calculate all measures of central tendency and dispersion.

2	5	3	4	3	2	6	1	3	3
4	3	8	3	5	2	3	4	4	3

6.11 An employee at the Purchasing Department claims that he and a few other employees do almost all the work. In support of his claim, he collects the accompanying data on the number of purchase orders cleared and processed by each of the 16 members of the department in a typical week. Calculate all measures of central tendency and dispersion for these data and evaluate this employee's claim. Do a few employees do almost all the work?

12	22	8	14	15	32	17	24
20	37	15	23	16	40	19	21

6.12 The director of the South Bloomington YMCA has become concerned about the health of the organization's employees. She issues a directive to all YMCA sites advising all managers to encourage employees to get at least 60 minutes of exercise per day. Following are the data on the number of minutes exercised per day (on the average) by the 10 employees of the South Bloomington YMCA site. Calculate all measures of central tendency and dispersion for these data. How well do these employees meet the standard for exercise recommended by the director of the YMCA?

75   20   15   95   30   100   40   10   90   120

6.13   Complaints have reached the city manager of Normal that it is taking too long to pay bills submitted to the city. You are assigned to check how long it takes by looking at a few bills. Following are the lengths of time in days that it has taken the city to pay seven bills. Calculate the mean, median, and standard deviation. Would you report the mean or the median? Why?

34   27   64   31   30   26   35

6.14   The Texas State Penitentiary is concerned about the number of violent incidents in its prisons. After examining the 10 prisons in the Texas system, a data analyst finds the following pattern of data for the number of violent incidents last month:

17   21   42   32   16   24   31   15   22   26

Calculate the mean, median, and standard deviation. Should the penitentiary use the mean or the median in its analysis? Why?

6.15   The city manager of Grosse Out Pointe wants to make sure that pay raises are distributed fairly to all employees. He asks his assistant to gather data on raises for a random sample of police and fire employees, because he has received complaints that raises are not being distributed fairly in one of the departments.

Police	Fire
610	570
590	580
650	700
650	600
640	480
580	690
550	740
550	450
$\mu = 603$	$\mu = 601$

The assistant calculates the mean for each group of employees. He tells the city manager that because the average pay raise is just about the same in each department, there is really no fairness issue to worry about. If you were the city manager, would you accept these results, or would you ask the assistant to provide you with more information? Explain.

PART

III

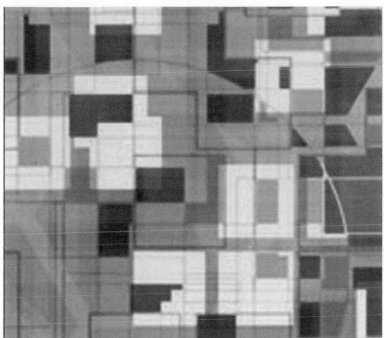

Probability

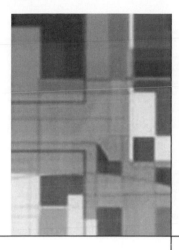

CHAPTER 7

Introduction to Probability

Probability is one of the most useful quantitative techniques available to public and nonprofit managers. **Probability** tells a manager how likely it is that certain events will occur. Using the rules of probability as discussed in this and the following chapters, public and nonprofit managers can diagnose and solve a variety of problems. For example, the head of maintenance in a city could use probability to determine how frequently major breakdowns will occur in the city's automobile and truck fleet and so could schedule maintenance personnel accordingly. A fire chief could use probability to allocate his workforce to the areas of the city where most fires occur. An affirmative action officer could use probability to determine whether an agency discriminates. A nonprofit manager could use probability to forecast demand for holiday meals to the homeless in a city. Another nonprofit agency might use probability to determine which areas of the county are most in need of services for the homebound elderly.

This chapter covers the basic rules and assumptions of probability. These rules and assumptions will permit us to treat some advanced probability techniques in the next two chapters.

Basic Concepts in Probability

The **basic law of probability** (which you should commit to memory) is this: Given that all possible outcomes of a given event are equally likely, the probability of any specified outcome is equal to the ratio of the number of ways that that outcome could be achieved to the total number of ways that all possible outcomes can be achieved. Now what does that mean? Equally likely events are events that all have an equal chance of occurring. If the events in question are equally likely, then the basic law of probability can be used, as follows:

Step 1: Determine the number of possible ways that the outcome you are interested in can occur.

Step 2: Determine the number of possible ways that every possible outcome can occur.

Step 3: Divide the first number by the second; the answer gives you the probability that the event in question will occur.

Let us look at some examples. Suppose you have an unbiased coin (an *unbiased* coin is one that has an equal probability of coming up heads or tails). What is the probability that the coin will land head side up if flipped? The number of possible ways a head can appear is one; there is only one head per coin. The number of total possible outcomes is two; a coin flip may come up either a head or a tail. Therefore, the probability of obtaining a head when flipping a coin is 1 divided by 2, or .5. Figure 7.1 shows the probability tree for one flip of a coin.

The probability of rolling a six on one roll of an unbiased die is .167. There are six sides to a die, all of which are equally likely to land that side up. Only one of those sides has a six on it, so the probability of rolling a six is 1 divided by 6, or .167. The probability of drawing a spade from a deck of 52 playing cards is the number of spades (13) divided by the total number of cards, or .25. Because a deck of playing cards has four suits each equally likely to occur, the probability of .25 (one out of four) makes good sense.

The same logic applies to events with more than one trial (that is, a flip, or a roll, or a draw). For example, what is the probability of obtaining two heads if an unbiased coin is flipped twice? This probability may be determined by a probability tree. On the first flip, a coin may land on either a head or a tail, as shown in Figure 7.1. If the result was a head on the first flip, the second flip could be either a head or a tail. If the coin was a tail on the first flip, then on the second flip it could be either a head or a tail. The probability tree in Figure 7.2 shows all possible results of two flips of a coin.

Examining the tree in Figure 7.2, you can see that the number of ways that two heads will appear is one. The number of ways that all possible outcomes can occur

Figure 7.1

Probability Tree for One Flip of a Coin

Figure 7.2

Probability Tree for Two Flips of a Coin

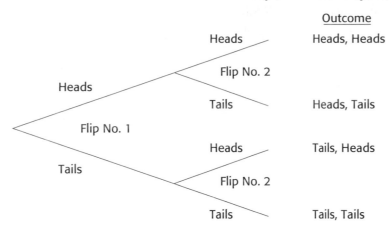

is four. Therefore, the probability of obtaining two heads on two flips of an unbiased coin is one out of four, or .25.

The same logic can be applied to more than two trials in any event. For example, draw the probability tree in the space provided for all possible outcomes when a coin is flipped three times.

What is the probability that you will obtain three heads on three consecutive flips of a coin? If your answer was .125 (or 1 ÷ 8), congratulations. If not, recheck your probability tree.

Using this same tree, determine the probability of obtaining two heads on three flips of a coin. Examining the tree reveals that the probability of two heads is three out of eight, or .375 (three combinations: head-head-tail, head-tail-head, or tail-head-head).

What is the probability of obtaining exactly two tails on three flips of a coin? Using the probability tree, you should find a probability of .375 (or three out of eight). What is the probability of obtaining three tails on three consecutive flips of an unbiased coin? The answer is one out of eight, or .125.

What is the probability of obtaining *two or more* heads on three flips of an unbiased coin? In this situation, you would add the number of ways of achieving three heads (one) to the number of ways of achieving two heads (three) and divide this number by the total number of possible outcomes (eight), for a probability of .5 (or four out of eight).

Finally, what is the probability of obtaining zero, one, two, or three heads on three flips of an unbiased coin? Because these are all the possible events, the answer is 1.0. This is one way to check that your probabilities are correct. The probability for all possible events should be 1.0.

Let us assemble these probabilities into a probability distribution. A **probability distribution** tabulates the probability of occurrence of each event or outcome in a particular domain. For example, the tables printed in the Appendix to this book are probability distributions. Table 7.1 presents a much simpler example, the probability distribution of the number of heads occurring in three flips of a fair coin. As the table shows, the basic law of probability is used to calculate the probability of each outcome (number of heads). In the table, *H* represents heads, and *T* corresponds to tails. You can use the probability distribution to check your answers to the questions asked above.

Now let us consider some definitions. Any probability that can be determined logically before an event actually occurs is called an **a priori probability.** The examples just given are a priori probabilities. With a priori probabilities, you do not have to carry out the experiment to determine the probabilities. By contrast, probabilities generated by numerous trials are called **posterior probabilities.** For example, if we do not know whether a coin is biased, we can flip it numerous times to find out. The ratio of heads to total flips is the posterior probability of flipping the coin and obtaining a head. An unbiased coin has a probability of .5 of coming up heads. Posterior probabilities may also be called *long-run probabilities.*

Although a priori probabilities present a good introduction to the subject, most of the probabilities that public managers calculate and use are posterior probabilities. The latter are based on obtaining the relevant data and calculating the relative frequency of occurrence of events of interest. For example, the probability of employees of the city public works department earning a promotion within 2 years of hiring—or requesting a transfer to another department, or having a statistical package program loaded on their microcomputer at work, or referring to this book to help them interpret results from it—are all posterior probabilities. The probabilities that a nonprofit agency in the state will have more volunteers than paid employees, or receive

Table 7.1

Probability Distribution of Number of Heads in Three Tosses of a Coin

Outcome: Number of Heads	(1): Number of Ways Outcome Can Occur	(2): Number of Possible Outcomes	(1) ÷ (2): Probability
0	1 (*TTT*)	8	.125
1	3 (*HTT; THT; TTH*)	8	.375
2	3 (*HHT; HTH; THH*)	8	.375
3	1 (*HHH*)	8	.125
			1.000

funding from government, or have interns from MPA programs are also posterior probabilities. These probabilities can only be determined by obtaining the relevant information from agency records, observation, surveys, and so forth, and performing the necessary calculations. Later in this chapter we show how to apply the rules of probability to the calculation and interpretation of posterior probabilities.

An Application to Game Theory

Probability forms the basis of most games of chance as well as of decision theory (see Chapter 25). Because more than half of the states operate state lotteries, and some jurisdictions have a variety of other forms of legalized gambling, understanding how such games work is useful for the public manager. Let us construct a simple game in which people pay $1 to play. A coin is flipped; if heads comes up, the person wins $2; if tails, the player wins nothing.

One thing a manager needs to do to assess whether a game will be profitable for her state or jurisdiction is to calculate the expected value of the game. The expected value of the game is nothing more than the average payoff per game played if the game were played *many times*. The expected value of any outcome is the probability that the outcome will occur multiplied by the payoff for that outcome. In Figure 7.3, for example, the probability of heads is .5, which yields a payoff of $2; the expected value is .5 × $2 = $1. The probability of tails is also .5, with a payoff of 0; the expected value is .5 × 0 = 0. For the entire game, the expected value is the sum of all the expected values for the individual options. The expected value for the game in Figure 7.3 is, thus, $1 + 0, or $1. An expected value of $1 means that, on the average, the game will pay $1 to a player every time the game is played. Such a game would generate no profits that could be used for public programs in the state or jurisdiction. The game can be altered in two ways to generate income. First, the probabilities of each occurrence can be changed (by using a computer rather than flipping a coin to set them), as shown in Figure 7.4.

Second, the payoff for the options can be changed, as shown in Figure 7.5.

The games in Figures 7.4 and 7.5 generate profits for the state or jurisdiction, but the problem is in getting people to play such simple games, since they can easily see

---

Figure 7.3

Simple Game of Chance

Outcome	Probability	Payoff	Expected Value
Heads	.5	$2	$1
Tails	.5	0	0

Game expected value = $1

Figure 7.4

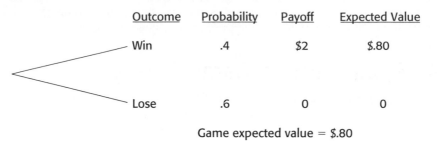

Simple Game of Chance with Probabilities Altered

Outcome	Probability	Payoff	Expected Value
Win	.4	$2	$.80
Lose	.6	0	0

Game expected value = $.80

Figure 7.5

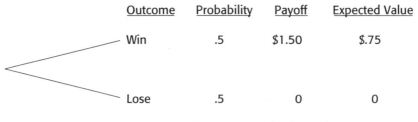

Simple Game of Chance with Payoff Altered

Outcome	Probability	Payoff	Expected Value
Win	.5	$1.50	$.75
Lose	.5	0	0

Game expected value = $.75

that they are better off by not playing. To get around this problem, we need to make a more complicated game, such as that in Figure 7.6.

With a $100 first prize, this game should attract more players yet produce revenue for the state or jurisdiction. What would happen if the price of playing increased to $2 and all the prizes were doubled? Calculate the expected value of this game in the space provided.

Doubling the playing price and doubling the payoff have no impact on the profitability of the game.

Figure 7.6

More Complex Game of Chance

Outcome	Probability	Payoff	Expected Value
First Prize	.001	$100	$.10
Second Prize	.25	$2	$.50
Lose	.749	0	0

Game expected value = $.60

Figure 7.7

Lottery-Style Game of Chance

Outcome	Probability	Payoff	Expected Value
First Prize	.0000003	$1,000,000	$.30
Second Prize	.00001	$1,000	$.01
Third Prize	.10	$2	$.20
Lose	.8999897	0	0

Game expected value = $.51

State lotteries tend to make the games attractive to play by offering a few very large prizes. Calculate the expected value of the game in Figure 7.7, which has a $1 million first prize (assume that the cost to play is $1).

Because of the large first prize, such a game is probably much more attractive to players than is the game in Figure 7.6. Is it a more profitable game for players? What does this tell you about the design of public lotteries?

A word of caution about expected values is in order. For expected values to be meaningful, a game or the options in a probability tree must be played/used many times. This is not a problem for a state government, since it can expect that millions of people might buy lottery tickets. It can be a problem for individuals, however. The game in Figure 7.8 illustrates this point.

Even though this game has an expected value of $12, an individual would be rational not to play this game. To achieve the expected value of $12 per play, an individual would have to play this game several million times. Few individuals would have the resources to convert this expected value into benefits or monetary returns from playing the game.

Figure 7.8

Game of Chance That Favors Long-Term Player

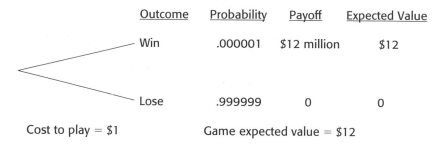

Outcome	Probability	Payoff	Expected Value
Win	.000001	$12 million	$12
Lose	.999999	0	0

Cost to play = $1   Game expected value = $12

Introduction to Probability Logic

To introduce you to the logic of probability, we will use Table 7.2, which lists data from the Flandreau income maintenance experiment. These data were collected to determine the impact of a guaranteed minimum income and other welfare options on the stability of welfare families. They are used to calculate posterior probabilities.

For the data on the Flandreau income maintenance experiment, what is the probability that a family in the experiment received workfare? We can apply the basic law of probability to find out. Table 7.2 shows that 40 families received workfare (outcome of interest) out of a total of 300 families (all possible outcomes). Thus, the probability that a family received workfare is the number of families that received workfare divided by the total number of families, or .133 (40 ÷ 300).

What is the probability that a family dissolved (*dissolved* is social science jargon for "the father abandoned the family")? Because 50 of the 300 families dissolved, the probability of a family dissolving is .167 (50 ÷ 300). If the situation that a family has dissolved is referred to as situation *D,* then the symbol for the probability of this event is $P(D)$.

Table 7.2

Preliminary Data, Flandreau Income Maintenance Experiment: Number of Families

Treatment	Impact on the Family		
	Family Dissolved	Family Stayed Together	Total
No welfare	5	20	25
Normal welfare	15	65	80
Guaranteed income	20	75	95
Income plus incentives	10	50	60
Workfare	0	40	40
	50	250	300

What is the probability that a family dissolved or that it did not receive any welfare at all? In this situation, we are asking for the probability that either of two events might have occurred. Determining this probability is the same as determining the earlier probabilities. It is the ratio of the number of families that received no welfare plus the number of families that dissolved to the total number of families. The number of families that received no welfare is 25, and the number of families that dissolved is 50, for a total of 75. This total, however, counts the 5 families that received no welfare *and* dissolved twice. Subtracting this number (5) and dividing the difference (70) by the total number of families yields a probability of .233 (70 ÷ 300). Statisticians refer to the probability of one event or another as the **union** of two probabilities. Symbolically, this is denoted as $P(A \cup B)$ (read as "*P* of *A* union *B*," or "the probability of *A* union *B*").

What is the probability that a family received a guaranteed income and that the family stayed together? In this situation, the logic is the same as used before. We divide the total number of families that received a guaranteed income and stayed together (75) by the total number of families (300). The probability that a family received a guaranteed income and stayed together is .25. The probability of two events occurring simultaneously is referred to as a **joint probability.** The symbolic representation of this is $P(A \cap B)$ (read as "*P* of *A* intersection *B*").

What is the probability that a family dissolved, given that it received an income plus incentives? Another way of expressing the "given" condition is to ask, Of the families that received income plus incentives, what is the probability that the family dissolved? The number of families receiving an income plus incentives that also dissolved is 10. The total number of families in this situation, however, is not 300. We are interested only in those families that received an income plus incentives, a total of 60 families. The probability that a family dissolved, given that it received an income plus incentives, is 10 ÷ 60, or .167. The probability of one event given that another event happened is called a **conditional probability.** The symbolic way of representing this is $P(A|B)$ (read as "the probability of *A* given *B*," or "*P* of *A* given *B*").

General Rules of Probability

To this point, we have discussed probability and its relationships intuitively. Now it is necessary to provide some general rules for understanding and calculating probabilities.

The General Rule of Addition

The **general rule of addition** applies whenever you want to know the probability that either of two events occurred. Statisticians express the general rule of addition symbolically as

$$P(A \cup B) = P(A) + P(B) - P(A \cap B)$$

Although this rule may appear complex, it is actually fairly simple. In English, the rule states that the probability of either of two events occurring $[P(A \cup B)]$ is equal to the probability that one event will occur $[P(A)]$ plus the probability that the other event will occur $[P(B)]$ minus the probability that both events will occur simultaneously $[P(A \cap B)]$. Remember that the probability of both events occurring at once is subtracted because this probability is contained in both the probability of the first event and the probability of the second event.

Perhaps the clearest way to illustrate the union of two probabilities is with a Venn diagram (see Figure 7.9). A *Venn diagram* pictures each event—for example, $[P(A)]$ with its own circle and can easily show intersection or overlap of different events— $P(A \cap B)]$. In Figure 7.9, it is clear that adding the probability of A to the probability of B counts the shaded area twice. For that reason, the shaded area [or $P(A \cap B)$] needs to be subtracted from the total.

The probability of any three events occurring $[P(A \cup B \cup C)]$ is a simple extension of the logic used for two events. Statisticians use the following formula:

$$P(A \cup B \cup C) = P(A) + P(B) + P(C) - P(A \cap B) \\ - P(A \cap C) - P(B \cap C) + P(A \cap B \cap C)$$

In other words, the probability of any of three events occurring $[P(A \cup B \cup C)]$ is equal to the probability of the first event $[P(A)]$ plus the probability of the second event $[P(B)]$, plus the probability of the third event $[P(C)]$, minus the probability that the first and the second event both occur $[P(A \cap B)]$, minus the probability that the first and third event both occur $[P(A \cap C)]$, minus the probability that the second and the third event both occur $[P(B \cap C)]$, plus the probability that all three events occur at once $[P(A \cap B \cap C)]$.

Again, it is easier to visualize this formula using Venn diagrams (see Figure 7.10). Adding the probability of A, the probability of B, and the probability of C together counts each of the lightly shaded areas twice and counts the darkly shaded area three times. Subtracting the intersection of A and B, the intersection of A and C, and the intersection of B and C removes each of the lightly shaded sections once. However, it also removes all three counts of the darkly shaded section ($A \cap B \cap C$), so this probability must be added back in.

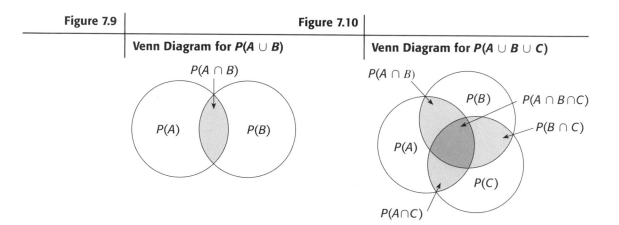

Figure 7.9

Venn Diagram for *P(A ∪ B)*

Figure 7.10

Venn Diagram for *P(A ∪ B ∪ C)*

Table 7.3

Results for England County Civil Service List

Exam Result	Pi Alpha Alpha Member			Not a Pi Alpha Alpha Member			Total
	College Degree	No Degree	Subtotal	College Degree	No Degree	Subtotal	
Passed exam	26	14	40	64	16	80	120
Failed exam	4	16	20	36	74	110	130
Subtotals	30	30	60	100	90	190	250
Totals	60			190			250

Clearly, an example will help here. Individuals can be placed on the England County civil service list in three ways: by passing the civil service exam, earning a college diploma, or being a member of Pi Alpha Alpha (a national public administration honorary society). Table 7.3 shows how the current list of eligibles qualified.

What is the probability that a person is on the England County eligibles list because he or she passed the exam, had a college degree, or was a member of Pi Alpha Alpha? The probability of passing the exam is .48(120 ÷ 250). The probability of having a college degree is .52(130 ÷ 250). The probability of being a member of Pi Alpha Alpha is .24(60 ÷ 250). (If you do not understand how these probabilities were derived, review the beginning of this chapter.) The sum of these probabilities is 1.24. From this number, we subtract the probability that someone passed the exam and had a college degree (90 ÷ 250 = .36), the probability that someone was a member of Pi Alpha Alpha and passed the exam (40 ÷ 250 = .16), and the probability that someone was a college graduate and a member of Pi Alpha Alpha (30 ÷ 250 = .12). Subtracting these probabilities from 1.24, we get a difference of .6. To this probability we add the probability that someone is a member of Pi Alpha Alpha, graduated from college, and passed the exam (26 ÷ 250 = .104), leaving us a probability of .704. Examining the table directly, we see that 176 persons were on the eligibles list (these three ways are the only ways to get on the list); the probability of being on the eligibles list, therefore, is .704 (176 ÷ 250).

You can calculate the probability that any of four or more events occurred by using the same logic that was used here. In practice, however, this calculation becomes fairly complex. If you are ever faced with such a problem, consult a statistics text or a statistician (or delegate to an exceptionally qualified and motivated intern!).

Whenever two events are mutually exclusive, a special rule of addition is used. Two events are **mutually exclusive** if the occurrence of A means that B will not occur. In other words, two events are mutually exclusive if only one of the events can occur at a time. As statisticians state it, if the probability of the intersection of A and B is zero, then A and B are mutually exclusive events. When two events are mutually exclusive, the probability of either A or B occurring is equal to the probability of A plus the probability of B (because there is no overlap to subtract).

The **special rule of addition for mutually exclusive events** is expressed symbolically as

$$P(A \cup B) = P(A) + P(B)$$

or as illustrated in the Venn diagram in Figure 7.11.

The General Rule of Multiplication

The **general rule of multiplication** is applied when you want to know the joint probability of two events (the probability that both events will occur). The general rule of multiplication is denoted symbolically as follows:

$$P(A \cap B) = P(A) \times P(B|A)$$
$$= P(B) \times P(A|B)$$

In other words, the joint probability of two events is equal to the probability of one event multiplied by the conditional probability of the other event, given that the first event occurs.

The Venn diagram in Figure 7.12 shows the intersection of *A* and *B,* which is equivalent to the probability of *A* times the probability of *B* given *A* (Figure 7.13), or the probability of *B* times the probability of *A* given *B* (Figure 7.14).

To illustrate the general rule of multiplication, let's use information supplied by the Bessmer (Michigan) Hospital, a nonprofit health care facility; the data are shown in Table 7.4. The hospital officials collected these data because they perceived that their workload was much higher in the summer months (reflecting the fact that babies are conceived in the winter months when recreation activities in Bessmer are fairly limited).

What is the probability that a woman is at least 3 months pregnant and it is winter? From the table, we can see the probability is .42 (216 ÷ 511). The general rule of multiplication says we can also find this probability by multiplying the probability that a woman is at least 3 months pregnant (.53, or 269 ÷ 511) by the probability that it is winter, given that a woman is at least 3 months pregnant (.80, or 216 ÷ 269). (Not every example can make sense!) The product of these probabilities is .42.

Figure 7.11 | **Figure 7.12** |

Venn Diagram for $P(A \cup B) = P(A) + P(B)$

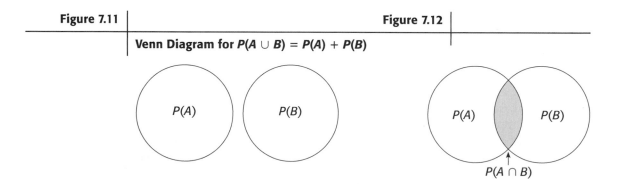

Figure 7.13   **Figure 7.14**

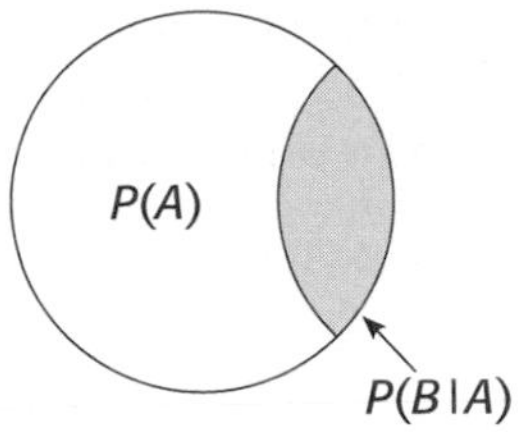

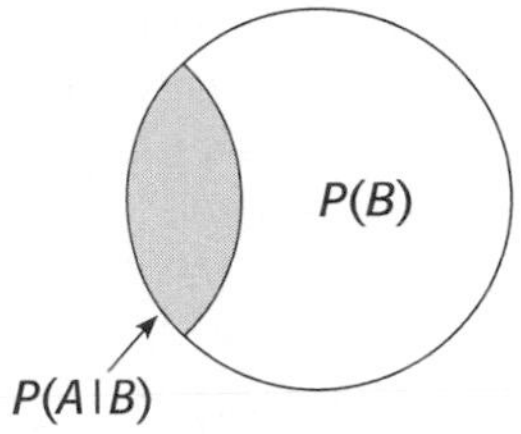

$P(A)$ $P(B|A)$ $P(A|B)$ $P(B)$

Table 7.4

Case Data on Bessmer Hospital Births

	Time of Year		
	October–March	April–September	Total
Women pregnant 3 months or more	216	53	269
Women pregnant less than 3 months	47	195	242
Total	263	248	511

From this information, should the Bessmer City Council authorize a cable TV system?

When two events are independent, a special rule of multiplication applies. Two events are **independent** if the probability of one event is not affected by whether or not the other event occurs. For example, when flipping a coin twice, the probability of obtaining a head on the second flip is independent of the result of the first flip. The probability remains .5 regardless of what happened on the first flip. Statisticians say two events A and B are *independent* if $P(A|B) = P(A)$. If the events are independent, it also follows that $P(B|A) = P(B)$.

When two events are independent, the probability of two events occurring is equal to the probability that one event will occur times the probability that the other event will occur. Or

$$P(A \cap B) = P(A) \times P(B)$$

If you think about it, the formula for the probability of two independent events occurring is an extension of the general rule of multiplication explained earlier. The multiplication rule states $P(A \cap B) = P(A) \times P(B|A)$. But when events are independent, $P(B) = P(B|A)$, so in this situation (only), the formula becomes easier: $P(A \cap B) = P(A) \times P(B)$.

This idea can be illustrated by the probability of obtaining two heads on consecutive flips of an unbiased coin. The probability of obtaining two heads is equal to the probability of obtaining a head on the first flip times the probability of obtaining a head on the second (.5 × .5 = .25). Note that the probability of a head remains the same on the second flip [$P(B|A) = P(B) = .5$], regardless of what happened on the first flip. Note, too, that these probabilities correspond to the ones you calculated earlier in the chapter for coin flips.

Chapter Summary

This chapter provides a basic introduction to probability. Probability provides a numerical estimate of how likely it is that particular events will occur. Concepts introduced include the basic law of probability, probability distribution, a priori probability, posterior probability, the union of two probabilities, joint probability, conditional probability, and the rules of addition and multiplication.

The basic law of probability (for equally likely events) states that the probability of an outcome is equal to the ratio of the number of ways that the outcome could occur to the total number of ways all possible outcomes could occur. A probability that can be determined before an event occurs is an a priori probability. Posterior probabilities are those generated by numerous trials. These are empirical probabilities, which require that the public or nonprofit manager gather the necessary data and calculate the relative frequency of occurrence.

The union of two probabilities is the probability that one event or the other will occur. The probability of two events occurring simultaneously is a joint probability. A conditional probability is the probability that one event will occur, given that another event has already happened.

The general rule of addition for two events A and B is as follows: The probability of either A or B occurring is equal to the probability of A plus the probability of B minus the joint probability of A and B (the subtraction is necessary to eliminate double counting). This rule can be extended to more than two events. The general rule of multiplication for two events A and B is this: The joint probability of A and B is equal to the probability of one event times the conditional probability of the other event, given that the first event has occurred. This rule can also be extended to more than two events.

Two events are independent if the probability of one event is not affected by whether or not the other event occurs. In that situation, the probability of both events occurring is found by multiplying the probability of one event times the probability of the other.

Problems

7.1   Answer the following questions by referring to the accompanying table, which lists the highway patrol's reasons for stopping cars and the number of tickets issued.

Reason for Stopping Car	Issued Ticket	Did Not Issue Ticket	Total
Speeding	40	170	210
No taillights	10	35	45
Failure to use signals	5	25	30
Careless driving	45	70	115
Total	100	300	400

Assume that a car was stopped.

(a) What is the probability that a ticket was issued?

(b) What is the probability that the car did not have taillights?

(c) What is the probability that a driver will get a ticket, given that he or she was stopped for careless driving?

(d) What is the probability that the person was stopped for speeding or for failure to use signals?

(e) Given that a ticket was not issued, what is the probability that the person was stopped for speeding?

7.2 David Morgan, the city manager of Yukon, Oklahoma, must negotiate new contracts with both the firefighters and the police officers. He plans to offer both groups a 7% wage increase and hold firm. Mr. Morgan feels that there is one chance in three that the firefighters will strike and one chance in seven that the police will strike. Assume that the events are independent.

(a) What is the probability that both will strike?

(b) What is the probability that neither the police nor the firefighters will strike?

(c) What is the probability that the police will strike and the firefighters will not?

(d) What is the probability that the firefighters will strike but the police will not?

7.3 What do we mean when we say that two events are independent?

7.4 In your own words, explain what mutually exclusive events are.

7.5 The probability that a smallpox case will be found in Metro City in any given week is .0034. In the week of July 17, four unrelated cases of smallpox are reported. If these are independent events, what is the probability that this would occur? Are these likely to be independent events?

7.6 The National Crop Reporting Service receives the accompanying information from the CIA on the Russian wheat harvest. Russian demand for wheat is approximately 210 million metric tons.

(a) What is the probability that the harvest will be adequate?

(b) If U.S. exports make up the difference, what is the probability that the United States will have to sell more than 20 million metric tons to the Russians?

Millions of Metric Tons	Probability
Less than 170	.05
170–180	.15
180–190	.23
190–200	.31
200–210	.15
210–220	.07
More than 220	.04

7.7 A successful launch of an ICBM requires three steps: the signal to fire must reach the missile team, the ignition mechanism must work properly, and the missile must not explode prematurely. The Department of Defense estimates that the probability that the signal to fire an ICBM will reach a missile team is .96. For any given missile, the probability that the ignition mechanism will work is .89. For missiles with operative ignition systems, 15 of every 100 will explode in the silo or before reaching orbit. Given the command to fire, what is the probability of a successful launch for any given missile?

7.8 From a survey of the households in Grayson, Missouri, the crime figures shown in the accompanying table were estimated.

Crime	Number Reported	Number Not Reported	Total
Murder	12	12	24
Robbery	145	105	250
Assault	85	177	262
Rape	12	60	72
Auto theft	314	62	376
Total	568	416	984

(a) What is the probability that a crime is reported?

(b) What is the probability that a crime is reported, given that an assault occurs?

(c) What is the probability that a nonreported crime is either a robbery or an assault?

(d) What is the probability that a crime is a rape and that it is reported?

(e) What is the probability that a crime is reported or that the crime is a robbery?

7.9 The city water department estimates that, for any day in January, the probability of a water main freezing and breaking is .2. For six consecutive days, no water mains break.

(a) What is the probability that this happens?

(b) Are the events independent?

7.10   Jane Watson is running a youth recreation program to reduce the juvenile crime rate. If Jane can get a Law Enforcement Assistance Administration (LEAA) grant to expand the program, she feels that there is a .9 probability that the program will work. If she fails to get the grant, the probability of success falls to .3. If the probability of getting the LEAA grant is .6, what is the probability that Jane's program will be successful?

7.11   Given $P(A) = .45$, $P(B) = .31$, and $P(A \cap B) = .26$, calculate:

   (a) $P(A \cup B)$.

   (b) $P(A|B)$

   (c) $P(B|A)$

7.12   Given $P(A) = .21$, $P(B|A) = .75$, and $P(A|B) = .41$, calculate:

   (a) $P(A \cap B)$

   (b) $P(B)$

7.13   Given $P(A) = .3$, $P(B) = .61$, and $P(A|B) = .3$, calculate:

   (a) $P(A \cap B)$

   (b) $P(A \cup B)$

7.14   Sheriff Joe Bob Stewart thinks the odds that any law enforcement grant is funded is .25. He believes that the decision to fund one grant is independent of the decision to fund any other grant.

   (a) Use a probability tree to tell Sheriff Stewart what the probability is that he can submit three grants and get none funded.

   (b) What is the probability of getting exactly one funded?

   (c) Exactly two?

   (d) Two or more?

CHAPTER 8

The Normal Probability Distribution

he most common probability distribution is the normal distribution. The normal distribution describes a great many phenomena: people's heights and weights, scores on numerous tests of physical dexterity and mental capability, psychological attributes, and so forth. Given this great range of phenomena, the normal probability distribution is very useful to managers in public and nonprofit organizations. This chapter elaborates the characteristics of the normal distribution and the calculation and use of standard normal scores or "z scores." It explains how to use the normal distribution table at the end of this book (Table 1) to determine and interpret probabilities, and the application of the normal distribution to problems of public and nonprofit administration.

Characteristics of the Normal Distribution

The normal probability distribution pertains to continuous variables. A **discrete variable** takes on a countable number of distinct values, such as 0, 1, 2, 3, ... The number of job classifications in an agency, the number of employees in a department, and the number of training sessions conducted are all examples of discrete variables. The binomial distribution, the subject of the next chapter, is a discrete distribution. It is used to calculate the probability that a certain number of events will occur in a given number of trials—for example, the number of defective binoculars purchased by the Pentagon in a sample of 10.

By contrast, a *continuous variable* can assume a countless number (or at least a very large range) of numerical values in a given interval; good examples are temperature, pressure, height, weight, time, and distance. Note that all of these variables can take on fractional values. Other characteristics, such as those measured in dollars (budgets, fringe benefit costs, income, and so forth) are not, strictly speaking, continuous. However, in a given interval, they have so many values, and the values are so close to one another (consider incomes of $30,101, $30,102, $30,103, . . .) that it makes sense to treat them as continuous variables.

The normal curve characterizes such continuous variables—provided that their distribution of scores takes on a certain shape. The general "bell shape" is well known and probably familiar to you. It is shown in Figure 8.1.

As Figure 8.1 illustrates, the **normal curve** is a mounded distribution centered around a single peak at the mean. The curve is perfectly symmetrical: Scores above and below the mean are equally likely to occur so that half of the probability under the curve (.5) lies above the mean and half (.5) below. Most values in a normal distribution fall close to the mean μ, and the curve tapers off gradually toward both of its ends or "tails." As values fall at a greater distance from the mean in either direction, the probability of their occurrence grows smaller and smaller. With respect to heights, weights, or other characteristics that have a normal distribution, most individuals cluster about the mean, and fewer and fewer individuals are found the farther one moves away from the central value in either direction. As shown in Figure 8.1, the normal curve does not touch the horizontal axis, which would indicate that a score at that point and beyond had zero probability of occurring. It is always possible, if not very likely, that a highly extreme value of a variable could occur. Nevertheless, as scores become more and more extreme, the probability of their occurrence becomes vanishingly small.

Figure 8.1

The Normal Distribution

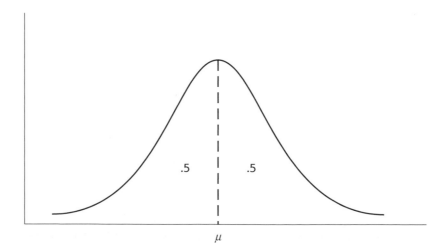

μ

The normal curve is completely determined by its mean μ and standard deviation σ (Chapters 5 and 6 discuss these statistics in detail). As shown in Figure 8.1, the height of the curve is greatest at the mean (where the probability of occurrence is highest). Figure 8.2 shows that the standard deviation governs the clustering of the data about this central value. In a normal distribution, approximately 68.26% of all values fall within one standard deviation of the mean in either direction, approximately 95.44% of all values fall within two standard deviations of the mean, and approximately 99.72% of all values fall within three standard deviations of the mean in either direction. The shaded areas in Figure 8.2(a), (b), and (c) illustrate this phenomenon.

Figure 8.2

The Normal Distribution and the Standard Deviation

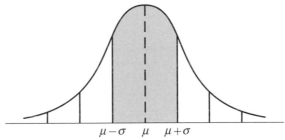

(a) 68.26% of all values lie within one standard deviation of the mean

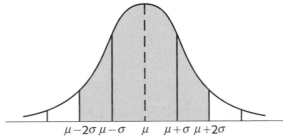

(b) 95.44% of all values lie within two standard deviations of the mean

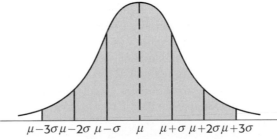

(c) 99.72% of all values lie within three standard deviations of the mean

Conversely, as shown by the unshaded areas in the figure, in a normal distribution only about 5% of the data values lie beyond two standard deviations of the mean in either direction $(1.0 - .9544 = .0456)$, and only about one-quarter of 1% of all values lie beyond three standard deviations $(1.0 - .9972 = .0028)$.

The normal distribution is measured in terms of its standard deviation. Given a normal distribution, we can use the curve to find the probability of a data value falling within any number of standard deviations from the mean (although the probability of a data value exceeding three standard deviations is very small). If all the public or nonprofit manager had to be concerned about was the probability of scores falling within one, two, or three standard deviations from the mean, or beyond each of these limits, this would be a very short chapter (and many statistical consultants would need to find other employment). Figure 8.2 displays these probabilities.

The manager has a much broader range of needs and interests for the normal curve, however. She or he is often interested in identifying the data values that demarcate the top 5% of applicants, or the bottom third of the work group, or the middle 75% of performers. For example, what score on the innovation inventory should be used to select the top 10% of nominees for the Municipal Innovation Award? If the nonprofit coordinating council wants to recognize the top 2% of nonprofit social service agencies in the state with respect to number of clients served, what numerical cutoff should it use? Or the manager may need to convert actual scores into their probability of occurrence. For instance, if scores on a test of typing proficiency have a normal distribution, what percentage of the applicant pool scored between the mean and a particular score of interest (say, the score of an applicant who performed well in other aspects of the job interview), or surpassed this score, or fell below it? If one nonprofit social service agency seemed to serve very few clients, what percentage of the agencies in the state did better—or worse? In what *percentile* did this applicant fall? Although none of these questions refer to data values that fall exactly one, two, or three standard deviations from the mean, the normal distribution can be used to answer them—as well as many other questions important for public and nonprofit management.

z Scores and the Normal Distribution Table

The way that the manager goes about addressing these questions is to calculate, and interpret, a z score. A **z score** is simply the number of standard deviations a score of interest lies from the mean of the distribution. Because the normal distribution is measured with respect to the standard deviation, one can use the z score to convert raw data values into their associated probabilities of occurrence with reference to the mean.

Let's call the score we are interested in X. To calculate the associated z score, first subtract the mean μ from the score of interest X, and then divide by the standard deviation σ to determine how many standard deviations this score is from the mean. Written as a formula:

$$z = \frac{X - \mu}{\sigma}$$

According to the formula (and the definition of the *z* score), a data value *X* exactly one standard deviation above the mean will have a *z* score of 1.0, a value two standard deviations above the mean will have a *z* score of 2.0, and a value three standard deviations above the mean will have a *z* score of 3.0. Referring to Figure 8.2, we see that the probability associated with a *z* score of 1.0 is .3413—that is, in a normal distribution, just over one-third of the data values lie between the mean and a value one standard deviation *above* it. The respective *z* score for a data value one standard deviation *below* the mean will be the same in magnitude but negative in sign, or −1.0. (Note that for scores of interest below or less than the mean in value, $X - \mu$ will be a negative number.)

Because the normal curve is symmetric about the mean, the negative sign poses no difficulty: The probability associated with a *z* score of −1.0 is also .3413 (again, just over one-third of the data values fall between the mean and one standard deviation below it). In a normal distribution then, .6826 of the data values lie within one standard deviation of the mean in either direction (.3413 + .3413), as shown in Figure 8.2(a). The associated probability for a *z* score of 2.0 (or −2.0) is .4772, and for a *z* score of 3.0 (or −3.0) the probability is .4986. Doubling these probabilities will yield the aggregate probabilities shown in Figure 8.2(b) and 8.2(c) of .9544 and .9972 for data values within two or three standard deviations from the mean, respectively.

How does the manager deal with the myriad of other *z* scores that she or he will encounter in everyday work life in public or nonprofit administration? It would be impractical to have a graph or picture for each one, as in Figure 8.2. Instead, for convenience, *z* scores are tabulated with their associated probabilities in a normal distribution table; the table appears as Table 1 in the Statistical Tables Appendix at the end of this book. As illustrated in Figure 8.3, the normal distribution table displays the percentage of data values falling between the mean μ and each *z* score, the area shaded

	Figure 8.3
Probability between a *z* Score and Mean	

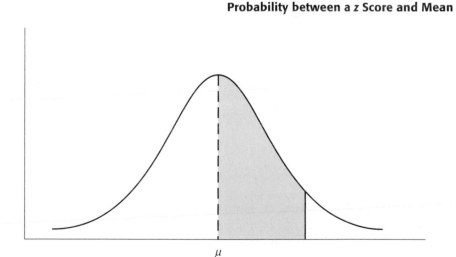

μ

in the figure. In the normal table, the first two digits of the z score appear in the far left column; the third digit is read along the top row of the table. The associated probability is read at the intersection of these two points in the body of the table.

For example, in a normal distribution, what percentage of the data values lie between the mean μ and a z score of 1.33? That question is the same as asking what percentage of the cases lie between the mean and a point 1.33 standard deviations away (that is, one and one-third standard deviations)? In the far left column of the table, locate the first two digits of the z score, 1.3, and read along this row until you reach the third digit, in the 0.03 column. The probability is .4082. In a normal distribution, 40.82% of the data values lie between the mean and a z score of 1.33.

Given this result, we can use our knowledge of the normal distribution to answer several questions of interest. For instance, what percentage of the data values lie between the mean and a z score 1.33 standard deviations *below* it? A negative z score, in this case -1.33, indicates a score of interest less than the mean. Because the normal curve is symmetric, this z score bounds the same amount of area (probability) under the normal curve as a z score of 1.33. The probability is identical: .4082.

What percentage of the data values lie *above* a z score of 1.33? This area of the normal curve is shaded in Figure 8.4. How can we find this probability? Recall that in a normal distribution, half (.5) of the probability lies above the mean and half below. We know that .4082 of all the values lie between the mean and a z score of 1.33. The shaded area beyond this z score can be found by subtracting this probability from .5, giving an answer of .0918. So 9.18% of the data values lie above this score.

In a normal distribution, what percentage of the data values lie below a z score of 1.33? This portion of the curve is shaded in Figure 8.5. We can proceed in either of two ways. The easier is to subtract from 1.0 (the total probability under the curve) the percentage of data values surpassing this z score (.0918); the answer is .9082. Or we know that the area under the curve between the mean and this z score is .4082 and that the area below the mean is equal to .5; add these probabilities to find the same total probability of .9082.

In the normal distribution table at the end of the book, practice finding the probabilities associated with the following z scores. Then, using the methods discussed earlier, calculate the percentage of data values in a normal distribution that fall above this z score and the percentage that fall below it:

z	Table Probability	Percentage above z	Percentage below z
1.62			
0.73			
2.40			
-1.50			
-0.48			
-3.16			

For further practice in using the normal distribution table, look up the probability associated with a z score of 1.0, that is, a score one standard deviation from the mean. For this z score the table displays the now familiar probability of .3413. Now,

Figure 8.4

Probability Greater Than a *z* Score

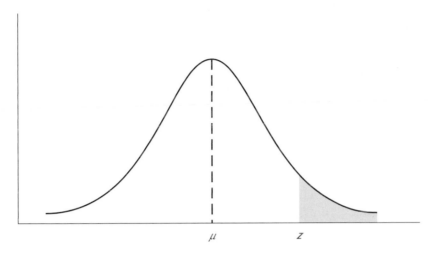

Figure 8.5

Probability Less Than a *z* Score

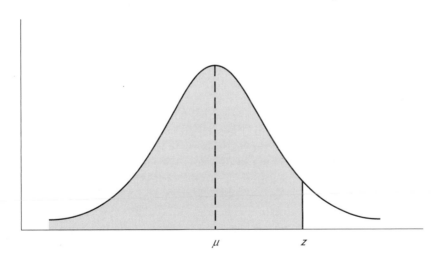

look up the probability for a *z* score of 2.0 (two standard deviations from the mean). No surprise here either: The probability is the equally familiar .4772. The probability for a *z* score of 3.0 also confirms our earlier understanding: The table shows that .4986 of the data values lie between the mean and a score three standard deviations above it.

Applications to Public Management

The police department in Jefferson, California, gives an exam to all applicants for their police academy. Scores on the Jefferson police exam have a normal distribution with a mean of 100 and a standard deviation of 10. (Any exam can be converted to one with a mean of 100 and a standard deviation of 10 by taking the raw scores, subtracting the mean from the score, and dividing by the standard deviation. This number is then multiplied by 10, and that number is added to 100. This process is called *standardization*.) Assume that the recruitment examiner gives the exam to an individual who scores 119.2. The next question is, How good is this score?

Another way of stating this question is to ask, what is the probability that a randomly selected individual would score 119.2 on the Jefferson police exam? To determine this probability, follow these steps.

Step 1: Convert the score on the exam into a *z* score. Recall that a *z* score is calculated by subtracting the mean test score from the score in question and dividing the difference by the standard deviation. Symbolically,

$$z = \frac{X - \mu}{\sigma}$$

In this case, subtract the mean, 100, from the score of interest, 119.2, to get 19.2; divide this number by the standard deviation, 10, to get a *z* score of 1.92. A *z* score tells you how many standard deviations (and in what direction) a score is from the mean. As explained earlier, values below the mean have negative *z* scores.

Step 2: Look up the value of a *z* score of 1.92 in a normal distribution table. Table 1 in the Appendix is a normal distribution table designed to convert *z* scores into probabilities. The numbers in the first column and across the top of the table represent the values of the *z* scores. The values inside the table represent the area of the normal curve that falls between the *z* score in question and the mean (the total area under the curve is 1.0). In this example, proceed down the first column until you find a *z* score of 1.9. According to the numbers across the top of the table, the first number next to the 1.9 represents a *z* score of 1.90; the second number is for a *z* score of 1.91; the third number represents a *z* score of 1.92 and is the one that interests us. The value found here is .4726. This means that 47.26% of the police exam scores fall between the mean (100) and a *z* score of 1.92 (119.2). Because 50% (or half) of the scores fall below the mean, a total of 97.26% of the scores fall below a score of 119.2. In probability terms, the probability that a randomly selected individual will score a 119.2 or better on the Jefferson police exam is .0274 (1.0 − .9726). Another way of stating this result is that the individual in question scored at the 97th percentile.

An important aspect of the normal distribution is its flexibility. The following examples illustrate some of the numerous applications of the normal distribution.

Suppose the police chief wants to know the percentage of job applicants who scored between 100 and 106 on the Jefferson police exam. Because the mean is 100 (and the standard deviation is 10), this question is equivalent to asking, what percentage of the applicants score between 106 and the mean? To answer, follow the two-step procedure discussed earlier and repeated here:

Step 1: Convert the score of interest into a z score. Use the formula for the z score:

$$z = \frac{X - \mu}{\sigma}$$

$$= \frac{106 - 100}{10}$$

$$= .60$$

The z score corresponding to a raw score of 106 is .60. In other words, this score is six-tenths of a standard deviation above the mean.

Step 2: Look up a z score of .60 in the normal distribution table (Table 1) at the end of the book. The police chief wants to know the percentage of job applicants who fall between this z score (raw score = 106) and the mean. We read this probability directly from the table; the table reveals a probability of .2257. Thus, about 22.6% of all applicants score between 100 and 106 on the exam. This area is shaded in Figure 8.6.

What percentage score above 106? This area, unshaded in Figure 8.6, is equal to .5 − .2257 = .2743. So, about 27.4% of job applicants surpass this criterion.

What percentage of applicants score between 88 and 112 on the exam? This problem is easy if you split it into two questions, with reference to the mean. First, what

Figure 8.6

Probability for z Score = .60

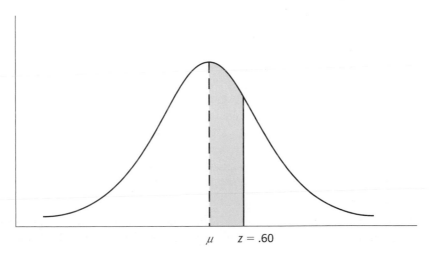

μ $z = .60$

percentage of applicants fall between the mean of 100 and a score of 112? Calculate z in the space provided. Then, look up the corresponding probability in the normal distribution table.

Step 1: Convert the score of interest into a z score:

$$z = \frac{112 - 100}{10}$$

$$= \frac{12}{10}$$

$$= 1.20$$

Step 2: Look up a z score of 1.20 in the normal distribution table. The percentage of job applicants who fall between this z score and the mean is .3849. Thus, 38.49% of all applicants score between 100 and 112 on the police examination.

Now, consider the second part of the question: What percentage of applicants score between 88 and the mean of 100? Note that 88 is the same distance from the mean as 112, but in the opposite (negative) direction. Therefore, it will yield the same absolute z value with a negative sign, -1.20. The associated probability is the same, .3849. To find the percentage of applicants who score between 88 and 112, add these probabilities, for an answer of about 77% (.3849 + .3849 = .7698). This area of the normal curve is shaded in Figure 8.7.

What is the probability that a randomly selected applicant will score between 117 and 122 on the Jefferson police examination? Note that the probability of scoring between these two values is equal to the probability of scoring between the mean and 122 *minus* the probability of scoring between the mean and 117; this difference is highlighted in Figure 8.8. To find this area of the normal curve, follow the two-step procedure presented earlier. First, calculate the z scores for the two scores of interest, 117 and 122:

$$z = \frac{117 - 100}{10} \qquad z = \frac{122 - 100}{10}$$

$$= \frac{17}{10} \qquad = \frac{22}{10}$$

$$= 1.70 \qquad = 2.20$$

Figure 8.7

Percentage between $z = 1.20$ and $z = -1.20$

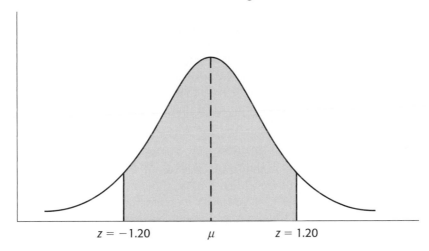

$z = -1.20$ μ $z = 1.20$

Figure 8.8

Probability between Two *z* Scores

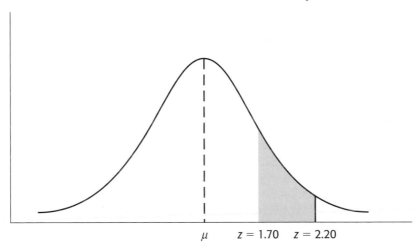

μ $z = 1.70$ $z = 2.20$

Next, look up the probabilities associated with *z* scores of 1.70 and 2.20 in the normal distribution table; .4554 of the area under the curve lies between 1.70 and the mean, and .4861 lies between 2.20 and the mean. As shown in Figure 8.8, the probability of scoring between 117 and 122, therefore, is equal to the difference between these two probabilities, or .0307 (.4861 − .4554).

What is the probability that an applicant will score 125 or more on the Jefferson police exam? Because we can calculate the probability that someone will score between the mean and 125, we can solve this problem. The probability of scoring between 100 and 125 (z score = ?) is .4938. Since 50% of all persons score below the mean, the probability of scoring 125 or below is .9938 (.50 + .4938). This means the probability of scoring 125 or above is .0062.

Calculating a probability when given a score or a range of scores is only one way the normal distribution is used. In public and nonprofit administration, the manager often needs to find the raw score that will cut off a certain percentage of the cases, for example, the top 10% or the bottom 25%. For example, the Jefferson police force has a policy of accepting only those who score in the top 20% of the persons taking the police exam. What raw score should be used as the cutoff point? This question can be answered by following these steps:

Step 1: The score associated with the top 20% is the same score that is associated with the bottom 80%. This problem is easier to solve for the bottom 80% than for the top 20%, so we will find the cutoff point for the bottom 80%. We know from the shape of the normal curve that 50% of the bottom 80% fall below the mean of 100. Another 30% fall between the cutoff value and the mean. To find the z score associated with this cutoff point, look up a probability of .3000 in the *body* of a normal distribution table. Then read to the far left column and top row of the table to find the corresponding z score. Note that this procedure reverses the one we have been following—that of calculating a z score from raw numbers and then finding the associated probability in the body of the table. Here, we know the probability we want to set off (.3000), and we need to find the associated z score. So, we start in the body of the table.

Scanning the body of the normal distribution table, we find that the closest probability to .3000, without going under it, is .3023. The z score associated with this probability is .85 and is the one we seek. (If we had chosen a z score with an associated probability less than .3000, we would cut off slightly more than the top 20% of scores on the police examination.)

Step 2: Convert this z score to a raw score. Recall that a z score is simply the number of standard deviations a score of interest is from the mean. We want the raw score associated with a z score of .85. So, multiply this z score times the standard deviation (10) to get 8.5; our score of interest is, thus, 8.5 above the mean. To complete the conversion, add this number to the mean to get 100 + 8.5 = 108.5. If the police academy class is limited to the top 20% of all applicants, only those who score 108.5 or above on the examination should be admitted.

One more example is in order. The Lower Slobovian Army recruits its officer corps from the Slobovian universities. To be admitted to Officer Candidate School (OCS), the college graduate must score in the top 75% of all those taking the exam. Last year, the mean exam score was 80, with a standard deviation of 6. Exam scores were normally distributed. At what value should the minimum passing score be set to admit only the top 75%?

Since we know 50% of the applicants will score above 80, we need to know the score below the mean that will contain 25% of the scores between it and the mean. Looking up a probability of .25 in the normal table, we find a value of .2486 associated with a z score of .67. Because we are interested in scores below the mean, this z score is $-.67$. Converting a z score of $-.67$ to a raw score, we get a minimum passing grade of 76 $[(-.67 \times 6) + 80 = 76]$.

A Measurement Technique Based on Standard Normal Scores

To this point in the chapter, we have used standardized scores or z scores to determine and interpret probabilities. We can also use z scores as an aid to measurement. In earlier examples, we showed how to use z scores to calculate the percentile in which a particular observation lies: Given a variable with a normal distribution and the resulting z scores, you can determine what percentage of observations lie above or below any score. If you had such information, for example, on the responsiveness of public relations departments to citizen inquiries in cities of greater than 100,000 population, you could use the normal distribution table to place the cities in percentiles on this variable.

You can also use normal scores to combine variables into scales or indexes. A **scale** or **index** is a composite measure combining several variables into a single, unified measure of a concept. Because variables are usually measured on different scales, you should not simply add scores together to create a new scale. For example, if you needed to create and report an overall measure of the physical fitness of military troops, their height (inches), weight (pounds), age (years), speed (time to run a mile), and personal habits (frequency of smoking, drinking, and so on) might all be important—but simply summing scores across the different variables would be meaningless. The measurement scales for the variables are not comparable.

You can use standard normal z scores to overcome the problem of different scales of measurement. A z score converts any variable to the same unit of measurement, hence, the name *standard* normal score. Regardless of the initial scale of measurement of a variable, all z scores are measured on the same normal curve or distribution and have the same probability interpretation. Thus, if variables are converted first to z scores to place them on the same measurement scale and then summed, the resulting scales or indexes will not be distorted by any initial differences in measurement: Each variable will contribute appropriately to the composite scale or index.

Let's look at an example. John Pelissero, a data analyst for the city of Evansville, feels that excellent performance by city garbage collection crews can be summarized by two variables: tons of trash collected and the number of complaints received from citizens. Mr. Pelissero would like to combine these data into a single measure of performance, but he realizes that the variables are based on very different units of measurement (tons of trash and number of complaints): Because the tons of trash are so much larger in magnitude, they will dwarf the number of complaints, which are relatively small numbers. He knows that to create a meaningful index of performance, something must be done to place the two variables on the same measurement scale.

Table 8.1

Performance of City Garbage Collection Crews in Evansville

Crew	Tons Collected	Complaints Against
A	127	6
B	132	8
C	118	4
D	170	9
E	123	3

Obviously, Mr. Pelissero has read this book and will go a long way in public management. In Table 8.1 he has assembled the data from each of the five city work crews on the number of tons of trash collected and the number of complaints they have received from citizens.

Mr. Pelissero wants to combine these two variables into a single measure of performance, so he follows these steps.

Step 1: Calculate the mean (μ) and standard deviation (σ) for each variable. They are shown in Table 8.2.

Table 8.2

Mean and Standard Deviation for Each Variable

	Tons	Complaints
μ	134	6
σ	18.6	2.3

Step 2: Convert each of the raw scores of trash collected and complaints received into z scores by taking the raw score, subtracting the mean, and dividing that difference by the standard deviation. The calculations are shown in Tables 8.3 and 8.4. Because complaints indicate poor performance (two complaints are worse, not better, than one complaint), the z scores for complaints were multiplied by -1 to reverse the scale.

Table 8.3

z Scores for Tons of Trash Collected

Tons $- \mu$	$(X - \mu) \div \sigma$	$= z$
$127 - 134 =$	$-7 \div 18.6 =$	$-.38$
$132 - 134 =$	$-2 \div 18.6 =$	$-.11$
$118 - 134 =$	$-16 \div 18.6 =$	$-.86$
$170 - 134 =$	$36 \div 18.6 =$	1.94
$123 - 134 =$	$-11 \div 18.6 =$	$-.59$

Table 8.4

z Scores for Complaints Received

Complaints $- \mu =$	$(X - \mu) \div \sigma = z$			$-z$
$6 - 6 =$	$0 \div 2.3 =$	0		0
$8 - 6 =$	$2 \div 2.3 =$	.87		$-.87$
$4 - 6 =$	$-2 \div 2.3 =$	$-.87$		.87
$9 - 6 =$	$3 \div 2.3 =$	1.30		-1.30
$3 - 6 =$	$-3 \div 2.3 =$	-1.30		1.30

Step 3: For each crew, add the z scores for trash collected and complaints received together, as shown in Table 8.5 to obtain performance scores. The performance scores can then be used to compare the trash collection crews with each other on a single measure. The z-score procedure simply converts each variable to a common base (standard deviations from the mean) so that the variables can be added appropriately. Note, as Table 8.3 shows, the highest-performing trash crew was fourth in total tons of trash collected but received the fewest complaints from citizens.

Table 8.5

Performance Scores for Garbage Collection Crews

Crew	Tons	Complaints	Performance
A	$-.38$	0	$-.38$
B	$-.11$	$-.87$	$-.98$
C	$-.86$	.87	.01
D	1.94	-1.30	.64
E	$-.59$	1.30	.71

This procedure weights both tons of trash collected and complaints received equally. If Mr. Pelissero felt that tons of trash was twice as important as complaints, he would multiply the z scores for tons of trash by 2 before adding them to the z scores for complaints, as shown in Table 8.6. Note that some of the trash crews change ranking when tons of trash collected is given a higher weighting (twice as important).

Table 8.6

Performance Scores When Tons Are Weighted Twice as Heavily as Complaints

Crew	Tons × 2		Complaints	Performance
A	$-.38 \times 2 =$	$-.76$	0	$-.76$
B	$-.11 \times 2 =$	$-.22$	$-.87$	-1.09
C	$-.86 \times 2 =$	-1.72	.87	$-.85$
D	$1.94 \times 2 =$	3.88	-1.30	2.58
E	$-.60 \times 2 =$	-1.20	1.30	.10

Table 8.7

Performance Scores When Tons and Complaints Are Weighted by One-Half

Crew	Tons × .5	Complaints × .5	Performance
A	−.38 × .5 = −.19	0 × .5 = 0	−.19
B	−.11 × .5 = −.055	−.87 × .5 = −.435	−.49
C	−.86 × .5 = −.43	.87 × .5 = .435	.005
D	1.94 × .5 = .97	−1.30 × .5 = .65	.32
E	−.59 × .5 = −.295	1.30 × .5 = .65	.355

A useful equal-weighting scheme is to weight the z scores for tons and the z scores for complaints by one-half or .5. This procedure is equivalent to calculating the mean performance score for each garbage collection crew. The resulting performance scores retain the value of a z score in indicating how many units (standard deviations) a score is above or below the mean. Positive scores indicate performance above the mean, and negative scores indicate performance below the mean. Performance scores calculated in this manner, as displayed in Table 8.7, show that crews A and B are below the mean in performance, crew C is at the mean, and crews D and E are above the mean.

A public or nonprofit manager can assign any weights to the variables so long as the variables have been converted to z scores first, and the weights can be justified. For example, the board of directors of a nonprofit food bank feels that dispensing meals is by far its most important activity. In comparing its performance with that of other food banks, it might weight meals served by a factor of 3.0, monetary donations by 2.0, and volunteer hours by 1.5. The number of variables that can be combined using the z-score method has no limit. A manager can use 2, 4, 6, or 50 indicators and combine them by adding z scores.

A note of caution is in order. The z-score technique should only be used when the manager believes that the concept being measured has only one dimension. If the concept has two or more dimensions (as the effectiveness of a receptionist is a function of efficiency and courtesy), then a more sophisticated statistical technique called *factor analysis* should be used to combine several indicators or variables. When you have multiple indicators of a multidimensional concept and want to combine some of the indicators, consult a statistician.

Chapter Summary

The normal distribution is a very common and useful probability distribution in public and nonprofit administration. The general bell shape of the curve describes the distribution of many phenomena of interest to the public or nonprofit manager.

The normal distribution is measured in terms of its standard deviation. In a normal distribution, 68.26% of all values lie within one standard deviation of the mean in either direction, 95.44% of all values fall within two standard deviations of the mean, and 99.72% of all values fall within three standard deviations.

To use the normal distribution, the manager must calculate and interpret a z score. A z score is defined as the number of standard deviations a score of interest lies from the mean of the distribution. It is used to convert raw data values into their associated probabilities of occurrence with reference to the mean. Denoting the score of interest X, the mean μ, and the standard deviation σ, the formula for the z score is

$$z = \frac{X - \mu}{\sigma}$$

The normal distribution table found in Table 1 in the Statistical Tables Appendix at the end of this book displays the percentage of cases falling between any z score and the mean of the distribution (or the probability that falls under this region of the curve). Using this information, the public or nonprofit manager can answer a variety of important questions, such as the probability of observing a score less than, or greater than, the score of interest or of falling between any two scores. She or he can also identify scores that will cut off portions of the curve of special interest, such as the top 5% of qualifiers.

One can also use standard normal scores to combine variables into a composite scale or index. This technique is very useful to public and nonprofit managers who often have several indicators of a concept (for example, performance) and need to combine them into a single measure.

Problems

8.1 Vince Yosarian works for the Bureau of Forms. His manager has reprimanded Vince because she feels that he has not performed up to standard for processing forms at the bureau, the crucial part of the job. At the bureau, the number of forms processed by employees is normally distributed, with a mean of 67 forms per employee per day, with a standard deviation of 7. His manager has calculated that Vince's average rate is 50 forms processed per day. What percentage of employees at the bureau process fewer forms than Vince? What percentage of employees at the bureau process more forms than Vince? Does the manager's complaint seem justified or not?

8.2 The average (mean) amount of time that a manager at the Mount Pleasant Department of Human Services spends in the annual performance review with an employee is 27.2 minutes, with a standard deviation of 4.9 minutes (normal distribution). What percentage of the annual performance reviews in the department take between 22.3 and 32.1 minutes? Between 17.4 and 37 minutes? Between 12.5 and 41.9 minutes? Explain your answers.

8.3 According to records kept by Compton County, the average (mean) amount of time that it takes for employees to be reimbursed for professional expenses incurred in service to the county is 36 days, with a standard deviation of 5 days. The distribution is normal. About 2 months ago, Marissa Lancaster attended a training conference for her job in the County Recreation Department. She filed for reimbursement for expenses that she had at the conference

42 days ago, but she has not received payment. What is the probability of receiving reimbursement within 42 days of filing? After 42 days? At this point, should Ms. Lancaster be apprehensive about receiving reimbursement?

8.4 Refer to Problem 8.3. The head of the Compton County Accounting Department wants to establish a standard regarding the length of time that employees can expect to wait to receive reimbursement for professional expenses. She wants to publish a standard that states the number of days it takes the department to process 95% of the claims filed. Help the department head find that standard.

8.5 Parnelli Jones, a vehicle manager for the northeast region of the forestry service, is charged with purchasing automobiles for service use. Because forestry service employees often have to drive long distances in isolated regions, Parnelli is very concerned about gasoline mileage for the vehicle fleet. One automobile manufacturer has told him that the particular model of vehicle that interests him has averaged 27.3 miles per gallon in road tests with a standard deviation of 3.1 (normal distribution). Parnelli would like to be able to tell his superiors at the forestry service that the cars will get at least 25 miles to the gallon. According to the road test data, what percentage of the cars can be expected to meet this criterion? Parnelli also thinks that his superiors might settle for cars that got 24 miles to the gallon or better. What percentage of the cars can be expected to meet this criterion?

8.6 Refer to Problem 8.5. During the negotiations with the automobile manufacturer, Parnelli gets a sinking feeling that some of the cars he is thinking of purchasing for the forestry service might average less than 20 miles to the gallon of gasoline. According to the road test data, what percentage of the cars can be expected to fall below this mileage level? Should Parnelli be very worried?

8.7 Butterworth, Missouri, is trying to increase its tourism, a great source of revenue. Among other things, Butterworth prides itself on its temperate climate. The tourism department would like to include in its glossy new brochure the middle range of temperatures that occur on 90% of the days there. A check with the National Weather Service finds that the average temperature in Butterworth is 76 degrees with a standard deviation of 5.7 (the temperatures were normally distributed). Help the tourism department by finding the two temperatures that cut off the middle 90% of temperatures in Butterworth.

8.8 The average (mean) paid by the Bureau of Indian Affairs for a 5-day training workshop contracted with the private sector is $1,500 (standard deviation = $280; normal distribution). Perk Morgan, a BIA employee, would like to attend a sensitivity training workshop in Bermuda (he feels that he must go to an exotic location to get in touch with his true feelings); the government rate for the training workshop is $2,400. What percentage of 5-day training workshops funded by the BIA exceed this amount? Perk has also inquired into a sensitivity training workshop to be held in Sausalito, California (less exotic location, but still able to get in touch with feelings); the cost for this workshop is $2,100. What percentage of BIA-sponsored training workshops exceed this cost? What would you advise Perk to do?

8.9 Ima Fastrack is a data analyst at the Oakmont Civil Service Commission. When she was first hired 3 months ago, she was satisfied with her salary of $24,832. In the time since she was hired, Ima has talked with several others in similar positions with the Oakmont city government; all earn more than she does. Ima has obtained data on the salaries of data analysts with the city. The distribution of salaries is normal, with an average salary of $25,301 and a standard deviation of $986. Ima has come to believe that she is seriously underpaid relative to others in her position. Do you agree or disagree with her? Use the normal curve to support your answer.

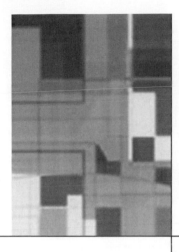

CHAPTER 9

The Binomial Probability Distribution

The **binomial probability distribution** provides a method for estimating probability when events that concern the public or nonprofit manager take on certain characteristics. It allows the manager to determine the probability that an event will occur a specified number of times in a certain number of trials. For example, if certain conditions are met, you can use the binomial distribution to estimate the probability that the mail will be delivered before a specified time every day for a week or the probability that a certain piece of equipment will remain operational throughout a 10-day inspection period. As these examples suggest, the binomial is a discrete distribution that deals with the probability of observing a certain number of events of interest in a set number of repeated trials. In this chapter, we discuss the characteristics and use of the binomial distribution.

Binomial Probabilities

The binomial probability distribution can be used when the process under consideration is what is called a Bernoulli process. The first characteristic of a **Bernoulli process** is as follows: The outcome of any trial (a trial being one attempt, whether or not successful) can be classified into one of two mutually exclusive and jointly exhaustive categories. One of these two categories (the one you want to examine) is referred to as a success; the other category is referred to as a failure.

Some examples are in order. Flipping an unbiased coin follows a Bernoulli process. Results of the flips can be classified as either a "head" or "not a head" (a tail). The solving of crimes by a police department can be described in a similar manner; a crime is either solved or not solved. Rolling a six on a die may be characterized as a six or not a six (any other number on the die).

The second characteristic of a Bernoulli process is that the probability of success must remain constant from trial to trial and be totally unaffected by the outcomes of any preceding trial. In short, each trial is independent of the previous trials (Chapter 7 discusses statistical independence). Examples of independent events include the probability of obtaining a head on any flip of a coin. The probability on any given flip is not affected by the number of heads obtained on previous flips. The probability of a fire occurring in a community on a given night is not affected by whether a fire occurred in a community the previous night (assuming that the city has no pyromaniacs).

Any process that meets these two characteristics is a Bernoulli process. When a Bernoulli process exists, the probability that any number of events will occur can be determined by using the binomial probability distribution. To determine a probability by using the binomial probability distribution, you must know three things. First, you must know the number of trials, that is, the number of times a certain event is tried. Second, you must know the number of successes—that is, the number of times you achieve or want to achieve a given event. Third, you must know the probability that the event in question will occur in any trial. This probability might be known a priori (such as rolling a six on a die), or you might have to calculate it (for example, from the rates of equipment failures).

With the knowledge of these three factors, the formula that follows can be used to calculate the probability of any one event for the binomial probability distribution.

$$C_r^n p^r q^{n-r}$$

where

$n =$ the number of trials

$r =$ the number of successes

$p =$ the probability that the event will be a success

$q = 1 - p$

Although this formula looks complex, in actuality it is not. The C_r^n is a symbol for something statisticians call a **combination** (read as "a combination of n things taken r at a time"). To illustrate a combination and its value, let us assume that we have four balls marked with the letters a, b, c, and d, respectively. We want to know how many different sets of three balls we could select from the four. In statistical language, we want to know the number of combinations of four balls taken three at a time. As the following illustration shows, a combination of four things taken three at a time equals 4; that is, there are 4 different combinations of four things taken three at a time.

Combination	Balls Selected
1	*a, b, c*
2	*a, b, d*
3	*a, c, d*
4	*b, c, d*

These four combinations of three balls represent all the possible ways that four items can be grouped into sets of three. In the space provided, use the same procedure to determine the value of a combination of four things taken two at a time.

If you found six combinations, congratulations (*ab, ac, ad, bc, bd, cd*).

Listing all possible combinations as a way to figure out the value of C_r^n often gets burdensome. For example, the following combination would take a long time to calculate by the combination-listing method:

$$C_6^{15}$$

The number of combinations of 15 things taken six at a time will be very large. To simplify, a shortcut method of determining combinations has been found using the formula

$$C_r^n = \frac{n!}{r!(n-r)!}$$

where $n!$ (called n factorial) is equal to $n \times (n-1) \times (n-2) \times (n-3) \times \cdots \times 3 \times 2 \times 1$; $r!$ and $(n-r)!$ have the same interpretation. For example, $6! = 6 \times 5 \times 4 \times 3 \times 2 \times 1 = 720$.

In the preceding example, we find

$$C_6^{15} = \frac{15!}{6!9!}$$

$$= \frac{\overbrace{15 \times 14 \times 13 \times 12 \times 11 \times 10 \times 9 \times 8 \times 7 \times 6 \times 5 \times 4 \times 3 \times 2 \times 1}^{15!}}{\underbrace{(6 \times 5 \times 4 \times 3 \times 2 \times 1)}_{6!} \times \underbrace{(9 \times 8 \times 7 \times 6 \times 5 \times 4 \times 3 \times 2 \times 1)}_{9!}}$$

$$= 5,005$$

The use of the binomial distribution can be best illustrated by working a problem. Assume that we are going to flip an unbiased coin three times, and we want to know the probability of getting exactly three heads. In this example, the number of trials (n) is equal to 3, the number of coin flips. The number of successes (r) is equal to 3, the number of heads. The probability of obtaining a head on one flip of a coin (p) is equal to .5; q, then, is equal to $1 - p$, or .5. Recall that in a Bernoulli process, only two outcomes are possible. If the probability of success is p, then the probability of failure must be $1 - p = q$. Substituting these numbers into the binomial probability distribution formula, we get the following:

$$C_r^n p^r q^{n-r} = \left(\frac{3!}{3!0!}\right) \times .5^3 \times .5^0 = .125$$

Calculating the combination term first, we find that the numerator (top) of the fraction is equal to 3! ($3 \times 2 \times 1$), or 6. This number is divided by the denominator (bottom) of the fraction, 3!, or 6, times 0!. To keep the universe orderly, *statisticians define 0! as equal to 1.* The combination term, therefore, is 6 divided by 6, or 1; that is, there is only one way in which you could flip a coin three times and get three heads (the sequence head-head-head). The probability terms are easily calculated: $.5^3$ is equal to $.5 \times .5 \times .5$, or .125, and $.5^0$ is equal to 1. Note again that *statisticians define any number to the 0 power as equal to 1* to maintain an orderly universe. The probability of obtaining three heads in three flips of an unbiased coin, then, is $1 \times .125 \times 1$, or .125.

To test yourself, calculate the probability that in four flips of an unbiased coin exactly two heads will occur. Calculate in the space provided.

You should have found a probability of .375 that two heads would occur on four flips of an unbiased coin. The problem may be defined as one where $n = 4$, $r = 2$, and $p = .5$ (the number of trials, the number of successes, and the probability of success, respectively). Again, q (probability of tails) $= 1 - p = .5$. The probability can be calculated as follows:

$$
\begin{aligned}
C_r^n p^r q^{n-r} &= \left(\frac{4!}{2!2!}\right) \times .5^2 \times .5^2 \\
&= \left(\frac{4 \times 3 \times 2 \times 1}{2 \times 1 \times 2 \times 1}\right) \times .25 \times .25 \\
&= 6 \times .25 \times .25 \\
&= .375
\end{aligned}
$$

Suppose you want to know the probability of obtaining *two or more* heads on four flips of an unbiased coin. In this situation, you would figure out the probability of obtaining four heads (.0625), the probability of obtaining three heads (.25), and the probability of obtaining two heads (.375). Because these three events are mutually exclusive, the probability of either two, three, or four heads is equal to the probability of two heads plus the probability of three heads plus the probability of four heads, or .6875. The calculations for two heads appear earlier; the calculations for three and four heads follow:

$$\text{Three heads: } C_3^4 \times .5^3 \times .5^1 = \left(\frac{4!}{3!1!}\right) \times .125 \times .5$$

$$= \left(\frac{4 \times 3 \times 2 \times 1}{3 \times 2 \times 1 \times 1}\right) \times .0625$$

$$= 4 \times .0625$$

$$= .25$$

$$\text{Four heads: } C_4^4 \times .5^4 \times .5^0 = \left(\frac{4!}{4!0!}\right) \times .0625 \times 1$$

$$= \left(\frac{4 \times 3 \times 2 \times 1}{4 \times 3 \times 2 \times 1 \times 1}\right) \times .0625$$

$$= 1 \times .0625$$

$$= .0625$$

An example of how the binomial probability distribution can be used in a public management setting is in order. Suppose that the Stermerville Public Works Department has been charged with racial discrimination in hiring practices. Last year, 40% of the persons who passed the department's civil service exam and were eligible to be hired were minorities. From this group, the public works department hired 10 individuals; 2 were minorities. What is the probability that, if the Stermerville Public Works Department did not discriminate, it would have hired two or fewer minorities? (Note that we assume, as a personnel analyst would have to in this situation, that anyone who passed the exam was capable of successful job performance. In other words, we assume that every individual had the same chance to be hired.)

The easiest way to figure out a problem of this nature is first to identify n, r, p, and q. In this case p, the probability that a minority is hired, is equal to the proportion of minorities in the job pool, or .4. And q, of course, is equal to $1 - p = 1 - .4 = .6$. The number of trials (n) in this case is equal to the number of persons hired, or 10. The number of successes (r) is equal to the number of minorities selected in this group, or 2. We are interested in the probability of two or fewer minorities selected, so we must calculate the binomial probability distribution for two minorities, one minority, and zero minorities.

The probability calculations for two minorities are as follows:

$$C_r^n p^r q^{n-r} = \left(\frac{10!}{2!8!}\right) \times .4^2 \times .6^8 = 45 \times .4^2 \times .6^8 = 45 \times .16 \times .6^8$$

$$= 7.2 \times .6^8 = 7.2 \times .0168 = .120$$

The probability calculations for one minority are as follows:

$$C_1^{10} \times .4^1 \times .6^9 = \left(\frac{10!}{1!9!}\right) \times .4 \times .6^9 = 10 \times .4 \times .6^9 = 4 \times .6^9 = 4 \times .010 = .040$$

The probability calculations for zero minorities are as follows:

$$C_0^{10} \, .4^0 \times .6^{10} = \left(\frac{10!}{0!10!}\right) \times .4^0 \times .6^{10} = 1 \times .4^0 \times .6^{10} = 1 \times 1 \times .6^{10} = .006$$

Statistically, a person can conclude that the probability that the Stermerville Public Works Department could select two or fewer minorities out of 10 individuals hired from a pool that consists of 40% minorities is .166 (.12 + .04 + .006 = .166) if the department shows no preference in regard to hiring minorities. In other words, a pattern such as this could happen about 1 time in 6.

This is a statistical statement. As a manager, you have to arrive at managerial conclusions. You need to know whether the department is engaged in discrimination. The statistical finding is only one piece of evidence that a manager uses in arriving at a conclusion.

After receiving statistical information, the manager should always ask whether anything else could have produced a result similar to this, other than discrimination (or whatever other question is involved). For example, perhaps more minorities were offered jobs, but they turned them down for some reason. Sometimes it is helpful to examine past behavior. If last year the department hired 42% minorities, you might not be too concerned. If they only hired 20% minorities last year, you might become more concerned. The manager's task at this point is to examine all potential reasons that explain why the statistical pattern occurred and to eliminate them. Can you think of other causes for these statistical results?

If no other reason (other than discrimination) can be found to account for the statistical pattern ($p = .166$), then the manager must decide how sure he or she wants to be. Because this pattern could have occurred by random chance 16.6% of the time, if the manager concludes that discrimination has occurred, there is a 1 in 6 chance that he or she is wrong. There is no magic number for how sure a manager should be. Social scientists often use a probability of less than 5% for making decisions. This is generally not a good idea for a manager. In some cases, a 5% risk is far too high. For example, would you authorize the launch of the space shuttle if there were a 5% chance of an explosion? Such a decision would mean that the manager would find it acceptable if 1 of every 20 launches resulted in an explosion. Alternatively, other decisions might not require levels as low as .05. A probability of .25, or even .35, might be acceptable in deciding between two alternative methods of collecting trash. In short, the manager must take the responsibility for establishing a level of risk based on how important the decision is. The manager should never let his or her statistical analyst set the probability level. This decision requires managerial judgment based on an individual's experience and willingness to take risks. Managers would do well to remember that statistical analysts are rarely fired when the manager they report to makes a bad decision. We return to the issue of how sure the manager should be in Chapter 12.

Although the binomial probability distribution provides a good method for estimating the probability that a given number of events will occur, often the task of calculating the binomial probability distribution becomes fairly complex mathematically. For example, suppose that instead of hiring 2 minorities out of 10 persons, the

Stermerville Public Works Department hired 43 minorities out of 150 persons. These figures would require the following probability to be estimated:

$$C_{43}^{150} \times .4^{43} \times .6^{107}$$

The estimation of this term for the probability of hiring exactly 43 minorities is complex. In addition, we would need to estimate the probability of hiring 42, 41, 40, and so on, minorities out of 150. Clearly the difficulty in estimating this probability exceeds the patience of most individuals. In situations like this, however, the binomial probability distribution can be estimated fairly well by using the normal distribution.

The Normal Curve and the Binomial Distribution

The utility of the binomial distribution is somewhat limited when the number of trials or the number of successes becomes large. For example, Bill Povalla, the head of the Chicago Equal Employment Commission, believes that the Chicago Transit Authority (CTA) discriminates against Republicans. The civil service records show that 37.5% of the individuals listed as passing the CTA exam were Republicans; the remainder were Democrats (for our purposes, let's assume no one registers as an independent in Illinois). CTA hired 30 people last year, 25 Democrats and 5 Republicans. What is the probability that this situation could exist if CTA did not discriminate?

Clearly the binomial distribution could be used to determine this probability, with the following information:

$p = .375$, the probability of randomly hiring a Republican

$q = 1 - p = .625$

$n = 30$, the number of persons hired

$r = 5, 4, 3, 2, 1,$ or 0, the number of Republicans hired (you need to know the probability of hiring five or fewer Republicans)

Calculating this probability would take the normal human being several hours. Using the normal curve is much faster.

To use the normal curve to determine a probability, you need to know the mean and the standard deviation of the population, as well as the raw score in question.

The mean of a probability distribution is equal to its expected value (see Chapter 7). If numerous clusters of 30 CTA eligibles were selected randomly, what would be the average number of Republicans selected? Obviously, the average is the number of persons selected (30) times the probability of selecting a Republican (.375), or 11.25. This is the mean (and the expected value).

The standard deviation of a probability distribution is defined by statisticians as

$$\sigma = \sqrt{np(1 - p)}$$

In this case, we have

$$\sigma = \sqrt{30 \times .375(1 - .375)} = \sqrt{11.25 \times .625} = \sqrt{7.03} = 2.65$$

To determine the probability that five or fewer Republicans would be selected if the CTA hiring were nonpartisan, simply convert the number actually hired into a z score. As shown in Chapter 8,

$$z = \frac{X - \mu}{\sigma}$$

$$= \frac{5 - 11.25}{2.65} = -2.36 \text{ or } 2.36$$

Looking up a z score of 2.36 in the normal table, we find a value of .4909, indicating that more than 49% of the values fall between a z score of 2.36 and the mean. Converting this to a probability (.5000 − .4909), we find the probability that 5 or fewer Republicans would be hired by the CTA if it were nonpartisan is .0091; that is, if the CTA does not discriminate, there is less than a 1% chance that it would hire 30 people and that 5 or fewer of them would be Republicans. In other words, the CTA probably gives preference to Democrats for its vacancies. If you were Mr. Povalla, what would you do with this information?

When to Use the Normal Curve

A word of caution is in order. The normal curve is a good approximation of the binomial distribution when $n \times p$ is greater than 10 and $n \times (1 - p)$ is greater than 10. If both these situations do not hold, the binomial distribution should be used. In addition, the normal curve tells you the probability only that r or fewer events occurred (or r or more). It does not tell you the probability of exactly r events occurring. This probability can only be determined by using the binomial distribution.

Chapter Summary

The binomial probability distribution can be used whenever the outcome of any trial can be classified into one of two mutually exclusive and jointly exhaustive outcomes (one outcome termed a success) and whenever each trial is independent of the other trials. To determine a probability by using the binomial probability distribution, you must know the number of trials (n), the number of successes (r), the probability of a success in any one trial (p), and the probability of failure ($q = 1 - p$). The probability of an event for the binomial probability distribution can be calculated by using the formula

$$C_r^n p^r q^{(n - r)}$$

where C_r^n is the number of combinations of n things taken r at a time. The formula for a combination is

$$C^n_r = \frac{n!}{r!(n-r)!}$$

In circumstances in which $n \times p > 10$ *and* $n \times (1-p) > 10$, the normal distribution can be used to approximate the binomial probability distribution. As explained in Chapter 8, the z score is used to find probabilities in the normal distribution. The formula for the z score is

$$z = \frac{X - \mu}{\sigma}$$

For the binomial probability distribution, the mean (μ) is equal to $n \times p$, and the standard deviation (σ) is equal to the square root of $n \times p \times (1-p)$. In the formula, X is the number of successes (r).

Problems

9.1   The state legislative council has been charged with sex discrimination in hiring. Last year it hired only 3 women out of 12 new employees. The civil service lists show that women comprise 40% of the qualified applicants for these jobs. What is the probability of hiring three or fewer women if the legislative council does not discriminate? Show all calculations.

9.2   The Armenian Navy gives all person who want to join the navy an intelligence test. Past tests had a mean of 90 and a standard deviation of 10.

   (a) What percentage of applicants scored between 82 and 104?

   (b) What percentage of applicants scored below 75?

   (c) What is the probability that a person taking the test will score 109 or more?

9.3   The foreign service exam gives a passing grade to only the top 10% of those taking the exam. The mean score is 84, with a standard deviation of 8. What should be the minimum passing grade?

9.4   In a grand jury case, a bookstore was indicted in Oklahoma County on several counts of selling an obscene book. The grand jury was composed of 22 Baptists and 8 other people. The defendant feels that Baptists are biased against free speech. What is the probability that 22 or more Baptists are selected on a jury if Oklahoma County is 40% Baptist?

9.5   Mary Doyle ran against Bernie Hobson for state senate. In one precinct, one of the two voting machines did not work, and 182 votes were cast on the broken machine. Mary needed to receive 177 of the 182 votes to win the election. On the other machine in the precinct, Mary received 51% of the votes. Assignment of voters to ballot boxes is independent. What is the probability that Mary won the election?

9.6   Traditionally, one-half of all cities that apply get job training grants. Four southern cities apply for grants, but none receive them. Assume all the cities were equally qualified. What is the probability that no southern city gets a grant?

9.7   Seaman David Brady is one of 16 seamen in Petty Officer Rickels's unit. Every day four seamen are assigned to chip paint, and the others are assigned to screen movies to see if they are suitable for viewing. Seaman Brady believes that Rickels does not like him because he has been assigned to the paint detail 16 times in the past 20 days. What can you tell Seaman Brady?

9.8   The Procurement Bureau runs tests on 30 brand X teletype machines. It finds that an average of three machines fail in any 1-day period. Against the bureau's advice, the Public Affairs Department purchased 140 of these machines for all state offices. On the first day, 26 machines fail. What is the probability that this would happen if the true failure rate were 10%?

9.9   This year, 620 persons are nominated to participate in the president's Management Internship Program. After screening, 212 are selected for the program. Maxwell George University nominates five persons, and all five receive awards. What is the probability that this event would occur if the events were independent and all nominees are equally qualified?

9.10   Refer to Problem 9.9. Of the 620 nominees, 211 are women; and of these, 91 are selected. Is there any preference with regard to sex?

9.11   Past experience has shown that 60% of all captains are promoted to major. The 819th Infantry Division has 48 captains who are eligible for promotion. Nine of these captains are West Point graduates. Eight of the nine West Pointers are promoted. Is there any reason to suspect that West Point graduates are given preferential treatment? Why? Show your work.

9.12   If one-third of the University of Wisconsin teaching assistants (TAs) sign a petition calling for a collective bargaining election, an election will be held. A survey of 50 TAs indicates that 40% will sign the petition. What is the probability that a sample such as this could have occurred if one-third or fewer of the TAs in the population will sign such a petition?

9.13   The area supervisor of the Occupational Safety and Health Administration has heard a story that a certain inspector is not enforcing safety regulations. Past statistics reveal that inspectors find safety violations in 91% of all inspections. The supervisor pulls the files for the eight most recent inspections for the inspector whose behavior is questioned. These files reveal that safety violations were cited in two of the eight cases. Analyze these data and present a statistical conclusion.

9.14   The BFOQ Job Training Corporation believes that is has a new program that will increase job placements. Essentially the corporation thinks that if it runs its trainees through a simulated interview before sending them out on a job interview, their likelihood of getting the job increases. BFOQ randomly selects 36 individuals of relatively equal skills on a matched pair basis. Eighteen of these individuals are run through the simulation. BFOQ then sends one pair, one person who went through the training and one person who did not, to interview for one of 18 different jobs. (These individuals are the only ones to interview for the jobs.) Thirteen of the 18 persons who went through the simulation get the jobs. What is the probability that 13 of the 18 would get jobs if there were no difference between the two sets of 18 persons? Show your work.

9.15 The Bureau of Paperwork wants to know whether agency personnel prefer to use HMOs for their health care benefits. If more than 25% favor using HMOs, then the bureau will begin to set up procedures for this type of health care. A sample of 100 of the bureau's personnel reveals that 29 favor the use of HMOs. What is the probability that less than 25% of the bureau's employees favor the use of HMO's? [**Hint:** If 25% (mean) or less of all bureau employees favor use of HMOs, what is the probability of obtaining a sample in which 29 out of 100 personnel are in favor?]

9.16 The Bluefield Regional Employment Service needs to place five individuals in jobs this week to meet its yearly quota. During the past several years, the service's track record is that every person sent to interview for a job has a .6 probability of getting the job. The placements appear to be independent of each other. The service decides to send seven individuals for interviews this week. Based on what you know, what is the probability that the service will make its yearly quota this week?

9.17 The Department of Treasury is concerned because one member of Congress has charged that, by normal accounting standards, one-third of all savings and loans in the country are bankrupt. To refute this claim, chief economist Tom Holbrook takes a sample of six savings and loans and finds that only one is insolvent (his staff had intended to gather a larger sample, but they were too busy processing S&L failures). If the true proportion of insolvencies is one-third, what is the probability that the Treasury Department would get the results that it did?

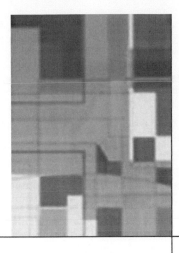

CHAPTER 10

Some Special Probability Distributions

lthough the binomial distribution and the normal curve cover a great many of the situations faced by nonprofit and public managers, in certain circumstances special probability distributions should be used. For example, assume that a finite number of persons apply for agency jobs and you want to know whether the agency discriminates. Or suppose that you need to determine the probability that an event will occur but have no idea about the number of trials. Or perhaps a fire department wants to know how long it can expect to wait between major fires. For situations similar to these, special probability distributions must be used. We will discuss three such distributions in this chapter.

The Hypergeometric Probability Distribution

The Andersonville City Fire Department contends that its civil service exam for firefighters is valid; that is, it feels that anyone who passes the exam is qualified to be a firefighter. Last year, 100 persons passed the firefighters exam, 66 men and 34 women. From this list of 100 persons, a fire academy class of 30 was chosen; 24 men and 6 women. One woman not selected filed a complaint with the federal Equal Employment Opportunity Commission (EEOC), alleging discrimination. Three years later, the EEOC decides it will hear the case. The question is, How probable is it that Andersonville does not discriminate against women and would by chance admit six or fewer women to the fire academy class in question?

Clearly, this question could be answered by using the normal curve to approximate the binomial distribution. The normal distribution, however, assumes that the population from which the trials are drawn is infinite. In the present situation, this is not the case. The population consists of those persons who passed the firefighters exam, and 100 is a long way from infinity. If the normal curve and the binomial probability distribution were used, the probability estimates would be conservative, that is, the test would be less likely to show discrimination.

With a finite population, the **hypergeometric probability distribution** should be used. To use the hypergeometric distribution, you need to know the same things that were needed for the normal curve plus the size of the population. The mean of the hypergeometric probability distribution is the distribution's expected value:

$$\mu = n \times p$$

In this case, μ equals 30 times .34 (the probability that a woman would be chosen at random), or 10.2. This mean is the same as the mean for the binomial distribution.

The standard deviation for the hypergeometric distribution is as follows:

$$\sigma = \sqrt{\left(\frac{\mathbf{N}_p - n}{\mathbf{N}_p - 1}\right)(np)(1 - p)}$$

where $\mathbf{N}_p$ is the size of the population, n is the number of trials, and p is the probability of success. The only difference between this standard deviation and the one for the binomial distribution is the ratio $[(\mathbf{N}_p - n)/(\mathbf{N}_p - 1)]$.

Substituting the values of this problem into the formula for the standard deviation, we have

$$\sigma = \sqrt{\left(\frac{100 - 30}{100 - 1}\right) \times 30 \times .34 \times .66}$$

$$= \sqrt{\frac{70}{99} \times 30 \times .34 \times .66}$$

$$= \sqrt{.71 \times 30 \times .34 \times .66}$$

$$= \sqrt{4.78} = 2.19$$

Given a mean of 10.2 and a standard deviation of 2.19, is it probable that Andersville could have randomly selected only six females for its firefighter class?

Converting 6 into a z score, we find

$$z = \frac{x - \mu}{\sigma} = \frac{6 - 10.2}{2.19} = -1.92$$

Using the z score of -1.92 and the normal distribution table, we find the probability (.0274) that Andersonville could select six or fewer women given that it had no preference in regard to sex.

Had we used the binomial distribution in this problem, the probability would have been higher. Calculate this probability in the space provided. Be sure to use the normal approximation to the binomial distribution with $n = 30$, $r = 6$ or less, and $p = .34$ (see Chapter 9).

If you found a probability of .0526, congratulations. If you found some other probability, reread Chapter 9. Because most social scientists require a probability of .05 or less to make a conclusion, why is it important to use the hypergeometric distribution in this situation?

The Poisson Distribution

The **Poisson distribution** is a probability distribution that describes a pattern of behavior when some event occurs at varying, random intervals over a continuum of time, length, or space. Such a pattern of behavior is called a *Poisson process.* For example, if we graphed the number of muggings in Chickasaw, Oklahoma, on a time dimension, we might find the following (where the X's represent muggings):

```
——+—— X —— X ———————————— XXX ————— X ————— X —+——
12:00 P.M.                                        12:00 A.M.
```

The number of potholes per foot on South Flood Street in Normal, Oklahoma, also follows a Poisson process, as shown in the following diagram.

```
——+—— XX —— XX —— X ————— XXXX—— X ————— X —— X —+——
0 feet                                          500 feet
```

In theory, each of these continuums can be divided into equal segments such that no more than one event (pothole, mugging) occurs in each segment. Every equal segment of Flood Street would either have a pothole or not have a pothole. In addition, for the process to be a Poisson process, the occurrence or nonoccurrence of any event must not affect the probability that other events will occur. That is, the fact that a pothole occurs at 621 South Flood does not affect whether or not a pothole occurs at 527 South Flood.

The process up to this point fits the description of a Bernoulli process: An event either occurs (success) or it does not (failure), and events are independent of each other. To determine the probability of any event when using the Bernoulli process, we need to know the probability of the event (*p*), the number of successes (*r*), and the number of trials (*n*). In the present situation, we could empirically determine the probability of a mugging occurring in Chickasaw during any time period (*p*). In this case, Chickasaw might experience .3 muggings per hour. Note that probabilities are based on time, length, or space. The number of successes (*r*) also could be determined. We can count the number of muggings in any period. *We do not, however, know, the number of trials.* How many potential muggings were there in Chickasaw? Clearly this information cannot be determined. The major difference between a Poisson process and a Bernoulli process, then, is that the number of trials is not known in a Poisson process.

The use of the Poisson distribution can best be illustrated with an example. The Elezar Rape Crisis Center wants to staff its crisis hot line so that a center member will always be present if a rape victim calls. The crisis center operates between the hours of 6:00 P.M. and 6:00 A.M. By examining the past records of the center, the director has determined that the mean number of rapes per hour is .05. This information can be found in police records.

The first question is, What is the probability that no rapes will occur on any given night? The steps in using the Poisson probability distribution are as follows:

Step 1: Adjust the mean to reflect the number of hours (length or space) you want to consider. In the present example, the mean number of rapes in an hour is .05. You want to know the mean number of rapes in 12 hours. Because these events are independent, the mean for a 12-hour period is .6 (.05 × 12). This new mean is called λ , the Greek letter lambda (some texts refer to it as λt, lambda *t*).

Step 2: To determine the probability of zero rapes, you turn to the Poisson distribution tables (Table 2 in the Appendix). For those of you who feel that using a table is cheating, exact probabilities can be calculated with the following formula:

$$y = \frac{\lambda^x e^{-\lambda}}{x!}$$

where λ is the probability of the event, *x* is the number of occurrences, *e* is a constant (2.71828), and *y* is the probability of *x* occurrences. If you are sane, turn to Table 2. Scanning across the top of the table, find λ equal to .6. You should find the following information:

X	$\frac{\lambda}{.6}$
0	.5488
1	.3293
2	.0988
3	.0198
4	.0030
5	.0004
6	.0000

This table gives a Poisson probability distribution for $\lambda = .6$. It tells you that if $\lambda = .6$, the probability of no rapes in a single night is .5488. The probability of exactly one rape is .3293. The probability of exactly two rapes is .0988, and so on.

How might this information be used in a management setting? Suppose that the director believes that (based on past experience) assisting a rape victim takes about 4 hours. One crisis center staff member remains with the victim for this period to assist with the medical treatment and police procedures. If the center had one staff member and two rapes occurred in a 4-hour period, than no one would be at the center to assist the second victim. The director wants to avoid this situation. How many staff members should be at the center?

Step 1: Adjust the mean to the time period. The mean is .05 for 1 hour, and you want to know about 4-hour periods (the amount of time a staff member will be away from the center). Therefore, λ is .2 (.05 $\times$ 4).

Step 2: Find the probabilities in the Poisson distribution table for 0, 1, 2, 3, 4, and 5 rapes when λ is .2.

Number of Rapes	Probability
0	.8187
1	.1637
2	.0164
3	.0011
4	.0001
5	.0000

To make the staffing decision, the director uses the preceding table. If 0 or 1 rape occurs in a 4-hour period, one staff member is sufficient. This will occur 98% of the 4-hour periods (.8187 + .1637 = .9824). Because the director wants to minimize the time during which the crisis center cannot respond, the probability is interpreted as follows: If the crisis center staffs only one employee, this will be inadequate 1.8% of the time periods. The 12-hour day is equivalent to three 4-hour periods, so a rape with no one present will occur on 5.4% (1.8% $\times$ 3) of the days (or once every 3 weeks). The director considers this risk unacceptable.

If two members are stationed at the crisis center, the probability of sufficient staff is .9988. Translating this into days when a rape will occur with no one at the crisis center (.0012 $\times$ 3 = .0036, or .36%) reveals that the staff will be inadequate .36% of the days, or once every 278 days (36 times in 10,000 days). The staff director feels that this risk is tolerable and decides to staff two persons.

(**Note:** Staffing three persons would increase the probability of sufficient staff to .9999. This means inadequate staff problems would occur once every 10,000 days.)

You may have noticed that the Poisson probability tables give values only for λ less than or equal to 20. Poisson tables for larger λ values are not presented because the normal distribution table provides fairly accurate probabilities when λ is greater than 20. The normal distribution of this magnitude has a mean of λ and a standard deviation equal to the square root of λ. For a λ value of 30, therefore, you would use the normal table with a mean of 30 and a standard deviation of 5.5 ($\sqrt{30} = 5.5$).

The Exponential Probability Distribution

The **exponential probability distribution** is used when you want to know the most probable length of time between independent events. For example, in the Elezar Rape Crisis Center case, the director might want to know the most probable length of time between rapes in order to plan center procedures. The exponential distribution is also used for scheduling. For example, it can be used to determine the time between arrivals at a municipal hospital, the time between fires in a city, the time between people's calls to the museum to find out how to volunteer, or the time between clients visiting the legal aid center. Clearly this information can be quite useful to a manager in scheduling his or her work force.

The calculation procedures for the exponential distribution are fairly complex. As a result, we will not discuss them in this book. But you should be aware that the exponential distribution exists and that it can be used to schedule activities when events occur randomly. If the need for this distribution ever arises, we suggest that a statistician be hired to program the problem. For large problems, such as scheduling police calls in a large city, computer programs are available [see also Neter, Wasserman, and Whitmore (1992)].

Chapter Summary

This chapter introduces three special probability distributions. The hypergeometric probability distribution is used, with finite populations, when one knows the number of trials (each trial is independent), the number of successes, and the probability of one success. Formulas for calculating the mean and the standard deviation are given for this distribution. The Poisson distribution is used whenever events are independent and events occur at varying random intervals of time, length, or space. The exponential probability distribution is used to estimate the length of time between independently occurring events.

Problems

10.1   One hundred cities (60 are northern cities) apply for CETA grants to train the unemployed. Fifty grants are awarded, 40 to northern cities. Is there any anti–Sun Belt bias?

10.2   The mean number of persons shot by the Metro City Police Department in an hour is .042. What is the probability that the MPD will shoot no one in a 24-hour period? What is the probability that the MPD will shoot one person? Two persons? More than two persons? Explain your work.

10.3   Police chief Lenny Lawnorder has heard through a normally reliable source that 30% of his officers are not using regulation handguns. To see whether this is true, Lenny randomly inspects 35 of his 200 officers. Seventeen have nonregulation handguns. If the true proportion is .3, what is the probability that this event will occur?

10.4   The mean number of major fires in Flandreau, South Dakota, is .057 on any given day. What is the probability of no major fires occurring in any given week? What is the probability of one major fire? Two major fires? Three or more major fires?

10.5   In the First Army, 150 first lieutenants were up for promotion to captain (35 of these are West Point graduates). Of these, 120 were promoted, including 24 West Pointers. Does the Army discriminate in promotions?

10.6   The mean number of teletype machines in the Bureau of Communications that break down is .625 in any given hour. If repairs take 8 hours, how many people should the Bureau of Communications staff?

10.7   Congressman Lester Asperin has charged that 50% of all IRS agents would fail a simple test on tax law. IRS Commissioner John Tight believes no more than 15% would fail. Of the 1,000 agents, 200 are randomly selected and given the test, and 60 fail. What is the probability that Asperin is correct? What is the probability that Tight is correct?

10.8   The mean number of murders reported in Metro City during the 8-hour graveyard shift is .5 for any hour. It takes two people 2 hours to investigate a homicide call. How many officers should be assigned to the homicide squad during these hours?

10.9   Refer to Problem 9.10 (Chapter 9), where 91 of the 211 women nominated for the president's Management Internship Program are selected and 212 of the 620 total nominees are accepted. Use what you have learned in this chapter to determine the probability of this happening if all persons are equally qualified. What can you say if you do not assume equal qualifications?

10.10   The mean number of contracts that consulting firms receive with the Department of Human Services is .4 for any given year. Ecosystems Inc., a heavy contributor to political candidates, receives three contracts in 1 year. What is the probability that this event would occur by chance? What is the probability that Ecosystems will receive six contracts in 2 years?

10.11   The Madison Fire Department's files reveal that an average of six firefighters a year suffer heart attacks while on duty. The personnel office is concerned about this because it must budget funds for disabilities. There are some concerns that the physical condition of firefighters is getting worse. This year, nine firefighters suffered heart attacks. What is the probability that an event this severe will occur? Given past history, what is the probability that no heart attacks will occur? Exactly one? Exactly two? Three or fewer?

10.12 The mean number of water main breaks is .4 per hour. In a 10-hour night shift, four mains break. What is the probability of exactly four mains breaking? Of four or more breaking? Which probability tells you the most about the chance of this situation happening?

10.13 The Nuclear Regulatory Commission estimates that the probability that a Westinghouse X-27 nuclear plant's warning system will fail in a year's time is .1. New York Power and Light operates six of the X-27 plants; last year one failed. What is the probability that one or more plants' warning systems will fail?

10.14 The mean number of fires per hour in Smallsville, Utah, is .1042. What is the probability that Smallsville will experience no fires on any given day? Five or more fires on any given day?

10.15 The Bureau of Paperwork has 1,000 employees, and the personnel division wants to know whether agency personnel prefer to use HMOs for their health care benefits. If more than 25% favor using HMOs, then the bureau will begin to set up procedures for this type of health care. A sample of 100 of the bureau's personnel reveals that 29 favor the use of HMOs. What is the probability that less than 25% of the bureau's employees favor the use of HMOs? [**Hint:** If 25% (mean) or less of bureau personnel favor use of HMOs, what is the probability of obtaining a sample in which 29 out of 100 are in favor?]

10.16 The University of Wisconsin employs 200 teaching assistants (TAs). If one-third of the TAs sign a petition calling for a collective bargaining election, an election will be held. A survey of 50 TAs indicates that 40% will sign the petition. What is the probability that a sample such as this could have occurred if one-third or fewer of the TAs in the population will sign such a petition?

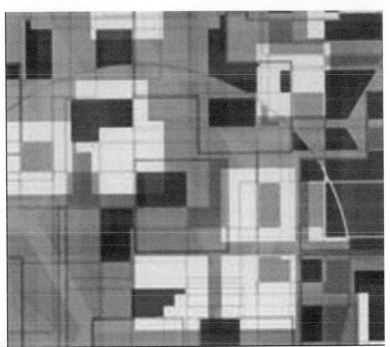

PART IV

Inferential
Statistics

CHAPTER 11

Introduction to Inference

When statistics are used to summarize the distribution of a given sample or population, we call this summarizing **descriptive statistics.** In descriptive statistics, we use statistical techniques to describe and to summarize data. **Inferential statistics** is the use of quantitative techniques to generalize from a sample to a population. In short, with inferential statistics, we hope to use a small subset of data to infer what all the data look like.

For example, the city fathers (and mothers) of Pittsburgh, Pennsylvania, would like to know how pleased Pittsburgh citizens are with their new bus service. The best way to do this would be to ask every citizen of Pittsburgh how he or she feels about the transit system. Because Pittsburgh has 370,000 people, this interviewing could take forever (not to mention that it would cost more to do that than to run the transit system). An alternative is to randomly select a subset of persons (say, 100) and ask them about the mass transit system. From this sample, we will infer what the people of Pittsburgh think.

In this chapter, we will begin the presentation of inferential statistics by reviewing some basic definitions and describing some simple inferential techniques.

Some Definitions

A **population** is the total set of items that we are concerned about. In the preceding example, the population is all the people who live in Pittsburgh, Pennsylvania.

A measure that is used to summarize a population is called a **parameter.** For example, the mean education level in Pittsburgh is 12.9 years. This measure is a parameter. Thus far in this book, we have discussed a variety of parameters including the mean, the median, and the standard deviation of the population.

A **sample** is a subset of a population. In this text, we will assume that all samples are selected randomly. A random sample is a sample in which every member of the population has an equal chance of being included. If a sample is not a random sample, then the rules of statistical inference introduced here do not necessarily hold.

A **statistic** is a measure that is used to summarize a sample. The mean, the standard deviation, and the median of a sample are all statistics.

To create a bit more complexity in the interests of clarity, statisticians use different symbols for the mean and the standard deviation, depending on whether they are parameters or statistics. Table 11.1 illustrates the symbols.

The mean is always calculated the same way whether the data are taken from a sample or a population. The standard deviation, however, is calculated differently. Recall that the formula for calculating the standard deviation is

$$\sigma = \sqrt{\frac{\sum\limits_{i=1}^{N}(X_i - \mu)^2}{N}}$$

The formula for the standard deviation of a sample is similar, with one slight twist:

$$s = \sqrt{\frac{\sum\limits_{i=1}^{n}(X_i - \overline{X})^2}{n-1}}$$

The difference here is that the sum of the squared deviations from the mean is divided by $n - 1$ rather than by $N.$ Later in this chapter, we will explain why this correction is made.

Table 11.1

Symbols for Parameters and Statistics

Measure	Population Parameter	Sample Statistic
Mean	μ	$\overline{X}$
Standard deviation	σ	s
Number of cases	N	n

Estimating a Population Mean

The best estimate of the population mean μ is the mean of the sample $\bar{X}$. To illustrate why this is true, we will use the data in Table 11.2, which lists the number of arrests by all 10 Yukon, Oklahoma, police officers in 2004.

The mean number of arrests by Yukon police officers is 15.0. But in circumstances where the population parameter cannot be calculated, either because the population is too large or because the data are not available, the mean of a sample can be used to estimate the population mean.

Assume that we took a random sample of five Yukon police officers and calculated the mean for those five as follows (the sample was selected by using a random number table):

Officers in Sample	Arrests	Mean
1, 3, 2, 8, 4	14, 10, 16, 20, 18	15.6

The sample mean is one estimate of the population mean. Note that although our estimate is close (15.6 compared with 15.0), it is not exact. This discrepancy occurs because of sampling error—that is, our sample is not perfectly representative of the population. We would expect, however, that if we took numerous samples of five, the average sample mean would approach the population mean. Let's try it. The data and calculations are shown in Table 11.3.[*]

Notice how the average sample mean quickly approaches the population mean and fluctuates around it. Statisticians have worked out this general problem and have logically demonstrated that the average sample mean over the long run will equal the population mean. The best estimate of the population mean, therefore, is the sample mean.

Table 11.2

Number of Arrests by Police Officers in Yukon, Oklahoma, 2004

Police Officer	Number of Arrests, 2004
1	14
2	16
3	10
4	18
5	8
6	15
7	17
8	20
9	19
10	13

[*]An entire field of statistics has developed around the idea of taking repeated samples with replacement. See Mooney and Duval (1993).

Table 11.3

Calculating the Average Sample Mean from Samples of Five

Officers in Sample	Number of Arrests	Sample Mean	Average of Means
1, 3, 2, 8, 4	14, 10, 16, 20, 18	15.6	15.6
1, 6, 8, 3, 4	14, 15, 20, 10, 18	15.4	15.5
7, 4, 1, 5, 9	17, 18, 14, 8, 19	15.2	15.4
2, 10, 7, 4, 6	16, 13, 17, 18, 15	15.8	15.5
7, 10, 3, 6, 5	17, 13, 10, 15, 8	12.6	14.9
10, 7, 2, 1, 4	13, 17, 16, 14, 18	15.6	15.0
10, 3, 7, 4, 2	13, 10, 17, 18, 16	14.8	15.0
10, 3, 8, 9, 4	13, 10, 20, 19, 18	16.0	15.1
6, 4, 8, 9, 10	15, 18, 20, 19, 13	17.0	15.3
2, 8, 4, 1, 5	16, 20, 18, 14, 8	15.2	15.3
8, 3, 9, 10, 5	20, 10, 19, 13, 8	14.0	15.2
2, 3, 7, 5, 1	16, 10, 17, 8, 14	13.0	15.0
10, 8, 5, 6, 4	13, 20, 8, 15, 18	14.8	15.0
9, 3, 6, 2, 7	19, 10, 15, 16, 17	15.4	15.0

Estimating a Population Standard Deviation

The best estimate of the population standard deviation σ is the sample standard deviation s. Remember that s has $n - 1$ as a denominator rather than **N**. Again, let's use the Yukon police arrests example to illustrate the estimating accuracy of the sample standard deviation. The population standard deviation is 3.7. (If you do not believe us, calculate it from the data in Table 11.2.)

Drawing a sample of five officers, we get the estimate of the standard deviation shown in Table 11.4 (note that we use the same sample in this illustration that we used before).

Our estimate of the population standard deviation is 3.85, which is close to the population value of 3.7. Note that had we divided by n rather than by $n - 1$, the standard deviation estimate would have been 3.4. Dividing by n gives us a consistently low estimate of the population standard deviation. For this reason, the estimate *always* is made with a denominator of $n - 1$. If you want to know why this is true, consult an advanced statistics text (Ott and Mendenhall, 1994).

Most statistical programs calculate the sample standard deviation, not the population standard deviation. When you use a statistical package, you need to be aware of this fact.

Table 11.4

Calculating *s* for a Sample of Five

Officer	Arrests	Arrests − Mean	Squared
1	14	−1.6	2.56
3	10	−5.6	31.36
2	16	.4	.16
8	20	4.4	19.36
4	18	2.4	5.76
			59.20 sum of squares

$$s = \sqrt{59.2 \div 4} = 3.85$$

The Standard Error

If you reported that the mean arrests per police officer in Yukon was 15.6, your superior might ask you if the mean was exactly 15.6. Your answer would be that you do not know but that your best estimate of the mean is 15.6. Your superior might then ask how good an estimate 15.6 is. Your superior really wants to know the range of values that the mean must fall within—that is, how much error can the mean estimate contain?

One way to answer this question is to take numerous samples, calculate a mean for each sample, and show the supervisor the range of mean estimates. If you wanted to be more sophisticated, you might calculate a standard deviation for all the mean estimates. The standard deviation for mean estimates has a special name; it is called the **standard error of the mean.**

Fortunately for the sanity of most management analysts, one does not need to take numerous samples, calculate a mean for each sample, and then calculate a standard deviation for the mean estimates to find the standard error of the mean. Statisticians have demonstrated that a good estimate of the standard error of the mean can be made with the following formula:

$$\text{s.e.} = \frac{\sigma}{\sqrt{n}}$$

where s.e. is the standard error of the mean, σ is the standard deviation of the population, and n is the sample size. Because we rarely know the population standard deviation, the estimated standard deviation can be used in computations:

$$\text{s.e.} = \frac{s}{\sqrt{n}}$$

Sometimes the symbol $S_{\bar{Y}}$ is used for the standard error of the mean to indicate it is the standard deviation of mean estimates.

In our current example, we have a mean estimate of 15.6, a standard deviation estimate of 3.85, and a sample size of 5. Substituting these values into the equation for standard error, we get

$$\text{s.e.} = \frac{3.85}{\sqrt{5}} = \frac{3.85}{2.236} = 1.7$$

How Sample Size Affects the Standard Error

The Yukon arrest data represent an ideal scenario as far as sampling is concerned. Because there were only 10 officers in the entire population, the chances of obtaining an accurate estimate of the population mean from a sample of 5 officers were very good. In the real world, we rarely have the time or resources to gather samples that are literally half the size of the population in question. For example, polling organizations typically use random samples in the range of 1,200 to 1,500 registered voters to make inferences about how tens of millions of voters are likely to vote in presidential elections. Because the goal of inference is to make a statement about the population using one sample, what impact can sample size have on our results?

Statisticians have determined that larger samples generally provide better estimates of the population mean than smaller samples (provided the sampling method is not arbitrary or biased). This is true because the size of the standard error for larger samples is typically less than it is for smaller samples.

An example with real data will help illustrate this point. One of the authors has data on grades for a population of 283 public administration students. The data are normally distributed, with a mean of 79.3 and a standard deviation of 11.4. Using these data, we generated six random samples: three samples where $n = 5$ (for each sample), and three samples where $n = 35$ (for each sample). Table 11.5 presents the means, standard deviations, and standard errors.

Notice how the means and standard deviations for the three larger samples are much closer to the true population values than the means and standard deviations for the smaller samples. The standard errors for the smaller samples are consistently larger than those for the larger samples. The results illustrate that larger samples typically do a better job capturing the characteristics present in the population than smaller samples.

Although there is no guarantee that we will always obtain a smaller standard error when using larger samples, well-known statistical principles called the **central limit theorem** and **law of large numbers** form the basis for the idea that larger samples are generally more reflective of population characteristics than smaller samples.

If using larger samples is more desirable, how does an analyst determine the appropriate sample size? Statisticians have found that beyond a certain point, adding additional cases to a sufficiently large sample will have a limited effect on the quality and accuracy of the inferences we make about a population. How do we know when

Table 11.5

The Impact of Sample Size on the Standard Error

Three Samples (**N** = 5 each)	Three Samples (**N** = 35 each)
Sample 1 $\bar{X}$ = 72.4	Sample 1 $\bar{X}$ = 77.9
s = 5.89	s = 10.88
s.e. = 2.64	s.e. = 1.84
Sample 2 $\bar{X}$ = 87.6	Sample 2 $\bar{X}$ = 78.43
s = 9.20	s = 11.55
s.e. = 4.11	s.e. = 1.95
Sample 3 $\bar{X}$ = 78.8	Sample 3 $\bar{X}$ = 75.37
s = 9.34	s = 11.22
s.e. = 4.18	s.e. = 1.89

we have a sufficiently large sample? We will elaborate the formulas and steps used to determine appropriate sample size in Chapters 12 and 13.

The *t* Distribution

Sample estimates of a population mean fit a probability distribution called the **Student's *t* distribution** or simply the ***t* distribution.** The *t* distribution is a sampling distribution. In other words, if we repeatedly took samples and calculated means for each sample and plotted them on a graph, the sample means would eventually take on a shape similar to that of the normal distribution.

The *t* distribution allows us to determine the probability of drawing a random sample with a particular mean and standard deviation, given a known or hypothesized population mean. In simpler terms, when we draw a random sample and calculate the mean, the *t* distribution enables us to evaluate which of the following statements is more likely to be correct:

The sample mean is statistically indistinguishable from the known (or hypothesized) population mean. As a result, there is a high probability that we could draw a sample with this mean from the given population.

The sample mean is statistically different from the known (or hypothesized) population mean. As a result, there is a low probability that we could draw a sample with this mean from the given population.

The interpretation of *t* scores is similar to that of *z* scores or "standard normal scores" (see Chapter 8). Recall that as *z* scores become larger, the data points associated with the scores fall increasingly away from the mean. As *t* scores become larger, the values for the sample means in question fall increasingly away from the population mean to which they are being compared. In other words, as the distance between the sample mean and the population mean grows, it becomes less likely that the sample mean could have come from a population with that population mean. When we interpret *t* scores, we use this information to make judgments about whether a sample mean is similar to or different from a population mean.

When a sample is 30 or more, the normal distribution can be used in place of the *t* distribution. The *t* distribution resembles the normal distribution but has a flatter shape. Unlike the normal distribution, the *t* distribution differs for each sample size. To use the *t* distribution, the public manager needs to know the *degrees of freedom* (df), which corresponds to sample size and identifies the appropriate *t* values. For a sample mean, the degrees of freedom are $n - 1$. In our earlier example, we have four degrees of freedom. The *t* distribution is found in Table 3 in the Appendix of Statistical Tables. Note that rather than printing a large table for every sample size, only key values of the *t* distribution are printed.

To illustrate, if we wish to know between what two numbers 95% of the mean estimates will fall, we calculate the following estimates:

$$\bar{X} \pm \text{s.e.} \times t$$

This formula is simply the mean estimate plus or minus the standard error times the appropriate *t* score. If we want the *t* score for a 95% **confidence limit,** we know that there must be 2.5% in each tail of the curve (to total 5%), so we look up the *t* score for .025 with four degrees of freedom. This figure is 2.78. The upper 95% confidence limit is 15.6 + (1.7 × 2.78), or 20.3. The lower limit is 15.6 − (1.7 × 2.78), or 10.9. We can be 95% sure ("confident") that the average number of arrests by Yukon police officers is between 10.9 and 20.3.

An Example

Several years ago, the Wiese school system was criticized because the average Wiese High School (WHS) graduate could only read at the ninth-grade level. After this report was made, a special reading program was established to upgrade skills. The WHS principal wants to know whether the reading program worked in improving reading scores. If it has, he will request that an accreditation team visit the school. If the program has not improved the reading level to at least 10.0 (sophomore level), the administrator would like to avoid the embarrassment of a poor review.

To determine the average reading level of the senior class, we select 10 seniors at random. We assume that reading scores are normally distributed. The reading scores for these 10 seniors are shown in Table 11.6. We proceed as follows:

Step 1: Estimate the population mean. Calculate the sample mean reading score in the space provided next to Table 11.6. The answer should be 10.6.

Step 2: Estimate the population standard deviation. In this case, the estimated standard deviation is 1.4. Calculate in the space next to the table.

Step 3: Calculate the standard error of the mean.

$$\text{s.e.} = \frac{s}{\sqrt{n}} = \frac{1.4}{\sqrt{10}} = \frac{1.4}{3.16} = .44$$

Table 11.6

Reading Scores

Senior	Reading Score
1	13.4
2	12.1
3	11.4
4	10.6
5	10.3
6	10.2
7	9.8
8	9.7
9	9.4
10	8.6

Step 4: Provide an **interval estimate** of the mean. An interval estimate is an interval such that the probability that the mean falls within the interval is acceptably high. The most common interval is the 95% confidence interval (we are 95% sure the mean falls within the interval). The t score (with 9 degrees of freedom) for 95% confidence limits is 2.262 (.025 in each tail; see Table 3 in the Appendix). Using this t score, we find that the 95% confidence interval is equal to

$$10.6 \pm 2.262 \times .44$$
$$10.6 \pm 1.0$$
$$9.6 \text{ to } 11.6$$

We are 95% sure that the mean reading level falls within the range of 9.6 to 11.6 years of school.

This answer bothers the principal because he wants to be certain that the mean is above 10.0. The principal wants us to calculate the probability that the population mean is 10.0 or less. The statistically correct way to ask this question is, if μ is 10.0 or less, what is the probability of drawing a sample with a mean of 10.6? This probability can be determined easily because we have both a mean and a standard error. We convert 10.6 into a t score:

$$t = \frac{\bar{X} - \mu}{\text{s.e.}} = \frac{10.6 - 10.00}{.44} = \frac{.6}{.44} = 1.36$$

Looking up a t score of 1.36 in Table 3, we find a probability greater than .10. In other words, the probability is greater than .1 that with a mean of less than 10.0 we could get a sample mean estimate of 10.6. Another way to say this is the chance of a sample mean of 10.6 if the true (population) mean is only 10.0 is greater than 10%. Computer programs can calculate and report the exact probability for a t score. A t score of

1.36 with 9 degrees of freedom has a probability of .103. To use the *t* table, one needs to know the degrees of freedom (in this case, 9) and compare the *t* scores with the listed values. A *t* score of 1.9, for example, is larger than 1.833 (the value for .05) and smaller than 2.262 (the value for .025), so the probability of a *t* score of 1.9 with 9 degrees of freedom is less than .05 (but more than .025).

The principal decides that he would like to be more certain. Greater certainty can be achieved if the standard error of the mean can be reduced. The formula for the standard error of the mean,

$$\text{s.e.} = \frac{s}{\sqrt{n}}$$

shows that the standard error can be reduced if the standard deviation can be reduced (not likely since this is a function of the population) or if the sample size can be increased. Let's increase the sample size to 100. By a quirk of fate, our sample of 100 has a mean of 10.6 and a standard deviation of 1.4. In the space provided, calculate the new standard error.

If you found the standard error to be .14, congratulations.

In the space provided, calculate the new 95% confidence limits for the Wiese High School senior class reading scores. (**Hint:** With 99 degrees of freedom, you may use the normal curve to approximate the *t* distribution.)

From this new information, what can you tell the principal?

Chapter Summary

Whenever someone wants to say something about a group of items or people based on a subset of those items or people, that person must engage in inference. Inferential statistics use quantitative techniques to generalize from a sample (with summary measures called *statistics*) to a population (with summary measures called *parameters*). We normally use samples because it is too difficult or too expensive to use the entire population. This chapter illustrates how to infer (by using estimates) population means and standard deviations from a sample. The standard error of the mean tells us how much error is contained in the estimate of the mean—that is, how good the estimate is. Larger samples tend to have smaller standard error values than smaller samples.

Problems

11.1 George Fastrack, head of the Bureau of Obfuscation's United Way drive, wants to know the average United Way pledge among Obfuscation Bureau employees (pledges are normally distributed). George takes a sample of 10 and gets the results shown in the accompanying table. What is George's best estimate of the mean donation? What is George's best estimate of the standard deviation of the donations? Between what two values can George be 95% sure the mean value lies?

Person	Pledge
1	$ 25
2	0
3	35
4	100
5	0
6	0
7	15
8	50
9	25
10	50

11.2 Captain E. Garth Beaver has been warned by Colonel Sy Verleaf that if the mean efficiency rating for the 150 platoons under Verleaf's command falls below 80, Captain Beaver will be transferred to Minot Air Force Base (a fate worse than Diego Garcias). Beaver wants to know in advance what his fate will be, so he knows whether to send change-of-address cards to all his magazine subscriptions. Beaver takes a sample of 20 platoons and finds the following:

$$\bar{X} = 85 \quad s = 13.5$$

Would you advise Beaver to send change-of-address cards? (Assume that efficiency ratings are normally distributed.)

11.3 Last year, sanitation engineer crews in Buffalo, New York, collected 124 tons of trash per day. This year, larger, more efficient trucks were purchased. A sample of 100 truck-days shows that a mean of 130 tons of trash were collected, with a standard deviation of 30 tons. What is the probability that a sample with this mean could be drawn if the new trucks are no improvement (i.e., the population mean = 124)?

11.4 Current Tinderbox Park water pumps can pump 2,000 gallons of water per minute. The park tests 10 new Fastwater brand pumps and finds a mean of 2,200 and a standard deviation of 500. What is the probability that the Fastwater pumps were selected from a population with a mean no better than that of the present pumps?

11.5 If the absenteeism rates for a school district rise above 10%, the state reduces its aid to the school district. Stermerville Independent School District takes a sample of five schools within the district and finds the following absenteeism rates: 5.4%, 8.6%, 4.1%, 8.9%, and 7.8%. What is your best estimate of the absenteeism rate in Stermerville? Is it likely that the absenteeism rate is greater than 10%?

11.6 The Department of Animal Husbandry at State University believes that adding cement to cattle feed will increase the cattle's weight gain. The average weekly gain for State U cattle last year was 12.7 pounds. A sample of 30 cattle are fed cement-fortified feed with the following results:

$$\bar{X} = 14.1 \text{ pounds} \quad s = 5.0$$

What can you tell the department?

11.7 Last year, Groton, Georgia, had 512 burglaries. The police chief wants to know the average economic loss associated with burglaries in Groton and wants to know it this afternoon. There isn't time to analyze all 512 burglaries, so the department's research analyst selects 10 burglaries at random, which show the following losses:

$550	$874
$675	$595
$324	$835
$487	$910
$1,246	$612

What is the best estimate of the average loss on a burglary? Place 80% confidence limits around this estimate.

11.8 Last year, the Department of Vocational Rehabilitation was able to place people in jobs with an average salary of $10,600. This year, placement is handled by a private agency that charges $200 per placement. Using the following placement figures for this year (sample of 100), what can you tell the department?

$$\bar{X} = \$10,900 \quad s = 2,000$$

11.9 The General Accounting Office is auditing Branflake International Airways, a company that flies numerous charters for the government. The contract with Branflake specifies that the average flight can be no more than 15 minutes late. A sample of 20 flights reveals the results in the accompanying table. Write a brief memo interpreting this information.

Flight Number	Status
217	On time
167	20 minutes late
133	17 minutes late
207	64 minutes late
219	On time
457	96 minutes late
371	30 minutes late
612	On time
319	6 minutes late
423	12 minutes late
684	11 minutes late
661	61 minutes late
511	On time
536	On time
493	17 minutes late
382	12 minutes late
115	6 minutes late
107	3 minutes late
19	26 minutes late
123	19 minutes late

11.10 The secretary of welfare hypothesizes that the average district office has 5% or fewer fraudulent or ineligible recipients. A sample of 10 offices reveals a mean of 4.7% with a standard deviation of 1.2%. What can be said about the secretary's hypothesis?

11.11 The Department of Health and Human Services wants to know the average income of general assistance recipients. A sample of 60 recipients shows a sample mean of $4,400 with a standard deviation of $2,500. (a) Place a 90% confidence limit around your best estimate of the average income of general assistance recipients. (b) What is the probability that the average income could be $6,000 or more? (c) What is the probability that the average might be as low as $4,000?

11.12 As an analyst for the Overseas Private Investment Corporation, you are required to report to Congress about guaranteed loans to companies doing business in Central American countries. You do not have time to find all the loans, so you take a sample of six loans. The loans have the following values, in millions of dollars:

223   247   187   17   215   275

Use this information to calculate a mean, and put 90% confidence limits around your estimate.

11.13 Complaints about how long it takes the city of Shorewood to pay its bills have reached the city manager. City policy requires that bills be paid within

30 days. A sample of 100 bills shows a mean of 34 days with a standard deviation of 15. Is it possible that a sample mean of 34 days could be generated from a population with a true mean of 30?

11.14   Last year, the Texas State Penitentiary averaged 14.1 violent incidents per day in its prisons. At the end of last year, the federal courts held that inmates could not supervise other inmates. Warden John Law thinks that this ruling will generate more violent incidents because, in the past, inmates used the supervision hierarchy to maintain a pecking order inside the prison. A sample of 40 days of records reveals a mean of 17.5 and a standard deviation of 2.0. What can you tell Warden Law?

11.15   The Metro City Bus system is concerned about the number of people who complain about the service. They suspect that many people do not know how to complain. Last year, complaints averaged 47.3 per day. This year, bus systems manager Ralph Kramden has posted a sign in all buses listing a number to call with complaints. Ralph would like to know whether this effort has generated any additional complaints. He takes a sample of 50 days and finds a mean of 54.7 and a standard deviation of 25.4. What can you tell Ralph?

CHAPTER 12

Hypothesis Testing

Public and nonprofit managers are often faced with decisions about program effectiveness, personnel productivity, and procedural changes. Decisions on such matters are based on the information relevant to them. Is the Chicago-area Head Start program upgrading the educational skills of its participants? Is Robert Allen an effective first-line supervisor? Will redesigning form SKL473/26 result in faster processing of equal employment complaints? A question that seeks information about managerial problems is called a **hypothesis.** When phrased as a statement rather than as a question, a hypothesis is nothing more than a statement about the world that may be tested to determine whether it is true or false. The following are examples of hypotheses:

Following the Connecticut Highway Patrol's crackdown on speeders, the number of highway accident fatalities dropped.

The average number of tons of trash collected by Jackson Hole, Wyoming, sanitation engineer crews is 247 tons per week.

After implementing the project team's management strategy, the productivity of the England County Welfare Department has increased.

Hypotheses are traditionally presented in the negative. For example,

Following the Connecticut Highway Patrol's crackdown on speeders, the number of highway accident fatalities *has not dropped.*

In the space provided, present the Jackson Hole and England County hypotheses in the negative.

A hypothesis expressed in the negative is referred to as the **null hypothesis** (the hypothesis that nothing happened). As this chapter will illustrate, null hypotheses are easier to use in inferential statistics than are other types of hypotheses.

You will notice that prior to stating these null hypotheses, you first had to interpret the original Jackson Hole and England County hypotheses. In order to test a null hypothesis, you must first state a **research hypothesis.** The research hypothesis is the opposite of the null. Put another way, if the null hypothesis is expressed in the negative, the research hypothesis is expressed in the positive. In policy evaluation, we often wonder whether policies have produced certain outcomes. Research hypotheses are generally constructed to reflect our expectations concerning policy outcomes.

For example, if a nonprofit organization institutes cost-cutting measures, the expectation is that costs will in fact go down. If a school district spends more money on teacher training, the expectation is that teacher performance should improve. If a state imposes tough new penalties on individuals convicted of driving under the influence, the expectation is that drunk driving arrests should go down.

Just because we have expectations about the effects of policies or managerial decisions does not mean that those effects will always be realized. The goal of testing hypotheses statistically is to determine whether the data support or fail to support the research hypothesis in question. A research hypothesis is always paired with a null hypothesis so we know what to conclude in those cases where the evidence fails to support the research hypothesis. Here are a few ways to conceptualize the difference between null and research hypotheses.

If the research hypothesis states that an outcome *has been realized,* the null hypothesis states that an outcome *has not been realized.*

If the research hypothesis states that a policy *had an effect,* the null states that the policy did *not have an effect.*

If the research hypothesis states that *a change has occurred,* the null states that *a change has not occurred.*

If the research hypothesis states that *a value will be greater than 50*, the null states that *a value will not be greater than 50*.

If the research hypothesis states that the score for the experimental group *is lower than the score for the control group*, the null states that *the score for the experimental group is not lower than the score for the control group.*

The practical implications of testing a null hypothesis are the following: If we are able to reject the null hypothesis, we accept the research hypothesis. If we are unable to reject the null hypothesis, we cannot accept the research hypothesis as true.

The research hypothesis is normally what the analyst believes is true and expects to find supported in the data analysis. The null hypothesis is the "foil" or comparison that facilitates this statistical test. When writing null and research hypotheses, it is helpful to label the research hypothesis as "H_1" and the null hypothesis as "H_0" to avoid confusion over which hypothesis is which. Stating a null hypothesis is easier if you state the research hypothesis first. It is usually less difficult to understand what the opposite of the research hypothesis is if we already know the meaning of the research hypothesis.

This chapter will cover the logic of hypothesis testing. It will also illustrate the process of testing hypotheses with both population parameters and sample statistics.

Steps in Hypothesis Testing

The logic of hypothesis testing is fairly simple:

Step 1: Formulate the hypothesis. Suppose that you have a research assistant, Thurman Truck, who is preparing a lengthy research report. Based on Truck's assurances, you develop the following hypotheses:

H_1 = Truck will complete the report by August.

H_0 = Truck will not complete the report by August.

Step 2: Collect data relevant to the hypothesis. You know that to complete the research report by August, Truck must complete a prospectus by January 15. On January 15, Truck tells you the prospectus will be done January 22. On January 21, Truck promises you the prospectus on January 28. On January 27, Truck swears that the prospectus will be on your desk by February 5. On February 4, Truck ceases to come to work.

Step 3: Evaluate the hypotheses in light of the data. Are the data consistent with the null hypothesis or the alternative hypothesis? Does Truck's behavior indicate that the research report will not be completed by August (the null hypothesis)?

Step 4: Accept or reject the null hypothesis. Remember that the research hypothesis typically states that a hypothesized change *has* taken place. The null hypothesis typically states that a hypothesized change has not taken place. We must accept the null hypothesis that Truck will not finish his research report by August. If we accept the null hypothesis, this tells us that the data do not support the research hypothesis.

Step 5: Revise your decision in light of this new information. In this case, you decide to transfer Truck to your regional office in Lubbock, Texas, as a punishment for nonperformance.

The Importance of Stating the Null and Alternative Hypotheses Correctly

The ability to state null and research hypotheses correctly is essential to public and nonprofit managers. The statistical techniques that we cover later in the chapter will have little meaning if you do not understand the difference between a null and a research hypothesis. Stating the null hypotheses for the Jackson Hole and England County examples was relatively easy since we provided the research hypotheses. Practice stating both the null and research hypotheses for the management questions that follow. Don't worry about numbers or statistical calculations at this point. Concentrate on identifying the research question in each example and correctly stating the hypotheses. Sample null and research hypotheses for each research question are presented at the end of the chapter. Exact wording is not important, so you should not be concerned if the hypotheses you write are stated a bit differently than the ones found at the end of the chapter.

Six months after the local newspaper ran a week-long series of articles on the Northlake, Virginia, Community Pride Center, the director wants to see whether this positive media coverage improved turnout at the center's after-school recreation programs, compared to turnout before the media coverage took place.

H_1

H_0

The head of the Alton, New York, Public Works Department has installed security cameras in the public yard in hopes of lowering the large number of illegal after-hours dumping incidents. After 90 days, officials want to assess the impact this measure has had on the number of illegal dumping incidents.

H_1

H_0

The director of philanthropy at the Art Institute of Cubs City, Illinois, is interested in assessing the impact recent changes in federal tax laws have had on donations. Because the changes gave potential donors favorable new tax benefits, the director would like to know whether the average donation amount is larger than it was prior to the change in the laws.

H_1
H_0

The principal of the Oaklawn Charter School claims that the "Oaklawn method" of mathematics instruction produces higher scores on standardized math skills tests compared to those of students in the district who are taught "the old math."

H_1
H_0

Now that you have gained some experience in stating hypotheses, we will demonstrate the statistical techniques used to test them.

Testing Hypotheses with Population Parameters

If the manager has access to population parameters, then hypothesis testing is as easy as deciding whom to start at center if Shaquille O'Neal plays for your team. As an illustration, suppose that Jerry Green, governor of a large eastern state, wants to know whether a former governor's executive reorganization has any impact on the state's expenditures. After some meditation, he postulates the following research and null hypotheses:

H_1: State expenditures decreased after the executive reorganization, compared with the state budget's long-run growth rate.

H_0: State expenditures did not decrease after the executive reorganization, compared with the state budget's long-run growth rate.

Governor Green stated the null hypothesis in this way so that the test would be fair. He reasoned that one could not expect an absolute decrease in expenditures because the state's population was growing (and thus generating greater demands for state services). The average growth rate of state expenditures appears to provide a reasonable test.

A management review shows that the state's expenditures grew at the rate of 10.7% per year before the reorganization and 10.4% after the reorganization. What do these figures say about the null hypothesis? Because 10.4% is less than 10.7%, we reject the null hypothesis and conclude that the growth rate in state expenditures declined after the reorganization.

You may have objected to the preceding conclusion, thinking that a 0.3% decrease in the growth rate of expenditures was not significant. If you meant statistically significant, you were incorrect. Since these are exact population parameters, statistical significance has no meaning (the probability that the state reduced its growth rate in expenditures is 1.0, or nearly so). If by significance you meant that the decrease was trivial, you are correct. Remember, however, that the hypothesis did not state that the change would be large, only that there would be a change.

Notice that we did not conclude that the reorganization resulted in a decline in the state budget's growth rate. That would be a causal statement. Statistics cannot come to this conclusion. Statistics can only determine whether the expenditure rate after the reorganization was less than the rate before the reorganization. To conclude that the reorganization resulted in the reduced rate, the manager must determine that no other variable could have caused the decline. This assessment is an evaluation of the research design (see Chapter 3). Finally, the manager must make a managerial assessment of this question based on the risks that the manager wishes to sustain.

To avoid overstepping the limits of statistics, we suggest you approach all statistical problems in three steps:

Step 1: The statistics step: Did the growth rate in the budget decline after the reorganization?

Step 2: The research design step: Could factors other than the reorganization have caused the decline?

Step 3: The managerial step: What can I confidently conclude about the reorganization and the budget growth rate?

Hypothesis Testing with Samples

In most managerial situations, population parameters are not available. This absence is the result of cost, inaccessibility, and a variety of other factors that prevent gathering data on the entire population. Although population parameters are the ideal data to use in hypothesis testing, circumstances almost always dictate the use of sample statistics. The Food and Nutrition Service of the Department of Agriculture, for example, may want to know the impact of food stamps on family nutrition. (The null hypothesis is that they have no impact.) Although the service might prefer data on all food stamp recipients, costs of gathering the data restrict the Food and Nutrition Service to testing with samples.

 Hypothesis testing with a sample can best be illustrated with an example. The police chief of Prudeville, Oklahoma, has received several complaints from the city council about prostitution in Prudeville. The council members all suggest a crackdown. The police chief issues orders to make more prostitution arrests and asks the department's research analyst to gather relevant data. After a month, the council is still upset and calls the police chief in to appear before the council. The chief asks his research assistant to assess the effectiveness of the crackdown so that the chief can present these data to the council.

Before the crackdown on prostitution, the Prudeville vice squad was making 3.4 prostitution arrests per day (arrests are normally distributed). The research assistant forms the following research and null hypotheses:

Table 12.1

Sample Data for Prostitution Arrests

Day	Prostitution Arrests
1	3
2	5
3	7
4	2
5	3
6	6
7	4
8	3
9	6
10	1

H_1: Following the Prudeville prostitution crackdown, prostitution arrests were greater than 3.4 per day.

H_0: Following the Prudeville prostitution crackdown, prostitution arrests were not greater than 3.4 per day.

How did we arrive at these hypotheses? If the research hypothesis states that the policy change had an effect, then the null hypothesis states that it did not have an effect. What is an effect in this case? The goal of the prostitution crackdown is to make more prostitution arrests. Accordingly, evidence of an effect would mean that prostitution arrests are rising above the precrackdown average of 3.4. If the policy did not have an effect, then we would expect to maintain the status quo of 3.4 arrests per day.

Because there is not enough time before the city council meeting to analyze all the data, the research analyst randomly selects 10 days of prostitution arrests for analysis. Table 12.1 presents the data.

The analyst proceeds by the following steps:

Step 1: Estimate the population mean after the crackdown. Because the best estimate of the population mean is the sample mean, the analyst calculates the mean. His figure is 4.0.

Step 2: Estimate the population standard deviation. In this example the estimated standard deviation is 1.94. (**Hint:** Divide by $n - 1$.)

Step 3: Calculate the standard error of the mean. Since we only have a sample, the mean estimate may be in error. As a result, we need to know how good an estimate of the mean we have. We use the formula

$$\text{s.e} = \frac{s}{\sqrt{n}} = \frac{1.94}{\sqrt{10}} = .61$$

The standard error is .61.

Step 4: Test the hypothesis. Answer the following question: What is the probability of drawing a sample of 10 with a mean of 4.0 if the population mean is 3.4? This question can be answered by converting 4.0 into a t score and using the t table (arrests are normally distributed).

$$t = \frac{\overline{X} - \mu}{\text{s.e.}} = \frac{4.0 - 3.4}{.61} = .98$$

Looking up a t score of .98 in the t table (df = 9), we find that the probability of a sample of 10 with a mean of 4.0 coming from a population with a mean of 3.4 is greater than .1. The research assistant has access to a computer program that provides an exact probability. This probability is .176.

Step 5: The research assistant decides to accept the null hypothesis because he feels .17 is too large a probability to reject the null hypothesis. The police chief overrules the research assistant because he wants to show positive results. He argues before the city council that this improvement in arrest rates has only a one-in-six chance of happening by chance. The research assistant is fired later that day.

Does the criterion used (arrest rates per day) accurately measure what the city council is concerned about? What does the city council want stopped? How could you measure this? How valid are the findings above given what you said about these measurements? Refer to Chapter 2, "Measurement." Apply the research design step to the alternate approach that you propose.

How Sure Should a Person Be?

In the preceding example, a research analyst felt that a probability of .17 was not sufficient to reject a null hypothesis, whereas the police chief felt that it was. Political considerations aside, how sure should a person be before rejecting the null hypothesis? In the words of Harvey Sherman, "It all depends." It all depends on how sure one needs to be to make a decision confidently.

When you make a decision about the probability for rejecting the null hypothesis, the general rule is that the t score obtained in testing the hypothesis must be larger than the t score associated with **alpha,** which is the probability you select for rejecting the null hypothesis. You should commit to memory the following decision rules for testing the null hypothesis:

If the t score generated exceeds the t score associated with alpha, we can reject the null hypothesis. This means we are able to accept the research hypothesis.

If the t score generated does not exceed the t score associated with alpha, we cannot reject the null hypothesis. This means we are unable to accept the research hypothesis.

Recall that the t score generated for the Prudeville arrests example is .98. If we decide to use an alpha of .05 for rejecting the null hypothesis (df = 9), the t score associated with alpha is 1.833. Since a *t* score of .98 is nowhere close to a score of 1.833, we clearly cannot reject the null hypothesis. In fact, the probability of .17 tells us that there is about a 17% chance that the null hypothesis is true in this case.

Social scientists routinely use a probability of .05 for rejecting the null hypothesis. But in many managerial situations, a .05 probability may be too great a risk. A rape crisis center may decide that the probability that one staff member cannot handle all the possible rape calls in any given day is .05. This means, however, that 1 day in 20, or once every 3 weeks, the rape crisis center will fail to meet a crisis. In this situation, a .05 level is too great a risk. A .001 level, one failure in 3 years, may be more acceptable.

A police department, on the other hand, may be able to accept a .05 probability that one of its cars will be out of service. But the fire department may require a probability of only .0001 that a fire hose will fail to operate (that is, 1 chance in 10,000).

When we assign a probability of .05 for rejecting the null hypothesis, we are saying that if our *t* score exceeds the *t* score associated with alpha and we reject the null, there is still a 5% chance that the null hypothesis is actually true. Why are we willing to tolerate error? Because sample data do not give us a perfect sense of what is true in the population, we must be willing to accept a certain amount of error when making inferences about the population. We do not have perfect, or sometimes even very good, information about most populations.

Keep in mind that when you test a hypothesis using a small sample, the *t* scores associated with alpha values will be higher than those for larger samples. This is because estimates of the population obtained from small samples contain more error than those obtained from larger samples. If you look closely at the table (Table 3, at end of book), you should see how alpha and degrees of freedom are related to sample size. Notice that as the number of degrees of freedom goes up, the *t* values for rejecting a null hypothesis go down. For example, if our sample contains 5 cases (df = 4), the *t* score for rejecting the null hypothesis with an alpha of .05 is 2.132. If our sample contains 25 cases (df = 24), the *t* score for rejecting the null hypothesis with an alpha of .05 is 1.711.

You may be wondering how to interpret the ∞ symbol at the bottom of the degrees of freedom column on Table 3. The symbol ∞ means infinity, a very large limitless number. When a sample is smaller than 30, we generally cannot assume that the distribution of sample means is normally distributed. When a sample is 30 or greater, we can have greater confidence that the distribution of sample means is normally distributed. As a result, all we need to know for samples larger than 30 is one particular *t* score for the alpha in question. For example, when assigning a .05 probability for rejecting the null hypothesis, we use a *t* score of 1.645 (one-tailed) whenever our sample contains more than 30 cases.

Recall that in Chapter 11, we stated that when a sample has more than 30 observations, the normal distribution can be used in place of the *t* distribution. To see how the *t* distribution and the normal (*z*) distribution begin to converge when the number of cases exceeds 30, you can compare the *t* table (Table 3) and the normal table (Table 1) at the end of the book. When a sample has more than 30 cases, the *t* score (one-tailed) for rejecting the null hypothesis at an alpha of .05 is 1.645. Turning to the normal distribution table, we find that a *z* score of 1.64 has a probability of .4495 and a

z score of 1.65 has a probability of .4505. Taking the mean of these two probabilities, we obtain a value of .4500 associated with a z score of 1.645. Subtracting .4500 from .50 (one-half of the normal distribution curve) yields an alpha value less than or equal to .05. Thus, we can say that 5% of the cases lie in one tail of the curve (that is, alpha = .05). The z and t values are giving us the same information about the percentage of observations found within the areas (assuming a one-tailed test) covered by the scores. In both cases, 5% of the data lie outside the range covered by the scores. The same logic applies for all of the other t score values at ∞.

The lesson here is that larger samples are more likely to converge on the true characteristics of the population than are smaller samples. The smaller t scores for alpha associated with larger samples reflect this fact.

Finally, remember that when you generate a t score to test a hypothesis, you must always use the score to evaluate whether the null hypothesis, not the research hypothesis, should be rejected. Understanding the difference between null and research hypotheses is key to making correct substantive conclusions in interpreting t scores.

The decision on how certain one must be to reject a null hypothesis depends on the importance of the question involved. A manager should never let his or her analyst make this decision. The analyst should provide the probability; it is the function of the manager to decide whether the probability is sufficient to reject the null hypothesis given the circumstances that are involved in the decision.

One- and Two-Tailed Tests

Determining the probability of an event is another way of assessing the statistical significance of an event. Another way of saying that the probability of event A is .01 is to say that A is statistically significant at the .01 level (that is, the probability that event A would occur by chance is .01). A significance test, therefore, is nothing more than a determination of the probability of an event.

Most statistics texts devote an extended discussion to one-tailed versus two-tailed tests of significance. This book will describe both briefly, but we will focus on the one-tailed test because it has much greater utility than the two-tailed test. A **one-tailed test** is applied whenever the hypothesis under consideration specifies a direction. In the previous Prudeville prostitution problem, the null hypothesis was that the arrest rate did not increase. We call this a one-tailed test because we are concerned with only one tail of the normal curve, the tail larger than 3.4 (see Figure 12.1).

A one-tailed test affects the probability assigned to the null hypothesis. Because we are interested only in values greater than 3.4, an $\bar{X}$ of 4.0 has a probability of .17. (**Reasoning**: If $\mu = 3.4$, 33% of all sample means fall between 3.4 and 4.0; 50% of all sample means fall below 3.4; this means 17% of all sample means fall at 4.0 or above; thus, the probability is .17.)

In rare circumstances, a public or nonprofit manager is interested in situations that differ greatly from the mean in either direction. For example, the Federal Railroad Administration is purchasing railroad ties to recondition a railroad line from Bessmer, Michigan, to Rolla, Missouri. (Many of Bessmer's finest serve at Fort Leonard Wood,

Figure 12.1

A One-Tailed Test

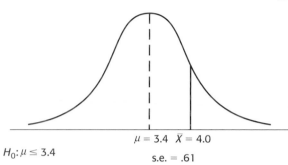

$\mu = 3.4$ $\bar{X} = 4.0$

$H_0: \mu \leq 3.4$

s.e. = .61

Missouri.) Because the railroad bed is unstable, only ties between 10 and 10 feet, 6 inches long can be used. The FRA administrator must inspect railroad tie shipments and decide whether they meet these standards. Because the FRA administrator cannot measure every tie, he decides to have a random sample of 10 pulled from every shipment. Any shipment of ties in which more than 20% of the ties are either too large or too small will be rejected. From past experience, the administrator knows that the standard deviation of machine-cut ties is 1 inch. Based on the mean of each sample of 10, how can the administrator decide whether or not to accept a shipment?

Because this problem does not specify a direction for the hypothesis, it requires a **two-tailed test.** The first step is to determine the maximum mean value so that less than 10% of all ties are more than 10 feet, 6 inches long. (We use 10% because, if 10% are too large and 10% are too small, 20% cannot be used.) To do this, look up a value of .1 in the t score table (Table 3) (df = 9). The t score is 1.383. If the mean sample is within 1.383 standard deviations of 10 feet, 6 inches, then the shipment should be rejected. Converting this figure to a length in feet, we have

$$X = 10 \text{ feet, 6 inches} - (1.383 \times 1 \text{ inch}) = 10 \text{ feet, 4.62 inches}$$

In any sample whose mean is greater than 10 feet, 4.62 inches, probably 10% of the ties are longer than 10 feet 6 inches.

Similarly, if the mean of the sample is 1.383 standard deviations from the lower limit of 10 feet, less than 10% of the ties will be too short. The lower limit for sample means then should be 10 feet, 1.383 inches. We now have a decision rule:

> If the mean length of 10 ties is between 10 feet, 1.38 inches and 10 feet, 4.62 inches, accept the shipment; if not, reject the shipment.

If shipments have a mean length of 10.3 inches and are normally distributed, using this decision rule will result in less than 20% of ties that are too long or too short. No more than 10% of the ties will be too long, and no more than 10% will be too short.

Although this problem uses both tails of the normal curve, it could easily be transformed into two separate problems, each with a one-tailed test. Because most management problems in the public sector and the nonprofit sector can be transformed into one-tailed problems, we suggest that you concentrate on learning how one-tailed tests are made. The only exception to this rule is when you want to know the optimal sample size so that you are 95% (or some other percentage) sure that a mean falls between two numbers (see below). *In sum, if your hypothesis specifies a direction, use a one-tailed test. If not, use a two-tailed test.*

Errors

When testing a null hypothesis, you can make two possible errors. You can reject the null hypothesis even though the null hypothesis is true. This is called a **Type I error.** For example, let us assume that the Federal Highway Administration wants to determine whether Colorado is enforcing the 65-mile-per-hour speed limit. If the average speed of Colorado cars is 65 or less, the FHA will concede that Colorado is enforcing the law. If the average speed is more than 65 miles per hour, then the FHA will begin proceedings to cut off Colorado's federal transportation funds. This is a serious step to take, so FHA officials want to be 99% certain before they act to cut off funds. Cost restrictions limit the sample of cars to be clocked to 100 cars.

Given this problem, the FHA analyst takes a preliminary survey and finds the standard deviation of Colorado car speeds to be 17.4 miles per hour. With a sample of 100, the standard error of any mean estimate would be

$$\text{s.e.} = \frac{s}{\sqrt{n}} = \frac{17.4}{\sqrt{100}} = \frac{17.4}{10} = 1.74$$

For a 99% confidence limit, the analyst scans the body of the normal table (to approximate a t table) for a probability value of .4900. This probability corresponds to a z score of 2.33. The analyst knows that if the sample mean of Colorado cars is 2.33 standard errors greater than 65, then he is 99% sure that Colorado cars' average speed exceeds 65 miles per hour.

Translating this into a decision rule, he finds

$$X = 65 + (2.33 \times 1.74) = 65 + 4.05 = 69.05$$

If the sample average speed of the sample of cars is 69.05 miles per hour or above, the FHA will conclude that Colorado cars' average speed is greater than 65 miles per hour and will begin withholding funds.

To illustrate the possibility of a **Type I error,** consider the following hypothetical situation. The average speed in Colorado is 65 miles per hour, but due to sampling error, the sample mean is 69.1. This situation will happen once every 100 samples. The hypothesis of 65 miles per hour was rejected when it was actually true.

The second type of error, called, quite appropriately, a **Type II error,** occurs when you accept the null hypothesis as true when in fact it is false. Suppose that in the preceding example the population mean is 67 miles per hour and a sample revealed a mean of 67 miles per hour. (Clearly this can happen.) In this situation, you would conclude that Colorado cars' average speed does not exceed 65 miles per hour when, in fact, it does.

Table 12.2

Calculations for Two Different Sample Sizes

Statistic	Sample 1	Sample 2
n	100	500
$\overline{X}$	67.0	67.0
s	17.4	17.4
s.e.	1.74	.78
probability $X < 65$	.119	.0051

The probability of committing either a Type I error or a Type II error always exists. The probability of committing a Type I error can be reduced by increasing the probability required to reject the null hypothesis (such as .001 or .0001). Unfortunately, this increases the probability of a Type II error. This trade-off is resolved by deciding whether it would be worse to make a Type I or a Type II error. Is it worse to cut off Colorado's federal aid when it is complying with the law or to continue to aid Colorado if it is violating the law? Clearly the former is more dangerous in a political sense, so one would try to minimize the probability of a Type I error.

A method of minimizing Type II errors is to increase sample size. All things being equal, the larger the sample size, the smaller is the standard error of the mean and, therefore, the smaller is the likelihood of rejecting a true hypothesis. The data in Table 12.2 illustrate this. The certainty of the analyst is increased by the larger sample. The probability of rejecting a true hypothesis with a sample mean of 67 is much less with a sample of 500 than with a sample of 100.

Determining Sample Size

Another research problem facing management analysts is deciding how large a sample is necessary to adequately test the hypothesis. For example, the Wisconsin State Welfare Department may want to know the average income of all Wisconsin welfare recipients. It would like to be 95% certain that its estimate of the average income is within $100 of the actual average (this information is needed for federal forms). Using a sample, we can get an estimate of the mean by using the sample mean. A 95% confidence interval can be placed around this estimate by adding and subtracting a number equal to 1.96 standard errors from the mean estimate (1.96 is the 95% confidence limit t score as n becomes large) and approaches infinity (see above):

$$\overline{X} \pm 1.96 \times \text{s.e.}$$

The amount of error in the estimate is represented by that part of the computation to the right of the plus or minus sign ($1.96 \times$ s.e.). Our problem is this: How large a sample is needed to reduce this error to $100? Mathematically, we can determine this by setting $1.96 \times$ s.e. equal to $100:

$$100 = 1.96 \times \text{s.e.}$$

But

$$\text{s.e.} = \frac{s}{\sqrt{n}}$$

so

$$100 = \frac{1.96s}{\sqrt{n}}$$

$$\sqrt{n} = \frac{1.96s}{100}$$

$$n = \left(\frac{1.96s}{100}\right)^2$$

These calculations show that, with an estimate of the standard deviation, we can calculate the desired sample size.

To estimate the standard deviation, the analyst takes a small sample of Wisconsin welfare recipients. The data of Table 12.3 result. In the space to the right of the data, calculate the standard deviation.

If you performed the calculations correctly, your answer should be 442. Substituting this value into the equation, we have

$$n = \left(\frac{1.96 \times 442}{100}\right)^2 = \left(\frac{866.3}{100}\right)^2 = (8.7)^2 = 75.7$$

The optimum sample size in this situation is 76 people. This size should provide an estimate of the average income of Wisconsin welfare recipients to within \$100.

To generalize this problem, the ideal sample size for any problem is a function of (1) the amount of error that can be tolerated, (2) the confidence one wants to have in

Table 12.3	

Data from a Sample of Wisconsin Welfare Recipients

Recipient	Income
1	\$1,500
2	1,700
3	2,600
4	1,800
5	1,200
6	2,400
7	1,300
8	1,700
9	2,000
10	1,800

the error estimate, and (3) the standard deviation of the population. Symbolically, this can be expressed as follows:

$$n = \left(\frac{t \times s}{E}\right)^2$$

where n is the sample size, t is the t score associated with the desired confidence limit, s is the estimated standard deviation, and E is the amount of error that can be tolerated.

For example, if you wanted to be 95% certain that the analyst's estimate in the previous example was within $50, you would perform the following calculations:

$$n = \left(\frac{1.96 \times 442}{50}\right)^2 = \left(\frac{866.3}{50}\right)^2 = (17.3)^2 = 300$$

The optimum sample size is 300 persons. (Always round up for sample sizes.)

Chapter Summary

Hypothesis testing is a statistical technique for evaluating whether a statement is more likely true or false. There are five steps involved: (1) formulate the hypothesis, (2) collect the relevant data, (3) evaluate the hypothesis in light of the data, (4) accept or reject the hypothesis, and (5) revise your decision in light of the new information.

Hypotheses can be tested by using population parameters or sample statistics, and hypothesis tests can be either one-tailed or two-tailed. When statistics are used, the techniques of inference are needed to test hypotheses. When conducting statistical inference, we always face a risk of error because we use sample data to make a guess about (unknown) population conditions.

Understanding the difference between research and null hypotheses is an essential part of testing hypotheses. When testing hypotheses, the statistical techniques described in the chapter are always used to assess whether the null hypothesis can or cannot be rejected. The t test, and the probabilities we interpret from these tests, are always used to evaluate the null, not research, hypothesis. If the null and research hypotheses are reversed or stated incorrectly, then the inferences made using t tests will be misleading.

This chapter also discusses the size of samples needed for ensuring only a given amount of error—that is, the sample size necessary to adequately test the hypothesis.

Problems

12.1   Last year, Normal, Illinois, had all car maintenance on the city's automobiles done by the city maintenance pool. The cost was $364 per car. This year, the city fathers fired all the workers in the maintenance pool and are using Jack's Crash Shop to perform the maintenance. They would like to know, without a complete audit, whether Jack is saving them money. A random sample of

36 cars showed a mean repair cost of $330, with a standard deviation of $120. What can you tell the city fathers?

12.2 The average grass maintenance engineer mows 1.4 acres of grass per day in Barron, Montana. Because labor costs are increasing, the city decides to try a new brand of mower. Ten randomly selected engineers are given these new mowers. After a test period, these 10 engineers cut an average of 2.1 acres per day, with a standard deviation of .6 acre. If the costs are similar, should the city purchase more new mowers?

12.3 It is contract negotiation time, and the Louisiana teachers union wants to argue that its salaries are the lowest in the region. Because the union has 20,000 members, it must rely on a survey. If the union wants to estimate its members' mean salary and be 95% sure that the estimate is within $200 of the real mean, how large a sample should the union use? Assume that a preliminary survey estimates the mean as $15,000, with a $1,000 standard deviation.

12.4 The departments at Bufford State University publish an average of 5.1 professional articles a year. The sociology department regularly averages about 3.5. The chairman of the sociology department, Steig Willick, feels her department does less well because it is harder to publish in sociology. Willick takes a survey of 12 other sociology departments and finds the following:

$$\overline{X} = 4.2 \qquad s = 1.6$$

What can Willick tell the dean?

12.5 The police chief of Kramer, Texas, reads a report that says the police clear 46.2% of all burglaries that occur in Kramer. The chief would like to know how good this figure is. She randomly selects 10 other Texas cities and asks them what percentage they clear. She gets the following numbers:

| 44.2% | 36.4% | 51.7% | 32.9% | 46.4% |
| 40.3% | 49.4% | 32.1% | 29.0% | 41.0% |

Is Kramer's clearance rate significantly different from those of other Texas cities?

12.6 The average per capita annual health care cost for a sample of U.S. cities (50,000-200,000 population) is $586, with a standard deviation of $116 ($n = 378$). Cavileer, Oregon (population 175,000), contends that its new outpatient treatment program reduces annual health care costs to $525 per person. Is this a significant improvement?

12.7 Refer to Problem 12.6. The average health care costs per year are $586. The Department of Health and Human Services has funded several Health Maintenance Organizations (HMOs). A sample of their average annual costs per person is as follows:

| $591 | $451 |
| $546 | $494 |

$437 $561
$527 $523
$602 $481

The hypothesis is that HMOs are an improvement. Are they?

12.8 The National Welfare Recipients Organization has charged that state case-workers are inexperienced. The Kansas State Welfare Department surveys its employees and finds that they have an average of 3.4 years of welfare experience ($s = 3.9$, $n = 200$). What can the Kansas State Welfare Department claim?

12.9 The Bureau of Forms has replaced 12 employees with 20 minicomputers. The 12 employees cost $204,500 per year in salaries and fringe benefits. The minicomputers cost $74,000. Operation and maintenance costs, however, are high; a sample of 10 machines reveals an average annual cost of $5,200, with a standard deviation of $2,000. What can be said about the decision to purchase minicomputers? (**Hint:** How much does the bureau save by replacing the employees with minicomputers? What is the savings per computer?)

12.10 The Whitehawk Indian Tribe wants to know the average number of absences for each student at the elementary school run by the Bureau of Indian Affairs (BIA). The tribe members believe that the number of absences is at least 12 per student. A sample of 150 students reveals

$$\overline{X} = 11.8 \qquad s = 4.3$$

What can you tell from this information about the Whitehawk hypothesis?

12.11 The Bureau of Administration is concerned with high levels of employee absenteeism. Last year, the average employee missed 12.8 workdays. This year, there is an experimental program in which the agency pays employees for each sick day or personal day that they do not use. A preliminary survey of 20 persons reveals a mean of 8.7 days missed and a standard deviation of 4.6. Present a hypothesis, a null hypothesis, and evaluate them. State a conclusion in plain English.

12.12 The state of Michigan has just changed one of its toll roads from human collection of tolls to machine collection. The idea behind the change was to allow traffic to flow more smoothly through the toll plaza. With human attendants, the mean number of cars passing through the toll plaza was 1,253 per hour. A random sample of 100 hours under the new machine system of toll collection shows a mean of 1,261, with a standard deviation of 59. Present a hypothesis, a null hypothesis, and evaluate them. State a conclusion in plain English.

12.13 The Iowa State University Agriculture Research Team is concerned about the impact of the recent drought on the productivity of the state's corn crop. During the last 10 years, Iowa's corn crop has averaged 32.4 bushels per acre per year. Final figures on this year's yields will not be in for another 6 months, but the team needs to estimate yields now in case the governor decides to apply for federal disaster aid. A sample of 100 acres reveals a mean of 22.4 bushels, with a standard deviation of 15.7. Based on this sample, present a hypothesis, a null hypothesis, and evaluate them. In plain English, state a conclusion of what you have found. Then place an 80% confidence limit around your best estimate of the mean yield.

12.14   The Heavenly Grace Christian Elementary School has decided to examine whether using biblical materials to teach reading has an impact on reading levels. Last year, a test revealed that the average sixth-grade student read at a 5.7 grade level. This year, after all secular humanist material was deleted from the curriculum, a 20-person sample of the sixth-grade student body was tested, with the following results:

$$\text{mean} = 6.4 \qquad \text{standard deviation} = 1.9$$

Present a hypothesis, a null hypothesis, and evaluate them. Present your conclusion in plain English.

12.15   The Wisconsin State Court system wants to assess the impact that punitive damages have on large tort awards. Using the court system's computer, 16 cases were selected at random from all those cases in which damages of $1 million or more were awarded. The sample revealed the following about the punitive damages in these cases:

$$\text{mean} = \$74,000 \qquad \text{standard deviation} = \$55,000$$

Place a 99% confidence limit around your best estimate of the punitive damages for this type of case. One concern is that punitive damages for these cases might be in excess of $100,000. Present a hypothesis, a null hypothesis, and evaluate your hypotheses. Finish with a conclusion that a judge could understand.

12.16   The director of philanthropy at the Fleckman Institute of the Arts is interested in assessing the impact that recent changes in federal tax laws have had on donations. The average donor gave $580 last year. A random sample of 50 donations reveals that in the 5 months since the laws were changed, the average donor gave $625, with a standard deviation of $97. Present a hypothesis, null hypothesis, and evaluate them. What can the director conclude about the effect the new tax laws are having on donations?

Answers to Sample Null and Research Hypotheses

Problem 1 H_1: Media coverage increased turnout at the Community Pride Center.

H_0: Media coverage did not increase turnout at the Community Pride Center.

Problem 2 H_1: The installation of security cameras has led to a decrease in the number of illegal dumping incidents.

H_0: The installation of security cameras has not led to a decrease in the number of illegal dumping incidents.

Problem 3

H_1: The size of the average donation has increased since the new tax laws were passed.

H_0: The size of the average donation has not increased since the new tax laws were passed.

Problem 4

H_1: Math scores at Oaklawn are higher than those at other schools in the district.

H_0: Math scores at Oaklawn are not higher than those at other schools in the district.

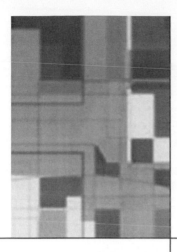

CHAPTER 13

Estimating Population Proportions

Often a manager does not want to know the mean score of some population but rather the percentage of some population that does something. A Department of Transportation official, for example, might want to know the proportion of motor vehicles that pass a state's vehicle inspection. A criminal justice planner might want to know what percentage of persons released from prison will be arrested for another criminal act within one year. A nonprofit manager might want to know the percentage of volunteers who show up when they are scheduled. All these situations require the analyst to estimate a population proportion rather than a population mean.

This chapter will illustrate the procedure for estimating population proportions and will demonstrate how to test hypotheses using proportions.

Estimating a Population Proportion

The procedure for estimating a population proportion and placing confidence limits around that estimate is relatively similar to that for estimating a population mean. We will illustrate this process with an example.

The warden of Ramsey Prison wants to know the prison's recidivism rate. The warden wants to know this information because he believes that the Ramsey rehabilitation program is a rousing success that others might want to copy. If the recidivism rate is fairly low (say, under 70%), the warden will write an article on the Ramsey re-habilitation program for the *Journal of Law 'n' Order*. (The Ramsey rehabilitation program involves teaching each inmate a skill, such as making license plates, and then finding the inmate a job making license plates in the outside world.)

Because Ramsey is a large institution, calculating the recidivism rate for all past inmates would be difficult. The warden takes a sample of 100 former inmates who went through the rehabilitation program. These inmates are traced through the FBI's data system to find out whether they were rearrested within a year of release. The warden considers anyone arrested within a year a failure. The FBI search reveals that 68 of the 100 inmates became inmates again.

Question 1: What is the best estimate of the proportion of recidivists in this situation? The sample of 100 can be interpreted as 100 samples of 1. The mean of these 100 samples is .68, which is the best estimate of the population proportion. In other words, the best estimate of a population proportion is the sample proportion.

Question 2: What is the standard deviation of the population? Recall that the standard deviation for a binomial probability distribution is

$$\sigma = \sqrt{n \times p \times (1 - p)}$$

where p is the probability and n is the number of trials.

If we treat this situation as a probability distribution, with $p = .68$ and 1 trial, the standard deviation is

$$\sigma = \sqrt{1 \times .68 \times .32} = \sqrt{.2176} = .47$$

The standard deviation is .47. In fact, this is how the standard deviation of a proportion is defined:

$$\sigma = \sqrt{p \times (1 - p)}$$

where σ is the standard deviation of the proportion and p is the proportion.

Since this is a sample, the formula is

$$s = \sqrt{p \times (1 - p)}$$

Actually, the standard deviation of a proportion makes no sense at all. All elements in the set have a value of 1 (recidivist) or 0 (not a recidivist). This means that the usual interpretation of a standard deviation as telling us the degree of clustering about the mean has little value. We calculate the standard deviation, however, because it permits us to calculate the standard error of the proportion.

Question 3: What is the standard error of the proportion? The standard error of a proportion has the same formula as the standard error of the mean:

$$\text{s.e.} = \frac{s}{\sqrt{n}}$$

where n is equal to the sample size. In our example we have

$$\text{s.e.} = \frac{.47}{\sqrt{100}} = \frac{.47}{10} = .047$$

Question 4: What are the 95% confidence limits of the proportion? (Although proportions cannot be normally distributed—since individuals are either recidivists or not—in this case the sample size is larger than 30, so the normal curve can be used to approximate the t distribution for 99 degrees of freedom.) With a mean (read "proportion") and a standard error of the estimate, we can easily construct a 95% confidence limit. In this situation, the 95% confidence limits are

$$p \pm t \times \text{s.e.}$$
$$.68 \pm 1.96 \times .047$$
$$.68 \pm .092$$
$$.59 \text{ to } .77$$

Question 5: Using the 95% confidence limit, should the warden submit an article to the *Journal of Law 'n' Order?*

Proportions

Proportions problems have the same logic as means problems, and both are solved in a similar manner. For example, city council member Liver Smith argues that a majority of the people in Worcester oppose the continued funding of the Worcester Transit Bus System. Liver bases this argument on a random sample of 30 Worcester residents. Twenty-one residents opposed continued funding of the bus system. For Liver's data, what is the probability that this sample could be drawn if a majority of residents favor continuing the bus system?

This problem can be interpreted as an example of hypothesis testing. Liver's hypothesis is that the proportion of Worcester residents opposing the bus system is greater than .5:

$$H_1: p > .5$$

The null hypothesis may be expressed as

$$H_0: p \leq .5$$

or "the proportion of Worcester residents who oppose the bus system is less than or equal to .5." Clearly this hypothesis can be tested.

Step 1: Estimate the population proportion. In this case, it is .7, or (21 ÷ 30).

Step 2: Estimate the population standard deviation. Because we are given a hypothetical population proportion ($p = .5$), that proportion (not the sample proportion) should be used to estimate the standard deviation:

$$\sigma = \sqrt{p \times (1 - p)} = \sqrt{.5 \times .5} = .50$$

Step 3: Estimate the standard error of the proportion.

$$\text{s.e.} = \frac{\sigma}{\sqrt{n}} = \frac{.50}{\sqrt{30}} = \frac{.50}{5.5} = .091$$

Step 4: Test the hypothesis. What is the probability that a sample of 30 would result in a proportion estimate of .7 or greater if the true proportion were .5? Use a t table, and convert .7 to a t score:

$$t = \frac{X - \mu}{\text{s.e.}} = \frac{.7 - .5}{.091} = \frac{.2}{.091} = 2.20$$

Looking up a t score of 2.20 in Table 3, we find a value of .025, which means that the probability is less than .025 of obtaining a sample that has a proportion of .7 or greater.

Step 5: Reject the null hypothesis. Accept the alternative hypothesis that the proportion of Worcester residents opposing the bus system is greater than 5.

A Digression

Before examining some other uses of proportions, a digression is in order. (Digressions are in order only after a t score of 2.0 or more.) The perceptive reader might have seen another way to solve the previous problem. Another way to phrase the problem is this: If the probability of finding a person opposed to the Worcester Bus System is .5, what is the probability that 21 or more of 30 randomly selected persons will oppose the bus system?

This problem is a binomial distribution problem, where $n = 30$, $r = 21$ or more, and $p = .5$. (If you need to refresh your memory regarding the binomial distribution, please see Chapter 9.) The mean in this case (or the expected value) is

$$\mu = n \times p = 30 \times .5 = 15$$

The standard deviation is

$$\sigma = \sqrt{n \times p \times (1 - p)} = \sqrt{30 \times .5 \times .5} = \sqrt{15 \times .5} = \sqrt{7.5} = 2.7$$

Converting r to a z score, we have

$$z = \frac{r - \mu}{\sigma} = \frac{21 - 15}{2.7} = \frac{6}{2.7} = 2.22$$

This z score corresponds to a probability of .0132 that 21 or more of 30 people oppose the bus system if $p = .5$. Although this probability is not the same as the probability found earlier (less than .025), the two probabilities are fairly close. The differences are the result of rounding error and the approximation of the t table.

Determining Sample Size

The director of the Office of Human Development wants to know the proportion of welfare recipients who own cars. She needs to know this information to refute the common myth about welfare Cadillacs. She wants to know the proportion within 2% and wants to be 95% certain. Determine the sample size necessary to find out this information.

This problem is identical to any other sample size problem. Remember from Chapter 12 that sample size is determined by the following formula:

$$n = \left(\frac{z \times \sigma}{E}\right)^2$$

where E is the amount of error tolerated. Because the director specified a 95% confidence limit and a 2% error, this formula becomes

$$n = \left(\frac{1.96 \times \sigma}{.02}\right)^2$$

The only thing we need to know in order to calculate sample size is the standard deviation. Although we could take a preliminary sample and estimate the standard deviation, there is an easier way. Statisticians have discovered that the standard deviation of a proportion is greatest when the proportion is equal to .5. You may verify this in a barefoot way by calculating the standard deviations for the listed proportions in Table 13.1. Those of you with a calculus background, feel free to present a proof.

If you calculated the correct standard deviations, the largest standard deviation is .50 for a proportion of .5. This fact means that if we do not know a population proportion and we need to estimate a sample size, .5 is the best proportion estimate to use. Because all other proportions have smaller standard deviations, they will require

Table 13.1

For What Proportion Is the Standard Deviation Greatest?

Proportion	Standard Deviation	Proportion	Standard Deviation
p	$\sqrt{p(1-p)}$	.5	
.1		.6	
.2		.7	
.3		.8	
.4		.9	

smaller samples to have the same accuracy. So, in this case, we assume a proportion of .5 and thus a standard deviation of .5. Substituting into the formula, we get

$$n = \left(\frac{1.96 \times .5}{.02}\right)^2 = \left(\frac{.98}{.02}\right)^2 = 49^2 = 2,401$$

To be 95% confident that the proportion of welfare Cadillacs is within 2% of the estimate, a sample of 2,401 is required.

To illustrate the need for a smaller sample if the proportion is smaller (or larger), assume that an earlier survey revealed that 10% of all welfare recipients owned Cadillacs. In this case, our estimate of the standard deviation is .3. Substituting this value into the sample size formula, we get

$$n = \left(\frac{1.96 \times .3}{.02}\right)^2 = (29.4)^2 = 864$$

If interview costs run approximately $20 per interview, why is it sometimes helpful to estimate the population proportion in advance?

Decision Making

John Johnson, the warden at the Maxwell Federal Penitentiary, is considering a novel rehabilitation program. He believes that if certain types of nonviolent offenders are released early, they will have a very low recidivism rate. John considers a recidivism rate of 50% an acceptably low rate. John would like to try the program for a few years and then, based on data from samples of inmates, decide whether or not to continue it. Because of the sensitive nature of experiments that release prisoners early, John wants to be 99% certain of his decision and can only afford a sample of 100. Given this information, construct a decision rule.

The procedure for a decision rule in this case is much like a decision rule based on means.

If $\mu > .5$, eliminate the program.

If $\mu < .5$, keep the program.

Translating this to a sample of 100 with 99% confidence, we have

If $\bar{X} + t \times$ s.e. $< .5$, keep the program.

(Note that we only need to consider the "keep the program" option because the greatest danger is in keeping a program that lets hardened criminals loose on the streets. This means that we are interested in only one tail of the curve, so we look up a probability of .01 in the t table. Because $n = 100$, we use the normal curve approximation to look up .49.)

Since a 99% confidence limit has a t score of 2.33, and since the largest standard deviation possible is for $p = .5$ ($\sigma = .5$), we can substitute in these values:

$$\bar{X} + 2.33 \times \left(\frac{.5}{\sqrt{100}}\right) < .5$$

$$\overline{X} + 2.33 \times .05 < .5$$
$$\overline{X} + .1165 < .5$$
$$\overline{X} < .3835$$

From these calculations, we can formulate a new decision rule in which we have 99% confidence. Stated in terms of percentages:

If $\overline{X} < 38.35$, keep the program.

If $\overline{X} > 38.35$, terminate the program.

Therefore, whenever a sample of 100 inmates reveals a recidivism rate of 38.35% or greater, the release program should be terminated.

Chapter Summary

Often the analyst will not have means but only proportions from the sample data. Proportions can be used to estimate parameters and to test hypotheses in processes very similar to those used for means. The problems and pitfalls remain basically the same. In addition, the sample size needed for a particular problem involving proportions can be determined in a manner similar to that shown in Chapter 12 for means.

Problems

13.1 The personnel department of a large government agency needs to know the percentage of employees who will retire this year. This information is essential to agency recruitment personnel. The agency determines this information with a random sample. If the agency wants to be 90% sure that its estimate of the retirement percentage is within 2%, how large a sample should it take?

13.2 If 33% of the members of the Sweetheart Union sign petitions to decertify the union, the National Labor Relations Board (NLRB) will call an election to determine whether Sweetheart will remain the exclusive bargaining agent. The union leadership takes a random sample survey of 40 and finds that 8 persons will sign the petition. What can you tell the union?

13.3 After a massive inventory, Central Library finds 12% of its volumes missing. As a result, Central institutes new procedures to prevent theft. After instituting these procedures for 1 year, Central Library wants to know whether they are working, but it cannot afford the cost of a complete inventory. The library takes a sample of 200 books and cannot locate 14 of them. These 14 are assumed to be lost to theft. What can you say about the new procedures?

13.4 Last year, 30% of all Wheezer School children missed class during March because of illness. This year, the school board requires all teachers to dispense vitamin C tablets during the morning milk break. A sample of 60 children reveals that only 12 missed school during March. What can be said about the differences in absentee rates?

13.5   According to the Department of Transportation, 74% of all cars on Interstate 35 were exceeding the 55-mile-per-hour speed limit. The department runs a series of public service ads, and then takes a sample of 2,000 cars. It finds that 72% of the cars are exceeding the speed limit. Write a memo discussing the possible impact of the department's ad program.

13.6   Bernie Belfry, the coordinator for Habitat for Humanity, wants to know the percentage of the population in substandard housing. Belfry wants to be 99% certain that he is within 10 percentage points of the population percentage. How large a sample does Belfry need?

13.7   Refer to Problem 13.6. If an earlier survey revealed that 30% of the population was in substandard housing, how large a sample should Belfry use?

13.8   The Department of Fish and Wildlife is under pressure to use poisons to kill coyotes. The department feels that poison will only kill those coyotes that would be killed by predators and harsh weather anyway. According to its records, an estimated 28% of all coyotes live through the winter. A pilot project is tried with poisons in the Lupus Wildlife Refuge. Of the 214 coyotes released there in the fall, 51 are found alive in the spring. What can you tell the department about the experiment?

13.9   Refer to Problem 11.9 (Chapter 11). What is your best estimate of the proportion of Branflake International flights that arrive on time?

13.10   VISTA manager William Phogbound suspects that 50% of his volunteers are over 65 years old. A survey of 16 volunteers reveals that 7 are over 65. What can be said about Phogbound's assertion?

13.11   If the error rate for TANF (Temporary Assistance to Needy Families) payments is greater than 5%, the federal government will cut off funding to the state of Utah. To see whether this is a problem, the agency director takes a sample of 250 welfare recipients and finds that errors have been made in 18 cases. What is your best estimate of the error rate in Utah? Place a 90% confidence limit around this estimate. Present a hypothesis, a null hypothesis, and evaluate them. State a conclusion in plain English.

13.12   The Milwaukee Independent School District is concerned with white flight—the withdrawal of white students from MISD. Last year, 63% of all MISD students were white. To get a quick reading of the situation this year, a sample of 100 students is selected: 52 of those students are white. What is your best estimate of the proportion of white students in MISD? Present a hypothesis, a null hypothesis, and evaluate them. Present a conclusion in plain English.

13.13   The village of Whitefish Bay uses a private insurance carrier to cover its automobile fleet. The carrier contends that it pays 90% of all claims within 30 days after the claims are filed. The department wants to check this out without going through a complete audit. Analyst Susan Medford takes a sample of 100 claims from last year and finds that 82 were paid within 30 days. Present a statistical evaluation of these results.

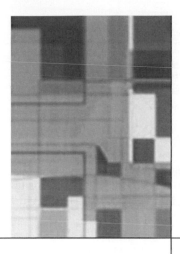

CHAPTER 14

Testing the Difference between Two Groups

Often a public or nonprofit administrator will have two samples and will want to know whether the values measured for one sample are different from those of the other sample. For example, a school administrator might want to know whether the reading levels of high school seniors improved after a special reading seminar was given: He wants a before-after comparison. A mental health counselor may want to know whether one type of treatment works better than another. A nonprofit executive may want to know whether agencies that contract with fund-raising firms net more donations than those that raise funds in-house. A librarian might want to know whether advertising affects circulation and thus might set up an experiment in which some branches advertise and others do not. In situations such as these, in which one wants to know whether two sample means are different or whether two sample proportions are different, the appropriate technique to use is a difference of means test.

Stating the Research and Null Hypotheses for Difference of Means Tests

In Chapter 11, we learned that when testing a hypothesis about a population using a single sample, the goal was to see whether a single sample with a particular mean could be drawn from a population with a known or hypothesized mean. The goal of testing hypotheses for two sample means is slightly different. When testing the difference between two sample means, the goal is to determine whether both sample means could have been drawn from the same population, or whether the two sample means are so different that they could not have been drawn from the same population.

For many management or policy evaluation issues, we expect the values for one sample to be different from those of the other sample. Research and null hypotheses are written to reflect this expectation. The general logic for the research hypothesis in a difference of means test is that one of the sample means is different (either smaller or larger) than the other sample mean. This is only a generic way of describing the underlying logic of a research hypothesis for a difference of means test. The actual hypotheses you write should be tailored to the specific research question at hand.

A thorough understanding of the research question helps clarify two important points necessary for carrying out a difference of means test: (1) the reason for hypothesizing a difference between the two groups (what makes one group different from the other?) and (2) the expected direction of the difference. For example, if we compare the academic performance of elementary school students who have participated in after-school learning programs to those who have not, it would be too vague simply to hypothesize that the performance of the two groups will be different. Instead, we would write the research hypothesis to reflect the expectation that the performance of program participants should be higher than that of nonparticipants.

Because we use samples to make inferences about larger populations, confirming the research hypothesis in a difference of means test indicates that the two population means are also different. In other words, there is a low probability that both samples could have been drawn from the same population. The general logic of the null hypothesis in a difference of means test is that the two sample means are not different. Failure to reject the null hypothesis indicates that the population means in question are not different.

Before examining the statistical issues involved in carrying out difference of means tests, we will illustrate how the process works using an example without any data. Officials at the Bureau of Forms want to examine the effect that continuing education seminars have on employee performance. Half of the employees at the bureau have participated in continuing education seminars, while the other half have not. To see whether continuing education seminars are having an effect on performance, agency officials randomly select 50 employees who have participated in seminars and 50 who have not. After administering job skills tests to each of the samples, agency officials want to evaluate whether the test scores for the two groups of employees are different. The research and null hypotheses are as follows:

H_1: Employees who have taken continuing education seminars will have higher job skills scores.

H_0: There is no difference in job skills scores between employees who have taken continuing education seminars and those who have not.

In this case, if we were unable to reject the null hypothesis, the substantive conclusion would be that the mean test scores for the two populations of workers (those attending seminars and those not attending seminars) are not different. In other words, the population mean for both groups is the same, indicating that seminars are not leading to higher job skills scores.

If we were able to reject the null hypothesis, the substantive conclusion would be that the mean test scores for the two populations of workers are different. In other words, the scores for the population of workers who have participated in continuing education seminars are higher than the scores for workers who have not. Thus, the two population means are different, indicating that seminars are leading to higher job skills scores.

Now that you have been introduced to the general logic of difference of means tests, we will present the statistical steps involved in the process.

Difference of Means Procedure

The best way to illustrate the difference of means test is with an example. The Ware County librarian wants to increase circulation from the Ware County bookmobiles. The librarian thinks that poster ads in areas where the bookmobiles stop will attract more browsers and increase circulation. To test this idea, the librarian sets up an experiment. Ten bookmobile routes are selected at random; on those routes, poster ads are posted with bookmobile information. Ten other bookmobile routes are randomly selected; on those routes, no advertising is done. In effect, the librarian has set up the following experiment:

Group	Treatment	Comparison
Experimental group	Place ads	Measure circulation
Control group	No ads	Measure circulation

After a week-long experiment, the information listed in Table 14.1 is available to the librarian.

The null hypothesis is that the mean circulation of the experimental group is not higher than the mean circulation of the control group. Testing the difference between two means tells us the probability that both groups could be drawn from the same population. More formally, the analyst wants to know if μ_e (the experimental mean) is greater than μ_c (the control mean) or, alternatively,

$$d = \mu_e - \mu_c$$

to test if $d = 0$. The procedure is as follows:

Table 14.1

Librarian's Data

	Experimental Group	Control Group
Mean	526 books	475 books
Standard deviation	125	115

Step 1: Calculate the mean and standard deviation for each group. This has already been done in Table 14.1. We use the sample means and standard deviations as estimates of the population parameters.

Step 2: Calculate the standard error of the mean estimate for each group.

$$\text{s.e.} = \frac{s}{\sqrt{n}}$$

Experimental group:

$$\text{s.e.} = \frac{125}{\sqrt{10}} = 39.5$$

Control group:

$$\text{s.e.} = \frac{115}{\sqrt{10}} = 36.4$$

Step 3: Calculate an overall or "pooled" standard error for both groups. The overall standard error is equal to the square root of the sum of the squared standard errors for each group. Symbolically, this can be expressed as

$$\text{s.e.}_d = \sqrt{\text{s.e.}_1^2 + \text{s.e.}_2^2}$$

For the present example, we have

$$\text{s.e.} = \sqrt{39.5^2 + 36.4^2} = \sqrt{1,560.25 + 1,324.96} = \sqrt{2,885.21} = 53.7$$

Step 4: Since we want to know the probability that the groups could be drawn from the same population, and since we have a mean estimate and a standard error, we can calculate the following t score:

$$t = \frac{\bar{X}_1 - \bar{X}_2}{\text{s.e.}_d}$$

where $\bar{X}_1$ is the control group mean, $\bar{X}_2$ is the experimental group mean, and s.e. is the overall standard error. In the present example we have

$$t = \frac{475 - 526}{53.7} = \frac{-51}{53.7} = -.95$$

Looking up a t score of $-.95$ in the t table [degrees of freedom (df) is $n_1 + n_2 - 2$, or 18 in this case], we find a probability of more than .1 (.18 if a computer is used). Statistically, we can say that there is more than 1 chance in 10 that the two samples could be drawn from the same population (that is, there is no difference).

Step 5: If the research design shows no other possible causes, what can the librarian say managerially about the program?

Understanding the Three Major Difference of Means Tests

The preceding formula for a difference of means test is actually only one of three such tests. It is the test that is used when the two samples are independent and the analyst is unwilling to assume that the two population variances are equal. There are two other tests: one for equal variances and one for dependent samples. To understand which test you should apply to a particular management question, you need to understand the difference between independent and dependent samples.

Independent samples are those in which cases across the two samples are not "paired" or matched in any way. The best procedure to obtain independent samples is through random sampling techniques. For example, if an analyst at the Internal Revenue Service randomly selects two samples from a national database, each consisting of 250 tax returns, there is no reason to expect a one-to-one linkage or pairing between individual cases across the two samples. Case 1 from sample A might be a tax return filed by a male from Arkansas. Case 1 from sample B might be a tax return filed by a female from Nevada. The remaining 249 tax returns for each sample should be similarly diverse in terms of the background characteristics of filers. Because each sample is drawn randomly, we have no reason to expect paired relationships (such as each person in sample A being matched with a close relative in sample B) between individual cases across the two samples.

Dependent samples exist when each item in one sample is paired with an item in the second sample. A before-after test would generate dependent samples if the same cases were used both before and after. For example, an agency could select 50 employees with low performance scores to attend mandatory performance workshops for a month. To see whether the workshops improve performance, the same 50 employees could be given performance exams after training has been completed. The scores for each employee are logically paired because each one has both a before and an after score.

The logic of dependent samples does not apply if the "before" and "after" cases are not paired. Let us assume that an agency with 1,000 employees has decided to select a random sample of 50 employees for drug testing. After obtaining the test results, agency officials undertake aggressive steps to reduce illegal drug usage among employees. Agency officials then draw a second random sample of 50 employees 3 months later to see whether the new policies are having an effect. The same 50 employees are not included in the before and after samples. Because cases for both samples were randomly selected, and there is no way to pair or connect the cases in the first sample with those in the second, the two samples are independent.

t Test Assuming Independent Samples with Unequal Variances

The independent samples unequal variances *t* test is the most conservative; that is, it is less likely than the other two *t* tests to reject the null hypothesis. Sampling error is one reason why samples often have unequal variances. The problem this poses for inference is that sampling error makes it harder to determine whether two sample means are truly different or different mainly because of different variances that result from sampling error. The *t* test for independent samples with unequal variances is conservative in the sense that the calculations for the standard errors are designed to takes large differences in sample variances into account. This helps clarify whether the sample means themselves are truly different. The calculations for degrees of freedom

---

Box 14.1

Calculating Degrees of Freedom When Using the *t* Test for Independent Samples and Unequal Variances

One reason the *t* test for independent samples and unequal variances is more conservative than other *t* tests has to do with the way degrees of freedom are calculated. The formula* for calculating degrees of freedom when using the independent samples unequal variances *t* test is as follows:

$$df = \frac{\left(\dfrac{s_1^2}{N_1} + \dfrac{s_2^2}{N_2} \right)^2}{\dfrac{\left(\dfrac{s_1^2}{N_1} \right)^2}{(N_1 - 1)} + \dfrac{\left(\dfrac{s_2^2}{N_2} \right)^2}{(N_2 - 1)}}$$

where: s = sample variance; N = number of cases in sample

This formula generally produces lower df values than the formula that we have been using up to this point, $df = (n_1 + n_2 - 2)$. The lower the degrees of freedom, the larger the *t* statistic must be when evaluating whether the null hypothesis can be rejected.

To simplify matters, we have used the less complex formula to calculate degrees of freedom for the problems at the end of the chapter. Although the degrees of freedom are sometimes the same using either formula (such as in the Stone Creek bureaus example), you should not assume that this will always be the case when you are analyzing your own data. Thus, you should familiarize yourself with the steps involved in calculating degrees of freedom for the independent samples unequal variances *t* test. Statistical software packages (such as SPSS) and spreadsheet programs (such as MS Excel) automatically calculate the correct degrees of freedom depending on the type of test (equal or unequal variances) that is selected.

---

*Formula for independent samples unequal variances test obtained from the National Institute of Standards and Technology Web site: *NIST/SEMATECH e-Handbook of Statistical Methods,* http://www.itl.nist.gov/div898/handbook/.

when using the *t* test for independent samples with unequal variances are also more conservative than those for other *t* tests, as explained in Box 14.1.

The independent samples, unequal variances *t* test is particularly useful when the number of cases in each sample is different or when the number of cases in one or both of the samples is small (less than 30 or so). For example, if one sample consists of 150 cases and the other 20, the amount of sampling error for the smaller sample might be much larger than that for the larger sample. If this were the case, the variances for the two samples would also be different.

While a *t* test that makes it harder to reject the null hypothesis might seem like a disadvantage, a more rigorous standard makes the occurrence of Type I errors less likely. A public or nonprofit manager could spend his or her entire life using this *t* test and make adequate decisions (similar to using the binomial probability distribution when the hypergeometric should be used). We will illustrate the use of this test with an example.

Sharon Pebble, the city manager of Stone Creek, South Dakota, wants to determine whether her new personnel procedures are decreasing the time it takes to hire an employee. She takes a sample of 10 city bureaus and calculates the average time to hire an employee in days before and after implementation of the new procedure. She gets the following results:

Bureau	Before	After
A	36.4	32.2
B	49.2	45.2
C	26.8	31.3
D	32.2	27.1
E	41.9	33.4
F	29.8	29.0
G	36.7	24.1
H	39.2	38.2
I	42.3	38.0
J	41.9	37.2

The hypothesis, that personnel are being hired in less time than they were before the adoption of the new procedures, is the same for all three tests. The null hypothesis is also the same: There is no difference between the time it takes to hire new personnel before and after implementation of the new procedures.

First, we discuss the independent samples and unequal variances procedure:

Step 1: Estimate the mean and standard deviation for the period before the adoption of the new procedures and the period after:

Period	Mean	*s*
Before	37.64	6.71
After	33.57	6.23

Step 2: Calculate the standard error for each group:

$$\text{Before} \quad \frac{6.71}{\sqrt{10}} = 2.12$$

$$\text{After} \quad \frac{6.23}{\sqrt{10}} = 1.97$$

Step 3: Calculate the overall standard error:

$$\sqrt{2.12^2 + 1.97^2} = 2.89$$

Step 4: Calculate the t score for the difference of means:

$$\frac{37.64 - 33.57}{2.89} = \frac{4.07}{2.89} = 1.41$$

Step 5: Look up a t score of 1.41 with df = 18. That value is significant at less than .1. So there is less than 1 chance in 10 that the samples could have been drawn from the same population and, thus, that the means are equal. The resulting t score is not large enough to safely reject the null hypothesis. Thus, Ms. Pebble could conclude that the new procedures had no impact.

t Test Assuming Independent Samples with Equal Variances

The t test for independent samples and equal variances is less conservative than the t test for independent samples and unequal variances, because the former generates smaller standard errors and larger t scores. There is nothing wrong with using the t test for independent samples and equal variances if you are certain that the two sample variances are equal. However, if you assume that the sample variances are equal and they really are not, the overall standard error produced using this test will usually be smaller than it should be. This increases the likelihood of making a Type I error when testing a hypothesis.

You can formally evaluate whether two sample variances are equal by performing the Levene test, which is an option available in most statistical software packages (see Box 14.2 for an explanation of how to interpret the Levene test). An even simpler approach is to always use the independent samples, unequal variances t test unless you are absolutely certain that the two sample variances are equal.

The t test for independent samples and equal variances operates as follows:

Step 1: Estimate the mean and standard deviation for the period before and the period after implementation of the new procedures, as shown in Step 1 in the prior example.

Step 2: Calculate an overall standard deviation by using the following formula:

$$s_d = \sqrt{\frac{[(n_1 - 1)s_1^2] + [(n_2 - 1)s_2^2]}{n_1 + n_2 - 2}}$$

This is essentially a weighted average of the two standard deviations:

$$\sqrt{\frac{(9 \times 6.71^2) + (9 \times 6.23^2)}{10 + 10 - 2}} = 6.47$$

Box 14.2

How to Interpret the Levene Test for Equality of Variances

When interpreting the Levene test, the null hypothesis is that the two sample variances are equal. The alternative (research) hypothesis is that the two sample variances are not equal. The test statistic in this case is an *F* statistic. If you use a statistical software package to run a difference of means test, the program will calculate the exact probability that the null hypothesis is correct. The following table is sample SPSS output for a difference of means test that includes results for the Levene test.

Independent Samples Test

| | Levene's Test for Equality of Variances | | *t* Test for Equality of Means | | | | | 95% Confidence Interval of the Difference | |
	F	Sig.	t	df	Sig. (two-tailed)	Mean Difference	Std. Error Difference	Lower	Upper
Equal variances assumed	87.392	.000	−15.386	1,038	.000	−6.2228	.4044	−7.0164	−5.4292
Equal variances not assumed			−14.921	790.145	.000	−6.2228	.4171	−7.0415	−5.4041

In the present example, $F = 87.392$. With a level of significance of .000, this result indicates that the probability the two sample variances are equal is extremely small. Thus, the null hypothesis should be rejected, and we should assume that the sample variances are not equal. Although a level of significance of .05 is commonly used to evaluate the test statistic, an analyst can also choose a more stringent threshold (such as .01) when testing the null hypothesis if necessary. For more information on how to calculate and interpret the Levene test, see Kurtz (1999, p. 185).

Step 3: Convert this overall standard deviation to a standard error with the following formula:

$$\text{s.e.} = s_d \sqrt{\frac{1}{n_1} + \frac{1}{n_2}}$$

$$6.47 \times \sqrt{\frac{1}{10} + \frac{1}{10}} = 2.89$$

In this case, the standard error is identical because the sample sizes are equal. If the after sample had 20 observations rather than 10, the final standard error would have been 1.99 for this method and 2.53 for the unequal variances method. The standard error for this method is always less than or equal to that of the other method; thus, the t score is always greater than or equal to the one for unequal variances. In the case of samples of 10 and 20, the t score for unequal variances would be 1.61 and for equal variances would be 2.05.

Step 4: Calculate the t score for the difference of means:

$$\frac{37.64 - 33.57}{2.89} = \frac{4.07}{2.89} = 1.41$$

Step 5: Look up a t score of 1.41 with df = 18. That value is significant at less than .1. So there is less than 1 chance in 10 that the samples could have been drawn from the same population and, thus, that the means are equal.

t Test Assuming Dependent Samples

Finally, the t test procedure for dependent samples is much different. In the present case, each of the items are paired because before and after data exist for each of the 10 bureaus. Because the items are paired, one simply subtracts one from the other to get d, the difference between the two items.

Step 1: Perform the pair-wise subtractions to obtain the differenc

Bureau	Before	After	Difference
A	36.4	32.2	4.2
B	49.2	45.2	4.0
C	26.8	31.3	−4.5
D	32.2	27.1	5.1
E	41.9	33.4	8.5
F	29.8	29.0	.8
G	36.7	24.1	12.6
H	39.2	38.2	1.0
I	42.3	38.0	4.3
J	41.9	37.2	4.7

The remaining steps are performed on the differences, rather than on the original data. The results are treated as a case of statistical inference on the differences.

Step 2: Calculate the mean and standard deviation of the differences. In this case, the mean is 4.07, and the standard deviation is 4.56.

Step 3: Calculate the standard error using the normal formula of dividing the standard deviation by the square root of the sample size. In this case, the standard error is

$$\text{s.e.} = \frac{4.56}{\sqrt{10}} = 1.44$$

Step 4: Calculate a t score with $n = 10$, or 9 degrees of freedom (df) to see whether the mean is different from zero:

$$t = \frac{4.07 - 0}{1.44} = 2.83$$

Step 5: This t score is significant at less than .01. The dependent samples t test produces the most significant results, but it can be used only when the samples are dependent. In this case, Ms. Pebble would likely conclude that there was a decrease in the time to hire new employees after the new procedures were implemented.

For the remainder of this chapter and the problems, we will assume independent samples and unequal variances unless otherwise specified.

Proportions

The t test is a technique that can be used both for the difference between two sample means and for the difference between two sample proportions. For example, the Morgan City parole board has been running an experimental program on one-third of their parolees. The parolees in the experimental program are placed in halfway houses run by nonprofit organizations that try to ease the readjustment to society. All other parolees are simply released and asked to check in with their parole officer once a month. The parole board wanted to evaluate the experimental program and decided that if the experimental program significantly reduced the recidivism rate of parolees, then the program would be declared a success. A random sample of 100 parolees who were placed in halfway houses is selected. These people's names are traced through the Nationwide Criminal Data System (NCDS); 68 have been arrested again and convicted. Two hundred randomly selected parolees who were not assigned to halfway houses were also traced through the NCDS, and 148 of these were in jail. Is the recidivism rate for parolees sent to halfway houses lower than the rate for other parolees?

The process of analysis of variance for proportions is identical to that for sample means:

Step 1: Calculate the sample proportions (means) and standard deviations. For the experimental group we have

$$p = \frac{68}{100} = .68$$

$$s = \sqrt{p(1 - p)} = \sqrt{.68 \times .32} = .47$$

For the control group, we have

$$p = \frac{148}{200} = .74 \quad \text{and} \quad s = \sqrt{.74 \times .26} = .44$$

Step 2: Calculate the standard error of the proportion estimate for each group.

$$\text{s.e.} = \frac{s}{\sqrt{n}}$$

Experimental group:

$$\text{s.e.} = \frac{.47}{\sqrt{100}} = .047$$

Control group:

$$\text{s.e.} = \frac{.44}{\sqrt{200}} = .031$$

Step 3: Calculate an overall standard error for both groups.

$$\text{s.e.}_d = \sqrt{\text{s.e.}_1^2 + \text{s.e.}_2^2} = \sqrt{.047^2 + .031^2} = \sqrt{.00317} = .056$$

Step 4: Convert the difference between the experimental and control groups into a t score with df $= 298$.

$$t = \frac{p_1 - p_2}{\text{s.e.}_d} = \frac{.74 - .68}{.056} = \frac{.06}{.056} = 1.07$$

The probability that the two samples could be drawn from a single population is .14.

Step 5: Because we are dealing with crime, a manager should be more certain before acting. A probability of .14 is not good enough. Conclude that the experimental program did not have lower recidivism rates.

Let us look at one more example. Suppose the Morgan City parole board had a second experimental parole program in which parolees did community service work with local charities before they are granted parole. A sample of 100 of these parolees reveals 60 recidivists. Is the second experiment successfully reducing the recidivism rate in comparison to the control group? The calculations follow:

Experimental Group	Control Group
$n = 100$	$n = 200$
$p = .60$	$p = .74$
$s = .49$	$s = .44$
s.e. $= .049$	s.e. $= .031$

$$\text{s.e.}_d = \sqrt{.049^2 + .031^2} = .058$$

$$t = \frac{.74 - .60}{.058} = 2.41$$

The probability that the samples could be drawn from the same population is .008. What can you say from a research design perspective? From a management perspective? What decisions would you make?

Chapter Summary

Often a manager has samples from two groups (experimental and control, before and after, and so on) and wants to determine whether the two samples could be drawn from the same population (and hence not be significantly different). This chapter illustrates the process of testing two sample means or two sample proportions to determine whether they could have been drawn from the same population. The procedure basically involves five steps. First, calculate the mean and standard deviation for each group. Second, calculate the standard error of the mean estimate for each group. Third, calculate an overall standard error for the groups. Fourth, calculate a t score and find its associated probability from the table. Finally, make an informed decision based on the analysis.

There are three major difference of means tests. The t test assuming independent samples with unequal variances is the most conservative because it consistently produces larger overall standard errors than the other two tests. The t test assuming independent samples with equal variances can be used if an analyst is sure that the sample variances in question are equal. The Levene test is a formal test of equality of sample variances and should be used if an analyst intends to use this difference of means test. The t test assuming dependent samples is most appropriate when values for the same cases occur at two different points in time. A thorough grasp of the difference between dependent and independent samples is needed to understand which of these tests should be used to examine a particular research or management question.

Problems

14.1   John Johnson, the local sheriff, suspects that many of his city's residents are operating motor vehicles without current inspection stickers. To determine whether this is true, John has his boys, John, H.R., and Charles, randomly stop 100 cars. Of these 100 cars, 43 do not have current inspection stickers. John decides to put some fear into drivers and launches a public relations campaign threatening to crack down. A month later, John wants to know whether the program worked. A random sample of 100 cars showed that 21 did not have valid inspection stickers. What can you tell John about the program (ask the statistical, research design, and management questions)?

14.2   The manager of the Houston Astros decides to see whether batting practice has any impact on the Astros' hitting. Twenty Astros take batting practice; they are randomly selected (the control group). Ten Astros, randomly selected, take no batting practice. After 25 games the figures shown in the accompanying table are available. What can you tell the manager about his experiment, statistically and managerially?

	Batting Practice Group	No-Practice Group
Mean	.212	.193
Standard deviation	.026	.047

14.3   The police chief wants to know whether the city's African Americans feel that the police are doing a good job. In comparison to whites' evaluations, this information will tell the police whether they have a community relations problem in the African American community. A survey reveals the information in the accompanying table. What can you tell the police chief?

Opinion	African American	White
Feel police do good job	74	223
Do not feel police do good job	76	73

14.4   General Kleinherbst is concerned with the VD (venereal disease) epidemic among soldiers in Europe. At a nonroutine inspection of 100 troops, 31 were found to have VD. Kleinherbst requires all troops to view the award-winning film *VD: Just between Friends*. At another inspection 180 days later, Kleinherbst finds that 43 of the 200 troops inspected have VD. What can you say about the program, statistically, managerially, and from a research design point of view?

14.5   Morgan City Fire Chief Sidney Pyro is concerned about the low efficiency scores that his firefighters receive at the state testing institute. Chief Pyro believes that these scores result because some firefighters are not in good physical condition. Pyro orders 75 randomly selected firefighters to participate in an hour of exercise per day. Another 200 firefighters have no required exercise. After 60 days, all firefighters are tested again by the state; the results are shown in the accompanying table. What can you tell the chief from this information?

	Exercise Group	No-Exercise Group
Mean	74.5	70.6
Standard deviation	31.4	26.3

14.6   Two hundred people on the welfare rolls in Deadbeat County are randomly selected. One hundred are required to do public service work for the county; the other 100 continue as before. After 6 months, 63 of the public service workers are still on welfare, as are 76 of the control group. What can you say about the effectiveness of this program? What facts may explain these results?

14.7   Ashville City Maintenance Chief Leon Tightwad wants to cut back the costs of maintaining the city automobile fleet. Knowing that city cars are kept for only 1 year, Leon feels that the city's periodic maintenance schedule may cost more than it is worth. Leon randomly selects 75 cars out of 300 and performs no maintenance on these cars unless they break down. At the end of the year, he finds the results shown in the accompanying table. What can you tell Leon about this experiment?

	Maintained Cars	No Maintenance
Mean	$625	$575
Standard deviation	150	200

14.8 Refer to Problem 14.7. Charlie Hustle is in charge of selling Ashville's cars after they have been used 1 year. He believes that Leon's policy costs the city money, and he presents the figures on the cars' sales prices, shown in the accompanying table. Does Charlie have an argument? On an overall basis, who will save the city the most money, Leon Tightwad or Charlie Hustle?

	Maintained Cars	No Maintenance
Mean	$3,456	$3,121
Standard deviation	250	200

14.9 Both the Brethren Charity and the Lost Soul's Mission are operating marriage counseling programs. The Brethren program has a man–woman team to counsel people, whereas Lost Soul's uses single counselors. Last year, 12 of 84 randomly selected couples receiving counseling at Brethren ended up divorced. Ten of the 51 randomly selected couples at Lost Soul's were divorced. As a policy analyst, what can you say about the programs?

14.10 The William G. Harding School of Public Affairs would like to evaluate its affirmative action program for students. After extended discussion, the faculty decides that all students will take the state civil service exam, and the scores on this exam will be used as the criterion of success. Write a memo discussing the results shown in the accompanying table.

	Regular Students	Affirmative Action Students
Mean	86.4	84.1
Standard deviation	17.3	28.2
n	44	19

14.11 A professor thinks that the MPA students at the University of Arizona (UA) are brighter than those at the University of Georgia (UGA). To examine this hypothesis, he gives the same midterm to UA students that he gave to UGA students the previous year. He finds the following results:

	UA	UGA
Mean	83.1	88.7
Standard deviation	11.4	7.8
n	36	24

Present a testable hypothesis, a null hypothesis, and evaluate them. Present a conclusion in plain English.

14.12 The state personnel bureau wants to know whether people resign if they are not promoted during the year. They take a sample of 30 people who are promoted and find that 6 of them resigned; a sample of 45 people who were not promoted includes 15 who resigned. State a hypothesis, a null hypothesis, and test them. State your conclusion in plain English.

14.13 Iowa has decided to run a quasi-experiment in regard to its workfare program and the program's impact on incentives. Officials think that workfare increases the incentives to individuals to earn more money in addition to welfare. Two hundred recipients are selected; 120 are randomly assigned to a workfare program, and 80 are assigned to a control group. By follow-up interviews, the state finds out how much outside income per week is earned by each individual with the following results:

	Workfare	Control
Mean	$142.50	$97.30
s	137.00	85.00

Present a hypothesis, a null hypothesis, and evaluate them. State a conclusion in plain English.

14.14 Wisconsin contracts with private organizations to operate its job placement program. The state needs to evaluate the quality of the program offered by one of its vendors, the Beaver Dam Job Placement Center. One hundred unemployed individuals are selected at random. Sixty of these are run through the Beaver Dam program; the others serve as a control group. Sixty percent of the Beaver Dam program group get jobs; the average salary of those jobs is $12,847 (with a standard deviation of $1,800). Of the control group, 30% get jobs; the average salary of those jobs is $14,567 (standard deviation $3,600). This program can be evaluated by two different criteria. Perform the calculations for both criteria, and present your conclusions.

14.15 Enormous State University has an MPS program. The MPA director is concerned with the small number of MPA students who are being awarded Presidential Management Internships. She thinks that this might be because MPA students lack interviewing skills. To experiment with this notion, 10 of the 20 PMI nominees are sent to a special interviewing workshop; the other 10 do not attend the workshop. Seven of the 10 attending the workshop receive PMIs, and 3 of those not attending the workshop receive PMIs. Present a hypothesis, a null hypothesis, and evaluate them. Present a conclusion in plain English.

14.16 The Department of Human Services has contracted with the Institute for Research on Poverty to run an experimental job training program. A group of 200 individuals are randomly selected from among the hard-core unemployed. A control group of 50 is selected at the same time. The 200 individuals in the experimental group are assigned to a program that attempts to place them in jobs. DHS has defined placement of the individual in a job for 6 months as a success. Of this group, 38 are still employed after 6 months. Of the control group, 11 are employed after 6 months. Present a hypothesis, a null hypothesis, and test them. Present a conclusion in plain English.

14.17   As a National Institutes of Health administrator, you wish to evaluate an experiment at the University of Illinois concerning the impact of exercise on individuals with high-cholesterol diets. The Illinois researchers take 25 pigs that have high-cholesterol diets; 10 of these are randomly selected and made to jog on a treadmill for 2 miles a day. The other 15 pigs do not jog (although they might play golf or get exercise in other ways). After 6 months, each pig is tested for cholesterol in the bloodstream (measured in parts per million) with the following results:

	Exercise Group	Others
Mean	160	210
Standard deviation	40	60

Present a hypothesis, a null hypothesis, and evaluate them. Present a statistical conclusion in plain English.

14.18   The Austin Independent School District wants to know whether the LBJ Magnet School for the Sciences is improving student performance. One hundred students were admitted as sophomores last year to the LBJ school. These students scored a mean of 14.7 on the junior year math achievement test (14 years, 7 months, or about a college sophomore level) with a standard deviation of 1.1. Twenty-three of these students play football. Education researcher Lana "Ein" Stein selects a control group of students who, in their sophomore year, performed comparably to the LBJ students in their sophomore year. These 144 students did not attend a magnet school. Their junior math achievement test produced a mean of 13.6 and a standard deviation of 2.9. Their mean IQ score was 117. Present a hypothesis, test this hypothesis, and present a conclusion in plain English regarding the magnet school students.

14.19   The Wisconsin legislature is considering a mandatory motorcycle helmet law. What legislators don't know is whether the law would encourage more people to use helmets. Senator I. C. Probability tells you that Minnesota has a law similar to the one that Wisconsin is considering. He would like you to compare the use of motorcycle helmets in Minnesota and Wisconsin. A survey is taken in both states resulting in the statistics presented below. Present a hypothesis, a null hypothesis, and test them. Present your conclusion in plain English.

	Minnesota	Wisconsin
n	75	110
Number using helmets	37	28

14.20   Paul Sabatier, a human relations theorist working for Warm and Fuzzy Inc., believes that workers who work in cooperatives are more satisfied with their jobs than workers who do not. He surveys 50 cab drivers who work in co-operatives and 30 cab drivers who do not work in cooperatives. All are asked whether they are satisfied with their job. From the data in the following table, what can you conclude?

Job Satisfaction	Cooperative	Noncooperative
Satisfied	21	17
Not satisfied	29	13

14.21 The Big State University's MPA program is running an experiment concerning the mental health of its students. Unknown to the students, they have been randomly assigned to two groups. Group A takes Statistics for Public Administration; there are 10 students in this group. Five suffer breakdowns before midterm. The 15 students in Group B take Sensitivity Training for Public Managers. Four students in this group suffer breakdowns. Is there a relationship between breakdowns and class assignments? Present a hypothesis, a null hypothesis, and evaluate them.

14.22 Madonna Lewis's job in the Department of Sanitary Engineering is to determine whether new refuse collection procedures have improved the public's perception of the department. Public opinion surveys were taken both before and after the new procedures were implemented. The results are as follows:

	Before	After
The department is doing a good job	23	47
The department is doing a poor job	79	73

Present a hypothesis, a null hypothesis, and evaluate the hypothesis.

14.23 Edinburg attorney J. L. "Bubba" Pollinard is collecting data for a discrimination suit. He asks 500 Latino people whether they believe that the city is biased against them; 354 say it is. Bubba asks 300 Anglo residents the same question, and 104 state the city is biased against them. Present a hypothesis, a null hypothesis, test the hypotheses, and present a conclusion in plain English.

14.24 The Postal Service recently compared newly hired employees who tested "drug-free" with those who tested "drug-positive" after 6 months on the job. They wanted to see whether more drug users than drug-free employees would be fired during their 6-month probation period. Research analyst Stephanie Larson presents a report with the following data:

	Total Hired	Total Fired	% Fired
Drug-free	3,340	319	9.5
Drug users	315	42	13.3

Present a hypothesis, a null hypothesis, and test them. What do these data mean? Could you design a more meaningful test?

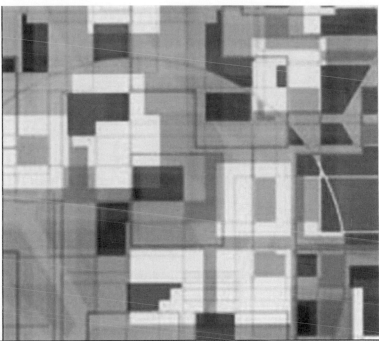

PART V

Analysis of Nominal and Ordinal Data

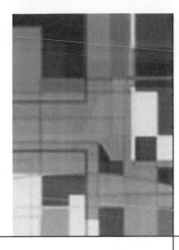

CHAPTER 15

Construction and Analysis of Contingency Tables

C hapter 2, on the topic of measurement, introduced the three levels of measurement—nominal, ordinal, and interval—and discussed the measures of central tendency that can be used to describe and summarize variables of each type. Although this information provides a useful guide to the treatment of single variables, ordinarily such univariate statistics constitute only the first step in data analysis—and in the job of the public or nonprofit administrator.

For example, imagine for a moment that you work in the department of public affairs for a large government or nonprofit agency. The department has just finished conducting its annual survey of public opinion toward the agency. Some of the initial results show that most of the people interviewed now feel that the agency is doing a "very poor job," and the median opinion is not very cheery, either—a "poor job." This assessment represents a dramatic downturn in public opinion compared with previous years. To be sure, this is important information, but obviously it is not the kind of news that you would want to give to your boss or to the mayor and the budget-minded city council or board of directors *without some idea of how the public image of the agency might be improved.* But how might this goal be attained?

One way to approach this question is to consider *why* public support has fallen. There may be several reasons. Perhaps the agency has cut a popular program that it used to administer in Avery County. If the loss of this program is responsible for the drop in public prestige, then you would expect to find a lower level of public favor in

Avery County than in the other counties, where it has not been necessary to cut programs. Or perhaps the fall in public esteem is a result of the recent appointment of a new director of the agency, "mean" Gene Medford, whose past political exploits received rough treatment in the local press. If so, then you would hypothesize that those citizens who disapproved of the appointment would be more critical of the job performance of the agency than would those who approved of the appointment. Fortunately, the survey of public opinion conducted by the agency elicited information pertaining to citizen residence and attitude toward the new director, so both of these ideas can be checked out.

These proposed explanations for the decline in public opinion carry different implications for public policy. If data analysis yielded support for the first explanation, then the chief executive could be informed (gently!) that, although public opinion of the agency is low, evidence indicates that it could be improved through restoration of the program that had been cut in Avery County. On the other hand, if the data showed support for the second explanation, the chief executive might advise Medford to clear the air about his past through public speeches and press conferences—or the chief executive might decide that less pleasant steps are necessary.

Regardless of which (if either) explanation proves to be correct, the important point to bear in mind is that data analysis has moved from a concern with a single variable—public opinion toward the performance of the agency—to a focus on *relationships between variables.* This sequence is typical in the analysis of data. Generally, we would like to know not only the distribution of scores or responses on a variable of interest but also an explanation for this distribution. Is there a relationship between the county of residence of a citizen and attitude toward the agency? Is there a relationship between citizens' attitudes toward the new director and their attitudes toward the agency? In other words, do the responses on one variable help explain or account for responses on a second variable?

This chapter begins with the development of statistical methods to answer such questions. It is concerned with relationships between variables measured at the nominal and ordinal levels. (Relationships between interval level variables are the subject of Part VI.) The method that is generally employed to examine these relationships is called *contingency table analysis* or the analysis of *cross-tabulations.* In this chapter, we show how to set up a contingency table—cross-tabulating the responses to a pair of nominal or ordinal variables—and how to interpret it. Subsequent chapters elaborate on this topic: Chapter 16 presents aids to the interpretation of contingency tables, such as "measures of association" between variables. Chapter 17 discusses a procedure called *control table analysis,* or *statistical controls,* through which the relationships among three or more variables can be examined.

Percentage Distributions

Before we can treat the construction and interpretation of contingency tables, we need to review *percentage distributions* (see Chapter 4). A contingency table is actually a bivariate (two-variable) percentage (or frequency) distribution. If you do not need the review, congratulations—please skip to the next section.

A percentage distribution is simply a frequency distribution that has been converted to percentages. It tabulates the percentage associated with each data value or group of data values. Consider the distribution of responses of a sample of individuals to a standard survey question that asks respondents to consider whether there are too many bureaucrats in the federal government. The distribution is shown in Table 15.1.

As it stands, this table is difficult to interpret. Although it is evident that the mode is "agree" (the data value that occurs with greatest frequency; see Chapter 5, on measures of central tendency), the table does not give a clear presentation of this opinion's popularity. Is it held by half of the people interviewed? A third? Nor does the table communicate the relative frequency of occurrence of the other opinions (strongly disagree, disagree, and so on). What proportion of the sample voiced these responses?

Without this information, it is difficult not only to comprehend this distribution of responses but also to compare it with other distributions of attitudes. For example, it would be interesting to know how this particular distribution of opinion toward federal bureaucrats compares with distributions obtained when the question was put to different samples of people, in different regions of the country, or at different times. Has there been a trend over time toward the view that there are too many federal bureaucrats? Does the public feel the same way about local bureaucrats or state bureaucrats?

The raw response figures displayed in Table 15.1 cannot answer these questions. In order to address them, data analysts conventionally convert the raw figures to percentages.

Steps in Percentaging

The procedure for converting raw figures to percentages involves three steps:

Step 1: Add the number of people (frequencies) giving each of the responses. In Table 15.1, this sum is equal to $686 + 979 + 208 + 436 + 232 = 2,541$.

Step 2: Divide each of the individual frequencies by this total and multiply the result by 100. For example, for the response "strongly agree" in Table 15.1, we divide 686 by 2,541 and obtain .26997. Then multiply this result by 100, yielding 26.997. This figure is the *percentage* of the people interviewed who

Table 15.1

Distribution of Responses

To what extent would you agree or disagree with the following statement? There are currently too many bureaucrats working for the federal government.

Response	Number of People
Strongly agree	686
Agree	979
Neutral	208
Disagree	436
Strongly disagree	232

Table 15.2

Percentage Distribution

To what extent would you agree or disagree with the following statement? There are currently too many bureaucrats working for the federal government.

Response	Frequency	Percentage	
Strongly agree	686	$(686 \div 2{,}541) \times 100 =$	27.0
Agree	979	$(979 \div 2{,}541) \times 100 =$	38.5
Neutral	208	$(208 \div 2{,}541) \times 100 =$	8.2
Disagree	436	$(436 \div 2{,}541) \times 100 =$	17.2
Strongly disagree	232	$(232 \div 2{,}541) \times 100 =$	9.1
Total	2,541		100.0

gave the response "strongly agree." Repeat the procedure for each of the other response categories.

Step 3:   Round each of the percentages to one decimal place. If the second place to the right of the decimal point is greater than or equal to 5, add 1 to the first place to the right of the decimal. In this procedure, .16 becomes .2, .43 becomes .4, and 26.997 becomes 27.0. Table 15.2 shows the percentage distribution. (You may prefer to express the percentages as whole numbers, with no decimal places. Follow these same rules for rounding.)

Displaying and Interpreting Percentage Distributions

The percentage distribution displays the percentage of respondents giving each of the responses to the survey item. The only frequency or raw number that should be presented in the table is the total number of cases, usually abbreviated **N**. The total frequency helps the reader evaluate the distribution of responses. In general, the larger the number of cases on which the percentages are based, the greater the confidence in the results. For example, you would normally have more confidence in a percentage distribution based on 2,541 respondents than in one based on 541 or 41. Table 15.3 shows the final percentaged table.

The percentage distribution facilitates interpretation and comparison. It is clear from the percentage distribution in Table 15.3 that approximately 40% of those interviewed (the mode) "agree" that there are currently too many federal bureaucrats and that 65.5% (27.0% + 38.5% = 65.5%), or nearly two-thirds, express agreement with this notion (either "strongly agree" or "agree"). The extent of agreement far outweighs the extent of disagreement—65.5% versus 26.3% (the percentage indicating either "disagree" or "strongly disagree"; 17.2% + 9.1% = 26.3%). Only a small proportion (8.2%) remain "neutral."

These percentages can be compared with those obtained in other surveys of public opinion, for example, surveys conducted at other points in time or administered to different groups, to assess how attitudes toward bureaucrats are changing. For instance,

Table 15.3

Percentage Distribution

To what extent would you agree or disagree with the following statement? There are currently too many bureaucrats working for the federal government.

Response	Percentage
Strongly agree	27.0
Agree	38.5
Neutral	8.2
Disagree	17.2
Strongly disagree	9.1
Total	100.0
	(**N** = 2,541)

if 5 years ago a similar survey of public opinion indicated that only 40% of the public expressed agreement that there are too many federal bureaucrats, it would be evident that public opinion is becoming more negative.

Collapsing Percentage Distributions

Often, public managers combine or *collapse* several of the original response categories in order to form a smaller number of new categories and to calculate percentages based on the new categories. For example, in the preceding discussion, the response categories "strongly agree" and "agree" and the categories "strongly disagree" and "disagree" were collapsed into broader categories of "agreement" and "disagreement," respectively.

To calculate percentages in a collapsed distribution, you employ the procedure elaborated earlier: (1) compute the total frequency, (2) divide the frequency of each of the new categories by this total and multiply by 100, and (3) round to the first decimal place. Alternatively, if the percentage distribution for the variable has already been computed based on the original response categories, the percentages for the new collapsed categories can be found by adding the percentages for the categories that have been collapsed. (The percentages for categories that have not been collapsed will not change.) The latter method was employed in the preceding discussion. For example, because 27.0% of the sample stated that they "strongly agree" that there are too many federal bureaucrats and 38.5% "agree," then a total of 65.5% fall into the new collapsed category of "agree." The first of these methods for percentaging a collapsed distribution is illustrated in Table 15.4.

There are two primary reasons for presenting the percentage distribution in collapsed form. First, it is easier to interpret a distribution based on a few response categories than one based on many. In many instances, such as the preparation of memoranda, the collapsed distribution presents all the information managers need to know, without burdening them with unnecessary complexity. Second, often in public and nonprofit administration, the data analyst or manager is not confident that the distinction between some response categories is very clear or meaningful; that is, you

Table 15.4

Collapsed Percentage Distribution

To what extent would you agree or disagree with the following statement? There are currently too many bureaucrats working for the federal government.

Original Response Categories	(Original) Frequency	Collapsed Response Categories	(Collapsed) Frequency	Percentage
Strongly agree	686⎤	Agree	1,665	$(1{,}665 \div 2{,}541) \times 100 =$ 65.5
Agree	979⎦			
Neutral	208	Neutral	208	$(208 \div 2{,}541) \times 100 =$ 8.2
Disagree	436⎤			
Strongly disagree	232⎦	Disagree	668	$(668 \div 2{,}541) \times 100 =$ 26.3
Total	2,541	Total	2,541	100.0

can generally be much more confident that, *in all,* 65.5% of those interviewed agree with a proposition than that *exactly* 27.0% "strongly agree" and *exactly* 38.5% "agree." In order to avoid communicating a false sense of precision, categories may be collapsed. Another good reason to get used to collapsed percentage distributions is that most contingency tables are based on this format (see below and Chapters 16 and 17).

When you collapse response categories of a variable, the collapsing must not pervert the meaning of the original categories. Response categories should be collapsed only if they are close in substantive meaning. Whereas the kind of collapsing we have done here—strongly agree and agree, strongly disagree and disagree—is justified, collapsing the categories of "disagree" and "neutral" would not be.

The major exception to this rule occurs in distributions of *nominal* variables that have many response categories. Frequently only a few of the categories will have a large percentage of cases, whereas most of the categories will have only trivial numbers. In this situation, the analyst may choose to present each of the categories containing a substantial percentage and a category labeled "other," formed by collapsing all the remaining categories. For example, consider the variable "religion." In a given sample, the distribution of religion may be 62% Protestant, 22% Catholic, 13% Jewish, 1% Shinto, .5% Buddhist, .6% Hedonist, .5% Janist, and .4% Central Schwenkenfelter. To summarize this distribution, the analyst may present the percentages as shown in Table 15.5.

An exercise may be helpful to illustrate these points. The Shawnee Heights Independent Transit Authority has commissioned a poll of 120 persons to determine where Shawnee citizens do most of their shopping. This is important information in determining future transit routes in Shawnee Heights. The transit planners receive the data shown in Table 15.6.

In the space provided, construct a collapsed percentage distribution of the data in Table 15.6. (**Hint**: Consider collapsing categories based on common locations.)

Table 15.5

Collapsed Percentage Distribution for Religion

Religion	Percentage
Protestant	62
Catholic	22
Jewish	13
Other	3
Total	100
	(**N** = 1,872)

Table 15.6

Data for Shawnee Heights Poll

Main Store Named	Number of Persons
Cleo's (neighborhood store)	5
Morgan's (downtown)	18
Wiese's (eastern shopping center)	12
Cheatham's (neighborhood store)	2
Shop City (eastern shopping center)	19
Food-o-Rama (western shopping center)	15
Stermer's (downtown)	7
Binzer's (neighborhood store)	2
England's (western shopping center)	1
Bargainville's (eastern shopping center)	26
Whiskey River (downtown)	13
	120

Contingency Table Analysis

Analysis of contingency tables or cross-tabulations is the primary method researchers use to examine relationships between variables measured at the ordinal and nominal levels. The remainder of the chapter discusses the construction and interpretation of contingency tables. As you will see, the methods for percentaging are instrumental to this type of analysis.

Constructing Contingency Tables

A **contingency table** or **cross-tabulation** is a bivariate frequency distribution. We have dealt with **univariate,** or single-variable, frequency distributions in examples in this chapter and in previous chapters. A univariate frequency distribution simply presents the number of cases (or frequency) taking each value of a given variable. By analogy, a **bivariate,** or two-variable, frequency distribution presents the number of cases that fall into each possible pairing of the values or categories of two variables simultaneously. This definition is more readily visualized in a concrete example.

Consider the cross-tabulation of the variables race (white, nonwhite) and sex (male, female) for volunteers to the Klondike Expressionist Art Museum. As these variables are defined here, there are four possible pairings: white and male, white and female, nonwhite and male, and nonwhite and female volunteers. Pairings across variables are easier to conceptualize if we first consider what the data look like prior to being summarized in a contingency table. For the Klondike volunteers, gender and race are coded as follows:

"Gender"	"Race"
1 = female	1 = white
2 = male	2 = nonwhite

Both variables are measured at the nominal level. Table 15.7 presents the raw data for 12 volunteers at the Art Museum.

The first row of data indicates that the respondent has a score of "1" for both variables. This indicates that the volunteer is a white female. The second row of data has values of "2" for both variables. This indicates that the volunteer is a nonwhite male. To make sure you understand the pairings for sex and race, interpret the entries for volunteers 3 through 12.

Table 15.7

Sample Data for Klondike Volunteers

Gender	Race
1	1
2	2
1	2
2	2
2	1
1	1
1	2
1	1
2	2
1	2
2	2
2	1

Table 15.8

Contingency Table: Race and Sex of Volunteers to Klondike Expressionist Art Museum

	Race		
Sex	White	Nonwhite	Total
Male	142	109	251
Female	67	133	200
Total	209	242	451

The cross-tabulation of these two variables displays the number of cases (volunteers) that fall into each of the race–sex combinations. In this sample of museum volunteers composed of 142 white males, 67 white females, 109 nonwhite males, and 133 nonwhite females, we obtain the contingency table displayed in Table 15.8. This type of table is called a *cross-tabulation* because it crosses (and tabulates) each of the categories of one variable with each of the categories of a second variable.

The numbers in each cell category simply represent the aggregate results compiled from all 451 rows of data on volunteers. Although the cells within contingency tables such as Table 15.8 sometimes contain large numbers that may "look" like interval level data, you should remember that these numbers represent total case counts for nominal or ordinal level variables. The data used to generate Table 15.8 look just like the data for the 12 volunteers displayed in Table 15.7, except that the data for all 451 rows (volunteers) are counted and summarized in Table 15.8.

At this point, some terminology is useful. The cross-classifications of the two variables—white-male, white-female, nonwhite-male, nonwhite-female—are called the **cells** of the table. The cell frequencies indicate the number of cases fitting the description specified by the categories of the row and column variables. The total number of respondents who are white or nonwhite is presented at the foot of the "white" and "nonwhite" columns, respectively. Similarly, the total number of respondents who are male or female is presented at the far right of the respective rows. In reference to their position around the perimeter of the table, these total frequencies are called **marginals** (or marginal frequencies). These totals are calculated by adding the frequencies in the appropriate column or row. Finally, the **grand total**—the total number of cases represented in the table (**N**)—is displayed conventionally in the lower right corner of the table. It can be found by adding the cell frequencies, or the row marginals, or the column marginals. You should satisfy yourself that all three of these additions give the same result. You should also make certain that you understand what each number in Table 15.8 means.

To ensure that you can assemble a cross-tabulation, fill in the cell, marginal, and grand total frequencies in Table 15.9. The variables of interest are "type of employment" (public sector, private sector, or nonprofit sector) and "attitude toward balancing the federal budget" (disapprove or approve). The cell frequencies are as follows: public-disapprove 126; public-approve 54; private-disapprove 51; private-approve 97; nonprofit-disapprove 25; nonprofit-approve 38.

Table 15.9

Relationship between Type of Employment and Attitude toward Balancing the Federal Budget

Attitude toward Budget Balancing	Type of Employment			
	Public	Private	Nonprofit	Total
Disapprove				
Approve				
Total				

Table 15.10

Relationship between Educational Level and Performance on Civil Service Examination

Performance on Civil Service Examination	Education		Total
	High School or Less	More Than High School	
Low	100	200	300
High	150	800	950
Total	250	1,000	1,250

Relationships between Variables

Researchers assemble and examine cross-tabulations because they are interested in the relationship between two ordinal or nominal level variables. A **statistical relationship** may be defined as a recognizable pattern of change in one variable as the other variable changes. In particular, the type of question that is usually asked is, As one variable increases in value, does the other also increase? Or, as one variable increases, does the other decrease?

The cell frequencies of a cross-tabulation provide some information regarding whether changes in one variable are associated statistically with (related to) changes in the other variable. The cross-tabulation presented in Table 15.10 of "education" (high school or less; more than high school) with "performance on the civil service examination" (low; high) illustrates this idea.

At first glance, the table seems to indicate that as education *increases* from high school or less ("low") to more than high school ("high"), performance on the civil service examination *decreases,* for twice as many individuals with high education (200) received low scores on the test than did those with low education (100). Because we would anticipate that education would *improve* scores on the examination, this initial finding seems counterintuitive. In fact, it is not only counterintuitive but also incorrect.

The reason for the faulty interpretation is that we have failed to take into account the *total number* of individuals who have low as compared with high education (that is, the marginal totals). Note that although this sample contained only 250 people with a high school education or less, 1,000 individuals—four times as many—had more than a high school education. Thus, when these figures are put in perspective, there are *four* times as many people with high education than low education in the sample—yet only *twice* as many of the former as the latter received low scores on the civil service examination. These data suggest that in contrast to our initial interpretation of the table, more highly educated people do earn higher scores on the civil service examination than do the less educated. This finding accords with intuition and is the primary conclusion supported by the table—when it has been analyzed correctly.

How does one do so? The analysis process has three major steps. The problem with the initial interpretation of the contingency table was that it overlooked the relative number of cases in the categories of education (that is, the marginal tools). This problem can be remedied by percentaging the table appropriately, which is the key to analyzing and understanding cross-tabulations. The steps in the analysis process are as follows:

Step 1: Determine which variable is *independent* and which is *dependent*. As explained in Chapter 3, the independent variable is the anticipated causal variable, the one that is supposed to lead to changes or effects in the dependent or response (criterion) variable. In the current example of the relationship between education and performance on the civil service examination, it is expected that higher education leads to improved performance on the test. Stated as a hypothesis: The higher the education, the higher the expected score on the civil service examination. Hence, education is the independent variable, and performance on the civil service examination is the dependent variable.

Step 2: Calculate percentages within the categories of the *independent* variable—in this case, education. We would like to know the percentage of people with high school education or less (low education) who received high scores on the civil service examination and the percentage of people with more than a high school education (high education) who received high scores. Then it would be possible to compare these percentages in order to determine whether those with high education receive higher scores on the examination than do those with low education. This comparison allows us to evaluate, on the basis of the data, whether the expectation or hypothesis stated previously is correct—that is, that education leads to improved scores on the civil service examination.

The procedure used to calculate percentages within the categories of education is the same as the univariate procedure elaborated earlier in the chapter. We are interested first in the percentage of people with high school education or less who received high scores on the civil service examination. Table 15.10 indicates that a total of 250 people fall into this category of education, and of these, 150 received high scores on the test. Thus, we find that

Table 15.11

Percentage Distribution for Data of Table 15.10

Performance on Civil Service Examination	Education	
	High School or Less	More Than High School
Low	$(100 \div 250) \times 100 = 40\%$	$(200 \div 1{,}000) \times 100 = 20\%$
High	$(150 \div 250) \times 100 = \underline{60\%}$	$(800 \div 1{,}000) \times 100 = \underline{80\%}$
Total	$(n = 250)$ 100%	$(n = 1{,}000)$ 100%

$(150 \div 250) \times 100 = 60\%$ of those with low education earned high scores on the civil service examination. (Note that this is also the probability of receiving a high score on the exam given low education; see Chapter 7.) The other 100 of the 250 people with low education received low scores on the test; converting to a percentage, we find that $(100 \div 250) \times 100 = 40\%$ of those with low education earned low test scores (the probability of a low test score given low education).

Moving to those with more than a high school education, Table 15.10 shows that 800 of the 1,000 people with this level of education—or 80% $[(800 \div 1{,}000) \times 100]$—received high scores on the civil service examination, and the other 200—or 20% $[(200 \div 1{,}000) \times 100]$—earned low scores. All percentages have now been calculated. Table 15.11 presents the cross-tabulation percentaged within the categories of education, including all calculations.

Step 3: Compare the percentages calculated within the categories of the *independent variable* (education) for *one* of the categories of the *dependent variable* (performance on civil service examination). For example, whereas 80% of those with high education earned high scores on the civil service examination, only 60% of those with low education did so. Thus, our hypothesis is supported by these data: In general, those with high education received higher scores on the examination than did those with low education. As hypothesized, the higher the education, the higher is the score on the civil service examination.

To summarize the relationship between two variables in a cross-tabulation, researchers often calculate a **percentage difference** across one of the categories of the dependent variable. In this case, the percentage difference is equal to 80% minus 60%, or 20 percentage points (the percentage of those with high education who earned high scores on the test minus the percentage of those with low education who did so). The conclusion, then, is that education appears to make a difference of 20 percentage points in performance on the civil service examination. As you will learn in Chapter 16, the percentage difference is a measure of the strength of the relationship between two variables.

Table 15.12

Automobile Maintenance Data

Automobile Breakdowns	Automobile Maintenance		Total
	None	Regularly Scheduled	
No breakdown	72	194	266
Breakdown	78	56	134
Total	150	250	400

Example: Automobile Maintenance in Berrysville

The city council of Berrysville, California, has been under considerable pressure to economize. Last year, the council passed an ordinance authorizing an experimental program for the maintenance of city-owned vehicles. The bill stipulates that, for 1 year, a random sample of 150 of the city's 400 automobiles will receive no preventive maintenance and will simply be driven until they break down. The other 250 automobiles will receive regularly scheduled preventive maintenance. The council is interested in whether the expensive program of preventive maintenance actually reduces the number of breakdowns. After a year under the experimental maintenance program, the city council was presented the data in Table 15.12, which summarizes the number of automobile breakdowns under the no maintenance and preventive maintenance conditions. Analyze the data for the city council, and help them by making a recommendation regarding whether the program should be continued (and/or expanded) or terminated.

Step 1: Determine which variable is independent and which is dependent. There should be no doubt that automobile maintenance is expected to affect the number of breakdowns. Therefore, "maintenance" is the independent variable, and "breakdowns" is the dependent variable. Stated as a hypothesis, we have the following: The greater the level of maintenance, the less the rate of breakdowns.

Step 2: Calculate percentages within the categories of the independent variable, "automobile maintenance." The calculations are shown in Table 15.13.

Table 15.13

Percentage Distribution for Data of Table 15.12

Automobile Breakdowns	Automobile Maintenance	
	None	Regularly Scheduled
No breakdown	$(72 \div 150) \times 100 = 48\%$	$(194 \div 250) \times 100 = 77.6\%$
Breakdown	$(78 \div 150) \times 100 = 52\%$	$(56 \div 250) \times 100 = 22.4\%$
Total	$(n = 150)$ 100%	$(n = 250)$ 100.0%

Step 3: Compare percentages for one of the categories of the dependent variable. Although more than half (52%) of the automobiles that received no maintenance broke down during the 1-year experimental program, only 22.4% of the automobiles that received regularly scheduled maintenance did so. This is a difference of 29.6% (52% − 22.4%). Thus, automobile maintenance appears to make nearly a 30% difference in the rate of breakdowns. The data show support for the hypothesis: As maintenance increases, the number of breakdowns decreases by almost 30%. From these data, should you recommend to the city council that they continue or terminate the experimental maintenance program?

Note: When these data were released to the public, the Berrysville press made great sport of the folly of the city council for experimenting with the "dang fool" (no) maintenance program. The members of the city council who had voted for the program were soundly defeated in the next election. In the first meeting of the new city council, the researcher who had compiled and analyzed the automobile maintenance data was awarded a substantial raise in salary. There may be a moral to this story.

Larger Contingency Tables

With a single exception, the examples of contingency tables presented in this chapter have consisted of "two-by-two" tables—cross-tabulations in which both the independent and the dependent variables comprise just two values or response categories. Cross-tabulations can and often do consist of variables with a greater number of response categories. For example, Table 15.14 presents the cross-tabulation of "income" (low, medium, and high) and "job satisfaction" (low, medium, and high)—How satisfied are you with your job?—for the employees of the Maslow City Post Office.

Although the analysis becomes more complicated, *contingency tables based on variables with many response categories are analyzed in the same way as are the smaller two-by-two tables.* Start by determining which variable is independent and which is dependent. In this example, you would expect income to lead to job satisfaction: The higher the income, the higher would be the job satisfaction. "Income" is the independent variable, and "job satisfaction" is the dependent variable. Therefore, the table

Table 15.14

Relationship between Income and Job Satisfaction

Job Satisfaction	Income			Total
	Low	Medium	High	
Low	100	30	10	140
Medium	60	80	15	155
High	40	40	50	130
Total	200	150	75	425

should be percentaged within the categories of income. Table 15.15 presents the cross-tabulation, percentaged according to the steps elaborated earlier.

The final step in the analysis of contingency tables is to compare percentages for one of the categories of the dependent variable. Although the choice of a category in two-by-two tables is not a critical decision—both categories of the dependent variable will yield the *same* percentage difference—in larger tables, the selection of a category of the dependent variable for purposes of percentage comparison requires more care. In general, you should *not* choose an *intermediate* category, such as "medium" job satisfaction, for this purpose. Choice of either of the *endpoint* categories—"low" or "high" job satisfaction—will result in clearer understanding and interpretation of the contingency table.

Once the (endpoint) category of the dependent variable has been selected, compare the percentages calculated for the *endpoint* categories of the independent variable. Again, avoid intermediate categories for this purpose. In Table 15.15, this rule suggests that we compare the percentage of those with low income who have high job satisfaction (20%) with the percentage of those with high income who have high job satisfaction (66.7%). Alternatively, we could compare the percentage of those with low income who express low job satisfaction (50%) with the percentage of those with high income who express low job satisfaction (13.3%)

Which percentage comparison(s) should the researcher use to summarize the relationship found in the cross-tabulation? The percentage difference calculation typically yields different results depending on the endpoint category of the dependent variable chosen. In the current case, the percentage difference based on high job satisfaction is 66.7% − 20.0% = 46.7%, whereas the percentage difference for low job satisfaction is 50.0% − 13.3% = 36.7%. These percentage differences suggest varying levels of support for the relationship.

Probably the best course of action for the public or nonprofit manager is to consider and report *both* figures. They show that those with high income indicated high job satisfaction more often than did those with low income (by 47%) and, conversely, that those with low income indicated low job satisfaction more often than did their counterparts (by 37%). Thus, income appears to make a difference of 37% to 47% in job satisfaction. These figures provide support for the hypothesis that the greater the income, the greater is the expected job satisfaction. Chapter 16 presents other techniques especially appropriate for the analysis of larger contingency tables.

Table 15.15

Percentage Distribution for Data of Table 15.14

	Income		
Job Satisfaction	Low	Medium	High
Low	$(100 \div 200) \times 100 = 50\%$	$(30 \div 150) \times 100 = 20.0\%$	$(10 \div 75) \times 100 = 13.3\%$
Medium	$(60 \div 200) \times 100 = 30\%$	$(80 \div 150) \times 100 = 53.3\%$	$(15 \div 75) \times 100 = 20.0\%$
High	$(40 \div 200) \times 100 = \underline{20\%}$	$(40 \div 150) \times 100 = \underline{26.7\%}$	$(50 \div 75) \times 100 = \underline{66.7\%}$
Total	$(n = 200)$ 100%	$(n = 150)$ 100.0%	$(n = 75)$ 100.0%

Displaying Contingency Tables

A set of conventions has been developed for presenting contingency tables. First, contingency tables are very rarely presented as bivarite frequency distributions. Instead, you should display the table in percentaged form; the percentages should be calculated and displayed according to the procedures described in the preceding section (do *not* show the percentage calculations). Second, the independent variable is placed along the *columns* of the table, and the dependent variable is positioned down the *rows*. Third, the substantive meaning of the categories of the independent variable should show a progression from least to most moving from left to right across the columns, and the categories of the dependent variable should show the same type of progression moving down the rows. In other words, the categories should be listed in the order "low," "medium," and "high"; or "disapprove," "neutral," and "approve"; or "disagree," "neutral," and "agree"; and so on. This procedure greatly facilitates the interpretation of measures of association (discussed in Chapter 16). See Table 15.15 for an illustration. Fourth, the percentages calculated within categories of the independent variable are summed down the column, and the total for each category is placed at the foot of the respective column. The sum should equal 100%, but because of rounding error, it may vary between 99% and 101%. *Do not add the percentages across the rows of the table; this is a meaningless operation.* Finally, the total number of cases within each category of the independent variable is presented at the foot of the respective column. Usually, these totals are enclosed in parentheses and contain the notation n = ___. Table 15.16 presents schematically a contingency table displayed according to the conventional rules.

Two problems arise regarding the conventional display of contingency tables. First, these rules are widely accepted—but not always. Thus, in reading and studying contingency tables presented in books, journals, reports, memoranda, magazines, newspapers, and so on, you should not assume that the independent variable is always

Table 15.16

Conventional Format for a Contingency Table

Dependent Variable	Independent Variable			
Substantive meaning of categories increases ↓	Substantive meaning of categories increases (e.g., "low," "medium," "high") ⟶			
	___%	___%	___%	___%
	___%	___%	___%	___%
	⋮	⋮	⋮	⋮
Total	100.0% (n = ___)	100.0% (n = ___)	100.0% (n = ___)	100.0% (n = ___)

along the columns or that the dependent variable is down the rows. Nor can you assume that the categories of the variables are ordered in the table according to the conventions. Instead, you should examine the table, decide which variable is independent and which is dependent, check to see whether the percentages have been calculated within the categories of the independent variable, and verify whether the author has compared percentages appropriately. You should recognize these procedures as the steps already elaborated for analyzing and interpreting cross-tabulations. Cultivation of this habit will not only increase your understanding of contingency table results but also sharpen your analytical skills.

The second problem arises as a consequence of computer utilization. On the job (or in class), you may be dealing with contingency tables constructed and percentaged by a computer. Not only is the computer oblivious to the distinction between independent and dependent variables, the ordering of response categories of variables, and so on, but computers are usually programmed to print out *three different sets of percentages:* percentages calculated (1) within categories of the row variable; (2) within categories of the column variable; and (3) according to the total number of cases represented in the contingency table, sometimes called *corner* or *total* percentaging. It is up to you as the data analyst to determine which set of percentages is most meaningful and, if necessary, to reconstruct the contingency table by hand from the computer printout according to the conventional form described here. If you follow the steps for the analysis of contingency tables developed in this chapter, this task should not be difficult.

This chapter has elaborated a general method for determining whether two variables measured at the nominal or ordinal levels are related statistically: contingency table analysis or cross-tabulation. However, it has not addressed the question of *how strongly* two variables are related. This question serves as the focus for the next chapter.

Chapter Summary

Contingency tables are used to display and analyze the relationship between two variables measured at the nominal or ordinal levels. The simplest and often most useful technique for analyzing contingency tables is to calculate percentages appropriately and to compare them.

This chapter illustrates the analysis of contingency tables. A contingency table is a bivariate—or two-variable—frequency distribution. It presents the number of cases that fall into each possible pairing of the values of two variables. There are three major steps in the analysis process. First, determine which variable is independent and which is dependent. Second, calculate percentages within the categories of the independent variable. Finally, compare the percentages calculated within the categories of the independent variable across one of the categories of the dependent variable, and interpret the results. Contingency tables for variables with more than two response categories are analyzed using the same basic approach as for two-by-two tables. You should calculate and report the percentage difference for both endpoint categories of the dependent variable.

Problems

15.1 The Lebanon postmaster suspects that working on ziptronic machines is the cause of high absenteeism. More than 10 absences from work without business-related reasons is considered excessive absenteeism. A check of employee records shows that 26 of the 44 ziptronic operators had 10 or more absences and 35 of 120 nonziptronic workers had 10 or more absences. Construct a contingency table for the postmaster. Does the table support the postmaster's suspicion that working on ziptronic machines is related to high absenteeism?

15.2 During last year's budget crunch, several deserving employees of the Bureau of Procedures were denied promotions. This year, an unusual number of BP employees retired. The bureau chief suspects that the denial of promotions resulted in increased retirements. Of the 115 employees denied promotion, 32 retired. Of the 58 employees promoted, 9 retired. Present a contingency table, and analyze this information.

15.3 The Egyptian Air Force brass believe that overweight pilots have slow reaction times. They attribute the poor performance of their air force in recent war games in the Sinai to overweight pilots. The accompanying data were collected for all pilots. Analyze these data for the Egyptian Air Force brass.

	Pilot Weight		
Reaction Time	Normal	Up To 10 Pounds Overweight	More Than 10 Pounds Overweight
Poor	14	36	45
Adequate	35	40	33
Excellent	46	25	15

15.4 Auditors for the Military Airlift Command (MAC) are checking the arrival times of the three charter airlines they used in the Pacific last year. Branflake Airways flew 135 flights and was late 78 times. Flying Armadillo Airlines flew 94 flights and was late 35 times. Air Idaho flew 115 flights, with 51 late arrivals. Set up a contingency table, and analyze it for MAC.

15.5 The state personnel office oversees the state's tuition assistance program, which pays the tuition of civil servants taking courses for an MPA. Only two schools offer an MPA degree in the state capital, Capital College of Law and East Winslow State University. Some concern is expressed by legislators that many tuition-assisted students do not graduate. Analyze the data in the accompanying table for the personnel office.

	Students Assisted For MPA Tuition	
Status	Capital	East Winslow
Did not graduate	69	83
Graduated	23	37

15.6 Hyram Drant, a research analyst for the city fire department, suspects that old water pumps are more likely to fail. From the data in the accompanying table, construct a contingency table and check Drant's suspicion. How else could this problem be analyzed?

Age of Pump in Years

Pump Failed	Pump Did Not Fail	
23	15	7
47	6	9
11	9	4
53	33	19
26	26	36
15	17	47
42	9	31
37	12	23
	31	6
	46	9
	15	3

15.7 As head scheduler of special events for the Incomparable Myriad (the city arena), your task is to schedule events that make a profit so that the city need not subsidize the arena. Analyze the data in the accompanying table, which is based on last year's data, and write a report to the city council.

	Type of Event				
Status	Hockey Games	Religious Rallies	Basketball Games	Rock Concerts	Public Administration Conventions
Not profitable	24	4	21	2	3
Profitable	18	32	6	8	0

15.8 As the newly appointed head of evaluation for the state agriculture experiment station, you are asked to evaluate the relative effectiveness of corn hybrids AX147 and AQ49. Of 32 test plots, AX147 had high yields on 21. AQ49 had high yields on 17 of 28 test plots. Construct a contingency table and make a recommendation.

15.9 The Cancer Institute is evaluating an experimental drug for controlling lip cancer. Eighty lip cancer victims are randomly selected and given the drug for 1 year. Sixty other lip cancer victims are randomly selected and given a placebo for a year. From the data in the accompanying table, what would you conclude?

Cancer Status	Drug Group	Placebo Group
Active	58	42
Remission	22	18

15.10   A supervisor in the Department of Rehabilitative Services is critical of the performance of one of her counselors. The counselor is expected to arrange job training for those in need of vocational rehabilitation so that they may find employment. Yet the counselor has managed to place just 35% of his clients. The counselor argues that he is actually doing a good job and that the reason for his overall low rate of placement is that most of his clients are severely disabled, which makes them very difficult to place. The counselor's caseload is presented in the accompanying table. Percentage the table appropriately, and evaluate who is correct—the supervisor or the counselor.

Job Placement	Not Severely Disabled	Severely Disabled
Not placed	17	118
Placed	47	26

15.11   A professor of public administration has kept records on the class participation of his students over the past several years. He has a strong feeling (hypothesis) that class participation is related to grade in the course. For this analysis he classifies course grades into two categories, fail and pass. He operationalizes class participation as "low" if the student participated in class discussion in fewer than 25% of class periods, and "high" if the student participated in 25% or more of the periods. Based on these definitions, he has assembled the cross-tabulation below. Does a relationship exist between class participation and course grades?

	Class Participation	
Grade in Course	Low	High
Fail	56	15
Pass	178	107

15.12   Susan Wolch and John Komer are interested in determining which of two books is more effective in teaching statistics to public administration students. They randomly assign a pool of 50 students to two groups of 25 students each. One group uses Meier, Brudney, and Bohte, *Applied Statistics for Public and Nonprofit Administration*. The other group uses Brand *X*. Their criterion for measuring success is student grades in the course. They get the results shown in the accompanying table. Evaluate these data and make a recommendation.

	Book Used in Class	
Grade	Brand *X*	Meier, Brudney, and Bohte
Students receiving C's, D's, or F's	18	9
Students receiving A's or B's	7	16

15.13   Madonna Lewis's job in the Department of Sanitary Engineering is to determine whether new refuse collection procedures have improved the public's perception of the department. A public opinion survey was taken both before and after the new procedures were implemented. The results appear in the accompanying table. Analyze the table, and evaluate whether public perception of the department appears to have improved over time.

Opinion	Before	After
Department is doing a poor job	79	73
Department is doing a good job	23	47

CHAPTER 16

Aids for the Interpretation of Contingency Tables

C hapter 15 developed a general method for constructing and analyzing contingency tables or cross-tabulations. It focused on procedures for percentaging these tables and determining whether two variables measured at the nominal or ordinal levels are associated statistically.

This chapter begins where the previous one concluded. It elaborates methods for assessing the strength of a relationship between a pair of nominal or ordinal variables in a contingency table. It is important to recognize that these techniques are not substitutes but *supplements* to those presented in Chapter 15. *All* of these procedures are useful for understanding the relationship between two variables measured at the nominal or ordinal levels.

The chapter is divided into three major segments. The first part is devoted to the chi-square test. The chi-square is a test of statistical significance for relationships between variables measured at the nominal or ordinal levels. Part IV, especially Chapters 11 and 12, discuss statistical inference. The chi-square test assesses whether the relationship observed in a cross-tabulation in a sample of data is sufficiently strong to infer that a relationship likely exists in the full population. The second part of the chapter develops methods for evaluating the strength of the relationship between two variables. The most straightforward of these techniques is the percentage difference, which was introduced in Chapter 15; it is discussed first. The final portion of the chapter explains measures of association: single statistics that summarize the strength of a relationship demonstrated in a cross-tabulation. The chapter presents a detailed development of frequently used measures of association: lambda and Cramér's V for nominal-level variables; and gamma, Kendall's tau-b and tau-c, and Somers's d_{yx} and d_{xy} for ordinal-level variables.

The Chi-Square Test: Statistical Significance for Contingency Tables

Chapter 11 introduced the issue of the correspondence between results obtained in a sample of data and the actual situation in the population that the sample is intended to represent. *Statistical significance* is a procedure for establishing the degree of confidence that one can have in making an inference from a sample to its parent population.

The **chi-square test** is a procedure for evaluating the level of statistical significance attained by a bivariate relationship in a cross-tabulation. The chi-square test procedure assumes that there is no relationship between the two variables in the population and determines whether any apparent relationship obtained in a sample cross-tabulation is attributable to chance. This procedure involves three steps. First, *expected frequencies* are calculated for each cell in the contingency table predicated on the assumption that the two variables are unrelated in the population. Second, based on the difference between the expected frequency and the actual frequency observed in each table cell, a test statistic called the *chi-square* is computed. Since the expected frequencies are premised on the assumption of no relationship, the greater the deviation between them and the actual frequencies, the greater is the departure of the observed relationship from the null hypothesis—hence the greater is the confidence in inferring the existence of a relationship between the two variables in the population. Third, the chi-square value computed for the actual data is compared with a table of theoretical chi-square values calculated and tabulated by statisticians. This comparison allows the analyst to determine the precise degree of confidence that he or she may have in inferring from the sample cross-tabulation that a relationship exists in the parent population.

Example: Incompetence in the Federal Government?

A disgruntled official working in the personnel department of a large federal bureaucracy is disturbed by the level of incompetence she perceives in the leadership of the organization. She is convinced that incompetence rises to the top, and she shares this belief with a coworker over lunch. The latter challenges her to substantiate her claim.

In order to do so, she selects from her personnel files a random sample of 400 people employed by the organization. From the formal education and civil service examination scores of these people, she classifies them into three levels of competence (low, medium, or high), and from their GS ratings and formal job descriptions, she classifies them into three categories of hierarchical position in the organization (low, medium, or high). The cross-tabulation of these two variables for the sample of employees appears in Table 16.1. She would like to know whether she can legitimately infer from

Table 16.1

Cross-Tabulation of Competence and Hierarchy

Hierarchy	Competence			
	Low	Medium	High	Total
Low	113	60	27	200
Medium	31	91	38	160
High	8	8	24	40
Total	152	159	89	400

this sample cross-tabulation that a relationship exists between competence and hierarchical position in the population of all workers in the organization. Accordingly, she decides to perform the chi-square test; the steps in this procedure follow:

Step 1: Compute **expected frequencies** for each cell of the cross-tabulation based on the null hypothesis that competence and hierarchical position are not related in the population. (**Note:** If the table has been percentaged, then the data must be converted to raw frequencies before calculation of the expected frequencies. Expected frequencies must be calculated on the basis of the raw figures.)

If these two variables were unrelated, then we would expect to find the same distribution of hierarchical position in each category of competence as in the sample as a whole. For each level of competence, the percentages of hierarchical position would be identical. In that case, competence would have no impact on hierarchy; there would be percentage differences of 0% for each category of the dependent variable, indicating that the two variables are totally unrelated.

Although calculation of the expected frequencies is a bit cumbersome, it is not difficult. Consider the distribution of hierarchical position. Of the 400 people in the sample, 200 (50%) rank low in position; 160 (40%) hold medium-level positions; and the remaining 40 (10%) are at the top. The hypothetical no-relationship cross-tabulation is displayed in Table 16.2. Assuming that the null hypothesis of no relationship between competence and hierarchy is true, we would expect to find this same distribution of hierarchical position in each of the categories of competence. For example, of the 152 employees ranking low in competence, you would expect to find 50%, or 76.0, in low hierarchical positions ($.50 \times 152 = 76.0$); 40%, or 60.8, in medium positions ($.40 \times 152 = 60.8$); and 10%, or 15.2, in high positions ($.10 \times 152 = 15.2$). These are the expected frequencies for the low-competence category.

The expected frequencies for the medium- and high-competence categories are found analogously. Table 16.3 presents the detailed calculations.

Table 16.2

Hypothetical No-Relationship Cross-Tabulation for Chi-Square

	Competence			
Hierarchy	Low	Medium	High	Total
Low	50%	50%	50%	50%
Medium	40%	40%	40%	40%
High	10%	10%	10%	10%

Table 16.3

Calculations for Expected Frequency and Chi-Square

Table Cell		Observed Frequency	Expected Frequency	(Observed − Expected)^2 ÷ Expected
Competence	Hierarchy			
Low	Low	113	.50 × 152 = 76.0	18.01
Low	Medium	31	.40 × 152 = 60.8	14.61
Low	High	8	.10 × 152 = 15.2	3.41
Medium	Low	60	.50 × 159 = 79.5	4.78
Medium	Medium	91	.40 × 159 = 63.6	11.80
Medium	High	8	.10 × 159 = 15.9	3.93
High	Low	27	.50 × 89 = 44.5	6.88
High	Medium	38	.40 × 89 = 35.6	.16
High	High	24	.10 × 89 = 8.9	25.62
	Total	400	400.0	89.20 = chi-square

Step 2: Compute the value of chi-square for the cross-tabulation. The **chi-square statistic** compares the frequencies actually observed with the expected frequencies (presuming no relationship between the variables) throughout the contingency table. The value of chi-square is found by (1) taking the difference between the observed and expected frequencies for each table cell, (2) squaring this difference, (3) dividing this result by the expected frequency, and (4) summing these quotients across all cells of the table. For example, in the low competence-low hierarchy cell of Table 16.1, the observed frequency is 113, as compared with an expected frequency of 76.0. Thus $(113 - 76.0)^2 \div 76.0 = 18.01$, as shown in the last column of Table 16.3. Although in themselves these calculations are not likely to make a great deal of sense to you, their virtue is that they yield a sum—the value of chi-square—whose theoretical distribution is well known and can be used to evaluate the statistical significance of the relationship found in the contingency table. Table 16.3 indicates that the value of chi-square for the competence–hierarchy cross-tabulation is 89.20.

Step 3: Compare the value of chi-square computed for the actual cross-tabulation with the appropriate value of chi-square tabulated in the table of theoretical values. The table of chi-square values is presented in Table 4 in the Appendix of this book.

To find the appropriate theoretical value of chi-square in this table for an actual contingency table, two pieces of information must be specified: (1) the *degrees of freedom* associated with the table and (2) the *level of statistical significance* desired. The **degrees of freedom** is simply a number that indicates some idea of the size of the empirical contingency table under study. It is found by multiplying one less than the number of rows in the table by one less than the number of columns (ignoring both marginal rows and columns). In the current example, the number of rows and the number of columns are both equal to 3, so there are $(3 - 1) \times (3 - 1) = 2 \times 2 = 4$ degrees of freedom. In the Appendix, Table 4, the degrees of freedom (df) are printed down the far left column of the table.

The **level of statistical significance** is determined by the public or nonprofit manager, according to his or her assessment of the decision-making situation (see Chapter 12). It is the exact probability of error that he or she is willing to tolerate in making an inference from the sample cross-tabulation to the parent population in the long run (i.e., if one were to use the same procedure over and over again to make decisions). For example, if the researcher selects the frequently used level of .05, then there is a probability of 5% that, in the long run, an incorrect inference will be made that a relationship exists in the population when in fact it does not. In the Appendix, Table 4, the level of statistical significance (abbreviated *P,* for probability) is printed along the top of the table; these values cut off the specified area of the curve. Turning to this table, you should find that the theoretical value of chi-square for 4 degrees of freedom, allowing a probability of error of 5% (i.e., a level of statistical significance of .05), is equal to 9.49.

Now that the appropriate theoretical value of chi-square has been determined, it is possible to make the critical decision whether, based on the sample cross-tabulation between competence and hierarchical position, the existence of a relationship can be inferred in the population of all agency employees. The table of theoretical values (Appendix, Table 4) consists of *minimum* values of chi-square that must be obtained in empirical contingency tables in order to infer, with a given level of confidence (statistical significance), that a relationship exists in the population. You should commit the following decision rules for chi-square to memory:

> If the value of chi-square exceeds the minimum value in the chi-square distribution table, you can reject the null hypothesis.
>
> If the value of chi-square does not exceed the minimum value in the chi-square distribution table, you cannot reject the null hypothesis.

In this case, because the value of chi-square calculated for the cross-tabulation (89.20) is far greater than the appropriate minimum value stipulated by Table 4 (9.49), allowing a 5% chance of error, we can infer that a relationship *does exist* between competence and hierarchical position in the population. Had the calculated value of chi-square failed to surpass this minimum, the null hypothesis of no relationship in the population could *not* be rejected.

Limitations of the Chi-Square Test

Although the chi-square test is very useful, the preceding example illustrates well one of its primary limitations. The test procedure led to the conclusion that a relationship does exist between competence and hierarchical position in the population of agency employees. However, recall that the researcher in this example hypothesized that this relationship is *inverse* or *negative:* that is, the less the competence of the employee, the higher is the level of the position attained in the hierarchy of the organization. In fact, when the cross-tabulation of these two variables in the sample of employees (Table 16.1) has been percentaged appropriately (see Chapter 15), the relationship between competence and hierarchical position is found to be *positive.* The percentaged cross-tabulation, presented in Table 16.4, shows that as competence increases, position in the hierarchy also increases. Thus, whereas the existence of a relationship can be inferred in the population, it is in the *opposite* direction of the one hypothesized by the researcher. Therefore, her hypothesis is incorrect.

The important point illustrated by this example is *not* that the chi-square test yields fallacious information but that it yields information of only a limited kind. The test is based solely on the deviation of an observed cross-tabulation from the condition of no relationship or statistical independence. A full treatment of statistical independence can be found in Chapter 7, which presents an introduction to probability. The chi-square test is totally insensitive to the nature and direction of the relationship actually found in the contingency table. Managers must be careful not to jump to the conclusion that a significant value of chi-square calculated in a table indicates that the two variables are related in the hypothesized manner in the population. It may—and it may not. Supplementary analytical procedures, such as percentaging the contingency table and computing a measure of association (as developed later in this chapter), are necessary to answer this question.

The other limitations of the chi-square test are typical of tests of statistical significance in general (see Part IV, "Inferential Statistics"). First, the chi-square test requires a method of sampling from the population—simple random sampling—that

Table 16.4

Percentaged Cross-Tabulation for Competence–Hierarchy Relationship

	Competence		
Hierarchy	Low	Medium	High
Low	74%	38%	30%
Medium	21%	57%	43%
High	5%	5%	27%
Total	100%	100%	100%
	($n = 152$)	($n = 159$)	($n = 89$)

sometimes cannot be satisfied. Second, the value of chi-square calculated in a cross-tabulation is markedly inflated by sample size. As a result, in large samples, relationships are sometimes found to be statistically significant, even when they are weak in magnitude. Hence, the test is not very discriminating.

Finally, although the chi-square test is frequently *misinterpreted* as a measure of strength of relationship, it does *not* assess the magnitude or substantive importance of empirical relationships. Instead, it provides information pertaining only to the probability of the *existence* of a relationship in the population. To be sure, this is valuable information, but it ignores the issue of size of relationship. (Later in this chapter, we present a measure of association derived from chi-square: Cramér's *V*.) For this reason, we strongly encourage you to use the chi-square test in conjunction with other statistical procedures, especially those designed to evaluate strength of relationship. We turn to those techniques now.

Assessing the Strength of a Relationship

The Percentage Difference

Two transportation planners are locked in debate regarding the steps that should be implemented to increase ridership on public transportation, particularly line buses. The first insists that the major reason that people do not ride the bus to work is that they have not heard about it. Thus, she argues that the way to increase ridership is to advertise the availability of public transportation. The second planner contends that the situation is neither that simple nor that inexpensive. He believes that the primary obstacle to the success of public transportation is that it is not readily accessible to great masses of potential riders. People will not leave their cars for a system they are unable to reach conveniently. From this point of view, the way to increase ridership is to expand existing bus routes and to design and implement new ones so that public transportation is more accessible.

The measures proposed by the two transportation planners carry dramatically different implications—as well as price tags—for public policy; therefore, the federal government has decided to fund a study to evaluate the relative validity of their claims. Data were collected from a random sample of 500 individuals. Among other questions, these individuals were asked whether they (1) rode the bus regularly to work, (2) had learned of the existence of public transportation through advertising, and (3) lived in close proximity to a bus stop (defined as within three blocks).

Table 16.5 presents the cross-tabulations between riding the bus to work and each of the other two variables. Both the raw, or nonpercentaged, tables and the percentaged tables are displayed. You should practice deriving the percentages from the raw figures. If any aspect of this process remains mysterious, you should review the steps for percentaging contingency tables elaborated in Chapter 15 before proceeding further.

Table 16.5 provides support for the hypotheses of both transportation planners. As hypothesized by the first, advertising is related positively to ridership. Whereas 33% of those who had heard advertising about public transportation rode the bus

Table 16.5

Data for Bus Survey

Raw Data

Heard Advertising				**Bus Accessible**			
Ride Bus	No	Yes	Total	**Ride Bus**	No	Yes	Total
No	225	134	359	No	269	90	359
Yes	75	66	141	Yes	81	60	141
Total	300	200	500	Total	350	150	500

Percentaged Cross-Tabulations

Heard Advertising			**Bus Accessible**		
Ride Bus	No	Yes	**Ride Bus**	No	Yes
No	75%	67%	No	77%	60%
Yes	25%	33%	Yes	23%	40%
Total	100%	100%	Total	100%	100%
	($n = 300$)	($n = 200$)		($n = 350$)	($n = 150$)

regularly to work, only 25% of those who had not heard such advertising did so. Thus, advertising was associated with an 8% increase in ridership. Similarly, as predicted by the second planner, accessibility is related positively to ridership; 40% of those living in close proximity to a bus stop rode the bus regularly, compared with only 23% of those for whom the bus was less convenient. Thus, accessibility was associated with a 17% increase in ridership.

These results raise the question of which proposal is likely to have the greater impact on increasing ridership of public transportation. Because accessibility seems to have made a difference of 17% in ridership and advertising appears to have made a difference of 8%, the former has the larger impact; that is, changes in accessibility apparently lead to a larger change in ridership than do changes in advertising. Stated another way, accessibility is related *more strongly* to ridership than is advertising. *In general, the greater the percentage difference, the stronger is the relationship between two variables.* Accordingly, if the federal government intends to adopt one or the other of the two proposals (but not both) as a measure to increase the ridership of public transportation, these data suggest that improving accessibility is to be preferred.*

---

*To have greater confidence in this conclusion, one must examine the effects on ridership of advertising and accessibility *simultaneously.* However, the techniques necessary to do so, called *statistical control table analysis,* lie beyond the scope of the present chapter. They are elaborated in Chapter 17.

Perfect and Null Relationships

In a cross-tabulation, as the independent variable changes categories, the percentage difference for a given category of the dependent variable may range from 0% to 100%. Percentage differences of 100 for each of the categories of the dependent variable indicate that the two variables are associated *perfectly*. If you are given the score of a case on the independent variable, you can predict the score on the dependent variable with certainty.

As shown in Table 16.6, the relationship between two ordinal variables is perfect if all cases are located in the diagonal cells of the contingency table. Two types of perfect relationship exist. First, if the categories of both variables are arranged in ascending order (such as low, medium, and high), the relationship is perfect in the *positive* direction if all cases fall into the diagonal cells sloping downward from the top-left cell to the bottom-right one. This pattern indicates that as scores on the independent variable increase, the scores on the dependent variable also increase. Second, as Table 16.6 shows, if all cases fall into the diagonal cells sloping downward from the top-right cell to the bottom-left one, the relationship is perfect in the *negative* direction. This pattern indicates that as scores on the independent variable increase, the scores on the dependent variable decrease. *The closer the observed cross-tabulation comes to either of these configurations, the stronger is the association between the two variables.* Because changes in the independent variable are hypothesized to be accompanied by changes in the dependent variable, this pattern is called the *covariation model* of relationship.

Table 16.6

Perfect Relationships

Perfect Positive Relationship

Dependent Variable	Independent Variable			
	Category 1	Category 2	...	Category k
Category 1	100%	0%	...	0%
Category 2	0%	100%	...	0%
⋮	⋮	⋮		⋮
Category k	0%	0%	...	100%
Total	100%	100%	...	100%

Perfect Negative Relationship

Dependent Variable	Independent Variable			
	Category 1	Category 2	...	Category k
Category 1	0%	0%	...	100%
Category 2	⋮	⋮		⋮
⋮	0%	100%	...	0%
Category k	100%	0%	...	0%
Total	100%	100%	...	100%

At the other extreme in a cross-tabulation, percentage differences of 0% within each of the categories of the dependent variable indicate that the two variables are *not* associated. The more similar the distribution of the dependent variable across each of the categories of the independent variable, the less strongly two variables are related. As was explained earlier in the discussion of the chi-square test, the strength of relationship between two variables reaches its lowest point when those distributions are identical. In that situation the variables are totally unrelated or statistically independent (see Chapter 7 for a discussion of statistical independence).

Table 16.2, which was developed in conjunction with the chi-square test, provides an example. Note that knowing the value of the independent variable (competence) in the table does not help in predicting values of the dependent variable (hierarchy) because the percentages are the same for each category of the independent variable. Even if you knew a person's level of competence, it would not help in predicting her or his position in the hierarchy. Table 16.7 illustrates that in contrast to the single model of perfect association, there are many empirical models of no association. As long as the percentages calculated on the dependent variable are identical for each category of the independent variable, no relationship exits.

In evaluating the strength of relationship between two variables, the critical question is, Where on the continuum between the poles of no association and perfect association do the actual data fall? Do they more closely resemble the model in Table 16.7 or the model in Table 16.6? The more that they correspond to the model of perfect association, the more strongly they are said to be related.

Table 16.7

No Relationship

No Association: General Model

($a\% + b\% + c\% = 100\%$)

Dependent Variable	Independent Variable		
	Category 1	Category 2	Category 3
Category 1	$a\%$	$a\%$	$a\%$
Category 2	$b\%$	$b\%$	$b\%$
Category 3	$c\%$	$c\%$	$c\%$
Total	100%	100%	100%

No Association: Empirical Examples

Dependent Variable	Independent Variable			Dependent Variable	Independent Variable		
	Category 1	Category 2	Category 3		Category 1	Category 2	Category 3
Category 1	50%	50%	50%	Category 1	7%	7%	7%
Category 2	25%	25%	25%	Category 2	90%	90%	90%
Category 3	25%	25%	25%	Category 3	3%	3%	3%
Total	100%	100%	100%	Total	100%	100%	100%

This discussion of extreme values of association raises a problem with respect to the percentage difference as a measure of strength of relationship. Since the models of perfect and null association are based on all cells of the cross-tabulation, it seems reasonable that a desirable quality of a measure intended to assess strength of relationship is that it take into account the configuration of data in the entire contingency table. Because it is based only on the endpoint categories of the dependent variable, the percentage difference does not satisfy this desideratum; it takes into account only a portion of the data in the table (see Chapter 15). As a result, in larger cross-tabulations, the choice of the dependent variable category not only is somewhat arbitrary but also can lead to *different* results representing the strength of relationship between two variables in the *same* table. Depending on one's point of view, the category selected may understate or overstate the actual degree of relationship in the cross-tabulation. Accordingly, we recommended (in Chapter 15) that you calculate and report both percentage differences.

It is important to place these points in perspective. In spite of its flaws, the percentage difference is perhaps the most widely used and certainly the most easily understood measure of strength of relationship. Used in combination with the other measures elaborated in this chapter, it can be extremely helpful for evaluating the nature and strength of relationship between two variables measured at the nominal or ordinal levels. It is a hard fact of quantitative life that all statistics have flaws. An inevitable consequence of describing or summarizing or distilling a distribution into a single representative number or statistic is that some features of the data are captured very well, whereas others are slighted or overlooked completely. For this reason, we encourage you to think of the measures presented for understanding bivariate relationships as complementary rather than exclusive. In actual data analysis situations, use those *measures* that best elucidate the relationship under study.

Measures of Association

Measures of association are statistics whose magnitude and sign (positive or negative) provide an indication of the extent and direction of relationship between two variables in a cross-tabulation. In contrast to the percentage difference, measures of association are calculated on the basis of—and take into account—all data in the contingency table. These statistics are designed to indicate where an actual relationship falls on the scale from perfect to null.

To facilitate interpretation, statisticians define measures of association so that they follow these four conventions:

1. If the relationship between the two variables is perfect, the measure equals +1.0 (positive relationship) or −1.0 (negative relationship).

2. If there is no relationship between the two variables, the measure equals 0.0.

3. The sign of the measure indicates the direction of the relationship. A value greater than zero (a positive number) corresponds to a positive relationship; a value less than zero (a negative number) corresponds to a negative relationship.

4. The stronger the relationship between the two variables, the greater is the magnitude of the measure. The absolute value of the statistic (ignoring sign) is what matters in assessing magnitude. A relationship measuring $-.75$ is larger than one measuring $-.25$.

Because the concept of direction (or sign) of relationship assumes that the categories of the variables are ordered (that is, they increase or decrease), this concept can be applied only to relationships between variables measured at the *ordinal* or *interval* levels. Direction of relationship has no meaning for nominal variables because the categories have no numerical ordering (for example, religion). Based on the properties of measurement for each type of variable (see Chapter 2), different measures of association have been developed. Thus, there are interval measures of association, ordinal measures, and nominal measures. Some interval measures are considered in Part VI, on regression analysis. The remainder of this chapter describes several ordinal and nominal measures of association and provides examples illustrating their use.

An Ordinal Measure of Association: Gamma

It is cumbersome to compute any of the ordinal measures of association by hand, even with the aid of a (nonprogrammable) calculator. If these measures are essential to a report or analysis, the best strategy is to obtain access to a computer or a programmable calculator.

We will illustrate the computation of one of the more easily calculated ordinal measures of association, gamma. As will be shown, several other of the most frequently used measures of ordinal association (the tau statistic of Kendall and the *d* statistics of Somers) have a similar development. Gamma will be used to assess the strength of relationship between education and seniority in a small sample of 50 employees in a nonprofit organization. These variables are cross-tabulated in Table 16.8.

To calculate the gamma statistic, we must first introduce the idea of **paired observations.** Consider two data cases in Table 16.8, one of an individual in the low education–low seniority cell, and the other of an individual in the high education–high seniority cell. (The data come from the Southeast Animal Rights Association.) With respect to one another, this pair of cases is ranked consistently on education and seniority—that is, for this pair of cases, as education increases, seniority increases. Thus, this pair provides support for the existence of a *positive* relationship between the two variables. If all cases were in these two cells of the table, we would have a perfect positive relationship (see Table 16.6). This situation is called a **concordant pair** of cases.

Now consider two different data cases in Table 16.8, one of an individual in the low education–high seniority cell, and the other of an individual in the high education–low seniority cell. In contrast to the first pair of cases, with respect to one another, this pair of cases is ranked inconsistently on education and seniority—that is, as education increases, seniority decreases, and vice versa. This pair provides support for the existence of a negative relationship between the two variables. It is called a **discordant pair.** If all cases fell in these two table cells, we would have a perfect negative relationship.

What **gamma** (and many other ordinal measures of association) does is to take the *difference* between the number of concordant or consistently ordered pairs and the

Table 16.8

**Cross-Tabulation of Education and Seniority for
Southeast Animal Rights Association**

Seniority	Education		Total
	Low	High	
Low	20	10	30
High	5	15	20
Total	25	25	50

number of discordant or inconsistently ordered pairs in the cross-tabulation. *This difference indicates the relative support in the contingency table for a positive as opposed to a negative relationship between the two variables.* If the number of concordant pairs exceeds the number of discordant pairs, then, on balance, there is greater support for a positive relationship in the table. In that case, the difference between them will be positive, and the gamma statistic will have this sign. On the other hand, if the number of concordant pairs is less than the number of discordant pairs, there is greater support for a negative relationship. The difference between them will be negative, and this will be reflected in the (negative) sign of gamma. Regardless of the direction of the relationship, the larger the difference between the number of concordant and the number of discordant pairs, the greater is the association between the two variables, and the greater is the magnitude of gamma.

With this understanding of concordant and discordant pairs, we are ready to calculate gamma. There are three steps:

Step 1: Calculate the number of concordant pairs and the number of discordant pairs of cases in the cross-tabulation.

In a small cross-tabulation, such as the one in Table 16.8, this calculation is not difficult. Consider first the concordant pairs. There are 20 cases in the low education–low seniority cell of the table. With respect to this group, the set of cases that is ordered consistently on both variables is the set of 15 observations in the high education–high seniority cell. Because each pairing of cases from these two table cells yields a concordant pair, in all there are $20 \times 15 = 300$ concordant pairs in Table 16.8.

The number of discordant pairs is found analogously. There are 10 cases in the high education–low seniority cell of Table 16.8. With respect to this set, the group of cases that is ordered inconsistently on the variables is the group of five observations in the low education–high seniority cell of the table. Because each pairing of cases from these two table cells gives a discordant pair, there are $10 \times 5 = 50$ discordant pairs in Table 16.8.

Step 2: Calculate the difference between the number of concordant pairs and the number of discordant pairs.

It is evident that the relationship between education and seniority in Table 16.8 is positive because there are more concordant than discordant pairs. The difference between them is $300 - 50 = 250$. However, this simple difference is not very meaningful for interpreting the relative strength of relationship. For example, it would be misleading to compare the difference obtained in this small contingency table with that obtained in a larger table or in tables with many more cases, for the latter will generate so many more pairs of cases.

For this reason, statisticians have *standardized* gamma (as well as most other measures of association) so that it will vary between -1.0 for a perfect negative relationship and $+1.0$ for a perfect positive relationship. Thus, the third and final step in calculating gamma is to standardize the measure.

Step 3: Divide the difference between the number of concordant pairs and the number of discordant pairs obtained in Steps 1 and 2 by their sum.

Division by the sum of the number of concordant pairs and the number of discordant pairs in the cross-tabulation ensures that gamma will vary between -1.0 and $+1.0$ (it will also follow the other conventions for measures of association discussed earlier). The three steps for calculating gamma can be summarized in a formula:

$$\text{gamma} = \frac{\text{number of concordant pairs} - \text{number of discordant pairs}}{\text{number of concordant pairs} + \text{number of discordant pairs}}$$

Accordingly, the value of gamma for Table 16.8 is equal to

$$\frac{300 - 50}{300 + 50} = \frac{250}{350} = .71$$

This value of gamma indicates a relatively strong positive relationship between education and seniority in the sample of employees of the Southeast Animal Rights Association. When the original cross-tabulation has been percentaged, as shown in Table 16.9, further support is found for this conclusion. The percentaged table shows that as education increases, employees were more likely to have high seniority by a difference of $60\% - 20\% = 40\%$.

Table 16.9

Percentaged Cross-Tabulation of Education and Seniority

Seniority	Education	
	Low	High
Low	80%	40%
High	20%	60%
	($n = 25$)	($n = 25$)

Other Ordinal Measures of Association: Kendall's tau-*b* and tau-*c* and Somers's d_{yx} and d_{xy}

Several other commonly used measures of association for ordinal-level variables have a derivation and interpretation similar to gamma's. These include Kendall's tau-*b* and tau-*c*, and Somers's d_{yx} and d_{xy}. These measures are similar and easy for the computer to calculate, and many statistical package programs have been designed to compute and show them routinely. Because they are very cumbersome to calculate by hand, however, we will not do so here but will only explain their use and interpretation.

Like gamma, all of these measures are based on comparing the number of concordant pairs with the number of discordant pairs in the contingency table. Yet they differ from gamma because they take into account pairs of observations in the table that are *tied* on one or both of the variables. For example, a case in the low education–low seniority cell of the table is tied with a case in the low education–high seniority cell with respect to education since both cases have the same rank on education. Similarly, a case in the low education–high seniority cell is tied with a case in the high education–high seniority cell with respect to seniority since they both have the same rank on seniority.

Gamma takes into account only concordant and discordant pairs; it ignores tied pairs completely. The other measures of association do not. Instead, they are based on a more stringent conception of the types of data patterns in a contingency table that constitute a perfect relationship. In particular, they will yield lower values for a contingency table to the extent that the table contains pairs of cases tied on the variables. For this reason, unless a contingency table has no tied pairs (a very rare occurrence), gamma will always be greater than tau-*b*, tau-*c*, d_{yx}, and d_{xy}.

Kendall's tau-*b* is an appropriate measure of strict linear relationship for "square tables"—tables with the same number of rows and columns. The calculation of tau-*b* takes into account pairs of cases tied on each of the variables in the contingency table. For the education-seniority cross-tabulation in Table 16.8, the calculated value of tau-*b* is .41. **Kendall's tau-*c*** is an appropriate measure of linear relationship for "rectangular tables"—tables with different numbers of rows and columns. Note that in such a cross-tabulation, no clear diagonal exists for either a perfect positive or a perfect negative relationship (see Table 16.6)—so a different measure of association is needed for this situation. In the current example, tau-*c* is .40 (tau-*b* is preferred because the table is square).

Somers's d_{yx} presumes that seniority is the dependent variable and yields lower values to the degree that cases are tied on this variable only. The logic is that a tie on seniority indicates that a change in the independent variable (education) does not lead to a change in seniority as a perfect relationship would predict. Here, Somers's d_{yx} is .40. Conversely, **Somers's d_{xy}** presumes that education is the dependent variable and yields lower values to the degree that cases are tied on education only. The reasoning is that a tie on the dependent variable (now education) indicates that a change in the independent variable (now seniority) does not lead to a change in education, as a perfect relationship would predict. In this example, Somers's d_{xy} is .42, but it would not be the statistic of choice because the hypothesis was that education (independent variable) leads to seniority (dependent variable), not the reverse.

Recall that the gamma calculated for Table 16.8 is .71, which is much greater than the calculated value of any of the other measures of association. The reason is the tied pairs of cases. This situation is not at all unusual in the analysis of contingency tables. Among the measures of association, gamma will typically yield the largest value, whereas the others will be more modest. Which measure(s) should you use and interpret? In general, the tau measures are used more commonly than are the Somers's *d* measures. Many managers prefer to use both gamma and either tau-*b* or tau-*c*, depending on whether the contingency table is square or rectangular, respectively. In this manner, the measures give a good idea of the magnitude of the relationship found in the table evaluated according to more stringent as well as less stringent standards of association.

A Nominal Measure of Association: Lambda

Ordinal measures of association are based on a covariation model of relationship. To the extent that two variables change together, or *covary*, they are considered associated or related. Measures of covariation such as gamma assess the extent to which increases in one variable are accompanied by increases (positive relationship) or decreases (negative relationship) in a second variable.

Because nominal variables do not consist of ordered categories (the categories lack any sense of magnitude or intensity), application of the covariation model of association to relationships between nominal variables is precluded. Therefore, a different model of association is required. A frequently used model of association for nominal variables is called the *predictability* model, or the model of *predictive association*. It is based on the ability to predict the category of the dependent variable based on knowledge of the category of the independent variable.

One of the most helpful and frequently used nominal measures of association premised on the predictability model is lambda. **Lambda** is defined as the proportional reduction in error gained in predicting the category of the dependent variable when the value of the independent variable is taken into account. That is, lambda evaluates the extent to which prediction of the dependent variable is improved when the value of the independent variable is known. Because the worst case is one in which the independent variable provides no (zero) improvement in predicting the dependent variable, lambda cannot be negative but ranges from 0.0 to +1.0. Measures of association that incorporate the proportional reduction in error interpretation are sometimes abbreviated *PRE statistics*.

An example will illustrate the calculation and interpretation of lambda. Consider the relationship between race (white; nonwhite) and whether an individual made a contribution to the Bureau of Obfuscation's United Way annual fund drive. These variables are cross-tabulated for a random sample of 500 employees in Table 16.10.

Step 1: Calculate the number of errors in predicting the value of the dependent variable if the value of the independent variable were not known.

To calculate the value of lambda for the relationship shown in Table 16.10, we first disregard totally the race of the employee (independent variable). If race is disregarded, how many errors will we make in predicting whether the employee made a contribution to the United Way (dependent variable)?

Table 16.10

Cross-Tabulation of Race and Contribution

Contribution	Race		Total
	White	Nonwhite	
No	100	125	225
Yes	200	75	275
Total	300	200	500

Because more employees made a contribution than did not, our best prediction is "contributed." This prediction is correct for 275 of the 500 employees in the sample who contributed, but it is in error for the remaining 225 who did not contribute. Thus, when the value of the independent variable is not taken into account (disregarded), the proportion of errors made in predicting the dependent variable is $225 \div 500 = .45$.

Step 2: Calculate the number of errors in predicting the value of the dependent variable, this time taking into account the value of the independent variable.

If the race of the employee is now introduced, how much better can we predict contributions to the United Way? If we knew that an employee was white, our best prediction would be that he or she made a contribution. We would be correct for 200 of the 300 whites in the sample who made a contribution, but we would make errors in predicting for the other 100 who did not. If an employee is nonwhite, we would predict that he or she did not make a contribution. We would be correct for 125 of the 200 nonwhites who did not contribute, leaving 75 errors in prediction for those who did. Thus, knowing the race of the employee, we would make a total of $100 + 75 = 175$ errors in predicting contributions to the United Way in a sample of 500 employees. This is a proportion of errors equal to $175 \div 500 = .35$.

Step 3: Calculate the rate of improvement in predicting the value of the dependent variable when the value of the independent variable is known (Step 2) over the original prediction in which the value of the independent variable was ignored (Step 1). In other words, by how much has the rate of error in predicting the dependent variable been reduced by introducing knowledge of the independent variable?

We began with a proportion of error in predicting the dependent variable of .45, not taking into account the independent variable. By introducing the independent variable, we were able to reduce the proportion of error to .35. How much of an improvement do we have? Compared with the original proportion, this is a rate of improvement in predicting the dependent variable—or proportional reduction in error—of

$$\frac{.45 - .35}{.45} = .22$$

which is the value of lambda for Table 16.10. This value suggests a moderate predictive relationship between race and contributions to the United Way.

An alternative way to understand and compute lambda is to consider that, without knowing the value of the independent variable, we made 225 errors in predicting the dependent variable; and knowing the independent variable, we made 175 errors, a reduction of 50 errors. Thus, errors in prediction were reduced by the proportion $50 \div 225 = .22$, which again is the value of lambda for Table 16.10. Based on this logic, the formula for lambda can be written

$$\text{lambda} = \frac{\left[\begin{array}{c}\text{number of errors in prediction}\\\text{not knowing value of}\\\text{independent variable}\end{array}\right] - \left[\begin{array}{c}\text{number of errors in}\\\text{prediction knowing value}\\\text{of independent variable}\end{array}\right]}{\left[\begin{array}{c}\text{number of errors in prediction}\\\text{not knowing value}\\\text{of independent variable}\end{array}\right]}$$

A Nominal Measure of Association Based on Chi-Square: Cramér's *V*

The chi-square test of statistical significance elaborated at the outset of this chapter is a measure of the existence of a relationship, not its strength. A variety of measures of association for nominal-level variables has been developed based on the chi-square. The measures include Pearson's contingency coefficient *C*, phi-square, Tschuprow's *T*, and Cramér's *V*. These measures are all related, and many computer statistical packages have been programmed to calculate and show them routinely.

Probably the most useful (and most often used) of the measures is **Cramér's *V*.** It is given by the formula

$$V = \sqrt{\frac{\text{chi-square}}{m\mathbf{N}}}$$

where chi-square = value of chi-square calculated for the contingency table; m = (number of rows in the table − 1) or (number of columns in the table − 1), whichever is smaller; and N = size of the sample. Although the formula may seem complicated, it is easy to calculate Cramér's *V*, and we do so now for the cross-tabulation in Table 16.1.

Step 1:　Calculate the value of chi-square for the cross-tabulation. For the data in Table 16.1, the value of chi-square is 89.20 (Table 16.3 shows the calculations).

Step 2:　Calculate m. Determine which is smaller, the number of rows or the number of columns in the cross-tabulation, and subtract 1 from this number. Because Table 16.1 has the same number of rows as columns (3), this choice does not matter in this example. Subtracting 1 from 3 yields a difference of 2, which is the value of m.

Step 3: The remainder of the formula indicates that we must multiply m times $\mathbf{N}$; divide chi-square (from Step 1) by this product; and take the square root of the result. In this example, $m = 2$ and $\mathbf{N} = 400$, so $m \times \mathbf{N} = 2 \times 400 = 800$. Dividing chi-square (89.20) by this product $= 89.20 \div 800 = 0.1115$; taking the square root of $0.1115 = 0.33$, which is the value of Cramér's V for Table 16.1.

Like all measures of association for nominal-level variables, Cramér's V is always a positive number (remember that the direction of relationship has no meaning for nominal data). The measure ranges from 0.0, indicating no relationship between the variables, to 1.0, indicating a perfect relationship.

Use of Nominal Measures of Association with Ordinal Data

For the analysis of relationships between variables measured at the ordinal level, researchers generally use ordinal measures of association. However, if the manager anticipates that the relationship is not one of covariation but of predictability, a nominal measure of association such as lambda can be employed. For example, one might hypothesize that, because jobs at the bottom of the organizational hierarchy tend to be low paying and those at the top tend to be quite stressful, middle-level officials may have the highest level of job satisfaction. An empirical example is presented in Table 16.11; the data are for staff members of the Inward Institute, a small liberal arts college in central Iowa.

Because the cross-tabulation in Table 16.11 does not demonstrate a consistent pattern of increase in job satisfaction (dependent variable) with an increase in hierarchy (independent variable), the value of an ordinal measure of association predicated on the covariation logic will be small. In contrast, because job satisfaction is highly predictable based on the categories of hierarchy, the value of lambda will be large. That is, if one knows an employee's level in the hierarchy, then a very good prediction can be made regarding job satisfaction. For example, for those low in hierarchy, predict low satisfaction—you would be correct 75% of the time. What would you predict for the middle level in the hierarchy? How often would you be correct? (High satisfaction—80%.) For high-level positions? How often correct? (Medium satisfaction—70%.) Although the relationship is not perfectly linear (see Table 16.6), it is quite predictable.

Table 16.11

Percentaged Cross-Tabulation of Hierarchy and Job Satisfaction

	Hierarchy		
Job Satisfaction	Low	Middle	High
Low	75%	10%	20%
Medium	15%	10%	70%
High	10%	80%	10%
Total	100%	100%	100%
	$(n = 200)$	$(n = 200)$	$(n = 200)$

Measures of Association for Larger Tables

We have illustrated the calculation and interpretation of measures of association for contingency tables with two rows and two columns, so-called two-by-two tables. The interpretation of the measures of association for larger tables is analogous, but the calculation is much more involved. Here we illustrate the calculation of gamma and lambda for the three-by-three cross-tabulation in Table 16.11. This example will show how useful it can be to apply different measures of association to a contingency table.

Even though the table is larger, calculation of gamma follows the same three-step procedure elaborated earlier. First, calculate the number of concordant pairs and the number of discordant pairs of cases in the cross-tabulation. Next, calculate the difference between the number of concordant pairs and the number of discordant pairs. Finally, divide this difference by the sum of the number of concordant pairs and the number of discordant pairs.

To begin, because measures of association are calculated from the raw frequencies rather than from percentaged data, we must convert the percentages in Table 16.11 to frequencies. Table 16.12 shows the result.

As explained before, *gamma* is based on the number of concordant pairs of cases versus the number of discordant pairs in the table; the concordant pairs demonstrate support for a positive relationship, whereas the discordant pairs show support for a negative relationship. To find the number of concordant pairs, work through the table, moving downward and to the right simultaneously. Begin with the cell in the top row and left column of the table. All table cells both below and to the right of this cell form concordant pairs with it. Four cells satisfy this condition: the middle-row–middle-column cell of the table, the middle-row–right-column cell, the bottom-row–middle-column cell, and the bottom-row–right-column cell. Sum the frequencies of the four cells (20 + 140 + 160 + 20 = 340); multiply the result by the frequency in the top-row–left-column cell (150). This multiplication gives the number of concordant pairs that can be formed with the top-row–left-column cell, $150 \times 340 = 51,000$ pairs [see part (a) of Figure 16.1].

Move to the top-row–middle-column cell of the table. Cells forming concordant pairs are again down and to the right: the middle-row–right-column cell and the bottom-row–right-column cell. Sum the frequencies in these two cells (140 + 20 = 160) and multiply by the frequency in the top-row–middle-column cell (20). This

Table 16.12

Cross-Tabulation of Hierarchy and Job Satisfaction (Frequencies)

| Job Satisfaction | Hierarchy | | | |
	Low	Medium	High	Total
Low	150	20	40	210
Medium	30	20	140	190
High	20	160	20	200
Total	200	200	200	600

Figure 16.1

Concordant and Discordant Pairs

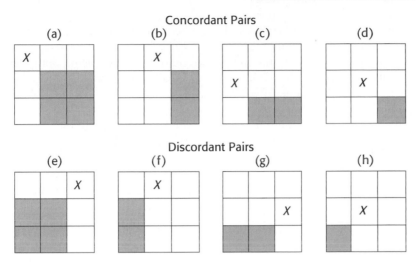

multiplication gives the number of concordant pairs that can be formed with the top-row–middle-column cell, $20 \times 160 = 3{,}200$ pairs [see part (b) of Figure 16.1].

Because no table cells are *both* to the right and below the top-row–right-column cell of the table, it forms no concordant pairs. Instead, move to the middle-row–left-column cell of the table. Concordant pairs are formed with the cells below and to the right: the bottom-row–middle-column cell and the bottom-row–right-column cell. Sum these two cell frequencies ($160 + 20 = 180$) and multiply by the frequency in the middle-row–left-column cell (30). This multiplication gives the number of concordant pairs that can be formed with this cell, $30 \times 180 = 5{,}400$ pairs [see part (c) of Figure 16.1].

Move to the middle-row–middle-column cell of the table. With which cells does it form concordant pairs? Just one—the bottom-row–right-column cell. Multiply the two cell frequencies to find the number of concordant pairs, $20 \times 20 = 400$ [see part (d) of Figure 16.1].

You may not realize it, but you have now found all concordant pairs in the table. Because no table cell is *both* below and to the right of the middle-row–right-column cell, no concordant pairs can be formed with it. Similarly, since no table cell is both below and to the right of the cells in the bottom row of the table, no concordant pairs can be formed with any of them. The total number of concordant pairs is equal to the sum of the four sets of concordant pairs that we have calculated: $51{,}000 + 3{,}200 + 5{,}400 + 400 = 60{,}000$ [see Figure 16.1, parts (a), (b), (c), and (d)].

To find the number of discordant pairs, the procedure is analogous to that for concordant pairs, except that you must start with the top-row–right-column cell of the table and move downward and to the left simultaneously to form the pairs.

Parts (e) through (h) of Figure 16.1 show the procedure schematically. To begin, multiply the frequency in the top-row–right-column cell (40) by the sum of the frequencies in the cells both below and to the left (20 + 30 + 160 + 20 = 230), yielding 9,200 pairs. Move to the top-row–middle-column cell; multiply this frequency (20) by the sum of the frequencies in the cells both below and to the left (30 + 20 = 50), giving 1,000 pairs. Move to the middle-row–right-column cell of the table, and multiply this frequency (140) by the sum of the cell frequencies below and to the left (160 + 20 = 180), yielding 25,200 pairs. Finally, the discordant pairs for the middle-row–middle-column cell are formed with the bottom-row–left-column cell only; multiplying the relevant cell frequencies yields $20 \times 20 = 400$ pairs. The total number of discordant pairs in the contingency table is the sum of these four sets of pairs: 9,200 + 1,000 + 25,200 + 400 = 35,800 pairs [see Figure 16.1, parts (e), (f), (g), and (h)].

Recall that gamma is equal to the difference between the number of concordant pairs and the number of discordant pairs in the contingency table, divided by their sum. Thus, for the cross-tabulation in Table 16.12, gamma is equal to

$$\frac{60,000 - 35,800}{60,000 + 35,800} = \frac{24,200}{95,800} = .25$$

This value of gamma suggests a modest degree of covariation or relationship between the level in the hierarchy and job satisfaction.

Note how important it is to set up the cross-tabulation in the standard format displayed in Table 15.15 in Chapter 15. Had the ordering of the categories for either variable in the contingency table been reversed, concordant pairs would have been misidentified as discordant pairs, and vice versa. For calculating measures of association, whether by hand or by computer, the presumption is that the table has been set up in the standard format shown in that chapter.

Lambda is a measure of association for nominal data based on the ability to predict values of the dependent variable. Like all statistics for nominal data, it can always be applied to higher levels of measurement, such as the ordinal variables cross-tabulated in Table 16.12.

Lambda is a proportional reduction in error statistic. The formula for lambda presented earlier indicates that we must (1) determine the number of errors in predicting the value of the dependent variable without knowledge of the independent variable, (2) subtract from this number the number of errors that we would make with knowledge of the independent variable to inform our predictions, and (3) see by what proportion the errors in predicting values of the dependent variable are reduced by introducing knowledge of the independent variable.

In Table 16.12, which category of job satisfaction would you predict that most employees have, if you did not know their level in the organizational hierarchy? Your best guess is low job satisfaction, because more employees gave this response than any other (210). You would make the correct prediction for these 210 employees, but you would be incorrect in making this prediction for employees with medium satisfaction (190) or high satisfaction (200). In all, you would make a total of 190 + 200 = 390 errors in predicting values of the dependent variable if you did not consider employees' position in the organizational hierarchy (the independent variable).

Now, introduce knowledge of the independent variable. For each category of hierarchy, select the category of the dependent variable that will minimize the number of errors in predicting employee job satisfaction. For employees who are low in the organizational hierarchy, what is your best guess of their level of job satisfaction? You should guess low satisfaction, because most employees low in the hierarchy gave this response (150). You would be correct in predicting the job satisfaction of these 150 employees, but you would make errors in prediction for the 30 employees low in the hierarchy who have medium job satisfaction, and for the 20 who have high satisfaction—a total of 50 errors in prediction.

Which category of job satisfaction yields the fewest errors in prediction for the employees in the middle ranks of the organizational hierarchy? The best prediction is high job satisfaction. This prediction would be correct for 160 of the employees in the middle ranks, but it would be in error for the 20 employees with medium job satisfaction and for the 20 with low satisfaction in the middle of the hierarchy—a total of 40 errors.

Finally, for employees high in the organizational hierarchy, the best prediction of job satisfaction is medium. The prediction is correct for 140 employees, but in error for 60 employees—the 40 with low job satisfaction and the 20 with high satisfaction in this category of hierarchy. In all, then, given knowledge of employees' standing in the organizational hierarchy (the independent variable), the total number of errors in predicting job satisfaction (the dependent variable) is $50 + 40 + 60 = 150$.

Lambda evaluates how much prediction of the dependent variable has improved by introducing knowledge of the independent variable. In this example, we began with 390 errors in predicting employees' levels of job satisfaction, absent knowledge of their position in the organizational hierarchy. Introducing this knowledge, we made only 150 errors in prediction. By what proportion has our prediction been improved? The formula for lambda provides the answer:

$$\frac{390 - 150}{390} = \frac{240}{390} = .62$$

This value of lambda suggests a much stronger relationship between hierarchy and job satisfaction than does the gamma value (.25). Because the percentaged cross-tabulation (Table 16.11) does not reveal a consistent pattern of increase or decrease in employee job satisfaction across levels of the organizational hierarchy, measures of association based on covariation—such as gamma—will be small (Kendall's tau and Somers's d would have been even smaller). By contrast, this relationship has high predictability, the model of association tapped by lambda. Given knowledge of employees' position in the organizational hierarchy, job satisfaction can be predicted very well. (See the discussion of predictability in relation to Table 16.11, which concluded the previous section.) As this example shows, a good strategy with table analysis is to use and interpret not only the percentaged cross-tabulation but also several measures of association.

Chapter Summary

This chapter introduces three aids for the analysis and interpretation of contingency tables. The chi-square test assesses whether the relationship observed in a cross-tabulation based on a sample of data is sufficiently large to reject the null hypothesis that in the population the variables are not related. The chi-square test involves three steps. First, compute expected frequencies for each cell of the cross-tabulation based on the null hypothesis that the variables are not related. Second, compute the value of chi-square for the cross-tabulation, which assesses the departure from statistical independence (or no relationship). Finally, compare the value of the computed chi-square with an appropriate value in the chi-square table of theoretical values to see whether it surpasses the threshold value necessary to reject the null hypothesis.

The strength of a relationship can be assessed by using percentage differences. The strength will range from a perfect relationship (percentage differences of 100) to a null relationship (percentage differences of 0).

Measures of association are statistics used to evaluate the extent and direction of a relationship between two variables in a contingency table. Gamma, which is based on pairs of observations, is a measure of association for ordinal data. It indicates the relative support in the contingency table for a positive, as opposed to a negative, relationship between the two variables. Related measures of association for ordinal-level variables are Kendall's tau-b and tau-c, and Somers's d_{yx} and d_{xy}. All of these measures employ a covariation model of relationship: As the independent variable increases, the dependent variable increases (positive relationship) or decreases (negative relationship).

A different model of relationship is used for nominal-level data. This model of predictive association or predictability underlies lambda. Lambda evaluates the extent to which prediction of the dependent variable is improved when the value of the independent variable is taken into account. Cramér's V, which is based on the chi-square, is another measure of association for nominal-level variables.

Analysts can also calculate and use nominal measures of association to assess the degree of relationship between ordinal variables in a cross-tabulation. Examining both covariation statistics such as gamma and predictability statistics such as lambda for a contingency table can help public and nonprofit managers understand and interpret the relationship.

Problems

16.1   The police chief wants to know whether the city's nonwhites feel that the police are doing a good job. In comparison to whites' evaluations, this information will tell the police whether they have a community relations problem in the nonwhite community. A survey reveals the data in the accompanying table. What can you tell the police chief? Base your statements on what you have learned in this chapter.

Attitude toward Police	Race		Total
	Nonwhite	White	
Police do not do good job	76	73	149
Police do good job	74	223	297
Total	150	296	446

16.2 For the competence–hierarchy example discussed earlier in the chapter, percentage the accompanying table and calculate gamma. Discuss the relationship between competence and level of organizational hierarchy.

Hierarchy	Competence			Total
	Low	Medium	High	
Low	113	60	27	200
Medium	31	91	38	160
High	8	8	24	40
Total	152	159	89	400

16.3 Compute the value of chi-square for the data in the accompanying table, and percentage the cross-tabulation. From these data, would you say that the relationship between proximity of residence to hospital and the frequency of visits to the hospital for care is weak or strong? Explain your answer.

Frequency of Visits	Proximity to Hospital		
	Close	Medium	Far
Low	1,000	1,030	1,050
Medium	525	520	515
High	475	450	435

16.4 Two scholars are locked in debate regarding the interpretation of the accompanying data. One insists that the relationship between the age of a child and the child's perception of the parents is very strong; the other argues that no relationship exists. Why do the two scholars reach different conclusions? Analyze the table and resolve the dilemma. Is there a relationship between the age of a child and the child's perception of the parents?

Child's Perception of Parents	Age of Child (Years)		
	5–15	16–27	28 and Older
Negative	11%	53%	23%
Neutral	18%	27%	59%
Positive	71%	20%	18%
Total	100%	100%	100%

16.5 Devise a hypothesis of interest to you. Using percentages, construct cross-tabulations that show (a) perfect support for the hypothesis and (b) no support for the hypothesis. Construct three additional tables that show (c) strong, (d) medium, and (e) weak support for the hypothesis. After you have constructed the percentaged tables, make up marginal frequencies for each category of the independent variable and convert the percentages in the table cells to frequencies.

16.6   The city parks commission has decided to redevelop a community park. Some members of the commission feel that refurbishment of existing park facilities is sufficient to meet the needs of the community; therefore, they advocate minimal redevelopment. Other members feel that such a small-scale project is pointless. They contend that improvement of the park will create greater public satisfaction with the park and thus will draw many more people than currently use it. An increase in patrons could exhaust existing facilities, thus necessitating further redevelopment. To resolve this disagreement, the commission hires a consultant to conduct a survey of community opinion. Among the questions asked are these: Do you regularly use the park? Do you consider park facilities satisfactory or unsatisfactory? From the cross-tabulation of these questions presented in the accompanying table, what should the consultant recommend to the commission?

	Park Facilities		
Use Park	Unsatisfactory	Satisfactory	Total
No	401	107	508
Yes	180	50	230
Total	581	157	738

16.7   The director of the state department of motor vehicles is concerned about the high level of employee dissatisfaction in the department. To alleviate this problem, he hires a statistical analyst to investigate the attitudes of employees. The analyst believes that the primary source of dissatisfaction is the type of job held by the employee—hourly wage or salary. To test this hypothesis, she obtains data pertaining to whether the employee is paid hourly or is salaried and whether he or she is satisfied or dissatisfied with the job. These data are cross-tabulated in the accompanying table. Percentage the table and calculate gamma. Is there a relationship between type of job and job satisfaction?

	Type of Job		
Attitude toward Job	Hourly	Salary	Total
Dissatisfied	194	54	248
Satisfied	278	85	363
Total	472	139	611

16.8   The data analyst from Problem 16.7 also obtained information regarding whether the employee was on a standard 8-hour shift or on flextime. The cross-tabulation between these two variables appears below. Percentage the table and calculate gamma. Is there a relationship between the employment status of employees (shift versus flextime) and job satisfaction?

Attitude toward Job	Employment Status		
	Shift	Flextime	Total
Dissatisfied	194	55	249
Satisfied	186	176	362
Total	380	231	611

16.9 The personnel department of a small city has compiled the accompanying data regarding city employees. The data consist of the age of employees and the probability of their receiving a job promotion. On the basis of these data, how should the department advise job applicants who seek employment with the city?

Probability of Promotion	Age		
	30 or Less	31–50	51 or Greater
Low	17%	9%	65%
Medium	56%	15%	22%
High	27%	76%	13%
Total	100%	100%	100%

16.10 A Ph.D. student in public administration has studied the relationship between the quality of municipal bureaucracy and the economic development of cities. She hypothesizes that the higher the quality of the city bureaucracy (as measured by such factors as innovativeness, efficiency, and responsiveness), the greater the economic development. By this hypothesis, she assumes that bureaucratic quality leads to economic development. To test this hypothesis, she sent out questionnaires to a random sample of 120 cities with a population between 50,000 and 100,000. Based on these data, she assembles the accompanying cross-tabulation.

Bureaucratic Quality	Economic Development		
	Low	Medium	High
High	6	8	16
Medium	12	16	22
Low	16	14	10

Percentage the table appropriately and calculate gamma. Is there a relationship between bureaucratic quality and economic development? (**Hint:** First reorganize the table according to the standard format for constructing and analyzing contingency tables presented in Chapter 15.)

16.11 In her dissertation, the Ph.D. student from Problem 16.10 writes that the relationship between the quality of a municipal bureaucracy and the economic development of a city is causal—that is, that higher-quality bureaucracy leads to higher economic development. Evaluate her claim of causality. What conditions would have to be met in order to establish that this relationship is causal? Does the cross-tabulation between the two variables (presented in standard format) bear on the question of causality? How? Explain your answer. (**Hint:** See Chapter 3, on research design and causal inference.)

16.12 Paul Sabatier, a human relations theorist working for Warm and Fuzzy, Inc., believes that workers who work in cooperatives are more satisfied than workers who do not. He surveys 50 cab drivers who work in cooperatives and 30 cab drivers who do not work in cooperatives. All are asked whether they are satisfied with their job. From the data in the accompanying table, calculate the percentage difference, gamma, lambda, and chi-square. What do you conclude?

	Type of Organization	
Job Satisfaction	Noncooperative	Cooperative
Not satisfied	13	29
Satisfied	17	21

16.13 Organizational analyst Paula McClain is examining the Peter Principle, which contends that people will rise in an organization until they reach their level of incompetence. She feels that this means that proportionately more competent people will be found at the lower level of the organization. To test this question, she decides to ask students to rate assistant professors, associate professors, and full professors; based on these ratings, she classified the competence of professors as high, medium, or low (deans are excluded to avoid biasing the results). Interpret the accompanying table; calculate any necessary statistics.

	Academic Rank			
Competence	Assistant	Associate	Full	Total
Low	27	38	24	89
Medium	60	91	8	159
High	106	38	8	152
Total	193	167	40	400

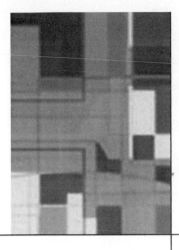

CHAPTER 17

Statistical Control Table Analysis

T he previous two chapters discussed methods for examining the relationship between two variables measured at either the ordinal or the nominal level. In that discussion, when a pair of variables were found to be associated statistically, we inevitably assumed that they were, in fact, related, in the sense that changes in one could be expected to lead to changes in the other. Conversely, when the variables were not associated statistically, we assumed that the opposite was true.

Unfortunately for the data analyst, this is not always a correct assumption. A simple example should persuade you how this assumption can lead you astray.

Suppose that you are a staff analyst working for the police department of a fairly large community. The mayor is concerned with a recent upsurge in juvenile crime and asks that you prepare a report advising him how the increase in crime can be combated. In researching the issue, you discover an interesting phenomenon. In those precincts of the city in which ice cream consumption is high, the rate of juvenile crime is low; and in the precincts in which consumption is low, juvenile crime reaches high levels. Thus, across the precincts of the city, the higher the ice cream consumption, the lower is the rate of juvenile crime. As Table 17.1 shows, according to any measure of association, this relationship is strong.

Table 17.1

Relationship between Juvenile Crime and Ice Cream Consumption

Rate of Juvenile Crime	Ice Cream Consumption	
	Low	High
Low	25%	80%
High	75%	20%
Total	100%	100%
	($n = 20$ precincts)	($n = 25$ precincts)

Using these data, should you advise the mayor that you have found the answer to the crime problem—to subsidize the sale of ice cream so that it may be offered at bargain prices to the rampaging juvenile hordes? Is satisfying their hunger for ice cream likely to appease their appetite for more costly antisocial behavior? After all, the data indicate that ice cream consumption and juvenile crime are strongly associated inversely.

Even though Table 17.1 would seem to support this policy response, somehow the proposed solution does not sit well. You would probably feel more than a little silly—not to mention fearful for your job—were you to inform the mayor that a scoop of chocolate (or perhaps rocky road or vanilla) is the answer to the problem of juvenile crime. But if ice cream is not the answer, then what is? And why are ice cream consumption and juvenile crime rates associated statistically, when, in fact, one almost certainly has nothing whatsoever to do with the other?

The answers to these two questions are interrelated. First, one variable that may bear on the rate of juvenile crime is the socioeconomic status (SES) of the precincts across the city. SES is a social science concept intended to assess the social status of a precinct based on the income, education, and occupational prestige of its residents (SES can also be measured at the level of individual respondents). For a number of reasons (such as stable home life, access to better education and job opportunities), juveniles living in high-SES precincts—those in which income, education, and occupational status are high—commit fewer crimes than do their peers living in less fortunate circumstances in low-SES precincts. As for the second question, in high-SES precincts parents and children have more money to purchase ice cream than do their counterparts living in low-SES precincts; therefore, ice cream consumption is higher in the former areas than in the latter. Note the circumstance created by these two relationships. In high-SES precincts, youths both eat more ice cream *and* commit fewer crimes than do youths living in low-SES precincts. Thus, because of the relationship of each variable to the SES of the precinct, ice cream consumption and the rate of juvenile crime *appear* to be related, when, in fact, they are quite independent of one another. These relationships can be depicted graphically:

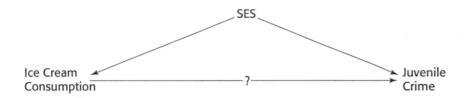

The type of reasoning illustrated in this example is typical of the data analysis process. The analyst finds that two variables are associated statistically (ice cream consumption and juvenile crime). She then tries to understand *why* the variables are associated. (Recall from Chapter 3 how important theory—a meaningful substantive explanation—is to understanding and interpreting a statistical relationship.) Are the two variables actually related in the sense that changes in one are likely to produce changes in the other, or is their apparent relationship attributable to the action of a *third* variable (SES of the precinct)? To address this question, the researcher must introduce the third variable explicitly into the analysis. She then reexamines the relationship between the original two variables, taking into account the effect of the third variable. The technique used to incorporate a third variable into the analysis is called *controlling for or holding constant* the third variable (controlling for SES or holding constant SES) or, more simply, **statistical controls,** and the third variable is often called the **control variable.**

This chapter elaborates statistical control techniques for the analysis of relationships among three or more variables measured at the ordinal or nominal levels. The chapter both explains the use of these techniques and illustrates several likely results of introducing a third variable into the examination of a two-variable relationship. Different possible results are illustrated in a series of examples.

Controlling for a Third Variable

The procedure by which the researcher controls for the effect of a third variable on a bivariate relationship is deceptively simple. *He or she examines the relationship between the original two variables within each of the categories of the control variable and compares the results across the categories of the control.* The examples that follow illustrate the procedure.

Example 1: Alcoholism in the Postal Service—The Effect of Hierarchical Position

The U.S. Postal Service has become alarmed by recent unsubstantiated reports from employees that the pressures of the workplace, such as large volumes of mail and very short time deadlines, contribute to alcoholism. The Postal Service has commissioned a blue ribbon panel to investigate the problem. The panel collected data from post

Table 17.2

Relationship between Hierarchy and Alcoholism

Raw Data

Alcoholism	Hierarchy		Total
	Nonsupervisor	Supervisor	
Nonalcoholic	115	60	175
Alcoholic	5	20	25
Total	120	80	200

Percentaged Data

Alcoholism	Hierarchy	
	Nonsupervisor	Supervisor
Nonalcoholic	96%	75%
Alcoholic	4%	25%
Total	100%	100%
	($n = 120$)	($n = 80$)

office employees working in offices in Ripple, Montana; Thunderbird, New Mexico; and Gallo, Mississippi.

As a first step the panel hypothesized a positive relationship between position of the employee in the post office hierarchy and rate of alcoholism. They reasoned that those holding supervisory positions were under greater pressure than those holding nonsupervisory jobs and, therefore, would be more likely to turn to alcohol to relieve tensions of work. The measure of alcoholism used by the study team is called the Harris Test. The test identifies with 95% accuracy whether the respondent is an alcoholic or a nonalcoholic. The relationship between hierarchical position (nonsupervisor or supervisor) and alcoholism (alcoholic or nonalcoholic) found by the study team is displayed in Table 17.2 in both raw (nonpercentaged) and percentaged form.

Because the table shows that supervisors are more likely than nonsupervisors to be alcoholics by a difference of 21% (25% − 4%), most members of the panel feel that these data offer support for the hypothesis that hierarchical position is related to alcoholism. However, one investigator is not convinced. He maintains that it is not hierarchical position at all that leads post office employees to drink; rather, it is whether they have been selected and are made to operate the ziptronic machine—a demonic device that puts high stress on the operator to identify zip codes printed on letters at an extremely rapid rate. Part of the process of selecting new supervisors is to identify employees who can succeed in this high-pressure job. Because supervisors operate the ziptronic more frequently than do nonsupervisors, he argues that it only appears that hierarchical position leads to alcoholism. In fact, if one were to control for the effects of operating the ziptronic, one would find no relationship between hierarchy and alcoholism. His argument can be depicted graphically:

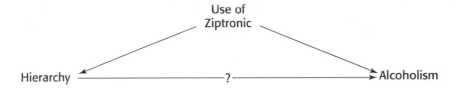

The statistical control process involves three major steps:

Step 1: Partition the sample according to the categories of the control variable. In the current example, 90 postal employees have operated the ziptronic, and the remaining 110 have not.

Step 2: Prepare the cross-tabulation between the original two variables for each of the subsamples defined by the control variable in Step 1. Percentage each of these tables separately (refer to Chapter 15 if you do not recall how to percentage a table). In this example, the researcher would construct two distinct cross-tabulations between hierarchical position and alcoholism: one for those employees who have operated the ziptronic and the second for those who have not operated the ziptronic. Table 17.3 presents the results obtained according to this procedure for the post office data. Both the non-percentaged and the percentaged cross-tabulations are displayed in the table.

Table 17.3

Cross-Tabulation of Subsamples

Employees Who Have Operated Ziptronic (*n* = 90)

Employees Who Have Not Operated Ziptronic (*n* = 110)

Raw Data

Alcoholism	Hierarchy Non-supervisor	Supervisor	Total	**Alcoholism**	Hierarchy Non-supervisor	Supervisor	Total
Nonalcoholic	29	45	74	Nonalcoholic	86	15	101
Alcoholic	1	15	16	Alcoholic	4	5	9
Total	30	60	90	Total	90	20	110

Percentaged Data

Alcoholism	Hierarchy Nonsupervisor	Supervisor	**Alcoholism**	Hierarchy Nonsupervisor	Supervisor
Nonalcoholic	97%	75%	Nonalcoholic	96%	75%
Alcoholic	3%	25%	Alcoholic	4%	25%
Total	100%	100%	Total	100%	100%
	(*n* = 30)	(*n* = 60)		(*n* = 90)	(*n* = 20)

It is important to recognize that the data presented in Table 17.3 are simply an *elaboration* of the cross-tabulation displayed in Table 17.2. Table 17.3 shows how the sample of 200 postal employees is distributed with respect to operation of the ziptronic (have operated the ziptronic, have not operated the ziptronic). For example, Table 17.2 shows that, in all, there are 175 non-alcoholics in the sample; Table 17.3 indicates that 74 of these employees have operated the ziptronic, and the remaining 101 have not. Similarly, of the total of 25 alcoholics in the sample (Table 17.2), 16 have operated the ziptronic; 9 have not (Table 17.3). With respect to hierarchical position, of the total of 120 nonsupervisors in the sample (Table 17.2), 30 have operated the ziptronic, whereas the other 90 have not (Table 17.3). Finally, of the 80 supervisors in the sample (Table 17.2), 60 have operated the ziptronic, and the remaining 20 have not (Table 17.3).

Because Table 17.3 elaborates the original cross-tabulation presented in Table 17.2, this research method is sometimes called the *elaboration model.* Make sure that you can follow the correspondences relating the two tables outlined in the previous paragraph. You should be able to see that the figures displayed in the cross-tabulations of Table 17.3 are perfectly consistent with those of Table 17.2.

Step 3: Interpret the cross-tabulations obtained for each of the categories of the control variable. This step is by far the most difficult in the statistical control procedure, but a modicum of reasoning will greatly simplify matters.

Consider the argument made by the investigator on the study team who introduced the issue of the ziptronic machines. If he is correct in his hypothesis that operating the ziptronic (rather than hierarchical position) is the actual cause of alcoholism among postal employees, then once the effect of the ziptronic has been taken into account, hierarchical position should make no difference in the rate of alcoholism. Another way of stating this conclusion is that, within the categories of the control variable (have operated the ziptronic; have not operated the ziptronic), one should find the same rate of alcoholism for supervisors and nonsupervisors. In other words, supervisory and nonsupervisory personnel who have operated the ziptronic *should not differ* in rate of alcoholism. Similarly, supervisors and nonsupervisors who have not operated the ziptronic also should not differ in rate of alcoholism. These data would indicate that after taking into account (controlling for) the effect of operating the ziptronic, hierarchical position bears no relationship to the rate of alcoholism.

This logic encapsulates one side of the picture. The expectation is that operating the ziptronic machine, rather than hierarchical position, is the actual cause of alcoholism among postal employees. What would one expect to find if the *opposite* is the case—that hierarchical position, rather than operation of the ziptronic, causes alcoholism? Since the operation of the ziptronic is not related to alcoholism, then one would expect to find the same relationship between hierarchical position and alcoholism as displayed in the original cross-tabulation (Table 17.2)—regardless of whether the employees have operated the ziptronic machine. Operationally, in each of the control tables (the separate tables cross-tabulating hierarchical position and alcoholism within each category of the control variable, operation of the ziptronic—Table 17.3), one should find that the relationship between hierarchical position and alcoholism is identical to that found in Table 17.2. These data would indicate that even when the effect of operating the ziptronic has been taken into account, hierarchical position and alcoholism remain related.

These two data expectations outline polar explanations for the causes of alcoholism among post office personnel. According to the first, if operation of the ziptronic machine (rather than hierarchical position) is the actual cause of alcoholism, then when the effect of operating the ziptronic is taken into account, the original relationship between hierarchy and alcoholism should disappear. That is, when use of the ziptronic is considered, hierarchical position is found to make no difference in the rate of alcoholism. According to the second, if hierarchical position (rather than operation of the ziptronic machine) is the actual cause of alcoholism, then when the effect of operating the ziptronic is taken into account, the original relationship between hierarchy and alcoholism should persist. Therefore, even when use of the ziptronic is considered, hierarchy continues to make a difference in the rate of alcoholism.

With these expectations in mind, we can interpret the data displayed in Table 17.3. To which polar situation do the percentaged cross-tabulations more closely correspond? These data show overwhelming support for the second explanation. When the effects of operation of the ziptronic have been controlled, hierarchical position is related to alcoholism in exactly the same manner as in the original, uncontrolled cross-tabulation in Table 17.2. Regardless of whether they have used the ziptronic machines, 25% of the supervisors are alcoholics, as compared with only 3% of the nonsupervisors, a difference of 22%. Because the relationship between hierarchy and the rate of alcoholism is unaffected by the introduction of the ziptronic variable into the analysis, these data lend support to the conclusion that hierarchical position (rather than operation of the ziptronic) is a cause of alcoholism among postal employees. This finding offers some evidence of a nonspurious relationship between these two variables (see Chapter 3, on causal inference).

Example 2: Performance on the Civil Service Examination— A Case of Favoritism in Blakely?

The *Daily Mirror,* the newspaper for Blakely, Vermont, has recently published a series of troublesome articles accusing the Blakely city government of favoritism in testing and hiring job applicants. The articles charge Blakely officials with giving hiring preference to those whom they know, rather than the most qualified applicants. One article quotes an unsuccessful job candidate: "Unless you know someone in Blakely city hall, you're not going to get a pass on the civil service examination. And without the pass, you don't make it onto the hire list. Check the list—most of the people on it have friends in city government. The key is to know somebody." Mayor Kent B. Fooled is disturbed by these charges and appoints his staff assistant, Evan Michael, to look into them.

To do so, Michael draws a random sample of 335 job applicants for analysis from the Blakely central personnel department. Fortunately, the application forms contained a number of questions useful for his purposes. One question asked whether the applicant knew anyone who worked for Blakely, and another gathered the usual background information on education. Department records also show whether the applicant has passed or failed the Blakely civil service examination.

Michael begins by cross-tabulating whether the applicant knew someone in Blakely city government (previous contact) with the information on whether she or he passed the civil service exam (test performance). Table 17.4 displays the cross-tabulation.

Like the mayor, Michael was disturbed by the results of the cross-tabulation. He had expected the charges aired in the newspaper articles to be unfounded, but in this sample, job applicants who did not know someone in city government failed the civil service examination at a rate 20% higher than did those without previous contact with a Blakely employee (54% − 34%). Michael, however, suspects that a third variable may be responsible for this surprising relationship: *education.* He reasons that level of education will certainly affect performance on the civil service exam. He feels

Table 17.4	

Relationship between Test Performance and Prior Contact

Raw Data

Test Performance	Prior Contact		
	No	Yes	Total
Fail	70	70	140
Pass	60	135	195
Total	130	205	335

Percentaged Data

Test Performance	Prior Contact	
	No	Yes
Fail	54%	34%
Pass	46%	66%
Total	100%	100%
	($n = 130$)	($n = 205$)

that the only reason that those with previous contact appear to fare better on the test is that they are more likely to have completed higher levels of education.

Michael knows that Blakely draws a lot of its job applicants from the local community college (Blakely Tech, home of the "Fighting Calculators," a perennial athletic power). He and other Blakely employees have attended several job fairs at the college and spoken before classes and other groups there; Blakely also works with the college on an internship program. Thus, college education puts potential job applicants in contact with Blakely city government, and higher education likewise helps them pass the civil service examination. To test these ideas empirically, Michael intends to introduce education (college graduate; not college graduate) into the analysis. The anticipated relationships among the three variables are shown in the following diagram:

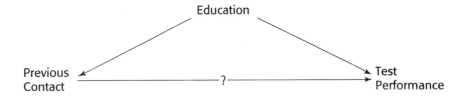

Michael then performs the following steps:

Step 1: Partition the sample according to the categories of the control variable. In this example, education is the control variable and consists of two categories: those who are college graduates and those who are not. Of the 335 individuals in the sample, 200 are college graduates and the remaining 135 are not.

Step 2: Assemble the cross-tabulation between the original two variables for each of the subsamples defined by the control variable in Step 1. Percentage each of these tables separately according to the procedure outlined in Chapter 15. In this instance, two cross-tabulations between previous contact and test performance would be obtained: the first based on those individuals who are college graduates and the second based on those individuals who are not. Table 17.5 displays the results obtained according to this procedure in the sample of applicants for positions in Blakely city government.

You should satisfy yourself that the elaboration of Table 17.4 presented in the cross-tabulations of Table 17.5 is perfectly consistent with the original data.

Step 3: Interpret the cross-tabulations obtained for each of the categories of the control variable. The logic of this process is precisely the same as that elaborated in the previous example (hierarchy–ziptronic–alcoholism).

If education (rather than previous contact) is the actual cause of performance on the civil service examination, then when the effect of education is taken into account, the original relationship between contact and test performance should disappear; that is, when the effect of education has been controlled, previous contact should make no difference in test performance. Conversely, if contact (rather than education) is the actual cause of performance on the

Table 17.5

Cross-Tabulation of Subsamples

Raw Data

College Graduates (n = 200)

Test Performance	Previous Contact		
	No	Yes	Total
Fail	10	40	50
Pass	30	120	150
Total	40	160	200

Not College Graduates (n = 135)

Test Performance	Previous Contact		
	No	Yes	Total
Fail	60	30	90
Pass	30	15	45
Total	90	45	135

Percentaged Data

Test Performance	Previous Contact	
	No	Yes
Fail	25%	25%
Pass	75%	75%
Total	100%	100%
	(n = 40)	(n = 160)

Test Performance	Previous Contact	
	No	Yes
Fail	67%	67%
Pass	33%	33%
Total	100%	100%
	(n = 90)	(n = 45)

examination, then when education is taken into account, the original relationship found between previous contact and test performance in Table 17.4 should persist; that is, even when the effect of education has been considered, contact should continue to make a difference in performance on the civil service examination.

The percentaged cross-tabulations presented in Table 17.5 show that once education has been controlled, those with and without previous contact fail the civil service examination with equal frequency. Among the college graduates, 25% of both groups fail the exam; and among the noncollege graduates, 67% of both groups fail. Thus, because within the categories of education previous contact makes no difference in test performance, these data warrant the conclusion that contact and performance on the civil service examination are not related. (If they were related, one would expect that previous contact would make a difference in test performance even when education was taken into account.)

Although prior contact with a Blakely city official *appeared* to affect test performance in the original bivariate cross-tabulation (Table 17.4), the introduction of the control variable (education) made the relationship disappear. Thus, in this example, contact is not a cause of test performance. Instead, previous contact is a *spurious* variable—one that initially appears to be related to the dependent variable but whose effect vanishes in the presence of the control variable.

Table 17.5 also demonstrates that, regardless of prior contact with a Blakely city official, the percentage of college graduates failing the examination (25%) is much smaller than the percentage of nongraduates who fail (67%). This finding indicates that it is *education* that leads to test performance. For both those who have and those who have not had prior contact, the higher the education, the better is the performance on the examination. The strength of this relationship can be seen in Table 17.6, which cross-tabulates education and performance on the civil service examination. This cross-tabulation is constructed from the control tables in Table 17.5. The relationship between education and test performance persists even when the effect of previous contact has been controlled.

Evan Michael reports these findings to the mayor. The mayor instructs him to write a letter to the *Daily Mirror* explaining that a careful look at all the data undermines the charges of favoritism in Blakely city government. Indeed, the results show that Blakely has a strong commitment to merit since those with college education pass the civil service examination at a much higher rate. The editors agree to publish a follow-up article, placing the earlier series of articles in the proper context. Impressed by the analytic power of multivariate methods, Michael returned to Blakely Tech to take more courses in applied statistics for public administration (these courses use a certain beloved textbook).

Table 17.6

Relationship between Education and Test Performance

Raw Data

Test Performance	Not College Graduate	College Graduate	Total
	Education		
Fail	90	50	140
Pass	45	150	195
Total	135	200	335

Percentaged Data

Test Performance	Not College Graduate	College Graduate
	Education	
Fail	67%	25%
Pass	33%	75%
Total	100%	100%
	($n = 135$)	($n = 200$)

Example 2½: Race, Education, and Complaints—
A Developmental Sequence

Suppose that as an employee of Lillian County government, you were interested in why whites seem to complain more often about road conditions than do nonwhites. Imagine further that the county administrator had assembled data in a cross-tabulation, based on a survey of county residents, to support this claim. The relationship in the cross-tabulation might closely resemble the pattern found in Table 17.4, with race (nonwhite versus white) as the independent variable and complaints about road conditions (no complaints versus complaints) as the dependent variable. In that case, whites would appear to complain at a much higher rate than nonwhites (66% − 46% = 20%). Why?

A good next step would be, as in the previous example, to control for *education*. You might reason that whites are more likely to have higher levels of education, and education leads to higher expectations concerning the level of services government should provide and more confidence to voice these demands for better services to county officials (a polite phrase for "complain"). Following this logic, if you were to introduce education (college graduate; not college graduate) as a control variable into the analysis (as in the previous example), you would probably find a data pattern very similar to the one displayed in Table 17.5: Race would no longer make a difference in the frequency of complaints from residents, but level of education would make a huge difference.

In contrast to the previous example, however, race is *not* a spurious variable in this case. Instead, race leads to differences in access to education, and these differences, in turn, lead to differences in the rate of complaining to county officials. Thus, this example illustrates a developmental sequence, in which education acts as an *intervening* variable.

The difference between the two examples lies in the underlying causal structure of the variables. In this example, we are sure that race leads to education, which leads to complaints. In the previous example, education led to *both* prior contact with Blakely city officials and passing the civil service examination. Hence, prior contact was not the reason that applicants passed the exam—this factor was actually obscuring the effect of the true causal variable, education. Once education was introduced as the control variable, it quickly became apparent that prior contact was spurious.

What lesson do these two examples hold for public and nonprofit managers? When the effect of an independent variable disappears with the introduction of a control variable, the reason may be either a spurious relationship or a developmental sequence. Both situations produce the same pattern of relationships in the control tables. To decide which situation is more likely, you must carefully review and logically analyze the causal structure underlying the independent, control, and dependent variables.

Example 3: Guaranteed Annual Income—A Case of Interaction

The previous two examples have illustrated polar data analysis situations. In the first, introduction of a control variable (operation of the ziptronic) into the analysis had no effect on the original bivariate relationship (hierarchy versus alcoholism). In the second, the control variable (education) was totally responsible for the apparent—but not actual—relationship originally found between two variables (previous contact with city officials and test performance).

A third situation that frequently occurs in the analysis of data is called *interaction* or *specification*. In this situation, the relationship between two variables changes markedly depending on the category of the control variable; that is, the categories of the control variable specify the nature of the relationship between the independent and dependent variables.

Several types of interactive relationships are possible. For example, in one category of a control variable, there may be no relationship between the independent and dependent variables; whereas in the second category of the control variable, there may be a strong positive or negative relationship. As an illustration, consider the likely effect on college major of attending career planning sessions, controlling for the year of the student in college. Among new students, one is likely to find a strong relationship between attending the meetings and choice of major; however, among graduating seniors, one is likely to find no relationship.

In a second type of interaction, the relationship between the independent and dependent variables can change direction (positive to negative or vice versa) contingent on the category of the control variable. The following example elaborates a three-variable relationship of this kind.

The federal government has been experimenting with a guaranteed annual income program (GAI). Volatile policy debate centers around the effects of this federal largesse. When people are guaranteed an income, are they more likely to spend all the money or to save at least a portion of it? To examine the effects of GAI, a staff analyst is appointed. He assembles data from 200 individuals who have participated in GAI and a matching sample of 200 who have not.

His first concern is whether those who participated in the GAI were more likely to save money than those who did not. Therefore, he cross-tabulates participation in GAI (no; yes) with money saved during the program (no; yes). The results are presented in Table 17.7.

This table reveals no relationship between participation in the GAI program and saving behavior. Those who participated in the program were just as likely to save (or not save) money as those who did not. However, the analyst is curious about the effect on this relationship of the individual's past history of saving money. He believes that the ability to save money is learned over time; therefore, he reasons that those who have a past history of saving money will do so again under the GAI. Those who lack this history (or "learning") will fail in this pursuit once again. This hypothesis calls for the introduction of the saving history of the respondent (have saved in the past, have not saved in the past) into the analysis as a control variable. We omit detailed elaboration of the first two steps of the control procedure and simply present in Table 17.8 the two cross-tabulations obtained when this control variable is introduced. (If these steps remain unclear to you, review the first two examples developed in the chapter.)

The control tables presented in Table 17.8 resemble neither of the polar situations developed in the first two examples. Instead, Table 17.8 shows that the past

Table 17.7

Relationship between GAI and Saving Money

Raw Data

Saved Money	Guaranteed Annual Income (GAI)		Total
	No	Yes	
No	100	100	200
Yes	100	100	200
Total	200	200	400

Percentaged Data

Saved Money	Guaranteed Annual Income (GAI)	
	No	Yes
No	50%	50%
Yes	50%	50%
Total	100%	100%
	($n = 200$)	($n = 200$)

Table 17.8

Cross-Tabulation of Subsamples

Raw Data

Have Saved in Past ($n = 220$)

Saved Money	GAI		Total
	No	Yes	
No	50	40	90
Yes	60	70	130
Total	110	110	220

Have Not Saved in Past ($n = 180$)

Saved Money	GAI		Total
	No	Yes	
No	50	60	110
Yes	40	30	70
Total	90	90	180

Percentaged Data

Saved Money	GAI	
	No	Yes
No	45%	36%
Yes	55%	64%
Total	100%	100%
	($n = 110$)	($n = 110$)

Saved Money	GAI	
	No	Yes
No	56%	67%
Yes	44%	33%
Total	100%	100%
	($n = 90$)	($n = 90$)

history of saving *specifies* the relationship between participation in the GAI program and saving money. Among the individuals who had a past history of saving money, participation in the program is related positively to saving. Note that program participants saved money more frequently over the period of the study than did nonparticipants. In the subsample of respondents with a past history of saving, 64% of participants in the GAI saved money, compared with 55% of the nonparticipants. These data suggest that for this subsample, the GAI encouraged and led to saving behavior.

In contrast, for those individuals who had no past history of saving money, participation in the GAI had exactly the opposite effect. In this subsample of respondents, participants in the program saved money less frequently than did nonparticipants, 33% versus 44%, a difference in saving behavior of 11%. Thus, among those who had not saved money in the past, participation in the GAI is related negatively to saving during the period of the study. In this subsample, the GAI seemed to discourage saving behavior. In an interactive relationship such as this one, the control variable must be taken into account in order to understand the relationship between the independent and dependent variables.

This example is important not only because it demonstrates an interactive relationship but also because it shows that a relationship between two variables may not be manifest *unless* a control variable is incorporated into the analysis. In the original, noncontrolled cross-tabulation displayed in Table 17.7, participation in the Guaranteed Annual Income program does *not* appear to be related to saving behavior. Participants in the program were just as likely to save (or not save) money as were nonparticipants. However, the controlled cross-tabulations presented in Table 17.8 indicate that, when the effect of past history of saving is considered, participation in the GAI is clearly related to saving behavior. Among individuals who had saved in the past, the GAI led to further saving; among those who had no past history of saving, just the opposite was true.

This example illustrates an important lesson in data analysis: Even when a bivariate cross-tabulation suggests that no relationship exists between two variables, the variables can still be related, but in a more complicated way. The introduction of a third, control variable can reveal a more subtle relationship. In the current example, failure to take into account a control variable suppressed the relationship between the independent and dependent variables. For this reason this type of situation is sometimes called a *suppressor* relationship.

The converse is also true: A cross-tabulation that demonstrates a statistical association between two variables cannot ensure that the two variables are actually related. It was on this point that the chapter began. Whereas ice cream consumption appeared to be related to juvenile crime, controlling for the socioeconomic status (SES) of the precinct will cause this relationship to disappear. In fact, SES—not ice cream consumption—is a cause of juvenile crime. Ice cream consumption only appeared to be related to crime, because individuals living in high-SES precincts are likely both to eat more ice cream and to commit fewer crimes than are those living in low-SES precincts. (Another example of such a spurious relationship was elaborated earlier, based on the relationships between previous contact, education, and performance on the civil service examination.) It is these kinds of complexities that make data analysis exciting and frustrating at the same time.

Example 4: Support for Performance-Based Pay— Evidence of Joint Causation

The mayor of the city of Athenia has proposed to the city council that Athenia change compensation systems. As do many cities in the southeastern United States, Athenia determines employee pay primarily on the basis of years (seniority) in government service, in a grade-and-step system. The mayor believes that motivation and productivity of city workers would improve if Athenia were to shift to a performance-based pay system. Under the mayor's plan, supervisors would meet annually with individual employees to set performance goals, employees would be evaluated 1 year later on accomplishment of the objectives, and pay increases would be tied to the performance evaluation. The city council is impressed with the pay plan, but before taking action, it authorizes the mayor to conduct a study of employee reaction to the plan and to report back with the results.

The mayor appoints two top MPAs in her office, Megan Samantha and Philip Joseph, to carry out the study. Because performance-based pay is thought to increase employee morale—because employees have greater involvement in establishing work goals and can move up the pay ladder more quickly than in a grade-and-step system—the mayor expects to find strong support for her plan. Samantha and Joseph decide to survey a representative sample of 212 Athenia employees to ascertain their attitudes and opinions toward the mayor's proposal. They are surprised to find that only a bare majority of city workers, 52% ($n = 111$), favor the mayor's plan, whereas 48% ($n = 101$) oppose it. Good analysts that they are, Samantha and Joseph decide to undertake further study.

They believe that prior experience in the private sector may help explain the results. Performance-based pay systems are much more common in private business than in government. Thus, Samantha and Joseph cross-tabulate support for performance-based pay (no or yes) in the Athenia sample by whether the employee has had work experience in the private sector (no or yes). They anticipate that city workers with a background in the private sector will be more favorable toward the new pay plan. Table 17.9 displays the cross-tabulation.

Just as Samantha and Joseph had expected, support for performance-based pay is higher by 9% for employees who have work experience in the private sector (57%) than for those who do not (48%). Still, the researchers would like to identify other factors that may account for the attitudes of Athenia workers and that would help them to devise a strategy for building employee acceptance.

One variable that occurs to them is job classification as either supervisory or non-supervisory personnel. The mayor's pay plan would add to the burden on supervisors by giving them a larger role in setting goals for employees and, especially, in evaluating their performance. Although Athenia supervisory personnel already have evaluation responsibilities, according to city records, more than 95% of the time, supervisors give employees performance ratings in the highest two categories. Samantha and

Table 17.9

Relationship between Employee Experience in the Private Sector and Support for Performance-Based Pay

Raw Data

Support for Performance-Based Pay	Private Sector Experience		
	No	Yes	Total
No	55	46	101
Yes	50	61	111
Total	105	107	212

Percentaged Data

Support for Performance-Based Pay	Private Sector Experience	
	No	Yes
No	52%	43%
Yes	48%	57%
Total	100%	100%
	($n = 105$)	($n = 107$)

Joseph would like to think that Athenia city government has a superior work force—but they doubt that it's that good. Instead, they suspect that, because performance appraisal is not tied strongly to pay, it has become largely a pro forma exercise for supervisors and employees. By linking pay raises to performance, however, the mayor's plan could radically alter the nature of evaluation: not only would it increase the workload on supervisors, but also (with pay at stake) it could make the process more confrontational and open the door to much-dreaded litigation. Of course, it might just as well produce greater teamwork and collaboration between supervisors and employees; yet Samantha and Joseph realize that when organizations introduce change without laying the appropriate groundwork, members often fear the worst. Their next step is to compare support for performance-based pay for supervisory versus non-supervisory personnel, again taking into account work experience in the private sector, which has been shown to have an effect on these attitudes (Table 17.9). Table 17.10 presents the cross-tabulation of support for performance-based pay and work experience in the private sector, controlling for employee status as supervisory or non-supervisory.

The percentaged data in the control tables lend insight into the attitudes of the Athenia employees. First, the tables show that even when job classification as supervisory versus nonsupervisory is taken into account (controlled statistically), prior

Table 17.10

Cross-Tabulation of Subsamples

Raw Data

Supervisory Personnel (*n* = 40)

Support for Performance-Based Pay	Private Sector Experience		
	No	Yes	Total
No	13	11	24
Yes	7	9	16
Total	20	20	40

Nonsupervisory Personnel (*n* = 172)

Support for Performance-Based Pay	Private Sector Experience		
	No	Yes	Total
No	42	35	77
Yes	43	52	95
Total	85	87	172

Percentaged Data

Support for Performance-Based Pay	Private Sector Experience	
	No	Yes
No	65%	55%
Yes	35%	45%
Total	100%	100%
	(*n* = 20)	(*n* = 20)

Support for Performance-Based Pay	Private Sector Experience	
	No	Yes
No	49%	40%
Yes	51%	60%
Total	100%	100%
	(*n* = 85)	(*n* = 87)

work experience in the private sector continues to have the same effect on support for performance-based pay. Whether the employee is a supervisor or not, private sector job experience increases support for the proposed pay system by 10% and 9%, respectively. These findings reinforce the original relationship investigated in Table 17.9, which also yielded a 9% difference. Thus, the control tables provide evidence that the relationship between private sector work experience and support for performance-based pay is *nonspurious;* that is, in the presence of a third variable, employee job classification, the relationship persists. (The control tables cannot prove nonspuriousness, however, because other variables may turn out to be responsible for the relationship observed in Table 17.9.)

What about the effect of the job classification variable on support for performance-based pay? Samantha and Joseph had anticipated that supervisors would be less receptive to the new pay plan than would nonsupervisory personnel. Comparing supervisors with nonsupervisors across the two control tables, Samantha and Joseph find that the latter group is considerably more favorable. Among those without background in the private sector, nonsupervisors are more supportive of performance-based pay 51% to 35%, a difference of 16%. Similarly, among city employees who have worked in the private sector, nonsupervisors are again more favorable than supervisors by a margin of 15% (60% − 45%). For job classification, too, the table gives evidence of a *nonspurious* relationship: Classification produces substantial differences in support for performance-based pay, both for employees who have and for employees who do not have prior work experience in the private sector. (As before, the control tables cannot prove that this relationship is nonspurious because other variables may account for the association found.) Stated in another (equivalent) way, controlling for private sector work experience, supervisory status appears to decrease support for performance-based pay—just as Samantha and Joseph had expected.

Samantha and Joseph could proceed with further analysis of the employee survey data, identifying other variables that may affect employee attitudes on this dimension. In this instance, the strength of the original relationship between prior work experience in the private sector and support for performance-based pay (Table 17.9) is maintained when supervisory status is introduced (Table 17.10): City employees with work experience in the private sector remained more favorable toward the mayor's pay plan by 9% to 10%. Had prior work experience (independent variable) been related to supervisory status (control variable), however, the control tables would very likely have shown an attenuation in the original relationship. In that case, the issue that the analyst would have to consider is whether the percentage differences produced by the independent variable on the dependent variable, though reduced, are still large enough to conclude that the independent variable has an effect on the dependent variable. If, when the control variable is introduced, these percentage differences should fall close to zero, the control tables give evidence of a spurious relationship (see, for example, Table 17.5), rather than of joint causation.

The difference between joint causation and interaction can sometimes be difficult to detect and interpret. Perhaps the easiest way to differentiate between the two situations is to note that if the relationship is one of joint causation, then the relationship between the independent variable and the dependent variable will be consistent in the control tables, and the relationship between the control variable and the dependent variable will also be consistent. In Table 17.10, for example, private sector experience had the same (positive) relationship to support for performance-based pay for both supervisory and nonsupervisory personnel. Similarly, nonsupervisory personnel, both those who have private sector experience and those who have not, were more supportive of performance-based pay. In contrast, if the relationship is one of interaction, these relationships will not be consistent. You can see in Table 17.8, for example, that for those who had saved in the past, the Guaranteed Annual Income tended to increase saving behavior, but for those who had not saved in the past, the GAI tended to reduce saving behavior. If the independent and the control variables interact in affecting the dependent variable, the relationships will be very different within and across the control tables.

Results and Implications of Control Table Analysis

It is now possible to summarize four sets of possible empirical results—and their implications for further data analysis—of introducing a third (control) variable into a bivariate relationship. These sets are explained in Table 17.11. Examples of all four types of three-variable relationships have been elaborated in this chapter.

Table 17.11

Effect and Interpretation of Introducing a Third (Control) Variable into a Bivariate Relationship

Example	Empirical Effect of Introduction of Control Variable	Substantive Interpretation	Implications for Further Analysis
1.	Relationship between independent and dependent variables remains virtually unchanged (evidence of nonspuriousness)	Evidence that independent variable is related to dependent variable and that control variable is not related to dependent variable.	Eliminate control variable from further analysis. Continue analysis of relationship between independent and dependent variables.
2.	Relationship between independent and dependent variables virtually disappears.	Evidence that independent variable is not related to dependent variable and that control variable is related to dependent variable; relationship between independent and dependent variables may be spurious.	Eliminate independent variable from analysis. Control variable becomes new independent variable in further analysis.
2½	Same as in Example 2.	Evidence that underlying causal structure may be developmental sequence linking independent, control, and dependent variables.	Independent variable affects control variable, which, in turn, affects dependent variable. Control variable becomes new independent variable in further analysis, but independent variable remains important in causal sequence.
3.	Relationship between independent and dependent variables changes markedly, depending on the category of the control variable (evidence of interaction).	Evidence that relationship between the three variables is interactive. Control variable specifies relationship between independent and dependent variables.	Both independent and control variables must be considered in further analysis.
4.	Relationship between independent and dependent variables persists or is only somewhat attenuated in each control table; control variable is related to dependent variable (evidence of joint causation).	Evidence that both independent and control variables are related to dependent variable.	Both independent and control variables must be considered in further analysis.

Limitations of the Control Table Technique

Multivariate Relationships

Control table analysis is a relatively tractable procedure for the analysis of three-variable relationships. However, beyond three variables, its utility as an analytical tool rapidly dissipates. For example, if a researcher is interested in the determinants of performance on the civil service examination, she might hypothesize that not only race and education but also sex and motivation might have an impact. To assess the effect of each of these variables on test performance, she would have to examine the relationship between performance and one of the independent variables—say, race—controlling simultaneously for the other two independent variables—sex and motivation. At a minimum, this procedure will generate four control tables: the cross-tabulation between race and test performance for (1) males with high motivation, (2) males with low motivation, (3) females with high motivation, and (4) females with low motivation. If the motivation variable consists of three categories (such as low, medium, and high) rather than two, six control tables will result. The number of control tables is equal to the product of the number of categories of each of the control variables. Just as in the three-variable case, which has been the focus of this chapter, each of these control tables must be analyzed, compared, and interpreted for evidence not only of the simple effects of independent variables but also of possible interactions among them. Obviously the number of control tables quickly becomes unwieldy. In addition, each control table requires sufficient cases for reliable analysis. As a result, the total number of cases necessary in the sample grows larger and, hence, more expensive to collect.

For these reasons, control table analysis is performed only rarely for more than three variables simultaneously and almost never for more than four variables. Instead, in the face of multivariate complexity, researchers typically turn to more powerful, parsimonious methods, especially regression analysis (see Part VI). Although regression analysis is predicated on the interval measurement of variables, many researchers feel that the advantages of this technique more than compensate for any problems occasioned by treating ordinal data as interval.

The Source of Control Variables

The examples presented in this chapter have begun with plausible relationships between two variables and then introduced sensible control variables. An issue that has been ignored in this process is, Where do control variables originate?

Without question, the best source of meaningful control variables is good theory. Substantive theory intended to explain a given phenomenon will identify the crucial variables that must be considered in data analysis. In Chapter 3, on research design, theory was discussed as an essential component in drawing correct causal inferences. Other valuable sources of control variables are creative intuition, experience, previous research and published literature in an area, and expert opinion—including your boss's or your instructor's, even if you do not consider them experts.

This issue should be put in proper perspective. The source of appropriate control variables is a limitation of not only control table analysis but also all other forms of data analysis. The most powerful statistical techniques cannot compensate for a lack of solid substantive ideas and insights. Statistics is an excellent tool for testing hypothesized substantive relationships, but it is a poor one for suggesting these hypotheses.

Chapter Summary

Control table analysis is used to determine how a third variable may affect the association between two variables. Control table techniques illustrated in this chapter use percentage differences. Basically, one examines the relationship between the original two variables within each of the categories of the control variable and compares the results across the categories of the control. The process involves three steps. First, partition the sample according to the categories of the control variable. Second, assemble the cross-tabulation between the original two variables for each of the subsamples defined by the control; percentage each of these tables separately. Third, interpret and compare the cross-tabulations obtained for each of the categories of the control variable.

The control table technique can help detect the major types of statistical effects emanating from the introduction of a control variable into a bivariate relationship: evidence of (1) nonspuriousness, (2) spuriousness or (2½) a developmental sequence, (3) interaction or specification, and (4) joint causation. The general approach can be used with other analysis aids discussed in Chapter 16, such as the chi-square test and measures of association.

Problems

17.1   General Halftrack suspects that Colonel Sy Verleaf is discriminating in his promotions by promoting more whites than nonwhites. The following table illustrates this hypothesis:

	Race		
Status	Nonwhite	White	Total
Passed over	23	14	37
Promoted	27	86	113
Total	50	100	150

When called in to explain, Colonel Verleaf presents the following table:

	Non–West Pointers' Race			West Pointers' Race	
Status	Nonwhite	White	**Status**	Nonwhite	White
Passed over	20	12	Passed over	3	2
Promoted	19	12	Promoted	8	74

Analyze the preceding tables, and present a brief statement to General Half-track about Colonel Verleaf's activities.

17.2 The Department of Defense is concerned about the number of Harrier crashes. The Air Force argues that the crashes result because many of these planes are piloted by marines. The data for this claim are shown in the following table:

| | Pilot | | |
Result	Marine	Air Force	Total
Crash	46	32	78
Did not crash	187	155	342
Total	233	187	420

When the number of flight hours of the pilot is controlled, the following pattern appears:

| | Pilot with Less Than 200 Hours | | | Pilot with More Than 200 Hours | | |
Result	Marine	Air Force	Total	Marine	Air Force	Total
Crash	36	26	62	10	6	16
Did not crash	62	51	113	125	104	229
Total	98	77	175	135	110	245

Analyze these tables and present your findings.

17.3 A health advocacy organization is trying to isolate the sources of health problems in the city. Some debate centers on whether health problems are related to family income or to frequency of city garbage collection. The accompanying tables display data for all neighborhoods in the city regarding average income of residents (low or high), frequency of city garbage collection (once per week or twice per week), and frequency of health problems reported in the neighborhood (low or high). Analyze these data and discuss the sources of health problems in the city.

| | Average Income | |
Frequency of Health Problems	Low	High
Low	103	180
High	147	120

Garbage Collection Once per Week

| | Average Income | |
Frequency of Health Problems	Low	High
Low	25	10
High	56	12

Garbage Collection Twice Per Week

| | Average Income | |
Frequency of Health Problems	Low	High
Low	78	170
High	91	108

17.4   A researcher is conducting an experiment to determine support for the feminist movement. The experimental procedure consists of playing a tape recording of a meeting of a feminist organization for a group of subjects, and then comparing their attitudes with those of a matched control group of subjects who are not exposed to the tape. At the conclusion of the experiment, the researcher is amazed to find that the tape recording apparently made no difference in attitude toward the feminist movement. Check this result in the following table:

Attitude toward Feminist Movement	Listened to Tape Recording	
	No	Yes
Not favorable	40	39
Favorable	40	41

The researcher then decides to take into account the sex of the subjects and obtains the following tables:

Men

Attitude toward Feminist Movement	Listened to Tape Recording	
	No	Yes
Not favorable	21	24
Favorable	19	16

Women

Attitude toward Feminist Movement	Listened to Tape Recording	
	No	Yes
Not favorable	19	15
Favorable	21	25

Did the tape recording have an effect on attitude toward the feminist movement? Explain your answer.

17.5   A national commission has been appointed to try to reduce crime in the United States. The commission has assembled data for 400 randomly selected cities. These data include whether police walk or do not walk a beat in the city, whether the city has fewer than the average number or more than the average number of streetlights for cities of the same size, and whether its crime rate is below the average or above the average for cities of the same size. For the accompanying data, what should the commission recommend in order to combat crime? Explain your answer.

Crime Rate	Streetlights	
	Below Average	Above Average
Below average	98	114
Above average	102	86

	Police Do Not Walk Beat	
	Streetlights	
Crime Rate	Below Average	Above Average
Below average	83	16
Above average	91	18

	Police Walk Beat	
	Streetlights	
Crime Rate	Below Average	Above Average
Below average	15	98
Above average	11	68

17.6 A consumer advocate is trying to get legislation passed that will protect the environment of a large city. To increase the probability of success, the advocate researches the history of all legislation introduced in the city council in the last 5 years. She records whether the bill was favorable or not favorable to industry, whether the bill was introduced by a member of the city council or by the mayor, and whether it passed or was defeated. These variables are cross-tabulated in the accompanying tables. From these cross-tabulations, whom should she try to persuade to introduce her legislation in the city council? Explain your answer.

	Favorable to Industry	
Bill	No	Yes
Defeated	132	43
Passed	138	87

	Bill Introduced by Mayor	
	Favorable to Industry	
Bill	No	Yes
Defeated	64	22
Passed	67	44

	Bill Introduced by Member of City Council	
	Favorable to Industry	
Bill	No	Yes
Defeated	68	21
Passed	71	43

17.7 A museum intends to construct a new wing. The board of directors is concerned that the new wing be a success in the sense of drawing many patrons. The museum staff has compiled data from 549 cities regarding how frequently museum collections are changed (infrequently or frequently), the size of the museum and surrounding grounds (small or large), and yearly attendance (low or high). From these data (see the accompanying cross-tabulations), what recommendations should be made to the board about constructing and maintaining the new wing?

	Size	
Attendance	Small	Large
Low	135	87
High	165	162

Infrequent Collection Changes				Frequent Collection Changes		
	Size				**Size**	
Attendance	Small	Large		**Attendance**	Small	Large
Low	78	47		Low	57	40
High	82	51		High	83	111

17.8 A state welfare department has commissioned a survey to investigate the attitudes of its clients toward the department. For one week, upon completing a visit to the department, clients were asked whether they thought that they had to complete too many forms, whether they had to wait too long in line for service, and whether they felt the agency was run efficiently or inefficiently. From the accompanying cross-tabulations of their responses, what can the welfare department do to improve its image with clients?

	Too Many Forms	
Opinion	No	Yes
Inefficient	192	182
Efficient	128	78

Not Too Long in Line				**Too Long in Line**		
	Too Many Forms				**Too Many Forms**	
Opinion	No	Yes		**Opinion**	No	Yes
Inefficient	96	62		Inefficient	96	120
Efficient	96	49		Efficient	32	29

17.9 A school district is experimenting with two different methods of instruction to improve the performance of elementary school students. The first "traditional" method emphasizes learning through memorization, and the second "modern" method emphasizes learning through individual discovery. As the first cross-tabulation indicates, the two methods seem to be equally effective in their impact on student performance. Some educators, however, dispute this result; they argue that the best method depends on the intelligence of the student. To test this hypothesis, they examine the relationship between instructional method and performance in each of three groups—students with low, medium, and high intelligence. Do the accompanying cross-tabulations support this hypothesis? Which method should the school district employ for which type of student? Explain your answer. (**Hint:** Although this example has three control tables, the procedures used in analysis are analogous to those used in the case of two control tables, which were discussed at length in this chapter. The analyst must examine the relationship between the original two variables within each category of the third or control variable and note how the control tables differ from one another and from the original table. You can interpret the result according to the guidelines presented in Table 17.11.)

	Method	
Performance	Traditional	Modern
Low	268	269
High	272	271

Low Intelligence

	Method	
Performance	Traditional	Modern
Low	68	120
High	102	70

Medium Intelligence

	Method	
Performance	Traditional	Modern
Low	78	79
High	102	101

High Intelligence

	Method	
Performance	Traditional	Modern
Low	122	70
High	68	100

17.10 The MPA director at a large university is interested in the factors that lead to successful placement of MPA students in employment. She defines successful placement of an MPA student as being offered the position that was his or her first choice for employment after completing the program. From student transcripts, she has classified students' grade point averages in the MPA program into two categories: 3.0 or below, and above 3.0 (on a 4.0 scale). From the transcripts, she also has determined whether the student took the courses in the quantitative concentration in the MPA program (which use a familiar statistics book). These data appear in the accompanying tables. Based on the data, how should the MPA director advise students about how to receive successful placements?

	Grade Point Average	
Placement	3.0 or Below	Above 3.0
Not successful	78	97
Successful	104	184

Did Not Take
Quantitative Concentration

	Grade Point Average	
Placement	3.0 or Below	Above 3.0
Not successful	44	58
Successful	44	79

Did Take
Quantitative Concentration

	Grade Point Average	
Placement	3.0 or Below	Above 3.0
Not successful	34	39
Successful	60	105

17.11 A researcher is interested in how agency and bureau directors can achieve stronger control over their organizations. Using data from 500 of these organizations, she finds a relationship between type of budget and control. By a large percentage difference, directors claim to have stronger control with a line-item budget than with any other type. This relationship persists even when she introduces the third (control) variables of size of agency or bureau and number of hierarchical levels in the organization. Accordingly, she concludes that the relationship between type of budget and director control must be causal. Explain why you agree or disagree with her conclusion.

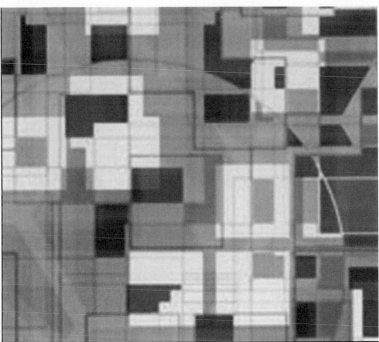

PART
VI

Regression
Analysis

CHAPTER 18

Introduction to Regression Analysis

O ften public or nonprofit managers want to know whether two variables are related but is unwilling to collapse information into categories (see Chapters 15–17). In general, an analyst should never take interval level data and use ordinal- or nominal-level techniques. Treating interval information as ordinal loses much of the information that the data contain. Just as the analyst should never calculate the mean and standard deviation for grouped data when the ungrouped data are available, an analyst should never take interval data (such as number of cars, revenue, highway speeds, hours volunteered, money donated, grant applications submitted, or crime rates) and collapse them into categories for analysis purposes. (Collapsing data to present simple tables is permissible.)

A variety of public and nonprofit management problems can be interpreted as relationships between two variables. For example, the director of the highway patrol might want to know whether the average speed of motorists on a stretch of highway is related to the number of patrol cars on that stretch of highway. Knowing this information would allow the director to decide rationally whether or not to increase the number of patrol cars. In other situations, the public manager might want to know the relationship between two variables for prediction purposes. For example, a northeastern state is considering a sales tax on beer and would like to know how much revenue the tax would raise in the state. An analyst's strategy might be to see whether a relationship exists between a state's population and its tax revenues from beer sales. If a relationship is found, the analyst could then use the state's population to predict its potential revenue from a beer sales tax. Similarly, Habitat for Humanity might be interested in knowing whether weather conditions (measured by inches of rainfall and so on) affect the number of construction volunteers.

This chapter will provide an introduction to the techniques of simple linear regression.

Relationships between Variables

Relationships between two variables can be classified in two ways: as causal or predictive *and* as functional or statistical. In our first example, the relationship between police cars on the road and motorists' average speed, we have a causal relationship. The implicit hypothesis is that increasing the number of patrol cars on the road will reduce average speeds. In the beer sales tax example, a state's population will predict, or determine, tax revenues from beer sales. The variable that is predicted or is caused is referred to as the *dependent* variable (this variable is usually called Y). The variable that is used to predict or is the cause of change in another variable is called the *independent* variable (this variable is usually called X).

In the following examples, determine which variable is the dependent variable and which is the independent variable:

A police chief believes increasing expenditures for police will reduce crime.

independent variable_____

dependent variable_____

A librarian believes that circulation is related to advertising.

independent variable_____

dependent variable_____

MPA candidates make good summer interns.

independent variable_____

dependent variable_____

The number of volunteers is affected by the weather.

independent variable_____

dependent variable_____

If you said the dependent variables were crime, circulation, good performance, and number of volunteers, congratulations.

Relationships may also be functional or statistical. A **functional relationship** is a relationship in which one variable (Y) is a direct function of another (X). For example, Russell Thomas, the longtime head of the city motor pool, believes that there is some type of relationship between the number of cars he sends over to Marquette's Tune-up Shop for tune-ups and the amount of the bill that he receives from Marquette's. Russell finds the information in Table 18.1 for the last five transactions with Marquette's.

Russell knows the first step in determining whether two variables are related is to graph the two variables. When graphing two variables, the independent variable (X)

Table 18.1

Data from Marquette's

Number of Cars	Amount of Bill
2	$ 64
1	32
5	160
4	128
2	64

is always graphed along the bottom horizontally, and the dependent variable (Y) is always graphed along the side vertically. See Figure 18.1.

On the axes presented in Figure 18.2, graph the points representing the two variables.

If you look carefully at the points you graphed in Figure 18.2, you will see that they fall without any deviation along a single line. This is a characteristic of a functional relationship. If someone knows the value of the independent variable, the value of the dependent variable can be predicted exactly. In the preceding example, Marquette's charges the city $32 to tune a car, so the bill is simply $32 times the number of cars.

Unfortunately, very few of the important relationships that public or nonprofit managers must consider are functional. Most relationships are statistical. In a statistical relationship, knowing the value of the independent variable lets us estimate a value for the dependent variable, but the estimate is not exact. One process of determining the exact nature of a statistical relationship is called *regression*. We will illustrate how regression can be used to describe relationships with an example.

Figure 18.1

The Horizontal Axis Is for *X*

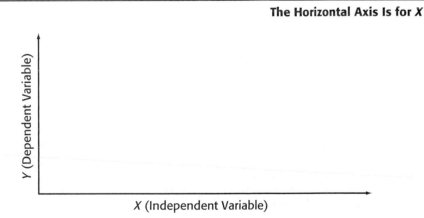

Figure 18.2

Graph Data Here

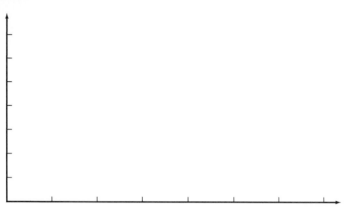

Table 18.2

Commissioner's Data

Number of Police Cars	Average Speed of Motorists
3	64
1	71
4	61
5	58
7	56

The Normal, Oklahoma, traffic commissioner believes that the average speed of motorists along Highway 35 within the city limits is related to the number of police cars patrolling that stretch. Average speed is measured by a stationary, unmanned radar gun. The experiment spans 2 months, with measurements taken daily. For a sample of 5 days, the results of the commissioner's experiment are as shown in Table 18.2.

The first step in determining whether a relationship exists is to plot the data on a graph. Plot the given data on the graph in Figure 18.2. After the data are plotted, the analyst can eyeball the data to see whether there is a relationship between the number of cars and the average speed. The graph of the data is shown in Figure 18.3.

Clearly, the graph shows a relationship between the number of police cars on this highway and the motorists' average speed: The more cars on the highway, the lower the average speed. This is termed a negative relationship because the dependent variable (speed) decreases as the independent variable increases.

Our hypothetical situation in which state population is compared with sales tax revenues from beer sales illustrates a positive relationship (see Table 18.3).

Figure 18.3

Graph of Traffic Speed Data

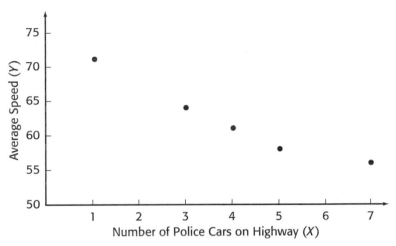

Table 18.3

Relationship between Tax Revenues and Population

State	Population (Millions)	Beer Revenue (Millions)
Texas	12.4	146
Louisiana	6.1	85
Arkansas	2.4	21
Kansas	4.3	47
Missouri	9.5	115
Colorado	7.6	90

The graph of these data is shown in Figure 18.4. From the graph, we see that as states' populations increase, so do the states' sales tax revenues from beer sales. Because both variables increase (or decrease) at the same time, the relationship is positive.

In many cases (far too many, for most managers), no relationship exists between the two variables. In Table 18.4, the number of police cars patrolling the streets of Normal, Oklahoma, is contrasted with the number of arrests for indecent exposure in Kansas City, Missouri.

A note of explanation is in order. On Wednesday, a regional public administration conference opened in Kansas City. Suspects are held for 24 hours, which also explains the Friday figures. Most of the Saturday incidents occurred at the airport.

Figure 18.4

Relationship between Population and Tax Revenue

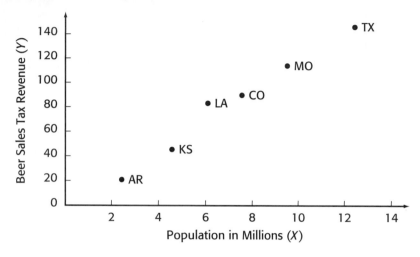

Table 18.4

Patrol Cars and Number of Arrests

Day	Cars on Patrol in Normal	Arrests for Indecent Exposure in Kansas City
Monday	2	27
Tuesday	3	12
Wednesday	3	57
Thursday	7	28
Friday	1	66
Saturday	6	60

The data are graphed in Figure 18.5. Clearly no relationship exists between the number of police cars patrolling the streets of Normal and arrests for indecent exposure in Kansas City.

Ode to Eyeballing

When an analyst has only a few data points, the relationship between two variables can be determined visually. When the data sets become fairly large, however, eyeballing a relationship is extremely inaccurate. What is needed are statistics that summarize the relationship between two variables. One variable, of course, can be summarized by a set of single figures, say, the mean and the standard deviation. *The relationship between two variables can be summarized by a line.*

Figure 18.5

Relationship between Number of Patrol Cars and Indecent Exposure Arrests

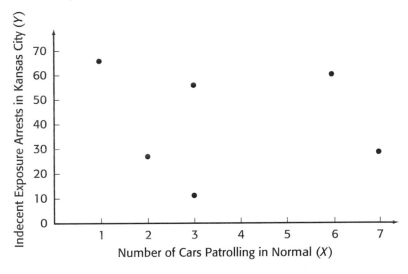

Figure 18.6

Straight Line for Data of Table 18.2

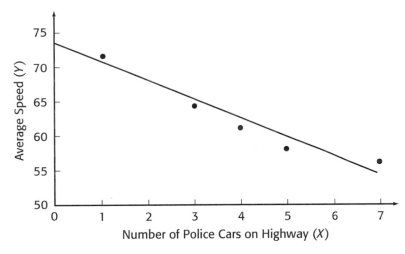

For our example of cars patrolling a stretch of Highway 35 and the average speed of traffic on that portion of highway, a straight line can be drawn that represents the relationship between the data (see Figure 18.6). The line generally follows the pattern of the data, sloping downward and to the right.

Figure 18.7

The Lines Differ in Their Slopes

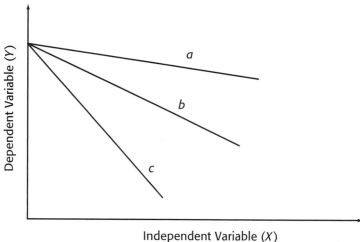

The slant of a line is referred to as its slope. The **slope** of any line is defined to be how much the line rises or falls relative to the distance it travels horizontally. Symbolically,

Any line can be described by two numbers, and the line describing the relationship between two variables is no exception. Lines *a*, *b*, and *c* in Figure 18.7 differ from each other in terms of how steeply the lines slant from left to right.

The slant of a line is referred to as its slope. The **slope** of any line is defined to be how much the line rises or falls relative to the distance it travels horizontally. Symbolically,

$$\beta = \frac{\Delta Y}{\Delta X}$$

where β (Greek letter beta) is the slope of a line, ΔY (Greek letter delta) is the change in the Y (dependent) variable, and ΔX is the change in the X (independent) variable.

Another way to express this formula is to say that the slope of a line is equal to the ratio of the change in Y for a given change in X (rise over run, for you geometry buffs). The graph in Figure 18.8 shows the slopes of several hypothetical lines.

The second number used to describe a line is the point where the line intersects the Y-axis (called the **intercept**). The graph in Figure 18.9 shows several lines with the same slopes but with different intercepts. The intercept, referred to as α (Greek letter alpha) by statisticians, is the value of the dependent variable when the independent variable is equal to zero.

Any line can be fully described by its slope and its intercept:

$$Y = \alpha + \beta X$$

A line describing the relationship between two variables is represented by

$$\hat{Y} = \alpha + \beta X$$

Figure 18.8

Several Different Slopes

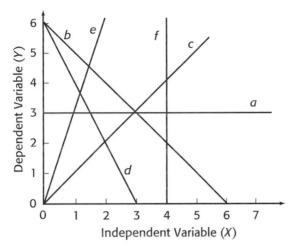

Line	Slope
a	0
b	−1
c	+1
d	−2
e	+3
f	∞

Figure 18.9

The Lines Have the Same Slope but Different Intercepts

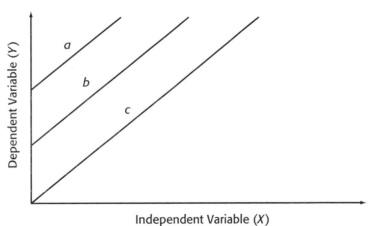

$\hat{Y}$ is a statistician's symbol for the **predicted value** of Y (called "Y hat"). $\hat{Y}$ for any value of X is a function of the intercept (α) and the slope (β), and it may or may not be equal to the actual value of Y.

To illustrate, let us return to our example of traffic speeds and patrol cars. The line drawn through the data in Figure 18.10 represents the relationship between the two variables. If we had only the line, what could we say about the expected average

Figure 18.10

Straight Line for Data of Table 18.2

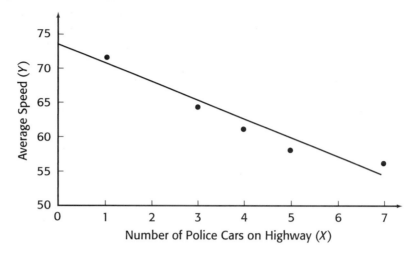

speed if three cars were on the road? $\hat{Y}$, the expected speed, is 65 miles per hour. (To find this number, draw a line straight up from the three-cars point to the relationship line. From the point where your line touches the relationship line, draw a line parallel to the X-axis to the speed limit line. Your line should touch the Y-axis at 65. This value is $\hat{Y}$.)

Note that the actual value of Y on the one day when three cars were on the road is 64 miles per hour. This fact illustrates the following:

$$\text{predicted value of } Y = \text{real value of } Y + \text{some error}$$

$$\hat{Y}_i = Y_i + e_i$$

or

$$e_i = (\hat{Y}_i - Y_i)$$

Another way of expressing this is that every value of Y is equal to some predicted value of Y based on X plus some error.*

Linear Regression

The pitfall of just drawing in a line to summarize a relationship is that numerous lines will look as if they summarize the relationship between two variables equally well. Statisticians have agreed that the best line to use to describe a relationship is the line

---

* We assume that error can be either negative or positive, so that it does not matter whether error is added to $\hat{Y}_i$ (or Y_i) or subtracted from $\hat{Y}_i$ (or Y_i).

that minimizes the squared errors—that is, makes the sum of all $(\hat{Y}_i - Y_i)^2$ the smallest possible number. This form of **regression** (or fitting a line to data) is called **ordinary least squares,** or you may call it just **linear regression.**

Linear regression using the principle of minimizing squared errors allows us to find one value of α and one value of β so that a unique regression line of the form $\hat{Y} = \alpha + \beta X$ can be determined. The calculations necessary to find α and β will be illustrated with an example.

Before progressing with the example, we should note that regression is a technique that is often used to make inferences from a sample to a population. Similar to other situations of inference, slightly different symbols are used. For a population regression, a line is denoted as

$$Y = \alpha + \beta X + \epsilon$$

Sometimes rather than simply using Y, statisticians use the symbol $\mu_{y|x}$ which stands for the mean of y given x, or the mean value of y given the use of x to try to predict y. The population intercept is denoted α and the slope β. The symbol ϵ represents an error term meant to capture any errors in prediction. In statistics we rarely work with populations but rather with samples. In that case, the symbols are

$$Y = a + bX + e$$

The sample intercept is represented by the symbol a, the slope by b, and the error term by e. Similar to the case with means, the best estimate of the population slope and intercept are the sample slope and intercept.

Through some heavy mathematics based on calculus, statisticians have found that the formula for b is as follows:

$$b = \frac{\sum(X_i - \overline{X})(Y_i - \overline{Y})}{\sum(X_i - \overline{X})^2}$$

Taken a piece at a time, this formula is not as intimidating as it looks. We will use the police cars and average speed data to calculate b (see Table 18.5).

Step 1: Calculate the mean for both the dependent variable (Y) and the independent variable (X). Do this in the space provided next to the table. If you have forgotten how to calculate a mean, reread Chapter 5. The mean for Y is 62, and the mean for X is 4.

Table 18.5

Relationship between Police Cars and Average Speed

Number of Police Cars (X)	Average Speed (Y)
3	64
1	71
4	61
5	58
7	56

Step 2: Subtract the mean of the dependent variable from each value of the dependent variable, yielding $(Y_i - \bar{Y})$. Do the same for the independent variable, yielding $(X_i - \bar{X})$.

$X_i - \bar{X}$	$Y_i - \bar{Y}$
$3 - 4 = -1$	$64 - 62 = 2$
$1 - 4 = -3$	$71 - 62 = 9$
$4 - 4 = 0$	$61 - 62 = -1$
$5 - 4 = 1$	$58 - 62 = -4$
$7 - 4 = 3$	$56 - 62 = -6$

Step 3: Multiply $(Y_i - \bar{Y})$ times $(X_i - \bar{X})$. That is, multiply the value that you get when you subtract the mean from Y_i by the value you get when you subtract the mean from X_i.

$(X_i - \bar{X}) \times (Y_i - \bar{Y})$			
-1	$\times$	2	$= -2$
-3	$\times$	9	$= -27$
0	$\times$	-1	$= 0$
1	$\times$	-4	$= -4$
3	$\times$	-6	$= -18$

Step 4: Sum all the values of $(Y_i - \bar{Y})(X_i - \bar{X})$. You should get a sum of -51. This is the numerator of the formula for b.

Step 5: Use the $(X_i - \bar{X})$ column in Step 3, and square each of the values found in the column.

$(X_i - \bar{X})$	$(X_i - \bar{X})^2$
-1	1
-3	9
0	0
1	1
3	9

Step 6: Sum the squared values of $(X_i - \bar{X})$. The answer is 20.

Step 7: Divide $\sum(Y_i - \bar{Y})(X_i - \bar{X})$, or -51, by $\sum(X_i - \bar{X})^2$, or 20. This number (-2.55) is the slope.

The intercept is much easier to calculate. Statisticians have discovered that

$$\alpha = \mu_y - \beta\mu_x$$

or

$$a = \bar{Y} - b\bar{X}$$

Substituting in the values of 62, -2.55, and 4 for $\bar{Y}$, b, and $\bar{X}$, respectively, we find

$$a = 62 - (-2.55) \times 4 = 62 - (-10.2) = 62 + 10.2 = 72.2$$

The regression equation that describes the relationship between the number of patrol cars on a stretch of Highway 35 and the average speed of motorists on that stretch of highway is

$$\hat{Y} = 72.2 - 2.55X$$

All sample regressions are of the general form

$$\hat{Y} = a + bX$$

In English, the predicted value of $Y(\hat{Y})$ is equal to X times the slope (b) plus the intercept (a). The slope and the intercept can be positive or negative.

Some Applications

The regression equation provides a wealth of information. Suppose the traffic commissioner wants to know the estimated average speed of traffic if six patrol cars are placed on duty. Another way of stating this question is, What is the value of $\hat{Y}$ (the estimated average speed) if the value of X (the number of cars) is 6? Using the formula

$$\hat{Y} = 72.2 - 2.55X$$

substitute 6 for X to obtain

$$\hat{Y} = 72.2 - 2.55 \times 6 = 72.2 - 15.3 = 56.9$$

The best estimate of the average speed for all cars on a stretch of Highway 35 is 56.9 if six patrol cars are placed on that stretch.

How much would the mean speed for all cars decrease if one additional patrol car were added? The answer is 2.55 miles per hour. The **regression coefficient** is the ratio of change in $\hat{Y}$ to the change in X. Where the change in X is 1 (car), the change in $\hat{Y}$ is -2.55 (miles per hour). In a management situation, this is how the slope should be interpreted. It is how much $\hat{Y}$ will change if X is changed (increased) one unit. Remember, though, that the regression line gives estimates, and there is error (e) in predicting actual Y scores.

What would the average speed be if no patrol cars were on the road? Substituting 0 into the regression equation for X, we find

$$\hat{Y} = 72.2 - 2.55X = 72.2 - 2.55(0) = 72.2$$

When X is 0, the value of $\hat{Y}$ is 72.2, or the intercept. The intercept is defined as the value of $\hat{Y}$ when X is equal to zero.

An Example

Most analysts rely on computer programs to calculate regression equations. We expect that you will do so, too. However, just for practice, we ask you to calculate the regression equation for the population and beer sales tax example. Recall that for six states,

Table 18.6

Relationship between Tax Revenues and Population

Population, X (millions)	Beer Revenue, Y (millions)
12.4	146
6.1	85
2.4	21
4.3	47
9.5	115
7.6	90

the data are as given in Table 18.6. In the space provided, calculate the slope and the intercept of the regression line.

$$\overline{X} = \underline{\hspace{3cm}} \qquad \overline{Y} = \underline{\hspace{3cm}}$$

$$X_i - \overline{X} \qquad\qquad (X_i - \overline{X})^2 \qquad Y_i - \overline{Y}$$

$$12.4 - \underline{\hspace{1.5cm}} = \underline{\hspace{1.5cm}} \qquad \underline{\hspace{1.5cm}} \qquad 146 - \underline{\hspace{1.5cm}} = \underline{\hspace{1.5cm}}$$

$$6.1 - \underline{\hspace{1.5cm}} = \underline{\hspace{1.5cm}} \qquad \underline{\hspace{1.5cm}} \qquad 85 - \underline{\hspace{1.5cm}} = \underline{\hspace{1.5cm}}$$

$$2.4 - \underline{\hspace{1.5cm}} = \underline{\hspace{1.5cm}} \qquad \underline{\hspace{1.5cm}} \qquad 21 - \underline{\hspace{1.5cm}} = \underline{\hspace{1.5cm}}$$

$$4.3 - \underline{\hspace{1.5cm}} = \underline{\hspace{1.5cm}} \qquad \underline{\hspace{1.5cm}} \qquad 47 - \underline{\hspace{1.5cm}} = \underline{\hspace{1.5cm}}$$

$$9.5 - \underline{\hspace{1.5cm}} = \underline{\hspace{1.5cm}} \qquad \underline{\hspace{1.5cm}} \qquad 115 - \underline{\hspace{1.5cm}} = \underline{\hspace{1.5cm}}$$

$$7.6 - \underline{\hspace{1.5cm}} = \underline{\hspace{1.5cm}} \qquad \underline{\hspace{1.5cm}} \qquad 90 - \underline{\hspace{1.5cm}} = \underline{\hspace{1.5cm}}$$

$$(X_i - \overline{X}) \times (Y_i - \overline{Y})$$

$$\underline{\hspace{1.5cm}} \times \underline{\hspace{1.5cm}} = \underline{\hspace{1.5cm}}$$

$$\underline{\hspace{1.5cm}} \times \underline{\hspace{1.5cm}} = \underline{\hspace{1.5cm}}$$

$$\underline{\hspace{1.5cm}} \times \underline{\hspace{1.5cm}} = \underline{\hspace{1.5cm}}$$

$$\underline{\hspace{1.5cm}} \times \underline{\hspace{1.5cm}} = \underline{\hspace{1.5cm}}$$

$$\underline{\hspace{1.5cm}} \times \underline{\hspace{1.5cm}} = \underline{\hspace{1.5cm}}$$

$$\underline{\hspace{1.5cm}} \times \underline{\hspace{1.5cm}} = \underline{\hspace{1.5cm}}$$

$$\sum (X_i - \overline{X})(Y_i - \overline{Y}) = \underline{\hspace{3cm}}$$

$$\sum (X_i - \overline{X})^2 = \underline{\hspace{3cm}}$$

$$\beta = \frac{\sum (X_i - \overline{X})(Y_i - \overline{Y})}{\sum (X_i - \overline{X})^2} = \underline{\hspace{3cm}}$$

$$\alpha = \overline{Y} - \beta \overline{X} = \underline{\hspace{3cm}}$$

Figure 18.11

Differences in Goodness of Fit

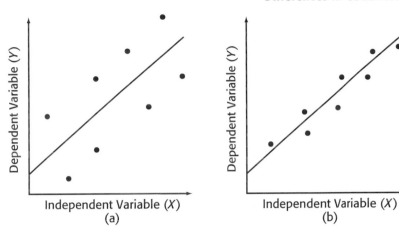

The answer to this exercise is presented at the end of the chapter, following the problems.

What would be the best estimate of Rhode Island's beer sales tax revenue if it had such a tax and had 5.5 million people?

Measures of Goodness of Fit

Any relationship between two variables can be summarized by linear regression. A regression line per se, however, does not tell us how well the regression line summarizes the data. To illustrate, the two sets of data in Figure 18.11 can both be summarized with the same regression line. In the graph of part (b), however, the data points cluster closely about the line; in the graph of part (a), the data points are much farther from the line. We can say that the regression line of (b) fits the data better than does the regression line of (a), even though the "best-fitting" regression line for the data in both Figure 18.11(a) and 18.11(b) is the same.

The distance a point is from the regression line is referred to as **error.** Recall that the regression line gives the value of $\hat{Y}_i$, whereas the data point represents Y_i. In the following sections, we will discuss various ways that statisticians have devised to measure the goodness of fit of the regression line to the data. All these methods are based on the error.

Error in the context of regression analysis means unexplained variance. A regression equation will almost always have some error, so trying to eliminate error entirely is not realistic. What are some causes of error in a regression equation?

First, a single independent variable rarely accounts for all of the variation in a dependent variable. For example, the unemployment rate might explain a substantial portion of the variation in demand for services at a local food bank, but other variables such as higher retail food prices and climate (such as cold weather) might also account for some of the variation in demand. Data values will not fall perfectly along a regression line if the independent variable only explains some of the variation in the dependent variable. This is why analysts often perform regression with several independent variables, a subject we cover in Chapter 21.

Second, individual cases within our data do not always conform to the overall relationships we find when using regression analysis. For example, if most drivers slow down when the number of police cars on patrol goes up, a small number of drivers may throw caution to the wind and continue traveling at a high rate of speed. Even when a regression equation reveals a relationship between an independent and dependent variable, deviations from the general pattern for individual cases are almost always inevitable.

The Standard Error of the Estimate

Statisticians commonly use three measures of fit in regression analysis. The first, called the **residual variation,** or the variance of the estimate, is equal to the sum of the squared error divided by $n - 2$. Symbolically,

$$S^2_{y|x} = \frac{\sum (Y_i - \hat{Y}_i)^2}{n - 2}$$

$S^2_{y|x}$ is called the residual variance of Y given X.

Another way of stating what $S^2_{y|x}$ represents is that it is the average squared error of the regression estimates. Although the residual variation is rarely used as a measure of fit, its square root $(S_{y|x})$ is. This measure, called the **standard error of the estimate** (or sometimes root mean square error), is an estimate of the variation in $\hat{Y}$, the predicted value of Y. The standard error of the estimate can be used to place confidence intervals around an estimate that is based on a regression equation.

To illustrate the utility of this measure of fit of the regression line, we need to calculate the residual variance for a set of data. We will use the police cars and speed data of Table 18.5. In the worked-out example presented earlier, we found that the number of patrol cars on the highway was related to the average speed of all cars and that

$$\overline{X} = 4 \qquad \overline{Y} = 62 \qquad \hat{Y} = 72.2 - 2.55X$$

To calculate the residual variation, follow these steps:

Step 1: Using the values of X and the regression equation, calculate a $\hat{Y}$ value for every X value.

$X \times$	b	Xb	$+ \ a$	$= \ \hat{Y}$
3 ×	−2.55	−7.65	+ 72.2	= 64.6
1 ×	−2.55	−2.55	+ 72.2	= 69.7
4 ×	−2.55	−10.2	+ 72.2	= 62.0
5 ×	−2.55	−12.75	+ 72.2	= 59.5
7 ×	−2.55	−17.85	+ 72.2	= 54.4

Step 2: Using the $\hat{Y}$ values and the Y values, calculate the total error for each value of Y.

$$\begin{array}{c} Y - \hat{Y} \\ \hline 64 - 64.6 = -0.6 \\ 71 - 69.7 = 1.3 \\ 61 - 62.0 = -1.0 \\ 58 - 59.5 = -1.5 \\ 56 - 54.4 = 1.6 \end{array}$$

Step 3: Square the errors found in Step 2, and then sum these squares.

$$\begin{array}{c} (Y - \hat{Y})^2 \\ \hline \left.\begin{array}{c} .36 \\ 1.69 \\ 1.00 \\ 2.25 \\ 2.56 \end{array}\right\} \Sigma(Y - \hat{Y})^2 = 7.86 \end{array}$$

Step 4: Divide the sum of the squared errors by $n - 2$ to find the residual variation (or average squared error).

$$S^2_{y|x} = \frac{7.86}{3} = 2.62$$

Step 5: Take the square root of this number to find the standard error of the estimate.

$$S_{y|x} = \sqrt{2.62} = 1.62$$

The standard error of the estimate may be interpreted as the amount of error that one makes when predicting a value of Y for a value of X. The standard error of the estimate, however, applies only to predicting error at the exact middle of the distribution [that is, where x is equal to the mean of x; to see a good explanation of why this is true, see Johnson (1992), pp. 667–669]. To predict a confidence limit around any single point, the following transformation of the standard error of the estimate is used:

$$S_{y|x} \times \sqrt{1 + \frac{1}{n} + \frac{(X_0 - \bar{X})^2}{(n-1)S^2_x}}$$

where X_0 is the value of X being predicted, $\bar{X}$ is the mean of X, S_x is the standard deviation of x, and n is the sample size. Confidence limits can be placed around any predicted value of Y by using the following formula:

$$Y \pm t \times S_{y|x} \sqrt{1 + \frac{1}{n} + \frac{(X_0 - \bar{X})^2}{(n-1)S^2_x}}$$

where t is the t score associated with whatever confidence limits that are desired.

Suppose the highway commissioner wanted to predict the average speed of all cars when three patrol cars were on the road. Using the regression equation, he would find

$$Y = 72.2 - 2.55(3) = 72.2 - 7.65 = 64.55$$

This estimate of the average speed is not exact; it can be in error by a certain amount. To put 90% confidence limits around this estimate (64.55) we need to know the t score associated with 90% confidence limits. Simple (bivariate) regressions have $n - 2$ degrees of freedom, so we check Table 3 in the Appendix for the .05 level (.05 + .05 = .10) with three degrees of freedom and find the value 2.35. Because we already know the value of x (it is 3), all we need is the standard deviation of x to do the calculations. That value is 2.23 (you need not believe us—you can calculate this yourself from the raw data). So the formula reduces to

$$64.55 \pm (2.35 \times 1.62) \times \sqrt{1.00 + (1/5) + [(3 - 4)^2/(5 - 1)(2.23)^2]}$$

$$64.55 \pm \quad 3.81 \times \sqrt{1.00 + .2 + .05}$$

$$64.55 \pm \quad 3.81 \times \sqrt{1.25}$$

$$64.55 \pm \quad 3.81 \times \quad 1.12$$

$$64.55 \pm \quad 4.27$$

$$60.28 \text{ to } 68.82$$

We can be 90% sure that the mean speed of all cars (when three patrol cars are on the road) is between 60.28 and 68.82 miles per hour.

The Coefficient of Determination

The second goodness of fit measure adjusts for the total variation in Y. This measure, the coefficient of determination, is the ratio of the explained variation to the total variation in Y. Explained variation is nothing more than the total variation in the dependent variable minus the error. Statisticians have defined the ratio of explained to unexplained variation as equal to

$$r^2 = \frac{\sum(\hat{Y}_i - \overline{Y})^2}{\sum(Y_i - \overline{Y})^2}$$

This measure is called the **coefficient of determination,** or r^2. In bivariate (one independent variable) regression, we use r^2. In multiple (more than one independent variable) regression, the symbol R^2 is used (see Chapter 21). The coefficient of determination ranges from zero (the data do not fit the line at all) to one (the data fit the line perfectly).

The best way to interpret the coefficient of determination is as follows. If someone wanted you to guess the next value of Y but gave you no information, your best guess as to what Y is would be $\overline{Y}$, the mean. The amount of error in this guess would be $(Y_i - \overline{Y})$. The total squared error for several guesses of Y would be $\sum(Y_i - \overline{Y})^2$. If someone asked you to guess the next value of Y and gave you both the corresponding value of X and a regression equation, your best guess as to the value of Y_i would be $\hat{Y}_i$.

Figure 18.12

Coefficient of Determination

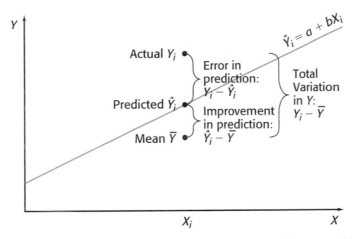

How much of an improvement would this be over just guessing the mean? Obviously, it is $(\hat{Y}_i - \overline{Y})$, or the difference between the estimated value of Y_i (or $\hat{Y}_i$) and the mean. The total improvement in squared error for several guesses would be $\Sigma(\hat{Y}_i - \overline{Y})^2$. As you can tell, the coefficient of determination is the ratio of the reduction of the error by using the regression line to the total error by guessing the mean. Figure 18.12 illustrates the improvement in prediction by using $\hat{Y}_i$ rather than $\overline{Y}$ to predict Y_i. The improvement in prediction is essential to calculating the coefficient of determination.

To calculate the coefficient of determination, follow these steps:

Step 1: Using the regression equation and each value of X, estimate a predicted value of $Y(\hat{Y})$. Such estimates were just made in the previous problem; they are

X	$\hat{Y}$
3	64.6
1	69.7
4	62.0
5	59.5
7	54.4

Step 2: From each value of $\hat{Y}$, subtract the mean value of Y (in this case 62), and square these differences.

$\hat{Y} - \overline{Y} = (\hat{Y} - \overline{Y})$	$(\hat{Y} - \overline{Y})^2$
$64.6 - 62 = \quad 2.6$	6.8
$69.7 - 62 = \quad 7.7$	59.3
$62.0 - 62 = \quad .0$	.0
$59.5 - 62 = -2.5$	6.3
$54.4 - 62 = -7.6$	57.8

Step 3: Sum these squared differences to find the numerator of the coefficient of determination. In this case, the answer is 130.2.

Step 4: Subtract the mean value of Y from the individual values of Y, and square these differences.

$Y - \bar{Y} = (Y - \bar{Y})$		$(Y - \bar{Y})^2$
64 − 62 =	2	4
71 − 62 =	9	81
61 − 62 =	−1	1
58 − 62 =	−4	16
56 − 62 =	−6	36

Step 5: Sum these squared differences to get the denominator of the coefficient of determination. The answer is 138.

Step 6: To find the coefficient of determination, divide the value found in Step 3 by the value found in Step 5.

$$r^2 = \frac{130.2}{138} = .94$$

To interpret the coefficient of determination, we can say that the number of patrol cars on a stretch of Highway 35 can explain 94% of the variance in the average speed of cars on that stretch of highway.

Although simpler ways of calculating r^2 exist, we will not discuss them here because most people will rely on computer programs to do these calculations. If you want to know the shortcut calculation methods, consult an applied statistics text, such as Ott and Mendenhall (1994).

The square root of the coefficient of determination is called the **correlation coefficient,** or r. The value of r ranges from -1.0 for perfect negative correlation to $+1.0$ for perfect positive correlation. Despite its frequent use in many academic disciplines, the correlation coefficient has no inherent value because it is difficult to interpret. The coefficient of determination is far more useful.

The Standard Error of the Slope

The third measure of goodness of fit is the standard error of the slope. If we took several samples with an independent and a dependent variable and calculated a regression slope (b) for each sample, the sample slopes would vary somewhat. The standard deviation of these slope estimates is called the **standard error of the slope** estimate. The formula for the standard error of the slope estimate is

$$s_b = \frac{S_{y|x}}{\sqrt{\sum(X_i - \bar{X})^2}}$$

The standard error of the slope can be used in the same manner as other standard errors—to place a confidence interval around the slope estimate. The standard error of the slope estimate is calculated as follows:

Step 1: Calculate $S_{y|x}$, the standard error of the estimate. If you turn back a few pages, you will find that $S_{y|x}$ for the data we have been considering is equal to 1.62.

Step 2: From each value of X, subtract the value of $\overline{X}$, and square these differences.

$X - \overline{X} = (X - \overline{X})$		$(X - \overline{X})^2$
3 − 4 =	−1	1
1 − 4 =	−3	9
4 − 4 =	0	0
5 − 4 =	1	1
7 − 4 =	3	9

Step 3: Sum all the squared differences: $\sum(X_i - \overline{X})^2 = 20$.

Step 4: Take the square root of the number found in Step 3: $\sqrt{20} = 4.47$.

Step 5: Divide the standard error of the estimate (1.62) by the number found in Step 4 to get the standard error of the slope estimate.

$$s_b = \frac{1.62}{4.47} = .36$$

The standard error of the slope estimate can be used just like any other standard error. We can place 90% confidence limits around the slope estimate. The procedure for using the sample slope to place a 90% confidence limit around the slope estimate is

$$b \pm t \times s_b \text{ (df = 3)}$$
$$-2.55 \pm 2.35 \times .36$$
$$-2.55 \pm .85$$
$$-3.40 \text{ to } -1.70$$

We can be 90% sure that the population slope falls between −1.70 and −3.40.

The standard error of the slope can also be used to answer the following question: What is the probability that one could draw a sample with a slope equal to the value of b obtained in a regression equation if the slope in the population equals zero? This is called *testing the statistical significance of the slope*. If $\beta = 0$, then there is no relationship between the variables in the population. If it is probable that the sample was drawn from such a population, we could not reject the null hypothesis that no relationship exists between the independent variable and the dependent variable.

To determine the probability in our example that a sample with a slope of −2.55 could have been drawn from a population where $\beta = 0$, we convert b into a t score by using 0 as the mean and by using the standard error of the slope

$$t = \frac{X - \mu}{s}$$

$$t = \frac{b - \beta}{s_b} = \frac{-2.55 - 0}{.36} = -7.1$$

A t value of 7.1 with 3 degrees of freedom is greater than the value for .005 ($t = 5.841$). The probability that a sample with a slope of -2.55 could have been drawn from a population with a slope of zero is less than .005. If there are no major research design problems (and there appear to be none), management would be justified in concluding that a relationship exists. (Research design is the subject of Chapter 3.)

Sometimes the entire population is used to calculate a regression line. In such cases, the preceding exercise of testing for statistical significance does not make theoretical sense. Many analysts do it anyway to illustrate that the relationship is not trivial. A manager must be aware that this is done.

Although you may not immediately see a link between the standard error of the slope and the coefficient of determination, the two are closely related. Think about why this is the case. The coefficient of determination reveals the amount of variation in the dependent variable that is explained by the independent variable. When we test the statistical significance of the slope and are unable to reject the null hypothesis ($\beta = 0$), the amount of variation in the dependent variable explained by the independent variable is typically small. In contrast, when we are able to reject the null hypothesis ($\beta = 0$), the coefficient of determination will be larger, since the independent variable does indeed explain variation in the dependent variable.

To illustrate this point, we will perform a regression using the data in Table 18.4. Recall that upon graphing these data, there was no evidence of a relationship between the number of police cars on patrol in Normal, Oklahoma, and arrests for indecent exposure in Kansas City, Missouri.

$$\hat{Y} = 4.24 - .0138X$$

$$s_b = .0541 \qquad r^2 = .017$$

$$t = \frac{-.0138 - 0}{.0541} = .26$$

The regression equation confirms our initial finding of no relationship between the two variables. The slope coefficient is clearly not statistically significant. A t value of .26 with 4 degrees of freedom fails to exceed the t value associated with alpha at .05 ($t = 2.132$). The r^2 for the model is .017, indicating that the number of police cars on patrol in Normal explains less than 2% of the variation in indecent exposure arrest rates in Kansas City.

Generally speaking, if the independent variable does a poor job explaining variation in the dependent variable, the r^2 value will also be quite low. A statistically insignificant slope and low r^2 are signs that the independent variable does a poor job explaining variation in the dependent variable.

Chapter Summary

Regression is a technique that can be used to describe the statistical relationship between two interval variables. This chapter illustrates the use of simple (bivariate) linear regression.

The relationship between two variables can be summarized by a line, and any line can be fully described by its slope and its intercept. The slope of a line is equal to the ratio of the change in Y for a given change in X. The intercept of the line is the point at which the line intersects the Y-axis. The technique of linear regression uses these concepts to find the best line to describe a relationship, which statisticians have agreed is the line that minimizes the squared errors about it. All regression equations are of the general form $\hat{Y} = \alpha + \beta X$, where α is the intercept and β is the slope. Calculations for slopes and intercepts are illustrated in the chapter.

Once the regression line has been found, we usually want to see how well that line summarizes the data. To do so, we use what statisticians call measures of the goodness of fit. Three common measures are used. The standard error of the estimate, $S_{y|x}$, is an estimate of the variation in $\hat{Y}$, the predicted value of Y. The coefficient of determination, r^2, adjusts for the total variation in Y and ranges between 0 (no relationship/fit) to 1 (perfect relationship/fit). The standard error of the slope, s_b, gives the standard deviation of the sample slope estimates. The standard error of the slope can also be used to test (with a t test) the statistical significance of the slope. Using this test, we can evaluate whether a sample b deviates from the null hypothesis that the sample was drawn from a population in which the two variables are not related (that is, $\beta = 0$).

Problems

18.1 The chief of automobile maintenance for the city of Normal feels that maintenance costs on high-mileage cars are much higher than those costs for low-mileage cars. The maintenance chief regresses yearly maintenance costs for a sample of 200 cars on each car's total mileage for the year. She finds the following:

$$\hat{Y} = \$50 + .030X \quad S_{y|x} = \$150 \quad s_b = .0005 \quad r^2 = .90$$
$$\bar{X} = 50,000 \quad s_x = 10,000$$

where Y is maintenance cost (in dollars) for the year and X is the mileage on a car.

(a) Is there a relationship between maintenance costs and mileage?

(b) What are the predicted maintenance costs of a car with 50,000 miles? Place a 95% confidence limit around this estimate.

(c) The maintenance chief considers $1,000 in maintenance a year excessive. For this criterion, how many miles will generate maintenance costs of $1,000?

18.2 James Jesse, the head of the Bureau of Animal Husbandry, perceives that several agencies received large increases in appropriations last year because they encouraged interest groups to testify for them before the House Appropriations Committee. The accompanying sample data for five agencies similar to Jesse's were gathered. Using regression analysis, calculate a regression equation. Does a relationship exist? The Bureau of Animal Husbandry could pressure 15 groups to testify for it. What percentage increase would this number of groups predict? Place a 90% confidence interval around that estimate. How large an increase is each additional interest group worth?

Interest Groups Testifying	Percentage Increase in Appropriation
25	22
14	17
7	8
18	19
10	12

18.3 Martina Justice, the head of the state Bureau of Criminal Justice, feels that she could significantly reduce the crime rate in the state if the state doubled expenditures for police. To support her argument, Martina runs a regression of state crime rates (Y) (in crimes per 100,000 population) on per capita police expenditures (in dollars). She finds the following:

$$\hat{Y} = 2{,}475 + 5.1X \quad S_{y|x} = 425 \quad s_b = 1.3 \quad r^2 = .63 \quad n = 50$$

What has Martina found? Interpret the slope, intercept, and r^2.

18.4 The South Dakota Department of Game and Fish (SDDGF) wants to lengthen the pheasant-hunting season to bring in more tourist revenue. SDDGF's thinking is that most pheasants are killed during the first 2 weeks of the season; therefore, a longer season will not deplete the bird population. Using sample data from all past hunting seasons, Rodney Ringneck, the SDDGF's data analyst, regresses the number of birds surviving the season on the length in days in the season. He finds

$$\hat{Y} = 547{,}000 - 214X \quad s_b = 415 \quad r^2 = .15 \quad S_{y|x} = 15{,}000 \quad n = 35$$

What is Rodney's hypothesis? What did he find?

18.5 Lieutenant Edgar Beaver believes that officers who take master's-level courses receive higher officer efficiency ratings (OERs). Using a sample of 100 officers, Beaver regresses OERs (Y—it ranges from 0 to 100) on the number of courses each officer took beyond the BA. He finds

$$\hat{Y} = 95 + .1X \quad S_{y|x} = 1.4 \quad s_b = .07 \quad r^2 = .4$$
$$\bar{X} = 5 \quad s_x = 8$$

What can Beaver say based on these results? Beaver has a 10-course master's degree. What is the best estimate of his OER? Place a 90% confidence limit around this estimate.

18.6 Caretakers, a local nonprofit organization, operates the concession stands for the Newland Baseball Park, home of the Newland Nuggets (a minor league baseball team). Doing so permits Caretakers to raise funds to operate its soup kitchen. Caretakers is concerned with waste in the concessions area. Too many precooked hot dogs are left over after a game. Heinz Canine, their research analyst, feels that hot dog consumption (and other concession sales) can be predicted by the number of advance sale tickets purchased for a game (attendance is usually twice advance sales). Heinz gathers the accompanying data for a sample of 10 days. Run the regression for Heinz and tell him whether his hypothesis is correct. Predict how many hot dogs will be sold if 1,000 advance tickets are sold.

Advance Sales	Hot Dog Sales
247	503
317	691
1,247	2,638
784	1,347
247	602
1,106	2,493
1,749	3,502
875	2,100
963	1,947
415	927

18.7 The Nome City Personnel Office suspects that employees are staying home on cold days during the winter. The personnel office regresses the number of absences on the low temperature of the preceding night. Using a sample of 60 days, it finds

$$\hat{Y} = 485 - 5.1X \quad s_b = 1.1 \quad S_{y|x} = 12.0 \quad r^2 = .86$$
$$\bar{X} = 20 \quad s_x = 35$$

Interpret the intercept, the slope, and r^2. Is the relationship significant? How many people will miss work if the overnight low is $-20°$? Place 90% confidence limits around this estimate.

18.8 Ridership on the North Salem Independent Transit System is increasing. The city's program evaluation office feels that the increase in the number of riders every day is due to the price of gasoline. Using data for the past 3 years, the evaluation office regresses daily ridership (Y) on the price of gasoline (in cents) for that day (X). It finds

$$\hat{Y} = 212 + 187X \quad s_b = 17.4 \quad S_{y|x} = 206 \quad r^2 = .91$$

Write a memo on the policy implications of a 50¢ increase in gasoline prices.

18.9 The Environmental Protection Agency believes that the air quality in a city is directly related to the number of serious respiratory diseases. The agency regresses the number of reported cases of respiratory diseases per 1,000 population on the city's air quality index (ranges from 0 to 100; high scores indicate pollution) for 150 cities. It finds

$$\hat{Y} = 15.7 + .7X \quad s_b = .04 \quad S_{y|x} = 5.1 \quad r^2 = .71$$

Write a memo interpreting these results. What other factors affect this relationship?

18.10 The Office of Gerontology Policy is considering a lawsuit against the Bureau of Investigations for age discrimination. OGP wants to base its suit on the following regression of civil service exam scores (Y) on age of applicant (X) for the Bureau of Investigations. Write a memo evaluating OGP's case.

$$\hat{Y} = 92.4 - .3X \quad s_b = .007 \quad S_{y|x} = 5.2 \quad r^2 = .45 \quad n = 500$$

18.11 The Wisconsin Association of School Districts is interested in the relationship between school district population and funding for schools. From a sample of 300 school districts, the association uses simple regression to predict total school district expenditures in dollars (Y) using the school district's population ($X =$ number of persons residing in the district). They find

$$\hat{Y} = \$4,566 - \$824X$$
$$s_b = 135 \quad S_{y|x} = 34,788 \quad r^2 = .78$$
$$t = 6.10 \quad p < .0001$$

Express in plain English what the substantive interpretations of the following are:

(a) the intercept

(b) the slope

(c) the coefficient of determination

(d) the *t* score and how it is calculated

18.12 Stanley Student is an MPA candidate at Big State University. Stanley is concerned about his performance in the BSU's quantitative methods class. The class has consisted of five quizzes and one midterm exam. Stanley is thinking of filing a civil rights suit against his professor because he did really well on the quizzes (a total of 45 points) but not as well on the midterm (75 points). He is thinking of using a unique application of the administrative law doctrine of collateral estoppel in his suit. Before filing suit, he needs to know whether there is a relationship between quiz grades and midterm grades. After stealing the instructor's grade book, Stanley runs the following regression, where Y is the midterm grade and X is the total points on the quizzes:

$$\hat{Y} = 52.5 + .78X$$
$$S_{y|x} = 8.46 \quad \overline{X} = 40$$
$$r^2 = .71 \quad s_b = .0049 \quad n = 40 \quad s_x = 5$$

Interpret this regression by explaining the meaning of the slope, intercept, and r^2, and test the slope for significance. Present, in plain English, a hypothesis concerning the relationship, and then a null hypothesis. What is your best estimate of the midterm grade that Stanley should have received given his quiz grade? Estimate the probability that Stanley would receive a 75 on the midterm given a quiz grade of 45.

18.13 The State Department of Mental Health is doing a study of the use of drugs to control violent behavior among its patients. The case histories of 75 patients are selected for analysis. For each patient two variables are collected: the number of violent incidents the patient was involved in during the previous 3 months and the daily dosage of Valium given to each patient in milligrams. A regression analysis results in the following:

$$\hat{Y} = 126.6 - .0138X$$
$$s_b = .0053 \quad S_{y|x} = 2.4 \quad r^2 = .46$$
$$\overline{X} = 500 \quad s_x = 200$$

What is the department's hypothesis? Interpret this regression. Is the hypothesis supported? Estimate the number of violent incidents that would be expected if a patient were given 1,000 milligrams of Valium per day. Put a 90% confidence limit around this estimate.

18.14 The Bureau of Personnel needs to predict how many employees will retire next month. Based on a sample of 35 past months, the bureau has run a regression using the number of employees older than age 60 as the independent variable and the number of retirements as the dependent variable. They calculate the following regression:

$$\hat{Y} = .21 + .04X$$
$$r^2 = .35 \quad S_{y|x} = 4.5 \quad s_b = .006 \quad \overline{X} = 540 \quad s_x = 90$$

Interpret the slope, intercept, and coefficient of determination, and test the slope for significance. What is your best estimate of the number of retirements next month if there are 620 employees older than 60? Could this number be as high as 30?

18.15 Dick Engstrom and Mike MacDonald are interested in the relationship between African American representation on city councils and the structure of the electoral system. Their independent variable is the percentage of African Americans in the population; their dependent variable is the percentage of seats on the city council that are held by African Americans. Engstrom and MacDonald want to compare representation under single-member district election systems and under at-large election systems. They get the following results:

At-Large Systems

$$\hat{Y} = .348 + .495X$$

$$r^2 = .34 \quad n = 128 \quad s_b = .061 \quad S_{ylx} = 2.4 \quad \overline{X} = 15 \quad s_x = 5.1$$

Single-Member District Systems

$$\hat{Y} = -.832 + .994X$$

$$r^2 = .816 \quad n = 36 \quad s_b = .075 \quad S_{ylx} = 2.1 \quad \overline{X} = 20 \quad s_x = 8$$

For each equation, interpret the slope, intercept, and coefficient of determination. Test the slope to see whether it could be zero. Get the predicted city council representation of a city with 25% African American population under both systems. Place a 95% confidence limit around your estimates. Present a hypothesis about the relative impact of electoral systems. What can you say about the relative representation of African Americans under each type of system?

18.16 Robert Stein of Brooklyn Associates argues that the per capita allocation of federal aid dollars to local governments is related to local needs. He measures *aid* as the number of dollars a city receives per person and *need* as the percentage of city residents that reside in poverty. For 1991, he gets the following results:

$$\hat{Y} = 27.81 + 339.10X$$

$$r^2 = .43 \quad n = 243 \quad s_b = 93.4 \quad S_{ylx} = 124.066$$

Interpret this equation. Present a hypothesis and a null hypothesis, and evaluate the hypotheses based on this equation.

18.17 Presidential candidate Rebecca Hendrick wants to know whether it would be worthwhile to challenge the incumbent next year. If she decides to run, she feels the key issue should be inflation, so she is interested in whether or not the inflation rate (X, in percentage increase in the Consumer Price Index) is related to the percentage of the vote received by the presidential candidate of the party in power. Using 12 elections, the following regression is found:

$$\hat{Y} = 54.3 - .84X \quad s_b = .24 \quad r^2 = .34 \quad S_{ylx} = 1.9 \quad \overline{X} = 6.7 \quad s_x = 3$$

Interpret this equation. Present a hypothesis and a null hypothesis, and test them. If inflation is 8%, predict the vote for the incumbent's party, and place an 80% confidence limit around it.

Answer to Regression Problem

$$\bar{X} = 7.1 \quad \bar{Y} = 84$$

$X_i - \bar{X}$	$(X_i - \bar{X})^2$	$Y_i - \bar{Y}$	$(X_i - \bar{X}) \times (Y_i - \bar{Y})$
$12.4 - 7.1 = \quad 5.3$	28.1	$146 - 84 = \quad 62$	$5.3 \times \quad 62 = 328.6$
$6.1 - 7.1 = -1.0$	1.0	$85 - 84 = \quad 1$	$-1.0 \times \quad 1 = -1.0$
$2.4 - 7.1 = -4.7$	22.1	$21 - 84 = -63$	$-4.7 \times -63 = 296.1$
$4.3 - 7.1 = -2.8$	7.8	$47 - 84 = -37$	$-2.8 \times -37 = 103.6$
$9.5 - 7.1 = \quad 2.4$	5.8	$115 - 84 = \quad 31$	$2.4 \times \quad 31 = 74.4$
$7.6 - 7.1 = \quad .5$	.3	$90 - 84 = \quad 6$	$.5 \times \quad 6 = 3.0$

$$\Sigma(X_i - \bar{X})(Y_i - \bar{Y}) = 804.7$$
$$\Sigma(X_i - \bar{X})^2 = 65.1$$
$$b = \frac{804.7}{65.1} = 12.4$$
$$a = \bar{Y} - b\bar{X} = 84 - 12.4 \times 7.1 = 84 - 88.0 = -4.0$$
$$\hat{Y} = -4.0 + 12.4X$$

CHAPTER 19

The Assumptions of Linear Regression

The presentation in Chapter 18 did not discuss the assumptions and limitations of linear regression. In the real world, analysts sometimes ignore these assumptions, but they do so at some managerial risk. All the uses of regression presented in the previous chapter become less reliable when any of the assumptions is not met.

In Chapter 18, recall that our highway patrol example found that

$$\hat{Y} = 72.2 - 2.55X \quad r^2 = .94$$

where $\hat{Y}$ is the predicted speed of all cars, and X is the number of patrol cars. In our discussion in Chapter 18, we found that $\hat{Y}_i$ did not exactly equal the real value of Y_i. According to the coefficient of determination, we only accounted for 94% of the variation in Y with $\hat{Y}$. What sort of other factors account for average car speed other than number of patrol cars on the road?

We can think of several factors. The weather conditions on any given day can slow traffic. The emergence and filling of potholes affect traffic speed. The number of other cars on the road restricts any one car's speed. The curves and hills on a stretch of highway affect traffic speed. These factors and others probably account for the difference between Y_i and $\hat{Y}_i$. We could express this symbolically as

$$\hat{Y} = \alpha + \beta X + \beta_1(X_1, X_2, X_3, X_4)$$

where X_1, X_2, X_3, X_4 are the other factors, and β_1 is some weight (slope).

To simplify matters, we generally refer to all the other factors as e, or error.

$$Y = \alpha + \beta X + e$$

That is, the value of Y is equal to some constant (α) plus a slope (β) times X plus some error (e).

We introduce this terminology because most assumptions about linear regression are concerned with the error component. In this chapter, we will discuss the assumptions and limitations of linear regression.

Assumption 1

For any value of X, the errors in predicting Y are normally distributed with a mean of zero.

To illustrate, let us assume that we continue the Normal, Oklahoma, patrol car experiment for an entire year. Every day between one and seven cars are sent out to patrol the local highway, and the average speed of all cars is measured. At the end of the year, let us assume that the overall regression equation remains the same:

$$\hat{Y} = 72.2 - 2.55X$$

By the end of the year, we probably have 50 days when four patrol cars were on the road. The average speed for each of these 50 days is listed in Table 19.1 in a frequency distribution.

Table 19.1

Frequency Distribution for Patrol Cars and Average Speeds (in mph)

Average Speed	Number of Days
58.5–59.0	1
59.0–59.5	2
59.5–60.0	2
60.0–60.5	4
60.5–61.0	4
61.0–61.5	6
61.5–62.0	6
62.0–62.5	6
62.5–63.0	6
63.0–63.5	4
63.5–64.0	4
64.0–64.5	2
64.5–65.0	2
65.0–65.5	1
65.5–66.0	0

Table 19.2

Error Calculations

Average Speed	−	Predicted Speed	=	Error	×	Frequency	=	Total Error
58.75	−	62	=	−3.25	×	1	=	−3.25
59.25	−	62	=	−2.75	×	2	=	−5.50
59.75	−	62	=	−2.25	×	2	=	−4.50
60.25	−	62	=	−1.75	×	4	=	−7.00
60.75	−	62	=	−1.25	×	4	=	−5.00
61.25	−	62	=	−.75	×	6	=	−4.50
61.75	−	62	=	−.25	×	6	=	−1.50
62.25	−	62	=	.25	×	6	=	1.50
62.75	−	62	=	.75	×	6	=	4.50
63.25	−	62	=	1.25	×	4	=	5.00
63.75	−	62	=	1.75	×	4	=	7.00
64.25	−	62	=	2.25	×	2	=	4.50
64.75	−	62	=	2.75	×	2	=	5.50
65.25	−	62	=	3.25	×	1	=	3.25

Using the midpoint of the frequencies to represent each interval, we can calculate the error for each prediction, because we know that the predicted speed for four patrol cars is 62 miles per hour ($72.2 - 2.55 \times 4 = 62$). The error calculations are given in Table 19.2. The mean error for all 50 cars is 0 (add the last column and divide by 50) and is distributed fairly close to normal.

Whenever e has a mean of zero and is normally distributed, statisticians have found that sample slopes (b) have a mean equal to the population slope (β) and are distributed like the t distribution with a standard deviation s_b. When the sample size is fairly large ($N > 30$), the t distribution resembles the normal distribution, and z scores can be used as estimates of t scores. Because the t distribution is flatter than the normal distribution (the t has greater probability in the tails), it behooves us to use large samples whenever possible.

Assumption 2

The variance of the error term is constant, regardless of the value of X. In other words, errors do not get larger as X gets larger. In Figure 19.1(a), errors have the same variance for all values of X_i; in Figure 19.1(b), the errors get larger as the value of X increases.

If this assumption of linear regression is violated—statisticians call it **homoscedasticity**—then the slope coefficient will appear to be significant when, in fact, it may not be. Techniques exist for handling many types of nonhomoscedasticity, but they are fairly advanced. The term *homoscedasticity* is a good one to know. The manager can always disturb her statistician by asking her whether the homoscedasticity assumption is met.

Figure 19.1

Errors and Their Variance

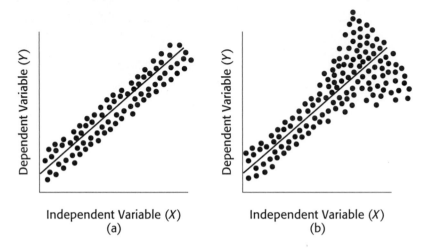

Independent Variable (*X*)
(a)

Independent Variable (*X*)
(b)

Although we have been discussing errors for which the size of the error is positively related to the value of X (as X increases, e increases), the opposite situation is just as severe. If e decreases as X increases, the data are still nonhomoscedastic.

Assumption 3

Assumption 3 is related to Assumptions 1 and 2. Assumption 3 is that the errors are independent of each other.

Another way of stating this assumption is to say that the size of one error is not a function of the size of any previous errors. We can test for nonindependent errors by examining the residuals (the predicted value of Y minus the actual value of Y). If they appear to be random with respect to each other, then the errors are independent, and we need not worry. Computer programs exist that can determine whether errors are not random. If this problem ever exists, find a statistician or consult a textbook [see Pindyck and Rubinfeld, (1997); Nelson, (1973)]. This problem usually causes difficulty only when time series data are used (see Chapter 20). Chapter 22 includes a test for nonrandom errors.

Assumption 4

Both the independent and the dependent variables must be interval variables (see Chapter 2).

The purist position is that regression cannot be performed with nominal or ordinal data. In a practical situation, however, regression with nominal or ordinal

Table 19.3

Mower Brand and Acres of Grass Mowed

Mower	Acres of Grass Mowed
Brand $A1$	52
Brand $A2$	63
Brand $A3$	71
Brand $B1$	54
Brand $B2$	46
Brand $B3$	38

$X_i - \bar{X} = (X_i - \bar{X})$	$(X_i - \bar{X})^2$	$Y_i - \bar{Y} = (Y_i - \bar{Y})$
$1 - .5 = \quad .5$	.25	$52 - 54 = \quad -2$
$1 - .5 = \quad .5$	.25	$63 - 54 = \quad 9$
$1 - .5 = \quad .5$	.25	$71 - 54 = \quad 17$
$0 - .5 = \quad -.5$	.25	$54 - 54 = \quad 0$
$0 - .5 = \quad -.5$	.25	$46 - 54 = \quad -8$
$0 - .5 = \quad -.5$	.25	$38 - 54 = \quad -16$

$$\sum(X_i - \bar{X})^2 = 1.50$$

$(X_i - \bar{X})$	$\times$	$(Y_i - \bar{Y})$	$=$	$(X_i - \bar{X})(Y_i - \bar{Y})$
.5	$\times$	-2	$=$	-1
.5	$\times$	9	$=$	4.5
.5	$\times$	17	$=$	8.5
$-.5$	$\times$	0	$=$	0
$-.5$	$\times$	-8	$=$	4.0
$-.5$	$\times$	-16	$=$	8.0

$$\sum(X_i - \bar{X})(Y_i - \bar{Y}) = 24$$

$$b = \frac{24}{1.5} = 16$$

$$a = \bar{Y} - b\bar{X} = 54 - (16 \times .5) = 46$$

$$\hat{Y} = 46 + 16X$$

dependent and independent variables is possible. First, we will illustrate regression with a nominal independent variable.

The Homegrove City Parks superintendent wants to determine whether brand A or brand B riding mowers are more efficient. He tries three of each riding mower, testing them over normal city parks; he finds the data given in Table 19.3.

If the independent variable (the type of mower) is coded 1 when brand A is used and coded 0 when brand B is used, we have a nominal variable (nominal variables with values of 1 or 0 are called **dummy variables**).

X	Y	$\bar{X} = .5$	$\bar{Y} = 54$
1	52		
1	63		
1	71		
0	54		
0	46		
0	38		

Recall from Chapter 18 that the formula for the slope of the regression line is

$$\frac{\sum(X_i - \bar{X})(Y_i - \bar{Y})}{\sum(X_i - \bar{X})^2}$$

The calculations follow.

Because X can be only two values, 0 and 1, $\hat{Y}$ can be only two values, 46 and 62. If we test for the significance of the regression slope, we will find whether the brand A mowers cut significantly more grass than do the brand B mowers. Recall that the formula for the standard error of the slope is

$$s_b = \frac{S_{y|x}}{\sqrt{\sum(X - \bar{X})^2}} = \frac{S_{y|x}}{\sqrt{1.5}} = \frac{S_{y|x}}{1.22}$$

Recall that $S_{y|x}$ can be calculated by the following formula:

$$S_{y|x}^2 = \frac{\sum(Y_i - \hat{Y}_i)^2}{n - 2}$$

The calculations follow.

$Y_i -$	$\hat{Y}_i =$	$(Y_i - \hat{Y}_i)$	$(Y_i - \hat{Y}_i)^2$
52 −	62 =	−10	100
63 −	62 =	1	1
71 −	62 =	9	81
54 −	46 =	8	64
46 −	46 =	0	0
38 −	46 =	−8	64

$$S_{y|x}^2 = \frac{\sum(Y_i - \hat{Y}_i)^2}{n - 2} = \frac{310}{4} = 77.5$$

$$S_{y|x} = 8.8$$

Substituting this value into the preceding formula yields

$$s_b = \frac{8.8}{1.22} = 7.2$$

Converting $b = 16.0$ to a t score, we have

$$t = \frac{16.0 - 0}{7.2} = 2.22$$

With a t score of 2.22, the probability of brand A being no better than brand B is approximately .05 (t test, df $= 4$).

When the mower problem was first presented, you may have thought that this problem could have been solved with a test of means (see Chapter 14). Indeed, it can.

Brand A	Brand B
$\bar{X} = 62$	$\bar{Y} = 46$
$s = 9.5$	$s = 8.0$
s.e. $= 5.48$	s.e. $= 4.61$

$$\text{s.e.}_d = \sqrt{5.48^2 + 4.61^2} = 7.2$$

$$t = \frac{62 - 46}{7.2} = \frac{16}{7.2} = 2.22$$

Notice that we get the same answer that we obtained using regression. This result occurs because a difference of means test is similar to regression with dummy variables (a dummy variable is a nominal variable with codes 1 and 0). You should also note that the regression intercept (46) is the same value as one of the means; the slope (16) is equal to the difference between the means; and the standard error of the slope (7.2) is equal to the overall standard error in the difference of means test.

Regression can also be performed with a nominal dependent variable. Suppose a personnel office tests the data entry skills of 10 job applicants, who are then hired. After 1 year, five of these processors have been fired. A personnel manager hypothesizes that the processors were fired because they lacked good keyboard skills. The job situation and data processing scores are listed in Table 19.4.

Table 19.4

	Job Situation and Data Processing Score
Job Situation, Y (0 = Fired; 1 = Not Fired)	Data Processing Score, X (Words per Minute)
1	85
0	48
1	63
0	57
1	94
0	56
1	65
0	58
0	72
1	82

After subjecting these data to a regression computer program, the analyst found the following relationship:

$$\hat{Y} = -1.19 + .0248X \quad s_b = .009$$

$$S_{y|x} = .4 \quad r^2 = .49$$

Clearly a relationship exists ($t = 2.8$, df = 8). To interpret this regression, we must interpret $\hat{Y}$ as the probability that a processor is not fired. For example, substituting the first person's data processing score into the regression equation, we find

$$\hat{Y} = -1.19 + .0248(85) = -1.19 + 2.11 = .92$$

The probability that the first person will not be fired is .92. Similar calculations could be made for all data processors, and confidence limits could be placed around the probability by using the standard error of the estimate.

Regression with dummy dependent variables does have some pitfalls. If we substitute the word processing score of the fifth person (94) into the regression equation, we find

$$\hat{Y} = -1.19 + .0248(94) = -1.19 + 2.33 = 1.14$$

The probability that this person will not be fired is 1.14, a meaningless probability. Using regression with dummy dependent variables often results in probabilities greater than 1 or less than 0. Managerially, we might want to interpret probabilities of more than 1.0 as equal to .99. Similarly, probabilities of less than 0 can be reset to .01. For most management situations, these adjustments will eliminate uninterpretable predictions. Special types of analysis called *probit and logit analysis* can be used to restrict probabilities to values between 0 and 1. These techniques are fairly sophisticated and, therefore, should not be used without expert assistance.

Assumption 5

The final assumption of regression is that the relationships are linear.

Linear relationships are those that can be summarized by a straight line (without any curve). If linear regression is used to summarize a nonlinear relationship, the regression equation will be inaccurate. To determine whether a relationship is linear, we must plot the data on a set of coordinate axes, just as we have been doing in this chapter and in Chapter 18. The data plotted in Figure 19.2 represent linear relationships.

Unfortunately, many relationships that a manager must consider are not linear. For example, the city manager may want to project city revenues for next year. The growth of city revenues may well look like the graph in Figure 19.3. Revenues increase in this example faster than a linear relationship would predict. The graph represents a **logarithmic relationship.** Such relationships and how they can be treated in regression are the subject of the next chapter.

Another relationship sometimes found in the public and nonprofit sectors is the *quadratic* relationship. In situations in which adding another worker will improve the productivity of all workers (because workers can then specialize and be more efficient),

Figure 19.2

Linear Relationships

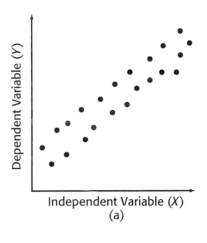
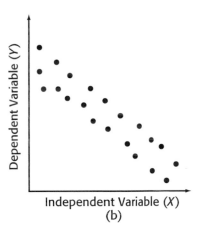

Figure 19.3

A Nonlinear Relationship

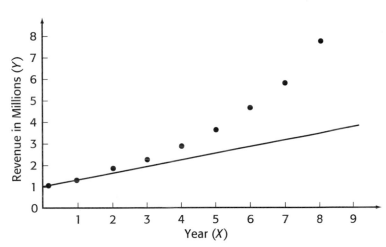

the relationship between the number of workers and total productivity may be quadratic. This idea is illustrated by the data in Table 19.5. Graphically, this relationship appears as shown in Figure 19.4. Quadratic relationships are discussed in Chapter 21.

Other relationships may be *cubic*. For example, the relationship of the total number of vice police to the number of prostitution arrests is probably cubic. The first few vice police will make very few arrests because they have so much territory to cover. Adding more vice police will raise the productivity of all vice police. As more and

Table 19.5

Data Representing a Quadratic Relationship

Number of Welfare Workers (X)	Number of Cases Processed per Day (Y)
1	1
2	4
3	9
4	16
5	25

Figure 19.4

A Quadratic Relationship

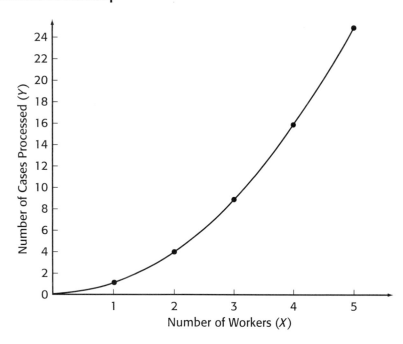

more vice police are added, the total arrests will level out (either because all possible prostitutes have been arrested or because they left town). The relationship would appear as shown in Figure 19.5. Cubic relationships will also be discussed in Chapter 21.

The important thing to remember about nonlinear relationships is that linear regression is not a good way to summarize them. Computers cannot (or, rather, usually do not) distinguish linear from nonlinear relationships; the onus is on the manager to discern nonlinear relationships.

Figure 19.5

A Cubic Relationship

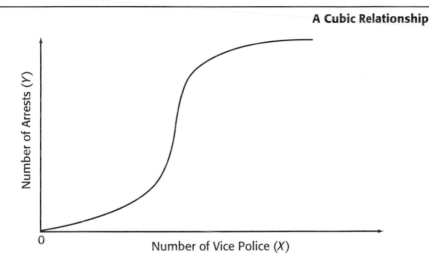

Chapter Summary

This chapter discusses five assumptions made by simple linear regression and presents some of the problems associated with violating these assumptions. The assumptions are as follows: (1) all errors in prediction are normally distributed, (2) the distribution of the errors is constant regardless of the value of X, (3) the errors are independent of each other, (4) both variables are measured at the interval level, and (5) the relationship is linear. Sometimes analysts ignore these assumptions in their day-to-day routine, but they do so at some managerial risk. All the analytical techniques of regression analysis presented in the previous chapter and in those following become less reliable when any of the assumptions is not met.

Problems

19.1   The Normal police chief wants to know whether police car cruising has any impact on crime rates. Of the city's 10 precincts, 5 are cruised regularly, and the other 5 are never cruised (police do respond to calls in these precincts). At the end of a test period, the police chief takes the crime rate (Y) in each precinct and regresses it on a dummy variable coded 1 for cruising and coded 0 for no cruising (X). From the following regression equation, what can you say about police cruising and crime rates in Normal?

$$\hat{Y} = 247.5 + 24X \quad s_b = 48 \quad S_{y|x} = 35.0 \quad r^2 = .12$$

19.2 Take each set of data in the accompanying table and graph it. Determine whether the relationships are linear or nonlinear. If nonlinear, state what type of relationship it is.

No. 1		No. 2		No. 3		No. 4	
X	Y	X	Y	X	Y	X	Y
2	1	2	1	1	5	1	15
5	3	5	3	4	8	2	11
7	6	8	5	7	11	4	6
9	10	11	9	10	14	6	4
14	15	14	14	13	17	9	3
17	16			16	20	15	2

19.3 The city parks chief is concerned about sprinkler systems corroding in parks and failing to operate. Using a sample of 100 sprinklers in operation the previous year, the parks department regresses whether a sprinkler failed (Y, coded 1 for failure and 0 for no failure) on the age of the sprinkler system. The department gets the following regression equation (X is age in years):

$$\hat{Y} = .06 + .016X \quad s_b = .0006$$
$$S_{y|x} = .04 \quad r^2 = .56$$

(a) Is there a relationship?

(b) The sprinkler system in Frolic Park is 52 years old. What is the probability that this sprinkler system will fail?

(c) A sprinkler system that is only two years old fails in Barren Park. What is the probability that this will happen?

(d) What is the probability that the 65-year-old sprinkler system in Choir-practice Park will fail?

19.4 Too many U.S. Army mechanics are failing their yearly skills tests. Colonel Maxwell Brown believes that this failure rate results because mechanics do not learn anything from experience. His hypothesis is that time spent in an occupational specialty is unrelated to performance on the exam. He regresses whether a mechanic failed the test ($0 =$ failure, and $1 =$ no failure) on the mechanic's time as a mechanic (X) in years. For a sample of 400 troops, he finds

$$\hat{Y} = .63 + .03X \quad S_{y|x} = .41 \quad s_b = .61 \quad r^2 = .09$$

Evaluate Brown's argument by interpreting the regression.

19.5 Refer to Problem 19.4. Sergeant Desk believes the failures are related to reading ability. She regresses whether these same 400 troops failed (Y) on their reading test scores (X, scored in terms of school grade levels). She finds

$$\hat{Y} = .15 + .071X \quad S_{y|x} = .06 \quad s_b = .011 \quad r^2 = .80$$

Interpret Desk's regression. Compare her argument with that of Brown's. Can you reconcile them?

19.6 Refer to Problem 19.5. What is the probability that a troop reading at the fifth-grade level will pass the mechanics' exam? To be 80% sure that 75% of the mechanics pass the exam, what would the reading level need to be raised to? Comment on the validity of the mechanics' exam.

19.7 The Department of Health and Human Services (HHS) wants to compare average per capita health care costs for four cities that have health maintenance organizations (HMOs) with four similar cities that do not have HMOs. Using the accompanying data, run a regression, and prepare a brief memo to HHS about the findings.

HMO CITIES	Non-HMO CITIES
$412	$516
$386	$250
$370	$409
$404	$460

19.8 The Intercity Bus Company is concerned with the high cost of fuel. The company believes that fuel is being wasted because drivers are exceeding the speed limit. A series of tests ($N = 85$) shows the following relationship between bus speed (X) and miles per gallon of fuel (Y) for speeds between 35 and 85 miles per hour (mph):

$$\hat{Y} = 12.4 - .11X \quad s_b = .007 \quad S_{y|x} = .41 \quad r^2 = .98$$
$$\bar{X} = 50 \quad s_x = 15$$

Intercity is considering placing a governor on all buses, limiting their speed to 55 mph. At an average speed of 55 mph, how many miles per gallon would a bus get? Place a 95% confidence limit around this estimate.

19.9 Refer to Problem 19.8. Intercity buses travel 8,200 miles a week. Current miles per gallon for buses is 5.1. Provide an estimate of the amount of money that could be saved in a week (with a 55-mph governor) if fuel costs $2 per gallon. Place 95% confidence limits around this estimate.

19.10 The White Hawk Indian Tribe wants to know whether their Head Start program is having any impact. To examine this question, an analyst regresses the reading scores in class grade equivalents of all fourth-grade students (Y) on whether the student was enrolled in a Head Start program (1 = enrolled; 0 = not enrolled). Interpret the following regression for the tribe.

$$\hat{Y} = 3.2 + .06X \quad s_b = .1 \quad S_{y|x} = 1.1 \quad r^2 = .16$$

19.11 The South Carolina Insurance Commission wants to know whether states that have no-fault insurance for automobiles have lower insurance rates. The commission takes a survey of 20 states and asks whether they have a no-fault insurance law (coded 1 if they do) and determines the cost (in dollars) of an automobile insurance policy for a 30-year-old male driver who drives 15,000 miles per year and owns a 1992 Dodge Omni. It gets the following results:

$$\hat{Y} = \$265.00 - 74.33X$$
$$s_b = 29.4 \quad S_{y|x} = 14.9 \quad r^2 = .34$$

Present a hypothesis, a null hypothesis, and evaluate them. Present a conclusion in plain English. Do not forget to interpret the regression.

19.12 A study by the Occupational Safety and Health Administration seeks to know whether the probability that an industrial plant is inspected is affected by the number of accidents at the plant. An analyst regresses whether a plant is inspected (1 = inspected) on the number of accidents resulting in a lost day of work (X). He finds:

$$\hat{Y} = .04 + .012X$$
$$s_b = .0021 \quad S_{y|x} = .19 \quad r^2 = .48 \quad n = 320$$
$$\bar{X} = 47 \quad s_x = 22$$

Interpret this regression. If Ace Manufacturing has 14 accidents resulting in lost work days, what can you say about whether it will be inspected?

CHAPTER 20

Time Series Analysis

Any public manager who can accurately predict the future will become a member of the Senior Executive Service before he or she is 35 years old. Any nonprofit manager who can do so is likely to become the executive director of an agency before he or she reaches that age. In many situations, a manager must make decisions today that will not be implemented until next year, and the success of those decisions will depend on factors unknown at the time of the decision. A personnel manager needs to know the agency's total employment for next year to negotiate health care plans with private insurers. A city budget officer needs to know next year's revenue to make current budget decisions. A public works planner needs to know the demand for sewage disposal over the next 20 years so that disposal systems can be designed and constructed. The director of volunteers at the local Red Cross needs to know when demand for volunteers is likely to be highest (or lowest) to plan a recruitment campaign for the coming year.

Projecting the future state of some managerially relevant variable is called **forecasting.** The major building block that permits data-based forecasting is called **time series analysis.** This chapter will illustrate a variety of time series techniques. First, the general principles of time series analysis will be presented. Second, simple time series linear regression models will be illustrated, followed by a more common logarithmic regression model. Third, the forecasting ability of these models will be illustrated. Finally, the bivariate time series model will be discussed.

Introduction to Time Series

A **time series** is nothing more than a sequence of observations on some variable (Y) when the observations occur at equally spaced time intervals. To illustrate the general principles of time series, we will use the following example. Kerry Jones, the head of the Flagler City Public Works Department, needs to know the number of absences by sanitation engineers. Kerry uses this information to hire substitutes, who are then assigned to refuse policing units (garbage crews) when a member of the crew does not show up for work. Substitutes are assigned because the efficiency of a crew drops dramatically when the crew is shorthanded. At the same time, Kerry announces an incentive program to reduce absenteeism. Any employee who does not use his or her sick leave by the end of the year will receive a cash payment. The graph in Figure 20.1 shows the number of absent sanitary engineers for the 6 weeks following the announcement of the incentive program.

The first noticeable aspect of the absenteeism graph is that a **cyclical pattern** based on the day of the week is present. Monday consistently has the second highest number of absentees. Absenteeism then drops on Tuesday and falls still further on Wednesday. After a slight increase on Thursday, absenteeism skyrockets to its weekly high on Friday. The cyclical pattern is the first important aspect that the analyst reports. It tells the analyst that absenteeism follows the same pattern for the public works department that it follows for most businesses, government, and nonprofits (that is, much absenteeism appears to result from long weekends).

A second, perhaps more important, question for Kerry Jones is, Did the absenteeism rate decline after the incentive system was introduced? This question is difficult to answer from the graph because the day-to-day fluctuations (*short-term variation*) obscure any long-term trend. If the short-term fluctuations could be removed from the data, however, the long-term trend would be visible.

Figure 20.1

Number of Absences for 6 Weeks

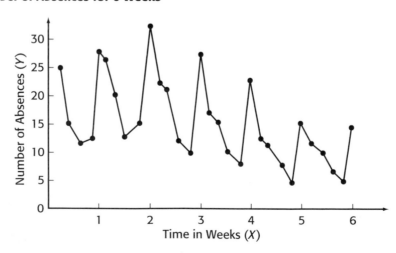

The accepted way to filter out a short-term fluctuation is by using a **moving average.** The first step is to determine how long the short-term cycle is. In this situation, the length of the short-term trend is obvious—5 days. Absenteeism follows a 5-day pattern, peaking on Mondays and Fridays. In this situation, then, a five-term moving average is needed.

To get a five-term moving average, simply take each day's number of absences and add the absences for the 2 previous days and the 2 following days. Divide this sum by 5. The resulting number is the five-term moving average. These calculations are performed in Table 20.1. (Note that the first 2 and the last 2 days in the

Table 20.1

Calculations for a Five-Term Moving Average

Week	Day	Day Number	Absences (Y)	Sum	Five-Term Average	Fluctuation
1	M	1	25			
	Tu	2	15			
	W	3	11	91	18.2	−7.2
	Th	4	12	92	18.4	−6.4
	F	5	28	97	19.4	8.6
2	M	6	26	98	19.6	6.4
	Tu	7	20	99	19.8	.2
	W	8	12	103	20.6	−8.6
	Th	9	13	99	19.8	−6.8
	F	10	32	100	20.0	12.0
3	M	11	22	100	20.0	2.0
	Tu	12	21	97	19.4	1.6
	W	13	12	93	18.6	−6.6
	Th	14	10	88	17.6	−7.6
	F	15	28	82	16.4	11.6
4	M	16	17	80	16.0	1.0
	Tu	17	15	78	15.6	−.6
	W	18	10	73	14.6	−4.6
	Th	19	8	68	13.6	−5.6
	F	20	23	64	12.8	10.2
5	M	21	12	61	12.2	−.2
	Tu	22	11	58	11.6	−.6
	W	23	7	50	10.0	−3.0
	Th	24	5	49	9.8	−4.8
	F	25	15	48	9.6	5.4
6	M	26	11	47	9.4	1.6
	Tu	27	10	47	9.4	.6
	W	28	6	46	9.2	−3.2
	Th	29	5			
	F	30	14			

Figure 20.2

Five-Term Moving Average and Absenteeism

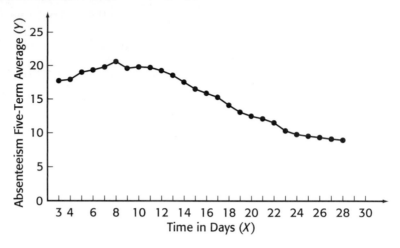

table do not have five-term moving averages.) The five-term moving average can then be graphed to determine whether the absenteeism rate is declining. See Figure 20.2.

From the graph in Figure 20.2, we can clearly see a trend in absences. If Kerry were interested in a further specification of the relationship, he could apply regression analysis to the data. This result would tell him how strong the relationship between time and absenteeism is (or, within the context of this problem, how great a decline in absenteeism followed the incentive program).

Whenever the length of a short-term fluctuation is an odd number, computing a moving average is easy. In our example, the value for the third observation was the average of observations 1, 2, 3, 4, and 5. For a three-term moving average, the value of the third observation is the average of observations 2, 3, and 4. For a short-term fluctuation of an even number of terms, we run into a problem. Using the previous data for a four-term moving average model, we find that the first moving average is 15.8—but this is the value for the 2½ observation. A 2½ observation does not make sense. In this situation, we first calculate the four-term moving average for the 3½ observation (16.5). Then we take the average of the 2½ observation and the 3½ observation and assign this value to the third observation [(15.8 + 16.5) ÷ 2 = 16.2]. We continue this procedure for all items, as illustrated here.

Observation:	1	2	3	4	5	6	7
Four-term average:		15.8	16.5	19.3	21.5	21.5	
Adjusted average:			16.2	17.9	20.4	21.5	

Forecasting without Fluctuation

The chief personnel officer of Blanchard needs to know approximately how many employees Blanchard will have each year for the next 5 years. The only information that Ms. Jean Cruncher, the head personnel analyst, has is the city's employment figures since 1992. These data appear in Table 20.2.

Ms. Cruncher assumes that the same factors that have caused employment to increase in the past 15 years (mandated federal programs, population growth, citizen demands for services, and so on) will continue to influence employment over the next 5 years. By assuming that the future will resemble the past, Ms. Cruncher can use some fairly simple techniques to forecast the city's employment in 2006, 2007, 2008, 2009, and 2010.

Step 1: The first step in time series analysis (just like the first step in any bivariate analysis) is to plot the data. Employment should be considered the dependent variable, and the year should be considered the independent variable. See Figure 20.3.

Step 2: Examine the plot of the data and determine whether any short-term fluctuations exist. The data show no appreciable short-term fluctuation, so go on to Step 4.

Step 3: If the data show a cyclical trend, as the absenteeism data did, you will need to determine the length of the short-term trend. Using this length (L), construct an L-term moving average model. Short-term fluctuations create some problems in the next few steps; the problems will be discussed later in this chapter.

Table 20.2

Blanchard Employment Data

Year	Blanchard City Employment Employees (thousands)
1992	35.7
1993	38.8
1994	40.9
1995	43.4
1996	44.9
1997	47.2
1998	48.8
1999	50.8
2000	50.8
2001	50.7
2002	55.0
2003	55.3
2004	58.6
2005	59.9

Figure 20.3

Blanchard Employment Data

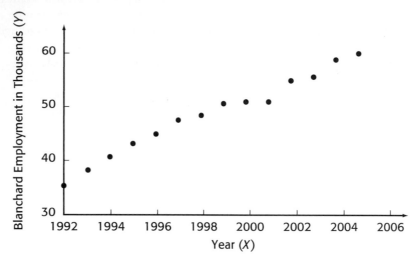

Step 4: Determine whether a relationship exists. From the data shown in Figure 20.3, you can discern a positive linear relationship between time and employment in Blanchard.

Step 5: Use linear regression to estimate the relationship between time and the variable that is being analyzed. To do this, label the first year (1992) as 1, the second year as 2, and so on. After this renumbering, we have the following data set:

X	Y
1	35.7
2	38.8
3	40.9
4	43.4
5	44.9
6	47.2
7	48.8
8	50.8
9	50.8
10	50.7
11	55.0
12	55.3
13	58.6
14	59.9

Now perform linear regression, with Y (employment) as the dependent variable. Because we will need the mean and standard deviation for X for confidence limits, calculate those also. A regression program produces the following results (if you do not believe us, feel free to calculate this yourself):

$$\hat{Y} = 35.69 + 1.73X$$

$$s_b = .07 \quad S_{y|x} = 1.11 \quad r^2 = .98 \quad \bar{X} = 7.5 \quad s_x = 4.2$$

This information tells us that a strong relationship exists between time and city employment.

Step 6: Using the regression equation, forecast employment figures for the years needed. Since 2005 is equivalent to an X value of 14, then 2006, the first year to forecast, has an X value of 15. Entering 15 into the regression equation, we get

$$\hat{Y} = 35.69 + 1.73 \times 15 = 35.69 + 25.95 = 61.64$$

Our best estimate of the Blanchard city employment for 2006 is 61.64. We can place 90% confidence limits around this estimate by using the standard error of the estimate, the correction for distance from the mean, and the t score for 90% confidence with 12 degrees of freedom:

$$61.64 \pm 1.78 \times S_{y|x} \times \sqrt{1 + \frac{1}{n} + \frac{(X_0 - \bar{X})^2}{(n-1)s_x^2}}$$

$$61.64 \pm 1.78 \times 1.11 \times \sqrt{1 + \frac{1}{14} + \frac{(15 - 7.5)^2}{(14-1)(4.2)^2}}$$

$$61.64 \pm 1.78 \times 1.11 \times 1.15$$

$$61.64 \pm 2.27$$

$$59.37 \text{ to } 63.91$$

The 90% confidence limits on the Blanchard city employment are 59.37 to 63.91.

A word of caution is in order. Forecasting forces us to go beyond the available data. Under normal circumstances, this process is to be avoided with regression models. Only if we can logically assume that the future will closely resemble the past can we forecast with confidence. In fact, the 90% confidence limits hold only if the future is an extrapolation of the past. If any major changes occur, the confidence limits are meaningless. Even so, the confidence limits are very wide.

The Blanchard city employment forecasts for 2007, 2008, 2009, and 2010 appear below.

Year	$X \times b$	$bX + a = \hat{Y}$
2007	16×1.73	$27.68 + 35.69 = 63.37$
2008	17×1.73	$29.41 + 35.69 = 65.10$
2009	18×1.73	$31.14 + 35.69 = 66.83$
2010	19×1.73	$32.87 + 35.69 = 68.56$

The 90% confidence limits of these forecasts are as follows:

2007: 61.04 to 65.70

2008: 62.71 to 67.49

2009: 64.37 to 69.29

2010: 66.02 to 71.10

Ms. Cruncher can now use these forecasts to plan a variety of personnel decisions, including size of health care benefits, amount of money that needs to be set aside for pensions, and affirmative action goals.

Forecasting an Exponential Trend

B. Tom Line, chief budgeting officer for Palmdale, Florida, needs to forecast city revenue for next year so that the city budget can be based on city revenue. The mayor also wants 5 years of revenue projections because he wants to know whether sufficient revenue will be generated to purchase a $100,000 park without a bond issue. The current year's budget is $2.1 million, and current revenues are $2.138 million. The mayor tells Mr. Line to assume that past revenue trends will continue and that expenditures will increase 7% per year for the next 5 years. The question to be answered is, can Palmdale accumulate $100,000 in excess revenue (revenue saved last year cannot be used as part of the $100,000)? The revenue data are shown in Table 20.3.

Before forecasting revenue, Mr. Line needs a forecast of expenditures. The mayor said to assume a 7% annual increase. This growth rate results in the projections shown in Table 20.4.

Table 20.3

Palmdale Revenue Data

Year	Revenue (thousands)
1992	678
1993	679
1994	743
1995	837
1996	949
1997	982
1998	1,081
1999	1,205
2000	1,317
2001	1,416
2002	1,479
2003	1,637
2004	1,968
2005	2,138

Table 20.4

Projected Expenditures

Year	Expenditures (millions)
2005	2.1 (actual)
2006	2.247
2007	2.404
2008	2.573
2009	2.753
2010	2.945

Figure 20.4

Yearly Revenue, City of Palmdale

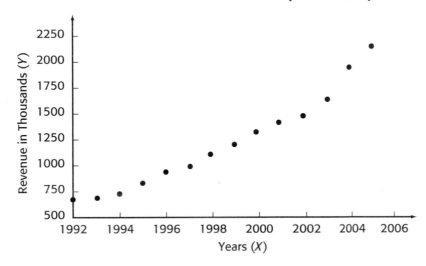

Given the data in Table 20.4, Mr. Line follows the forecasting procedure outlined previously.

Step 1: First, Mr. Line plots the data. The plot is shown in Figure 20.4.

Step 2: Does a short-term fluctuation exist? None is apparent in the graph, so Mr. Line assumes that no short-term fluctuations exist. He skips to Step 4.

Step 4: Does a time series relationship exist? Clearly one does. Unfortunately, the data do not appear to be linear; rather, they appear to increase a greater amount each year. For the moment, Mr. Line decides to ignore this fact and to proceed to Step 5.

Step 5: Using linear regression, Mr. Line estimates the equation for the line. To do this, he converts 1992 to year 1 and numbers all following years accordingly (2005 is year 14). He estimates the following regression line:

$$\hat{Y} = 412 + 108.1X$$
$$s_b = 7.29 \quad S_{y|x} = 110 \quad r^2 = .95$$

Step 6: Using the regression equation, Mr. Line forecasts revenues for 2006 through 2010:

Year	$X \times b$	$bX + a = \hat{Y}$
2006	15×108.1	$1621.5 + 412 = 2{,}033.5$
2007	16×108.1	$1729.6 + 412 = 2{,}141.6$
2008	17×108.1	$1837.7 + 412 = 2{,}249.7$
2009	18×108.1	$1945.8 + 412 = 2{,}357.8$
2010	19×108.1	$2053.9 + 412 = 2{,}465.9$

Clearly something is wrong with the forecasts. Revenue for 2006 is forecast to be $105,000 less than 2005 revenue. When a time series that is not linear, such as this one, is estimated with linear regression, the forecasts will generally be underestimations. This results because linear regression cannot account for the upswing in revenues for the most recent few years. If Mr. Line's forecasts are compared with expenditures, the mayor will receive quite a shock (see Table 20.5).

The correct procedure to follow when the time series increases at a constant rate is to convert the time series variable into logarithms. [Those not familiar with logarithms should see Neter, Wasserman, and Whitmore (1988).] This conversion is done in Table 20.6.

Performing regression on the values of X and Y in Table 20.6, Mr. Line finds

$$\hat{Y} = 2.767 + .0389X$$
$$s_b = .0011 \quad S_{y|x} = .016 \quad r^2 = .99$$

Notice that r^2 increased when a log transformation of Y was regressed on time. This occurs because a log transformation bends the line upward to fit the values of the data.

How can the preceding regression line be interpreted? If we convert the regression slope into an antilog (in this case, the antilog of .0389 is 1.094), and subtract 1

Table 20.5

Revenue and Expenditures

Projected Revenue	Expenditures	Debt
2,033.5	2,247	214
2,141.6	2,404	262
2,249.7	2,573	323
2,357.8	2,753	395
2,465.9	2,945	479

Table 20.6

Converting to Logarithms

Year, X	Revenue	Log (revenue), Y
1	678	2.831
2	679	2.832
3	743	2.871
4	837	2.923
5	949	2.977
6	982	2.992
7	1,081	3.033
8	1,205	3.081
9	1,317	3.120
10	1,416	3.151
11	1,479	3.170
12	1,637	3.214
13	1,968	3.294
14	2,138	3.330

from the antilog, the resulting number tells us the percentage that Y increases every year.

$$1.094 - 1.0 = .094, \text{ or } 9.4\%$$

Palmdale city revenues are increasing at a rate of 9.4% per year.

To forecast city revenues with a logarithmic regression, follow the usual procedure to get predicted logarithms of expenditures.

Year	$X \times$ b	bX + a = $\hat{Y}$
2006	15 × 0.0389	0.584 + 2.767 = 3.351
2007	16 × 0.0389	0.622 + 2.767 = 3.389
2008	17 × 0.0389	0.661 + 2.767 = 3.428
2009	18 × 0.0389	0.700 + 2.767 = 3.467
2010	19 × 0.0389	0.739 + 2.767 = 3.506

The predicted values of Y must now be converted from logarithms to regular numbers. This can be done with a calculator that has a power key. One merely takes 10 to the $\hat{Y}$ power to get the regular number (see Table 20.7).

Contrasting the revenue projections in Table 20.7 with expenditure predictions, we find the results shown in Table 20.8. The surplus figures show that Palmdale, Florida, will accumulate the needed $100,000 for the park sometime near the middle of year 2008. The figures also show that the city will run a budget surplus of $262,000 if no new programs are added and taxes are not cut. Why might this information be valuable to the mayor?

Table 20.7

Converting $\hat{Y}$ to Revenue

Year	$\hat{Y}$	Projected Revenue
2006	3.351	2,241
2007	3.389	2,451
2008	3.428	2,681
2009	3.467	2,932
2010	3.506	3,207

Table 20.8

Revenues and Expenditures

Year	Revenues	Expenditures	Surplus
2006	2,241	2,247	−6
2007	2,451	2,404	47
2008	2,681	2,573	108
2009	2,932	2,753	179
2010	3,207	2,945	262

Forecasting with a Short-Term Fluctuation

To this point, we have illustrated two fairly simple forecasts of trends. Neither set of data had any noticeable short-term fluctuation. To illustrate how forecasting is done when a time series contains some short-term fluctuation, let us return to our example of Flagler Public Works Department absences introduced at the beginning of this chapter. Refer to Figure 20.5, which shows the number of absences from work for a 6-week period.

Step 1: The first step is to plot the data, as is done in Figure 20.5.

Step 2: By examining the graph, determine whether any short-term fluctuation exists. In this instance, absences peak on Friday, remain high on Monday, drop on Tuesday and Wednesday, and show a slight increase on Thursday. Clearly a short-term trend exists.

Step 3: Determine the length of the short-term fluctuation. In this example, the length of the short-term fluctuation is 5 days. To remove this short-term fluctuation, calculate a five-term moving average. These calculations, explained earlier in this chapter, are shown in Table 20.9.

Step 4: Graph the five-term moving average, because this figure represents the number of absences that occur each day when the short-term fluctuation is removed. Examining the graph in Figure 20.6, we see that a negative relationship exists between time and absenteeism. The absenteeism rate is clearly downward.

Table 20.9

Calculations for a Five-Term Moving Average

Week	Day	Day Number	Absences (Y)	Sum	Five-Term Average	Fluctuation
1	M	1	25			
	Tu	2	15			
	W	3	11	91	18.2	−7.2
	Th	4	12	92	18.4	−6.4
	F	5	28	97	19.4	8.6
2	M	6	26	98	19.6	6.4
	Tu	7	20	99	19.8	.2
	W	8	12	103	20.6	−8.6
	Th	9	13	99	19.8	−6.8
	F	10	32	100	20.0	12.0
3	M	11	22	100	20.0	2.0
	Tu	12	21	97	19.4	1.6
	W	13	12	93	18.6	−6.6
	Th	14	10	88	17.6	−7.6
	F	15	28	82	16.4	11.6
4	M	16	17	80	16.0	1.0
	Tu	17	15	78	15.6	−.6
	W	18	10	73	14.6	−4.6
	Th	19	8	68	13.6	−5.6
	F	20	23	64	12.8	10.2
5	M	21	12	61	12.2	−.2
	Tu	22	11	58	11.6	−.6
	W	23	7	50	10.0	−3.0
	Th	24	5	46	9.8	−4.8
	F	25	15	48	9.6	5.4
6	M	26	11	47	9.4	1.6
	Tu	27	10	47	9.4	.6
	W	28	6	46	9.2	−3.2
	Th	29	5			
	F	30	14			

Step 5: Using linear regression, estimate the relationship between time and the five-term moving average. In this case, use all values of X from $X = 3$ to $X = 28$. The regression estimate of the relationship is

$$\hat{Y} = 23.3 - .508X$$

$$s_b = .0392 \quad S_{y|x} = 1.497 \quad r^2 = .87$$

where X is the day and Y is the number of absences.

Figure 20.5

Number of Absences for 6 Weeks

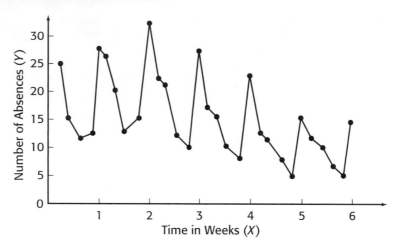

Figure 20.6

Five-Term Moving Average

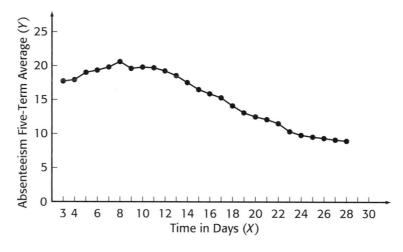

You now have a forecast for the moving average of the number of absences. At this point, if you want to forecast specific days, the short-term fluctuation must be put back into the model. This procedure is fairly advanced and needs to be done with the assistance of a statistician [see Neter, Wasserman, and Whitmore (1988); Nelson (1973)].

Bivariate Forecasting

In the previous three examples of forecasting, the independent variable was always time. This need not be the case. The independent variable can, in fact, be a variable that causes the dependent variable to vary. This section will illustrate forecasting when the independent variable is not time. Such forecasting is called **bivariate forecasting.**

Stermerville is a bedroom suburb located 15 miles north of Jackson. J. R. "Dusty" Rhodes, the Stermerville director of sewage treatment, wants to forecast the volume of sewage per day his plant will need to treat for the next 5 years. The Stermerville Treatment Plant has a capacity of 500 tons of sewage per day. At this time, the plant is treating 375 tons per day. To expand the plant, it will take about 4 years (counting funding, EPA clearance, construction, and testing). For this reason Mr. Rhodes needs to forecast future demands on his sewage treatment plant. If demand will exceed 500 tons per day in the next 5 years, Mr. Rhodes must begin the process to expand the plant now.

Because Stermerville is a bedroom community with no industry and little commercial development, the volume of sewage is highly correlated with the number of households in Stermerville. Dusty's data analyst, Morticia "Severe" Storms, has discovered that she can accurately predict next year's sewage demand by combining the present number of houses in Stermerville with 90% of the number of building permits issued for new houses (90% is used because 10% of new houses for which permits are issued are not built). Severe gathers the data given in Table 20.10.

Severe explains what she wants to do. She wants to forecast next year's sewage demand in tons per day. Because the actual number of houses is highly correlated with sewage use, Severe needs an estimate of next year's number of houses to forecast next year's sewage use. This value appears in the "Projected Houses" column. Projected houses for 1993 (1,370) is equal to the number of houses in 1992 (1,100) plus 90% of the building permits ($300 \times .9 + 1,100 = 270 + 1,100 = 1,370$). Note that "Projected Houses" fairly accurately predicts the next year's total housing. Severe then aligns the variables in two columns so that sewage use for a given year is lined up with next year's projected houses for the previous year (that is, the value for 1992 projected houses is actually the projected number of houses for 1993; see Table 20.11). The number of projected houses for 2005 is withdrawn from the data set for the moment.

Severe then runs a regression of sewage in tons (Y) on the projected number of houses, with the following results:

$$\hat{Y} = 125.2 + .0367X$$
$$s_b = .0016 \quad S_{y|x} = 10.5 \quad r^2 = .98 \quad \bar{X} = 4,069 \quad s_x = 1,923$$

Severe has no trouble using this information to project sewage demand for 2006 because she has a projected housing value for 2006 (7,578). Substituting this value for X, Severe gets the following projection for 2006:

$$\hat{Y} = 125.2 + .0367X = 125.2 + .0367(7,578) = 403.3$$

Table 20.10

Stermerville Data

Year	Tons of Sewage per Day	Houses	Building Permits	Next Year's Projected Houses
1992		1,100	300	1,370
1993	158	1,370	150	1,505
1994	188	1,500	570	2,013
1995	192	2,000	600	2,540
1996	230	2,510	511	2,970
1997	234	3,000	754	3,679
1998	252	3,700	310	3,979
1999	285	4,050	680	4,662
2000	293	4,620	318	4,906
2001	315	4,885	815	5,619
2002	335	5,500	510	5,959
2003	353	6,040	603	6,582
2004	358	6,580	590	7,111
2005	375	7,150	475	7,578

Table 20.11

Sewage and Projected Houses

Tons of Sewage per Day (Y)	Projected Houses (X)
158	1,370
188	1,505
192	2,013
230	2,540
234	2,970
252	3,679
285	3,979
293	4,662
315	4,906
335	5,619
353	5,959
358	6,582
375	7,111

Using the standard error of the estimate and the correction factor for distance from the mean of X, Severe can place 90% confidence limits around this estimate (df $= 11$).

$$403.3 \pm t \times S_{y|x} \times \sqrt{1 + \frac{1}{n} + \frac{(X_0 - \bar{X})^2}{(n-1)S_x^2}}$$

$$403.3 \pm 1.796 \times 10.5 \times \sqrt{1 + (1/13) + \frac{(7,578 - 4,069)^2}{(13-1)(1,923^2)}}$$

$$403.3 \pm 1.796 \times 10.5 \times 1.16$$

$$403.3 \pm 21.9$$

381.4 to 425.2

How can Severe forecast sewage demand for 2007 to 2010? Severe needs the estimated number of houses in Stermerville. The estimated number of houses is the current number plus 90% of the building permits issued. If Severe could estimate the number of building permits for the next 5 years, then she could extrapolate the number of houses. Severe consults several local builders, who tell her that they expect to reduce new starts to about 450 per year for the next 4 years. Severe makes the following estimates of housing:

Projected Houses	=	Last Year's Projection	+	.9 ×		Permits
Projected 2007 houses	=	7,578	+	(.9 × 450) =		7,983
Projected 2008 houses	=	7,983	+	(.9 × 450) =		8,388
Projected 2009 houses	=	8,388	+	(.9 × 450) =		8,793
Projected 2010 houses	=	8,793	+	(.9 × 450) =		9,198

Severe then used these estimates to project future sewage demand.

Year	$X \times b$	$Xb + a = \hat{Y}$
2007	7,983 × .0367	293.0 + 125.2 = 418.2
2008	8,388 × .0367	307.8 + 125.2 = 433.0
2009	8,793 × .0367	322.7 + 125.2 = 447.9
2010	9,198 × .0367	337.6 + 125.2 = 462.8

The projections show that Stermerville will not exceed its capacity of 500 tons per day in the next 5 years. Severe shows these data to Mr. Rhodes. Mr. Rhodes asks Severe how sure she is that demand in 2010 will not exceed 500 tons per day. Severe uses the standard error of the estimate and the adjustment for the value of X to determine the probability that the 2010 estimate exceeds 500. This is

$$10.5 \times \sqrt{1 + (1/13) + \frac{(9,198 - 4,069)^2}{(13-1)(1,923^2)}}$$

$$10.5 \times \sqrt{1 + .08 + .59}$$

$$10.5 \times 1.29$$

13.6

This figure can be used as a standard error to calculate a t score in the following formula:

$$t = \frac{Y - \hat{Y}}{s} = \frac{500 - 462.8}{13.6} = 2.74$$

Looking up this value in the t table (df $=$ 11), Severe concludes that the probability is less than .01. She reports this information to Mr. Rhodes.

Rhodes then wants to know what year to expect the demand to exceed 500 so that he can plan. Severe substitutes a value of 500 for Y into the regression equation:

$$500 = 125.2 + .0367X$$
$$374.8 = .0367X$$
$$10{,}212 = X$$

Severe finds that when projected housing exceeds 10,212, then sewage will exceed 500 tons per day. When will this be? Severe consults her builder friends who tell her that 450 new starts will hold for the next 10 years. Using this figure, Severe projects the following housing figures:

2011: 9,603
2012: 10,008
2013: 10,413

These figures indicate that the capacity of the sewage treatment plant will be adequate until 2013. Forecasts involve greater risks the farther that they extend into the future; therefore, 2011 or 2012 may well be a more appropriate year for plant expansion to be completed. Note that any changes in building permits should be monitored; any change in permits will require new forecasts.

Chapter Summary

Forecasting is an attempt to predict the future, usually through some reliance on statistical techniques. This chapter introduces some simple forecasting techniques based on linear regression.

The foundation on which data-based forecasting rests is time series analysis. A time series is a sequence of observations on some variable when the observations occur at equally spaced time intervals. Most time series will have some short-term fluctuations, which can be filtered out by using a moving average.

There are six basic steps in a time series analysis. First, plot the data. Second, examine the plot and determine whether any short-term fluctuations exist. Third, if the data show a cyclical trend, determine the length of the short-term trend and filter the trend. Fourth, determine whether a relationship exists. Fifth, use linear regression to estimate the relationship between time and the variable being analyzed. Sixth, make a forecast by using the regression equation.

When the forecast involves an exponential trend—that is, the time series increases at a constant rate—the time series variable must be converted to logarithms. If the forecast involves short-term fluctuations, a moving average must be calculated.

When the independent variable in a set of observations is not time, the forecasting is called bivariate forecasting. The analysis process for this situation is somewhat similar to that for time series analysis; again, linear regression techniques are used.

Problems

20.1   John Johnson, warden of Ramsey Prison, believes that a relationship exists between the size of the state's population between the ages of 18 and 35 and the number of inmates assigned to Ramsey. John has his trusty analyst, Marc Wallace, go down to the Census Bureau's local office to get census estimates for the past 50 years. Marc then regresses Ramsey's prison population on the size of the state's 18- to 35-year-old population. He finds the following:

$$\hat{Y} = -14 + .0005X$$
$$s_b = .0000003 \quad S_{y|x} = 12.6 \quad r^2 = .93$$

   (a)   The Census Bureau estimates that next year's population between the ages of 18 and 35 will be 934,000. What is the projected prison population?

   (b)   Ramsey's capacity is 500 persons. The old wing of the prison contains room for 100 persons. John would like to close this wing to save on maintenance. How small would the state's 18- to 35-year-old population need to be to do this?

20.2   The Indiana State Department of Agriculture is concerned about the number of acres of farmland being withdrawn from farming. The department would like to propose new legislation to prevent this but would like to show the legislature what would happen if it does not act. Dewey Compost, the department's statistician, regresses the number of acres used for farming in the state on time (1945 = year 1). Dewey finds the following:

$$\hat{Y} = 2.743 - .027X$$
$$s_b = .0007 \quad S_{y|x} = .013 \quad r^2 = .89 \quad s_x = 16 \quad \bar{X} = 29 \quad n = 61$$

   (a)   How strong is the relationship?

   (b)   If $\hat{Y}$ is in millions of acres, how many acres of farmland will be lost in the next 10 years if the legislature does not act and if past practices continue?

   (c)   How many acres will be used for farming in 2006? Place a 90% confidence interval around this estimate.

20.3   I. L. Iterate High School is the only high school in Milward, Iowa. The superintendent hires you to forecast future school enrollments so that the school can plan ahead. Using the accompanying data, what can you tell the superintendent?

Year	Students
1991	810
1992	1,094
1993	1,402
1994	1,893
1995	2,205
1996	2,687
1997	3,115
1998	3,324
1999	3,496
2000	3,531
2001	3,412
2002	3,174
2003	2,963
2004	2,810
2005	2,794

20.4 The Chelsea City Police budget appears to be increasing at a rate of 10% per year. Could the city use linear regression to forecast this budget? What percentage will the budget increase in 10 years?

20.5 The Aurora city economist, I. C. Recession, uses the previous year's growth in the money supply (in percent) to forecast the inflation rate (in percent) for Aurora. Using data for 35 years, Recession has built the following regression model (Y is inflation in percentage; X is money supply growth in percentage):

$$\hat{Y} = -5.4 + 2.1X$$
$$s_b = .007 \quad S_{y|x} = 2.0 \quad r^2 = .99 \quad X = 3.2 \quad s_x = 3.0$$

Interpret this regression equation; then forecast next year's inflation rate whether the money supply grows 8.2%. Place 90% confidence limits around this estimate. What is the probability that the rate of inflation will be over 15%?

20.6 The Fifth Division of the U.S. Army wants to forecast personnel costs for the next 5 years. A search of the records reveals the accompanying data. Using these data, forecast personnel costs for 2006, 2007, 2008, 2009, and 2010. Place 90% confidence limits around these estimates.

Year	Costs (thousands)
2005	51,576
2004	49,015
2003	40,845
2002	34,497
2001	28,625
2000	25,376
1999	21,163

Year	Costs (thousands)
1998	18,468
1997	14,992
1996	13,633
1995	12,069
1994	11,452
1993	10,321
1992	9,329
1991	7,982
1990	7,877
1989	7,648
1988	7,071
1987	6,411
1986	5,409
1985	4,657
1984	4,017

20.7 The number of patients at the Bluefield State Mental Hospital (Y) appears to be related to the state's population (X):

$$\hat{Y} = .07 + .0031X$$
$$s_b = .00013 \quad S_{y|x} = 46 \quad r^2 = .99 \quad \mathbf{N} = 35$$

Interpret the regression and forecast the number of patients if the state's population is predicted to be 876,451. How many additional patients would a population increase of 20,000 bring?

20.8 From the accompanying data on the Yanktoni Sioux Indian Tribe, project the tribal population for 2006 and 2011. Place a 90% confidence limit around both projections.

Year	Population
1996	812
1997	831
1998	863
1999	901
2000	925
2001	963
2002	989
2003	1,016
2004	1,037
2005	1,062

20.9 Metro City Police believe that the number of domestic disputes on any summer night is highly correlated with the temperature that night (the hotter the night, the more family fights there are). If the number of disputes can be forecast, the police department can use the results to allocate personnel. Research analyst Silvia Saint regresses the number of domestic disputes (Y) on the

Fahrenheit temperature at 4:00 in the afternoon (X). Interpret this regression for the Metro City Police.

$$\hat{Y} = 216 + 3.1X$$
$$s_b = 1.5 \quad S_{y|x} = 18 \quad r^2 = .81 \quad \mathbf{N} = 150$$

Forecast, with appropriate confidence limits, the number of disputes if the temperature is 95° at 4:00 P.M.

20.10 Using the number of traffic fatalities for the 30-year period beginning in 1976 (1976 = year 1), a western state wants to forecast traffic fatalities for 2006, 2007, and 2008. Using the following regression, make these forecasts, and place an 80% confidence limit around the forecasts.

$$\hat{Y} = 1,246 + 36.4X$$
$$s_b = 1.9 \quad S_{y|x} = 24 \quad r^2 = .97 \quad \bar{X} = 15.5 \quad s_x = 8.8$$

20.11 The city building permit agency is concerned about its future workloads. Initially, the agency thinks that it can predict the number of building permits that will be issued next year by simply using the year as the independent variable (1954 is year 1). This regression results in the following:

$$\hat{Y} = 2,256 + 234.6X$$
$$s_b = 23.1 \quad S_{y|x} = 154 \quad r^2 = .65$$

The agency then uses the unemployment rate (percentage of unemployed), rather than the year, as the independent variable to predict building permits. This produces the following:

$$\hat{Y} = 13,413 - 678X$$
$$s_b = 21.4 \quad S_{y|x} = 108 \quad r^2 = .78$$

Interpret each of these regressions. For each regression, predict the number of building permits that will be issued in 2006 if unemployment is 7.2%. Which of these equations is the better one from a managerial perspective?

20.12 The Mansfield school district wants to predict student enrollments for next year. They hire Daniel Mazmanian Educational Consultants to do this work. Using data from 1983 through 2005 (1983 = year 1), the consultants assume that all past trends will continue and use a time series regression to predict the total number of students enrolled (Y). They get the following:

$$\hat{Y} = 781 + 28.8X$$
$$s_b = .68 \quad S_{y|x} = 6.2 \quad \mathbf{N} = 23 \quad r^2 = .9955 \quad \bar{X} = 10 \quad s_x = 6$$

Interpret the slope, intercept, and r^2. Is there a relationship between time and enrollments? Predict the number of students for 2006, and place an 80% confidence limit around it. What is the probability that enrollments might be as high as 1,400 next year?

20.13 The president needs to predict future expenditures on Medicaid. Office of Management and Budget analyst, Alex Pacek, undertakes the task. With Medicaid expenditures expressed in millions of 1967 dollars and using data from 1964 (year 1) to 2005, the OMB gets the following regression:

$$\hat{Y} = -669.9 + 306X$$
$$s_b = 10.77 \quad S_{y|x} = 320 \quad \mathbf{N} = 42 \quad r^2 = .98$$

Interpret this regression. What is your best guess as to Medicaid expenditures in 2006? In 2007?

20.14 The Department of Labor's division of workers' compensation programs believes that it is unfair to charge that rising medical costs for workers' compensation programs are the result of program expansion. The department believes that costs rise because medical costs in general rise. Using the total amount of money spent for workers' compensation medical benefits in millions of dollars (Y), the department runs a regression using the Consumer Price Index for medical care as the independent variable (CPIMED $= 100$ in 1967). This produces the following regression:

$$\hat{Y} = -927.60 + 17.71X$$
$$s_b = .22 \quad S_{y|x} = 106.2 \quad \mathbf{N} = 45 \quad r^2 = .9949$$

Interpret this regression. Present a hypothesis, a null hypothesis, and evaluate the hypotheses. State your conclusions in plain English.

20.15 Expenditures for the Women, Infants, and Children (WIC) program in millions of 1971 dollars are regressed on time (year 1 = 1971):

$$\hat{Y} = 40.19 + 45.46X$$
$$s_b = 3.87 \quad S_{y|x} = 20.5 \quad \mathbf{N} = 35 \quad r^2 = .97 \quad \bar{X} = 16 \quad s_x = 9$$

Interpret this regression. Predict 2006 expenditures, and calculate 90% confidence limits.

CHAPTER 21

Multiple Regression

In the three preceding chapters, all regression problems were solved with simple regression (regression with only one independent variable). By contrast, in many management situations, a dependent variable will have more than one cause. Under such circumstances, simple regression is an inadequate technique. **Multiple regression** is a statistical procedure designed to incorporate more than one independent variable. In this chapter, we will discuss the techniques of multiple regression.

Recall from our discussion of causality in Chapter 3 that one of the key issues in demonstrating a causal relationship between two variables is taking other explanatory variables into account as possible causes of variation in the variable being explained. The chief limitation of bivariate regression is that only one independent variable is used to explain variation in the dependent variable. Assuming that one variable is the cause of another without thinking about other possible explanatory variables is usually not a wise research strategy. Multiple regression is a valuable research tool because it allows for the inclusion of several independent variables to explain a dependent variable.

Bivariate regression is a good starting point for constructing causal relationships. If statistically significant results are obtained in a bivariate regression, it may seem like the task of constructing a causal model is complete. Yet, the results obtained from bivariate models are often just the starting point for constructing more inclusive causal models.

When statistically significant results are obtained using bivariate regression, the next logical step is to select other relevant independent variables and perform multiple regression. But what if we really don't care about other independent variables and are only interested in finding out whether the initial independent variable we selected is related to the dependent variable? Should we still consider multiple regression in cases like this?

The answer is yes. Causal explanations are stronger when we include control variables in our analyses. *We can have more faith in the idea that a particular independent variable explains variation in a dependent variable if, after generating a multiple regression that includes other relevant explanatory variables, the original independent variable remains statistically significant.* If we end our modeling efforts after performing a bivariate regression and finding statistically significant results, we run the risk of attributing too much explanatory power to one variable. Sometimes statistically significant relationships from bivariate models "wash out" in the presence of other explanatory variables (see "The Logic of Controls" in this chapter). Bivariate regression is a very useful tool, but one should take care before making definitive statements about the existence of causal relationships using this technique alone.

An Example

The best way to illustrate the use of multiple regression is with an example. Charles Pyro, fire chief of Stermerville, has divided Stermerville into nine fire districts of approximately equal size. Pyro's problem is that Stermerville is planning to offer fire service to Boonsville, a neighboring town about the size of one of Stermerville's fire districts. Pyro would like to know how many fires a month he can expect to fight in Boonsville so that he can allocate his firefighters accordingly.

As an old hand at firefighting, Chief Pyro knows that older houses are more likely to burn than are newer houses. He decides to see whether he can predict the number of monthly fires in a fire district by using the average age of district housing. Pyro has the data shown in Table 21.1.

Table 21.1

Stermerville Fire Data

District	Number of Fires (Y)	Average Housing Age (X)
1	44	23
2	94	35
3	38	4
4	65	49
5	95	48
6	57	12
7	20	14
8	52	33
9	64	25

After graphing these data, Pyro performs a regression analysis on them to get the following results:

$$\hat{Y} = 28.6 + 1.12X$$

$$s_b = .41 \quad S_{y|x} = 18.4 \quad r^2 = .51 \quad \bar{X} = 27.0 \quad s_x = 15.7$$

Using this information to predict the number of fires in Boonsville, which has an average housing age of 42 years, Pyro finds

$$\hat{Y} = 28.6 + 1.12(42) = 28.6 + 47.02 = 75.6$$

Placing a 90% confidence limit around this prediction (df $=$ 7), Pyro receives a shock.

$$75.6 \pm t \times S_{y|x} \times \sqrt{1 + \frac{1}{n} + \frac{(X - \bar{X})^2}{(n-1)s_x^2}}$$

$$75.6 \pm 1.895 \times 18.4 \times 1.11$$

$$75.6 \pm 38.7$$

$$36.9 \text{ to } 114.3$$

The confidence interval on this estimate is so wide that it is of little value to Chief Pyro.

One way to interpret a regression with a low (in terms of need) r^2 is to conclude that some factors in addition to or perhaps instead of the independent variable explain the variation in Y. To identify these factors, one uses experience, intuition, theory, or even trial and error. In the present instance, Chief Pyro knows that fewer fires occur in homes that are owner occupied than in homes that are rented. Pyro believes that he could accurately predict fires if he knew both the average age of housing in a fire district and the percentage of houses that are owner occupied. In short, Pyro would like a prediction equation of the following form:

$$\hat{Y} = \alpha + \beta_1 X_1 + \beta_2 X_2$$

where $\hat{Y}$ is the number of fires, X_1 is the average age of housing, X_2 is the percentage of owner-occupied housing, α is the intercept, and β_1 and β_2 are weights or slopes.

Obviously, Pyro could set up the prediction equation just stated; the key is the selection of the weights. Pyro would like to select weights so that his predictions of Y are as accurate as possible. In short, Pyro would like to minimize the squared error, or $(\hat{Y}_i - Y_i)^2$. This is the familiar principle of least squares that we use in simple regression (see Chapter 18). In fact, multiple regression is nothing more than the assignment of weights so that $(\hat{Y}_i - Y_i)^2$ is minimized.

We will consider specifically how these regression coefficients are calculated shortly. But first we will discuss the interpretation of a multiple regression. Pyro's data analyst runs a multiple regression on the data in Table 21.2.

The regression program provides the following information:

$$\hat{Y} = 38.1 + 1.57X_1 - .49X_2$$

$$s_{b_1} = .087 \quad s_{b_2} = .036 \quad S_{y|x} = 3.55 \quad R^2 = .98$$

Table 21.2

Fire Data Including Owner Occupied Homes

Fire District	Fires per Month (Y)	Housing Age (X_1)	Housing Percentage Owned (X_2)
1	44	23	70
2	94	35	3
3	38	4	10
4	65	49	96
5	95	48	40
6	57	12	4
7	20	14	80
8	52	33	78
9	64	25	15

The interpretation of this regression equation focuses on the estimated values of β_1 and β_2. These are the values of slopes, just as β was in simple regression, only now the slopes are in three dimensions (and thus difficult to graph) rather than in two dimensions. The regression coefficient for age of housing (b_1) is equal to the increase in the number of fires in a district if the average age of all housing in the district increases by 1 year *and* the percentage of owner-occupied housing remains the same. In other words, b_1 is the increase in the number of fires resulting from increases in housing age, controlling for the percentage of owner occupied housing. In this case, a district will have 1.57 more fires for every year older its houses are if the percentage that are owner occupied remains the same. Statisticians often refer to this slope as a **partial slope.**

The regression coefficient for percentage of housing that is owner occupied (b_2) has a similar interpretation. For every percentage point increase in owner-occupied housing in a district, the district will have .49 fewer fires if the average age of houses remains the same.

Although the intercept remains the value of $\hat{Y}$ if both average age and percentage of owner-occupied houses are zero, $\hat{Y}$ can also have a value of 38.1 for numerous other values of X_1 and X_2. For example, if X_1 is equal to 10 and X_2 is equal to 32, $\hat{Y}$ is also equal to 38.1.

A variety of other factors must also be considered when interpreting a multiple regression. If all the assumptions of regression hold (see Chapter 19), sample estimates of the regression slopes are *t*-distributed. This means that each slope will have its own standard error. Note that two standard errors of the slope estimates have been presented. These standard errors can be used to determine the probability that the data came from a population with slopes equal to 0. When a partial slope equals 0, it means that the *X* value in question is unrelated to *Y* when the other *X* values are controlled.

For b_1 the probability that the data came from a population with slope = 0 can be found as follows:

$$t = \frac{b_1 - 0}{s_{b_1}} = \frac{1.57 - 0}{.087} = 18.0$$

To look up this t value in Table 3 of the Appendix, you need to know the number of degrees of freedom. For a multiple regression, the degrees of freedom is equal to the number of cases (in this case, 9) minus the number of parameters estimated (in this case, 3—one intercept and two slopes). Using 6 degrees of freedom, this t value has a probability of less than .0005. We can be fairly sure the slope in question is not zero. In the space provided, calculate the probability that b_2 came from a population with slope = 0.

If you found a probability of less than .0005 ($t = 13.6$), congratulations.

In the results just reported, you might have noticed this equality: $R^2 = .98$. R^2 is the symbol for the *multiple coefficient of determination*. R^2 is the percentage of variance in Y that is explained by X_1 and X_2. Another interpretation of R^2 is that it is equal to the r^2 between Y and $\hat{Y}$. Notice that R^2 is larger than r^2 in the simple regression of fires on age. This will always happen. When more variables are used to explain or predict the dependent variable, the coefficient of determination will increase.

Because of the way it is calculated, R^2 goes up even if we add independent variables that have little or no explanatory power. In other words, even if the partial slope for the independent variable equals zero, the value of R^2 will still go up. If R^2 is low, we could essentially add variables at random, with each one pushing R^2 higher, even if each new partial slope was statistically insignificant. This obviously can give a false sense of the real explanatory power of a model.

To remedy this problem, statistical programs generate something called an **Adjusted R^2**. The Adjusted R^2 provides a more accurate picture of the explanatory power of a model because it adjusts for the presence of partial slopes with insignificant t values. If a model includes both statistically significant and insignificant partial slopes, the Adjusted R^2 will be lower than the R^2 itself. If a model includes only partial slope coefficients with significant t values, the Adjusted R^2 and R^2 values will typically be quite similar. There are valid reasons for including partial slopes with insignificant t values, so you should not automatically remove independent variables from your model simply because they lower the Adjusted R^2. We will explain the reasons for this later in the chapter.

Finally, notice that the value of the standard error of the estimate has dropped. If Boonsville has housing that is 42 years old on the average and is 80% owner occupied, the number of fires per month can be predicted:

$$\hat{Y} = 38.1 + 1.57X_1 - .49X_2$$

For Boonsville, $X_1 = 42$ and $X_2 = 80$:

$$\hat{Y} = 38.1 + 1.57(42) - .49(80) = 38.1 + 65.9 - 39.2 = 64.8$$

Notice that this estimate is different from the simple regression estimate of 75.6.

Unfortunately, putting a confidence limit around an estimate for a multiple regression is fairly difficult. Many advanced statistics books do not even cover its calculation because the formula is highly complex and, for more than two variables, requires the use of matrix algebra. The standard error of the estimate is a reasonably good estimate for the amount of the error when the sample size is large and the X values are close to their respective means. So, for practical purposes, managers can often use plus or minus twice the standard error of the estimate to approximate 95% confidence limits. The actual limits are likely to be somewhat larger than this, especially if the X values are far from their means. Some computer programs are designed to automatically calculate confidence limits on predictions. When these limits are available, they should be used. Using the two times rule of thumb, Chief Pyro gets confidence limits of

$$64.8 \pm 2 \times 3.55$$

$$57.7 \text{ to } 71.9$$

This narrower range of confidence (in comparison to simple regression with a standard error of 18.4) is one that Chief Pyro can use with some confidence.

Calculating Partial Slopes

If we wish to calculate the slope values in a multiple regression, it is helpful to change the standard designation of a regression line to the following:

$$\hat{X}_1 = a + b_{12.3}X_2 + b_{13.2}X_3$$

where $b_{12.3}$ means the regression slope of X_1 on X_2 controlling for X_3 and $b_{13.2}$ means the regression slope of X_1 on X_3 controlling for X_2. Statisticians, using the principles of least squares, have found that

$$b_{12.3} = \frac{b_{12} - (b_{13})(b_{32})}{1 - (b_{23})(b_{32})}$$

If we performed all the simple regressions indicated on the right side of the equation using the Stermerville fire data, we would find that

$$b_{12} = 1.12 \quad b_{13} = -.24 \quad b_{23} = .16 \quad b_{32} = .92$$

If you do not believe that these are the correct slopes, feel free to calculate them yourself. Substituting these values into the equation for $b_{12.3}$, we find

$$b_{12.3} = \frac{1.12 - (-.24)(.92)}{1 - (.16)(.92)} = \frac{1.12 + .22}{1 - .15} = \frac{1.34}{.85} = 1.57$$

For $b_{13.2}$, the calculations are

$$b_{13.2} = \frac{b_{13} - (b_{12})(b_{23})}{1 - (b_{32})(b_{23})} = \frac{-.24 - (1.12)(.16)}{1 - (.92)(.16)} = \frac{-.41}{.85} = -.49$$

To calculate the value of the intercept, we use the following formula:

$$a = \bar{Y} - b_1\bar{X}_1 - b_2\bar{X}_2 = 58.8 - 1.57(27.0) - (-.49)44$$
$$= 58.8 - 42.4 + 21.6 = 38$$
$$\hat{Y} = 38 + 1.57X_1 - .49X_2$$

In the real world, very few analysts calculate the slopes and intercepts in multiple regression by hand. Several excellent computer programs can do this far more quickly and accurately than can any normal human being. The role of a manager, after all, is to make decisions based on the information available rather than to calculate regression coefficients.

The Logic of Controls

In Chapter 17, we introduced the logic of controls for nominal and ordinal data. The logic of control relationships applies equally well to interval-level data and multiple regression.

A Spurious Relationship

The head statistician for North Zulch City Police, Mr. A. Nalist, has discovered a startling new finding. When Mr. Nalist regresses the number of juvenile crimes in a precinct on the number of household pets in that precinct, he finds the following:

$$\hat{Y} = 15.4 - .075X \quad s_b = .009 \quad r^2 = .70$$

Pet ownership in a precinct appears to be a fairly good predictor of juvenile crimes. While Mr. Nalist was drafting a memo advocating the free distribution of pets to prevent crime, I. C. Fallacy (a research assistant) suggested that a multiple regression with both pet ownership (X_1) and median income in the precinct (X_2) be used to predict juvenile crime (Y). A multiple regression reveals the following:

$$\hat{Y} = 16.5 - .003X_1 - .32X_2$$
$$s_{b_1} = .047 \quad s_{b_2} = .006 \quad R^2 = .85$$

Note that the regression slope for pet ownership in a precinct has fallen to zero (t score $= .06$), whereas median income is strongly related to juvenile crime

($t = 53.3$). Whenever a relationship is spurious, the regression slope between these two variables will fall to zero if one includes a variable that causes both the other variables (in this case, high income causes pet ownership and low crime rates).

A Specification

A relationship is specified if two variables appear unrelated but become related in the presence of a third variable (see Chapter 17). For example, when absenteeism rates (Y) are regressed on the age of letter carriers (X) for the Ripple, North Dakota, Post Office, no relationship exists:

$$\hat{Y} = 8.6 + .03X$$
$$s_b = .58 \quad r^2 = .01$$

But when an analyst controls for the length of routes (X_2) by entering it into the regression equation, the following pattern emerges:

$$\hat{Y} = 4.7 + .18X_1 + 2.1X_2$$
$$s_{b_1} = .021 \quad s_{b_2} = 1.1 \quad R^2 = .50$$

When length of routes (in miles) is controlled, a relationship exists between absenteeism and age. Obviously, older letter carriers with longer routes have higher absenteeism rates. In the best of all possible worlds, the Ripple postmaster would reassign routes so that older letter carriers would have shorter routes. In theory, the result would be lower absenteeism and, thus, higher productivity.

Dummy Variable Regression

In Chapter 19, simple regression with a dichotomous independent variable was demonstrated. The results were identical to a difference of means test. Can regression be used with nominal independent variables when the independent variable has more than two categories? Yes, but only when the analyst constructs the regression carefully.

Suppose a police chief wants to see whether precinct crime rates are related to different areas of the city. The chief is particularly concerned about the crime rates in the inner city, downtown, and middle-class residential areas. One way to determine whether the area of the city affects precinct crime rates is to regress crime rates in each precinct on area of the city. To do this, create a dummy variable X_1 that is coded 1 if the precinct in question is in the inner city and is coded 0 if it is not. Another dummy variable, X_2, is created that is coded 1 if the precinct is downtown and coded 0 if it is not.

Do not create a third dummy variable for middle-class areas. Two dummy variables account for all three types of precincts, as illustrated here:

If $X_1 = 1$ and $X_2 = 0$, then precinct is *inner city.*

If $X_1 = 0$ and $X_2 = 1$, then precinct is *downtown.*

If $X_1 = 0$ and $X_2 = 0$, then precinct is *middle class.*

A regression of precinct crime rates on X_1 and X_2 might reveal the following:

$$\hat{Y} = 5{,}463 + 2{,}471X_1 - 1{,}362X_2$$
$$s_{b_1} = 236 \quad s_{b_2} = 147$$

This regression equation can be interpreted as follows. The intercept, 5,463, is the mean crime rate of all middle-class precincts ($X_1 = 0$ and $X_2 = 0$). The mean crime rate for all inner-city precincts is $a + \beta_1$, or 7,934. The mean crime rate for downtown precincts is $a + \beta_2$, or 4,101. The standard errors of the regression slopes indicate that crime rates in the inner city and downtown are significantly different than those in the middle-class precincts. These results would match those for analysis of variance and are much easier to interpret.

Regression with Three Independent Variables

Multiple regression can be used with an unlimited number of independent variables. Regression with three or more independent variables is nothing more than a straightforward extension of the two-variable case.

An Example

Jack Sixgun, the police chief of Metropolis, is concerned about the number of assaults made on police officers in Metropolis. Chief Sixgun asks his data analysts to study the assaults on Metropolis police over the past 10 years. As the dependent variable, the analysts use a dummy variable coded 1 if a police officer was assaulted in a year and coded 0 if he or she was not.

Chief Sixgun suggests that the analysts use three independent variables. The first is the height of the police officer: Chief Sixgun feels that taller officers command more authority and, therefore, are less likely to be assaulted. The analysts operationalize this variable as the number of inches in height a police officer is over the 5-foot, 4-inch minimum. Second, Chief Sixgun believes that officers are less likely to be assaulted if they are operating in teams. This is a dummy variable coded 1 if the officer was teamed with another officer and coded 0 if the officer was not. Third, Chief Sixgun believes that rookies are more likely to make mistakes that will result in assaults. This variable was operationalized as the number of years the officer has served on the force.

Using a multiple regression computer program, Sixgun's analysts find the following:

$$\hat{Y} = .11 + .05X_1 + .21X_2 - .03X_3$$
$$s_{b_1} = .016 \quad s_{b_2} = .062 \quad s_{b_3} = .008 \quad S_{y|x} = .08 \quad R^2 = .73 \quad \mathbf{N} = 200$$

where X_1 is the police officer's height, X_2 is the team variable, and X_3 is the number of years on the force.

The regression equation is interpreted in the same way as was the equation for the two-variable case. The regression coefficient for height (.05) shows that the amount the probability of assault increases (Y is a dummy variable; thus, $\hat{Y}$ becomes a probability) with each inch in height over 5 feet, 4 inches if teams and time on the force are held constant. This finding shocks Chief Sixgun, because a 6-foot, 6-inch police officer has a .7 greater probability of being assaulted than does a 5-foot, 4-inch police officer.

The second regression coefficient is the increase in the probability of assault by being assigned to a team (.21) if height and time on the force remain constant. Again Chief Sixgun is surprised, because officers in teams are more likely to be assaulted than officers alone.

Finally, the third regression coefficient indicates that the probability of being assaulted drops .03 for every year the officer serves on the force (all other things being equal).

The intercept (.11) is the probability of being assaulted when X_1, X_2, and X_3 are all zero. In other words, our best estimate is that a 5-foot, 4-inch police officer who is not teamed with another officer and is a rookie (0 years) has a .11 probability of being assaulted in the line of duty in a year's time.

Note that all three regression coefficients have standard errors. By determining the probability that each could be drawn from a population where $\beta = 0$, the strength of the relationships can be assessed. Do this in the space provided.

The preceding regression equation can be used in the same way that any other regression equation can be used. For example, we can predict the probability that a 6-foot-tall officer with three years on the force assigned to a team would be assaulted. We substitute the values of 8 (inches over 5 feet, 4 inches), 1, and 3 for X_1, X_2, and X_3, respectively.

$$\hat{Y} = .11 + .05(8) + .21(1) - .03(3)$$
$$= .11 + .40 + .21 - .09 = .51 + .12 = .63$$

This officer has a .63 probability of being assaulted this year. Using the same standard error of the estimate (.08), we could place a rough 95% confidence limit around this estimate (a t value of 2.0 will provide a good approximation).

$$.63 \pm t \times S_{y|x}$$
$$.63 \pm 2.0 \times .08$$
$$.63 \pm .16$$
$$.47 \text{ to } .79$$

Chief Sixgun can also use the regression equation to make management decisions. Because teams increase the probability of assaults by .21, he may decide to eliminate team patrols. Because taller officers are more likely to be assaulted, he may decide to relax the height requirement for police officers.

Calculating Regression Coefficients

When you, as an analyst, must perform a regression with three or more independent variables, we strongly recommend that you use one of numerous computer programs to calculate the regression. Most programs will provide the values for all slopes, the intercept, all slope standard errors, the standard error of the estimate, and the coefficient of determination. For those who prefer to calculate regression slopes by hand, use the following formula:

$$b_{12.34} = \frac{b_{12.3} - (b_{14.3})(b_{42.3})}{1 - (b_{24.3})(b_{42.3})}$$

Note that this is only one slope needed for a regression with three independent variables. Other formulas for the intercept and the standard errors can be found in statistics texts (see Blalock, 1972).

Testing a Hypothesis

Several minority groups have charged that the Capers City civil service exam discriminates against minorities. In fact, whites are twice as likely to pass the exam as are minorities. Harlan Fitzgerald, Capers civil service commissioner, counters these claims with the argument that minorities taking the exam have less education, less job-related experience, and lower school grades and thus are more likely to fail for these reasons. Minority groups contend that even when these factors are considered, the exam still discriminates against minorities.

The dispute could be resolved if we could test Mr. Fitzgerald's hypothesis:

H_0: When education, job experience, and grades are controlled, race is unrelated to performance on the Capers City civil service exam.

Regression can be used to test this hypothesis. For each civil service applicant, the following information must be gathered:

Y = score on the civil service exam
X_1 = number of years of formal education
X_2 = years of relevant job experience
X_3 = grade point average in college
X_4 = minority status (1 = minority, 0 = nonminority)

A regression line estimated for this information would be as follows:

$$\hat{Y} = \alpha + \beta_1 X_1 + \beta_2 X_2 + \beta_3 X_3 + \beta_4 X_4$$

Mr. Fitzgerald's hypothesis can be restated as follows:

H_0: β_4 is equal to zero.

β_4 is the relationship of race to civil service exam scores when education, experience, and grades are controlled. If β_4 equals zero, then race is unrelated to exam scores when the other factors are controlled. As Mr. Fitzgerald would say, the relationship between race and civil service exam scores is spurious. One can test whether β_4 is equal to zero by calculating a t score and finding the probability of this t score in Table 3 of the Appendix.

For the minority groups to prove their contention, not only would β_4 have to not be equal to zero, but it would also have to have a negative value. A negative slope demonstrates that minorities do worse on the exam than whites do when education, experience, and grades are controlled. If β_4 is positive, Mr. Fitzgerald still wins his argument (at least in regard to minority groups).

Two Additional Regression Assumptions

Recall our discussion of the assumptions of regression analysis in Chapter 19. Each of the assumptions for bivariate regression also applies in the case of multiple regression. Multiple regression differs from bivariate regression in that two additional assumptions must be considered when developing equations with more than one independent variable.

Assumption 1: Model is Specified Correctly

An important assumption in multiple regression is correct model specification. In simple terms, a well-specified regression equation contains all or most of the independent variables known to be relevant predictors of the dependent variable.

As a starting point in specifying a model, it is quite common to look at existing research on a topic to see what others examining the same (or a similar) question have used as explanatory variables. The more substantive knowledge you possess about the topic in question, the better your ability to select relevant independent variables.

Although existing research can help inform the selection of explanatory variables, there is hardly ever a case where one objectively "correct" set of explanatory variables for a particular regression model exists. Model specification involves good judgment. Above all, you should have sound reasons for choosing the explanatory variables used in a multiple regression analysis and should be prepared to defend your choices. As a beginning data analyst, you should think about a few fairly obvious questions when selecting explanatory variables for a multiple regression equation.

Have Key Variables Been Omitted from the Equation?

Given our knowledge of the factors that affect the dependent variable, does it appear that key explanatory variables have been omitted from the model? If so, why? The reason might be something as simple as an inability to locate data for the variable. Input from a colleague or supervisor who might see things from a different point of view can be helpful when an analyst wonders whether she or he has considered all relevant explanatory variables.

How do we know whether our model is "underspecified"—that is, does not contain enough important independent variables? One way to spot an underspecified model is by looking at the R^2 and Adjusted R^2. The closer either of these values is to zero, the lower the explanatory power of the model. The omission of key independent variables results in the error term absorbing much of the variance that would otherwise be explained by missing independent variables. The size of the error term tends to decrease as relevant explanatory variables are added to the equation. The following example illustrates the problem of an underspecified model.

The director of the Westville, Tennessee, homeless shelter wants to obtain a better understanding of program costs. He has data on operating costs for the last 15 weeks. The director knows that when unemployment is high, demand for services tends to increase. Accordingly, he obtains weekly data on new unemployment claims from the state unemployment office and uses the number of new claims as the first independent variable. At times, the shelter experiences a dropoff in volunteers, which results in paid employees working more hours. The director decides to include the number of volunteer hours worked per week as the second independent variable. He generates the following regression equation:

$$\hat{Y} = 9{,}780 + 2.44X_1 - 55.14X_2$$

$$s_{b_1} = 1.5 \quad s_{b_2} = 31.8 \quad R^2 = .34 \quad \text{Adj. } R^2 = .23$$

where X_1 is the number of new unemployment claims and X_2 is the number of hours worked by volunteers.

The director is somewhat disappointed that his model explains only about a third of the variation in operating costs. He meets with his staff and asks for feedback on the results. One member of the staff notices that the director seems to have missed the most obvious determinant of operating costs—the number of clients served. The director reruns the regression equation using the number of clients served per week as the third independent variable:

$$\hat{Y} = 8{,}540 + 1.98X_1 - 9.91X_2 + 44.51X_3$$

$$s_{b_1} = 1.2 \quad s_{b_2} = 5.8 \quad s_{b_3} = 6.5 \quad R^2 = .87 \quad \text{Adj. } R^2 = .84$$

where X_1 is the number of new unemployment claims, X_2 is the number of hours worked by volunteers, and X_3 is the number of clients served.

By including the number of clients served per week, the R^2 and Adjusted R^2 values for the model rose dramatically. In addition to increasing the explanatory power of a model, the inclusion of important omitted variables results in more accurate estimates of the effects on the dependent variable of all the independent variables included in the regression equation.

Can I Explain Why I Selected Each Independent Variable?

Theory should always guide the choice of possible explanatory variables. "Fishing" for results by haphazardly adding independent variables to, or subtracting them from, the regression equation in hopes of obtaining statistically significant findings is not sound practice. The chances of finding spurious relationships increase when little forethought is put into model specification. In Chapter 3, we discussed theory as a key component used to determine causality. A good data analyst should always be prepared to explain (in English) the substantive rationale for the statistical relationship between an independent and dependent variable. Maximizing the number of statistically significant slopes or maximizing R^2 for the sake of obtaining impressive-looking results is not the goal of multiple regression.

You should keep in mind, however, that fishing for results and searching for novel explanations are very different things. You should not be afraid to test different model specifications if you have sound reasons for adding or removing explanatory variables from an equation. Sometimes the theories guiding our research are poorly developed, which opens the door to innovative attempts at model specification. The key is to have a rationale underlying the choice of each independent variable used in a regression equation.

When Should a Variable Be Dropped from an Equation?

A common belief among data analysts is that after performing a multiple regression and finding a variable with an insignificant slope coefficient, the variable should be removed and the regression rerun. Statistically, this may help improve the "fit" of the model because a variable with low explanatory power has been removed from the equation. The Adjusted R^2 value typically goes up when statistically insignificant slope coefficients are removed from a model.

Removing independent variables with insignificant slope coefficients has value, especially when selecting a final set of explanatory variables to be included in a model. If the partial slope for a particular variable is not statistically significant, removing the variable and rerunning the regression may provide a more accurate depiction of the relationships between the remaining independent variables and the dependent variable.

However, a crucial point to keep in mind is that statistically insignificant slope coefficients can be very significant substantively from a managerial standpoint. In policy analysis, knowing what is *not* statistically significant is often as important as knowing what is statistically significant.

For example, a program analyst for Ohio is interested in determining the factors that shape student performance. She performs a multiple regression in which student test scores are the dependent variable. The analyst selects average class size, teacher experience (in years), and average state aid per pupil as independent variables. She generates the following regression equation:

$$\hat{Y} = 78 + .41X_1 + .28X_2 + .14X_3$$

$$s_{b_1} = .11 \quad s_{b_2} = .09 \quad s_{b_3} = .98 \quad R^2 = .81 \quad \text{Adj. } R^2 = .70$$

where X_1 is average class size, X_2 is teacher experience, and X_3 is state aid per pupil.

The t values for the first two partial slopes are significant at the .05 probability level. With a t value of .143, the partial slope coefficient for the state aid per pupil variable is not statistically significant. Does this mean that the analyst should automatically drop the variable from the equation and rerun the model in hopes of increasing the Adjusted R^2? If the analyst takes this route, she may be throwing away very important information about how a policy is working. Knowing that state aid per pupil is unrelated to student performance (at least in terms of statistical significance) may be useful information for revising policy in the future.

A negative connotation sometimes is associated with the term *statistically insignificant.* Statistical significance or insignificance should not trigger automatic response sets when interpreting partial slopes in a regression equation. It is perfectly acceptable to remove independent variables from a model if they lack explanatory power. Yet care and judgment should be used to assess the substantive importance of findings, regardless of whether the results are statistically significant. If gaining knowledge about the effects of a particular independent variable is important, it is a good idea to leave the variable in the equation even if the partial slope coefficient is not statistically significant. If gaining knowledge about the effects of a particular independent variable is not central to the research question at hand, then removing a statistically insignificant variable may be appropriate. A manager should always interpret the substantive meaning of partial slope coefficients before dropping independent variables from a regression equation.

Assumption 2: Low Multicollinearity

A second important assumption in multiple regression is low **multicollinearity.** This term refers to a case in which two or more independent variables are highly correlated (have a linear relationship). Examples of variables that can be expected to be highly correlated are agency budget size and number of agency employees, or population size and number of traffic accidents.

Multicollinearity makes it difficult for the regression equation to estimate unique partial slopes for each independent variable. Partial slope estimates and the associated *t* values can be misleading if one independent variable is highly correlated with another. Not only is it difficult to distinguish the effect of one independent variable from another, but high multicollinearity also typically results in partial slope coefficients with inflated standard errors, thus making it hard to obtain statistically significant results.

Multicollinearity can be diagnosed in a regression equation by looking for two things: the equation may produce a high Adjusted R^2 but slope coefficients that are not statistically significant. Or, the value of the coefficients may change (sometimes dramatically) when independent variables are added and subtracted from the equation. The unstable variables are likely to be collinear.

One of the simplest ways to avoid or address multicollinearity is to assess logically whether each independent variable included in a model is really measuring something different than the others. If you think one independent variable might be measuring the same thing as another, you can test this by calculating a correlation coefficient (with a computer program, if possible) for the variables in question. Values for correlation coefficients range from -1.0 (perfect negative correlation) to $+1.0$ (perfect positive correlation). The closer values are to either end of the range, the more closely the two variables move or covary together. Alternatively, if you suspect that multicollinearity between two independent variables is a problem, you can run a bivariate regression in which one of the explanatory variables is used to explain the other. The closer the R^2 value for the equation is to 1.0, the more likely multicollinearity is a problem.

The effects of multicollinearity are best illustrated with an example. Frank Watson, the director of the Arizona State Audit Bureau, is interested in finding out why some auditors perform better on annual auditor skills tests than others. Dr. Watson selects three independent variables to explain exam scores for a random sample of 19 auditors. Years of job experience at the bureau is selected as the first independent variable because the director feels that more experienced employees should possess a deeper knowledge of auditing procedures than their less experienced counterparts. Dr. Watson selects employee age as the second independent variable because he believes that there is no substitute for life experience when dealing with complex program evaluation issues. Finally, Dr. Watson feels that salaried workers should have more knowledge about auditing procedures than hourly workers, so a dummy variable coded 1 if an employee is salaried and 0 if not is included in the analysis. The following regression equation is generated:

$$\hat{Y} = 75.2 + .56X_1 + .25X_2 + 1.36X_3$$

$$s_{b_1} = .66 \quad s_{b_2} = .35 \quad s_{b_3} = .90 \quad R^2 = .81 \quad \text{Adj. } R^2 = .79$$

where X_1 is employee experience, X_2 is employee age, and X_3 is a salaried/hourly dummy variable.

The director is puzzled by the results. The R^2 and Adjusted R^2 values indicate that the model explains approximately 80% of the variation in employee exams scores, yet none of the partial slope coefficients are statistically significant. The director's assistant points out that multicollinearity may be affecting the results because employee age and years of job experience are probably correlated with each other to some extent. To confirm her hunch, the assistant calculates a correlation coefficient and finds a .95 correlation between employee experience and employee age. Upon regressing years of job experience on employee age, an R^2 value of .91 is obtained. Based on these results, the assistant recommends that Dr. Watson remove one of the independent variables from the equation. Dr. Watson decides to remove employee age from the model because he feels that years of experience at the bureau provides a more precise measure of actual job skills. The new regression equation is as follows:

$$\hat{Y} = 80.9 + 1.03X_1 + 1.32X_2$$

$$s_{b_1} = .13 \quad s_{b_2} = .79 \quad R^2 = .80 \quad \text{Adj. } R^2 = .77$$

where X_1 is employee experience and X_2 is the salaried/hourly dummy variable.

The results of the second regression model indicate that employee experience in years has a positive and statistically significant effect on employee exam scores. Recall that in the first model, the partial slope coefficients for both the employee experience and age variables were not statistically significant because of high multicollinearity.

Although logical reasoning can be helpful for identifying which of the independent variables are affected by multicollinearity, sometimes an analyst will not have prior knowledge about relationships between or among particular independent variables. Because we often do not know ahead of time whether multicollinearity might be a problem, it is always a good idea to generate the correlations between each pair of independent variables included in a regression equation (called a *correlation matrix*). An even more advanced approach for detecting multicollinearity is analysis of variance inflation factors (VIFs), which most statistical software programs provide.

It may seem that the obvious solution to high multicollinearity is the removal of one or more independent variables from the regression equation, but a manager should not let his or her statistician make such changes automatically. Changing how a model is specified requires sound judgment because removing important independent variables may make it more difficult to study the management question at hand. Sometimes a loss of precision in estimating partial slope coefficients is preferable to removing highly correlated independent variables from a model. Other options commonly pursued by analysts include combining the collinear variables into an index or transforming a suspect variable using a mathematical calculation (such as taking the logarithm of each value). All options must be carefully considered to ensure that the concept each variable represents (for instance, age, budget size, numbers of employees, or test scores) is not lost in the transformation. Diagnosing and reducing multicollinearity is a fairly advanced topic, so if you suspect it is a problem, you should consult a statistician or statistical textbook (see Fox, 1991).

Polynomial Curve Fitting

Linear regression is only appropriate where the relationship between variables is linear. In Chapter 20, nonlinear regression with logarithms was demonstrated. Two other forms of nonlinear regression, also called **polynomial curve fitting,** are important to know: quadratic relationships and cubic relationships.

Quadratic Relationships

Boomtown, Wyoming, a fast-growing new town in the western coal fields, has also experienced a phenomenal increase in its crime rate as the city's population has skyrocketed. The data in Table 21.3 show this increase.

The county sheriff, Seymour "Tex" Critter, would like to forecast the number of crimes in Boomtown so that he can decide how many deputies to assign to Boomtown. Tex begins his analysis by graphing the data. Do this on the graph in Figure 21.1.

Table 21.3

Crime Rate in Boomtown

Year	Number of Crimes
1998	1
1999	3
2000	10
2001	31
2002	69
2003	124
2004	183
2005	234

Figure 21.1

Graph Data Here

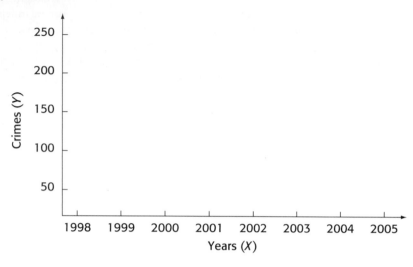

Table 21.4

Calculations for Boomtown Data

Year	X	X^2	Y
1998	1	1	1
1999	2	4	3
2000	3	9	10
2001	4	16	31
2002	5	25	69
2003	6	36	124
2004	7	49	183
2005	8	64	234

When Tex examines the graph of the data, he sees that the relationship is not linear; crime is increasing at an increasing rate. This is the general form of a quadratic relationship. To fit a curved line to these data, Tex must convert years to regular numbers for new X values. Then these X values must be squared. See Table 21.4.

To calculate a regression equation that will accurately describe the data, Tex must estimate the following regression:

$$\hat{Y} = \alpha + \beta_1 X + \beta_2 X^2$$

Notice that both X and X^2 are included in the equation.

Performing a regression on the data, Tex finds

$$\hat{Y} = 8.9 - 15.1X + 5.5X^2$$
$$s_{b_1} = 5.0 \quad s_{b_2} = .54 \quad S_{y|x} = 7.04 \quad R^2 = .996$$

From this information, Tex can determine whether the relationship is, in fact, quadratic. If the slope for X^2 does not equal zero, then the regression has a quadratic shape ($5.5 \div .54 = 10.2 = t$ score). In this case, the coefficient is significant, and the relationship is quadratic. To the novice, the individual slope coefficients have little meaning; do not worry about them. Our objective is only to forecast, so we need not interpret these coefficients.

Tex attempts to forecast 2006 crime in Boomtown by substituting in the value 9 for X and the value 81 for X^2.

$$\hat{Y} = 8.9 - 15.1(9) + 5.5(81) = 8.9 - 135.9 + 445.5 = 318.5$$

Tex's forecast of 318.5 crimes appears reasonable given the pattern of the data. Using the standard error of the estimate, Tex could place a rough confidence limit around this estimate. Do this for Tex.

To illustrate the utility of the quadratic forecast, Tex determined a straight linear forecast for crime in Boomtown.

$$\hat{Y} = -74.1 + 34.7X$$
$$s_b = 4.6 \quad S_{y|x} = 30.0 \quad r^2 = .90$$

Notice that, for the linear regression, r^2 is lower and the standard error of the estimate is higher. Forecasts with this model would be less accurate than would be those with the quadratic model. The forecast for 2006 would be as follows:

$$\hat{Y} = -74.1 + 34.7(9) = -74.1 + 312.3 = 238.2$$

The linear forecast for 2006 is only five crimes more than the 2005 figure. Clearly this forecast would not be accurate if past trends continued.

Cubic Regression

The city of Xenith has been experimenting over the past year with the number of officers assigned to the vice squad. For the past 11 months, the city has gathered the information on prostitution arrests shown in Table 21.5.

Currently, the city council wants the police department to double its vice squad to drive prostitution off the streets. The police chief would rather use these additional

Table 21.5

Xenith City Data on Prostitution Arrests

Arrests	Number of Vice Squad Officers
25	1
34	2
43	3
98	4
123	5
194	6
253	7
271	8
294	9
292	10
298	11

Figure 21.2

Graph Data Here

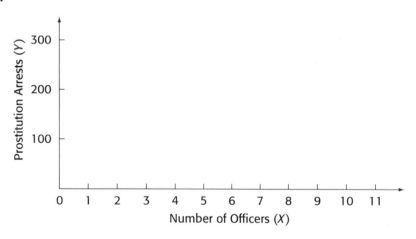

officers on homicide, because she believes that any increase in vice squad officers would have no impact on prostitution arrests.

The police chief begins her analysis by graphing the data. Do this for the police chief on the graph in Figure 21.2.

The police chief recognizes the pattern of a cubic relationship, as illustrated in Chapter 19. She then decides to run three regressions, one with X, one a quadratic, and one a cubic, as follows:

$$\text{linear:} \quad \hat{Y} = a + \beta X$$
$$\text{quadratic:} \quad \hat{Y} = a + \beta_1 X + \beta_2 X^2$$
$$\text{cubic:} \quad \hat{Y} = a + \beta_1 X + \beta_2 X^2 + \beta_3 X^3$$

Table 21.6

Calculations for Xenith City Data

Y	X	X²	X³
25	1	1	1
34	2	4	8
43	3	9	27
98	4	16	64
123	5	25	125
194	6	36	216
253	7	49	343
271	8	64	512
294	9	81	729
292	10	100	1,000
298	11	121	1,331

To do this, the police chief squares and cubes the X values, as shown in Table 21.6. The following regressions result:

linear:

$$\hat{Y} = -22.8 + 33.0X$$

$$s_b = 2.8 \quad S_{y|x} = 29.0 \quad r^2 = .94$$

quadratic:

$$\hat{Y} = -55.3 + 48.0X - 1.3X^2$$

$$s_{b_1} = 11.7 \quad s_{b_2} = .95 \quad S_{y|x} = 27.9 \quad R^2 = .95$$

cubic:

$$\hat{Y} = 43.9 - 34.0X + 15.1X^2 - .91X^3$$

$$s_{b_1} = 15.4 \quad s_{b_2} = 2.9 \quad s_{b_3} = .16 \quad S_{y|x} = 12.6 \quad R^2 = .991$$

Notice the increase in the coefficient of determination for the cubic equation and the decrease in the standard error of the estimate. These results plus the standard errors of the slopes indicate that the relationship is cubic.

The real advantage of the cubic form is in forecasting. If the police chief forecasts the number of arrests with 11 officers by using the linear and cubic models, she finds

$$\text{linear: } \hat{Y} = -23.4 + 33(11) = 340.2$$
$$\text{cubic: } \hat{Y} = 43.9 - 34.0(11) + 15.1(121) - .91(1,331)$$
$$= 42.8 - 374 + 1,827 - 1,211 = 285$$

Notice that not only is the cubic forecast more accurate, but the linear forecast is far too high. This result is important in decision making, because a linear forecast of 22 police officers would show a large increase in arrests, whereas the cubic forecast would not. (Note that forecasting arrests by 22 officers is extremely risky when data only contain information for 1 to 11 officers.)

Chapter Summary

Multiple regression is a technique used for interval-level data when the analyst has more than one independent variable. This chapter discusses the interpretation of multiple regression and the application of regression to two or more independent variables.

Two concepts involved in multiple regression are partial slopes and the multiple coefficient of determination. Each is analogous to its counterpart, the (bivariate) slope and coefficient of determination (r^2), in simple linear regression based on a single independent variable. Adjusted R^2 values reveal the reduction in explanatory power of a model after taking statistically insignificant partial slope coefficients into account. This chapter illustrated the interpretation of these terms when a dependent variable is regressed on two or more independent variables.

The logic of control relationships, introduced in Chapter 17, applies equally well to multiple regression. Dummy variable regression can be used with nominal independent variables having more than two categories.

Multiple regression can be used to test hypotheses involving more than one independent variable. Multiple regression can also be used to estimate relationships that are not linear, a technique known as polynomial curve fitting. In addition to all the assumptions for bivariate regression (see Chapter 19), in multiple regression analysis, sound and valid results depend on two further assumptions: that the regression equation includes all of the independent variables that theory or experience suggest will influence the dependent variable (specification), and that the predictor variables are not so closely related that their independent effect on the dependent variable cannot be distinguished (multicollinearity).

Problems

21.1 Forrest Tucker, the head statistician for the National Parks Service, believes that park usage as measured by number of visitors (Y) is a function of the number of people who live within 200 miles of the park (X_1), the number of camping hookups available (X_2), and the mean annual temperature at the park (X_3). For a sample of 200 parks under Forrest's supervision, the following regression is calculated (Y is number of visitors):

$$\hat{Y} = 147 + .0212X_1 + 15.4X_2 + 186X_3$$

$$s_{b_1} = .0157 \quad s_{b_2} = 12.4 \quad s_{b_3} = 10.4 \quad R^2 = .50 \quad \text{Adj. } R^2 = .43$$

For this regression, what can you tell Forrest? Write a one-page memo with your assessment.

21.2 If Janice Position-Classification, personnel officer for the Bureau of Forms, can forecast agency separations 6 months from now, she can plan recruitment efforts to replace these people. Janice believes that separations 6 months from now are determined by the number of agency people passed over for promotion (X_1), the number of agency people 64 years old or older (X_2), and the ratio of government salaries to private sector salaries (X_3). Using regression, Janice finds the following:

$$\hat{Y} = 27.4 + .35X_1 + .54X_2 - 271X_3$$

$$s_{b_1} = .0031 \quad s_{b_2} = .0136 \quad s_{b_3} = 263 \quad S_{y|x} = 54$$
$$R^2 = .89 \quad \text{Adj. } R^2 = .85 \quad \mathbf{N} = 214$$

Write a one-page memo explaining the results, and then forecast the number of separations if 418 people are passed over for promotion, 327 people are 64 years old or older, and government salaries equal those in the private sector.

21.3 The Forest Service believes that it can predict the number of forest fires per month in a forest, knowing the amount of rainfall that fell the previous month (X_1) and the average daily temperature for that month (X_2), taken from historical records. A regression yields the following:

$$\hat{Y} = 2.0 - 1.1X_1 + .14X_2$$

$$s_{b_1} = .021 \quad s_{b_2} = .003 \quad S_{y|x} = 1.4$$
$$R^2 = .96 \quad \text{Adj. } R^2 = .96 \quad \mathbf{N} = 136$$

(a) Write a brief memo interpreting the slopes, the intercept, and R^2.

(b) Barren National Forest has had 4 inches of rain in the last month and has a historical mean temperature of 84 degrees for this month. What is the best estimate of the number of fires in Barren this month?

21.4 The McKeesport Fire Department wants to know how likely it is that a truck pump will fail. The fire chief, George Pyro (no relation), thinks pump failure is a function of age (X_1) and water hardness (X_2, measured on a scale of 1 to 10). The department statistician runs a regression on a dummy variable (coded 1 for failure and 0 for no failure) for 217 pumps. She finds the following:

$$\hat{Y} = .14 + .01X_1 + .05X_2$$

$$s_{b_1} = .0002 \quad s_{b_2} = .025 \quad S_{y|x} = .04 \quad R^2 = .93 \quad \text{Adj. } R^2 = .92$$

Write a memo explaining what the regression means. If the average water hardness is 3, and the chief would like to replace any pump with a probability of failing of .80 or more, at what age should pumps be replaced?

21.5 Lieutenant Colonel Syl Verleaf is placed in charge of base security at all 240 military bases in Europe. Verleaf believes that the crime rate is positively correlated to the size of the base, the percentage of troops without high school degrees, and the number of women on base. Verleaf's statistician finds the following:

$$\hat{Y} = 47.3 + .031X_1 + 2.4X_2 - .065X_3$$

$$s_{b_1} = .0021 \quad s_{b_2} = 3.0 \quad s_{b_3} = .0027 \quad S_{y|x} = 17.1$$
$$R^2 = .80 \quad \text{Adj. } R^2 = .78$$

where X_1 is the number of troops on the base, X_2 is the percentage of troops without high school degrees, X_3 is the number of women on the base, and Y is the number of serious crimes in a month. Interpret all the regression coefficients, R^2, and the intercept. What is the most important independent variable? Ramstein Air Base has 15,000 troops, 42% of its troops have no high school degree, and there are 3,000 women on base. What is your best estimate of the number of crimes per month for this base?

21.6 Refer to Problem 21.5. The information for Rathesberg Base and Krasmic Kaserne appears in the accompanying table.

Statistic	Rathesberg	Krasmic
X_1 (troops)	12,000	14,000
X_2 (% without high school degree)	34	28
X_3 (women)	2,000	3,000
Y (number of crimes)	517	290

Calculate $\hat{Y}$ for each base. Why might it be interesting to study both bases in depth?

21.7 The Missouri Department of Education has hired a program evaluation team to investigate why the average reading scores for all seniors vary from 9.4 to 13.1 for different high schools ($N = 326$). The program evaluation team believes that reading scores are affected by pupil–teacher ratios (X_1) and per-student spending on education in a school district (X_2). Using regression analysis, the team finds

$$\hat{Y} = 10.6 - .091X_1 + .0031X_2$$
$$s_{b_1} = .017 \quad s_{b_2} = .00061 \quad S_{y|x} = .17 \quad R^2 = .75 \quad \text{Adj. } R^2 = .74$$

Interpret this equation for the department of education. The education department's budget has enough money to lower the pupil–teacher ratio by 5 or to increase the per-student spending by $50. Which should it do?

21.8 Several states have argued that the 65-mph speed limit has no justification and have refused to enforce it. The federal Department of Transportation (DOT) believes that the 65-mph limit saves lives. To illustrate its contention, the department regressed the number of traffic fatalities last year in a state (Y) on the state's population (X_1), the number of days of snow cover (X_2), and the average speed of all cars (X_3). It found

$$\hat{Y} = 1.4 + .00029X_1 + 2.4X_2 + 10.3X_3$$
$$s_{b_1} = .00003 \quad s_{b_2} = .62 \quad s_{b_3} = 1.1 \quad S_{y|x} = 36.1$$
$$R^2 = .78 \quad \text{Adj. } R^2 = .78 \quad N = 50$$

Does reducing the average speed of cars have an impact? All other things being equal, how many lives would be saved in a state if the average speed were reduced from 75 to 65 mph?

21.9 Redlands Blue Cross wants to hold down hospital costs in the area hospitals. It regresses the average cost of a hospital stay (Y) on the number of days the person stayed in the hospital (X_1), the number of lab tests made (X_2), and the number of prescription drugs ordered (X_3). Interpret the following regression and decide whether any policy changes can be recommended.

$$\hat{Y} = 25.36 + 96.40X_1 + 24.90X_2 + 1.41X_3$$

$$s_{b_1} = 6.4 \quad s_{b_2} = 3.2 \quad s_{b_3} = 2.0 \quad S_{y|x} = 12.50$$
$$R^2 = .96 \quad \text{Adj. } R^2 = .93 \quad N = 75$$

21.10 The Buford State University chapter of the American Association of University Professors (AAUP) regressed the salaries of all BSU faculty (Y) on the number of articles each faculty member published (X_1) and the number of years the person has served on the faculty (X_2). Interpret the following regression:

$$\hat{Y} = 15,200 + 250X_1 + 750X_2$$

$$s_{b_1} = 180 \quad s_{b_2} = 52 \quad S_{y|x} = 524$$
$$R^2 = .91 \quad \text{Adj. } R^2 = .87 \quad N = 517$$

21.11 New Mexico is concerned about rising costs of health care for employees. Ten years ago, it shifted all employees to HMOs. Now it would like to evaluate the impact of the HMOs on the cost of health care to the state on a per-person basis. Average health care costs are the dependent variable in a time series analysis that covers the years 1940 to 1995. The three independent variables are X_1 (a trend variable, a counter starting at 1 for 1940 and increasing by one per year), X_2 (a variable coded 0 before the introduction of the HMOs and coded 1 afterward), and X_3 (a variable coded 0 before the introduction of the HMOs and coded as a counter afterward—for example, 1, 2, 3, 4, . . .). Costs are in dollars. Interpret the following regression, and present a brief analysis of the impact of the HMOs on the cost of health care.

$$\hat{Y} = \$45.00 + \$51.45X_1 - \$123.69X_2 - \$7.25X_3$$

$$s_{b_1} = 5.43 \quad s_{b_2} = 49.67 \quad s_{b_3} = 1.14 \quad S_{y|x} = 93.50$$
$$R^2 = .99 \quad \text{Adj. } R^2 = .98$$

21.12 Ohio has had an urban enterprise zone program in operation for the past 5 years. Local governments are free to set up three types of zones to attract new industry: zone A (businesses are exempt from taxes for 10 years), zone B (industries are exempt from taxes for 10 years, and they may use tax-free industrial development bonds), and zone C (the local government contributes to the capital investment of the industry). Local governments can set up one and only one type of urban enterprise zone. The state wants to know the impact of the zones on local unemployment rates (Y). To do this, it set up a dummy variable X_1 (coded 1 if the zone is a B-type zone and coded 0 otherwise) and another dummy variable X_2 (coded 1 if the zone is a C-type zone and 0 otherwise). It wants to control for the following variables: X_3, the percentage of unemployment in the counties surrounding the urban area with the zone; X_4, the median education level of the urban area in years; and X_5, the percentage of the urban area's employed population that is employed in services. Y is measured in percentage unemployed. A regression for 136 cities reveals the following results:

$$\hat{Y} = 5.4 + 1.32X_1 - .64X_2 + .82X_3 - .07X_4 - .13X_5$$
$$s_{b_1} = .31 \quad s_{b_2} = .32 \quad s_{b_3} = .03 \quad s_{b_4} = .13 \quad s_{b_5} = .031$$
$$S_{y|x} = .62 \quad R^2 = .53 \quad \text{Adj. } R^2 = .51$$

Interpret all slopes, the intercept, and the R^2. Analyze the slopes, including tests of significance, and express in clear English what this regression reveals. Youngstown has a zone C enterprise zone, with unemployment in the surrounding counties of 8.9%, median education of 10.8 years, and 31% of the city's employed working in services. What is your best guess of the percentage of unemployment in Youngstown?

21.13 The Strategic Air Command is concerned about the possibility that missiles will not launch successfully. Utilizing test data, they regress X_1 (the temperature at launch in degrees Fahrenheit), X_2 (the number of months since the last overhaul of the launch mechanism), and X_3 (the number of ICBMs sited within 800 meters). They get the following results with Y (a dummy variable that is coded 1 if the launch fails):

$$\hat{Y} = .06 - .012X_1 + .006X_2 - .094X_3$$
$$s_{b_1} = .0021 \quad s_{b_2} = .0015 \quad s_{b_3} = .087 \quad S_{y|x} = .034$$
$$R^2 = .69 \quad \text{Adj. } R^2 = .65 \quad \textbf{N} = 214$$

Interpret the slopes, intercept, and R^2, and test the slopes for significance. SAC wants the probability of failure to be no more than 20%. If launches will proceed at -10 degrees with no other missiles within 800 meters, how often should launch mechanisms be serviced?

21.14 At Eastern State University, a study of sex discrimination in salaries is undertaken. The analyst regresses the salary of each teaching professional on the number of years of experience (X_1), the number of publications (X_2), and the sex of the person (X_3, a dummy variable with male coded as 1). She gets the following results:

$$\hat{Y} = \$18,563 + \$2,235X_1 + \$65X_2 + \$1,150X_3$$
$$s_{b_1} = 386 \quad s_{b_2} = 39 \quad s_{b_3} = 316 \quad S_{y|x} = 2,690$$
$$R^2 = .68 \quad \text{Adj. } R^2 = .67$$

Interpret the slopes, intercept, and R^2. Estimate the salary of a male professor with 7 years of experience and three publications.

21.15 The U.S. Department of Human Services research team has submitted a report to you on the infant mortality rate. The team uses a regression equation in which infant mortality (the number of infants who die per 1,000 live births) is a function of the year (X_1, where 1960 = 1), Medicaid expenditures (X_2, in millions of dollars), and the expenditures on Women, Infants, and Children (WIC) supplemental food programs (X_3, also in millions of dollars). Interpret the following regression. Then predict the infant mortality rate for 2002 if $4,536 million is spent on Medicaid and $774 million is spent on WIC. Which of the variables is the most important predictor? If you had $1 million to spend, what would be the most effective use of that money?

$$\hat{Y} = 28.32 - .239X_1 - .001476X_2 - .003266X_3$$

$$s_{b_1} = .029 \quad s_{b_2} = .000143 \quad s_{b_3} = .00137 \quad S_{y|x} = .32$$
$$R^2 = .99 \quad \text{Adj. } R^2 = .98$$

21.16 The state tax division is evaluating the money raised by state sales taxes. Using data from all states, division members regress the amount of money raised by the sales tax per capita on the average per-capita income (X_1) and a dummy variable coded 1 if the state taxed the sale of groceries (X_2). They get the following results:

$$\hat{Y} = .03 + .0218X_1 + 147.18X_2$$

$$s_{b_1} = .0043 \quad s_{b_2} = 36.3 \quad S_{y|x} = 31.40 \quad R^2 = .86 \quad \text{Adj. } R^2 = .85$$

Interpret this regression. Present a hypothesis about placing a tax on the sale of groceries and evaluate this hypothesis. How much could a state with a per-capita income of $11,947 and a tax on groceries raise per capita with a sales tax?

21.17 The Massachusetts State Personnel Board wants to know whether merit system salaries are based on job responsibilities, education, or seniority. The board regresses the current annual salaries of employees (Y) on the number of Hay Points (X_1, a job responsibility scale that ranges from 0 = no responsibility to approximately 1,500 = agency heads), the number of years in the agency (X_2), and the number of years of formal education (X_3). The board finds

$$\hat{Y} = \$4,195 + \$26.08X_1 + \$149X_2 + \$226X_3$$

$$s_{b_1} = 1.19 \quad s_{b_2} = 20.9 \quad s_{b_3} = 58.0 \quad S_{y|x} = \$2,755$$
$$R^2 = .70 \quad \text{Adj. } R^2 = .69 \quad N = 458$$

Interpret the slopes, intercept, and R^2. Test to determine whether each of the partial slopes is significant. What is your best guess as to the salary of a newly hired administrative assistant (270 Hay Points) with a 2-year MPA who supervises three people?

21.18 The Department of Economic Development in Grundy County wants to evaluate the economic development program that it started in 1983. Its measure of success is the total number of persons employed in Grundy County. Independent variables are X_1, a trend variable starting as 1 in the first year of the data, 1969; X_2, the percentage of persons unemployed at the national level; and X_3, a dummy variable coded as a counter variable after the start of the economic development program. A regression produces the following results:

$$\hat{Y} = 215{,}400 - 2{,}400X_1 - 4{,}235X_2 + 1{,}421X_3$$

$s_{b_1} = 746 \quad s_{b_2} = 625 \quad s_{b_3} = 419 \quad S_{y|x} = 4{,}300 \quad R^2 = .99 \quad \text{Adj. } R^2 = .98$

Interpret this regression. Predict the number of jobs in Grundy County in 2002 if unemployment is 5.1%.

21.19 You have been hired by the U.S. Supreme Court to find out whether there is any racial bias against persons receiving the death penalty. Your data are 194 persons who were convicted of murder in six southern states. The dependent variable is a dummy variable coded 1 if the person received the death penalty and coded 0 otherwise. The independent variables are X_1, the number of persons killed by the convictee (ranges from 1 to 8); X_2, a dummy variable coded 1 if the person was able to pay for his or her own attorney (rather than having a court-assigned public defender); X_3, the number of years of formal education the person has; and X_4, a race variable coded 1 if the convictee was white and coded 0 otherwise. A regression analysis finds the following:

$$\hat{Y} = .54 + .05X_1 - .23X_2 - .02X_3 - .31X_4$$

$s_{b_1} = .042 \quad s_{b_2} = .083 \quad s_{b_3} = .006 \quad s_{b_4} = .012 \quad S_{y|x} = .14$
$$R^2 = .52 \quad \text{Adj. } R^2 = .49$$

(a) Interpret this regression, including slopes, intercept, and R^2. Are the slopes significant? What does this regression say about the research question?

(b) How likely is it that a white man with a college degree, who paid for his own attorney, and who killed two people will get the death penalty?

(c) How likely is it that a nonwhite man with an eighth-grade education, who had a public defender, and who killed one person will receive the death penalty?

(d) How would you change this study to find out whether the victim's race mattered?

21.20 Tax expert Bob Erikson is interested in the reliance of state governments on "sin taxes"—taxes on alcohol, tobacco, and gambling. The dependent variable is the percentage of state revenue that is raised from sin taxes. Three research hypotheses guide Bob's analysis. First, Bob believes that Catholics are generally "good-time" people who drink, smoke, and play bingo a lot; X_1 is the percentage of the state population who are Catholic. Second, Bob notes that Republicans seem less concerned than Democrats do that sin taxes might be regressive; X_2 is the percentage of the state legislature who are Republicans. Third, Bob suspects that sin taxes could be used to hold down the level of property taxes; X_3 is the per-capita property tax in thousands of dollars. A regression program produces the following results:

$$\hat{Y} = 5.4 + .23X_1 + .11X_2 - 1.41X_3$$

$$s_{b_1} = .04 \quad s_{b_2} = .087 \quad s_{b_3} = .15 \quad S_{y|x} = .74$$

$$R^2 = .74 \quad \text{Adj. } R^2 = .71$$

(a) Interpret the slopes, intercept, and R^2.

(b) What are the research hypotheses? Evaluate these hypotheses.

(c) Michigan has 20% Catholic constituents, 47% Republicans in the state legislature, and a property tax of $2.5 per thousand. What is your best guess as to the sin tax rate in Michigan?

(d) The actual sin tax rate in Michigan is 16.1%. What would you conclude about that?

CHAPTER 22

Interrupted Time Series: Program and Policy Analysis

n many cases, public or nonprofit managers or policymakers introduce a new program or policy to change a pattern of behavior. For example, the Whitefish Bay Sanitary Engineering Department believed that it costs too much to collect trash. The department introduced new trucks that could be operated by two people rather than by three, and the department provided incentives for the workers to collect trash faster. A program analyst might then want to know whether current trash collections cost less than they did before the changes. A variety of other examples of this kind of analysis exists. For instance, the state of Wisconsin adopted a "learnfare" program that denied welfare benefits to families whose school-age children were not attending school; the objective was to increase school attendance. A nonprofit organization might predict that using radio ads would increase the number of volunteers it recruits. As another example, proponents of a capital gains tax suggest that it will increase tax collections by providing an incentive to sell capital assets.

This chapter provides an introduction to a set of techniques, called *interrupted time series analysis,* that are useful in evaluating changes in policies or programs. Interrupted time series analysis assumes that a person has a time series of observations such as the following:

$$O_1 \; O_2 \; O_3 \; O_4 \; O_5 \; X \; O_6 \; O_7 \; O_8 \; O_9 \; O_{10}$$

Figure 22.1

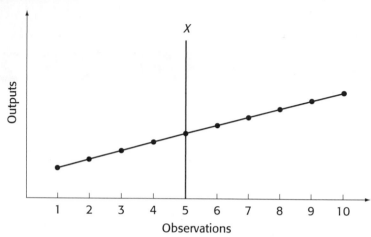

Continuation of Trend

where each O is an observation on an output variable of interest (garbage collected, class attendance, tax collections, and so on), the subscripts refer to time points, and where X is the implementation of a new program or policy.

In many cases, analysts simply compare observation 5 (O_5) with observation 6 (O_6) using a comparison of means or a comparison of proportions test (see Chapter 14). Such a comparison can be misleading because the output measure might have been increasing or decreasing before the new program, and observation 6 might just be the continuation of a trend. Figure 22.1 illustrates this problem using the Whitefish Bay trash collection experiment.

Observation 6 falls along a trend line that is simply the continuation of the line from observation 1 to observation 5. In this case, the new trucks made no difference that would not have occurred if past practices had simply continued. The pattern in Figure 22.1 represents the null hypothesis in interrupted time series. This is not the only "no impact" pattern, however; each of the trend lines in Figure 22.2 is also a trend consistent with the null hypothesis of no impact.

Short-Term Impacts

Using interrupted time series analysis is a matter of recognizing a few basic patterns, and then knowing how to use multiple regression to provide a statistical test for the results. One common pattern is a short-term impact (or what analysts call a change in intercept). As Figure 22.3 shows, a short-term impact is one in which the output variable makes an immediate change (drop or rise), but the underlying trend of the data remains the same. Other patterns that reveal a short-term impact are shown in Figure 22.4.

Figure 22.2

No Impact Patterns

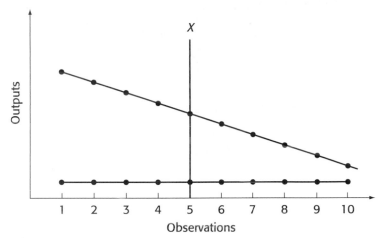

Figure 22.3

Short-Term Impacts

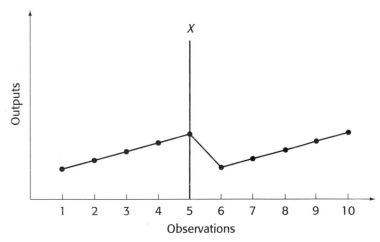

Although the use of graphs to judge policy impact is both inexpensive and easy, at times it can be misleading when the graphs become complex. As a result, most analysts use multiple regression for their interrupted time series designs. We will illustrate this with an example. In 1974, as a result of the Arab oil embargo, the United States adopted a 55-mph speed limit. Although designed to save gasoline, a side benefit of

Figure 22.4

Additional Short-Term Impacts

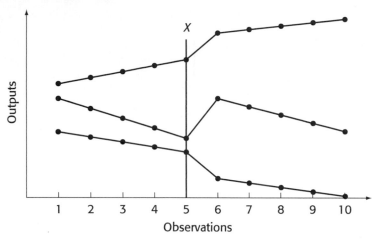

Table 22.1

Traffic Fatalities in Arkansas

Year	Fatalities (Y)	Time (X_1)	Program (X_2)
1968	412	1	0
1969	437	2	0
1970	428	3	0
1971	453	4	0
1972	449	5	0
1973	463	6	0
1974	384	7	1
1975	395	8	1
1976	414	9	1
1977	406	10	1

the new speed was a decrease in traffic fatalities. Bob Savage, a policy analyst for the state of Arkansas, gathered the data listed in Table 22.1 on traffic fatalities in Arkansas.

To determine whether a short-term impact occurred, two new variables are created. The first is a time variable similar to the time variables in Chapter 20. This variable (X_1) is coded 1 in the first year of the study and is increased by 1 for every year thereafter. The second variable (X_2), called the *program variable,* is a dummy variable coded 1 if the 55-mph speed limit is in effect (1974 and after) and coded 0 if it is not. Treating fatalities as the dependent variable and both time and program as independent variables, analyst Savage runs a regression to get the following results:

$$\hat{Y} = 409 + 8.9X_1 - 85.1X_2$$
$$s_{b_1} = 1.67 \quad s_{b_2} = 9.82 \quad S_{y|x} = 7.94 \quad R^2 = .93$$

Examining this equation, Savage focuses on the regression coefficients. The first coefficient tells him that there is an annual increase in traffic fatalities in Arkansas of 8.9 per year. This increase is statistically significant as shown by a t score of 5.33 ($t = 8.9 \div 1.67 = 5.33$) with 7 degrees of freedom. (If you have forgotten about t scores, reread Chapter 18.) More important for Bob, the second slope reveals that traffic fatalities dropped by 85.1 in the year following the adoption of the 55-mph speed limit; this is a statistically significant drop (t score $= 8.67$ with df $= 7$).

As an analyst, Bob can conclude that a statistically significant drop in traffic fatalities occurred in Arkansas after the adoption of the 55-mph speed limit. Because he is a good analyst, Bob knows that he cannot conclude that the 55-mph speed limit caused this drop. A major threat to validity in an interrupted time series design is history (see Chapter 3). Any event that occurred at the same time as the 55-mph speed limit (the gasoline shortage, the adoption of new license plates, and so on) might also have caused this drop. Bob's next task is to seek out these alternative factors and to attempt to eliminate them as causes of the drop in fatalities.

Long-Term Impacts

Short-term impacts are dramatic events. In most cases, we do not expect programs or policies to have such an immediate impact. Rather, when implementing a new management program, we often think that what will occur is some gradual improvement in efficiency over a relatively long period of time as employees get used to the program. Similarly, in designing policies, we often expect change to be slow and to occur over an extended period of time as the program is implemented. Let us use an example. The city of Stewartville is concerned about the rising insurance costs that the city has to pay for health insurance, life insurance (for employees), workers' compensation insurance, and liability insurance (for auto accidents, accidents on city property, and other damages). Mayor Betty Sue Jaworski decides that the city needs a risk manager to oversee all insurance operations and to see whether some cost savings can be made. Billy Joe Bob Zimmerman, the new risk manager, knows that it is unrealistic to expect a dramatic drop in insurance costs. What he hopes to achieve is a reduction in the long-term rate of growth in insurance costs. Figure 22.5 shows such an impact.

This pattern is called a *long-term* impact or a *change in slope* impact because the slope of the line changes after the program is implemented. Similar to short-term impacts, long-term impacts can take a variety of forms. Some of these forms are shown in Figures 22.6 and 22.7.

Determining a long-term impact using interrupted time series is similar to assessing a short-term impact, but with a slightly different twist. Table 22.2 shows the insurance costs data gathered by risk manager Billy Joe Bob Zimmerman to evaluate the impact of consolidating the insurance programs and hiring the risk manager (in 1996).

Figure 22.5

Long-Term Impacts

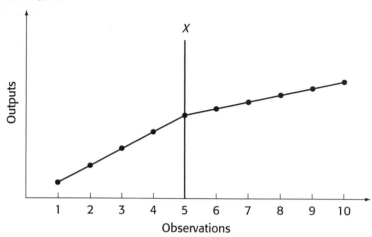

Figure 22.6

More Long-Term Impacts

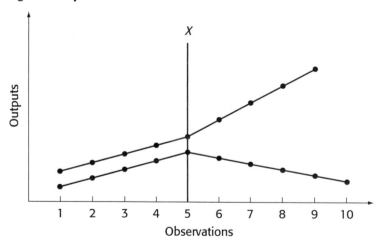

The dependent variable in this analysis is insurance costs. The first independent variable is a time variable that accounts for any trend in the data, just as the time variable does in the short-term impact analysis. The second dependent variable is used to assess any long-term changes in the slope of the trend. This variable is coded 0 before the change in policy and is coded as a countervariable after the change (1,2,3,4,5,. . .).

Figure 22.7

Additional Long-Term Impacts

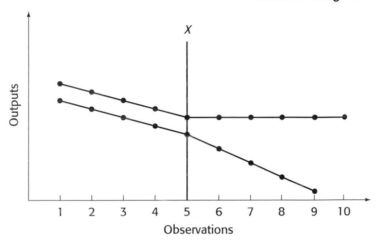

Table 22.2

Insurance Costs in Stewartville

Year	Insurance Costs (Y)	Time (X₁)	Program (X₂)
1991	423,700	1	0
1992	516,900	2	0
1993	593,200	3	0
1994	684,300	4	0
1995	751,200	5	0
1996	814,300	6	1
1997	867,200	7	2
1998	941,300	8	3
1999	995,800	9	4
2000	1,056,700	10	5

Billy Joe Bob can then use these variables in a regression analysis to assess any long-term change in the growth of insurance costs. He gets the following results:

$$\hat{Y} = 348,857 + 81,381X_1 - 21,329X_2$$

$$s_{b_1} = 1,800 \quad s_{b_2} = 2,869 \quad S_{y|x} = 6,510 \quad R^2 = .99$$

An examination of the two slopes tells Billy Joe Bob what he wants to know about the change in insurance programs. The first slope tells him that insurance costs were increasing at a rate of $81,381 ($t = 45.2$) per year before he was hired as risk manager.

The second slope of $21,329 tells Billy Joe Bob that the trend in insurance costs was reduced by $21,329 per year ($t = 7.44$) after he was hired. This does not mean that insurance costs are actually declining but rather that they are increasing at a slower rate than they were before the change. By adding the two slopes together [$81,381 + ($-$21,329)], Billy Joe Bob can find the rate of increase after the change ($60,052). This means that insurance costs increased at a rate of $60,052 following the program changes. Although this still represents an increase, it is a statistically significant decrease from the trend that existed before Billy Joe Bob was hired.

Again, remember that what was found here was a statistical result. The analysis did not prove that hiring a risk manager and consolidating programs lowered insurance costs. The same threats to validity that were of concern for short-term effects remain a concern for long-term effects. To conclude that the changes made produced the insurance savings, Billy Joe Bob would have to examine all the other potential causes of this change and eliminate them as possibilities (see Chapter 3).

The reader should be aware that short- and long-term effects apply to the rate of change. A short-term effect should not be interpreted as a temporary effect. It is a permanent effect, but its impact is immediate (in the short term). A long-term effect is also permanent, but its impact takes place over a longer period of time.

Both Short- and Long-Term Effects

In many cases, our theoretical understanding of how public policy affects individuals and outputs is only modest. For example, despite the fact that a great deal of effort is focused on understanding how the U.S. economy works, the impacts of various tax and spending policies are not completely understood. If an area such as macroeconomics is marred with theoretical uncertainty, so are most areas of concern to public and nonprofit managers. As a result, the manager might not know whether he or she should expect a program change to have a short-term effect or a long-term effect. Or the program manager might expect that a program will have both long- and short-term impacts.

Figure 22.8 illustrates one possible combination of short- and long-term effects. In this case, a short-term drop in the output occurs immediately; in addition, the long-term slope of the trend decreases. A variety of other short- and long-term impacts are shown in the graphs in Figures 22.9 and 22.10.

To illustrate the technique for estimating both short-term and long-term impacts, we present an example from Goose Pimple, Vermont. Police Chief Cynthia Weather has been receiving a lot of complaints from merchants about people who park illegally but do not get parking tickets. Chief Weather feels that this is a problem that can be solved. Rather than having regular officers take time away from law enforcement duties, she decides to hire and train a group of officers specifically for this task. She decides that these officers should wear cute uniforms and be called "meter boys." Chief Weather thinks that the new team will have an immediate impact on the number of parking tickets issued, and it will also have a long-term impact as the meter boys get used to their jobs.

Figure 22.8

Short- and Long-Term Impacts

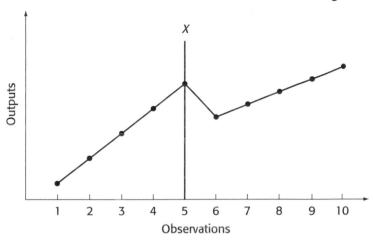

Figure 22.9

More Short- and Long-Term Impacts

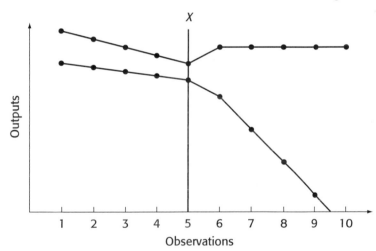

After implementing the new approach, Chief Weather waits 8 weeks to let enough time pass to expect the program to have some impact. She then tells her trusty assistant, Cat Mandu, to determine whether the program has had an impact. Mandu collects data on parking tickets both before and after the new program started; the data are presented in Table 22.3.

Figure 22.10

Additional Short- and Long-Term Impacts

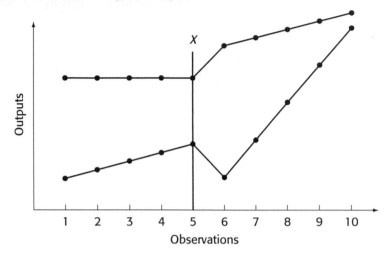

Table 22.3

Parking Tickets Issued in Goose Pimple, Vermont

Week (X_1)	Parking Tickets (Y)	Short-Term (X_2)	Long-Term (X_3)
1	46	0	0
2	39	0	0
3	39	0	0
4	52	0	0
5	55	0	0
6	48	0	0
7	51	0	0
8	54	0	0
9	65	1	1
10	71	1	2
11	74	1	3
12	77	1	4
13	74	1	5
14	82	1	6
15	87	1	7
16	93	1	8

Because the weeks are already expressed as a number, Mandu uses this variable as a time trend variable. She then creates two more variables, as shown in Table 22.3: one for a short-term impact (X_2) and one for a long-term impact (X_3). These data are then used in a multiple regression to get the following results:

$$\hat{Y} = 40.18 + 1.74X_1 + 7.88X_2 + 1.80X_3$$

$$s_{b_1} = .63 \quad s_{b_2} = 4.10 \quad s_{b_3} = .88 \quad S_{y|x} = 4.05 \quad R^2 = .96$$

Mandu makes the following interpretation based on the three slopes. First, the number of parking tickets was increasing by 1.74 per week even before the new program went into effect ($t = 2.78$). With the implementation of the new program, the number of parking tickets issued jumped immediately by 7.88 ($t = 1.92$). In addition, after implementation of the new program, the rate of increase in parking tickets increased by 1.80 per week ($t = 2.03$), for a total weekly increase after the new program of 3.54 (or 1.80 + 1.74).

Pulse Effects

In some cases, policies will have only a short-term temporary effect on some policy output. Crackdowns on drunk driving, for example, appear to have a significant impact on traffic deaths (a 10% reduction or so) for approximately 6 months. Such a short-term temporary effect is known as a *pulse effect*. Illustrations of pulse effects are shown in Figure 22.11.

An illustration is in order. Bart Hawkins, chief administrator of Our Lady of Mercy Hospital, thinks that his city's month-long imported beer festival affects the

Figure 22.11

Pulse Effects

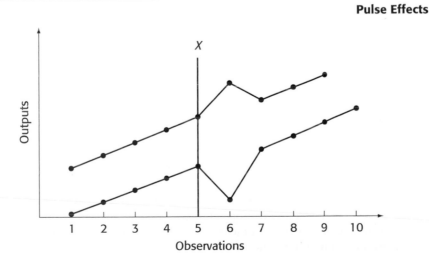

Table 22.4

Absences at Our Lady of Mercy Hospital

Month	Number Absent	Trend (X_1)	Pulse Effect (X_2)
January	46	1	0
February	52	2	0
March	55	3	0
April	60	4	0
May	66	5	0
June	68	6	0
July	70	7	0
August	76	8	0
September	79	9	0
October	105	10	1
November	81	11	0
December	86	12	0

number of staff who are absent from work. The beer festival begins October 1 and lasts for the entire month. Curious about this hypothesis, Bart uses his handy microcomputer to call up the number of absences for the past year. The data in Table 22.4 result.

Bart creates two independent variables. The first is a trend variable (X_1) that will reflect any long-term gain or loss in absences. The second variable (X_2) is a dummy variable, coded 1 for the month of interest and coded 0 otherwise. A multiple regression produces the following result:

$$\hat{Y} = 45.4 + 3.52X_1 + 24.4X_2$$
$$s_{b_1} = .19 \quad s_{b_2} = 2.4 \quad S_{y|x} = 2.2 \quad R^2 = .99$$

Bart's only real concern is whether there is a pulse effect; thus, he immediately examines the second regression coefficient. He finds that there are 24.4 more absences in October than would be predicted from a simple trend. This increase is statistically significant ($t = 10.2$).

Some Considerations

Generally, when examining a program, you should decide whether to look for a short-term, long-term, or pulse impact based on theory—if any exists. Without theory, you can always graph the data and make a guess as to whether to estimate short-term, long-term, or pulse impacts. When you are not sure, you can estimate all three effects (although usually just a short- and a long-term effect are estimated). When proceeding in this manner, if you find that one of these impacts is not significant, then the regression should be rerun without the insignificant impact. This process will give you a more precise estimate of the impact that does exist.

A second consideration is that in time series analysis, the way the series of interest is measured can play a big role in assessing the impact of a policy intervention. Generally, the finer the time interval, the better the resolution of the data. Quarterly data tend to reveal trends and patterns better than annual data. Monthly data tend to reveal trends and patterns better than quarterly data, and so on.

Let's explore the logic of measurement intervals in time series analysis with the following example. Officials in Wisconsin want to analyze the impact of a law that imposed tougher penalties on drunk drivers who cause traffic accidents. The law was passed in March 1998. In March 2004, the state legislature instructs its program evaluation division to analyze the effect that the tougher laws have had on drunk driving arrest rates. Susan Smith, the chief program analyst, has both annual and monthly data on arrest rates from the beginning of 1997 to the end of 2003. If you were Ms. Smith, would you use the annual or monthly data to study the impact of this policy change?

If we constructed our series for drunk driving arrests using annual data, the series would only have seven time points (one for each year). If we used the monthly data instead, the series would consist of 84 time points. Assessing the impact of an intervention using the monthly data would give us a much clearer picture of the impact of the policy change on arrest rates. Why is this the case? Let's review some basic points we discussed in Chapter 3 concerning research design and causality.

First, a narrower time interval addresses the problem of "history" or alternative explanations to the intervention of interest. It is generally easier to demonstrate causality using narrower rather than broader time intervals. A time series constructed using broader time intervals, such as annual data, makes it harder to rule out other factors as possible explanations for any change we see at a particular point in the series. With annual data, a variety of events aside from the hypothesized intervention might have occurred over the course of 1998 (the year when the laws were changed). Assuming we see a change in the series, how can we rule out other events that took place during the year as potential causes?

With monthly data, ruling out other possible explanations becomes an easier task. We know the policy change took place in March 1998, meaning that we only have to look for other possible explanations that occurred around this month, not the entire year. Accounting for alternative explanations is easier when the data show the precise time point the intervention took place, but much harder when we can only place the intervention within a broad interval of time.

A narrower time interval also makes it easier to see pre- and postintervention changes in a data series. Time series intervention techniques work best when there are many pre- and postintervention data points. On the preintervention side, having a limited number of data points makes it difficult to see the underlying trend in the data prior to the intervention. In the current example, constructing the time series using annual data would provide us with only one time point prior to the intervention that took place in 1998. This hardly gives us a chance to determine whether the intervention caused a change in the underlying mean of the series, simply because one data point does not provide a sense of the underlying trend in the data. If we construct the series using monthly data, we would have 14 data points prior to the intervention

(12 months of data from 1997 and 2 months of data from 1998), giving us a better idea of any preintervention trends in the data. On the postintervention side, having too few data points can make it difficult to determine whether an intervention has had a short- or long-term impact on the level of the series.

The basic lesson here is that time series analysis is about comparing pre- and postintervention *trends*. You cannot know what a trend looks like if you do not have enough data either before or after the policy intervention.

Realistically, a manager sometimes may not have the ability to obtain data that are broken down in very narrow time intervals. Yet when a manager does have the option, he or she should seriously consider the merits of choosing a narrower time interval when constructing a time series.

Although breaking a time series down into narrower time intervals has distinct advantages, one disadvantage is greater data volatility (compared to data collected at broader time intervals). Sometimes month-to-month fluctuations in an indicator can be very large. Skewness can become a problem in these cases. Data transformations such as converting data into logarithms (see Chapter 20) may be necessary to correct the problem. In contrast, when a time series is constructed with annual data, month-to-month fluctuations that occur over the course of any given year are smoothed out to a certain degree.

When deciding whether to use a broader or narrower time interval, you should keep the following points in mind. First, if you know that a variety of alternative explanations to the intervention of interest exist, annual data may not provide the necessary resolution to disentangle the influence of potentially competing causal explanations. Constructing a time series using a narrower time interval may be necessary.

Second, does a narrower time interval match the natural flow of the data? For instance, constructing a multiyear time series using monthly data on the number of applications processed by a state licensing board makes good sense because applications are processed every month. In contrast, constructing a multiyear time series using monthly data on the number of income tax returns filed with the state of Michigan makes less sense, simply because returns are only filed over the course of a few months each year. Over the course of a year, most returns would probably be concentrated in 4 or 5 months, with almost no returns filed during the remaining months. If observations at a narrower time interval only occur sporadically, the statistical problems that result may outweigh any advantages gained from this approach.

A third consideration that you, as an analyst, should be aware of is autocorrelation. Recall that Chapter 19 stated that one of the assumptions of regression is that the errors are not correlated. Correlated errors or autocorrelation is usually a problem only in time series analysis. The problem created by autocorrelation is that the standard errors of the slopes are underestimated. In practical terms, autocorrelation can result in slopes that appear to be significant when, in fact, they are not. This means that a manager might conclude that a program has an impact when in fact it does not.

Dealing with autocorrelation is a fairly complex undertaking. Fortunately, there is a relatively simple test to see whether a regression equation has significant autocorrelation. This test is based on a statistic called the Durbin-Watson. Most regression programs will calculate a Durbin-Watson for you, if you ask it nicely. For the Goose

Pimple, Vermont, parking regression (Table 22.3), the Durbin-Watson statistic is 1.85. Durbin-Watson statistics are close to 2.0 if there is no autocorrelation, equal to 0 if there is perfect positive autocorrelation, and equal to 4.0 if there is perfect negative autocorrelation.

Table 5 in the Appendix provides the Durbin-Watson table to test for autocorrelation at the .05 level of confidence. To use a Durbin-Watson table, you need to know the number of independent variables (in this example, 3) and the number of cases (in this example, 16). Using the table for $k = 3$ independent variables and $n = 16$ cases, we find two numbers, .857 and 1.728. The higher number, 1.728, is known as the upper limit (denoted d_U); the lower number is the lower limit (d_L). If the Durbin-Watson is greater than 1.728, you can reject the existence of autocorrelation with .05 confidence. If the number is less than .857, you can reject the hypothesis that there is no autocorrelation with .05 confidence. For numbers between .857 and 1.728, you cannot be certain whether autocorrelation exists. Because our Durbin-Watson is 1.85, we can be reasonably confident that autocorrelation is not a problem. If autocorrelation is a problem in any of your analyses, you should consult an advanced statistics text, such as Nelson (1973) or Pindyck and Rubenfeld (1997). Better yet, find a trained statistician to help you correct for this problem.

Using Data to Represent Program Changes

With all the interrupted time series models presented so far in this chapter, the independent variables have been a trend variable, a dummy variable, or some type of countervariable. A dummy variable is a fairly crude indicator of a change in a policy or in a new program. Often the analyst will have a better measure of the policy change. For example, Michael Lewis-Beck and John Alford in the 1979 *American Political Science Review* analyzed the impact of government regulation on coal mine safety. Their dependent variable is coal mine safety deaths; their independent variable used to measure government regulation is federal expenditures for coal mine regulation. Although they could have used a dummy variable to measure when the federal government created a coal mine safety program, the use of budget figures was a more precise estimate of how much effort the federal government was putting into government regulation.

For example, let us suppose that the federal government wants to know whether the Medicaid program (a health care program for low-income people) has had any impact on infant mortality. The infant mortality rate (number of infant deaths per 1,000 live births) is the dependent variable; the analysis will cover the years 1950 to 1988. The infant mortality rate in the United States was declining before the Medicaid program was started (1965), as a result of general improvements in nutrition and medical care. To represent this general trend of improvement, a trend variable (X_1) is included that is coded as 1 for 1950 and increases by 1 each year after that. A traditional interrupted time series would create two new independent variables: one for a short-term effect, coded 1 after the Medicaid program was started (1965) and coded 0 before it started (X_2); and one for a long-term effect, coded 0 before Medicaid and coded as a countervariable afterward (X_3). This interrupted time series regression is shown as follows:

$$\hat{Y} = 28.3 - .250X_1 - .871X_2 - .409X_3$$

$$s_{b_1} = .05 \quad s_{b_2} = .50 \quad s_{b_3} = .05 \quad S_{y|x} = .76 \quad R^2 = .96$$

According to this equation, the infant mortality rate was dropping at the rate of .25 per year ($t = 5.0$), a significant drop. The introduction of the Medicaid program had an immediate short-term impact of a drop of .871 in the infant mortality rate ($t = 1.74$) and a long-term drop of .409 per year after the program's introduction ($t = 8.18$).

An alternative way to examine the impact of Medicaid on infant mortality would be to use total Medicaid expenditures (in millions of constant dollars). This interrupted time series is presented here:

$$\hat{Y} = 28.5 - .250X_1 - .0159X_2$$

$$s_{b_1} = .028 \quad s_{b_2} = .00013 \quad S_{y|x} = .539 \quad R^2 = .99$$

This equation is more informative than the previous equation. The first slope still means that infant mortality rates dropped at a rate of .25 per year after 1951 ($t = 8.93$). The interpretation of the second coefficient, however, is the real difference. For every $1 million spent on Medicaid, the U.S. infant mortality rate drops by .0159. This regression gives the analyst a more precise linkage between the Medicaid program and infant mortality rates, suggesting that it is the total money spent on Medicaid rather than just the existence of the Medicaid program that affects infant mortality rates. In addition, this is a better prediction of infant mortality rates in the United States than was the previous equation, that is, the standard error of the estimate is smaller.

Controlling for Other Variables

One advantage of interrupted time series analysis is that it allows the analyst to control for other factors that might influence the dependent variable by including these factors as additional independent variables. For example, in 1983, the federal government was very concerned about the rising level of health care costs being paid as part of Medicare and Medicaid. In that year, the federal government implemented something called Diagnostic Review Groups, which were designed to hold down the costs of health care. To determine whether this change had an impact on Medicaid costs, you might use Medicaid costs in millions of dollars as a dependent variable and include a trend variable (X_1) that increases by 1 each year and a short-term impact variable (X_2) for the Diagnostic Review Groups program. One problem with this estimation is that it does not take into account the rapid rise in health care costs as a result of inflation. Interrupted time series analysis can handle this problem simply by including a measure of inflation in the equation. In this case, a measure of medical prices (the medical price index, which equals 100 in 1967) is included as the third independent variable (X_3). A regression yields the following results:

$$\hat{Y} = 5,200 - 122X_1 - 4,117X_2 + 8,936X_3$$

$$s_{b_1} = 23 \quad s_{b_2} = 567 \quad s_{b_3} = 299 \quad S_{y|x} = 547 \quad R^2 = .99$$

The large positive coefficient for medical prices reveals that a one-point increase in the medical price index is associated with an $8,936 million increase in Medicaid costs controlling for the year and whether the Diagnostic Review Groups program was in effect ($t = 29.9$). The second coefficient is the one that is of most concern. This coefficient reveals that the implementation of the Diagnostic Review Groups program resulted in a $4,117 million reduction in Medicaid costs controlling for the year and rising medical care costs ($t = 7.25$).

This example contains a single control variable. Additional control variables could be added if the analyst believes that these variables could affect Medicaid costs. For example, total Medicaid recipients or the national unemployment rate could be used as a measure of demand for this program.

Chapter Summary

This chapter examined a technique used to evaluate the impacts of programs and policies when time series data are available. Interrupted time series analysis is an approach to estimate the impact of a policy or a program while controlling for any underlying trends in the data. This chapter showed how an analyst using multiple regression could estimate the short-term impact, the long-term impact, and a short-term temporary (pulse effect) impact of a policy or program. Because interrupted time series analysis uses multiple regression, the technique is very flexible. An analyst can use program expenditures as an independent variable and can control for a variety of variables that might also affect the dependent variable of interest.

Problems

22.1 The city of Madison, Wisconsin, needs to squeeze a bit more tax revenue out of its citizens. The city decides to charge $200 for each ambulance call. It knows that health and automobile insurance companies will pay this fee for those individuals who carry insurance. One concern is that people will not use the ambulance after it arrives when they are informed of the charge; this is called a *dry run*. To assess the impact of the new fee on the percentage of dry runs, monthly data for 80 months is gathered. The dependent variable is the percentage of dry runs. The independent variables are X_1, a monthly fluctuation variable (ambulance calls are more frequent in the summer); X_2, a trend variable coded 1 in the first month and coded 80 in the last; and X_3, a long-term impact variable coded 0 before the $200 charge and coded as a countervariable (e.g., 1, 2, 3, 4, . . .) after the charge. The following regression is produced:

$$\hat{Y} = 1.82 + 21.29X_1 + .026X_2 + .55X_3$$

$$s_{b_1} = 3.14 \quad s_{b_2} = .0095 \quad s_{b_3} = .15 \quad S_{y|x} = 1.74 \quad R^2 = .57$$

Ignore the first independent variable. Interpret the remaining slopes and R^2.

22.2   Jack "Crash" Craddock, the chief analyst for the Federal Aviation Administration, wants to know whether airline deregulation had any impact on airline safety. As a measure of airline safety, he uses the number of near misses (a *near miss* is when planes come within a certain number of feet of each other) for each year. Using data from 1960 to 1992, Craddock collects the following independent variables: X_1, a countervariable coded 1 in 1960 and increasing by 1 each year; X_2, a long-term impact variable coded 0 before deregulation (1978) and increasing by 1 each year thereafter; and X_3, a control for the state of the economy, percentage growth in gross national product over the previous year (people fly more during good economic times). A regression shows the following:

$$\hat{Y} = 137.1 + 15.9X_1 + 12.3X_2 + 26.1X_3$$
$$s_{b_1} = 1.2 \quad s_{b_2} = 14.6 \quad s_{b_3} = 3.2 \quad S_{y|x} = 20.1 \quad R^2 = .93 \quad N = 33$$

Interpret the slopes, intercept, and coefficient of determination. Test each slope for significance. What can you say about airline deregulation?

22.3   Sheriff S. Norton Koch wants to know if the number of drug arrests in Weed County has increased since the 1984 passage of a tough new state law on drug possession. His dependent variable is the number of drug arrests. He has three independent variables: X_1 is a trend variable coded 1 in the first year and increasing by 1 each year thereafter; X_2 is a short-term impact variable coded 0 before 1984 and coded 1 afterward; and X_3 is a long-term impact variable coded 0 before 1984 and increasing by 1 each year afterward. A regression produces the following results:

$$\hat{Y} = 546.5 - 5.1X_1 + 67.2X_2 + 4.3X_3$$
$$s_{b_1} = .92 \quad s_{b_2} = 17.3 \quad s_{b_3} = 1.3 \quad S_{y|x} = 34.1 \quad R^2 = .99 \quad N = 32$$

Interpret the slopes and coefficient of determination. Test the slopes for significance, and explain what this equation says about the drug law.

22.4   Roberta Refuse, the head sanitation engineer for the metropolis of Cramer, would like to assess the impact that a statewide recycling law on trash collection has in Cramer. The law prohibits the disposal of yard waste in trash cans. If this law is having an impact, the amount of trash collected would drop. Weekly trash collection data are available. The dependent variable is total tons of trash collected. The independent variables are X_1, the number of inches of rainfall the previous week (grass grows more when it rains); X_2, the mean Fahrenheit temperature for the previous week (grass grows better when it is warm); and X_3, a short-term impact variable coded 0 before the recycling law went into effect and coded 1 afterward. She gets the following results:

$$\hat{Y} = 12,405 + 140X_1 + 7.4X_2 - 575X_3$$
$$s_{b_1} = 31 \quad s_{b_2} = 2.0 \quad s_{b_3} = 45 \quad S_{y|x} = 327 \quad R^2 = .63 \quad N = 75$$

Interpret the slopes, intercept, and coefficient of determination. Test the slopes for significance, and explain what this equation says about the recycling law.

22.5 The infant mortality rate is considered a good indicator of overall health care in a country. The following regression uses the infant mortality rate in the United States from 1951 to 1989 (number of infant deaths per 1,000 live births) as the dependent variable. The independent variables are X_1, a trend variable coded 1 in the first year and increasing by 1 for each year thereafter; X_2, the amount of money spent in the federal Medicaid program (a health care access program) in millions of dollars; and X_3, the amount of money spent in the federal supplemental program for women, infants, and children (WIC, a nutrition program).

$$\hat{Y} = 28.32 - .26017X_1 - .00138X_2 - .00211X_3$$

$$s_{b_1} = .00365 \quad s_{b_2} = .00017 \quad s_{b_3} = .00113$$

$$S_{y|x} = .12 \quad R^2 = .99 \quad N = 39$$

Interpret the slopes, intercept, and coefficient of determination. Test the slopes for significance, and explain what this equation says about the impact of Medicaid and WIC on the infant mortality rate.

22.6 Florida has adopted a new sentencing law to increase the penalties for drug-related crimes. The state legislative research bureau is interested in knowing whether courts are upholding this law. The dependent variable that the bureau uses is the average number of months in prison that first-time drug offenders receive if convicted for sale of drugs. The independent variables are X_1, a trend variable coded 1 in the first month of the study and increasing by 1 each month thereafter; X_2, a short-term impact variable coded 0 before the new law and coded 1 afterward; and X_3, a long-term impact variable coded 0 before the law and coded as a countervariable (1,2,3, . . .) afterward. A regression shows the following results:

$$\hat{Y} = 24.52 - .13X_1 + 27.4X_2 + 2.15X_3$$

$$s_{b_1} = 3.15 \quad s_{b_2} = 2.36 \quad s_{b_3} = 4.53 \quad S_{y|x} = 5.4 \quad R^2 = .88 \quad N = 75$$

Interpret the slopes and coefficient of determination. Test the slopes for significance, and explain what this equation says about the impact of the new sentencing law.

CHAPTER 23

Regression Output and Data Management

I n Chapters 18 through 22, we presented the results of various regression analyses in equation form to illustrate how a relationship between an independent and dependent variable can be expressed in terms of a slope, intercept, and error term. You should be aware that most statistical software packages do not present regression results this way. To show you how regression output is displayed using statistical software, we have generated computer output for some of the examples presented in Chapter 18 using SPSS.

Bivariate Regression Output

Example 1

Computer-generated regression reports typically contain a lot of information, including some terms and statistics not discussed in the body of the chapter. You generally do not need to discuss all of the information displayed on the output when describing regression results. However, we feel it is important for beginning analysts to know what all of these data mean. Our first sample SPSS output page in Table 23.1 is for

Table 23.1

SPSS Output for Police Cars and Average Speed Regression

Model Summary

Model	R	R^2	Adjusted R^2	Std. Error of the Estimate
1	.971[a]	.942	.923	1.62788

[a] Predictors: (Constant), CARS.

ANOVA[b]

Model		Sum of Squares	df	Mean Square	F	Significance
1	Regression	130.050	1	130.050	49.075	.006[a]
	Residual	7.950	3	2.650		
	Total	138.000	4			

[a] Predictors: (Constant), CARS.
[b] Dependent variable: SPEED.

Coefficients[a]

Model		Unstandardized Coefficients		Standardized Coefficients	t	Significance
		B	Std. Error	Beta		
1	(Constant)	72.200	1.628		44.352	.000
	CARS	−2.550	.364	−.971	−7.005	.006

[a] Dependent variable: SPEED.

the police cars and average speed data from Table 18.2. We will explain each section of the output, moving from the bottom of the table to the top.

Coefficients

The coefficients section of the output displays the values for the intercept and slope. Many statistical programs use the term *constant* instead of *intercept,* but they mean the same thing.

The first thing you should notice is that the values for the constant and slope (the CARS variable) are the same as those found in the equation in the "Some Applications" section in Chapter 18. However, they are not presented in actual equation form on the computer output. If we wanted to present these or any regression results in equation form, we have all the information necessary to do so. We simply take the unstandardized regression coefficients from the rows labeled "Constant" and "CARS" and produce the equation below:

$$\hat{Y} = 72.2 - 2.55X$$

Remember that a negative sign in front of the slope coefficient indicates a negative relationship. This is why the equation is stated as an intercept minus a slope. Statistical packages do not print out positive signs in front of positive slope coefficients. In cases like these, the equation will be stated as an intercept plus a slope.

Notice that the standard error of the slope is displayed to the right of the slope coefficient. If you divide the slope coefficient by the standard error of the slope, the result is the t statistic seen in the column labeled "t." The level of significance for rejecting the null hypothesis is provided on the output itself, which means we do not have to consult a t table to interpret the probability associated with the t value for the slope. The "Sig." column reveals that the level of significance for the cars variable is .006. This means that there is less than a 1% chance that the null hypothesis of no relationship is actually true. So, you should reject the null hypothesis of no relationship.

Although information for the standard error and t score is also provided for the intercept, most analysts do not report these data (other than the intercept itself). Because the goal of regression analysis is usually determining whether an independent variable is statistically related to a dependent variable, it is far more important to interpret tests of significance for the slope coefficient. The final column heading is for standardized coefficients. Standardized coefficients are more relevant in the case of multiple regression; we will discuss the meaning of this term when we consider multiple regression output later in the chapter.

Anova

The "ANOVA" (analysis of variance) section of the output provides information on the percentage of explained versus unexplained variance for the regression model. The "Sum of Squares" column provides information for both the independent variable and the error term. If you look at the row labeled "Regression," you will see a value of 130.05. If we divide this number by the total sum of squares, we can determine the proportion of variance explained by the model. Notice that when we divide 130.05 by 138, the result is .942. If you look at the "Model Summary" section of the output, you will find that the R^2 value is also .942. This is no coincidence. When you divide the sum of squares for the regression by the total sum of squares, the result will always be equal to R^2.

We did not show you a real error term in Chapter 18, so those of you who eagerly awaited one will now be rewarded. The row labeled "Residual" provides important information about the error term. Recall that the error term refers to the amount of variance in the dependent variable that cannot be explained by the independent variable. The value for the sum of squares for the residual is 7.95. If we divide this number by 138, the result is .058. How is this number related to R^2? If we subtract the R^2 of .942 from 1, we obtain a result of .058. This tells us that approximately 6% of the variation in the dependent variable remains unexplained.

While analysts traditionally report R^2 instead of ANOVA output, information from the "Sum of Squares" column is useful for evaluating the fit of a model. If the sum of squares for the residual is low in relation to the sum of squares for the regression, this suggests that the independent variable explains at least some of the variation in the dependent variable. An easy way to spot weak results is if the sum of squares for the residual approaches the total sum of squares itself.

The column labeled "Mean Square" is simply the data from the sum of "Sum of Squares" column divided by the degrees of freedom (df). In general, analysts rarely interpret the output in this column. However, you should be aware that it is undesirable for the value for the "Regression" df to be anywhere near the value for the "Total" df. Each time we add an explanatory variable to a model, the df value for the regression increases by one. If the degrees of freedom for the regression approaches the degrees of freedom for the entire model, this means we have included almost as many independent variables as there are total observations for the dependent variable.

The column labeled "F" displays the F statistic. The F statistic is more relevant to multiple regression, so we will explain the meaning of this term later in the chapter.

Model Summary

This section provides information about the overall "fit" of the model.

The column labeled "R" displays the correlation coefficient. As we noted in Chapter 18, we rarely interpret the correlation coefficient when analyzing regression output. It is much more common to report the R^2, which appears in the column to the right of the "R" column. Remember that you can calculate the value for R^2 by using the data from the "Sum of Squares" column found in the ANOVA section. While an adjusted R^2 value appears on the output, it has far more meaning in the context of multiple regression models.

Finally, the standard error of the estimate (see Chapter 18) appears in the last column.

Example 2

The regression output for the police cars and average speed example was ideal for demonstrating the results of a statistically significant relationship. Table 23.2 displays regression results for the data in Table 18.4, where the independent variable is the number of police cars on patrol in Normal, Oklahoma, and the dependent variable is the number of indecent exposure arrests in Kansas City, Missouri. Common sense tells us that it is silly to hypothesize a relationship between these two variables. We are generating a regression with these data to give you a sense of what output looks like when there is no relationship between the independent and the dependent variables.

This should also serve as a reminder of a point we made in Chapter 3 regarding the use of statistical tools for testing causal relationships. Computers and statistical software packages will generate output, even if the hypothesized relationship examined is completely ridiculous. The fact that computers can quickly generate results does not mean you should use them in place of common sense. As an analyst, you should always have a sound rationale for studying particular research questions.

Coefficients

The results from the coefficients section clearly indicate that a relationship does not exist between the number of police cars in Normal and indecent exposure arrest rates in Kansas City. The t score for the slope is $-.263$, with a probability of .805. This

Table 23.2

SPSS Output for Police Cars and Arrests Data

Model Summary

Model	R	R^2	Adjusted R^2	Std. Error of the Estimate
1	.130[a]	.017	0	24.51462

[a] Predictors: (Constant), CARS.

ANOVA[b]

Model		Sum of Squares	df	Mean Square	F	Significance
	Regression	41.467	1	41.467	.069	.806[a]
1	Residual	2,403.866	4	600.966		
	Total	2,445.333	5			

[a] Predictors: (Constant), CARS.
[b] Dependent variable: ARRESTS.

Coefficients[a]

Model		Unstandardized Coefficients		Standardized Coefficients	t	Significance
		B	Std. Error	Beta		
1	(Constant)	46.183	19.894		2.321	.081
	CARS	−1.232	4.689	−.130	−.263	.806

[a] Dependent variable: ARRESTS.

means there is about an 81% chance that the null hypothesis of $B = 0$ (that is, no relationship) is true.

Anova

An easy way to determine whether an independent variable does a good job of explaining variation in a dependent variable is to look at the sum of squares values. In this case, the sum of squares for the residual or error is 2,403.86. The total sum of squares is 2,445.33. When we divide the first number by the second, we get a result of .983: this means that over 98% of the variation in the dependent variable remains unexplained. The sum of squares for the regression is 41.46. When we divide this number by the total sum of squares, the result is .017. This indicates that the "police cars" variable explains less than 2% of the variation in the dependent variable "indecent exposure arrests."

Model Summary

The R^2 and adjusted R^2 values mirror the results found in the ANOVA section. The R^2 of .017 shows that the number of police cars on patrol in Normal explains less than 2% of the variance in arrest rates in Kansas City.

If the two variables are unrelated, you may be wondering why the R^2 is greater than zero. Even though the slope coefficient is not significant, the independent variable still absorbs 1 df. In cases like this, R^2 values above zero are possible simply because of the way R^2 is calculated. The adjusted R^2 of zero indicates that the small amount of explanatory power indicated by the R^2 is purely the result of the insignificant independent variable absorbing a degree of freedom, rather than having any meaningful explanatory power.

Multiple Regression Output

For the next example, we will explain multiple regression output. The legislative audit bureau for the state of Arkansas has gathered data for 15 community mental health centers across the state. State officials want to obtain a better understanding of differences in employee satisfaction rates across branch locations. Employee satisfaction is measured as the percentage of total employees at each branch who are satisfied with their jobs.

Three independent variables are included in the regression equation. The number of clients served per year is used to see how differences in workload affect satisfaction rates. The second variable is the average years of experience of supervisory and managerial employees. State officials hypothesize that more experienced managers are better able to motivate their employees. Finally, the age of the facility is used to assess whether the setting itself affects employee satisfaction rates. The results for this regression are displayed in Table 23.3. Because we have already explained what the terms displayed on the output mean, we will move directly to interpretation.

Coefficients

The value for the intercept is 110. Sometimes the intercept term takes on unrealistic values. In the present case, the literal interpretation is that if the number of clients, managerial experience, and age of facility were all equal to zero, 110% of employees would be satisfied with their jobs. This is clearly impossible, given that the maximum percentage of satisfied employees cannot exceed 100%. Unrealistic values for the intercept are not uncommon, so you should not be concerned when you come across cases like this.

The coefficients for the independent variables indicate that the number of clients served and manager experience are statistically significant. The coefficient for age of facility is not statistically significant, as indicated by the t score of $-.48$. The "Significance" column shows the probabilities associated with each partial slope. With the level of significance at .64, the partial slope for facility age is clearly not even close to the traditional .05 cutoff for statistical significance. Remember that in each case, the t statistics for the partial slopes are calculated by dividing the partial slope coefficient by its standard error.

As we noted in Chapter 21, model specification issues should be considered before automatically removing statistically insignificant variables from a regression equation. In this case, the knowledge that the age of the facility does not seem to affect

Table 23.3

SPSS Multiple Regression Output

Model Summary

Model	R	R^2	Adjusted R^2	Std. Error of the Estimate
1	.965[a]	.930	.911	4.117

[a] Predictors: (Constant), AGEFACT, JOBEXPR, CLIENTS.

ANOVA[b]

Model		Sum of Squares	df	Mean Square	F	Significance
1	Regression	2,490.459	3	830.153	48.970	.000[a]
	Residual	186.475	11	16.952		
	Total	2,676.933	14			

[a] Predictors: (Constant), AGEFACT, JOBEXPR, CLIENTS.
[b] Dependent variable: SATISF.

Coefficients[a]

Model		Unstandardized Coefficients		Standardized Coefficients	t	Significance
		B	Std. Error	Beta		
1	(Constant)	110.093	27.846		3.954	.002
	CLIENTS	−.127	.055	−.461	−2.317	.041
	JOBEXPR	3.230	1.114	.543	2.900	.014
	AGEFACT	−.037	.076	−.045	−.480	.641

[a] Dependent variable: SATISF.

employee satisfaction rates could be valuable by pointing state officials toward other variables that are more likely to improve performance.

Of course, the other option is simply to remove the age of facility variable and reestimate the equation. If you drop insignificant variables from a model, you should be aware that the audience who sees the final results might ask why certain variables were left out. For example, legislators who read a summary report might assume that age of facility was never considered at all when conducting the analysis. To ensure the intended audience knows which independent variables were used in the final equation, you may want to report and briefly discuss the results for the original model briefly or in a footnote.

Standardized Coefficients

The standardized coefficients column presents the partial slopes and intercept values in standard deviation units. Standardized coefficients are more commonly referred to as *beta weights*. Beta weights are more useful in the case of multiple regression than they are for bivariate regression.

Beta weights are used to assess the relative effect of each partial slope coefficient. From our discussion of standard normal scores in Chapter 8, you may remember that when variables are measured on different scales, they are often difficult to compare. In the present case, the number of clients served ranges from 320 to 502, while managerial experience ranges from 3 to 9 years. Determining the relative impact of each variable can be difficult because the scales are so different. Beta weights address this problem by transforming the values for each partial slope into a common metric: standard deviation units.

A beta weight reveals the amount of change in the dependent variable (expressed in standard deviations) for every one standard deviation change in the independent variable. For example, the beta weight for the number of clients is $-.46$. This means that a one standard deviation change in the number of clients will result in a $-.46$ standard deviation decrease in employee satisfaction. The beta weight for managerial experience is .54, indicating that a one standard deviation change in this variable leads to a $-.54$ standard deviation increase in employee satisfaction.

Regarding the unstandardized coefficients for these two variables, the coefficient for managerial experience is much larger than the coefficient for the number of employees. When the variables are expressed as beta weights, the magnitude of change for managerial experience is still larger than it is for the number of employees, but not by nearly as much. A one standard deviation change in either variable results in approximately a half standard deviation change in the dependent variable.

While beta weights can be useful for assessing the relative impact of independent variables in a regression equation, analysts often report unstandardized coefficients because they are easier to interpret. Even when the beta weight for a particular variable is larger than the beta weights for all of the other variables in an equation, you have not necessarily discovered the independent variable that will always be most influential in explaining variation in the dependent variable. The independent variable with the largest beta weight is only larger relative to the other independent variables *currently* in the equation. The magnitude of beta weights can change when new variables are added or existing variables are removed from an equation. Values for beta weights can also change when the number of observations in a data set changes. For example, the number of cases in a data set might change if an analyst is updating a data set after new data have become available.

The *F* Statistic

In multiple regression, the *F* statistic shows whether the partial slope coefficients for all of the independent variables taken together are equal to zero. If all of the partial slope coefficients in a multiple regression lack explanatory power, the *F* statistic will be very low. The significance column next to the *F* statistic reveals the probability of all partial slope coefficients in the equation being equal to zero. The larger the *F* statistic, the more likely it is that at least one of the independent variables is statistically significant. In the current example, the *F* statistic of 48.97 indicates that there is virtually no chance that all of the partial slopes are equal to zero.

The *F* statistic is useful for assessing whether multicolinearity (see Chapter 21) is a problem. If the value for the *F* statistic indicates a low probability that all partial slopes are equal to zero, but none of the partial slope coefficients are statistically significant, this often indicates the presence of high multicolinearity between two or more of the independent variables.

Anova

The ANOVA section for multiple regression is interpreted the same way as it is for bivariate regression. The overall explanatory power of the model can be assessed by comparing the sum of squares for both the regression and residual to the total sum of squares. When we divide the sum of squares for the regression, 2,490, by the total sum of squares value, 2,676, the result is .93. This indicates that all three independent variables together explain about 93% of the variation in employee satisfaction rates. The sum of squares for the residual is 186. When we divide this number by the total sum of squares, the result is 6.95. This indicates that about 7% of the variation in employee satisfaction rates remains unexplained.

Model Summary

Although R^2 and adjusted R^2 values are provided for both bivariate and multivariate regression equations, the adjusted R^2 is more useful for interpreting the latter. The R^2 of .93 indicates that the number of clients, managerial experience, and age of facility explain about 93% of the variation in employee satisfaction rates. Earlier we found that the partial slope coefficient for the age of facility variable was not statistically significant. The slightly lower adjusted R^2 of .91 reflects this finding.

The dropoff in explanatory power for this model is not very dramatic. When the adjusted R^2 is substantially lower than the R^2, it is usually a good idea to identify the partial slope coefficients with insignificant t scores to determine whether these variables should remain in the model.

Time Series and Dummy Variable Regression Output

For the final example, we will interpret the results of multiple regression output for the Goose Pimple Vermont data in Chapter 22, Table 22.3. The dependent variable is the number of parking tickets issued per week. In addition to the time trend, short-term, and long-term impact variables, the model also includes a dummy variable, coded 1 if an extra patrol was on duty during the week and 0 if not. The results for this model appear in Table 23.4.

Coefficients

The coefficients for each of the independent variables are statistically significant ($p < .05$). Because we already covered the interpretation of interrupted time series variables in Chapter 22, we will focus on the interpretation of the dummy variable. A *dummy variable* is a two-category variable that is usually coded 1 if a condition is met

Table 23.4

SPSS Regression Output Containing Time Series and Dummy Variables

Model Summary[a]

Model	R	R^2	Adjusted R^2	Std. Error of the Estimate
1	.994[a]	.988	.984	2.204

[a] Predictors: (Constant), EXTRAOFA, LNGTERM, STERM, WEEK.

ANOVA[b]

Model		Sum of Squares	df	Mean Square	F	Significance
	Regression	4,365.490	4	1,091.372	224.614	.000[a]
1	Residual	53.448	11	4.859		
	Total	4,418.938	15			

[a] Predictors: (Constant), EXTRAOFA, LNGTERM, STERM, WEEK.
[b] Dependent variable: PTICK.

Coefficients[a]

Model		Unstandardized Coefficients		Standardized Coefficients	t	Significance
		B	Std. Error	Beta		
	(Constant)	37.523	1.786		21.013	.000
	WEEK	1.295	.350	.359	3.704	.003
1	STERM	7.173	2.234	.216	3.210	.008
	LNGTERM	2.329	.491	.389	4.744	.001
	EXTRAOFA	7.436	1.368	.194	5.434	.000

[a] Dependent variable: PTICK.

(for example, an organization is nonprofit) versus 0 if the condition is not met (the organization is not nonprofit). The value for the extra patrol dummy coefficient is 7.44. To properly interpret this or any other dummy variable, an analyst always needs to record how the variable was originally coded.

When working with a dummy variable in a statistical software package, remember that the slope coefficient will always express the effect of the variable in terms of the category that is coded as a "1." In the present case, the coefficient indicates that when an extra patrol is on duty, the number of tickets issued goes up by 7.44 per week. Because the t statistic is significant ($p < .05$), this indicates that there is a difference in the number of traffic tickets issued with an extra patrol versus no extra patrol.

How would the results be affected if an analyst decided to code the presence of an extra patrol as 0 and the absence of an extra patrol as 1? Each version of the dummy variable is presented in Table 23.5. Each row represents one case or observation.

Table 23.5

Different Ways to Code a Dummy Variable

Original Dummy	New Dummy
1 = extra patrol	1 = no extra patrol
0 = no extra patrol	0 = extra patrol
1	0
0	1
0	1
1	0
1	0
0	1
1	0
1	0
1	0
1	0
1	0
1	0
0	1
1	0
1	0
1	0

The SPSS output with the new version of the extra officer dummy variable appears in Table 23.6.

The only thing that changes in the regression output when the new version of the dummy variable is used is the direction or sign (positive or negative) of the coefficient. The magnitude is still exactly the same as it was in the first equation. Because "no extra patrol" is coded as 1 in this case, the substantive interpretation of the coefficient is that the number of parking tickets issued per week goes down by 7.44 when no extra patrol is assigned (rather than up with an extra patrol).

For consistency purposes, we recommend that the values for the "1" category in a dummy variable be reserved for cases that possess a particular attribute, or where a condition does exist. The values for the "0" category should be reserved for cases that do not possess a particular attribute, or where a condition does not exist. If an analyst uses several dummy variables and does not stick to a consistent definition for whether the "1's" or "0's" indicate the presence or absence of an attribute, this can make the interpretation of the results very confusing.

You should never interpret or report standardized regression coefficients for regression equations containing dummy or interrupted time series counter variables. Unstandardized coefficients should always be reported when a regression model contains dummy variables or time series counter variables (see Chapter 23).

Table 23.6

SPSS Regression Output with Recoded Dummy Variable

Model Summary

Model	R	R^2	Adjusted R^2	Std. Error of the Estimate
1	.994[a]	.988	.984	2.204

[a] Predictors: (Constant), EXTRAOFB, LNGTERM, STERM, WEEK.

ANOVA[b]

Model		Sum of Squares	df	Mean Square	F	Significance
	Regression	4,365.490	4	1,091.372	224.614	.000[a]
1	Residual	53.448	11	4.859		
	Total	4,418.938	15			

[a] Predictors: (Constant), EXTRAOFB, LNGTERM, STERM, WEEK.
[b] Dependent variable: PTICK.

Coefficients[a]

Model		Unstandardized Coefficients		Standardized Coefficients	t	Significance
		B	Std. Error	Beta		
	(Constant)	44.959	1.930		23.298	.000
	WEEK	1.295	.350	.359	3.704	.003
1	STERM	7.173	2.234	.216	3.210	.008
	LNGTERM	2.329	.491	.389	4.744	.001
	EXTRAOFB	−7.436	1.368	−.194	−5.434	.000

[a] Dependent variable: PTICK.

What to Report When Discussing Regression Output

The short answer to what you should report when discussing regression output is to report anything your supervisor asks you to report. In the problems presented in Chapters 18 through 21, we focused on interpreting values for the intercept, slopes, and partial slopes. When summarizing regression results, you should be able to discuss the meaning of these coefficients in plain English. You should also note whether the slope or partial slope coefficients are statistically significant. Finally, you should discuss the R^2 or adjusted R^2 values to provide a sense of the overall explanatory power of the model.

Data Management Issues

At this point, you are probably eager to perform some statistical analyses using a computer software package such as SPSS, SAS, or Stata. A statistical package program can produce regression output for a data set containing thousands of observations in seconds. Although you may be tempted to move immediately to advanced statistical analyses, you should first take some important data management issues into account.

Managing Variables

It is always good practice to have both a working and master data set. Considerable time, effort, and money can be wasted if you make irreversible changes to a data set only to find later that you need a copy of the data set in its original form. To make a working data set, you can simply save your working data set using a name that is different than the name for the master data set.

Creating a working file is important because you may find it necessary to recode or transform variables in the master (original) data set. For example, you may decide to recode an interval-level variable into an ordinal variable to create a contingency table. Or you may decide to collapse an ordinal-level variable with 10 categories into an ordinal variable with only three categories.

If you overwrite a variable when recoding data, this could pose a problem if you save the data set and later find that you need the variable in its original form. Aside from recoding variables only in a working file, it is good practice not to overwrite existing variables in a database. Instead, you should leave variables in their original form and create new recoded variables.

Creating subsets of larger data sets is another reason for having both working and master data sets. Analysts sometimes find it necessary to truncate data sets to include only a subset of cases. For example, if an analyst has a large data set with thousands of observations for dozens of branch offices, he or she may want to conduct an analysis using only cases for one or two specific branch locations. It would be very risky and ill advised for an analyst to delete large numbers of cases in the master data set while trying to remember not to click on the "save file" button as he or she is working with the data set. A large number of cases could be lost if an error were made in saving.

Missing Values

Missing values for a variable are those for which no legitimate responses or scores are available. SPSS refers to nonmissing cases as "valid cases." Missing values occur for a variety of reasons: a respondent refuses to answer a question in a survey, data are lost or miscoded, the data may not be available for all cases, and so forth. Note that the amount of missing data and the particular cases with missing data usually vary across the variables in a data set. For example, gender may be available for all cases, education level may be available for most cases, but a more sensitive variable on age has a large amount of missing data.

Missing data values should always be addressed before conducting statistical analyses. For example, only 65% of clients who complete a survey administered by a social services agency might answer the question "What is your annual income?" Or when working with a time series data set that contains 20 variables covering 72 months, all 72 data points for all 20 variables may not be available.

Identifying missing data values prior to analysis is important for several reasons. First, if a key variable has a substantial number of missing values, making valid conclusions about statistical relationships becomes more difficult. For example, if the values for a key variable consist mostly of missing values, it may be difficult to make inferences or study causal relationships with so few cases. If an analyst performs multiple regression analysis using SPSS, the default setting is to include only those cases with nonmissing values for each variable. SPSS will produce an equation based only on those cases for which all data are available for all variables. This means that in a data set where many variables have missing data, the number of cases that are actually analyzed could be substantially reduced. For example, in a data set with 100 cases, where the variable for gender has 100 cases, the variable for education has 85 cases, and the variable for age has 60 cases, you are likely to end up with fewer than 60 valid cases (the cases with missing data on some variables may be different from the cases with missing data on other variables).

Second, identifying missing values is especially useful for spotting potential problems with survey questions. If a small percentage of survey respondents provide answers to certain questions, the large number of missing responses might be due to the questions being poorly worded. The individuals filling out surveys may simply leave confusing or ambiguous questions blank. In a situation like this, an analyst may need to send out new survey forms with different questions in order to increase response rates.

Different statistical software packages treat missing observations differently, so you should never assume that the software package you are using will automatically recognize or adjust for missing observations. Many software packages require that missing values be defined as a number, such as "9" or "99" (depending on the number of digits in data values for a variable) before the observations are defined as missing. You should not define missing values as "0's" because in many cases zero values are legitimate responses. Prior to performing any statistical analyses, you should familiarize yourself with the procedures employed to recognize and label missing data values in the particular statistical package you use.

The Importance of Examining Descriptive Statistics Prior to Using More Advanced Statistical Techniques

One of the biggest mistakes beginning analysts make is jumping straight to techniques such as contingency tables or regression analysis without first running descriptive statistics for the variables used in the analysis. Running descriptive statistics is important because doing so can help identify outliers or data entry errors.

The Range and Other Descriptive Statistics

The range is one of the most useful diagnostic tools for spotting outliers or data entry errors. Spotting data entry errors would be easy if data sets contained only 10 to 15 rows of data and only a few variables. However, what happens when a data set contains several thousand rows of data and dozens of variables? "Eyeballing" the data is not practical in such instances.

The range is useful because it provides information about the lowest and highest values for a variable. This is extremely helpful for discovering miscoded data or outliers. The utility of identifying the highest and lowest values for the variables in a data set is that we usually know ahead of time the legitimate range of values a variable can take. For example, two of the authors of this text were once working with data on average teacher salaries for a set of public schools. When we calculated the range for this variable, the minimum value was $29,000 and the maximum value was $360,000. Before you decide to quit your MPA program to become a public school teacher, you should realize that what really happened in this case was that an extra zero was accidentally added to the numbers for some school districts. After correcting the data errors, the actual range was $29,000 to $36,000.

As an analyst in a government or nonprofit setting, you may have to work with data that have passed through several hands. For example, clients or citizens fill out forms, which are then processed by administrative clerks, which are then matched with other data to create a data set. In other cases, you may be working with a data set that was originally put together by another party, such as a state or federal agency. As data pass through many hands, data entry errors can be made along the way. The point is that you should confirm, rather than assume, that your data set is free of errors before undertaking any statistical analyses.

When outliers have been identified, it is important not to delete or change outlying observations without first knowing the reason why the values are so extreme in relation to the other data points. Sometimes outliers are not the result of data coding errors but are instead substantively important observations that should not be deleted or recoded.

Aside from using the range to detect outliers, you should calculate descriptive statistics for all variables prior to doing more advanced data analysis techniques. If the values for a particular measure of central tendency or measure of dispersion seem abnormally high or low, a closer look at the data may be warranted. Analysts sometimes accompany the results obtained from more advanced statistical techniques such as regression analysis with a table that lists the means and standard deviations for all of the variables used in the analysis.

The Importance of Plotting Data before Analysis

An analyst can get a better idea of the shape of a data distribution or relationship by plotting the data on a set of coordinate axes prior to analysis. Data plots provide analysts with two useful pieces of information. First, data plots can be used to locate outliers. Even when the number of observations is large, extreme values tend to stand out on graphs.

Second, plotting variables helps an analyst get a sense of the functional form of a relationship. Although regression analysis should be used to formally assess whether an actual relationship exists between an independent variable and a dependent variable, plotting the variables beforehand can provide clues about whether the relationship (if any) is linear. Recall from Chapter 19 that one of the assumptions of regression analysis is that the relationship between an independent and dependent variable should be linear. If the relationship is quadratic, cubic, or logarithmic, traditional regression analysis without the necessary adjustments will provide misleading results. A graphical plot is a simple tool that can tell you whether nonlinear estimation methods or transformation of the data may be necessary.

Chapter Summary

When regression analysis is performed using statistical software packages such as SPSS or SAS, the output generated will provide a large amount of information about each regression equation. At a minimum, analysts usually report and describe the substantive meaning of regression coefficients and R^2 values.

The ANOVA section of regression output allows an analyst to assess the amount of error present in a model and the proportion of variance in the dependent variable that is explained by the independent variables. Although ANOVA output provides useful information about the overall fit of a regression model, analysts more commonly report and discuss R^2 and adjusted R^2 values.

Standardized regression coefficients are useful for multiple regression output. Standardized coefficients or beta weights make it possible to compare the relative magnitude of partial slope coefficients within a model by expressing results in terms of standard deviation units. Analysts generally prefer reporting unstandardized rather than standardized coefficients because the former are easier to interpret.

A good analyst will always run descriptive statistics and look for data entry errors or missing values prior to performing regression analysis or any other advanced data analysis techniques. Missing data, outliers, or miscoded data can affect the quality of the results obtained from more advanced statistical analysis techniques—which can affect the quality of the inferences and conclusions made using statistical output. Statistical software packages can calculate all of these key diagnostic tools very quickly, so an analyst should never jump straight to more advanced techniques before taking these basic preliminary steps.

Problems

23.1   The Director of Economic Development in Potto Gulch, Wisconsin, is interested in studying the relationship between business activity and spending on social welfare programs. Specifically, she hypothesizes that as business activity increases, the boost to the local economy (mainly through job creation) should result in lower spending on programs for the poor. To test this hypothesis, the director gathers annual data for the last 11 years on three variables. The dependent variable is annual spending on social welfare programs (in millions of dollars). The director feels that the number of business permits issued each year is a good indicator of economic activity and selects this as the first independent variable (BPRMT). The second independent variable is the number of residents in Potto Gulch (POP). The regression output is displayed below.

Model Summary

Model	R	R^2	Adj. R^2	Std. Error of the Estimate
1	.791[a]	.626	.532	800,770.013

[a] Predictors: (Constant), BPRMT, POP.

ANOVA[b]

Model		Sum of Squares	df	Mean Square	F	Significance
	Regression	8,568,393,095,762.110	2	4,284,196,547,881.058	6.681	.020[a]
1	Residual	5,129,860,913,328.790	8	641,232,614,166.099		
	Total	13,698,254,009,090.910	10			

[a] Predictors: (Constant), BPRMT, POP.
[b] Dependent variable: EXPENDIT.

Coefficients[a]

Model		Unstandardized Coefficients		Standardized Coefficients	t	Significance
		B	Std. Error	Beta		
	(Constant)	3,655,278.783	8,482,054.890		.431	.678
1	POP	109.855	100.721	.293	1.091	.307
	BPRMT	−5,049.119	2,339.638	−.581	−2.158	.063

[a] Dependent variable: EXPENDIT.

(a) Interpret the slopes and intercept for this model. What substantive conclusion can the director make about the relationship between business activity and spending on social welfare programs?

(b) The director is concerned about the drop in the explanatory power of the model indicated by the adjusted R^2 value. What is the likely explanation for why the adjusted R^2 is lower than R^2?

(c) The director has located data on the actual number of Potto Gulch citizens receiving social welfare assistance each year. If the director includes this new variable in the model, which of the current independent variables should be removed from the model? Explain.

23.2 The head of philanthropy at the Shady Hills, Michigan, Institute of Fine
Arts has asked her assistant to come up with some statistical evidence on the
causes of variation in member renewal rates (measured as the percentage of
members who renew each year). The assistant hypothesizes that new exhibits
are essential to keeping members interested and selects the number of new
exhibits each year as the first independent variable (EXHIBITS). The assistant selects the number of mail or telephone contacts with members (per
year) as the second independent variable (CONTACTS) because she feels
that members may become annoyed and lose interest if they are contacted
too many times over the course of a year. Using data for the last 15 years, the
assistant generates the following regression output:

Model Summary

Model	R	R^2	Adj. R^2	Std. Error of the Estimate
1	.949[a]	.901	.885	1.29298

[a] Predictors: (Constant), CONTACTS, EXHIBITS.

ANOVA[b]

Model		Sum of Squares	df	Mean Square	F	Sig.
1	Regression	183.538	2	91.769	54.892	.000[a]
	Residual	20.062	12	1.672		
	Total	203.600	14			

[a] Predictors: (Constant), CONTACTS, EXHIBITS.
[b] Dependent variable: RENEWAL.

Coefficients[a]

Model		Unstandardized Coefficients		Standardized Coefficients		
		B	Std. Error	Beta	t	Sig.
1	(Constant)	45.348	2.265		20.022	.000
	EXHIBITS	1.078	.252	.562	4.271	.001
	CONTACTS	−1.434	.410	−.460	−3.496	.004

[a] Dependent variable: RENEWAL.

(a) Interpret the slopes, intercept, and R^2 for this model. Write a short
memo to the head of philanthropy discussing these results. What potential changes in policy would you recommend based on these results?

(b) Compare the unstandardized and standardized regression coefficients.
How does the relative impact of each independent variable vary across
the two sets of coefficients?

23.3 In an attempt to boost performance, Officials at the Bureau of State Licensing in New York have decided to purchase new computer workstations equipped with simpler database programs for all staff members. Eight weeks after the changes were adopted, the director wants to assess their impact on performance. The director selects the number of forms processed per week as the dependent variable. Because 16 weeks of data are available, the director decides that interrupted time series variables are appropriate for the analysis. The first independent variable is a time trend variable which starts at 1 and increases by 1 for each week in the analysis (WEEK). The second independent variable is a short-term impact variable, coded 0 from Weeks 1 through 8, and 1 thereafter (STERM). A long-term impact variable is coded 0 for the first 8 weeks and switches to a time trend variable for the remaining weeks (LNGTERM). The director would also like to know what impact the presence of an unpaid intern from a nearby MPA program has on performance. This variable is a dummy variable coded 1 if an intern worked during the week and 0 if not (INTERN). The results are displayed below:

Model Summary

Model	R	R^2	Adj. R^2	Std. Error of the Estimate
1	.996[a]	.992	.989	17.355

[a] Predictors: (Constant), INTERN, LNGTERM, STERM, WEEK.

ANOVA[b]

Model		Sum of Squares	df	Mean Square	F	Significance
1	Regression	425,280.464	4	106,320.116	352.979	.000[a]
	Residual	3,313.286	11	301.208		
	Total	428,593.750	15			

[a] Predictors: (Constant), INTERN, LNGTERM, STERM, WEEK.
[b] Dependent variable: FORMS.

Coefficients[a]

Model		Unstandardized Coefficients		Standardized Coefficients	t	Sig.
		B	Std. Error	Beta		
1	(Constant)	386.130	14.060		27.463	.000
	WEEK	12.688	2.754	.357	4.608	.001
	STERM	86.730	17.591	.265	4.930	.000
	LNGTERM	20.845	3.865	.353	5.394	.000
	INTERN	66.835	10.773	.177	6.204	.000

[a] Dependent Variable: FORMS.

Interpret the slopes, intercept, and R^2. Write a short memo discussing the effects of the new computers and software as well as the presence of MPA interns on agency performance.

23.4 The director of the Northern Tennessee Association of Local Governments is conducting a study on differences in average property taxes (in thousands of dollars) residents in 15 local communities pay on their homes. The director believes that variations in property taxes are a function of two variables: the number of government employees on staff in each city (EMPLOYEES) and city size, measured in square miles (SIZE). The director uses SPSS to generate the following regression where the average property tax per residence is the dependent variable:

Model Summary

Model	R	R^2	Adj. R^2	Std. Error of the Estimate
1	.983[a]	.967	.961	112.85532

[a] Predictors: (Constant), SIZE, EMPLOYEES.

ANOVA[b]

Model		Sum of Squares	df	Mean Square	F	Significance
	Regression	4,421,115.713	2	2,210,557.857	173.563	.000[a]
1	Residual	152835.887	12	12,736.324		
	Total	4,573,951.600	14			

[a] Predictors: (Constant), SIZE, EMPLOYEES.
[b] Dependent variable: PTAX.

Coefficients[a]

Model		Unstandardized Coefficients		Standardized Coefficients		
		B	Std. Error	Beta	t	Significance
	(Constant)	938.736	336.866		2.787	.016
1	employees	8.225	2.631	.564	3.126	.009
	size	47.532	19.974	.430	2.380	.035

[a] Dependent Variable: PTAX.

(a) Interpret the intercept, slopes, and R^2 values.

(b) Interpret the standardized coefficients. Explain how the standardized coefficients differ in magnitude from the unstandardized coefficients.

23.5 The director of exhibits at the Grosse Out Pointe Institute of Modern and Trashy Art wants to know what drives monthly attendance figures. She believes that the number of new exhibits each month (EXHIBITS) is an important variable, because the public has a large appetite for new and inno-vative trashy art. For the second independent variable, the director decides to study the impact of the season on attendance, reasoning that in cold-weather months, residents are more likely to attend the museum since there are fewer outdoor and recreational options available. The director creates a dummy variable (SEASON), coded 1 if the month is a cold-weather month (November through March) and 0 if not. The director uses SPSS to generate the following regression, where monthly attendance is the dependent variable.

Model Summary

Model	R	R^2	Adj. R^2	Std. Error of the Estimate
1	.925[a]	.857	.783	311.53355

[a] Predictors: (Constant), SEASON EXHIBIT.

ANOVA[b]

Model		Sum of Squares	df	Mean Square	F	Significance
	Regression	6,953,045.135	2	3,476,522.568	35.821	.000[a]
1	Residual	1,164,637.798	12	97,053.150		
	Total	8,117,682.933	14			

[a] Predictors: (Constant), SEASON, EXHIBIT.
[b] Dependent variable: ATTEND.

Coefficients[a]

Model		Unstandardized Coefficients		Standardized Coefficients	t	Significance
		B	Std. Error	Beta		
	(Constant)	2,659.058	304.018		8.746	.000
1	Exhibit	360.714	42.860	.942	8.417	.000
	Season	153.784	168.032	.102	.915	.378

[a] Dependent Variable: ATTEND.

(a) Interpret the intercept, slopes, and R^2.

(b) Interpret the adjusted R^2 value. What is the likely reason why the adjusted R^2 is somewhat lower than R^2?

23.6 Refer to the EDUCATION data set stored on the CD-ROM. Use the following set of independent variables: SALTEACH, REVPUP, CLASS, and PECD to explain teacher turnover rates, or TETURN.

(a) Interpret the slopes, intercept, and R^2 for the model.

(b) Based on your interpretation of the standardized regression coefficients, which independent variable has the greatest impact on teacher turnover rates?

23.7   Refer to the EDUCATION data set located on the CD-ROM. Use the following set of independent variables—PAFR, PHISP, CLASS, and TETURN—to explain overall student pass rates, or PASSALL.

(a) Interpret the slopes, intercept, and R^2 for the model. Based on your interpretation of R^2, does it seem like relevant explanatory variables might be missing from the model? Explain.

(b) Add ATTEND to the existing set of independent variables and generate a second regression. Interpret the slopes, intercept, and R^2 for the model. Has the addition of a new independent variable improved the explanatory power of the model? Explain.

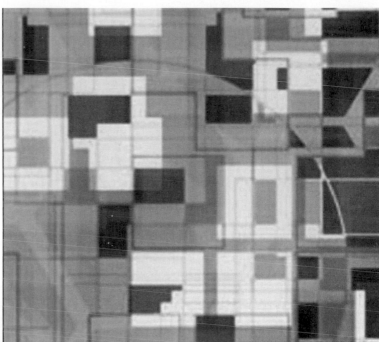

PART
VII

Special Topics
in Quantitative
Management

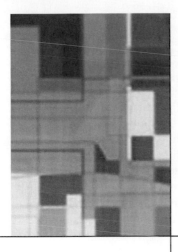

CHAPTER 24

Performance Measurement Techniques

Performance measurement has become increasingly important in both government and nonprofit settings. Performance measurement yields information necessary for explaining program results to external constituencies. Donors to nonprofit organizations want to see evidence that their contributions are being spent on worthwhile activities. Citizens want to know that government agencies are putting their tax dollars to good use. The efficient use of funding is only one dimension of performance. External constituencies also want to know whether government and nonprofit organizations are making progress toward stated goals. Is a government agency adequately addressing the problem it was created to address? Is a nonprofit organization generating results consistent with its mission statement, or is it having problems meeting key objectives?

In addition to presenting program operations before external constituencies, performance measurement provides organizations with information that can be used to adjust internal operations. Performance measurement can reveal how efficiently resources such as time and money are being used. Performance data can also help managers spot problems such as inconsistencies in how policies are being applied.

This chapter provides an overview of statistical tools useful in performance measurement. If you have read and followed the earlier chapters, you will see that performance measurement is an application that brings together several different statistical procedures for effective use by public and nonprofit managers.

Defining Inputs, Outputs, and Outcomes

To apply statistical tools to performance measurement, you first need to know what to measure and why. In Chapter 3, you learned about independent and dependent variables. If performance is the dependent variable we wish to explain, we obviously need to consider independent variables that might account for variations in performance.

There are also validity and reliability issues in selecting performance measures. Just because an activity is measurable does not mean it will be a valid or reliable performance indicator. *Inputs, outputs, outcomes,* and *efficiency* are common terms used in performance measurement. We discuss each of these in the following sections.

Inputs

Inputs generally refer to resources an organization has been given to achieve its goals. Common examples of inputs include the following:

Annual appropriations

The dollar amount of donations received annually

The number of employees

The number of hours worked by employees

The number of volunteers

The number of hours worked by volunteers

Organizations are endowed with resources so that they can achieve certain goals. Collecting data on resource variables like these is crucial if we want to see how resources affect performance. Having data on inputs does not mean that you will be able to explain 100 percent of the variation in organizational performance. Yet information about core resources like money and the work of employees should provide a solid foundation for understanding and explaining at least some of the variation in performance.

Outputs versus Outcomes

How do we measure or operationalize the concept of performance? To understand performance, we must first explain the difference between outputs and outcomes. *Outputs* are tangible indicators used to show how resources are being employed. Common examples of outputs include the following:

The number of cases processed per employee

The number of forms processed per day

The number of clients each employee has served

The number of overtime hours worked per week

The number of times an agency stays within its spending targets

The average cost of serving a client

The average amount of time (minutes, hours, days) spent per client.

Outputs are sometimes called *workload measures* because they show what organizations have produced with the inputs that have been provided to them. Are outputs indicators of performance? They can be, but measuring performance solely in terms of outputs has some serious drawbacks. Although outputs provide tangible evidence of what inputs such as money or employees produce, they generally provide little information about quality. For example, an agency that processes 25% more forms than it did last month might appear to be making impressive gains in efficiency, but if the error rate in processing forms has tripled as a result, the higher output would not be very impressive. No organization wants to live by the motto "We may make a lot of errors, but at least we're fast."

When employees are sensitized to the fact that performance is being measured in terms of outputs, they may also feel pressured to produce desirable levels of output while ignoring the larger question of whether organizational goals are actually being achieved. For example, if counselors of a domestic abuse shelter are evaluated primarily by how quickly they serve each client, they may feel pressure to move from one client to the next without adequately assessing the circumstances of each client. If teachers feel pressure to produce high scores on standardized achievement tests, they may "teach to the test" instead of focusing on broader learning objectives. When too much attention is placed on outputs, we sometimes lose sight of whether key organizational goals are actually being achieved.

Outcomes are more precise indicators of performance than outputs because the former focus more on quality than quantity. Impressive output or workload statistics are not necessarily evidence that organizational goals are being achieved. For example, an output for a parole officer is the number of parolees supervised per year. An outcome is the recidivism rate for the parolees being supervised. If a parole officer is supervising a large number of parolees but more than 90% go back to jail within a year, it is questionable whether progress toward core organizational goals is being made.

How do we determine outcomes? A nonprofit organization can identify important outcomes by looking at its mission statement. Foundations and major grantmakers sometimes define outcomes that must be measured to ensure continued funding. In the case of government agencies, legislative bodies, such as city councils and state legislatures, often select outcomes. Public officials appropriate funds to agencies with the expectation that certain goals will be achieved.

Examples of outcomes include the following:

The percentage of cases processed correctly

The percentage of job training participants (out of all program participants) who receive full-time jobs

The percentage of alcohol treatment patients who remain sober for 2 years after completing the program

The percentage of low-income students who graduate college

The percentage of new immigrants who pass an English-language test after 1 year

Outcomes are usually more important in the case of human services organizations that deal with complex social problems. Examples of human services organizations include domestic abuse shelters, alcoholism treatment centers, homeless shelters, unemployment offices, agencies for the blind or disabled, and other social welfare agencies. When dealing with complex social problems, the number of clients processed usually is not as important as whether the cases have been handled correctly.

Defining performance in terms of outputs is usually more acceptable for "bottom-line" organizations, where tasks are very clear, and little controversy exists over the meaning of performance. For example, a municipal recycling yard is an organization whose tasks are well defined (collecting and processing recyclable material) and not very complex. A public transit department may have slightly more complicated performance goals, but the outputs—riders transported and fares collected—are still fairly easy to measure.

Both outputs and outcomes are valid indicators of organizational performance, but outputs are generally much easier to measure than outcomes. We raise the distinction between the two to emphasize that performance evaluations for organizations addressing complex social problems typically need to go beyond simple output or workload measures. Measurement validity means we are actually measuring what we think we are measuring (see Chapter 2). You should always be clear on whether you are actually measuring the extent to which goals have been achieved or just workload.

Inputs, Outputs, and Efficiency

Organizations often measure efficiency using data on inputs and outputs. One of the most common methods for evaluating efficiency involves dividing outputs by inputs to determine the average level of inputs per output (sometimes referred to as *unit cost*). For example, if a drug abuse treatment facility spends $750,000 in staff time and supplies to serve 580 patients, the average cost per patient is $1,293 ($750,000 ÷ 580). A public works department that spends $340,000 in salaries and supplies to complete 297 minor patching and repair jobs on city streets spends an average of $1,144 per job ($340,000 ÷ 297).

Efficiency measures provide information about changes in costs on a per-client or per-event basis over time. For example, if a drug abuse treatment center spent $1,293 per client last year and $1,480 per client this year, officials would likely want to examine the factors responsible for the change.

Relying heavily on efficiency measures to evaluate performance has some serious drawbacks. First, efficiency measures generally cannot measure quality. If the cost of treating a client decreases from $1,293 to $920, but the percentage of cases successfully resolved also goes down, the improvement in efficiency comes at a high price. Average cost data can also be misleading if the level of resources employed varies dramatically per client or event. Costs for minor street repairs might vary from $200 to $4,900. Small changes in the number of high- or low-cost repairs from year to year could result in substantial fluctuations in the average cost per job.

Measuring efficiency is important because doing so can help a manager determine whether resources are being wasted. However, efficiency is rarely *the* central focus of most nonprofit and government organizations. If the average cost of putting out a fire goes up from one year to the next, it would be silly to tell the fire department to find a cheaper way to fight fires. If the average cost of treating a mental health patient increases by 10% from one year to the next, cutting corners to improve efficiency may result in reduced quality of care. Organizations charged with protecting public health and safety should be evaluated primarily on whether they get the job done right, rather than on how inexpensively work is completed.

Outcome Measures from External Sources

One limitation of outcome measures generated by organizations is that employees may overstate the number of successes and understate the number of failures to portray themselves and their agencies in a better light. An advantage of externally generated outcome measures is that individuals who do not have a vested interest in the success of an organization may provide more honest assessments of organizational performance. Externally generated outcome measures can be compared to those generated internally to see if major discrepancies exist.

For example, if counselors at a community mental health agency file reports indicating that less than 2% of clients are dissatisfied with services received, the director of the agency could send surveys to former clients to get a sense of how accurate this figure really is. If the surveys reveal that the percentage of dissatisfied clients is much higher than 2%, agency officials might want to investigate whether counselors are understating the rate of client dissatisfaction. Additional survey questions might focus on how promptly services were provided, whether the client would be willing to use agency services in the future, and whether counselors did a good job explaining agency policies and answering client questions. Similarly, the head of a public works department could validate job completion data reported by snow-plowing crews by asking citizens when and how often their streets were plowed and whether the crews did a good job clearing the roads.

Survey data can provide a wealth of information about performance because clients may have different viewpoints about an agency than its employees. Clients can raise awareness of problems that managers might not even know exist. A variety of important methodological issues need to be addressed when writing survey questions and administering surveys. If you want to learn more about how to construct and administer surveys, consult a textbook on the topic (see Fowler, 2001).

In addition to survey data, other examples of outcome measures based on external data might include the number of complaints an agency receives each month, the number of newspaper articles about an organization that take a negative tone, certification by an accreditation agency, any awards or citations received, or the number of deficiencies in performance identified by an outside auditor.

The Importance of Using Multiple Output and Outcome Measures

A single output or outcome measure is rarely adequate for assessing the performance of an entire organization. Organizations typically address a variety of problems and thus have a variety of goals. Inputs are spread across different departments or subunits in organizations. Separate input, output, and outcome measures are necessary to track the performance of individual subunits and programs in large organizations.

For example, if a department of public works is made up of several different sub-units, each subunit will be allocated a share of the budget. Trying to establish a link between the department's total budget and the performance of one of its subunits would not be a very sound approach. A much more accurate understanding of how inputs affect performance would be gained by constructing output and outcome measures that are specific to each subunit, then measuring the fractional share of total organizational inputs directed toward each subunit.

Having multiple output and outcome measures also makes it possible to spot inconsistencies in performance. If we know that two output measures should be highly correlated but the data reveal they are not, performance problems may exist. For example, if a social services agency asks both agency staff and clients to answer the question "Was the problem adequately solved?" large differences in the response patterns across the two groups would be undesirable. Public schools often measure performance in terms of the percentage of students who pass state-mandated standardized tests. A comparison performance measure in this case would be dropout rates. Increasing pass rates accompanied by increasing dropout rates might mean that performance gains are taking place not because the quality of education is improving, but because weak test takers are dropping out of school.

Finally, performance is usually a multidimensional concept. Organizations sometimes have short-, medium-, and long-term performance goals. If a nonprofit is receiving grant money from several different foundations, each foundation may require information on different outputs and outcomes. Defining performance using multiple measures helps avoid an all-or-nothing mentality, where success is determined by looking only at a single criterion.

Techniques for Presenting Performance Data

Many of the statistical techniques presented in earlier chapters are applicable to performance data. Contingency tables are useful for analyzing client surveys. For example, a manager might want to see whether client attributes such as gender or race are statistically related to client satisfaction with services.

Regression and time series techniques are valuable tools for testing causal relationships among inputs, outputs, and outcomes. For example, we could regress organizational outputs on appropriations to see how differences in funding levels affect performance. Interrupted time series techniques can be used to determine whether a change in strategy or procedures results in improved performance from the pre- to postintervention time period. We will illustrate how more advanced statistical techniques can be used in performance measurement in the problems section at the end of the chapter.

There is certainly nothing wrong with using advanced statistical techniques to evaluate performance, but you need to remember the audience in mind. If the goal is describing performance patterns to a general audience, sophisticated statistical analyses may confuse rather than clarify. Political officials, boards of directors, the media, and the public may not understand what to make of significance tests or regression output. If the results are not clearly explained, the audience might even conclude that complex statistics are being used to hide poor performance. If you choose to analyze and describe performance to general audiences using more advanced statistical methods, remember that the results have to be explained in plain English rather than statistical jargon.

Public managers must know how to effectively summarize performance to external audiences. Summary performance documents for government and nonprofit organizations typically do not present performance using advanced statistical techniques. If you review a municipal budget, a Comprehensive Annual Financial Report (CAFR), or an annual report issued by a nonprofit organization, you are far more likely to find discussions of performance based on graphical presentations, trend analysis, and benchmarking techniques. Graphical presentations are often coupled with trend analysis to illustrate how performance indicators have changed over time. Benchmarking techniques involve performance comparisons between an organization and its peers. The goal of these techniques is to present performance information in a manner that external audiences can easily understand. We review each of these techniques below.

Graphical Presentations

You know that "a picture is worth a thousand words." In performance measurement, graphical displays can often convey findings just as effectively as paragraphs of written commentary on performance. Although graphs can be a simple and effective way to summarize performance, you need to consider several issues involving presentation of the data.

Selecting the Content

Graphical presentations are best for summarizing relatively straightforward performance measures that do not need a lot of explanation beyond what already appears on the graphs. For example, the use of transformed variables should be avoided since a general audience is unlikely to understand how to interpret variables expressed as Z scores (see Chapter 8) or logarithmic units (see "Forecasting an Exponential Trend" in Chapter 20 for a review of log transformations).

Although you may present several performance measures on the same graph to illustrate their interrelationship, the more variables summarized on a single graph, the more likely the target audience will be confused over how to interpret the graph. For example, if a graph summarizes trends for employee health care, overtime, fringe benefit, and training costs with four separate trend lines, keeping track of each variable could be difficult.

Scaling issues also need to be considered when presenting multiple variables on the same graph. When the scales for two variables are not comparable, it may be difficult to illustrate changes for each variable. For example, if the values for one variable are measured in the tens of thousands and the values for another are well below 100, the dramatic differences in scale will likely obscure trends for the variable with the much smaller scale.

In addition to using multiple graphs to present data for several variables, another approach is to express two closely related variables in ratio terms. For example, a common measure of financial performance for nonprofit organizations is the current ratio. The current ratio is calculated by dividing current assets by current liabilities. Presenting the current ratio, instead of both assets and liabilities, makes it possible to summarize information about two related variables with a single measure. Similarly, an organization could summarize information about the number of employees and the number of clients served by tracking changes by means of an employee–client ratio.

Selecting the Format

Spreadsheets and statistical software packages offer a wide variety of formats for presenting data graphically. Ideally, the format you choose should be suited to the dimension of performance you wish to highlight. For example, pie charts work well for breaking down aggregate categories into component parts. If an organization's budget is broken down into several functional areas, a pie chart can show the percentage of the total budget allocated to each area. Line graphs are useful if the goal is presenting changes in performance measures over time. Histograms or bar graphs are useful for ranking data or making comparisons across different observations. For example, a city manager who wants to illustrate how low the property tax burden in her city really is could use a bar graph to compare average property taxes per person in her city to averages for five neighboring cities.

You should review the section titled "Graphic Presentations" in Chapter 4 to refresh your memory about some of the different formats that can be used to present data. If you want an in-depth examination of the different options for summarizing data with graphical tools, see Tufte (2001).

We will illustrate the use of line graphs and histograms with an example. Joe Copp is the police chief of Groton, Georgia. In early 2003, Chief Copp asked the mayor and city council for more funding so that the police department could initiate a "click it or ticket" campaign to combat the problem of drivers who do not wear seat belts. The extra funds would be used to beef up patrols and run public service campaigns about the penalties for not wearing seat belts. The chief's funding request was approved for the 2004 fiscal year (which begins in October 2003). To show the mayor and city council the effect of increased funding, the chief asks his assistant to construct a histogram for the number of citations issued for drivers not wearing seatbelts from June 2003 through May 2004. Figure 24.1 displays the graph.

The graphical evidence reveals a general downtrend in the number of citations issued for seat belt violations. Chief Copp believes that this graph will help him make a convincing case to the mayor and city council that the increase in funding has helped the police department address the problem more effectively.

Selecting the Scale

If the default settings used by the graphics software do not fit the actual range of the data in question, there is nothing wrong or deceptive about changing the scale to better fit the data. Inappropriate scales can obscure changes in performance, which negates the benefits of using graphs to summarize performance in the first place. This is

Figure 24.1

Groton Click It or Ticket Output Data

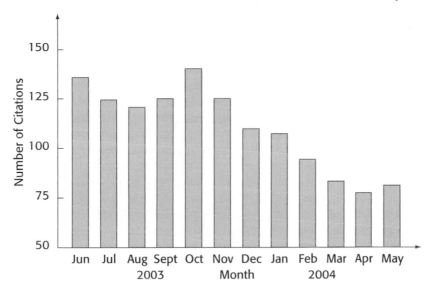

especially true in cases where the values for a performance measure are in a relatively narrow range. For instance, if the values for a variable range from 10 to 25, performance changes might be difficult to spot if the scale of the graph ranges from 0 to 100.

To illustrate the effects of differences in scale, we will present the Groton "Click It or Ticket" program data using two different line graphs. In Version A (Figure 24.2), the scale for the Y-axis ranges from 0 to 175. In Version B (Figure 24.3), it ranges from 50 to 150.

Notice how differences in scale affect the presentation of results. Although the data are the same in both cases, the effect of the program looks more pronounced in Version B than it does in Version A. An important point to remember about spreadsheets and other computer graphics tools is that these programs often apply default settings that do not necessarily fit the data in question. In the present case, the data values range from 77 to 140, but the graphics program automatically selected a scale of 0 to 175. Is a range of 0 to 175 necessary? The data range from 77 to 140, so there is really no need to choose a minimum value of 0 and a maximum value of 175 for the Y-axis. Assessing changes in performance is easier when the minimum and maximum points on a scale more closely match the actual range of the data.

Graphical performance summaries are often used in conjunction with trend analysis and benchmarking, two techniques we discuss next.

Trend Analysis

Temporal context is important in performance measurement. Input, output, and outcome measures typically have clearest meaning when they are compared over time. It is difficult to determine whether performance at the present time is adequate without

Figure 24.2

Groton Click It or Ticket Data Using a Scale of 0 to 175

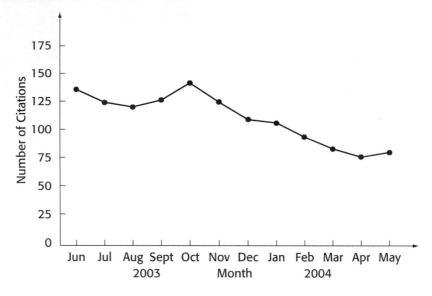

Figure 24.3

Groton Click It or Ticket Data Using a Scale of 50 to 150

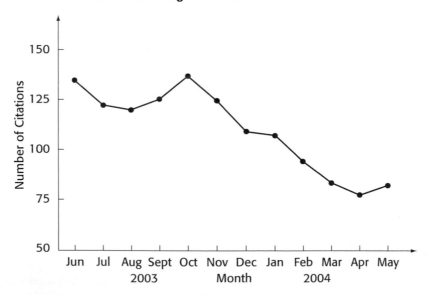

having past performance data as a baseline. We can better gauge success by looking at current performance relative to past performance. Additionally, current outputs or outcomes are often the result of trends that started several time periods earlier. For example, a nonprofit might be experiencing performance problems at the present time because donations started to fall off 10 months earlier.

Moreover, analyzing performance trends makes it easier to identify and define unusual changes in performance. If historical data reveal that the number of inspections an agency conducts rarely varies by more than 3% from month to month, a change of 10% might require some investigation. After analyzing trends, a manager can establish thresholds for when performance should be more carefully scrutinized.

Data on inputs, outputs, and outcomes are commonly presented in documents such as municipal budgets and the annual reports of nonprofit organizations. Input measures themselves are not indicators of performance, so performance summaries typically focus more on outputs and outcomes. However, data on inputs can be relevant if a manager wants to make the case that declining inputs are the reason for negative trends in outputs or outcomes.

Summarizing performance trends is a good way to succinctly present information about what an organization has accomplished and how these accomplishments compare to those of earlier time periods. Here are the basic steps for summarizing performance trends:

Step 1: Select the inputs, outputs, or outcomes you wish to summarize. Be sure that historical data for each indicator are available.

Step 2: Select a time period for summarizing trends. Annual performance data are often presented in municipal budgets and the annual reports of nonprofit organizations. A manager might use monthly or quarterly intervals if seasonality is an issue. Seasonality refers to data patterns that vary substantially depending on the time of year (see Chapter 20). For example, demand at a homeless shelter might increase dramatically over the winter months but then drop to much lower levels during the spring and summer months.

Construct a table that includes totals for the performance measure for each year (or month, or quarter).

Step 3: Calculate the rate of change in the performance measure from one time period to the next. A rate of change is calculated as follows:

$$\text{Change} = \left(\frac{P_t - P_{t-1}}{P_{t-1}} \right) * 100$$

where

P_t = Performance measurement at time t

P_{t-1} = Performance measurement at time $t - 1$

For example, in 2003, the Eastville Soup Kitchen received $72,800 in donations. In 2002, the shelter had received $68,390. The percentage change from 2002 to 2003 is calculated by first subtracting the totals for 2002 from the totals for 2003, which yields a difference of $4,410. This number is then divided by $68,390 for a result of .0645. To determine the percentage change, multiply this number by 100. The result is a 6.45 percent increase in donations from 2002 to 2003.

The number of percentage changes will always be one less than the total number of time periods, since the first time period is a baseline. For example, if we have performance data from 1995 to 2003, there will be eight individual percentage changes for 9 years of data. Because data for 1994 are not available, we would not be able to calculate the rate of change from 1994 to 1995. The first percentage change would be from 1995 to 1996. To calculate the average percentage change for the time period, sum the individual percentage changes and divide by the total number of percentage changes.

We typically summarize performance trends in terms of percentages because it is often difficult to spot trends in raw numbers, especially when the numbers are quite large. For example, identifying performance changes in a city clerk's office that processes tens of thousands of documents a year may be difficult if we only see the raw data on the number of forms processed.

More important, if you are comparing two or more performance measures that differ in scale, raw numbers can make comparisons across indicators more complicated. If the values for one indicator are generally much larger than those for another, the values for the first indicator may "swamp" or overwhelm the values for the second. For example, monthly donations for the Eastville Soup Kitchen average $4900. The number of meals served per month averages 1,900. Due to differences in scale, it may be difficult to spot how one indicator moves with the other simply by looking at the raw data.

Step 4: Establish performance targets. A performance target is the desired rate of change for a performance indicator. Increasing donations by 4% from the prior year could be a performance target for a nonprofit. A decrease in drunk driving arrests of 10% could be a performance target used to evaluate a police department's public service campaign against drunk driving. A manager obviously needs to have a strategy for achieving a performance target, so developing a plan of action should come before a target rate of change is selected.

Historical data on performance measures are useful for providing reasonable estimates of change when selecting performance targets. If the data reveal that donations have been rising at an average of 7% a year for the past 5 years, a 2% increase for the current year would probably be too low a target.

Step 5: Evaluate progress toward the performance target. If a target has not been met, analyze what went wrong. The original target may have been unrealistic. A lack of resources could also be to blame. If a target has been met, analyze the factors that contributed to success so this knowledge can be used in the future.

Table 24.1

Donations and Meals Served at the Eastville Soup Kitchen

Month	Total Donations	Percentage Change	Number of Meals Served	Percentage Change
January	$3,090		2,210	
February	$2,950	−4.5%	2,197	−.58
March	$2,800	−5.1%	2,080	−5.3
April	$2,788	−.42%	2,031	−2.4
May	$2,650	−4.9%	1,957	−3.6
June	$2,320	−12.5%	1,938	−.97
July	$1,997	−13.9%	1,853	−4.4
August	$1,795	−10.1%	1,784	−3.7
September	$1,590	−11.4%	1,540	−13.7
October	$1,798	13.1%	1,790	16.2
November	$2,190	21.8%	2,250	25.7
December	$2,890	32.0%	2,490	10.7

An example should help illustrate how this process works. Joan Smith, the director of the Eastville Soup Kitchen, decides to present information about performance trends in the upcoming newsletter. Ms. Smith selects monthly donations as her major input measure and the total number of meals served per month as her output measure. She produces a table on monthly donations and the number of meals served per month for 2004 (Table 24.1).

Ms. Smith is concerned about the trend in donations. Because the soup kitchen's primary source of funding is individual donations, her ability to meet demand in the spring and summer is hurt by declining donations. Ms. Smith hypothesizes that donations drop off in the spring and summer months because the public assumes that the soup kitchen's workload declines as weather conditions start to improve. She believes that many potential donors may not be aware of the fact that from the late spring and early summer to the end of summer, the soup kitchen serves a large number of children who would normally receive free meals at school.

Ms. Smith believes that presenting this information in the soup kitchen's quarterly newsletter will provide valuable guidance to donors. She intends to highlight the fact that during the spring and summer months in particular, an unfavorable gap exists between donations and the number of meals served. Although the kitchen's workload does decline somewhat in the spring and summer months, the fact that it does not drop off dramatically should help illustrate the point that hunger is not a seasonal phenomenon. The number of meals served only dropped sharply in September as students went back to school. Ms. Smith feels this evidence should help persuade existing and potential donors to make more frequent contributions during the spring and summer months.

In addition to the table, Ms. Smith presents a line graph comparing donation and workload data. Notice that the graph uses percentage changes, rather than the raw

Figure 24.4

Eastville Soup Kitchen Donation and Workload Data

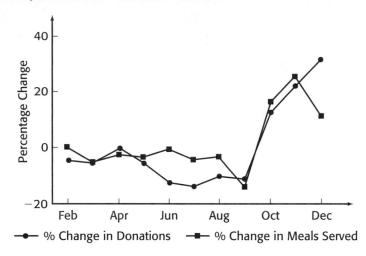

data on donations and the number of meals served. Because the monthly data for donations are always larger than the total number of meals served per month, the line representing donations on the graph would always look much larger than the line representing the number of meals served. Similarly, if the raw data were represented using a bar graph, the bars for donations would always be much higher than the bars for the number of meals served. In both cases, this might give donors the impression that the soup kitchen has more than enough resources to serve its mission. The percentage changes for each variable provide a more accurate picture of the underlying trends.

Having seen the trends for 2004, Ms. Smith establishes a performance target for 2005 of no monthly declines in donations greater than 5%. Because the data for 2004 reveal that donations began to drop off around March, Ms. Smith's strategy is to run a series of public service announcements beginning in late February 2005 to better inform people about the soup kitchen's spring and summer programs.

As this example shows, tracking performance measures over time can provide a manager with a wealth of information useful for planning purposes. You may have noticed that no formal statistical tests for a causal relationship between donations and the number of meals served were presented. Performance reports are usually prepared for outside audiences who have limited familiarity with advanced statistical techniques such as regression analysis. Thorough discussion and analysis of trends are much more important than tests of statistical significance for explaining performance to a general audience. Individual donors, foundations, legislators, and the media are more likely to understand explanations for performance that make intuitively plausible links between inputs and outputs than those relying on elaborate statistical procedures to get the message across.

Table 24.2

Smoke Detector Intervention Program Data, City of Cul-de-Sac

Year	Number of Detectors Installed	Percentage Change	Fire-Related Hospitalizations	Percentage Change
1998	1,100		359	
1999	1,140	3.6	341	−5.0
2000	1,200	5.3	322	−5.6
2001	1,219	1.6	305	−5.3
2002	1,190	−2.4	281	−7.9
2003	1,271	6.8	253	−9.9

$$\mu = -6.74$$

In the next example, we will illustrate what a performance evaluation using outcome data might look like. Martha Jones is the chief of the Fire Department for the city of Cul-de-Sac. Chief Jones has been informed that due to a tight fiscal environment, the state has decided to phase out funding for the Smoke Detector Intervention Program. This program allows the fire department to install free smoke detectors and replace batteries in existing smoke detectors in homes across the city. Chief Jones believes that if she and other fire department chiefs provide state officials with information about how successful this program has been, these officials may reconsider their decision.

The chief selects the number of smoke detectors installed and batteries replaced as her output indicator. To make a convincing case to state officials, she feels that data on program outcomes are necessary as well. The goal of the smoke detector program is protecting the lives of citizens. The chief measures this outcome by collecting data on the number of fires in dwellings without a working smoke detector where one or more residents were hospitalized. Because the size of the state grant has remained at $10,000 for each of the past 5 years, Chief Jones only includes program outputs and outcomes in the table (see Table 24.2).

Chief Jones is not overly concerned about the rate of change in the number of detectors installed per year, because the data reveal that outputs dropped slightly for only one of the five time periods. The bounce-back in program activity from 2002 to 2003 is evidence that demand for the program is still strong (see Figure 24.5).

The chief is far more interested in the outcome data, because they reveal a consistent decline in hospitalizations involving residents who live in homes with malfunctioning smoke detectors or no smoke detectors. The average annual decline in hospitalizations for the 6-year time period was 6.74%. The installation and repair of thousands of smoke detectors seem to be improving public safety. Chief Jones knows that she will have to discuss other factors, such as the severity of particular fires and the total number of fires each year, in explaining these results. However, because the outcome measure pertains to the specific subset of fires that are most logically linked to the need for the smoke detector program, she believes she can make a strong case to state officials.

Figure 24.5

City of Cul-de-Sac Fire Department Program Results

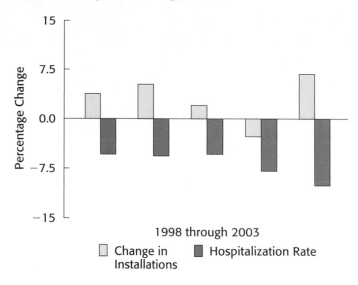

1998 through 2003

☐ Change in Installations   ■ Hospitalization Rate

Reliability Issues in Measuring Performance Over Time

Reliability is a major concern when tracking trends in performance measures. Changing the way an output or outcome indicator is measured can lead to significant reliability problems if you plan to compare performance measures over time. If you consistently measured an indicator the same way for many time periods but then decide to change the way it is measured, data for the old and new versions of the indicator may not be directly comparable.

For example, if a state includes special education students in calculating student pass rates on standardized reading skills exams for 10 years but decides to exclude special education students from the calculations for the current year, the measurement of the indicator is not consistent over time. As another example, a police department that has for years counted rental car thefts as part of a larger "auto theft" category stops including rental cart thefts and, instead, recategorizes them as instances of "credit card fraud." Although the reported number of auto thefts would decline as a result, we cannot be sure about the actual rate of thefts.

Output and outcome measures are sometimes changed solely to boost apparent performance and not because the existing definitions were somehow flawed. Even in cases where there are valid reasons for changing how an indicator is measured over time, confusion and controversy arise when researchers fail to make clear that such changes have taken place. Have pass rates suddenly improved because students are performing better, or have they improved because a subset of test takers was suddenly excluded from the calculations? Have auto theft rates suddenly dropped because of improved policing or because the definition of auto theft has changed? It is critical to know whether changes in the underlying trends performance indicators display are the result of changes in measurement or meaningful changes in performance.

Analyzing trends is a central part of performance measurement. You should always be attentive to any changes in how performance indicators have been measured over time. Problems in consistency can be overcome if information is provided on how older data can be recoded to fit the new measuring scheme, or vice versa. Changing how an output or outcome measure is defined to clarify or enhance the understanding of performance is perfectly acceptable. Changing a performance measure to obscure poor performance is not.

Benchmarking

Trend analysis focuses mainly on measuring performance data for an individual organization over time. The logic of benchmarking is that an organization can gain a better understanding of its own performance by comparing itself to similar organizations. The following examples illustrate the logic of benchmarking:

> A police department for a city of 500,000 residents compares its crime clearance rate to those of police departments in 10 similarly sized cities.

> A sanitation department compares its average cost for collecting a ton of trash to cost data for five other municipal sanitation departments within the county.

> A drug treatment center compares its success rate in treating patients to those of three other drug treatment facilities across the state.

> A YMCA branch compares its customer satisfaction rates to those of 10 other branch locations across the state.

Comparative performance data allow an organization to determine how well it is doing relative to its peers. Once top performers have been identified, organizations with performance problems can study the strategies used by their more successful peers and adopt similar strategies themselves. The term *best practices* is often used in conjunction with benchmarking because the process can provide organizations with strategies that can lead to better performance. The steps involved in the benchmarking process are as follows:

Step 1: Select the output or outcome measure to be used as a benchmark. Benchmarking is not feasible if data for a performance measure are unavailable for the organizations in the peer group. Data availability issues should be examined prior to selecting the measures to be used as benchmarks.

Because the results obtained from benchmarking are often presented to external audiences, benchmarks should be defined in formats that are easily understood. For example, an aggregate total such as total expenditures in millions of dollars is more difficult to interpret than average expenditures per person.

Descriptive statistics are useful in benchmarking because oftentimes, we want to know how close or far values for a performance indicator are from a desired value. Averages and standard deviations convey summary information about performance in ways that most people understand.

Step 2: Select a peer group of organizations. You should always be prepared to explain why particular organizations have been chosen. Benchmarking is about making comparisons, so the peer group should consist of similar organizations. For example, a police department in a rural Illinois town of 5,000 people would not want to benchmark its performance against that of the police department in the city of Chicago, because the scale and nature of policing in a large metropolitan area is much different than it is in a small rural town. Similarly, a homeless shelter that handles 25,000 clients a year might have unique scale advantages in purchasing food and supplies over a shelter that only serves 2,500 people a year. If the circumstances of different organizations vary dramatically, it can be difficult to make valid comparisons.

Some examples of criteria that can be used to select peer organizations include the number of employees (such as organizations with 1,000 employees or more), size in dollars (cities with annual budgets between $10 and $15 million), function (human services), and location (urban, suburban, or rural).

Step 3: Collect the benchmark data for each member in the peer group. You may need to consult a variety of sources to obtain information about outputs, outcomes, and organizational characteristics. Budgets and Comprehensive Annual Financial Reports (CAFRs) provide detailed information about the activities of city and county governments. References such as the *Statistical Abstract of the United States,* the *Book of the States,* and the *Municipal Yearbook* provide a wide variety of data useful for benchmarking purposes. Detailed information on the financial performance of nonprofit organizations can be obtained from annual reports and IRS Form 990 returns.

Step 4: Assess where your organization ranks in the peer group. The data for each member of the peer group should be summarized and displayed in a table. Comparing your organization's score to the average score for the peer group can be helpful.

Step 5: Determine what steps (if any) should be taken to correct performance deficiencies. Look to better-performing peers for strategies that might help improve performance.

Benchmarking is best illustrated with an example. A group called Citizens against Taxing and Spending (CATS) has gone before the media to complain about the "bloated bureaucracy" in the city of Dorchester, Michigan. The group feels that the city employs too many people compared to similar cities in the area.

Mayor Sandra Jackson believes that CATS's claims are exaggerated and that staffing levels in Dorchester are quite reasonable. She decides to benchmark Dorchester against nearby cities using the number of government employees for every 1,000 citizens as the performance measure.

The mayor uses two criteria in choosing the other cities for comparison: population and size in square miles. Mayor Jackson decides that the population of each city should be within 10% above or below 52,000, the population of Dorchester. The size

Table 24.3

Comparison of Government Employees per 1,000 Residents for Five Cities

City	Number of Residents	Number of City Employees	Employees per 1,000
Auburn Park	49,000	298	6.08
Nova City	51,000	280	5.49
Dorchester	**52,000**	**290**	**5.58**
Royal Pine	53,900	299	5.55
Southville	55,000	340	6.18

Average employees per 1,000 residents for cities in peer group = 5.78

of the city also must be within 10% of Dorchester's 42.5 square miles, since geographic size has a major impact on the number of police and fire employees a city needs.

The mayor's assistant reviews the annual budgets and CAFRs for 12 nearby cities and finds 4 that meet the above criteria. Data on the number of employees were also obtained from each city's annual budget.

The assistant divides the number of employees by the total residents for Dorchester and obtains a result of .0056. He sees nothing wrong with presenting the results in terms of the number of employees per resident, but the mayor explains that .0056 employees per resident is not a number the average citizen is likely to find very meaningful. He agrees and multiplies the results for all cities by 1000 to facilitate interpretation. The results are displayed in Table 24.3.

The mayor is pleased with the results because they support the view that Dorchester is not that much different than nearby cities when it comes to the ratio of city employees to residents. In fact, Dorchester is slightly below the average of 5.78 employees per 1000 residents for cities in the peer group (see Figure 24.6). The mayor's assistant comments that "it looks like CATS has been declawed," but the mayor expects CATS to raise other questions. She begins thinking about additional benchmarks that would help illustrate how fiscally responsible her administration has been.

Causality Issues in Explaining Performance

The purpose of trend analysis and benchmarking techniques is to identify potential performance problems. Once problems are discovered, the underlying causes responsible for performance deficiencies need to be explored. Internal factors are usually more controllable than external factors. Internal factors include organizational policies and strategies that are under the control of management. For example, if performance is suffering because of issues with staffing patterns, staff can be reassigned to programs or projects that require more attention. Funds could also be allocated differently to meet more pressing needs.

External factors are more difficult to adjust because government and nonprofit organizations sometimes have little control over the number of cases they process or

Figure 24.6

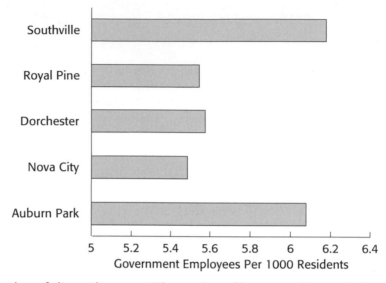

Results for Government Employee Benchmarking Exercise

Government Employees Per 1000 Residents

the number of clients they serve. The number of hours a public works department spends on snow plowing will vary from year to year depending on the severity of weather conditions. Exceeding spending ceilings is largely uncontrollable if the number of snowstorms is unusually high for a particular year. If recidivism rates increase, it may be the result of parole officers being assigned more cases than they can adequately handle. Losses in personnel or funding due to the actions of political officials are largely out of a government agency's control. In the case of nonprofit organizations, conditions imposed on the use of funds by grantors may reduce the flexibility managers have to meet desired goals. Or, a sharp rise in immigration may exacerbate the demand for nonprofit social services, such as housing and job training.

The solutions for fixing performance problems are not always quick and easy, but it helps if a manager knows whether variations in a key performance measure are due more to internal or external factors. Taking corrective action may be easier if the problem is largely the result of internal factors under the control of management. Improving performance when outside forces are responsible is a more difficult task. Poor performance due to factors outside of an organization's control may actually help make the case that more resources are needed by the agency to achieve desired goals.

Chapter Summary

Government and nonprofit managers must know how to communicate with outside audiences. Performance measurement techniques provide organizations with the tools that are necessary for effective communication. There is not one "right" way to present performance data. Analysts may have differing opinions about how performance data should be presented, but the overriding concern is to make sure that the information is presented in a fair, accurate—and comprehensible—manner.

Managers must be aware of validity issues when measuring performance. Variations in performance can only be understood when inputs, outputs, and outcomes are identified. Outputs or workload measures are not necessarily the same as outcomes. Managers need to be clear on whether they are really measuring outcomes or simply outputs.

Graphical presentations, trend analysis, and benchmarking are three commonly used techniques for summarizing performance data. Managers need to understand these techniques in order to describe their agencies' performance effectively to outside audiences.

Problems

24.1 The finance director for North Dakota has established a toll-free tax assistance helpline due to the large number of complaints citizens have made about the complexity of the state's income tax forms. To determine the effectiveness of the tax assistance program, she collects a random sample of 500 tax forms early in the tax season.

Usage is coded as a dummy variable where 1 = filer used helpline and 0 = filer did not use helpline. Error is coded as a dummy variable where 1 = no errors found on tax return and 0 = one or more errors found on tax return. The director generates the following contingency table:

Error Found on Tax Return	Used Tax Assistance Helpline	
	No	Yes
No	139	190
Yes	93	78

Present the research and null hypotheses, percentage the table, and calculate chi-square. What can you tell the director about the effect the tax assistance helpline is having on error rates?

24.2 Tex Anderson has just been appointed director of the Roads Department in Gak, Texas. He knows that the last director was "urged to explore other career opportunities" due to performance problems in the department. The former director never collected data on performance, frequently exceeded spending ceilings, and rarely followed up on citizen complaints. Tex asks his staff to come up with performance measures for the following key program areas:

Minor Street Repairs and Pothole Patching

Street Signage and Traffic Light Repair

Animal Carcass Removal

Tex tells his staff that the mayor will "chew him up and spit him out like a bad piece of brisket" if performance does not improve. Help Tex develop two output indicators and two outcome indicators for each of these programs.

24.3 The chief of fiscal services for Piney Hills, North Carolina, has data on unreserved fund balances from 1998 through 2004. Unreserved fund balances are a key measure of financial performance because they measure the capability of a government to keep spending under control and build up reserves for emergencies or revenue shortfalls.

In preparing financial data for an upcoming debt review by a major debt ratings agency, the chief asks you to present a summary table showing the annual rate of change in general fund balances. She also asks you to calculate the average annual rate of change in fund balances from 1998 through 2004. The end of fiscal year data on fund balances (in millions of dollars) appear in the following table:

Year	General Fund Balance	Percentage Change in Fund Balances
1998	$9,067	
1999	$9,688	
2000	$10,090	
2001	$10,445	
2002	$11,140	
2003	$11,490	

The chief feels that an average annual increase in fund balance of 5% for the time period in question would be very impressive. What can you tell the chief about her target goal?

24.4 The head of economic development for Nutria Haven, Louisiana, has been criticized by the mayor for doing too little to stimulate business activity. The mayor claims that fluctuations in the number of building permits each year point to a pattern of incompetence in the economic development office. The head of economic development has countered that variations in business activity are largely the result of changes in the economy.

To see whose viewpoint is more accurate, the chief fiscal analyst regresses the number of building permits for each of the last ten years on two variables. Because the mayor has argued that the office has always had the resources needed to stimulate business activity, he selects the annual budget for the economic development office (X_1, in millions of dollars) as one independent variable. To see whether external forces are responsible, he selects the average prime lending rate for each year (X_2) as the second independent variable, because fluctuations in interest rates are known to affect business activity. He obtains the following results in the regression analysis:

$$\hat{Y} = 2,659 - .00003X_1 - 195X_2$$

$$s_{b_1} = .00004 \quad S_{b_2} = 77.95 \quad R^2 = .82 \quad \text{Adj. } R^2 = .76$$

Interpret the slopes, intercept, R^2, and adjusted R^2. Based on the regression results, are variations in performance due more to internal factors under the control of the economic development director or external factors beyond his control?

24.5 A major foundation has asked the Woodbridge Domestic Abuse Shelter to send a summary report on how the foundation's grant money is being spent. This report will be used to evaluate a pending grant proposal for the upcoming fiscal year. The director of the shelter is not sure whether the foundation wants output or outcome data, but she assumes she will need to provide measures for both. Since the current grant is restricted to patient counseling and housing needs, the director focuses her attention on these two areas. Help the director by answering the following questions:

(a) Which variables would you select as output measures?

(b) Which variables would you choose as outcome measures?

(c) Since the summary evaluation plays a key role in the foundation's evaluation of the pending grant proposal, would you place more emphasis on presenting output or outcome measures in summarizing performance? Explain.

24.6 The beleaguered mayor of Dorchester, Michigan, whom you met earlier, has now received complaints about the city's "outrageously high" levels of general obligation debt (debt backed by the full faith and credit of the city). She asks her assistant to obtain data on the dollar amount of outstanding general obligation debt for four nearby cities so she can benchmark Dorchester's debt burden. The assistant produces the following table:

City	Debt	Population
Auburn Park	$38,665,200	49,000
Nova City	$36,464,000	51,000
Dorchester	$41,801,025	52,000
Royal Pine	$44,856,200	53,900
Southville	$45,485,175	55,000

Upon reviewing the table, the mayor comments, "If the numbers speak for themselves, this must be a foreign language." She tells her assistant that few people will understand the meaning of the table if they are forced to interpret all of these large numbers. She asks her assistant to calculate one summary benchmark measure using both the data on debt and population.

(a) Create a summary measure that is based on both the total debt and population data. What is the common sense interpretation of the measure? How does Dorchester compare to the other cities on this measure?

(b) The mayor asks her assistant to create a graph or chart summarizing the results based on the new measure. What would be a good graphical format for presenting the findings on the new measure?

24.7   What are some ways a police department could assess progress toward important goals through the use of performance measures? Specifically, come up with performance measures for the following areas:

Preventing crime

Promoting good relations with citizens

Controlling abusive policing tactics

Explain the rationale underlying your choice of measures. Be sure to explain whether your performance measures are outputs or outcomes.

24.8   John Patrick Vannelli, the mayor of Snowy Bluffs, Florida, is concerned about the number of complaints his office has received concerning service at the public library. Most of the complaints center on the long wait times and slow service when checking out books. The director of the library has been asked to explain why complaints are increasing. He argues that the trend in complaints is due to the continued growth in the number of patrons using library services, coupled with budget constraints that prevent him from hiring more employees. The data on the number of complaints received and patrons served for the last 10 quarters appear below:

	Number of Complaints	Number of Patrons Served
2002		
Q1	26	1,141
Q2	25	1,130
Q3	28	1,205
Q4	35	1,190
2003		
Q1	33	1,170
Q2	37	1,240
Q3	41	1,251
Q4	44	1,358
2004		
Q1	45	1,404
Q2	50	1,490

(a) Because the highest number of patrons served per quarter is below 1,500, the director feels that the number of complaints per 100 patrons each quarter is a reasonable way to present the data. Assist the director by performing the calculations and tabulating the results.

(b) Based on the results, which argument—if either—do the data support?

24.9   The board of directors of Earth Rocks!, a nonprofit organization focused on environmental protection, hypothesizes that individuals are more likely to donate if they see evidence that their donations are used primarily for program activities, rather than administrative and fundraising costs. To get a

sense of how its own cost structure compares to other groups, the board decides to benchmark the financial performance of Earth Rocks! against several
other environmental organizations. The data for Earth Rocks! and the other
environmental organizations appear below:

	Program Expenditures	Fund-raising Costs	Administrative Costs	Total Costs
Earth Rocks!	$374,900	$98,000	$121,400	$594,300
Weed Lovers	$421,000	$104,300	$98,350	$623,650
Flora and Fauna	$353,400	$97,600	$71,840	$522,840
Leave It Be	$501,900	$89,000	$109,750	$700,650
Nature's Gift	$455,470	$71,000	$ 82,450	$608,920

Use these data to benchmark Earth Rocks! against the other environmental
organizations. How does Earth Rocks! compare to the other environmental
groups?

24.10   The mission statement of the Teen Crisis Center reads:

"The mission of the Teen Crisis Center is to assist troubled youth
through counseling and educational programs designed to make positive
changes in their lives. We strive to help teens cope with legal, medical, and
emotional difficulties."

The director of the Teen Crisis Center knows that foundations and
donors will want to see evidence regarding the extent to which the goals laid
out in the mission statement are being met. Provide several performance
measures that would help the director track the center's progress.

CHAPTER 25

Decision Theory

A ccording to Nobel prize–winning economist Herbert Simon, the essence of management is decision making. Managers must make decisions on how to organize an office, how to evaluate a program, the necessary skills needed in an agency position, how to motivate employees, and numerous other tasks in a public or nonprofit organization. A large body of literature has sprouted around the idea of management as decision making. This chapter overviews decision theory and its uses for public and nonprofit managers. Many of the approaches outlined in this chapter can be used to solve problems found in other chapters.

The Rational Decision-Making Model

An ideal type of decision making has surfaced in a variety of management areas. Planning, program evaluation, performance appraisal, and budgeting are often structured to meet the ideal, **rational decision-making** goal. Many management theorists argue that good managers attempt to attain this ideal decision-making pattern. Although this position is not without challenge, rational decision making should be part of every manager's skills.

There are five steps in rational decision making:

Step 1: Identify the problem. Although this first step appears simple, in many situations it is not. The U.S. Army, for example, has noted increased disciplinary problems, including drug usage, among its troops. The immediate problem is discipline, but the underlying problem may be something else. Inadequate training, lack of meaningful work assignments, absence of effective supervision, inadequate leadership, or recruitment problems generated by the volunteer army may be the real problem. Failure to identify the problem correctly may lead to a poor decision. If inadequate training is the problem and it results in less discipline, increasing punishments may have no impact on the discipline of troops. One secret of good management is to be able to diagnose problems correctly.

Step 2: Specify goals and objectives. Given a specific problem, exactly what does the organization wish to achieve? A state welfare office may have a problem if its payments are too high given the agency's resources. How the agency responds to this problem depends on its goals. If the goal is simply to lower costs, then word can be passed to deny more claims. If the goal is to restrict the amount of waste, control mechanisms to catch fraud could be implemented. If the goal is to make welfare recipients self-sufficient, then providing recipients with needed job skills might be an alternative. Without carefully specified goals, the rational decision-making model cannot function.

Specifying goals, although it seems a rational and commonsense thing to do, is not without its problems. First, whenever more than one person must accept a goal (normally the case in a public organization), agreement on goals becomes problematic. An individual's perception of agency goals will be a function of that person's role in the organization and that person's individual values and preferences. City planners, for example, may feel that the goal of an urban renewal project is to beautify the city. The chief fiscal officer may see the project as a way to increase the city's tax base. The community development director may see the project as a means of increasing employment opportunities through construction jobs. The public works head may see the project's goal as providing city government office space. These and numerous other goals can logically be offered as the goal of an urban renewal project. Without agreement on the goal of the project, decision making becomes difficult.

Second, as illustrated before, any one project or agency can have numerous goals. Even so simple a task as refuse collection can have several goals. Refuse is collected to avoid health problems that occur when garbage sits in alleys. Refuse collection also has cost goals; city managers would like to collect trash as cheaply as possible. Refuse collection has service goals; city residents may want garbage collected twice a week so that it does not pile up in yards. Multiple objectives mean several goals must be sought simultaneously, and this restriction creates problems for decision makers.

Third, where multiple goals exist, some are bound to conflict. In our example of urban renewal, maximizing employment opportunities may well conflict with the goal of holding down costs. Increasing the city's tax base conflicts with increasing the available city government office space. If conflicts between goals cannot be resolved, rational decision making is not possible.

Fourth, goal expression raises the specter of **suboptimization.** A single subunit of an agency maximizing its goals or a single agency of government maximizing its goals may produce results detrimental to the overall organization's goals. An audit division, for example, that is overzealous in its effort to prevent the waste of taxpayers' money may place such restrictions on operating agencies that the agencies spend more time responding to fiscal control than they spend delivering services. Although this situation may be rational for the audit agency, it is not rational from a governmentwide perspective. Similarly, a volunteer coordinator for a nonprofit organization might recruit more volunteers than the organization can use.

Step 3: Specify all alternatives available to attain the goals. Once goals have been established, the decision maker must then specify all the alternative options that he or she has to attain the goals. This does not mean the decision maker must list every alternative no matter how ridiculous; rather, some judgment is exercised to limit the alternatives considered to those that are politically and managerially feasible. The Florida State director of welfare, for example, when faced with the goal of reducing welfare costs, does not consider the alternative of simply forcing welfare recipients to move to another state.

Step 4: Evaluate the alternatives in light of the goals. Each alternative is examined to see whether it will attain the goals in question. All alternatives capable of attaining the ends in question are then compared to determine which alternative is the most likely to achieve the goals. At this stage of decision making, a variety of analytical tools can be used to contrast alternatives. Cost-benefit analysis, in which program costs are contrasted with program benefits, is the favorite of many program evaluators. Direct and indirect, as well as present and future, costs and benefits must be included. Creative analysis is needed to include the unanticipated second-order costs and benefits (a successful drug rehabilitation program, for example, will reduce the crime rate for robbery and burglary). Other offshoots of cost-benefit analysis, including system analysis, risk analysis, and feasibility analysis, are also used.

The evaluation of alternatives need not be a sophisticated mathematical assessment. Alternatives may be judged on the basis of past experience, political information, and so on. In fact, these **extrarational analysis** methods of analyzing options are often the only methods available to the decision maker. Even when sophisticated methods of analysis exist, the manager must determine how realistic the evaluation models are. As many Defense Department officials have learned from sad experience, a manager cannot defend a failure by blaming a cost-benefit model (at least not more than once).*

Step 5: Select the optimal alternative. From the alternatives considered in Step 4, the best alternative in terms of the goals established should be selected and then implemented. The last step is crucial; a brilliant decision that is not implemented is worse than no decision at all. At least if there is no decision, the agency personnel did not waste their time in a futile exercise.

A Brief Critique

The rational decision model has been heavily criticized as an inaccurate description of how decisions are made. Herbert Simon, for example, argues that decision makers "satisfice" rather than maximize. When faced with a problem, decision makers do not specify goals or list all the alternatives. Rather, they consider one or two alternatives that are not too different from current agency policy. If one alternative appears to satisfactorily solve the problem, it is implemented. If the alternative does not yield satisfactory utility, a few more alternatives are examined.

Simon's **satisficing** model and other incremental models probably do portray decision making as it actually occurs in many organizations. In many circumstances in which the benefits of two alternatives do not differ greatly, the decision costs of the rational model are not justified. In other situations, however, in which sufficient information is available to the decision maker, the rational model is a useful tool for the manager. The task of the manager is to determine whether a problem has the characteristics that permit the application of the rational model and to use this model where appropriate.

Decision Making under Certainty

Any important variables that affect the outcome of a decision but are not under the control of the decision maker are **states of nature** (the conditions that exist when a decision is made). The major variation in decision theory concerns the decision maker's knowledge about the various possible states of nature. When the states of nature are known before the decision is made, a state of **certainty** exists. When states of nature are unknown but can be assigned probabilities, decision making is under **risk.** When probabilities cannot be assigned, decision making under **uncertainty** is required.

---

*A book as long as this one should have at least one lengthy footnote, and this is it. Some management theorists will be offended by our model of rational decision making because we have modified it to fit the real world. Such theorists would require the rational decision maker to analyze all possible costs and benefits for all possible alternatives. Management theorists who do this set up a straw man that is easily demolished as unrealistic. See Herbert Simon, *Administrative Behavior* (New York: Free Press, 1947) or David Braybrooke and Charles Lindblom, *A Strategy of Decision* (New York: Free Press, 1970). We believe that in many management decisions under certainty, the rational model is appropriate. In many decisions under risk, it is a useful model.

Decision making under certainty means that the decision maker's knowledge of the environment is complete, the problem is clearly identified, and goals are uniformly accepted and explicitly defined. Under such conditions, one best alternative exists that will attain the goals in question.

An example will illustrate the ideas. The Aberdeen Fire Department has two fire stations—one on the north side of town and one on the south side. When a fire call comes in, the dispatcher must decide whether to send a fire truck from the north-side station or the south-side station. The informal decision rule has been that any fire call north of the railroad tracks will be answered by the north-side station. The south-side station handles all other calls.

The goal of the Aberdeen Fire Department is to respond to fire calls as quickly as possible (this will help it attain a goal of minimum fire losses). For every point in the city, two alternatives exist: dispatch from the north-side station or dispatch from the south-side station. Because traffic congestion has increased around the south-side station, trucks from the north-side station may be able to reach some locations in the southwest part of town faster than could the south-side trucks.

The fire chief authorizes a series of practice runs to determine which station can respond faster to various parts of the city. After numerous runs, the results are transferred to a map. A line is drawn that divides the city into two parts—a part from which the north-side station can respond faster and a part from which the south-side station can respond faster. The dispatcher's decision rules are changed so that any call north of the dividing line is assigned to the north-side station and vice versa. (In larger cities, dispatchers use an alphabetized Rolodex of street names. The Rolodex lists the station to be used plus all backup stations.)

Note the characteristics of the Aberdeen Fire Department problem. First, the goal was clear and unambiguous—to dispatch fire trucks so that they reach the scene of the fire as fast as possible. Second, only a limited number of alternatives were available (in this case, two). Third, each alternative could be directly evaluated in terms of the goal. Fourth, the states of nature were certain. Once a fire call is received, its location in the city can be pinpointed. Under such conditions of certainty, a rational decision model is appropriate. (An entire class of such problems, called linear programming problems, are discussed in Chapter 26.)

Decision Making under Risk

A decision under risk exists when the decision maker cannot tell before a decision is made exactly what the state of nature is. The decision maker can, on the basis of logic or past experience, assign probabilities to the various states of nature. Decision making under risk is best illustrated with an example.

The city of Reginald, Ohio, must choose between one of three types of employment programs. The effectiveness of each program depends on the level of unemployment (the state of nature). What are the city's options?

Option 1:   Do nothing. Reginald can simply ignore any unemployment problems and hope that the marketplace will correct any problems. Option 1 works best if unemployment is low since the city will not spend any funds. If unemployment reaches moderate levels (5% to 9%), then costs to Reginald in terms of countercyclical aid and political unrest will be moderate. If unemployment is high (greater than 9%), Option 1 becomes a disaster, with reduced demand for goods catapulting the Reginald area into a major recession.

Option 2: Operate a job placement center to locate jobs for persons currently out of work. Option 2 incurs minor fixed costs if unemployment is low, but returns major benefits where unemployment is moderate (5% to 9%). Under moderate unemployment the service still has sufficient jobs to place most temporarily out-of-work persons. If unemployment is high, however, the placement program will be inadequate.

Option 3: Implement a job training program. If unemployment is less than 5%, this program's high fixed costs make it an unattractive alternative. Under moderate unemployment (5% to 9%), the program incurs some minor costs. The job training program works best under conditions of high unemployment because it absorbs surplus labor and alters the work force's skills.

Reginald's choice of employment programs can be analyzed as a decision under risk. To do so, the following steps must be implemented.

Step 1: Set up a **decision table.** Place each of the states of nature (in this case low, moderate, and high unemployment) across the top of the table. Note that the states of nature must cover all conceivable possibilities. Place each of the decision options down the left side of the table. The decision table of Table 25.1 results.

Table 25.1

Decision Table for Reginald, Ohio

Decision Options	Unemployment		
	Low	Moderate	High
Do nothing			
Placement			
Job training			

Step 2: Calculate the **payoff** to the city for each cell in the decision table. That is, what is the cost or benefit to Reginald if unemployment is low and the city does nothing? What is the cost to the city if unemployment is low and the city runs a placement service? Payoffs may be calculated in a variety of ways. The manager may assign payoffs based on past experience, cost-benefit calculations can be done for each option, and so on. The mayor of Reginald,

Joyce Caruthers, asks Thomas Malthus, a labor economist at Reginald State University, to calculate the costs and benefits for each cell. Professor Malthus turns the project over to his graduate student, who produces the costs and benefits shown in Table 25.2 (where K = $1,000).

Table 25.2

Costs and Benefits for Reginald

Decision Options	Unemployment		
	Low	Moderate	High
Do nothing	$20K	−$5K	−$120K
Placement	−$10K	$50K	−$30K
Job training	−$110K	$10K	$140K

To interpret this table, one merely assigns the value listed to the decision option given a certain state of nature. For example, if unemployment is high and the city does nothing, the cost to the city will be $120,000.

Step 3: Determine the probability that each state of nature will occur; that is, for the period that the decision will cover, what is the probability of low unemployment (less than 5%), moderate unemployment (5% to 9%), or high unemployment (greater than 9%)? Mayor Caruthers asks Calvin Kent, a local economics consultant, to forecast the probability of low, moderate, or high unemployment. Kent predicts a .2 probability of low unemployment, a .3 probability of moderate unemployment, and a .5 probability of high unemployment. These figures are placed in the table next to the states of nature (see Table 25.3).

Table 25.3

Probabilities for States of Nature

Decision Options	Unemployment		
	Low (.2)	Moderate (.3)	High (.5)
Do nothing	$20K	−$5K	−$120K
Placement	−$10K	$50K	−$30K
Job training	−$110K	$10K	$140K

Step 4: Calculate the expected value for each decision option. The **expected value** of any choice (decision option) is the sum of all the values that can be attained times the probability that each of the values will be attained; that is,

$$EV = \sum P_i V_i$$

where EV is a choice's expected value, V is the value that can be attained, the P is the probability associated with each of the values. Expected values were introduced earlier, in Chapter 7, in relation to probability.

To illustrate, some of the authors of this text are avid joggers who are known to consume a barley-based beverage (in fact, we were once charged with the crime of jogging only to make the beverage taste better). After jogging, both authors retire to a local establishment and drink several beverages. One author proposes that each day they flip a coin. If it comes up heads, he will buy a drink for both authors (a cost of $3.20); if it is tails, the other author will buy the refreshments. What is the expected value of this choice? It is the probability that a person will buy the drinks (.5 if the coin is unbiased) times the cost of that option ($3.20) plus the probability that the same person will buy no drinks (.5) times the cost of that option ($0), or

$$EV = (\$3.20 \times .5) + (\$0 \times .5) = \$1.60 + \$0 = \$1.60$$

The expected value of this choice is $1.60.

Returning to our Reginald problem, we see that the expected value of doing nothing (Option 1) is the sum of the products of each of the three payoffs associated with this option times their respective probabilities. In other words, the value of doing nothing is equal to $20,000 if unemployment is low, $-$5,000 if unemployment is moderate, and $-$120,000 if unemployment is high. Because the respective probabilities of each of these states of nature are .2, .3, and .5, the expected value of doing nothing is

$$EV = (.2 \times \$20,000) + (.3 \times -\$5,000) + (.5 \times -\$120,000)$$
$$= \$4,000 + (-\$1,500) + (-\$60,000) = -\$57,500$$

The expected value of doing nothing is a loss of $57,500.

The expected value for Option 2, the placement option, is as follows:

$$EV = (.2 \times -\$10,000) + (.3 \times \$50,000) + (.5 \times -\$30,000)$$
$$= -\$2,000 + (+\$15,000) + (-\$15,000) = -\$2,000$$

Notice that the probabilities for the states of nature remain the same; only the values associated with each state change.

For the third option, the training program, the expected value is

$$EV = (.2 \times -\$110,000) + (.3 \times \$10,000) + (.5 \times \$140,000)$$
$$= -\$22,000 + \$3,000 + \$70,000 = \$51,000$$

Mayor Caruthers's decision should be obvious. The expected value of doing nothing is a loss of $57,500. The expected value of placement is a loss of $2,000, and the expected value of job training is a benefit of $51,000. The mayor selects the job training program.

For using this procedure, we should provide a caveat: Decision making under risk makes some assumptions that may not be attractive to decision makers. First, it assumes that the decision maker has the same attitude toward risk regardless of the size of benefit involved. The expected value of a decision with a .25 probability of a $10,000 loss is the same as the expected value of a decision with a .0025 probability of a $1 million loss. A manager might well be willing to take the first risk yet find the second one unacceptable. Decision theory in the form presented earlier cannot incorporate this willingness to take risks. Second, the model assumes that expected value covers all the values the decision maker wants to maximize. A public sector decision maker may want to incorporate different values. If Milton Friedman were mayor of Reginald, he might wish to err on the side of less government and do nothing—or at most run only a placement program. Other public managers might echo Franklin Roosevelt's sentiments when he conceded that his policies might be wrong but that it was better to try and fail than not to try at all. Both the amount of risk tolerated and the additional values considered are political criteria. These criteria, in addition to the results of the decision table, must be considered by public managers and policy analysts.

The Value of Perfect Information

Mayor Caruthers is visited by J. Barringford Tipton of Chaste Econometrics, a well-known economic forecasting firm. Tipton tells Caruthers that Chaste can accurately forecast the unemployment rate in Reginald for the next year. Caruthers is enthused until Tipton tells her that the forecast will cost Reginald $25,000. Should Caruthers hire Chaste to forecast for her?

Another way of asking this question is to ask, What is the value of **perfect information?** (Perfect information means that you can specify the exact state of nature in advance.) Without any information concerning the states of nature (except their probabilities), Caruthers selected Option 3, the job training program, with a value of $51,000. This figure needs to be compared with the expected value if the city had perfect information.

Refer to the payoff table, Table 25.4. If the city knew that unemployment would be low, it would do nothing and reap a benefit of $20,000. Because low unemployment will occur 20% of the time, the expected value of this occurrence is $4,000 ($20,000 × .2). If the city knows that unemployment will be moderate, the best decision would be a placement program with a payoff of $50,000. Because moderate unemployment will occur 30% of the time, the expected value of this occurrence is

Table 25.4

Probabilities for States of Nature

Decision Options	Unemployment		
	Low (.2)	Moderate (.3)	High (.5)
Do nothing	$20K	−$5K	−$120K
Placement	−$10K	$50K	−$30K
Job training	−$110K	$10K	$140K

$15,000. Finally, if the city knew that unemployment would be high, it would run a job training program and receive $140,000 in benefits. Discounting this figure by its probability (.5) yields an expected value of $70,000. The expected value of decisions based on perfect information is the sum of all three payoffs:

$$(.2 \times \$20{,}000) + (.3 \times \$50{,}000) + (.5 \times \$140{,}000)$$
$$= \$4{,}000 + \$15{,}000 + \$70{,}000 = \$89{,}000$$

With perfect information, the city could expect a long-run benefit of $89,000 every time this decision was made. Comparing this with the next best alternative (selecting Option 3 without perfect information), the city's payoff is $89,000 versus $51,000. The difference ($38,000) is the value of perfect information. In other words, Reginald should purchase the forecast because its cost ($25,000) is less than its value ($38,000).

Decision Making under Risk: Decision Trees

Many times decision making under risk becomes far more complicated than indicated by the simple tables presented up to now. A decision maker will have several decisions to make in a variety of states of nature. In special circumstances, these states of nature are determined by other factors. Under complex conditions, decision analysts often represent decisions with **decision trees** rather than with a simple payoff table. One such tree is shown in Figure 25.1.

Consider the strategic possibilities of the United States in the Cold War era of the late 1970s and early 1980s. The example illustrates how useful the analysis of decision trees can be.

The decision facing the analyst in the question represented in Figure 25.1 is whether to deploy the MX missile (a mobile U.S. strategic missile). The initial decision point on the far left is the deployment decision. Any decision that the decision maker can resolve is referred to as a **decision node** and is designated with a box. Sometime after the United States decides whether to deploy the MX, the Soviets will decide whether to deploy their Backfire bomber (a tactical bomber with strategic capabilities). Because this decision cannot be controlled by the United States, it is designated as a **chance node** and is represented by a circle on the decision tree. For every chance event (or state of nature), a probability is listed. These probability estimates were made by national security analysts based on the information that they have at their disposal. Note that the probability that the Soviets will deploy the Backfire bomber is .7 if the United States deploys the MX missile and .4 if the United States does not deploy the MX.

After the Soviet decision has been made about deploying the Backfire bomber, the United States must decide whether to deploy the Cruise missile. This decision node is again denoted with a box. The final decision, which belongs to the Soviets, is whether to build up and modernize forces in Europe. These states of nature and the probabilities associated with them are represented to the right of the last column of circles.

Figure 25.1

A Decision Tree

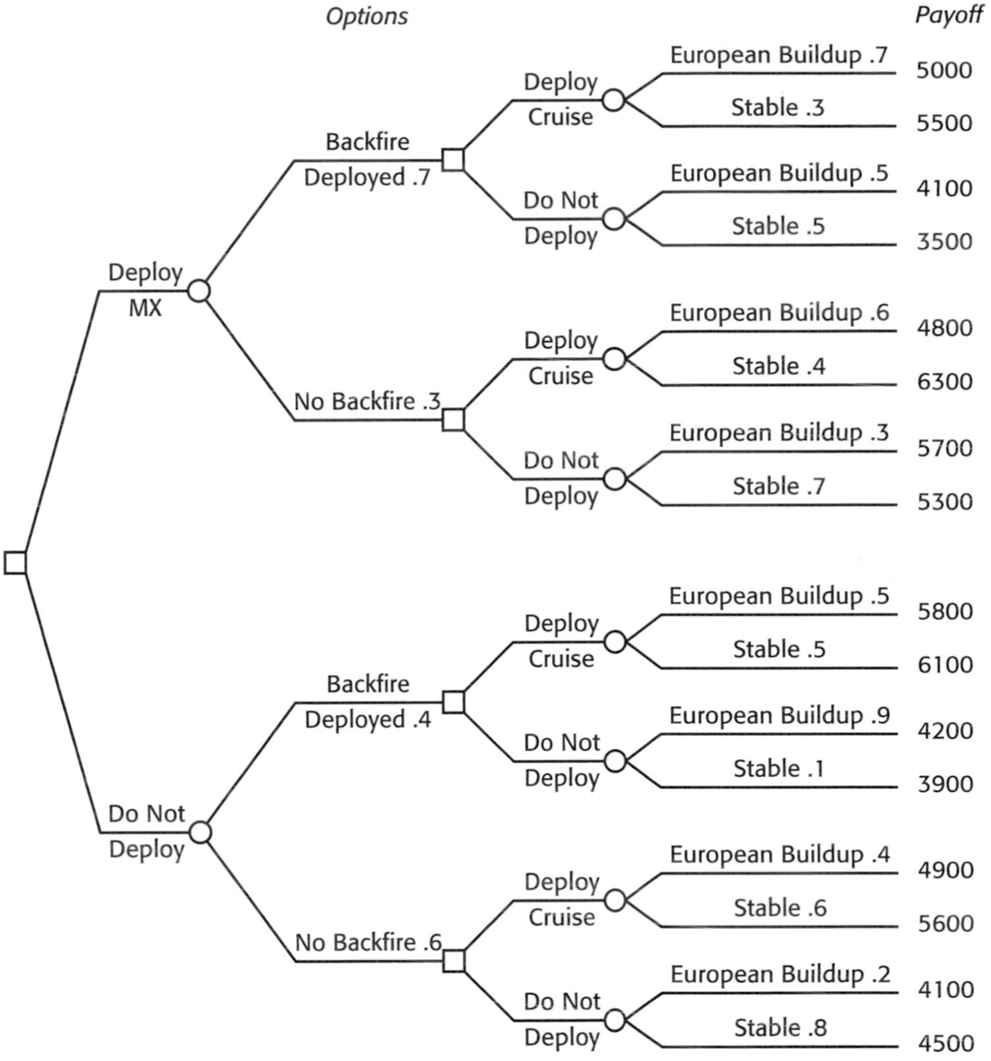

Options

Payoff

The figures on the extreme right of the decision tree under the heading "Payoff" are the numbers of nuclear warheads that the United States will have available for a second strike if the events associated with limbs of the tree hold. For example, if the United States deploys both the MX and the Cruise and the Soviets deploy the Backfire and build up forces in Europe, then an estimated 5,000 strategic nuclear warheads will survive a Soviet strike and be available for a U.S. second strike. The objective is to decide whether to deploy the MX and the Cruise missile so that the number of second-strike warheads is maximized.

Decision trees are solved by working backward from the branches of the tree to the trunk. Because each pair of branches representing the Soviet decision on building up forces in Europe has both probabilities and payoffs for both states of nature, an expected value can be calculated. For example, for the branch where the United States deploys the MX, the Soviets deploy the Backfire, and the United States deploys the Cruise, the expected value is as follows:

$$(.7 \times 5{,}000) + (.3 \times 5{,}500) = 3{,}500 + 1{,}650 = 5{,}150$$

The United States could expect to have 5,150 remaining warheads if this option is pursued.

The remaining expected values are presented on the truncated tree in Figure 25.2. You may wish to calculate these expected values yourself to gain some practice with decision trees.

Once the expected values are calculated, the decision to deploy the Cruise missile is easy. Simply select the option that yields the greatest expected value. In Cases 1, 3, and 4, the Cruise should be deployed, because this option has the greatest expected value. Only in Case 2, in which the MX is deployed but the Backfire is not, should the United States not deploy the Cruise. These decisions reduce the decision tree to the tree shown in Figure 25.3.

For the expected value calculated previously and the assigned probabilities, the Soviet decision to deploy the Backfire can be reduced to expected values of warheads remaining. For the Deploy MX option, the expected value is

$$(.7 \times 5{,}150) + (.3 \times 5{,}420) = 3{,}605 + 1{,}626 = 5{,}231$$

For the Do Not Deploy option, the expected value is

$$(.4 \times 5{,}950) + (.6 \times 5{,}320) = 2{,}380 + 3{,}192 = 5{,}572$$

According to the information presented, the United States should not deploy the MX missile. Then, no matter what the Soviets do regarding the Backfire bomber, the United States should deploy the Cruise missile. These two decisions maximize the expected number of warheads available for a second strike.

Decision trees often get more complex than the ones presented here. In many circumstances, so many options must be considered that only a computer can solve the resulting trees. Any manager or policy analyst who is basing a decision on a decision tree must remember that the key to using decision trees is to set up a tree that accurately reflects the real world. If all the probabilities and the payoffs are correct, the solution is easy. If they are not correct, the tree is less useful. Managers and analysts are paid to design acceptable decision trees where they are appropriate. Once this is done, the decision tree can be solved by a technician.

Decision Making under Uncertainty

In conditions of uncertainty, the decision maker has less information than is available under conditions of risk. Under uncertainty, the decision maker can specify the possible states of nature but cannot objectively assign probabilities to these states of

Figure 25.2

Remaining Decision Tree

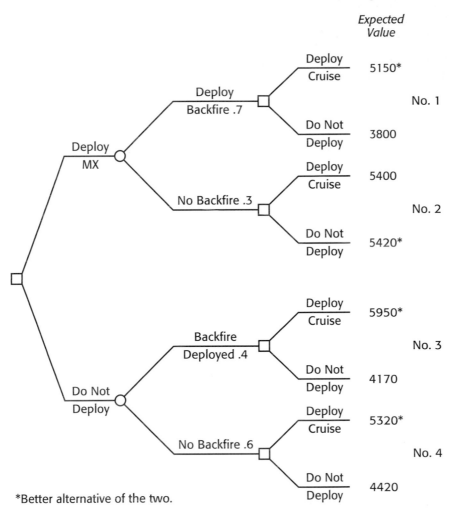

*Expected
Value*

Deploy
Cruise — 5150*

No. 1

Do Not
Deploy — 3800

Deploy
Cruise — 5400

No. 2

Do Not
Deploy — 5420*

Deploy
MX

Deploy
Backfire .7

No Backfire .3

Deploy
Cruise — 5950*

No. 3

Do Not
Deploy — 4170

Deploy
Cruise — 5320*

No. 4

Do Not
Deploy — 4420

Do Not
Deploy

Backfire
Deployed .4

No Backfire .6

*Better alternative of the two.

nature. For example, R. E. Gressum, the head of research for Bayville, Iowa, must decide whether to write a federal grant to fund a halfway house for drug addicts. Gressum feels that it would cost the city about $5,000 in time and materials to apply for
the grant. If the application is successful, the city will receive $100,000. If Gressum
does not apply for this grant, she is sure that the time could be used to write a Title I
grant for training for $25,000 that would be funded. If the rehabilitation grants are
funded, however, no money will be left for Title I grants, so Gressum could receive
nothing if the first grant is funded. The decision table facing Gressum is as shown in
Table 25.5.

Figure 25.3

Decisions Remaining

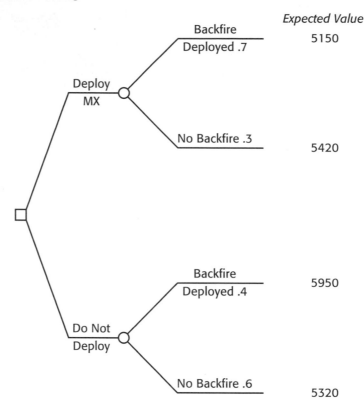

Expected Value

Backfire Deployed .7	5150
No Backfire .3	5420
Backfire Deployed .4	5950
No Backfire .6	5320

Deploy MX

Do Not Deploy

Notice that the optimal decision for Gressum depends on what the federal government does. If the federal government funds the grant, Gressum should apply for the funds. If the federal government will not fund the grant, Gressum would be better off not applying and trying to fund the Title I grant. Since the probability that the federal government will fund the grant is unknown, Gressum cannot unambiguously decide whether to submit the grant.

Table 25.5

Decision Table for Gressum

	Federal Action	
Gressum's Options	Fund	Do Not Fund
Write grant	$100K	−$5K
Do not write grant	$0K	$25K

Decisions under uncertainty *can* be resolved through a variety of decision strategies. The five most common strategies are discussed next.

Strategy 1: The Bayesian Approach

Bayesian statisticians believe that subjective judgments ought to be incorporated into any statistical analysis for which objective assessments are not available. In the present situation, if Gressum's analyst were a Bayesian, the analyst would urge Gressum—on the basis of her experience, knowledge, and intuition—to assign a probability that the federal government will fund the halfway house grant. After some thought, Gressum believes that the probability that the federal government will fund the halfway house grant is .2; this means that the probability of not funding is .8. A Bayesian would then use these probabilities to calculate expected values for both of Gressum's options:

write grant: $\quad (.2 \times 100K) + (.8 \times -5K) = 20K - 4K = \$16K$

do not write grant: $\quad (.2 \times 0K) + (.8 \times 25K) = 0K + 20K = \$20K$

Using these expected values, Gressum should not write the grant, but rather, should concentrate her efforts on the Title I training grant.

Strategy 2: The Insufficient Reason Approach

The principle of **insufficient reason** attempts to define order from uncertainty. If Gressum has no idea whether the federal government will fund the grant and has no idea whether the probability is large or small, the principle of insufficient reason holds the best estimate of the probability of one of two events is .5. In other words, if we have no way of establishing otherwise, we should assume that events are equally probable. (If three events were involved, the principle of insufficient reason would offer equal probabilities of .33.) With equal probabilities, expected values can be calculated for each option:

write grant: $\quad (.5 \times 100K) + (.5 \times -5K) = 50K - 2.5K = \$47.5K$

do not write grant: $(.5 \times 0K) + (.5 \times 25K) = 0K + 12.5K = \$12.5K$

Under the principle of insufficient reason, Gressum should write the grant.

Strategy 3: The Maximin Principle

The **maximin** principle was discovered by a pessimist. Under maximin, Gressum should assume the worst that could happen. Examining the payoff table (Table 25.5), Gressum sees that the worst that could happen if she wrote the grant would be that the federal government would not fund it and that she would lose $5,000 in expenses.

Gressum's Options	Federal Action	
	Fund	Do Not Fund
Write grant	$100K	−$5K
Do not write grant	$0K	$25K

If Gressum does not write the grant, the worst that could happen is that the federal government will fund the grant. In this case, Gressum would receive nothing. Maximin then requires that the worst cases be compared and the best of the worst cases be selected.

Options	Worst Case
Write grant	−$5K
Do not write grant	$0K

The best option, according to this criterion, is clearly to not write the grant and thus not lose any money. (Maximin gets its name from the logic it uses; the decision maker selects the *maxi*mum of the *mini*mum payoffs.)

Strategy 4: Minimax Regret

The **minimax regret** principle is based on opportunity costs. It asks the question, if we decide a certain way and make the wrong decision, what opportunity has been lost? For example, if Gressum does not write the grant and the grant would have been funded, Gressum would lose $100,000 in opportunity costs. If she writes the grant and it is funded, she loses nothing in opportunity or regret costs. If the grant is not funded, writing the grant is associated with an opportunity cost of $30,000; not writing the grant has no opportunity costs. Combining these opportunity costs into a single decision table, we get the results of Table 25.6.

Next, the maximum opportunity cost associated with each alternative is noted:

Options	Maximum Opportunity Cost
Write grant	$30K
Do not write grant	$100K

The minimax regret principle then designates the minimum opportunity cost as the best alternative. In this case, the best alternative is to write the grant, because the greatest opportunity cost is only $30,000 versus $100,000 for the other alternative. (Minimax regret gets its name because one selects the *mini*mum of the *max*imum regrets.)

Table 25.6

Opportunity Costs

Gressum's Options	Federal Action	
	Fund	Do Not Fund
Write grant	$0K	$30K
Do not write grant	$100K	$0K

Strategy 5: Maximax

Maximax is a decision principle supported by the same people who, in April, bet that the Chicago Cubs will win the World Series. Maximax is the principle of the optimist. The decision maker takes the position that the best will happen. In this situation, Gressum will assume that if she writes the grant, it will be funded (a gain of $100,000), and if she does not write the grant, the Title I project will be funded (a gain of $25,000). One simply compares the best that can happen with each option and selects the *maxi*mum *max*imum. In this case, Gressum would write the grant to get the $100,000 project funded.

How to Decide?

Decision rules are everywhere, but which to use? In a situation of uncertainty, should you select Bayesian, insufficient reason, maximin, minimax regret, or maximax? That decision should be based on two factors. First, how important is the decision? U.S. defense planners favor the maximin rule. They assume that the worst will happen and plan accordingly. That way, if less than the worst happens, the U.S. defenses are in better shape than necessary. In such a life-and-death situation, pessimism may be the best decision rule. If the decision has few consequences (such as which of three grants we should apply for in our spare time), then maximax might be more appropriate. If the manager has confidence in his or her subjective probability estimates, then perhaps Bayesian decisions would work best. Second, the appropriate decision rule depends on the manager's attitude toward risk. Some of the decision rules require greater risks (maximax) in hopes for greater payoffs; other rules are conservative. A manager who thrives on risk may select one rule, whereas a risk avoider may select another. The appropriate decision rule, therefore, is a management decision.

Game Theory

Often in a managerial or policy situation, states of nature are not naturally occurring; rather, they result from decisions made by others. When the other actor seeks to maximize his or her position and these actions affect us, a game situation exists. Game theory was developed to analyze competitive situations.

Zero-Sum Games

The simplest game is the two-person, zero-sum game. A two-person game obviously involves two people, and a **zero-sum game** is one in which one player's gains are the other person's losses, and vice versa. An illustration is in order.

Joe Atobelly, the personnel chief for the parks department, wants to increase his hiring level. Joe's opponent is Melvin Merit, the civil service commissioner, who wants to make sure that employee levels are kept as low as possible. Melvin has two options: he can insist that all applicants take and pass all civil service exams, or he can suspend tests and use a quicker temporary screening. Joe has three options: He can send over employees as regular employees, as special affirmative action employees, or as temporary employees. Joe sends over five employee names at a time.

If Joe sends over five names as regular employees, four will be hired if Melvin uses regular procedures, but only one will be hired if Melvin uses temporary procedures. If Joe uses the affirmative action option, two will be hired under regular procedures, but three will be hired if temporary procedures are used. If Joe uses the temporary strategy, only one will be hired if regular procedures are used, and two if the temporary procedures are. The payoff table for Joe is shown in Table 25.7. The values are the number of people hired.

Because Melvin wants to hold down employment, his payoff table looks like Table 25.8. Joe's gains are Melvin's losses.

What strategy should Joe decide to use? At first glance, he notices that no matter what Melvin decides, Joe would always be better off stressing affirmative action rather than using the temporary strategy. When this situation exists, game theorists say that the affirmative action choice *dominates* the temporary choice. As a result, Joe need not consider the temporary help strategy. Joe then assumes that Melvin is out to hold down employment (which he is) and decides to act on a worst-case basis and use maximin. Under maximin, Joe would get one employee under regular procedures and two under affirmative action. He opts for affirmative action. Melvin also applies maximin because he distrusts Joe. Under maximin, Melvin could hold Joe to a maximum of four employees with regular procedures or to a maximum of three with temporary procedures. Melvin decides on temporary procedures.

The result of the two independent decisions means that Joe will get three employees of every five applicants sent to Melvin. Joe cannot improve this record because he would only get one employee if he tried regular employees and if Melvin

Table 25.7

Joe's Payoff Table

Melvin's Choice	Joe's Choice		
	Regular	Affirmative Action	Temporary
Regular	4	2	1
Temporary	1	3	2

Table 25.8

Melvin's Payoff Table

Melvin's Choice	Joe's Choice		
	Regular	Affirmative Action	Temporary
Regular	−4	−2	−1
Temporary	−1	−3	−2

(rationally) stayed with temporary procedures. Melvin, however, notices that he could hold Joe to two employees if he invoked regular procedures. Melvin also sees that if he always had regular procedures, Joe would use regular employees and hire four of every five persons. So Melvin begins to act randomly, sometimes using regular procedures, sometimes temporary ones. Joe continues his affirmative action strategy and gets only an average of 2.5 employees every time. Melvin has finessed Joe out of 1 employee out of every 10. Melvin can do this because the present game does not have a *saddle point*—a single solution that yields the optimum for both actors.

Can Joe counteract Melvin's randomness? No, because if Joe occasionally sent people over as regular employees, half of the time four would be hired and half of the time one would be hired, for an average of 2.5. In this situation, random action is a rational choice, but only for one of the actors.

Positive-Sum Games

A city police union must decide whether it should push for moderate demands or make strong demands on the city. The city manager must decide whether to settle quickly or to tolerate a strike. If the city settles quickly, the police will do better if they have high demands. If the city tolerates a strike, high demands reflect unfavorably on the union, and it will do less well. Although this situation looks much like the zero-sum game described before, the city has the option of turning it into a **positive-sum game** in which everyone benefits.

Let us say that the police union contract expires in an election year. As a result, the mayor does not want a strike and tells the city manager to avoid one. He also tells the city manager to hold down salary costs. The manager has an idea. He tells the union that if it will moderate wage demands, he will give the union more than it wants in pensions. This offer translates the game into a positive-sum game. The union is happy because it received everything it asked for, although not all of it in wages. The manager avoids a strike; and since the pensions will cost future managers rather than his administration, the manager is happy. Neither participant lost; hence the game is positive sum. (The only losers are future city managers and the taxpayers.)

The Prisoner's Dilemma

A special two-person game is called the **prisoner's dilemma.** The Equal Employment Opportunity Commission (EEOC) is investigating the Ajax Rubber Goods Company and its union for racial discrimination. The EEOC believes that the company and the union conspired to deny employment to minorities. The EEOC tells the union and Ajax separately that if both admit guilt and provide all needed information, both will be fined $10,000. If one of the two admits guilt and provides the information that will implicate the other party, the admitting party will be fined $2,000. The noncooperating party will then be prosecuted in court and in all probability, will be fined $20,000. If neither party admits guilt, EEOC will begin court proceedings that will cost both parties $5,000 each to defend the suits.

For Ajax Rubber Goods Company, its decision table appears as shown in Table 25.9. The Ajax manager reasons as follows: If the union does not plead guilty, the

Table 25.9

Cost to Ajax

	Union Action	
Ajax Option	No Plea	Pleads Guilty
No plea	$5K	$20K
Guilty plea	$2K	$10K

Table 25.10

Cost to Union

	Ajax Action	
Union Option	No Plea	Pleads Guilty
No plea	$5K	$20K
Guilty plea	$2K	$10K

company would be better off if it pled guilty and implicated the union ($2,000 versus $5,000). If the union pleads guilty, the company would save $10,000 in fines if it also pled guilty ($10,000 versus $20,000). No matter what the union does, the company would always be better off by pleading guilty. Ajax notifies the EEOC it would like to plead guilty.

The union faces the decision table shown in Table 25.10. The union faces the same payoff table that Ajax faced. The union by similar reasoning decides to plead guilty and notifies the EEOC.

The EEOC then fines both the union and the company $10,000. Why is this a prisoner's dilemma? For a simple reason: Had the union and the company talked to each other, they could have both said nothing. This action would cost each unit $5,000 rather than $10,000. Therein lies the dilemma. Cooperation would make both the union and the company better off, but rationality leads to a less than optimal solution.

A manager faced with a prisoner's dilemma should seek to turn the game into a positive-sum game through collusion with the other players. If the players trust each other, then all parties will be better off than if they were caught on the horns of the dilemma.

A Final Comment

This section limits its discussion to two-person games. Game theory has developed beyond simple two-person games to three-, four-, and n-person games. Although these topics are too advanced for this introductory text, when gamelike situations exist in the real world that are not just two-person games, more complex models should be used. Consult any management science text for a treatment of more complex games [see Singleton and Tyndall (1974)].

Chapter Summary

Decision theory is a set of decision approaches used to resolve managerial problems. For ideal conditions, five steps have been identified in the rational decision-making procedure. First, identify the problem. Second, specify goals and objectives. Third, specify all available alternatives. Fourth, evaluate the alternatives in light of the goals. Fifth, select the optimal alternative.

When all the crucial aspects (states of nature) of a decision are known, decision making takes place under certainty. When the environment of a decision can only be assigned probabilities, then decisions are made under risk. Decisions under risk involve decision tables, payoff tables, cost-benefit calculations, probability calculations for each state of nature, and expected value computations. In very complex situations, decision analysts often represent decisions under risk with decision trees rather than with a simple payoff table.

When nothing is known about the environment, decision making under uncertainty uses one of several strategies. Bayesian probabilities incorporate subjective judgments into the statistical analysis. The principle of insufficient reason attempts to define order from uncertainty. Under the maximin principle, the decision maker selects the maximum of the minimum payoffs (the best of the worst). Using minimax regret, one selects the minimum of the maximum regrets. Under the maximax principle, the decision maker selects the maximum of the maximum payoffs (the best of the best).

Often in a managerial situation, the states of nature result from decisions made by others. Game theory was developed to analyze these competitive situations. In a zero-sum game, one player's gains are the other's losses, and vice versa. In a positive-sum game, everyone benefits.

Problems

25.1 The department of social services is considering three programs to vocationally train people with disabilities: a contract for teaching the unskilled labor skills, provided by a private vendor (program A); a proposal to train the disabled as computer operators, provided by the state data processing center (program B); and a program to teach clerical skills, provided by a local business school (program C). Three states of nature affect the success of each program. State A is a pool of disabled people in which less than 20% are severely disabled; state B is 20% to 40% severely disabled; and state C is more than 40% severely disabled. The accompanying payoff table shows the number of disabled who could be successfully rehabilitated in a year with the three programs and the three states of nature.

	State of Nature		
Program	A	B	C
A	20	70	30
B	40	35	35
C	30	10	100

(a) Using the maximin criterion, what program would you select and why?

(b) Using the maximax criterion, what program would you select and why?

(c) Is maximin or maximax the more appropriate criterion in this case?

25.2 Refer to Problem 2.1 in Chapter 2.

(a) With minimax regret, what is the best decision?

(b) Using the principle of insufficient reason, what program would you select and why?

25.3 Refer to Problem 25.1. You are a Bayesian, and your analyst tells you that she believes that the probability of each state of nature is .6 for A, .2 for B, and .2 for C.

(a) With this information, what is the best program?

(b) How much would the expected value of rehabilitated cases be affected by a survey that told you the exact number of severely disabled?

(c) Would you pay $30,000 for such a survey?

25.4 A. Rookie, an assistant professor of human relations at the Jackson School of Public Affairs, wants to teach his class the value of cooperation. He divides the class into three teams. Each team must select a color, either red or green. If all three teams select green, Rookie will pay each team a dollar. If two teams select green, these two teams will pay the other team a dollar each. If one team selects green, it must pay $2 to each of the other teams. If all three teams select red, each team pays Rookie a dollar. After 10 rounds of the game, Rookie discovers himself $24 richer. What has happened?

25.5 Ray Wiley decides that he wants to live a life of crime since it is the only way he can support himself in the style to which he has become accustomed. Ray finds the figures shown in the accompanying table in the FBI crime statistics. What specialization should Ray select? Why?

Crime	Average Taken	Probability of Not Being Caught
Bank robbery	$30,640	.46
Robbing convenience store	850	.75
Corporate theft	15,474	.93
Street robbery	345	.87
Burglary	1,247	.98

25.6 Stanley E. Konomist, the chief financial officer for Breverham State University, must decide how to invest this year's private contributions. Stanley has four options. He can invest in corporate bonds, in the stock market, in treasury notes, or in land. The payoff is affected by the rate of inflation for the next year, as the accompanying table shows. Using maximin, maximax, minimax regret, and the principle of insufficient reason, what should Stanley do? Which is the most appropriate criterion?

	Inflation Rate		
BSU Options	0%–4%	4%–10%	10%+
Corporate bonds	$75K	$70K	$70K
Stock market	$60K	$120K	$45K
Treasury notes	$100K	$80K	$60K
Land	$30K	$90K	$150K

25.7 Refer to Problem 25.6. Pretend that you are a Bayesian. Assign subjective probabilities for each state of nature, and then select the best option. What would you pay for an accurate forecast of the inflation rate?

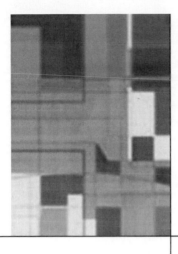

CHAPTER 26

Linear Programming

Linear programming is a quantitative technique that can optimally allocate an agency's resources under conditions of certainty. The agency may be in the public or nonprofit (or for-profit) sector. Before discussing the techniques for linear programming, some situations in which it could be used will be noted. A prison nutritionist needs to determine the proper mix of foods to buy so that a given level of nutrition is met at the least cost. An Air Force logistics officer needs to supply six bases in Europe from four supply depots at the minimum cost to the Air Force. A parks supervisor wants to assign her personnel to various parks so that she can maximize productivity given her budget constraints. The local food bank wants to transport food to homeless shelters throughout the city so that nutritional requirements are met at each shelter at the least cost.

These are all linear programming problems. In each case, we want to find the optimal mix of resources. Variables that the manager can control—which foods to buy, which depots to use, where to assign personnel—are called **decision variables** because the manager can decide how to allocate these variables. **Constraints** are variables that limit the choices of the manager: in the previous examples, a given nutrition level must be met; all six bases must be supplied; the park supervisor only has X men. Some constraints are in the form of inequalities: For example, vitamin C intake level must be at least 5 milligrams; no more than 247 people can be used. Finally,

output variables are those that the manager seeks to maximize or minimize—cost, productivity, and so on.

Linear programming seeks to optimize output variables by manipulating decision variables, subject to the restrictions of the constraints. Linear programming can only work under conditions of certainty. The manager must know the constraints and the exact relationship among all decision variables and the output variables. The Air Force officer must know, for example, the number of items each base needs, the number of items each depot has, the cost of transporting an item from every depot to every base, and so on. Unless such certainty exists, linear programming can be used only as a way of thinking about problems.

Linear programming is a special form of programming in which all the relationships are linear. Other, more advanced forms of programming are available, but they are well beyond the scope of this text. Linear programming assumes, as we noted, that all relationships are linear (or proportional). If one apple and a sandwich contain 100 units of B-14, then two apples and two sandwiches contain 200 units of B-14. Linear programming also assumes that all inputs and outputs are infinitely divisible. Mowing the grass in one-half of a park or feeding every prisoner one-fourth of an apple are solutions that linear programming models find. Finally, linear programming assumes that the processes are interchangeable. If the parks department can either mow 1,200 acres of grass or trim 4,000 feet of hedges, it can also mow 600 acres of grass and trim 2,000 feet of hedges.

In this chapter, we introduce you to the techniques of linear programming.

An Example

The Ware County Library maintains a book repair division in the basement of its central library. The repair unit has two functions: It puts hardcover bindings on paperback books, and it reconditions damaged hardcover books. The unit has more work than it can handle. Any excess work is farmed out to Orva's Bindery. Orva charges $12 to cover a paperback and $15 to repair a hardcover book.

The repair unit has four processes. Labeling is the process of writing the call numbers on the spine of the book. The labeling people can label 500 books a month; the distinction between hardcover and paperback does not affect them. The binding people can bind 400 paperback books a month or rebind (an easier process) 600 repaired hardbacks. The cover-cutting people can cut 350 covers a month; covers are only used on the paperback books. The repair people can process either 1,000 paperbacks or 450 hardback books a month.

Step 1: Decide what the agency wants to maximize or minimize. Since at Orva's, covering a paperback costs $12 and repairing a hardback costs $15, the value of the repair unit's activities is $12 for every paperback re-covered and $15 for every hardback repaired. So let

$$X_1 = \text{the number of paperbacks covered}$$
$$X_2 = \text{the number of hardbacks repaired}$$

The Ware County Library would like to maximize

$$\$12X_1 + \$15X_2$$

The decision will tell the library how many paperbacks to re-cover and how many hardbacks to repair to maximize the payoff.

Step 2: Determine the constraints on each process. If the labeling people only label newly bound paperbacks, they can label 500 per month. Each paperback they label takes 1/500 of their total time. Similarly, each re-bound paperback requires 1/400 of the binding time, 1/350 of the cover-cutting time, and 1/100 of the repair time. Each repaired hardcover requires 1/500 of the labeling time, 1/600 of the binding time, and 1/450 of the repair time. The labeling constraint on the repair unit can be expressed as

$$\left(\frac{1}{500}\right)X_1 + \left(\frac{1}{500}\right)X_2 \leq 1$$

That is, the number of paperbacks re-bound and the number of hardbacks repaired cannot exceed total labeling capacity. The other constraints are as follows:

$$\text{binding: } \left(\frac{1}{400}\right)X_1 + \left(\frac{1}{600}\right)X_2 \leq 1$$

$$\text{cover cutting: } \left(\frac{1}{350}\right)X_1 + 0X_2 \leq 1$$

$$\text{repair: } \left(\frac{1}{100}\right)X_1 + \left(\frac{1}{450}\right)X_2 \leq 1$$

Two other constraints must be noted, particularly if one uses computer routines to do linear programming. Both the number of paperbacks covered and the number of hardbacks repaired must be greater than or equal to zero (this may be logical to you, but it is not to the computer). Thus,

$$X_1 \geq 0 \quad X_2 \geq 0$$

Step 3: Give the problem to your linear programmer to solve. In the current situation, with only two output variables (paperbacks and hardbacks), the problem can be solved by graphing. Draw a graph with one axis (say, the horizontal) representing the number of paperbacks and the other axis representing the number of hardbacks (see Figure 26.1). This graph will be used to graph the constraints on the repair unit.

To graph the labeling constraint, note that labeling can either process 500 paperbacks and 0 hardbacks or 0 paperbacks and 500 hardbacks. Find these two points on the graph, and connect them with a straight line. See Figure 26.2. This line represents the labeling constraints on the repair unit. Every point on the graph below and to the left of the line (including points on the line) is within the capacity of the repair unit. Point A, for example—300 hardbacks and 200 paperbacks—is within the capacity of the repair unit.

Figure 26.1

Axes Labels

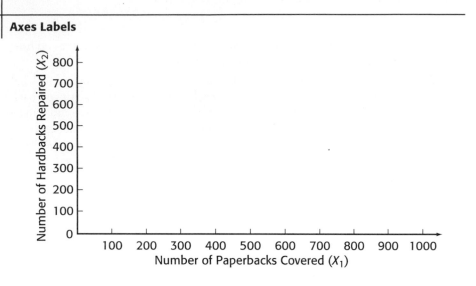

Figure 26.2

Line for the Labeling Constraint

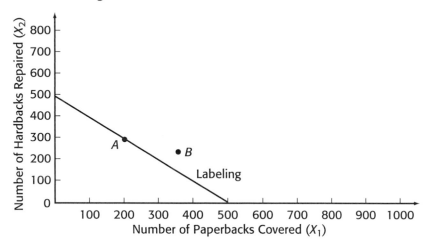

Point *B*, however—250 hardbacks and 350 paperbacks—exceeds the repair unit's capacity.

The next step is to graph all the constraints on the same graph. This is done in Figure 26.3.

On the constraints graph, the only options that are open to management are those in the shaded area of the graph. One point within this area is the optimal ratio of hardbacks to paperbacks. The question is, which one? We will find the optimal point much as the computer does—by trial and error.

Figure 26.3

Constraints Graph

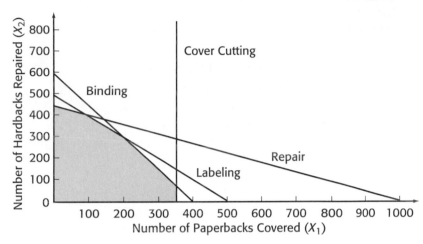

Start the trial-and-error process by setting the equation $\$12X_1 + \$15X_2$ equal to some value, say, $4,200.

$$\$4,200 = \$12X_1 + \$15X_2$$

The repair shop could produce $4,200 worth of repairs by either covering 350 paperbacks (4,200 ÷ 12) or 280 hardbacks. These values are plotted on the graph in Figure 26.4 and are connected with a line. Any value above and

Figure 26.4

Finding the Optimal Ration

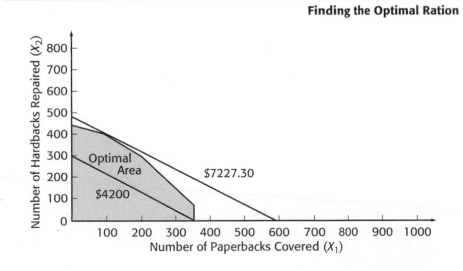

to the right of this line will yield a greater payoff than any value on this line. Because many of the values above and to the right of this line are within the shaded area, a production value of more than $4,200 is possible. The computer tries several lines until it finds a line that has only one point within the shaded area. In this problem, the only line with only one point within the shaded area is

$$\$7{,}227.30 = \$12X_1 + \$15X_2$$

This line touches the shaded area only where the labeling and the repair constraints intersect (see Figure 26.4). The optimal point will always be at the intersection of two or more constraints.

The next step is to determine the values of X_1 and X_2 at the optimal point. The labeling constraint is

$$\left(\frac{1}{500}\right)X_1 + \left(\frac{1}{500}\right)X_2 \leq 1$$

The repair constraint is

$$\left(\frac{1}{1{,}000}\right)X_1 + \left(\frac{1}{450}\right)X_2 \leq 1$$

Multiply the repair constraint by 2 to get

$$\left(\frac{2}{1{,}000}\right)X_1 + \left(\frac{2}{450}\right)X_2 \leq 2$$

$$\left(\frac{1}{500}\right)X_1 + \left(\frac{2}{450}\right)X_2 \leq 2$$

Subtract the labeling constraint from the new repair constraint.

$$\left(\frac{1}{500}\right)X_1 + \left(\frac{2}{450}\right)X_2 \leq 2$$

$$-\left(\frac{1}{500}\right)X_1 - \left(\frac{1}{500}\right)X_2 \leq -1$$

$$0X_1 + \left(\frac{2}{450}\right)X_2 - \left(\frac{1}{500}\right)X_2 \leq 1$$

$$\left(\frac{40}{9{,}000}\right)X_2 - \left(\frac{18}{9{,}000}\right)X_2 \leq 1$$

$$\left(\frac{22}{9{,}000}\right)X_2 \leq 1$$

$$X_2 \leq 409.1$$

To find the value for X_1, simply substitute 409 for X_2 in the labeling constraint.

$$\left(\frac{1}{500}\right)X_1 + \left(\frac{1}{500}\right)409 \leq 1$$

$$\left(\frac{1}{500}\right)X_1 + \frac{409}{500} \leq 1$$

$$\left(\frac{1}{500}\right)X_1 + .818 \leq 1$$

$$\left(\frac{1}{500}\right)X_1 \leq .182$$

$$X_1 \leq 91$$

The optimal production point is to repair 409 hardcover books per month and to bind 91 paperbacks per month. This will return a value of $7,227.

If the mathematics to solve this problem is intimidating, you can always use the graph to eyeball the answer. A linear programming problem solved by a computer program, however, would print out the optimal values.

Linear Programming with More Than Two Variables

Rarely will a linear programming problem be so simple that a solution can be found graphically. But a public or nonprofit manager's function is not to solve linear programming problems. The manager's first function is to recognize problems that can be solved through linear programming. Any time a manager wants to maximize or minimize some value that is determined by some mix of inputs subject to constraints and the manager is operating under certainty (in regard to costs, relationships, and so on), then linear programming is a useful technique. The second managerial function in linear programming is to identify the constraints and relationships for the analyst. The third managerial function is to determine whether the optimal solution is feasible. Certain political constraints that could not be incorporated into the model, for example, might make the optimal solution impossible to obtain. In short, linear programming is a tool that provides valuable inputs into a manager's decision; it is not a decision-making device. After all, when was the last time a linear programming model was fired?

Chapter Summary

Linear programming is used to allocate inputs in order to maximize some outputs within constraints when conditions of certainty exist. This chapter illustrates a very elementary version of linear programming that can be instructive in public and nonprofit management.

Variables that the manager can control are called decision variables. Constraints are variables that limit the choices of the manager. Output variables are those that the manager wishes to maximize or minimize. Linear programming seeks to optimize output variables by manipulating decision variables, subject to the restrictions of the constraints.

Three basic steps are involved in linear programming. First, decide what it is you wish to maximize or minimize. Second, determine the constraints on each process. Third, if the problem is simple enough, solve it by graphing (otherwise an analyst trained in linear programming must be brought in to solve the problem). Note that the public or nonprofit manager's function is not to solve linear programming problems, but rather to recognize that a problem can be solved by using these techniques and to identify the constraints and the relationships for the analyst.

Problems

26.1 An Air Force logistics officer has to transport 850 planes in the United States (500 at Minot Air Force Base and 350 at Offutt) to the Pacific. Of these 850 planes, 200 must go to Kadena, 150 to Guam, 400 to Osan, and 100 to Hickham. The costs of flying between each of these points are listed in the accompanying table. How can the officer transport these planes at the least cost? Set up the variables you want to minimize and the constraints on these variables.

	From	
To	Minot	Offutt
Kadena	$600	$900
Guam	700	600
Osan	800	1,100
Hickham	400	300

26.2 Beaver Falls City Hall has two incinerators to burn city hall trash. Together they burn 100 tons of trash per day, but the city hall produces 200 tons. The remaining trash is buried—a more expensive method. Incinerator X can burn 40 tons of trash per day, but it releases 5 pounds of particles per ton and 12 units of hydrocarbons per ton. Incinerator Y can burn 60 tons of trash per day, and it releases 3 pounds of particles and 16 units of hydrocarbons per ton. If the EPA will allow city hall to emit no more than 40 pounds of particles and 130 units of hydrocarbons, what is the most efficient use of the incinerators?

26.3 The Conrad, North Carolina, Parks Department has been allocated 50 Comprehensive Employment and Training Act (CETA) employees for three months. These employees will be used to trim hedges and mow lawns. Normally these functions are contracted out to Greenthumb Lawn Care

Company at a cost of $12 per acre of grass and $8 per 50 feet of hedges. One person can mow 6.5 acres of grass per day or trim 500 feet of hedges. The city has 38 lawn mowers and 35 hedge trimmers. How can the city use its CETA employees to its best advantage if there is more grass and there are more hedges than 50 workers can possibly service? Set up this problem and solve it graphically.

26.4   Several years ago, an economist applied a linear programming model to a university. The output the university was to maximize was the earning power of its graduates, subject to constraints of money, faculty, buildings, and so on. Is this an appropriate use of linear programming? Why or why not?

26.5   The General Services Administration's Office of Typewriters stores brand X and brand Y typewriters at four locations as follows:

Location	Brand X	Brand Y
Boston	2,400	1,200
Atlanta	1,200	3,000
Seattle	6,000	200
Dallas	3,000	2,000

Numerous typewriters must be shipped from these offices to the federal regional office centers. The centers' needs are as follows:

Center	Brand X	Brand Y
Kansas City	3,500	800
Denver	1,500	700
Chicago	2,700	2,400
Cincinnati	4,600	1,100

The typewriters cost the same amount to ship, regardless of whether they are brand X or brand Y, as follows:

From	To			
	K.C.	Denver	Chicago	Cincinnati
Boston	$18	$24	$13	$9
Atlanta	21	32	17	11
Seattle	17	10	18	24
Dallas	4	14	12	15

Set up the linear programming problem to move the brand X typewriters from the four warehouses to the four regional centers at the least cost.

26.6   Refer to Problem 26.5. Set up the problem to move the brand Y typewriters from the four warehouses to the four regional centers at the least cost.

Annotated Bibliography

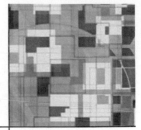

Ammons, David N. *Tools for Decision Making: A Practical Guide for Local Government* (Washington, DC: Congressional Quarterly Press, 2002). A clear and concise overview of a wide variety of analytical tools with useful public management applications.

Babbie, Earl R. *The Practice of Social Research,* 10th ed. (Belmont, CA: Wadsworth, 2003). An excellent introductory guide to the design, conduct, and evaluation of research.

Babbie, Earl R. *Survey Research Methods,* 2nd ed. (Belmont, CA: Wadsworth, 1990). Focuses on the design of surveys and the analysis of results. Contains a chapter on survey ethics.

Bingham, Richard D., and Marcus E. Ethridge, eds. *Reaching Decisions in Public Policy and Administration: Methods and Applications* (New York: Longman, 1982). An interesting collection of readings illustrating various approaches to data collection and decision making in public administration.

Blom, Barry, and Salomon A. Guajardo. *Revenue Analysis and Forecasting* (Chicago, IL: Government Finance Officers Association, 2001). An excellent overview of applied forecasting techniques. A practical guide for the beginner that does not contain a lot of advanced math or complex formulas.

Campbell, Donald T., and Julian C. Stanley. *Experimental and Quasi-Experimental Designs for Research* (Boston: Houghton Mifflin, 1975). Classic presentation of the strengths and weaknesses of important research designs.

Cook, Thomas, and Donald T. Campbell. *Quasi-Experimentation* (Boston: Houghton Mifflin, 1979). A thorough discussion of the analysis of public programs in field settings.

Cooley, William W., and Paul R. Lohnes. *Multivariate Data Analysis* (Melbourne, FL: Krieger, 1985). An advanced text with emphasis on factor analysis and similar techniques.

Fowler, Floyd. *Survey Research Methods,* 3rd ed. (Newbury Park, CA: Sage, 2001). A good overview of how to prepare and administer surveys.

Fox, John. *Regression Diagnostics: An Introduction.* (Newbury Park, CA: Sage. Sage University Paper Series on Quantitative Applications in the Social Sciences, 07-079, 1991). An excellent overview of how to diagnose and address violations of regression assumptions. Provides practical advice on how to deal with multicolinearity, errors in model specification, heteroskedasticity, and other issues related to the assumptions of regression analysis.

Frankfort-Nachmias, Chava, and David Nachmias. *Research Methods in the Social Sciences,* 6th ed. (New York: Freeman, 2000). A good introductory book on research methods and statistics. Emphasizes social science problems.

Graybill, Franklin A., and Hariharan K. Iyer. *Regression Analysis: Concepts and Applications* (Belmont, CA: Duxbury Press, 1994). An advanced text with emphasis on regression applications. A good reference book.

Greene, William H. *Econometric Analysis,* 5th ed. (New York: Pearson Education, 2002). The cadillac of econometric regression books, it is an excellent reference, but remember to bring your matrix algebra skills.

Hamilton, James D. *Time Series Analysis* (Princeton, NJ: Princeton University Press, 1994). A nice overview of a wide variety of techniques for analyzing time series data.

Hamilton, Lawrence. *Regression with Graphics* (Pacific Grove, CA: Brooks/ Cole, 1995). The hands-down best advanced book for using exploratory data analysis, graphics approaches, and regression diagnostics. One of the authors uses it for his advanced class along with Pindyck and Rubinfeld.

Hanushek, Eric A., and John E. Jackson. *Statistical Methods for Social Scientists* (New York: Academic Press, 1977). An advanced book on regression techniques designed for social science researchers.

Hays, William L. *Statistics,* 5th ed. (Fort Worth, TX: Harcourt Brace, 1994). A very complete, basic treatment of statistics.

Iman, Ronald L. *A Data-Based Approach to Statistics* (Belmont, CA: Duxbury Press, 1995). A good introduction with computer examples in four different software packages.

Johnson, Janet Buttolph, Richard A. Joslyn, and H. T. Reynolds. *Political Science Research Methods,* 4th ed. (Washington, DC: CQ Press, 2001). An excellent introduction to research methods and statistics, with some public administration examples.

Johnson, Robert. *Elementary Statistics,* 7th ed. (Belmont, CA: Duxbury Press, 1996). A classic, well-written introduction to statistics. A valuable reference.

Kennedy, Peter. *A Guide to Econometrics,* 4th ed. (Cambridge, MA: MIT Press. 1998). For those who want a nice intuitive description of some of the most advanced statistical procedures in economics.

Kerlinger, Fred N. *Foundations of Behavioral Research,* 4th ed. (Belmont, CA: Wadsworth, 1999). A classic text in research methods for the social sciences.

King, Gary. *Unifying Political Methodology: The Likelihood Theory of Statistical Inference* (New York: Cambridge University Press, 1989). A sustained argument that the logic of least squares may be inappropriate, and that statistics based on maximum likelihood estimators are more appropriate in most instances. Advanced book that should be required reading for doctoral students in public administration and other fields.

Kleinbaum, David G., Lawrence L. Kupper, and Keith E. Muller with Azhar Nazita. *Applied Regression Analysis and Other Multivariate Methods,* 3rd ed. (Belmont, CA: Brooks/ Cole, 1997). For those advanced students who want a detailed discussion of regression and analysis of variance.

Kurtz, Norman. *Statistical Analysis for the Social Sciences.* (Needham Heights,

MA: Allyn & Bacon. 1999). Provides in-depth and straightforward coverage of hypothesis testing and difference of means tests. A good source for those seeking in-depth knowledge of the principles of statistical inference.

Maddala, G. S. *Introduction to Econometrics,* 3rd ed. (New York: Wiley, 2001). The most readable, but not all that readable for the novice, econometric book on the market.

Manheim, Jarol B., Richard C. Rich, and Lars Willnat. *Empirical Political Analysis: Research Methods in Political Science,* 5th ed. (New York: Longman, 2001). A readable discussion of how to plan, conduct, and write up a data-based study.

McKenna, Christopher K. *Quantitative Methods for Public Decision-Making* (New York: McGraw-Hill, 1980). An intermediate-level presentation of useful managerial techniques, such as cost-benefit analysis, linear programming, and program evaluation review technique/critical path method (PERT/CPM). Has good examples.

McLaughlin, Thomas A. *Streetsmart Financial Basics for Nonprofit Managers,* 2nd ed. (New York: Wiley, 2002). Hands down, the clearest treatment of quantitative management techniques useful for nonprofit financial management. Topics include financial ratio analysis, break-even analysis, and basic accounting. One of the best books for students who want to gain practical knowledge of how to analyze and interpret financial data for nonprofit organizations.

Meier, Kenneth J., and Jeff Gill. *What Works? A New Approach to Program and Policy Analysis* (Boulder: Westview Press, 2000). An innovative approach to analysis that argues that most traditional regression approaches do not meet the needs of managers. The book merges optimization techniques with regression.

Mendenhall, William, James E. Reinmuth, and Robert J. Beaver. *Statistics for Management and Economics,* 7th ed. (Belmont, CA: Duxbury Press, 1993). Focuses on parametric statistics. Good reference on probability and applied regression.

Michel, R. Gregory. *Decision Tools for Budgetary Analysis* (Chicago: Government Finance Officers Association, 2001). An excellent overview of quantitative techniques useful for evaluating financial aspects of policy decisions. Topic coverage includes cost-effectiveness analysis, net present value analysis, and break-even analysis among others. A nice compliment to more theory-based discussions of decision-making techniques.

Miller, Delbert C., and Neil J. Salkind. *Handbook of Research Design and Social Measurement,* 6th ed. (Newbury Park, CA: Sage, 2002). An excellent, comprehensive reference on the research process, especially study design, measurement, data collection, and reporting results.

Mills, Terence C. *Time Series Techniques for Economists* (Cambridge: Cambridge University Press, 1991). Provides thorough coverage of the techniques used to analyze time series data. Topics include data transformations, forecasting, intervention analysis along with more advanced topics such as ARIMA modeling and Vector Autoregression.

Heavy use of advanced econometrics, so parts of the text may be difficult for students with limited backgrounds in statistics.

Mooney, Christopher Z., and Robert D. Duval. *Bootstrapping: A Nonparametric Approach to Statistical Inference* (Newbury Park, CA: Sage, 1993). A primer on a computationally intensive alternative to classical statistics.

Morrow, James D. *Game Theory for Political Scientists* (Princeton, NJ: Princeton University Press, 1994). Provides a thorough overview of game theory. Not quite as technical as more advanced texts on the topic, so this is a good choice for those who want to learn more about game theory but have limited backgrounds in the area.

Nachmias, David. *Public Policy Evaluation* (New York: St. Martin's Press, 1979). A program evaluation book with some statistics included. Excellent for public policy research design and measurement. Statistics concentrate on regression.

Neter, John, William Wasserman, and G. A. Whitmore. *Applied Statistics,* 4th ed. (Boston: Allyn & Bacon, 1993). A solid applied statistics text with business applications. Excellent on probability, inference, and introduction to time series.

Ott, Lyman, and Michael Longnecker. *An Introduction to Statistical Methods and Data Analysis,* 5th ed. (Belmont, CA: Brooks/Cole, 1999). Text contains a wide variety of problems from agriculture, politics, medicine, and so on. Fairly brief for the beginning student.

Ott, Lyman, and William Mendenhall. *Understanding Statistics,* 6th ed. (Belmont, CA: Duxbury Press, 1994). A well-written introductory statistics book with a variety of examples.

Paulos, John A. *Innumeracy: Mathematical Illiteracy and Its Consequences* (New York: Farrar, Straus & Giroux, 2001). Provides an intuitive overview of various principles in probability using clever and amusing examples.

Paulos, John A. *A Mathematician Reads the Newspaper* (New York: Doubleday, 1996). An entertaining and informative look at the misuse of statistical data by the media. A good intuitive guide on how to evaluate probabilities and other statistical evidence.

Pindyck, Robert S., and Daniel L. Rubinfeld. *Econometric Models and Economic Forecasts,* 4th ed. (New York: McGraw-Hill/Irwin, 1997). A good advanced book especially on time series.

Poister, Theodore H. *Public Program Analysis* (Baltimore: University Park Press, 1978). Comprehensive statistics text with emphasis on public policy research problems. Good reference for public sector managers.

Poister, Theodore H. *Measuring Performance in Public and Nonprofit Organizations* (San Francisco: Jossey-Bass, 2003). A thorough overview of key issues in performance measurement, including the development of program logic models, guidelines for creating performance indicators, techniques for analyzing performance data, and the applications of performance measurement to strategic management. General theories are illustrated with data and examples from a variety of governmental and nonprofit organizations.

Rea, Louis M., and Richard A. Parker. *Designing and Conducting Survey Research: A Comprehensive Guide,* 2nd ed. (San Francisco, CA: Jossey-Bass, 1997). A good, nontechnical guide to survey construction and implementation.

Secrest, Lee, Donald Campbell, and Richard D. Schwartz. *Unobtrusive Measures,* vol. 2 (Newbury Park, CA: Sage, 1999). A discussion of measurement under circumstances where good measures are difficult to find.

Singleton, Robert R., and William F. Tyndall. *Games and Programs* (San Francisco: Freeman, 1974). For students who want a more in-depth treatment of game theory and decision analysis.

Stokey, Edith, and Richard Zeckhauser. *A Primer for Policy Analysis* (New York: Norton, 1978). Not a statistics text. Shows how some statistics can be used in policy analysis. One of the best introductions to linear programming.

Tufte, Edward R. *The Visual Display of Quantitative Information,* 2nd ed. (Englewood Cliffs, NJ: Graphics Press, 2001). A classic text on how to effectively describe and summarize data using graphical techniques.

Welch, Susan, and John C. Comer. *Quantitative Methods for Public Administration: Techniques and Applications,* 3rd ed. (Mason, OH: Thomson/South-Western, 2000). The second-best public administration/public policy statistics book. Primarily uses policy examples.

Statistical Tables

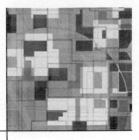

Table 1

The Normal Distribution

Each entry in the table indicates the proportion of the total area under the normal curve contained in the segment bounded by a perpendicular raised at the mean and a perpendicular raised at a distance of *z* standard deviation units.

To illustrate: 40.99% of the area under a normal curve lies between the maximum ordinate and a point 1.34 standard deviation units away.

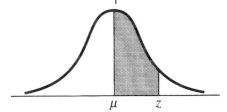

z	0.00	0.01	0.02	0.03	0.04	0.05	0.06	0.07	0.08	0.09
0.0	0.0000	0.0040	0.0080	0.0120	0.0160	0.0199	0.0239	0.0279	0.0319	0.0359
0.1	0.0398	0.0438	0.0478	0.0517	0.0557	0.0596	0.0636	0.0675	0.0714	0.0753
0.2	0.0793	0.0832	0.0871	0.0910	0.0948	0.0987	0.1026	0.1064	0.1103	0.1141
0.3	0.1179	0.1217	0.1255	0.1293	0.1331	0.1368	0.1406	0.1443	0.1480	0.1517
0.4	0.1554	0.1591	0.1628	0.1664	0.1700	0.1736	0.1772	0.1808	0.1844	0.1879
0.5	0.1915	0.1950	0.1985	0.2019	0.2054	0.2088	0.2123	0.2157	0.2190	0.2224
0.6	0.2257	0.2291	0.2324	0.2357	0.2389	0.2422	0.2454	0.2486	0.2518	0.2549
0.7	0.2580	0.2612	0.2642	0.2673	0.2704	0.2734	0.2764	0.2794	0.2823	0.2852
0.8	0.2881	0.2910	0.2939	0.2967	0.2995	0.3023	0.3051	0.3078	0.3106	0.3133
0.9	0.3159	0.3186	0.3212	0.3238	0.3264	0.3289	0.3315	0.3340	0.3365	0.3389
1.0	0.3413	0.3438	0.3461	0.3485	0.3508	0.3531	0.3554	0.3577	0.3599	0.3621
1.1	0.3643	0.3665	0.3686	0.3708	0.3729	0.3749	0.3770	0.3790	0.3810	0.3830
1.2	0.3849	0.3869	0.3888	0.3907	0.3925	0.3944	0.3962	0.3980	0.3997	0.4015
1.3	0.4032	0.4049	0.4066	0.4082	0.4099	0.4115	0.4131	0.4147	0.4162	0.4177
1.4	0.4192	0.4207	0.4222	0.4236	0.4251	0.4265	0.4279	0.4292	0.4306	0.4319

Table 1

The Normal Distribution (continued)

z	0.00	0.01	0.02	0.03	0.04	0.05	0.06	0.07	0.08	0.09
1.5	0.4332	0.4345	0.4357	0.4370	0.4382	0.4394	0.4406	0.4418	0.4429	0.4441
1.6	0.4452	0.4463	0.4474	0.4484	0.4495	0.4505	0.4515	0.4525	0.4535	0.4545
1.7	0.4554	0.4564	0.4573	0.4582	0.4591	0.4599	0.4608	0.4616	0.4625	0.4633
1.8	0.4641	0.4649	0.4656	0.4664	0.4671	0.4678	0.4686	0.4693	0.4699	0.4706
1.9	0.4713	0.4719	0.4726	0.4732	0.4738	0.4744	0.4750	0.4756	0.4761	0.4767
2.0	0.4772	0.4778	0.4783	0.4788	0.4793	0.4798	0.4803	0.4808	0.4812	0.4817
2.1	0.4821	0.4826	0.4830	0.4834	0.4838	0.4842	0.4846	0.4850	0.4854	0.4857
2.2	0.4861	0.4864	0.4868	0.4871	0.4875	0.4878	0.4881	0.4884	0.4887	0.4890
2.3	0.4893	0.4896	0.4898	0.4901	0.4904	0.4906	0.4909	0.4911	0.4913	0.4916
2.4	0.4918	0.4920	0.4922	0.4925	0.4927	0.4929	0.4931	0.4932	0.4934	0.4936
2.5	0.4938	0.4940	0.4941	0.4943	0.4945	0.4946	0.4948	0.4949	0.4951	0.4952
2.6	0.4953	0.4955	0.4956	0.4957	0.4959	0.4960	0.4961	0.4962	0.4963	0.4964
2.7	0.4965	0.4966	0.4967	0.4968	0.4969	0.4970	0.4971	0.4972	0.4973	0.4974
2.8	0.4974	0.4975	0.4976	0.4977	0.4977	0.4978	0.4979	0.4979	0.4980	0.4981
2.9	0.4981	0.4982	0.4982	0.4983	0.4984	0.4984	0.4985	0.4985	0.4986	0.4986
3.0	0.4986	0.4987	0.4987	0.4988	0.4988	0.4989	0.4989	0.4989	0.4990	0.4990
3.1	0.4990	0.4991	0.4991	0.4991	0.4992	0.4992	0.4992	0.4992	0.4993	0.4993
3.2	0.4993	0.4993	0.4994	0.4994	0.4994	0.4994	0.4994	0.4995	0.4995	0.4995
3.3	0.4995	0.4995	0.4995	0.4996	0.4996	0.4996	0.4996	0.4996	0.4996	0.4997
3.4	0.4997	0.4997	0.4997	0.4997	0.4997	0.4997	0.4997	0.4997	0.4998	0.4998
3.5	0.4998	0.4998	0.4998	0.4998	0.4998	0.4998	0.4998	0.4998	0.4998	0.4998
3.6	0.4998	0.4998	0.4999	0.4999	0.4999	0.4999	0.4999	0.4999	0.4999	0.4999
3.7	0.4999	0.4999	0.4999	0.4999	0.4999	0.4999	0.4999	0.4999	0.4999	0.4999
3.8	0.4999	0.4999	0.4999	0.4999	0.4999	0.4999	0.4999	0.5000	0.5000	0.5000
3.9	0.5000	0.5000	0.5000	0.5000	0.5000	0.5000	0.5000	0.5000	0.5000	0.5000

Source: Table F (p. 774) in *Statistical Analysis: A Decision-Making Approach,* Second Edition by Robert Parsons. Copyright © 1978 by Robert Parsons. Reprinted by permission of Harper & Row, Publishers, Inc.

Table 2

Poisson Probability Distributions

Entry is probability mass $f(x)$ corresponding to $X = x$, where $f(x) = \lambda^x \exp(-\lambda)/x!$.

	λ								
x	.1	.2	.3	.4	.5	.6	.7	.8	.9
0	0.9048	0.8187	0.7408	0.6703	0.6065	0.5488	0.4966	0.4493	0.4066
1	0.0905	0.1637	0.2222	0.2681	0.3033	0.3293	0.3476	0.3595	0.3659
2	0.0045	0.0164	0.0333	0.0536	0.0758	0.0988	0.1217	0.1438	0.1647
3	0.0002	0.0011	0.0033	0.0072	0.0126	0.0198	0.0284	0.0383	0.0494
4	0.0000	0.0001	0.0003	0.0007	0.0016	0.0030	0.0050	0.0077	0.0111
5	0.0000	0.0000	0.0000	0.0001	0.0002	0.0004	0.0007	0.0012	0.0020
6	0.0000	0.0000	0.0000	0.0000	0.0000	0.0000	0.0001	0.0002	0.0003

	λ								
x	1.0	1.5	2.0	2.5	3.0	3.5	4.0	4.5	5.0
0	0.3679	0.2231	0.1353	0.0821	0.0498	0.0302	0.0183	0.0111	0.0067
1	0.3679	0.3347	0.2707	0.2052	0.1494	0.1057	0.0733	0.0500	0.0337
2	0.1839	0.2510	0.2707	0.2565	0.2240	0.1850	0.1465	0.1125	0.0842
3	0.0613	0.1255	0.1804	0.2138	0.2240	0.2158	0.1954	0.1687	0.1404
4	0.0153	0.0471	0.0902	0.1336	0.1680	0.1888	0.1954	0.1898	0.1755
5	0.0031	0.0141	0.0361	0.0668	0.1008	0.1322	0.1563	0.1708	0.1755
6	0.0005	0.0035	0.0120	0.0278	0.0504	0.0771	0.1042	0.1281	0.1462
7	0.0001	0.0008	0.0034	0.0099	0.0216	0.0385	0.0595	0.0824	0.1044
8	0.0000	0.0001	0.0009	0.0031	0.0081	0.0169	0.0298	0.0463	0.0653
9	0.0000	0.0000	0.0002	0.0009	0.0027	0.0066	0.0132	0.0232	0.0363
10	0.0000	0.0000	0.0000	0.0002	0.0008	0.0023	0.0053	0.0104	0.0181
11	0.0000	0.0000	0.0000	0.0000	0.0002	0.0007	0.0019	0.0043	0.0082
12	0.0000	0.0000	0.0000	0.0000	0.0001	0.0002	0.0006	0.0016	0.0034
13	0.0000	0.0000	0.0000	0.0000	0.0000	0.0001	0.0002	0.0006	0.0013
14	0.0000	0.0000	0.0000	0.0000	0.0000	0.0000	0.0001	0.0002	0.0005
15	0.0000	0.0000	0.0000	0.0000	0.0000	0.0000	0.0000	0.0001	0.0002

Table 2

Poisson Probability Distributions (continued)

					λ				
x	5.5	6.0	6.5	7.0	7.5	8.0	9.0	10.0	11.0
0	0.0041	0.0025	0.0015	0.0009	0.0006	0.0003	0.0001	0.0000	0.0000
1	0.0225	0.0149	0.0098	0.0064	0.0041	0.0027	0.0011	0.0005	0.0002
2	0.0618	0.0446	0.0318	0.0223	0.0156	0.0107	0.0050	0.0023	0.0010
3	0.1133	0.0892	0.0688	0.0521	0.0389	0.0286	0.0150	0.0076	0.0037
4	0.1558	0.1339	0.1118	0.0912	0.0729	0.0573	0.0337	0.0189	0.0102
5	0.1714	0.1606	0.1454	0.1277	0.1094	0.0916	0.0607	0.0378	0.0224
6	0.1571	0.1606	0.1575	0.1490	0.1367	0.1221	0.0911	0.0631	0.0411
7	0.1234	0.1377	0.1462	0.1490	0.1465	0.1396	0.1171	0.0901	0.0646
8	0.0849	0.1033	0.1188	0.1304	0.1373	0.1396	0.1318	0.1126	0.0888
9	0.0519	0.0688	0.0858	0.1014	0.1144	0.1241	0.1318	0.1251	0.1085
10	0.0285	0.0413	0.0558	0.0710	0.0858	0.0993	0.1186	0.1251	0.1194
11	0.0143	0.0225	0.0330	0.0452	0.0585	0.0722	0.0970	0.1137	0.1194
12	0.0065	0.0113	0.0179	0.0263	0.0366	0.0481	0.0728	0.0948	0.1094
13	0.0028	0.0052	0.0089	0.0142	0.0211	0.0296	0.0504	0.0729	0.0926
14	0.0011	0.0022	0.0041	0.0071	0.0113	0.0169	0.0324	0.0521	0.0728
15	0.0004	0.0009	0.0018	0.0033	0.0057	0.0090	0.0194	0.0347	0.0534
16	0.0001	0.0003	0.0007	0.0014	0.0026	0.0045	0.0109	0.0217	0.0367
17	0.0000	0.0001	0.0003	0.0006	0.0012	0.0021	0.0058	0.0128	0.0237
18	0.0000	0.0000	0.0001	0.0002	0.0005	0.0009	0.0029	0.0071	0.0145
19	0.0000	0.0000	0.0000	0.0001	0.0002	0.0004	0.0014	0.0037	0.0084
20	0.0000	0.0000	0.0000	0.0000	0.0001	0.0002	0.0006	0.0019	0.0046
21	0.0000	0.0000	0.0000	0.0000	0.0000	0.0001	0.0003	0.0009	0.0024
22	0.0000	0.0000	0.0000	0.0000	0.0000	0.0000	0.0001	0.0004	0.0012
23	0.0000	0.0000	0.0000	0.0000	0.0000	0.0000	0.0000	0.0002	0.0006
24	0.0000	0.0000	0.0000	0.0000	0.0000	0.0000	0.0000	0.0001	0.0003
25	0.0000	0.0000	0.0000	0.0000	0.0000	0.0000	0.0000	0.0000	0.0001

Table 2

Poisson Probability Distributions (continued)

					λ				
x	12	13	14	15	16	17	18	19	20
0	0.0000	0.0000	0.0000	0.0000	0.0000	0.0000	0.0000	0.0000	0.0000
1	0.0001	0.0000	0.0000	0.0000	0.0000	0.0000	0.0000	0.0000	0.0000
2	0.0004	0.0002	0.0001	0.0000	0.0000	0.0000	0.0000	0.0000	0.0000
3	0.0018	0.0008	0.0004	0.0002	0.0001	0.0000	0.0000	0.0000	0.0000
4	0.0053	0.0027	0.0013	0.0006	0.0003	0.0001	0.0001	0.0000	0.0000
5	0.0127	0.0070	0.0037	0.0019	0.0010	0.0005	0.0002	0.0001	0.0001
6	0.0255	0.0152	0.0087	0.0048	0.0026	0.0014	0.0007	0.0004	0.0002
7	0.0437	0.0281	0.0174	0.0104	0.0060	0.0034	0.0019	0.0010	0.0005
8	0.0655	0.0457	0.0304	0.0194	0.0120	0.0072	0.0042	0.0024	0.0013
9	0.0874	0.0661	0.0473	0.0324	0.0213	0.0135	0.0083	0.0050	0.0029
10	0.1048	0.0859	0.0663	0.0486	0.0341	0.0230	0.0150	0.0095	0.0058
11	0.1144	0.1015	0.0844	0.0663	0.0496	0.0355	0.0245	0.0164	0.0106
12	0.1144	0.1099	0.0984	0.0829	0.0661	0.0504	0.0368	0.0259	0.0176
13	0.1056	0.1099	0.1060	0.0956	0.0814	0.0658	0.0509	0.0378	0.0271
14	0.0905	0.1021	0.1060	0.1024	0.0930	0.0800	0.0655	0.0514	0.0387
15	0.0724	0.0885	0.0989	0.1024	0.0992	0.0906	0.0786	0.0650	0.0516
16	0.0543	0.0719	0.0866	0.0960	0.0992	0.0963	0.0884	0.0772	0.0646
17	0.0383	0.0550	0.0713	0.0847	0.0934	0.0963	0.0936	0.0863	0.0760
18	0.0255	0.0397	0.0554	0.0706	0.0830	0.0909	0.0936	0.0911	0.0844
19	0.0161	0.0272	0.0409	0.0557	0.0699	0.0814	0.0887	0.0911	0.0888
20	0.0097	0.0177	0.0286	0.0418	0.0559	0.0692	0.0798	0.0866	0.0888
21	0.0055	0.0109	0.0191	0.0299	0.0426	0.0560	0.0684	0.0783	0.0846
22	0.0030	0.0065	0.0121	0.0204	0.0310	0.0433	0.0560	0.0876	0.0769
23	0.0016	0.0037	0.0074	0.0133	0.0216	0.0320	0.0438	0.0559	0.0669
24	0.0008	0.0020	0.0043	0.0083	0.0144	0.0226	0.0328	0.0442	0.0557
25	0.0004	0.0010	0.0024	0.0050	0.0092	0.0154	0.0237	0.0336	0.0446
26	0.0002	0.0005	0.0013	0.0029	0.0057	0.0101	0.0164	0.0240	0.0343
27	0.0001	0.0002	0.0007	0.0016	0.0034	0.0063	0.0109	0.0173	0.0254
28	0.0000	0.0001	0.0003	0.0009	0.0019	0.0038	0.0070	0.0117	0.0181
29	0.0000	0.0001	0.0002	0.0004	0.0011	0.0023	0.0044	0.0077	0.0125
30	0.0000	0.0000	0.0001	0.0002	0.0006	0.0013	0.0026	0.0049	0.0083
31	0.0000	0.0000	0.0000	0.0001	0.0003	0.0007	0.0015	0.0030	0.0054
32	0.0000	0.0000	0.0000	0.0001	0.0001	0.0004	0.0009	0.0018	0.0034
33	0.0000	0.0000	0.0000	0.0000	0.0001	0.0002	0.0005	0.0010	0.0020
34	0.0000	0.0000	0.0000	0.0000	0.0000	0.0001	0.0002	0.0006	0.0012
35	0.0000	0.0000	0.0000	0.0000	0.0000	0.0000	0.0001	0.0003	0.0007
36	0.0000	0.0000	0.0000	0.0000	0.0000	0.0000	0.0001	0.0002	0.0004
37	0.0000	0.0000	0.0000	0.0000	0.0000	0.0000	0.0000	0.0001	0.0002
38	0.0000	0.0000	0.0000	0.0000	0.0000	0.0000	0.0000	0.0000	0.0001
39	0.0000	0.0000	0.0000	0.0000	0.0000	0.0000	0.0000	0.0000	0.0001

Source: From J. Neter, W Wasserman, and G. A. Whitmore, *Applied Statistics.* Copyright © 1978 by Allyn and Bacon, Inc., Boston. Reprinted with permission.

Table 3

The *t* Distribution

df	.10	.05	.025	.01	0.005	.001	.0005
1	3.078	6.314	12.71	31.821	63.657	—	636.619
2	1.886	2.920	4.31	6.965	9.925	—	31.598
3	1.638	2.353	3.19	4.541	5.841	—	12.941
4	1.533	2.132	2.78	3.747	4.604	7.18	8.610
5	1.476	2.015	2.57	3.365	4.032	5.90	6.859
6	1.440	1.943	2.45	3.143	3.707	5.21	5.959
7	1.415	1.895	2.37	2.998	3.499	4.79	5.405
8	1.397	1.860	2.31	2.896	3.355	4.51	5.041
9	1.383	1.833	2.27	2.821	3.250	4.30	4.781
10	1.372	1.812	2.23	2.764	3.169	4.15	4.587
11	1.363	1.796	2.20	2.718	3.106	4.03	4.437
12	1.356	1.782	2.18	2.681	3.055	3.93	4.318
13	1.350	1.771	2.16	2.650	3.012	3.86	4.221
14	1.345	1.761	2.15	2.624	2.977	3.79	4.140
15	1.341	1.753	2.13	2.602	2.947	3.74	4.073
16	1.337	1.746	2.12	2.583	2.921	3.69	4.015
17	1.333	1.740	2.11	2.567	2.898	3.65	3.965
18	1.330	1.734	2.10	2.552	2.878	3.62	3.922
19	1.328	1.729	2.09	2.539	2.861	3.58	3.883
20	1.325	1.725	2.09	2.528	2.845	3.56	3.850
21	1.323	1.721	2.08	2.518	2.831	3.53	3.819
22	1.321	1.717	2.07	2.508	2.819	3.51	3.792
23	1.319	1.714	2.07	2.500	2.807	3.49	3.767
24	1.318	1.711	2.06	2.492	2.797	3.47	3.745
25	1.316	1.708	2.06	2.485	2.787	3.45	3.725
26	1.315	1.706	2.06	2.479	2.779	3.44	3.707
27	1.314	1.703	2.05	2.473	2.771	3.43	3.690
28	1.313	1.701	2.05	2.467	2.763	3.41	3.674
29	1.311	1.699	2.05	2.462	2.756	3.40	3.659
30	1.310	1.697	2.04	2.457	2.750	3.39	3.646
∞	1.282	1.645	1.96	2.326	2.576	3.08	3.291

Level of Significance for One-Tailed Test

Source: Adapted from *Applied Regression Analysis and Other Multivariable Methods* by David G. Kleinbaum and Lawrence L. Kupper. Copyright © 1978, Wadsworth, Inc., Belmont, CA. Reprinted by permission of the publisher, Duxbury Press. Figures for .025 and .001 calculated by Kenneth J. Meier using NCSS statistical software.

Table 4

The Chi-Square Distribution

p	0.10	0.05	0.025	0.01	0.005	df
	2.71	3.84	5.02	6.63	7.88	1
	4.61	5.99	7.38	9.21	10.60	2
	6.25	7.81	9.35	11.34	12.84	3
	7.78	9.49	11.14	13.28	14.86	4
	9.24	11.07	12.83	15.09	16.75	5
	10.64	12.59	14.45	16.81	18.55	6
	12.02	14.07	16.01	18.48	20.3	7
	13.36	15.51	17.53	20.1	22.0	8
	14.68	16.92	19.02	21.7	23.6	9
	15.99	18.31	20.5	23.2	25.2	10
	17.28	19.68	21.9	24.7	26.8	11
	18.55	21.0	23.3	26.2	28.3	12
	19.81	22.4	24.7	27.7	29.8	13
	21.1	23.7	26.1	29.1	31.3	14
	22.3	25.0	27.5	30.6	32.8	15
	23.5	26.3	28.8	32.0	34.3	16
	24.8	27.6	30.2	33.4	35.7	17
	26.0	28.9	31.5	34.8	37.2	18
	27.2	30.1	32.9	36.2	38.6	19
	28.4	31.4	34.2	37.6	40.0	20
	29.6	32.7	35.5	38.9	41.4	21
	30.8	33.9	36.8	40.3	42.8	22
	32.0	35.2	38.1	41.6	44.2	23
	33.2	36.4	39.4	43.0	45.6	24
	34.4	37.7	40.6	44.3	46.9	25
	35.6	38.9	41.9	45.6	48.3	26
	36.7	40.1	43.2	47.0	49.6	27
	37.9	41.3	44.5	48.3	51.0	28
	39.1	42.6	45.7	49.6	52.3	29
	40.3	43.8	47.0	50.9	53.7	30
	51.8	55.8	59.3	63.7	66.8	40
	63.2	67.5	71.4	76.2	79.5	50
	74.4	79.1	83.3	88.4	92.0	60
	85.5	90.5	95.0	100.4	104.2	70
	96.6	101.9	106.6	112.3	116.3	80
	107.6	113.1	118.1	124.1	128.3	90
	118.5	124.3	129.6	135.8	140.2	100

Source: Adapted from *Applied Regression Analysis and Other Multivariable Methods* by David G. Kleinbaum and Lawrence L. Kupper. Copyright © 1978, Wadsworth, Inc., Belmont, CA. Reprinted by permission of the publisher, Duxbury Press.

Table 5

Durbin-Watson Statistic Test Bounds

Probability = .05

n	k = 1		k = 2		k = 3		k = 4		k = 5		k = 6	
	d_L	d_U	d_L	d_U	d_L	d_U	d_L	d_U	d_L	d_U	d_L	d_U
6	0.610	1.400	—	—	—	—	—	—	—	—	—	—
7	0.700	1.356	0.467	1.896	—	—	—	—	—	—	—	—
8	0.763	1.332	0.559	1.777	0.368	2.287	—	—	—	—	—	—
9	0.824	1.320	0.629	1.699	0.455	2.128	0.296	2.588	—	—	—	—
10	0.879	1.320	0.697	1.641	0.525	2.016	0.376	2.414	0.243	2.822	—	—
11	0.927	1.324	0.758	1.604	0.595	1.928	0.444	2.283	0.316	2.645	0.203	3.005
12	0.971	1.331	0.812	1.579	0.658	1.864	0.512	2.177	0.379	2.506	0.268	2.832
13	1.010	1.340	0.861	1.562	0.715	1.816	0.574	2.094	0.445	2.390	0.328	2.692
14	1.045	1.350	0.905	1.551	0.767	1.779	0.632	2.030	0.505	2.296	0.389	2.572
15	1.077	1.361	0.946	1.543	0.814	1.750	0.685	1.977	0.562	2.220	0.447	2.472
16	1.106	1.371	0.982	1.539	0.857	1.728	0.734	1.935	0.615	2.157	0.502	2.388
17	1.133	1.381	1.015	1.536	0.897	1.710	0.779	1.900	0.664	2.104	0.554	2.318
18	1.158	1.391	1.046	1.535	0.933	1.696	0.820	1.872	0.710	2.060	0.603	2.257
19	1.180	1.401	1.074	1.536	0.967	1.685	0.859	1.848	0.752	2.023	0.649	2.206
20	1.201	1.411	1.100	1.537	0.998	1.676	0.894	1.828	0.792	1.991	0.692	2.162
21	1.221	1.420	1.125	1.538	1.026	1.669	0.927	1.812	0.829	1.964	0.732	2.124
22	1.239	1.429	1.147	1.541	1.053	1.664	0.958	1.797	0.863	1.940	0.769	2.090
23	1.257	1.437	1.168	1.543	1.078	1.660	0.986	1.785	0.895	1.920	0.804	2.061
24	1.273	1.446	1.188	1.546	1.101	1.656	1.013	1.775	0.925	1.902	0.837	2.035
25	1.288	1.454	1.206	1.550	1.123	1.654	1.038	1.767	0.953	1.886	0.868	2.012
26	1.302	1.461	1.224	1.553	1.143	1.652	1.062	1.759	0.979	1.873	0.897	1.992
27	1.316	1.469	1.240	1.556	1.162	1.651	1.084	1.753	1.004	1.861	0.925	1.974
28	1.328	1.476	1.255	1.560	1.181	1.650	1.104	1.747	1.028	1.850	0.951	1.958
29	1.341	1.483	1.270	1.563	1.198	1.650	1.124	1.743	1.050	1.841	0.975	1.944
30	1.352	1.489	1.284	1.567	1.214	1.650	1.143	1.739	1.071	1.833	0.998	1.931

Table 5

Durbin-Watson Statistic Test Bounds (continued)

Probability = .05

n	$k=1$ d_L	d_U	$k=2$ d_L	d_U	$k=3$ d_L	d_U	$k=4$ d_L	d_U	$k=5$ d_L	d_U	$k=6$ d_L	d_U
31	1.363	1.496	1.297	1.570	1.229	1.650	1.160	1.735	1.090	1.825	1.020	1.920
32	1.373	1.502	1.309	1.574	1.244	1.650	1.177	1.732	1.109	1.819	1.041	1.909
33	1.383	1.508	1.321	1.577	1.258	1.651	1.193	1.730	1.127	1.813	1.061	1.900
34	1.393	1.514	1.333	1.580	1.271	1.652	1.208	1.728	1.144	1.808	1.080	1.891
35	1.402	1.519	1.343	1.584	1.283	1.653	1.222	1.726	1.160	1.803	1.097	1.884
36	1.411	1.525	1.354	1.587	1.295	1.654	1.236	1.724	1.175	1.799	1.114	1.877
37	1.419	1.530	1.364	1.590	1.307	1.655	1.249	1.723	1.190	1.795	1.131	1.870
38	1.427	1.535	1.373	1.594	1.318	1.656	1.261	1.722	1.204	1.792	1.146	1.864
39	1.435	1.540	1.382	1.597	1.328	1.658	1.273	1.722	1.218	1.789	1.161	1.859
40	1.442	1.544	1.391	1.600	1.338	1.659	1.285	1.721	1.230	1.786	1.175	1.854
45	1.475	1.566	1.430	1.615	1.383	1.666	1.336	1.720	1.287	1.776	1.238	1.835
50	1.503	1.585	1.462	1.628	1.421	1.674	1.378	1.721	1.335	1.771	1.291	1.822
55	1.528	1.601	1.490	1.641	1.452	1.681	1.414	1.724	1.374	1.768	1.334	1.814
60	1.549	1.616	1.514	1.652	1.480	1.689	1.444	1.727	1.408	1.767	1.372	1.808
65	1.567	1.629	1.536	1.662	1.503	1.696	1.471	1.731	1.438	1.767	1.404	1.805
70	1.583	1.641	1.554	1.672	1.525	1.703	1.494	1.735	1.464	1.768	1.433	1.802
75	1.598	1.652	1.571	1.680	1.543	1.709	1.515	1.739	1.487	1.770	1.458	1.801
80	1.611	1.662	1.586	1.688	1.560	1.715	1.534	1.743	1.507	1.772	1.480	1.801
85	1.624	1.671	1.600	1.696	1.575	1.721	1.550	1.747	1.525	1.774	1.500	1.801
90	1.635	1.679	1.612	1.703	1.589	1.726	1.566	1.751	1.542	1.776	1.518	1.801
95	1.645	1.687	1.623	1.709	1.602	1.732	1.579	1.755	1.557	1.778	1.535	1.802
100	1.654	1.694	1.634	1.715	1.613	1.736	1.592	1.758	1.571	1.780	1.550	1.803
150	1.720	1.746	1.706	1.760	1.693	1.774	1.679	1.788	1.665	1.802	1.651	1.817
200	1.758	1.778	1.748	1.789	1.738	1.799	1.728	1.810	1.718	1.820	1.707	1.831

Source: Reprinted with permission from *Biometrica,* Vol. 38 (1951: 159–178).

Glossary

a priori probability   probability based on reasoning rather than on a series of trials.

adjusted R^2 (coefficient of determination)   a measure of goodness of fit in regression which adjusts for the inclusion of variables with little or no explanatory power in a model.

alpha   the probability level selected as the cutoff point for rejecting the null hypothesis.

assumptions   untested propositions (usually within a theory).

asymmetric distribution   a frequency or percentage distribution that is not perfectly balanced about its midpoint.

average deviation   the average difference between the mean and all other values in a set of data.

bar chart   a bar graph for a variable that can take on only a very limited set of values.

basic law of probability   states that if all possible outcomes of an event are equally likely, the probability of any outcome is equal to the ratio of the number of ways that the outcome could occur to the total number of ways that all outcomes could occur.

Bayesian   an approach to statistics and decision making that relies on subjective probabilities.

benchmarking   a technique used to compare an organization's performance

on a particular criterion to performance of similar organizations on the same criterion.

Bernoulli process   a process in which the outcome of any trial can be classified into one of two mutually exclusive and jointly exhaustive outcomes and each trial is independent of all other trials.

bimodal distribution   a data distribution with two distinct peaks where observations tend to cluster.

binomial probability distribution   a discrete probability distribution for phenomena that can be described by a Bernoulli process.

bivariate   using two variables; contingency tables are bivariate presentations; simple regression is a bivariate technique.

bivariate forecasting   a time series in which the independent variable is a real variable rather than time.

case study   an in-depth examination of an event or locale, usually undertaken after something dramatic has transpired.

cells   the cross-classifications of two variables in a contingency table.

central limit theorem   a foundational concept in statistical inference which states that if a sampling distribution is made up of samples containing more than 30 cases (each), the sample means will be normally distributed.

certainty in decision theory, the situation in which the states of nature are known before the decision is made.

chance node in decision theory, a decision that cannot be controlled by the decision maker.

chi-square statistic the calculated value of chi-square that is compared with the chi-square distribution table (see statistical tables in the appendix) to determine statistical significance.

chi-square test a measure of statistical significance for contingency tables.

class one of the group categories used to cluster data in a frequency distribution.

class boundary the lowest or highest value of a variable that falls within a class or grouping of a variable.

class frequency the number of items in any given class in a frequency distribution.

class interval the distance between the upper class boundary and the lower class boundary in a frequency distribution.

class midpoint the point halfway between the lower and upper boundaries of a class.

coefficient of determination a measure of goodness of fit for a regression line based on the ratio of explained variation to total variation.

combination the number of ways a group of items can be clustered into subsets of similar size (such as a combination of five things taken three at a time).

concept the basic building block of research or theory that abstracts or summarizes a critical characteristic or aspect of a class of events.

concordant pair used in some measures of association for a contingency table, a pair of observations that provides support for the existence of a positive relationship between two variables.

conditional probability the probability that one event will occur given that another has occurred.

confidence limits the upper and lower boundaries that one is X percent sure the estimate falls within (as in 95% confidence limits).

consensual validity an indicator has consensual validity when numerous researchers accept the indicator as valid.

constraints in linear programming, the variables that restrict the options open to managers.

context in research design, the setting in which a study is conducted, important for external validity.

contingency table a table that shows how two or more variables are related by cross-tabulating the variables.

continuous variable a variable that can take on values that are not whole numbers (fractional values).

control variable a third variable introduced to determine if the relationship between two other variables is spurious.

convergent validity if indicators of a concept produce similar results, the indicators have convergent validity.

correlational validity validity established when an indicator correlates strongly with other accepted valid indicators.

correlation coefficient the square root of the coefficient of determination with a plus or minus sign the same as that for the slope.

covariation a statistical relationship between variables, necessary (but not sufficient) to infer causality.

Cramér's V a measure of association based on chi-square for cross-tabulations that include variables measured at the nominal or higher levels of measurement.

cross-sectional (correlational) study a quasi-experimental research design in which data are obtained for one point in time, often from a large sample of subjects.

cubic relationship a relationship between two variables that resembles an S-shaped curve.

cumulative frequency distribution a frequency distribution in which one column contains the cumulative percentage of items and below in a given class.

cumulative percentage distribution a percentage distribution that progressively adds the percentages of observations that fall above or below a certain standard.

cyclical pattern in time series analysis, a trend or cycle in the data points that repeats regularly over time.

decision node in decision theory, any decision that the decision maker can resolve.

decision table in decision theory, a table that pairs the various states of nature with the decision options open to the decision maker.

decision tree a method of analysis for analyzing a series of decisions.

decision variable in linear programming, the variables that the manager can affect or change.

degrees of freedom a measure needed to use many probability distributions, such as the chi-square or the t distributions.

dependent samples samples where individual cases from one sample are paired or matched with cases from the second sample.

dependent variable the variable that is caused or predicted by the independent variable (in regression the Y variable).

descriptive statistics statistics used to summarize a body of data; contrasted with inferential statistics.

discordant pair used in some measures of association for a contingency table, a pair of observations that provides support for the existence of a negative relationship between two variables.

discrete variable a variable that has a minimum-sized unit that cannot be further subdivided.

discriminant validity if an indicator distinguishes one concept from another similar but different concept, it has discriminant validity.

dispersion (measures of) numerical designations of how closely data cluster about the mean or other measure of central tendency (see *standard deviation*).

dummy variable   a nominal level variable coded with values of 1 and 0 and used in a regression.

error   in regression analysis, the distance a data point is from the regression line.

expected frequencies   in calculating the chi-square statistic, the hypothetical frequencies that would be predicted for each cell of the contingency table if the two variables were not related.

expected value   the sum of the products of all the values that can be attained and their respective probability of attainment.

experimental design   research design with rigid controls in a laboratory setting.

exponential probability distribution   a probability distribution used to estimate the length of time between events.

external validity   the degree to which research findings or results can be generalized to hold true in other populations, settings, or times.

extrarational analysis   analysis that goes beyond rational models and incorporates judgment, experience, and so on.

face validity   an indicator has face validity when the researcher accepts the indicator as valid.

forecasting   the use of statistical techniques—usually time series regression—to predict the future.

frequency distribution   a table that shows a body of data grouped according to numerical values.

frequency polygon   a graphic method of presenting a frequency distribution.

functional relationship   a relationship in which one variable is an exact weighted combination of one or more variables or constants (a relationship without statistical error).

gamma   an ordinal measure of association sensitive to curvilinear relationships.

general rule of addition   a probability rule that tells one how to calculate the probability of the union of two events.

general rule of multiplication   in probability, the formula used to calculate the joint probability of two events, that is, the probability of both events occurring.

grand total   the total number of cases contained in a contingency table.

grouped data   data that are grouped into classes, such as in a frequency distribution.

histogram   a bar graph representing a frequency distribution.

homoscedasticity   an assumption of linear regression that the size of the errors is not affected by the size of the independent variables.

hypergeometric probability distribution   a probability distribution used when trials are independent and the universe is finite.

hypothesis   a statement about the world that can be either true or false.

independent events   in probability, the situation in which the probability of one event occurring is not affected by whether or not the other event occurs.

independent samples   samples where individual cases across two samples are not paired or matched.

independent variable   the variable that causes or predicts the dependent variable (in regression, the X variable).

indicator   a measurable aspect of a concept.

inferential statistics   using sample statistics to infer characteristics about the population.

insufficient reason   a principle that holds that events are equally probable unless one can establish otherwise.

intercept   the point at which the regression line crosses the Y-axis.

internal validity   the degree to which research findings or results satisfy all conditions for establishing causality.

interpolation   a procedure used to calculate how far into a class or interval of a variable a particular value lies.

interquartile deviation   in a frequency or percentage distribution, the two data values that cut off the middle 50% of all values.

interrater reliability   a technique used to assess the degree of consistency among individuals who are applying a measurement scheme to collect and code data.

interval estimate   in statistical inference, a range or interval determined so that the probability that a parameter falls within it is acceptably high (for example, 95%).

interval level   a highly precise level of measurement based on a unit or interval accepted as a common standard.

joint probability   the probability of two events both occurring.

Kendall's tau-*b* and tau-*c*   measures of association based on covariation for cross-tabulations that include variables measured at the ordinal level; tau-*b* is appropriate for square tables, and tau-*c* is appropriate for rectangular tables.

lack of precision   a threat to the reliability of measurement arising from the use of small samples or measurement scales lacking sufficient gradations.

lambda   a nominal measure of association based on the principle of proportionate reduction in error.

law of large numbers   a concept in probability theory that states that large samples are more likely to approach normality than small samples.

least squares   in regression analysis, the principle of minimizing the sum of squared errors to fit the regression line to the data.

level of statistical significance   the probability of error (i.e., type 1 error) the researcher is willing to tolerate in making an inference from the sample to the population.

levels of measurement   the precision inherent in the measurement of different types of variables.

linear programming   a management technique that allocates inputs to maximize outputs subject to constraints under conditions of certainty.

linear regression   regression in which the relationship between the variables is assumed to be linear.

logarithmic relationship   a relationship between two variables in which one increases at a constant rate.

marginals   the row or column frequency totals in a contingency table.

maximax a criterion for decision making under uncertainty that assumes that the best situation will happen.

maximin a criterion for decision making under uncertainty that is based on expecting the worst to happen.

mean the arithmetic average for a group of data.

measurement the systematic assignment of numbers or categories to some phenomenon of interest for purposes of analysis.

measurement reliability an indicator is reliable if it consistently assigns the same numbers to similar phenomena.

measurement validity does the measure tap what the research analyst thinks it measures?

measures of association statistics designed to measure the magnitude and direction of the relationship between two variables in a cross-tabulation.

measures of central tendency statistics designed to represent the average or middle in a distribution of data.

measures of dispersion statistics designed to reveal how much the data do or do not cluster around the mean.

median the middle item in a group of data when the data are ranked in order of magnitude.

minimax regret a criterion for decision making under uncertainty that maximizes opportunity costs.

mode the most common value in any distribution.

model a simplified version of a theory that captures its key components and is amenable to empirical testing.

model specification the idea in multiple regression that relevant explanatory variables are included, while irrelevant ones are excluded, when predicting variation in a dependent variable.

moving average in time series analysis, a procedure based on averaging contiguous observations to filter out short-term fluctuations, especially cycles.

multicolinearity a case in multiple regression analysis where two independent variables significantly overlap, affecting the accuracy of slope estimates.

multiple causation the social science position that an event or phenomenon can have several causes.

multiple indicators a strategy of measurement in which several indicators are used to measure a single concept.

multiple regression an interval level statistical technique that uses several independent variables to predict or explain one dependent variable based on minimizing squared error.

mutually exclusive events are mutually exclusive if they both cannot happen at the same time.

negatively skewed data a frequency distribution that has a few extremely low numbers or data values that distort the mean.

nominal definition defines a concept in terms of other concepts.

nominal level a measurement level that allows only a determination that phenomena are the same or different, lacking any sense of relative size or magnitude.

nonspuriousness a criterion for a causal relationship requiring that a covariation or association between two variables or phenomena cannot be explained by a third factor.

normal curve a classic bell-shape curve or distribution indicating that observations at or close to the mean occur with highest probability, and that the probability of occurrence progressively decreases as observations deviate from the mean.

normal distribution a bell-shape curve that describes the distribution of many phenomena.

null hypothesis the hypothesis that there is no impact or change (nothing happened); the working hypothesis phrased negatively.

objective indicators indicators that are based on reports or documents and do not require any judgment on the researcher's part.

ogive a graphic presentation of a cumulative frequency distribution.

one-tailed test a significance test in which the hypothesis specifies a direction (and, therefore, uses only one tail of the normal curve or some other probability distribution).

operational definition a definition that specifies that a concept will be measured in a given way for purposes of the study in question.

ordinal level a level of measurement at which it is possible to say the one object (or event or phenomenon) has more or less of a given characteristic than another, but not how much more or less.

outlier an extreme value in a frequency distribution; can have a disproportionate influence on the mean.

output variables in linear programming, variables that the manager wants to maximize or minimize.

paired observations a procedure used in the calculation of some measures of association for contingency tables that relates observations in different cells of the table.

panel study a type of study in which a series of cross-sectional studies is conducted on the same sample of individuals over time; that is, a group of individuals is surveyed at repeated intervals over time.

parallel forms reliability the correlation between responses obtained on two sets of items measured for reliability.

parameter a measure used to summarize characteristics of a population based on all items in the population (such as a population mean).

partial slope another name for regression coefficients in a multiple regression.

payoff in decision theory, the benefit or cost to the decision maker of selecting a particular course of action, contingent on the states of nature or the actions of another decision maker.

percentage difference in contingency table analysis, an elemental measure of association based on calculating and comparing percentages in appropriate cells of the table.

percentage distribution a frequency distribution that contains a column listing the percentage of items in each class.

perfect information information that allows one to specify in advance the state of nature that will occur.

Poisson distribution   a probability distribution used when events occur at varying intervals of time, space, or distance.

polynomial curve fitting   the use of regression to estimate nonlinear relationships.

population   the total set of items that one wants to analyze (all bus users, all citizens of a city, and so on).

positive-sum game   a game that everyone can win.

positively skewed data   a frequency distribution that has a few extremely high numbers or data values that distort the mean.

posterior probability   probabilities generated by numerous trials; also called long-run probability.

predicted value   in regression analysis, the expected (predicted) value of the dependent variable for a given value of the independent variable based on the calculated regression line.

predictive validity   a type of measurement validity based on the degree to which an indicator correctly predicts a specified outcome in the future.

prisoner's dilemma   a game theory situation where rationality results in a suboptimal situation.

probability   expresses the likelihood of a given event occurring over the long term.

probability distribution   an exhaustive listing of all possible outcomes of a phenomenon or event with their associated probabilities of occurrence.

quasi-experimental designs   research designs that lack the requirements of experimental designs but are structured in a similar fashion.

random assignment   in research design, a procedure that gives each subject an equal chance of placement in the experimental group or the control group so that no systematic difference exists between the groups prior to administration of the treatment.

range   a measure of dispersion calculated by subtracting the smallest value in a distribution from the largest value.

rational decision making   decision making following these steps: (1) identify the problem, (2) specify goals, (3) specify alternatives to reach goals, (4) evaluate alternatives in light of goals, and (5) select the optimal alternative.

regression   a statistical technique used to describe the relationship between two variables based on the principle of minimizing errors in prediction.

regression coefficient   the weight assigned to independent variables in a regression (the beta or slope).

reliable indicator   an indicator that consistently assigns the same scores to some phenomenon that has not, in fact, changed, regardless of who is doing the measuring, where the measuring is conducted, or other extraneous factors.

research design   a systematic program for testing empirically, proposed causal relationships that guides the collection, analysis, and interpretation of the relevant data.

research hypothesis   the opposite of the null hypothesis, typically phrased positively (impact or change rather than no impact or no change).

residual variation   the average squared error in prediction with a regression equation.

risk   a condition that exists when probabilities can be assigned to states of nature before a decision is made.

sample   a subset of the population usually selected randomly. Measures that summarize a sample are called sample statistics.

satisficing   selecting an alternative in decision making that will work rather than looking for the best alternative.

scale   a composite measure that combines several variables into a single unified measure of a concept.

slope   the degree that a regression line rises or falls as one moves along it from left to right (often called beta or the regression coefficient).

Somers's d_{yx} and d_{xy}   measures of association based on covariation for cross-tabulations that include variables measured at the ordinal level.

special rule of addition for mutually exclusive events   in probability theory, when two events are mutually exclusive, the probability of one or the other of them occurring is equal to the probability of one of the events plus the probability of the other (addenda to the "general rule of addition").

split-half reliability   measure of reliability in which the set of items intended to measure a given concept is divided into two parts.

spurious relationship   a relationship between two variables that is caused by a third variable.

standard deviation   a measure of dispersion, the square root of the average squared deviation from the mean.

standard error of the estimate   an estimate of the error (equivalent to one standard deviation) in an estimate of Y derived from a regression equation; a measure of goodness of fit.

standard error of the mean   an estimate of the amount of error in a sample estimate of a population mean.

standard error of the slope   a measure of goodness of fit in a regression; a measure of error in a slope estimated from sample data.

states of nature   in decision theory, any important variables that affect the outcome of a decision but are not under the control of the decision maker (the conditions that exist when a decision is made).

statistic   a measure that is used to summarize a sample of data.

statistical controls   a procedure used to check and evaluate the relationship between an independent variable and a dependent variable by introducing a third, control variable into the analysis.

statistical relationship   a recognizable pattern of change in one variable as the other variable changes.

Student's t distribution   a sampling distribution used for testing hypotheses on small samples.

subjective indicators   indicators that are based on the judgment of one or more persons.

subjective measure a measure that relies on the judgment of the analyst or of a respondent in a survey.

suboptimization a subunit of an organization maximizing its goals in a manner detrimental to the goals of the entire organization.

symmetric distribution a frequency or percentage distribution that is perfectly balanced about its midpoint.

test–retest reliability method for assessing measurement reliability by measuring the same phenomenon or set of variables twice over a reasonably short time period.

theory an integrated set of propositions intended to explain or account for a given phenomenon.

time order a criterion for a causal relationship requiring that the independent variable or phenomenon must precede the dependent variable or phenomenon in time.

time series a variable measured at regular time intervals.

time series analysis a variety of statistical techniques for analyzing and forecasting the observations of a variable measured at equally spaced intervals over time.

total frequency the total number of observations or cases in an analysis, usually denoted by the symbol **N**.

trend study studies that monitor and attempt to account for shifts over time in various indicators, usually highly aggregated (e.g., gross national product).

***t* test** a statistical test based on the t distribution used for slopes and

for means when n is less than 30 and the population is not normally distributed.

two-tailed test a significance test in which the hypothesis does not specify direction (and, therefore, uses both tails of a probability distribution).

Type I error rejecting the null hypothesis when it is true.

Type II error accepting the null hypothesis when it is false.

uncertainty a condition in which the probability of any given state of nature is unknown.

uniform distribution a frequency (percentage) distribution in which each data value or set of values occurs with equal frequency (percentage).

union in probability theory, for two events, the probability that one event occurred or the other event occurred.

univariate referring to the presentation or analysis of one variable at a time; for example, frequency distributions and measures of central tendency.

unobtrusive indicator a variable or measure collected without the knowledge or reactivity of the subject, such as fingerprint smudges on museum display cases to evaluate the popularity of different exhibits.

unobtrusive measures nonreactive measuring instruments in which the act of measuring a phenomenon does not alter the behavior or attribute being assessed.

valid indicator an indicator that accurately measures the concept it is intended to measure.

variable   a measured quantity or characteristic that can take on a variety of values (that is, varies).

variance   the average squared deviation from the mean; the square of the standard deviation.

zero-sum game   a game in which one person's winning means another person lost.

z score   the number of standard deviations an item is from the mean; z scores can be calculated for raw data, means, slopes, regression estimates, and so on.

Answers to Odd-Numbered Computational Problems

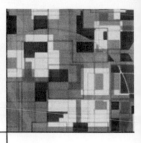

The following are the answers to selected problems in which computations play an important role. Where the answers to questions are based on interpretation (for example, Chapters 1–4) or management judgment, the answers are not included.

For Chapters 11–14, exact probabilities for the answers have been calculated using a statistical software package. Because the t distribution table only provides seven levels of significance ranging from .10 to .0005, exact probabilities cannot be calculated by hand. When working out the problems for these chapters, it is sufficient to evaluate whether the t statistic obtained falls above or below a particular level of significance (such as < or > .05).

Chapter 2

2.9 A different number should be selected to represent each category. Because there are 4 categories, numbering the categories 1 through 4 is logical, but other numbers are acceptable.

$1 =$ Friend
$2 =$ Silver
$3 =$ Gold
$4 =$ Platinum

Interval Version	Ordinal Version
$25	1
$150	2
$75	1
$450	3
$100	2
$750	4
$90	1
$175	2
$250	3
$50	1

2.11 Translating the numbers into words yields the following results for each employee

Employee   1: female, full-time, and professional.

                2: male, full-time, general labor

                3: female, part-time, administrative

                4: male, full-time, administrative

                5: female, part-time, professional

                6: female, part-time, professional

                7: male, part-time, general labor

                8: female, full-time, general labor

Chapter 5

5.1 Mean = 59; median = 59

5.3 Mean = 7.87; median = 9.32. On average, public works department employees use more sick leave than other Normal, Oklahoma, employees.

5.5 Mean = \$1,330; median = \$1,391.30

5.7 Mean = 24.16; median = 19.91. Since data are positively skewed, the median age is more appropriate.

5.9 Mean = 52.5; median = 44; both are correct

5.11 Mean = 15.47; median = 16.28

5.13 Mean = 3.48; median = 3.55

5.15 Percentage distribution

To a very great extent	37.8%
To a great extent	27.9%
To a moderate extent	17.1%
To some extent	10.8%
Not at all	6.3%

Level of measurement = ordinal; median = to a great extent; mode = to a very great extent. Department appears to have a problem with waste and inefficiency.

5.17 Percentage distribution

Far above expectations	11.5%
Above expectations	16.8%
Meets expectations	58.8%
Below expectations	6.9%
Far below expectations	6.1%

Level of measurement = ordinal; median = meets expectations; mode = meets expectations. Only 28.3% of recreation department employees, rather than the 90% desired by the department head, fall into the top two categories.

Chapter 6

6.1   Brand B has greater variation despite its higher mean; it may not be as useful as Brand A.

6.3   Some crews are hauling a lot less garbage than others and skewing the distribution in a negative direction.

6.5   Standard deviation = 43.23.

6.7   Select System A. System A is better than System C because it has a smaller mean and standard deviation. System A is also better than System B because System B is erratic.

6.9   On average (mean) it takes 193 days to close a case, but mean is inflated by some especially long closures.

6.11   Mean = 20.94; median = 19.5; mode = 15; standard deviation = 8.55. Evidence suggests that a few employees do much more work than all of the others.

6.13   Mean = 35.29; median = 31; standard deviation = 12.12. Report median because data are positively skewed (one case is nearly twice as large as the next largest case).

Chapter 7

7.1   (a) .25 (b) .1125 (c) .3913 (d) .6 (e) .5667

7.5 $p < .0000000001336$

7.7   .726

7.9   .262, unlikely

7.11 $P(A \cup B) = .45 + .31 - .26 = .50$

$P(A \mid B) = .84$, (Hint: use general rule of multiplication)

$P(B \mid A) = \mathbf{.51}$

7.13 $P(A \cap B) = .61 \times .3 = .18$

$P(A \cup B) = .3 + .61 - .18 = .73$

Chapter 8

8.1 $z = (50 - 67) \div 7 = -17 \div 7 = -2.43$. $p\ (z = 2.43) = .4925$. $.5 - .4925 = .0075$. So, 0.75% process fewer forms, and 99.25% process more forms. Complaint seems justified.

8.3 $z = (42 - 36) \div 5 = 6 \div 5 = 1.20$. $p\,(z = 1.20) = .3849$. So the probability of reimbursement within 42 days $= .5 + .3849 = .8849$. The probability of reimbursement after 42 days $= 1 - .8849 = .1151$. Since score is only slightly more than one standard deviation above mean, probably should not be apprehensive.

8.5 For 25 mpg, $z = (25 - 27.3) \div 3.1 = -2.3 \div 3.1 = -0.74$. $p\,(z = 0.74) = .2704$. The probability of cars that will get at least 25 mpg $= .2704 + .5 = .7704$, or 77.04%. For 24 mpg, $z = (24 - 27.3) \div 3.1 = -3.3 \div 3.1 = -1.06$. $p\,(z = 1.06) = .3554$. The probability of cars that will get at least 24 mpg $= .3554 + .5 = .8554$, or 85.54%.

8.7 .90 criterion corresponds to $z\,(p = .45)$. $z\,(p = .45) = 1.65$. Convert z to actual scores: lower limit $= 76 - (1.65 \times 5.7) = 76 - 9.4 = 66.6$; upper limit $= 76 + (1.65 \times 5.7) = 76 + 9.4 = 85.4$.

8.9 $z = (24{,}832 - 25{,}301) \div 986 = -469 \div 986 = -0.48$. $p\,(z = 0.48) = .1844$. Ima's salary is within one-half of one standard deviation of average salary. She is not seriously underpaid.

Chapter 9

9.1 $n = 12$, $p = .4$, $r = 3$ or less; $p(3) = .141894$, $p(2) = .063852$, $p(1) = .017414$, $p(0) = .002177$; answer $= .225337$ or $.23$

9.3 94.32

9.5 $n = 182$, $p = .51$, $r = 177+$, normal curve method; mean $= 92.82$, standard deviation $= 6.74$, $z = 12.49$, $p < .0001$

9.7 $n = 20$, $p = .25$, $r = 16+$; answer $= .0000003865$

9.9 $n = 5$, $p = .34$ (or 212/620), $r = 5$, $p = .00467$

9.11 $n = 9$, $p = .6$, $r = 8, 9$; $p(8) = .060$, $p(9) = .010$, $p(8,9) = .07$

9.13 $n = 8$, $p = .91$, $r = 2$ or less, $p = .000013$

9.15 $n = 100$, $p = .25$, $n = 29+$, normal curve method; mean $= 25$, standard deviation $= 4.23$, $z = .92$, $p = .1588$

9.17 $n = 6$, $p = .33$, $r = 1, 0$; $p(1) = .27$, $p(0) = .09$, $p(0,1) = .36$

Chapter 10

10.1 $n = 50$, $p = .6$, $r = 40+$, $Np = 100$; mean $= 30$, standard deviation $= 2.46$, $z = 4.07$, $p < .0001$

10.3 $n = 35$, $p = .3$, $r = 17+$, $Np = 200$; mean $= 10.5$, standard deviation $= 2.47$, $z = 2.63$, $p = .0043$

10.5 $n = 120$, $p = .23$, $r = 24+$, $Np = 150$; mean 27.6, standard deviation $= 2.07$, $z = 1.74$, $p = .0409$

10.7   Asperin; $n = 200$, $p = .5$, $r = 60$ or less, $Np = 1,000$; mean $= 100$, standard deviation $= 6.33$, $z = 6.32$, $p < .0001$

10.9 $n = 211$, $p = .34$, $r = 91+$, $Np = 620$; mean $= 71.74$, standard deviation $= 5.59$, $z = 3.44$, $p = .0003$

10.11 $\lambda = 6.0$ (a) .1526 (b) .0025 (c) .0149 (d) .0446 (e) .1512

10.13 $\lambda = .1$; .0954

10.15 $n = 100$, $p = .25$, $r = 29+$, $Np = 1,000$; mean $= 25$, standard deviation $= 3.97$, $z = 1.01$, $p = .1562$

Chapter 11

11.1   s.e. $= 9.83$; mean $= \$30$; standard deviation $= \$31.10$; 95% confidence, $\$7.78$ to $\$52.22$ using $t = 2.26$ for 9 df

11.3   s.e. $= 3.0$, $t = 2.0$, $p = .0228$

11.5   Best estimate $= 6.96$, $s = 2.1$, s.e. $= .94$, $t = 3.22$ with 4 df, $p < .025$

11.7   Best estimate $= \$710.80$, $s = \$262$, s.e. $= 82.85$, 80% confidence limits (using $t = 1.38$ with df $= 9$) $= \$596.47$ to $\$825.13$

11.9   Mean $= 20.0$, $s = 25.3$, s.e. $= 5.66$

11.11   (a) s.e. $= 323$, confidence limits $4,400 \pm 1.65 \times 323$, or 3,867 to 4,933

   (b) $z = 4.95$, $p < .0001$

   (c) $z = 1.24$, $p = .1075$

11.13   s.e. $= 1.5$, $t = 2.67$, $p = .0038$

11.15   s.e. $= 3.6$, $t = 2.06$, $p = .0197$

Chapter 12

12.1   Hypothesis: Jack costs less than $\$364$ per car.

   Null hypothesis: Jack does not cost less than $\$364$ per car.

   s.e. $= 20$, $t = 1.7$, $p = .0445$; possible discussion points: inflation, quality of repairs, costs of terminating public employees.

12.3   Survey of 96

12.5   Best estimate $= 40.34\%$, $s = 7.68$, s.e. $= 2.43$, $t = 2.41$ (9 df), $p < .025$

12.7   Hypothesis: HMO costs are less than $\$586$ per year.

   Null hypothesis: HMO costs are not less than $\$586$ per year.

   Mean $= \$521.30$, $s = \$55.80$, s.e. $= 17.65$, $t = 3.67$ (9 df), $p < .005$

12.9   Subtract the cost of purchasing the computers ($\$74,000$) from the annual employees' cost of $\$204,500$. Divide this number by 20 to get a number

($6,525) to compare with the computer cost of $5,200 each. s.e. = 632.45, $t = 2.10$ (9 df), $p < .05$; before concluding that the computers are saving money, some consideration of maintenance costs and replacement costs should be considered.

12.11 Hypothesis: Absenteeism is less than 12.8 workdays.

Null hypothesis: Absenteeism is not less than 12.8 workdays.

s.e. = 1.03, $t = 3.98$ (19 df), $p < .005$; conclusion: reject the null hypothesis. This would happen by chance only rarely so the number of absences is probably less than 12.8.

12.13 Hypothesis: This year's corn crop yields are less than 32.4 bushels/acre.

Null hypothesis: This year's corn crop yields are not less than 32.4 bushels/acre.

s.e. = 1.57, $t = 6.37$, $p < .0001$; 80% confidence limits = 22.4 ± 1.28 × 1.57, or 20.4 to 24.4.

12.15 s.e. = 13,750; 99% confidence limits = 74,500 ± 2.95 × 13,750, or 115,063 to 33,938.

Hypothesis: Punitive damages average less than $100,000 per case.

Null hypothesis: Punitive damages do not average less than $100,000 per case. $t = 1.85$

$p < .05$; conclusion: punitive damages are not likely to average more than 100,000 per case.

Chapter 13

13.1 1,702

13.3 $s = .32$, s.e. = .023, $t = 2.17$, $p = .015$

13.5 Hypothesis: After the public service ads, less than 74% of drivers violate the speed limit.

Null hypothesis: After the public service ads, 74% (or more) of drivers violate the speed limit.

$s = .44$, s.e. = .0098, $t = 2.04$, $p = .0207$; note that this finding is statistically significant yet substantively trivial.

13.7 140

13.9 Best estimate = .25

13.11 Best estimate of error rate 7.2%, $s = .258$, s.e. = .016; 90% confidence .072 ± 1.65 × .016, or .0984 to .0456.

Hypothesis: The error rate is greater than 5% or .05.

Null hypothesis: The error rate is not greater than 5% or .05.

Need to calculate new deviation and s.e.: they are .218 and .014, $t = 1.57$, $p = .0582$

13.13 Best estimate of paid is 82% or .82.

What is the probability that this percentage could result if the population proportion were .9 or larger? Standard deviation = .3 (use square root of .9 × .1), s.e. = .03, $t = 2.67$, $p = .0038$

Chapter 14

14.1 Hypothesis: After the PR campaign, fewer people do not have inspection stickers.

Null hypothesis: After the PR campaign, there is no change in the number of people lacking inspection stickers.

	Proportion	s	s.e.	s.e.$_d$	t	p
Before	.43	.50	.050			
After	.21	.41	.041	.065	3.38	.0004

14.3 Hypothesis: African Americans are less likely to feel that the police are doing a good job.

Null hypothesis: There is no difference in the proportion of African Americans and whites who feel the police are doing a good job.

	Proportion	s	s.e.	s.e.$_d$	t	p
African Americans	.49	.5	.041			
Whites	.75	.43	.025	.048	5.42	<.0001

14.5 Hypothesis: The exercise group will perform better than the nonexercise group.

Null hypothesis: There is no difference in performance between the exercise and nonexercise groups.

Exercise s.e. = 3.63, nonexercise group = 1.86, s.e.$_d$ = 4.08, $t = .96$, $p = .1685$

14.7 Hypothesis: Maintenance costs will be less on cars that do not get routine maintenance.

Null hypothesis: There is no difference in maintenance costs for cars that receive service and those that do not.

Maintained s.e. = 10, not maintained s.e. = 23.1, s.e.$_d$ = 25.2, $t = 1.99$, $p = .0239$

14.9 Hypothesis: Brethren will have a lower divorce rate.

Null hypothesis: There is no difference in divorce rates for Brethren and Lost Souls.

	Proportion	s	s.e.	s.e.$_d$	t	p
Brethren	.14	.35	.038			
Lost Souls	.196	.39	.055	.067	.84	.2005

14.11 Hypothesis: UA students score higher than UGA students.

Null hypothesis: There is no difference in the scores of UA and UGA students.

(**Note:** This hypothesis is rejected by the results since UGA students have a higher mean.)

UA s.e. = 1.9, UGA s.e. = 1.6, s.e.$_d$ = 2.48, t = 2.26, p = .0122

14.13 Hypothesis: People on workfare earn more money.

Null hypothesis: There is no difference in earnings for those on workfare and those not on workfare.

Workfare s.e. = 12.5, control s.e. = 9.50, s.e.$_d$ = 15.7, t = 2.88, p = .0020

14.15 Hypothesis: Workshop students are more likely to receive PMIs.

Null hypothesis: Workshop attendance has no effect on the likelihood of receiving PMIs.

	Proportion	s	s.e.	s.e.$_d$	t	p
Workshop Group	.7	.46	.145			
Control Group	.3	.46	.145	.205	1.95	<.0.5
					(df = 18)	

14.17 Hypothesis: Jogging pigs have lower cholesterol levels.

Null hypothesis: The cholesterol levels of jogging and nonjogging pigs are not different.

Joggers s.e. = 12.65, control s.e. = 15.49, s.e.$_d$ = 20.0. t = 2.5 with 23 df, p = .01

14.19 Hypothesis: Seat belt use is higher in Minnesota.

Null hypothesis: There is no difference in the proportion of residents using seat belts in Minnesota and Wisconsin.

	Proportion	s	s.e.	s.e.$_d$	t	p
Minnesota	.49	.5	.058			
Wisconsin	.25	.44	.042	.072	3.33	.0004

14.21 Hypothesis: More students in statistics suffer breakdowns.

Null hypothesis: There is no difference in the proportion of statistics and sensitivity training students having breakdowns.

	Proportion	s	s.e.	s.e.$_d$	t	p
Statistics	.5	.5	.158			
Sensitivity Training	.27	.44	.114	.195	1.18	ns
					(df = 23)	

14.23 Hypothesis: Latinos are more likely to feel the city is biased.

Null hypothesis: There is no difference in the proportion of Latino and Anglo residents who feel the city is biased.

	Proportion	s	s.e.	s.e.$_d$	t	p
Latinos	.71	.45	.020			
Anglos	.35	.48	.028	.034	10.59	<.0001

Chapter 15

15.1 Cross-tabulation (frequencies):

	Work on Ziptronic?	
Number of Absences	No	Yes
Less than 10	85	18
10 or more	35	26
Total	120	44

Cross-tabulation (percentaged):

	Work on Ziptronic?	
Number of Absences	No	Yes
Less than 10	71%	41%
10 or more	29%	59%

Conclusion: Hypothesis is supported. Employees who operate ziptronic are more likely to have 10 or more absences than those who do not by 30%.

15.3 Cross-tabulation (percentaged):

Reaction Time	Normal	Pilot Weight up to 10 Pounds Overweight	More than 10 Pounds Overweight
Poor	15%	36%	48%
Adequate	37%	40%	36%
Excellent	48%	25%	16%

Conclusion: Egyptian Air Force brass is correct. Overweight pilots are more likely to have poor reaction time than normal-weight pilots by 33% (48% − 15% = 33%). Overweight pilots are also less likely to have excellent reaction time than normal-weight pilots by 32% (48% − 16% = 32%).

15.5 Cross-tabulation (percentaged):

	Students Assisted for MPA Tuition	
	---	---
Status	Capital	East Winslow
Did not graduate	75%	69%
Graduated	25%	31%

Conclusion: Legislators have reason for concern. Most tuition-assisted students do not graduate. East Winslow does slightly better than Capital in graduation rate (by 6%), but 72% of these students do not graduate.

15.7 Cross-tabulation (percentaged):

	Type of Event				
	---	---	---	---	---
Status	Hockey Games	Religious Rallies	Basketball Games	Rock Concerts	Public Administration Conventions
Not Profitable	57%	11%	78%	20%	100%
Profitable	43%	89%	22%	80%	0%

Conclusion: Religious rallies rank highest with respect to the rate of profitable events (89%), followed closely by rock concerts (80%). Hockey games (43%) and basketball games (22%) lag far behind, and public administration conventions (0%), alas, rank dead last.

15.9 Cross-tabulation (percentaged):

Cancer Status	Drug Group	Placebo Group
Active	72%	70%
Remission	28%	30%

Conclusion: Virtually no difference between drug group and placebo group in achieving remission. The drug does not appear to be effective.

15.11 Cross-tabulation (percentaged):

	Class Participation	
	---	---
Grade in Course	Low	High
Fail	24%	12%
Pass	76%	88%

Conclusion: Professor's hypothesis is supported. Students who had a high rate of class participation were more likely to pass the course than students with a low rate of participation by 12%.

15.13   Percentage cross-tabulation:

Opinion	Before	After
Department is doing a poor job	77%	61%
Department is doing a good job	23%	39%

Hypothesis: New refuse collection procedures have improved the public's perception of the Department of Sanitary Engineering.

Null hypothesis: New refuse collection procedures have not improved the public's perception of the Department of Sanitary Engineering.

Conclusion: New refuse collection procedures appear to have improved the public's perception of Department of Sanitary Engineering. The second (after) survey shows that 39% feel that the department is doing a good job, compared with 23% in the first (before) survey, a difference of 16%.

Chapter 16

16.1   Percentaged cross-tabulation:

	Race	
Attitude toward Police	Nonwhite	White
Police Do Not Do Good Job	51%	25%
Police Do Good Job	49%	75%

Conclusion: The police have a community relations problem in the nonwhite community.

16.3   Percentaged cross-tabulation:

	Proximity to Hospital		
Frequency of Visits	Close	Medium	Far
Low	50%	52%	53%
Medium	26%	26%	26%
High	24%	23%	22%

Chi-square = 3.13; not statistically significant.

Conclusion: Percentaged table and chi-square show that no relationship exists between these variables.

16.7   Percentaged cross-tabulation:

	Type of Job	
Attitude toward Job	Hourly	Salary
Dissatisfied	41%	39%
Satisfied	59%	61%

For gamma, C = 16,490; D = 15,012:

$$\frac{16,490 - 15,012}{16,490 + 15,012} = .05$$

No relationship exists between type of job and job satisfaction.

16.9 Probability of promotion is much greater for younger employees (age 30 or less), and especially for middle-age employees (age 31–50), than for the oldest group of employees (age 51 or greater).

16.11 The four conditions of causality are covariation, time order, nonspuriousness, and theory (see Chapter 3). Cross-tabulation satisfies covariation condition, and theoretical justification probably exists for this relationship. However, Ph.D. student gives no evidence that she has satisfied time order condition (does bureaucratic quality lead to economic development or the reverse?), and nonspuriousness condition (might third variables be responsible for the observed covariation?).

16.13 Percentaged cross-tabulation:

	Rank		
Competence	Assistant	Associate	Full
Low	14%	23%	60%
Medium	31%	54%	20%
High	55%	23%	20%

Conclusion: McClain's hypothesis gains support. Assistant professors (55%) have the highest percentage of high competence, with associate professors (23%) and full professors (20%) far behind. Associate professors (54%) have the highest percentage of medium competence, with professors (20%) again far behind. Professors (60%) lead in only one category—low competence!

Chapter 17

17.1 Percentaged cross-tabulation (no control variable):

	Race	
Status	Nonwhite	White
Passed Over	46%	14%
Promoted	54%	86%

Percentaged control tables:

	Non–West Pointers			**West Pointers**	
Status	Nonwhite	White	**Status**	Nonwhite	White
Passed Over	51%	50%	Passed Over	27%	3%
Promoted	49%	50%	Promoted	73%	97%

Conclusion: Original table suggests discrimination because whites promoted at a much higher rate than nonwhites, 86% versus 54%. Control tables show that Non–West Pointers—whether nonwhite or white—have 50–50 chance of promotion (no discrimination). However, among West Pointers, whites have much higher rate of promotion than nonwhites, 97% versus 73%. This finding again suggests racial discrimination, although a larger sample of nonwhite West Pointers would have been desirable.

17.3 Percentaged cross-tabulation (no control variable):

	Average Income	
Frequency of Health Problems	Low	High
Low	41%	60%
High	59%	40%

Percentaged control tables:

Garbage Collection Once per Week

	Average Income	
Frequency of Health Problems	Low	High
Low	31%	45%
High	69%	55%

Garbage Collection Twice per Week

	Average Income	
Frequency of Health Problems	Low	High
Low	46%	61%
High	54%	39%

Conclusion: Original cross-tabulation shows that higher income have lower rate of health problems by 19%. Control tables show that both income and frequency of garbage collection affect rate of health problems: High income have lower rate of health problems than low income by 14% to 15%, and those with garbage collected twice per week have lower rate of health problems than those with once-per-week collection by 15% to 16%.

17.5 Percentaged cross-tabulation (no control variable):

	Streetlights	
Crime Rate	Below Average	Above Average
Below Average	49%	57%
Above Average	51%	43%

Percentaged control tables:

Police Do Not Walk Beat

	Streetlights	
Crime Rate	Below Average	Above Average
Below Average	48%	47%
Above Average	52%	53%

Police Walk Beat

	Streetlights	
Crime Rate	Below Average	Above Average
Below Average	58%	59%
Above Average	42%	41%

Conclusion: Original table suggests that cities with above-average streetlights are more likely to have below-average crime rates by 8%. However, control tables show that when control for police walking (or not walking) beat, streetlights have no effect on crime rate. Instead, cities that have police walking a beat more often have below-average crime rates than cities without police on the beat by 10% to 12%. According to these data, cities are better advised to increase beat-walking than streetlights to reduce crime.

17.7   Percentaged cross-tabulation (no control variable):

	Size	
Attendance	Small	Large
Low	45%	35%
High	55%	65%

Percentaged control tables:

Infrequent Collection Changes				**Frequent Collection Changes**		
	Size				Size	
Attendance	Small	Large		**Attendance**	Small	Large
Low	49%	48%		Low	41%	26%
High	51%	52%		High	59%	74%

Conclusion: Original cross-tabulation suggests that large-size museums are more likely to have high attendance by 10%. However, control tables show that if the museum collection changes infrequently, size makes no difference with respect to attendance. By contrast, if the collection changes frequently, attendance tends to be high, especially for large-size museums. Recommend that the city change the collection frequently, regardless of size of new museum, and, if possible, build large museum.

17.9   Percentaged cross-tabulation (no control variable):

	Method	
Performance	Traditional	Modern
Low	50%	50%
High	50%	50%

Percentaged control tables:

	Low Intelligence	
Performance	Traditional	Modern
Low	40%	63%
High	60%	37%

Performance	Medium Intelligence	
	Traditional	Modern
Low	43%	44%
High	57%	56%

Performance	High Intelligence	
	Traditional	Modern
Low	64%	41%
High	36%	59%

Conclusion: Original cross-tabulation suggests no relationship between method of instruction and student performance. However, control tables show that if student has low intelligence, traditional method of instruction more often leads to high performance than does modern method by 23%. If student has medium intelligence, traditional and modern methods are equally effective in achieving high performance. If student has high intelligence, modern method is more effective in achieving high performance by 23%. These data support the hypothesis that the best method of instruction depends on the intelligence of the student.

Chapter 18

18.1 **(a)** Yes, a relationship exists, $t = 60$; for each additional mile driven, maintenance costs increase by 3 cents.

(b) $\$1,550 \pm \$295$ or $\$1,845$ to $\$1,295$

(c) If $Y = 1,000$, then what is X?

Substitute into the equation and solve, $X = 31,667$

18.3 Slope = for each increase of $\$1.00$ in per capita police expenditures, the state crime rate *increases* by 5.1. Intercept = if per capita police expenditures are equal to 0 (not a likely situation), then the best guess as to the crime rate is 2,475. Coefficient of determination = if you know the per capita expenditures for crime, you can explain 63% of the variation in crime rates. There is a positive correlation between crime rates and expenditures; this probably exists because states increase budgets to combat crime whenever crime increases.

18.5 Beaver can say the following:

(a) For every additional course taken the OER increases by .1.

(b) If a person takes 0 courses, the best estimate of the OER is 95.

(c) Knowing the number of courses taken can explain 40% of the variation in OERs.

(d) $t = 1.43$, $p = .6778$; a relationship exists, but it is weak.

Estimate of Beaver's OER = $96 \pm (1.65 \times 1.4 \times 1.05)$, or 98.43 to 93.57.

18.7 Intercept = if the temperature is 0 degrees, our best guess as to the number of absent workers is 485. Slope = for each increase of 1 degree in temperature, absences drop by 5.1. Coefficient of determination = if you know the low temperature for the preceding night, you can explain 86% of the variation in absences. The relationship is significant; $t = 4.63$; workers absent = $587 \pm (1.65 \times 12 \times 1.02)$, or 607 to 567.

18.9 Slope = an increase of 1 in the air quality index is associated with a .7 increase in respiratory diseases per 1,000 population. Intercept = if the air quality index is 0, the best guess as the number of respiratory diseases per 1,000 population is 15.7. If you know the air quality index for city, you can explain 71% of the variation in respiratory disease rates. The relationship is significant; $t = 17.5$.

18.11 Intercept = the best guess of the expenditures in a school district even if the district had no people is $4,566 (an unlikely situation). Slope = for each person in the school district, expenditures increase by $824. Coefficient of determination = if you know the number of people in the school districts, you can explain 78% of the variation in school expenditures. t score = calculated by dividing the slope by the standard error of the slope; it indicates a statistically significant relationship.

18.13 Hypothesis: There is a negative relationship between Valium-administered and violent behavior. Intercept = the best estimate of the number of violent incidents during the previous 3 months is 126.6 for patients who received no Valium. Slope = each milligram of Valium reduced the number of violent incidents by .0138; $t = 2.60$. Coefficient of determination = knowing the Valium dosage permits you to explain 46% of the variation in the number of violent incidents; $112.8 \pm (1.65 \times 2.4 \times 1.10)$, or 117.2 to 108.4. This does not seem to produce a major improvement.

18.15 In an at-large system: Intercept = in a city with no African Americans, our best estimate is that African Americans will hold .348% of the city council seats. Slope = for each increase of 1 percentage point in African American population, African American representation on the city council increases by .495 percentage points; $t = 8.11$; it is significant. Coefficient of determination = if you know the African American population percentage, you can explain 34% of the variation in the African American council percentage.

Single-member district systems: Intercept in a city with no African Americans, our best estimate is that African Americans will hold − .832% of the city council seats (not a likely situation, this might indicate a threshold effect). Slope = for each increase of 1 percentage point in the African American population, African American representation on the city council increases by .994 percentage points; $t = 13.25$. Coefficient of determination = if you know the African American population percentage, you can explain 82% of the variation in the African American council percentage.

Predictions: At-large 12.7% $\pm$ (1.96 $\times$ 2.4 $\times$ 1.02), or 17.5 to 7.9

Single-member 24.0% $\pm$ (1.96 $\times$ 2.1 $\times$ 1.02), or 28.2 to 19.8

Hypothesis: African Americans receive more representation in single-member district cities.

18.17 Hypothesis: Vote for the incumbent president is negatively related to inflation. Intercept = if the inflation rate is 0, our best guess is the incumbent will receive 54.3% of the vote. Slope = for each increase of 1 percentage point in inflation, the incumbent president's vote percentage decreases by .84. If you know the inflation rate, you can explain 34% of the variation in vote for the incumbent president. $t = 3.5$ with 10 degrees of freedom, $p < .005$. Prediction: 47.6 $\pm$ (1.37 $\times$ 1.9 $\times$ 1.06), or 44.8 to 50.4.

Chapter 19

19.1 There is a positive but nonsignificant relationship between cruising and crime rates ($t = .5$ with 8 df). The analyst should conclude that cruising is unrelated to crime rates.

19.3 Yes, there is a relationship; $t = 26.67$.

Frolic Park, $p = .892$; Barren Park, $p = .092$, Choirpractice Park, $p = 1.10$. (This should be interpreted as a probability of .99; in other words, the sprinkler in this park should be replaced immediately.)

19.5 Desk is correct. This is a strong relationship between reading ability and test scores ($t = 6.45$). In fact, reading scores can explain 80% of the variation in test scores. The slope shows that the probability of passing the exam increases by .071 for each increase of one grade in reading ability. Both persons can be correct since their hypotheses are compatible. Brown does not find a relationship between experience and exam scores because exam scores are strongly affected by the reading ability of the troop.

19.7 $Y = \$408.75 - \$15.75X$, $r^2 = .012$, $S_{ylx} = 82$, $s_b = 58$. There is no relationship between HMOs and health care costs.

19.9 At 6.35 miles per gallon, buses consume 1,291 gallons per week rather than 1,608 per week. But using the 95% confidence limits of 5.55 to 7.15, the consumption of fuel range is 1,477 to 1,147; this means a savings of between 131 gallons, or $262, and 461 gallons, or $922.

19.11 Hypothesis: States with no-fault laws have lower insurance costs. Intercept = the average cost for a policy of this nature in states without no-fault insurance is $265. Intercept = no-fault insurance states have policy costs of $74.33 less. $t = 2.53$ with 18 df, $p < .05$.

Chapter 20

20.1   **(a)** $453 \pm (2.58 \times 12.6)$, or 485.5 to 420.5

(b) If $Y = 400$, what is X? $X = 828,000$

20.3   The relationship is not linear. Forecasting enrollments from these data would result in predictions that are not particularly useful.

20.5   Intercept = if the money supply grows at a rate of 0%, then your best guess as to the inflation rate would be -5.4 (or deflation of 5.4%). Slope = a 1 percentage point increase in the money supply is associated with a 2.1 percentage point increase in inflation. The relationship is significant; $t = 300$. If you know the change in the money supply you can explain 99% of the variation in the inflation rate. Inflation rate of $11.82 \pm (1.65 \times 2 \times 1.05)$, or 15.29 to 8.35.

Could the rate be 15%? $t = (11.82 - 15)/2.1 = 1.51$, $p = .0655$.

20.7   Slope = for every additional person in the state population, the patients at Bluefield State will increase by .0031 (or by 31 for every 10,000 persons); this relationship is significant; $t = 23.85$. (a) 2,718 (b) 62.

20.9   Intercept = your best guess as to the number of domestic disputes on a night when the temperature at 4:00 P.M. is 0, is 216. Slope = for each degree increase in temperature, the number of domestic disputes increases by 3.1; $t = 2.07$, which is significant. If you know the temperature at 4 P.M. you can explain 81% of the variation in the number of domestic disputes in Metro. $510.5 \pm (t \times 18)$.

20.11   Regression 1: Intercept = if the year is 1953, your best guess as to the number of building permits issued is 2,256. Slope = for each year that passes, building permits issued will increase by 234.6; $t = 10.16$. If you know the year, you can explain 65% of the variation in the number of building permits issued.

Regression 2: If the unemployment rate is 0, your best guess as to the number of building permits issued is 13,413. Slope = for each 1 percentage point increase in unemployment, building permits drop by 678; $t = 31.68$, which is significant. If you know the percent unemployment, you can explain 78% of the variation in the number of building permits.

Prediction; Equation 1: 13,751.4; Equation 2: 8,531.4. The second equation is more useful. It has a lower overall standard error of the estimate.

20.13   Intercept = if the year is 1963, your best guess as to Medicaid expenditures is $-\$669.9$ million (this does not make sense). Slope = for each year that passes, Medicaid expenditures increase by \$306 million. $t = 28.41$; the relationship is significant. If you know the year, you can explain 98% of the variation in Medicaid expenditures. \$10,958 million in 2001; \$11,264 million in 2002.

20.15   Intercept = if the year is 1970, your best estimate of the expenditures on WIC is \$40.19 million. Slope = for each year that passes, WIC expenditures increase by $45.46 million. $t = 11.75$ with 24 df. If you know the year, you can explain 97% of the variation in WIC expenditures. $1,494.91 million $\pm$ (1.65 $\times$ 20.5 $\times$ 1.06), or $1,459.06 to $1,530.76.

Chapter 21

21.1 All regression interpretations are fairly similar, so 20.1 will be done in depth. Intercept = if the number of people who live within 200 miles of the camp is 0, the number of camping hookups is 0, and the mean annual temperature at the park is 0 (not a likely situation), then your best estimate of park usage will be 147 (people). Slope 1 = for each additional person living within 200 miles of the park, an additional .0212 persons will visit the park, controlling for hookups and temperature. $t = 1.35$; this relationship is barely significant. Slope 2 = for each additional camping hook-up available, an additional 15.4 people will visit the camp, controlling for residents within 200 miles and temperature. $t = 1.24$; this relationship is barely significant. Slope 3 = for each additional degree higher the mean annual temperature is, a park can expect an additional 186 visitors if you control for residents within 200 miles and temperature. $t = 17.55$; this relationship is significant. Coefficient of determination = knowing the number of residents within 200 miles, the number of camping hookups, and the mean annual temperature at the park allows one to explain 50% of the variation in park usage. The assessment should note that weather conditions seem to be the major influence on park usage.

21.3 The t scores are 52.4 for rainfall and 46.7 for temperature. Best estimate for Barren is 9.36.

21.5 t scores are 14.76 for troops, .8 for education, and 24.1 for women. Note that education is not significant. Best estimate of number of crimes = 418.1.

21.7 t scores are 5.35 for pupil-teacher ratios and 5.08 for spending. Decreasing the pupil-teacher ratio by 5 improves reading scores by .455, while increasing spending by $50 improves them by. 155.

21.9 t scores are 15.06 for days stayed, 7.78 for lab tests, and .71 for prescription drugs. Costs could be controlled by holding down the length of hospital stay or the number of lab tests. Restricting the number of prescription drugs would not likely have any impact.

21.11 Costs increase about $51.45 per person per year ($t = 9.48$). With the introduction of HMOs, costs drop $123.69 from this trend line ($t = 2.49$). HMOs also hold down the future increase in costs by $7.25 per year (or the yearly increase in costs becomes $51.45 − $7.25 or $44.20; $t = 6.36$).

21.13 t scores are 5.71 for temperature, 4.0 for time since overhaul, and 1.08 for number of closes by ICBMs (not significant). Set $y = .2$, temperature = −10, missiles = 0, and solve for overhaul time. Answer: 43.3 months.

21.15 t scores are 8.24 for time trend, 10.32 for Medicaid expenditures, and 2.38 for WIC expenditures. The best predictor is Medicaid expenditures. The 2002 estimate of infant mortality is 8.82. Spend the money on WIC since $1 million for WIC has more of an impact on infant mortality than $1 million on Medicaid.

21.17 Test of partial slopes: job responsibility, $t = 21.92$; years in the agency, $t = 7.13$; number of years of formal education, $t = 3.90$. All are significant. Best estimate of salary if $X_1 = 270$, $X_2 = 0$, and $X_3 = 18$, is $15,304.60.

21.19 Test of slopes: number of persons killed, $t = 1.19$; ability to pay for attorney, $t = 2.77$; number of years of formal education, $t = 3.33$; race, $t = 25.83$. The regression clearly shows that the race of the convicted is associated with receiving the death penalty. Whites are less likely to receive the death penalty, all other things being equal. If $X_1 = 2$, $X_2 = 1$, $X_3 = 16$, and $X_4 = 1$, then $Y = -.22$. Since a probability cannot be less than 0, one should conclude that there is little chance that such a person would receive the death penalty. Second person: if $X_1 = 1$, $X_2 = 0$, $X_3 = 8$, and $X_4 = 0$, then $Y = .43$. To find out if the race of the victim mattered, gather data on a fifth variable, the race of the victim, and add this variable to the equation.

Chapter 22

22.1 Slope 2 = the percentage of dry runs is increasing at a rate of .026 per month before the introduction of the fee. $t = 2.74$, $p = .0031$. Slope 3 = after the introduction of the fee, the percentage of dry runs is increasing by .55 per month more than it was before the fee (an increase of .55 per month over the previous trend line). $t = 3.67$, $p = .0001$. If you know the monthly fluctuation, the value of the trend variable, and how many weeks it is after the introduction of the fee, you can explain 57% of the variation in the percentage of dry runs.

22.3 Slope 1 = the number of drug arrests in Weed County declines by 5.1 per year before the new state law. $t = 5.54$. Slope 2 = the number of drug arrests jumps by 67.2 over the preexisting trend and the new slope in the first year of the new drug law. $t = 3.88$, $p < .0001$. Slope 3 = after the adoption of the new drug law, the annual change in drug arrests increases by 4.3 per year over the previous trend [the new slope is $(-5.1 + 4.3$ or $-.8)$]. If you know the year you can explain 99% of the variation in drug arrests. The law appears to have had a significant short-term impact and had a significant impact on reducing the trend toward declining arrests.

22.5 Intercept = your best guess as to the infant mortality rate in 1950 is 28.32 (note that this is before either Medicaid or the WIC program start). Slope 1 = for each year that passes, the infant mortality rate declines by .26017 if you control spending on Medicaid and WIC. $t = 71.3$, $p < .0001$.

Slope 2 = for each $1 million spent on Medicaid, the infant mortality rate drops by .00138 if you control for year and WIC spending. $t = 8.12$, $p < .0001$. Slope 3 = for each $1 million spent on WIC, the infant mortality rate drops by .00211 if you control for year and Medicaid spending. $t = 1.87$, $p = .0307$.

Chapter 23

23.1   **(a)** Intercept: If population and the number of business permits were both equal to zero, Potto Gulch would spend about $3.65 million on social welfare programs each year.

Slopes: The slope coefficient for population is not statistically significant. For every additional business permit issued, social welfare expenditures go down by $5,049. There is a relationship between new business permits and social welfare expenditures ($t = 2.16$), but the overall impact is rather small.

(b) The adjusted R^2 is lower than the R^2 due to the presence of the insignificant population variable.

(c) Because the population variable is not statistically significant, replacing this variable with the actual number of residents receiving social welfare assistance is an appropriate strategy.

23.3   **(a)** Intercept: If all of the independent variables were equal to zero, the agency would process 386 forms per week.

Slopes: The coefficient for WEEK indicates that the number of forms processed is increasing by about 12.7 per week ($t = 4.61$). The STERM coefficient indicates that after the change in computers was implemented, there was a short-term increase in the number of forms processed of about 87 forms ($t = 4.93$). The LNGTERM coefficient indicates a long term change in the number of forms processed of about 21 forms per week ($t = 5.39$). The INTERN dummy coefficient indicates that when an MPA intern is working, the number of forms processed per week increases by about 67 ($t = 6.2$).

The memo should explain that the new computers are having a positive impact on performance. The memo should also point out that the bureau processes more forms when an MPA intern is working.

23.5   **(a)** Intercept: If the number of new exhibits was equal to zero and it is a warm-weather month, the average number of visitors would be 2,659.

Slopes: For every one additional new exhibit, the number of visitors goes up by about 361 per month. The season coefficient is not statistically significant.

(b) The R^2 of .857 indicates that these two variables explain about 86 percent of the variation in the number of visitors. The likely reason the adjusted R^2 is lower than R^2 is because the coefficient for the season dummy variable is not statistically significant.

23.7 **(a)** Intercept: If class size, teacher turnover, percentage of African American students, and percentage of Hispanic students were all equal to zero, the expected pass rate would be 94.5%.

Slopes: For every 1 percent increase in the percentage of African American students, overall student pass rates decline by $-.194$ of a percentage point (about 2/10 of a percentage point). For every 1% increase in the percentage of Hispanic students, overall student pass rates decline by $-.116$ of a percentage point (about 1/10 of a percentage point). For every 1% increase in the teacher turnover rate, overall student pass rates decline by $-.184$ of a percentage point. All three slope coefficients are significant at the .05 level. The coefficient for class size is not statistically significant at the .05 level.

The R^2 value indicates that the model explains about 30% of the variation in pass rates on state mandated tests. With only 30% of the variance explained, other variables are likely not currently included in the model that affect pass rates.

(b) When attendance is included as an explanatory variable ($t = 10.5$), the R^2 rises to .37. This is a clear improvement in explanatory power over the original model.

Chapter 24

24.1 Percentaged cross-tabulation:

Error found	Used Tax Helpline	
	No	Yes
No	60%	70.9%
Yes	40%	29.1%

For chi-square, the expected frequencies are as follows:

Error found	Used Tax Helpline	
	No	Yes
No	152.67	176.34
Yes	79.34	91.66

Chi-square $= 6.67$; this chi-square (1 degree of freedom) is statistically significant ($< .05$).

Conclusion: The tax helpline is improving error rates somewhat. From a performance standpoint, the program seems to be a success.

24.3

Year	General Fund Balance	Percentage Change in Fund Balances
1998	$9,067	
1999	$9,688	6.85
2000	$10,090	4.15
2001	$10,445	3.51
2002	$11,140	6.65
2003	$11,490	3.14

Average Annual Increase in Fund Balance = 4.86%

Conclusion: The city is very close to its target of 5% annual growth in the general fund balance. Because that calculations show that the performance target is generally being met, officials should not be overly concerned about falling short of the stated performance target.

24.9 One way to benchmark Earth Rocks! against the other organizations is to divide program expenditures by total expenditures to see how much each organization spends on program activities.

				Percentage of Total Expenditures for Program Activities
Earth Rocks!	**$98,000**	**$121,400**	**$594,300**	**0.63**
Weed Lovers	$104,300	$98,350	$623,650	0.68
Flora and Fauna	$97,600	$71,840	$522,840	0.68
Leave It Be	$89,000	$109,750	$700,650	0.72
Nature's Gift	$71,000	$82,450	$608,920	0.75

Based on the benchmarking exercise, Earth Rocks! does not compare favorably with its peers in terms of the percentage of expenditures devoted to program activities. Earth Rocks! devotes 63% of expenditures to program activities, which is the lowest of all the groups.

Because data on fund-raising and administrative costs are also provided, we could also benchmark Earth Rocks! against its peers by examining the proportion of total expenditures taken up by either (or both) of these expenditure categories.

Chapter 25

25.1 Maximin = B, maximax = C

25.3 **(a)** C

(b) Increases expected rehabilitation by 16

(c) What is a rehabilitation worth?

25.5 Corporate theft has the greatest expected value.

25.7 Answer depends on the probabilities selected.

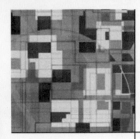

Index